International Financial Management: Theory and Application

International Financial Management: Theory and Application

Second Edition

Edited by
Donald R. Lessard
Sloan School of Management
Massachusetts Institute of Technology

John Wiley & Sons
New York Chichester Brisbane Toronto Singapore

Library of Congress Cataloging in Publication Data

Main entry under title:

International financial management.

Includes bibliographical references and index.

1. International business enterprises—Finance—Addresses, essays, lectures. 2. Investments, Foreign—Addresses, essays, lectures. 3. Foreign exchange problem—Addresses, essay, lectures. I. Lessard Donald R.

HG4027.5.I574 1985 658.1'5 84-15378
ISBN 0-471-88026-4

Printed in the United States of America

10 9 8 7 6 5 4 3 2 1

Preface

Few areas of finance have undergone such rapid change as international financial management. The international economic environment and the theoretical base of financial management have changed radically in the last ten years. A relatively predictable international monetary system has become a flexible and volatile exchange system. New institutions and markets, particularly the Eurocurrency markets, have integrated hitherto segmented national capital markets. A series of events beginning with the creation of OPEC have shifted wealth among countries and have increased the demand for international financial intermediation. Governments have taken a more active role in regulating and intervening in both domestic and international financial markets. These factors have caused managements to become more aware of the international financial environment but have also increased significantly the necessary level of sophistication.

Capital market theory has made substantial strides and has increased the ability to develop rigorous models that reflect the complexities of international finance. Empirical evidence regarding the efficiency of markets has significantly altered the traditional perspectives on foreign exchange markets and international financial transactions.

Advances in international financial management have resulted from both sets of forces. The requirements of the new international economic environment have led to substantial innovation at the practical level, and advances in capital market theory have led to new insights concerning corporate financial management. However, as yet there has been relatively little integration of the emerging theoretical perspectives deduced from capital market theory and the advances in practice that have come about through necessity.

International financial management is in much the same position today as the entire field of financial management was a decade ago. On the one hand, there exists a body of capital market theory that has had little practical impact; on the other hand, there exists a substantial body of institutional knowledge and normative theory that has not yet been linked to a positive economic base. This situation is both exciting and frustrating. It is exciting because there is great scope for advancement in the field and important conceptual breakthroughs are possible. It is frustrating because many of the practical problems at hand remain beyond the reach of existing theoretically based approaches. Further, the standard of rigor that has been applied in recent years in the field of finance often is unattainable in the international area at its current, relatively early level of development.

It is precisely when a field is at this stage of development that the identification and synthesis of existing research is most important. In selecting the readings to be included in this second edition, I have chosen articles that lie on the frontier of international financial management and display rigor, relevance, and accessibility. The majority of the articles are new, reflecting the substantial growth in the international finance literature in recent years. Many of the articles replace earlier pieces by the same authors, reflecting changes not only in the environment but also in the sophistication of the approach. The normative management section is considerably stronger, although many issues relating to investment and financing choices have, as yet, not been treated adequately in the literature.

A major problem in compiling a book of readings for an emerging field lies in drawing boundaries. Whereas a few topics belong uniquely to the area of international financial management, others are traditionally treated in international macroeconomics, corporate finance, accounting, and planning and control. It is impossible for any single work to draw together all these disciplines. One criterion used in deciding what areas to cover in this book, as well as which specific articles to include, was to exclude topics that are treated in depth elsewhere. For example, I have omitted a comprehensive treatment of the international monetary system, the balance of payments or the determinants of exchange rates, and descriptions of foreign exchange markets and foreign and international money and capital markets. These topics have been treated extensively within the more traditional disciplines. When material on exchange rates and foreign exchange markets is included, it emphasizes those aspects that bear directly on international financial management. The book does not discuss the relevance of fixed versus floating exchange rates for national monetary policy or the problems of integrating external goals with internal goals at the level of the macroeconomy. The themes of purchasing power parity and the linkages between interest rates, forward rates, and spot exchange rates, however, are included, since these form the building blocks for international financial management.

This book includes discussions both of the positive theory of international investment and valuation and of normative models and approaches to specific international financial decisions. Both perspectives are highly relevant to management. The first approach provides the necessary understanding of the forces underlying international investment and valuation, while the second demonstrates the application of these basic concepts to specific management decisions.

The first two parts of the book deal primarily with the positive theory of international corporate finance, while the last two cover the normative theory of this field. Part I covers the theory of international investment, with an emphasis on financial aspects. The first section introduces the theory of international capital flows. The second section provides an overview of the theory of direct investment, which includes, but clearly is not limited to, the theory of capital flows. This is followed by sections bringing together theoretical and empirical perspectives on the degree of international integration of capital markets and its implications for the valuation of capital assets in the international context. Part II singles out the currency factor. The first section provides an overview of the theory of exchange rate determination, with special emphasis on the role of asset markets. The second section deals with financial parity relationships and the efficiency of exchange markets, and the last section covers purchasing power parity and the real exchange rate.

The normative theory of international financial management is broken down into short- and medium-run tactical aspects and long-run strategic aspects. Part III focuses on the tactical aspects, including international working capital management and the broad and ill-defined area of exposure management. The subject of long-term aspects, treated in Part IV, is divided into sections on financing and investment considerations. The emphasis in both sections is on unique factors in the international arena, including multiple currencies, tax differentials, and capital flow restrictions.

Each major part of the book begins with an introduction and overview that integrate the various selections and place them in a common context. It is hoped that these introductions go well beyond the scope of the individual readings in providing a conceptual framework for international financial management.

As editor, my greatest debt is to the authors and publishers who gave permission to reprint their works. I also am grateful to Michael Adler, Raj Aggarwal, Gunter Dufey,

Gene Flood, Jacob Frenkel, Ian Giddy, Laurent Jacque, Richard Levich, Dennis Logue, and James Paddock for valuable suggestions regarding the content of the book, and to David Sharp and Betsy Springer for their assistance in preparing the volume.

Donald R. Lessard

Contents

Contents

Part I

Theories of International Investment and the Multinational Firm

INTRODUCTION

In order to choose among the investment and financing options facing a firm that operates across national boundaries, it is useful to have a theoretical understanding of the reasons for international investment, whether undertaken by individuals or corporations, as well as an understanding of the specific motivations for international expansion by corporations. This requires a focus both on the markets for goods and real factors of production in which a specific firm, because of its previous experience, scale, and scope, faces investment opportunities not readily available to other firms, and on financial markets which provide the basis for valuing such opportunities. Since financial markets work relatively well while individual firms are most likely to be able to develop substantial competitive advantages in goods and factor markets, most value will be added by appropriate identification and exploitation of real investment opportunities rather than by clever financial transactions. Nevertheless, finance plays an important role in enhancing the value of the firm since it provides the bench mark by which individual opportunities should be judged. The purpose of this first section is to provide a broad understanding of the reasons for international portfolio and direct investment and of models of asset valuation in an international context.

The emphasis given to financial factors in the theory of direct investment (DFI) has shifted substantially in recent years. In the classical view, which dominated academic literature through the early 1960s, international investment of a portfolio or a direct nature was viewed primarily as a capital flow, motivated by differences in interest rates. In the late 1960s, in light of the upsurge in DFI by U.S. firms, theorists shifted their emphasis and argued that direct foreign investment belonged to the realm of industrial organization and had little, if anything, to do with traditional capital flow theory. By now, the pendulum appears to have swung back part way, with a recognition that financial factors are relevant even to direct investment, although they are often secondary in importance to the real market factors addressed by industrial organization theorists. Further, modern capital market theory provides a basis for the valuation of international activities whether these are motivated by real or by financial considerations.

One of the reasons why financial motivations for international investment fell into disrepute is that, in their classical form, they could not explain several readily observed phenomena, specifically the industry specificity of DFI flows and the existence of cross-flows of both direct and portfolio investment. Interest differentials can explain flows in only one direction and provide no basis for industry-specific movements. Modern capital market theory, in contrast, with its emphasis on the efficient allocation of risks through investor diversification, provides a powerful motivation for international capital flows above and beyond the flows called for by differences in the balance between investment opportunities and investable resources in various countries. Further, these flows resulting from the diversification motive will be in many directions and will often cross. However, unless there are barriers to portfolio capital flows, capital market theory cannot explain DFI.

When a firm invests internationally, it typically transfers capital as well as management and technology. Even when it borrows locally to finance the expansion, DFI almost always involves a transfer of risk capital. Thus, in investing internationally, the multinational corporation (MNC) serves as a financial intermediary. In a world with no barriers to capital flows, this intermediation could take place through a variety of channels, including bank loans and portfolio investment, and the MNC's ability to diversify internationally would not result in a competitive advantage. Thus, only when there are impediments or costs to market-mediated international financial transactions are financial considerations a motive for DFI. This argument parallels the generally accepted view that imperfections in markets for technology or other real factors of production are what make these factors relevant to multinationalism. In each case, there are underlying economic forces which motivate an international transfer of some factors and barriers or impediments to market-mediated transfers of these factors which make DFI the most attractive channel.

Financial markets by and large are among the most efficient of all markets since there are many possible transactors, information is widely disseminated, and transactions costs tend to be quite low. Nevertheless, there are a number of impediments to international capital flows. The obstacles may include formal or informal barriers to international flows or imperfections in domestic capital markets.[1]

The distinction between financial and real factors is not absolute, but can be thought of in terms of the simple valuation formula,

$$V = \sum_{t=0}^{T} \frac{\overline{CF}_t}{(1 + \rho)^t}$$

or with perpetual cash flows,

$$V = \frac{\overline{CF}}{\rho}$$

where V is the value of the firm (project), $\overline{CF}$ is the expected cash flow in period t, and ρ is the required rate of return.

Real market imperfections typically will be reflected in the cash flows, while financial factors will be reflected in the discount rate, that is, in the valuation of a particular cash flow stream because of the way in which the project is financed and the market(s) in which the securities are placed.[2]

OUTLINE OF PART I

International Portfolio Investment

The first group of articles deals with the theory of international portfolio investment. Black (Article 1) outlines the determinants of capital flows from the perspective of capital market theory. His approach parallels the classical approach in leaving aside real factors which distinguish investment opportunities faced by different firms or individuals, but goes beyond classical theory in two important regards. First, he shows that if financial markets work well, interest differentials will never appear, and, thus, the theory must be

[1]These are discussed in the introduction to Part III.

[2]The valuation of projects, taking into account explicit financial factors, is discussed in Articles 33 and 34.

based on underlying phenomena. Second, he stresses the potential for international risk diversification which requires cross-flows of capital, in contrast to the one-way flows predicted by classical theory.

Lessard (Article 2) again outlines the case for international diversification, but also discusses the potential obstacles to cross-border investment including currency risk; cross-border political risk; limits to the scope, depth, and efficiency of particular national markets; and taxes and other explicit constraints on cross-border investment. He argues that these will influence the composition of desired international holdings by investors based in different countries, but are unlikely to rule out cross-border investment altogether.

Ibbotson, Carr, and Robinson (Article 3) provide an extensive review of the relative magnitude of U.S. and non-U.S. equity and bond markets and of historical returns and risk in those markets. Their results show that while international investors may expect gains from diversification, imperfections in international capital markets may provide them with further profit opportunities.

Direct Investment

The second group of articles focuses on direct international investment. Vernon (Article 4) reassesses his classical product-life cycle perspective in the context of modern firms that possess global scope and experience and of a convergence of desired product attributes in industrialized countries. In doing this, he reviews the motivations for global expansion by firms that have gained an edge through product or process technology that is transferable across national boundaries. Kogut (Article 5) extends this line of analysis by focusing on factors that cause multinationals to gain incrementally vis-à-vis single-country firms rather than on the reasons for going abroad in the first place. In particular, he stresses the "option" to engage in arbitrage given distortions in markets for goods and financial assets that is provided by a multinational network.

Capital Market Integration and Asset Valuation

Models of asset valuation are the hallark of modern financial economic theory. They provide the basis for understanding how risk and return are traded off in alternative capital market regimes and for virtually all normative rules in corporate finance. Asset valuation in an international context is significantly more complex than in a single country setting. In the first place, there are many currencies in which assets may be denominated or in which returns may be measured. Further, because of physical and legal barriers to trade as well as differences in taste, the consumption preferences of individuals domiciled in different countries are likely to differ and hence their asset demands are likely to differ as well. Further, the existence of national tax systems and controls over access to capital markets give rise to barriers or implicit taxes to cross-border financial transactions, raising the possibility that investors domiciled in different countries not only have differing consumption preferences, but also will face different investment opportunity sets. This potential for partial market segmentation is enhanced by the existence of some outright controls on cross-border capital flows as well as basic limits to the enforceability of contracts across national jurisdictions. Taken together, these considerations suggest that it is unlikely that a world-level analogue to the single country capital asset pricing model, where all investors hold the same portfolio of risky securities, will be a reasonable representation of equilibrium. Unfortunately, modeling many of these complications is exceedingly complex and the financial economics literature has seen a burgeoning of alternative international valuation models.

Stulz (Article 6) provides an overview of recent financial economic models of international asset valuation. Drawing on basic theoretical work by himself and others, he outlines international valuation under three different sets of circumstances. First, he explores asset valuation where there are multiple currencies, but no barriers to trade and no differences in consumption preferences. In this simple case, Stulz shows that the international valuation problem becomes the same as that treated by Black in a single country with no riskless asset. Returns on assets that are riskless in terms of the various currencies are not riskless in real terms and, hence, are likely to include non-zero risk premia. However, all investors face the same opportunity set and hence continue to hold the same portfolios of risky assets. The second case that Stulz treats is that of multiple currencies and differing consumption preferences across national boundaries. In this context, investors in different countries will want to hold different portfolios that are hedged to reflect their desired consumption patterns. Nevertheless, they are likely to hold similar portfolios of risky assets so long as other assets, such as money-fixed claims and commodity-linked claims, are available to perform the hedging functions. In treating this case, Stulz shifts from the class of asset valuation models that relate the risk of a security to its covariance with the market portfolio to a class of models that relate the risk of a security to its covariance with aggregate consumption. While such models have yet to be put to extensive empirical testing, they provide a more fundamental understanding of the valuation process and are likely to be increasingly important in state-of-the-art theoretical work. In his third section, Stulz treats the case of barriers to cross-border investment. He, like Black and others, abstract from many of the institutional differences in the form of cross-border barriers and treat them as taxes on cross-border investment flows. With barriers, he shows investors in different countries will hold different portfolios of risky assets and that specific securities will be either on the relevant domestic security market line or the international security market lines depending on whether or not they are traded internationally in equilibrium.

Theoretical models of the implications of international capital market integration are well and good, but to make judgments regarding their validity and relevance, it is important to have some idea of the extent to which markets in fact appear to be integrated.

Kohlhagen (Article 7) reviews the extensive literature on the international integration of financial markets and finds that most of the evidence is inconclusive. The major problem, he notes, is that any test of integration is a test of a joint hypothesis of a particular model of asset valuation and the extent to which that model holds. Given the broad range of potential asset valuation models, it is not surprising that it is difficult to specify a test. Further, as is now well known in the case of testing the single country capital asset pricing model, equilibrium models with respect to risky assets are specified in terms of expected returns, but the validity of these models can only be inferred from realized returns. Since it is unlikely that the structure of returns will be stable for a long enough period to provide the types of observations required, such models must be taken largely on the basis of the correspondence of their logic to observations regarding the institutional character of markets and the behavior of investors within them. Kohlhagen, not surprisingly, finds substantially greater evidence regarding the integration of fixed income markets especially in the case of short term Eurocurrency deposits. This is as it should be, since institutionally the markets for various currencies exist within a single jurisdiction and the relationship being tested involves arbitrage rather than one that requires measurement of expected returns. Turning to relationships between short-term interest rates in domestic markets, Kohlhagen finds that there is weaker, but nevertheless impressive, evidence regarding market integration, but little evidence regarding integration of markets for long-term bonds. Again, this is not terribly surprising, since long-term assets denominated in different currencies should react quite differently to a variety of factors in addition to the spot exchange rate and hence require the joint test of a rather complex model of how they behave, how they are valued, and whether they adhere to such a model.

International Portfolio Investment

1

The Ins and Outs of Foreign Investment*

Fischer Black

This article attempts to lay out the basic economic influences on investment across national boundaries. It assumes throughout that investors and corporate managers attempt to take advantage of any profit opportunities they see: They attempt to maximize the value of and income from the portfolios and firms they own or control, net of any taxes they must pay, and taking account of any government controls or possible expropriation.

The approach it takes could be called neoclassical economics. It also draws heavily on the modern theory of finance, which assumes that investors choose their portfolios in the light of both risk and expected return. It contrasts with the kind of analysis that assumes supply and demand for goods or labor can be out of balance because prices don't move fast enough to bring them into line. Prices are unlikely to move slowly (except by government edict) with profit-maximizing investors and managers around.

WHY FOREIGN INVESTMENT EXISTS

Why do investors hold assets in other countries? They may have saved more than they can invest profitably at home. Or their governments may tax capital heavily or threaten to take it away. Perhaps they want the advantages of international diversification or feel more optimistic about the prospects for foreign assets than foreigners are. A more relevant question might be, "Why don't investors hold more assets in other countries?"

THE DISTRIBUTION OF WEALTH

If a country's residents are wealthier than the country, they will hold assets in other countries. Suppose that the residents of country A are worth \$150 billion, but that investments in country A are worth only \$100 billion. The residents of country B, however, are worth only \$50 billion, while investments in country B are worth \$100 billion.

If A and B are the only countries in the world, there is bound to be foreign investment. In general, the residents of A must hold \$50 billion of B's assets, plus an added amount equal to the value of assets in A held by residents of B. If residents of B hold \$10 billion of A's assets, the residents of A must hold \$60 billion of B's assets, since they have \$150 billion in assets, only \$90 billion of which is invested within their own country. (We define assets broadly, as including real assets, financial assets, deposits and money held by individuals.)

Other things being equal, the thriftier a country's residents, the more they are likely to

*This article is reprinted, with permission, from *Financial Analysts Journal,* May-June 1978, pp. 1–7.

own of other countries' assets. Conversely, when a country's residents spend more than they earn, they are likely to find that foreign ownership of their assets increases. Thus increasing foreign investment can be sign of changes in the spending habits of a country's citizens, rather than a sign of any change in foreigners' investment preferences.

The fact that an uneven distribution of wealth may lie behind much foreign investment may go unnoticed by investors or even by the countries receiving the foreign investment. Any single investor of country A is unlikely to feel the constraints that necessitate $50 billion of his country's wealth being invested in Country B. He feels free to invest his whole portfolio in A, or to invest his whole portfolio in B, or to divide it in any way between A and B. He may even be able to sell short some of A's securities, or borrow in A, and invest an amount in A or B greater than the value of his portfolio.

It may also go unnoticed that an increase in foreign investment in one country means, if nothing else has changed, an equal increase in that country's residents' investments outside the country. If a resident of B, deciding to invest in A, sells an asset in B and buys an asset in B, and if no assets move from A to B or from B to A, then a resident of A must simultaneously decide or agree to invest in B. In this situation, we can say that, for every investment by B's residents in A, there is a simultaneous investment by A's residents in B. The residents of B, as a group, exchange ownership of assets in B for ownership of assets in A with the residents of A, as a group. Gross foreign investment increases, but net foreign investment stays the same.

When a foreigner invests in the U.S., he must give something up. Normally, either he gives up a claim on a foreign asset or he imports goods or services. To understand one side of the transaction, we must understand the other. Most increases in gross foreign investment in the U.S. are accompanied by increases in gross U.S. investment abroad.

THE DISTRIBUTION OF INVESTMENT OPPORTUNITIES

We have assumed that assets change hands without changing locations. In fact, however, real assets can move between countries. This section assumes that the assets moving between countries are investment goods—machines, tools, industrial and agricultural chemicals and the like.

The owner of an investment good will place it where it will earn the highest rental (net of taxes and other government levies). When he transfers the asset to another country, foreign investment in that country will go up. Thus a country that has improved investment opportunities (or that lowers its taxes on capital or investment goods) will find that foreign investment in the country is higher than it would otherwise have been.

For example, suppose that the residents of our countries A and B have the same wealth—each group owns $100 billion in assets. If investment opportunities are greater in B, the assets will be distributed unevenly: There will be, say, $150 billion of assets in B and only $50 billion of assets in A.

The fact that investment opportunities are greater in B than in A will not show up in the form of a higher interest rate or higher expected return on assets in B. If investors are on their toes, they will shift assets between countries in anticipation of any changes in interest rates or expected return. Sometimes they will shift too much or too soon, and assets will flow into the country that turns out to have the lower interest rate or expected return. Since this is about as likely to happen as the reverse, we should see no particular correlation between asset flows and the pattern of interest rates and expected returns among countries. The fact that expected returns on risky assets are not observable creates another obstacle to seeing a correlation between differences in expected return and flows of physical capital.

Similarly, the specific sectors within a country that have more attractive investment opportunities will not show up as sectors with higher returns to investors. They will show up as sectors attracting investment of physical capital. But the flows of physical capital into these sectors will keep the returns to investors at about the same levels as, sometimes higher and sometimes lower than, the returns to investors in other sectors.

TAXES AND THE THREAT OF EXPROPRIATION

Taxes and other government levies can have an important effect on investment between countries. If one country increases its taxes on capital (the corporate income tax, for example), and other countries do not, then capital goods will leave the country with the higher tax rate. If a country reduces its taxes on capital, then capital goods will come in and net foreign investment in the country will increase. Similarly, if a country has a habit of expropriating capital goods without compensation at market value (by nationalizing certain industries, for example) or if there is a threat of such expropriation in the future, then capital goods will leave the country and net foreign investment in the country will decline.

A change in taxes on foreign investors or foreign investments will affect the ownership of assets in different locations and the locations of the assets. If the government of A or the government of B imposes a tax on the holdings of A's residents in B, residents of A will want to do one of two things—transfer capital goods from B to A, or exchange ownership of assets in B for ownership of assets in A. If they transfer capital goods to A, the return on assets in A will fall, and residents of B who own assets in A will transfer some of them back to B. The net effect will be reduced foreign investment by residents of A in B, reduced foreign investment by residents of B in A, and a flow of capital goods into A.

Changes in the likelihood of expropriation of foreign investments will have similar effects. Expropriation can take various forms. When a country imposes interest rate ceilings on bank deposits, the depositors may view the act as expropriation. Limits on the freedom of an investor to transfer assets out of the country are a form of expropriation. A new government that takes away some of the wealth of members of the old government, or of groups that prospered under the old government, is, in effect, expropriating that wealth.

If country B changes to a government that favors taking assets within country B away from residents of other countries, capital goods will be transferred out of country B and both inward and outward foreign investment will decline. Residents of B will reduce their holdings of assets outside B because assets inside B will become more attractive as residents of other countries reduce their holdings of them.

Thus an increase in taxes on foreign investment or in the likelihood of expropriation of foreign investment will tend to reduce both gross and net foreign investment in a country. An increase in taxes on capital or in the likelihood of expropriation of capital without regard for who owns it will tend to reduce net inward foreign investment, while increasing gross outward foreign investment: Even the residents of the country will tend to shift the capital they own to other countries.

Although all kinds of taxes and controls will affect both net and gross foreign investment, lower taxes are not necessarily better than higher taxes, as we will see.

INTERNATIONAL DIVERSIFICATION

Suppose that both country A and country B have assets worth \$100 billion, partly because investment opportunities are the same in both. Suppose further that both the residents of A and the residents of B own \$100 billion in assets. Finally, suppose that the taxes on residents of A are just like the taxes on residents of B. In this situation, the residents of A may own only assets in A, while the residents of B may own only assets in B. But it will almost always be better for the residents of A to own some assets in B and for the residents of B to own some assets in A because of the benefits of international diversification.

The benefits to an investor of diversifying his portfolio across assets in different countries are similar to the benefits of diversifying his portfolio across assets in different industries within a country. A decline in the value of assets in one country may be offset by an increase in the value of assets in another country. For a given level of expected return, an investor who diversifies across countries will find that he has less risk than an investor who diversifies only within his own country.

We are not talking here about the investor's ability to concentrate his portfolio in a country that is likely to do better than other countries in the short run, and to switch his holdings successfully from one country to another as his expectations change. There is no evidence that investors are able to do this, and investors as a group can't switch their portfolios from one country to another because all assets in each country must always be held by someone.

We are talking about keeping a portfolio invested in assets of different countries. Normally, this strategy implies that an investor will not sell his investments in a given country to buy assets in another country. He may sell them to get money to spend, or to avoid or take advantage of a change in tax laws. But he does not have to have high turnover in his investment portfolio to get the benefits of international diversification.

In fact, in the absence of special taxes on investment across national boundaries and of the threat of expropriation, if investors agree on the prospects for investments in each country they should hold a piece of the same portfolio—the world market portfolio of risky assets. The world market portfolio contains all risky assets in every country. If the U.S. has risky assets worth 10 times as much as the risky assets in Japan, then both a U.S. investor and a Japanese investor would have 10 times as much invested in U.S. risky assets as in Japanese risky assets. The Japanese investor would invest much more abroad than at home.

In practice, of course, there are many reasons why an investor will hold a share of the world market portfolio. Many countries have taxes or controls that restrict inward or outward foreign investment. And many assets, such as personal property and claims on an individual's future income, are not for sale.

Nevertheless, the amount of international investment we would expect in an unrestricted world is enormous. To get the benefits of international diversification, most investors would keep most of their wealth in foreign risky assets. This is why we say that, what we have to understand is not why foreign investment occurs, but why it isn't much more common.

THE DISTRIBUTION OF INFORMATION

Investors may not agree about the prospects for assets in different countries.* In particular, there may be systematic differences between investors within a country and investors outside the country.

For example, at a given point in time investors outside the U.S. may think U.S. assets are going to do better than other assets, while investors within the U.S. think other assets are going to do better than U.S. assets. Thus foreigners will hold an unusually large share of U.S. assets, while U.S. residents will hold an unusually large share of foreign assets. In other words, gross foreign investment, both inward and outward, will be higher than usual. Similarly, if foreigners think the relative prospects for U.S. assets are worse than U.S. residents think they are, gross foreign investment will be reduced. Either way, there will be no obvious effect on net foreign investment.

Of course, it is not possible for everyone to think that the prospects for U.S. assets are infinitely better than the prospects for foreign assets. The price of U.S. assets would rise and the price of foreign assets would fall until investors were willing to hold all of both kinds of assets.

One important factor affecting systematic differences between investors is the distribution of information. Residents are generally more familiar with assets inside their country than with assets outside their country. Investors tend to concentrate their holdings in assets they are familiar with. Thus U.S. residents tend to hold more U.S. assets, and U.K. residents tend to hold more U.K. assets.

Ignorance about assets in other countries acts like a tax on investment in other countries: It tends to reduce both gross and net foreign investment. This effect is probably stronger than it should be. Since investors within a country usually have all available information about a company that operates in that country, their trading will cause the stock price to reflect all of the available information. Investors outside all the country can safely buy the stock; even if they don't have much information on the company, they can rely on those investors who do to keep the price fair.

So long as investors insist on buying the stock of familiar companies, they will benefit less than they should from international diversification (and from other kinds of diversification as well).

WILLINGNESS TO BEAR RISK

If investors in country A are more willing to bear risk than investors in country B, the former may hold most of the risky assets in both countries. We may find investors in A borrowing to buy risky assets and investors in B lending so they won't have to hold risky assets. In effect investors in A will borrow from investors in B, directly or indirectly, and will use the money to buy risky assets in B.

This in itself will have no obvious effect on net investment between A and B. It will, however, affect gross foreign investment and the composition of foreign investment in both countries. The existence of differences in willingness to bear risk will tend to increase

*We assume that investors judge investments in terms of both expected return and risk. When we say the prospects for a country's assets are better than the prospects for another country's assets, we mean the expected return compares more favorably with the return commensurate with the assets' risk levels.

gross foreign investment: The countries more tolerant of risk will tend to hold foreign equity assets, while the countries more averse to risk will tend to hold foreign debt assets.

If this tendency is extreme, the residents of B may hold short-term notes issued by the government of A, while the residents of A make direct investments in B and hold common stock of companies in B. Such a pattern implies nothing more nor less than differences in willingness to tolerate risk; the fact that equity investments may be classed as "long term" while government bills are classed as "short term" has no significance. The only broad economic effect this pattern will have is that residents of A will gain in wealth relative to residents of B in good times, while residents of B will gain in wealth relative to residents of A in bad times. Investors choosing between debt and equity assets, between direct and portfolio investment, or between various sectors of an economy are in effect exercising choices of taste that have no other identifiable economic consequences.

The fact that residents of A may be more willing to bear risk than residents of B does not mean they will do it for free. It merely means the expected return needed to induce residents of A to hold assets with a given amount of risk is lower than the expected return needed to induce residents of B to hold the same assets.

SHOULD FOREIGN INVESTMENT BE CONSTRAINED?

The biggest question of broad economic significance related to foreign investment is the choice between the benefits of free international investment and trade and the benefits of the government revenues derived from taxing inward or outward foreign investment and imports or exports. Sometimes constraints—in the form of direct or indirect taxation, expropriation or outright banning of foreign investment—will benefit a country's economy. At other times, the country that imposes constraints will find itself their victim.

FOREIGN INVESTMENT AND THE TRADE BALANCE

Suppose that an American oil billionaire retires to an island off the coast of France. All the food, jewels and other things that he buys are imported to the island. Since he continues to hold his wealth, which is located entirely outside of the island, he is a large outward foreign investor. Since goods and services flow into the island, but rarely flow out, the island shows a large trade deficit. Will he worry about this trade deficit? Probably not.

Foreign investment and changes in foreign investment are closely tied in with a country's trade balance. A country that holds large net outward foreign investments and consumes the return from these investments will tend to show a trade deficit. But since this deficit occurs because the country is so wealthy, it is hardly cause for alarm. Similarly, a country with large inward foreign investment may find itself with a large trade surplus. Since this is a result of the fact that the country is poorer than other countries, it is nothing to be pleased about.

Changes in foreign investment may also affect the trade balance. If a country raises its taxes on capital, capital goods will tend to flow out of the country, leading to a trade surplus. If a country's residents go through a period during which they save much more than residents of other countries, they will tend to export more (because they consume less of what they produce) and import less. This too will lead to a trade surplus. This surplus may turn to a deficit, however, when the country starts consuming the fruits of its foreign investment.

In general, when a resident of A acquires ownership of an asset in B, he must give up something in exchange. If he gives up a claim on an asset in A, then there is a change in gross foreign investment, but not in net foreign investment. This is true whether the claim he gives up is a common stock, a government bill or a claim on a demand deposit in one of A's banks. If he gives up goods or services, however, there will be a change in net foreign investment, and the transaction will form part of the trade balance. His country will have more of a surplus or less of a deficit than otherwise.

FREE TRADE AND INVESTMENT

The benefits of free foreign investment into or out of a country are like the benefits of free trade—often illusory. The potential benefits are there, if most countries negotiate a balanced reduction in barriers to free trade and investment. But if a single country unilaterally reduces its barriers to trade or investment, other countries may gain more than all the benefits: The country that made the move may end up worse off.

A country can profit from such trade restrictions as taxing foreign investment or expropriating property. The clearest example of this is the oil exporting nations. Until recently, they had relatively free trade and investment, and they were poor. Now they have heavy export taxes and have discouraged inward foreign investment by expropriating foreign property without adequate compensation. And they are rich.

How can we induce them to lower their barriers to free trade and investment? We can't because we have nothing to offer in exchange, except perhaps outright cash grants. To be in a position to negotiate, we must set up barriers ourselves. The most direct way to do that is to start taxing imports of oil. (While it would be nice to tax investments in oil exporting countries, it would be impossible because these investments can be made indirectly.)

If we put a tax on imports of oil equal to the export tax imposed by the producing countries, we will have something to bargain with. If other consuming countries impose a similar tax, we would have a good collective bargaining position. The tax would hurt some individuals and some sectors of the economy, but would permit general tax cuts that would benefit most individuals and most sectors.

The natural countermeasure to someone else's tax is a tax of your own on exactly the same transaction. If France taxes exports of wine, the U.S. can tax imports of wine. If Canada taxes investments by U.S. residents in Canada, the U.S. can tax the same investments. Countertaxing, by increasing the damage done by taxation, should make it easier to negotiate reductions in both taxes. You can't win a tariff war by refusing to fight. If someone else imposes a tax in spite of your warnings, you must impose one too, (or threaten to do so) to show you mean business. Only then can you negotiate a general reduction in taxes on international transactions.

If another country subsidizes foreign investment or exports, however, you should not retaliate: You should rejoice and pretend not to notice. If it bans certain types of foreign investment, you will not have to impose a tax or a ban of your own to have a basis for negotiation. A ban will not, as a tax does, yield any direct benefits for the country imposing it.

Taxation of international trade and investment causes distortions but, then, any taxation causes distortions. It is not obvious that modest levels of taxation of international transactions are always worse than low or no taxes.

EMPLOYMENT, INFLATION AND THE BALANCE OF PAYMENTS

Employment, inflation and the balance of payments are three subjects generally irrelevant to discussions of foreign investment. We don't know enough about the relation between these factors and foreign investment to be able to take them into account.

We can make a few partial statements about employment. If, by imposing a tax on capital, a country drives physical capital out, thus reducing net inward foreign investment, it will probably reduce wages and employment. The less capital per worker, the less certain his employment and the lower his wages are likely to be. Offsetting this effect, however, will be the proceeds of the tax on capital. It may be hard to say which of these effects is more important.

Since we don't know what causes increases or decreases in the rate of inflation, we don't know how foreign investment fits into the picture. All existing theories of inflation violate the assumption that investors constantly try to take advantage of any profit opportunities they see. Furthermore, it is not at all clear what harm inflation does, or what harm changes in the rate of inflation do. We know that some people gain at the expense of others, but that is common to all economic phenomena. We don't know if there are any general gains from better control of inflation, in the sense that there are general gains from free trade and investment.

The balance of payments is the most mysterious concept of all. We don't even know how to define it meaningfully, let alone how to measure it. And for every proposed definition, we are uncertain about whether we would rather have a surplus, a deficit or neither. If accumulation of gold represents a balance of payments surplus, is that good? Do we want to hold gold rather than productive assets? If we don't have gold, can we settle our international accounts? Should we count foreign securities of some sort as reserves along with gold? If so, where do we draw the line, and why? Why not include all foreign securities? Why not domestic securities, too? Why not the ability to issue domestic securities in the future? The list of questions is endless.

OBJECTIVES OF DIRECT VERSUS PORTFOLIO INVESTMENT

In a world where investors try to maximize the returns on their investments, the objectives of direct and portfolio investment will be the same. An investor will want to maximize the value of the enterprise in which he holds shares, whether he holds two shares or all shares.

If foreigners gain control of a U.S. company and then try to hurt U.S. residents by interfering in some way with the operations of the company, they will almost always hurt themselves more than they hurt the company's customers. The customers can go to a competitor, but the value of the company will decline sharply, costing the foreigners much of the value of their investment.

If foreigners gain control of a U.S. company and move some of its operations abroad, despite the fact that those operations can be done at lower cost in the U.S., the foreigners will again be the biggest losers. The company will lose sales to its competitors, and the value of its shared will decline.

On the other hand, if some of the company's operations can be done at lower cost abroad, and the previous managers did nothing about it, then both the company's customers and its owners will be better off if the shifts are made. A transfer of ownership to foreigners may have the same benefits any transfer of ownership may have. When old ways are thrown out and new ways brought in, the company, its customers and its competitors' customers sometimes gain.

Of course, it is possible that foreign owners will try to appropriate some of the company's assets to their own benefit; this will hurt the company and the other shareholders. But this is a problem common to any company with minority shareholders who do not share in effective control of the company. The law provides solutions, at least in part, to problems of this kind. And foreign owners of shares in a U.S. company cannot usually escape U.S. law.

It is sometimes claimed that foreign investors take their profits home rather than reinvesting them. Whether they do or not depends on whether net inward foreign investment is increasing or decreasing. If it is increasing, profits are being reinvested. The more relevant point is that, with all foreign investment, foreigners *own* their profits. Even if they reinvest them, they continue to own them and the further profits they earn on them. But there is no difference between direct and portfolio investment in this respect. Foreign investors own their profits whether they come from majority or minority ownership of a firm.

INVESTMENT IN SPECIFIC SECTORS

Foreign investment will often be concentrated in certain industries or sectors of an economy, partly because foreigners will be more familiar with certain sectors and partly because they may be more optimistic about certain sectors. This concentration of foreign investment will tend to displace U.S. investment in those sectors but, if investors act sensibly, it will not increase the total amount invested in any sector.

Concentration of foreign investment within a sector does not have any apparent consequences. It is similar in its impact to concentration of investment in the shares of a single company. Foreigners can disrupt the sector in which they have large investments if they have sufficient control over the companies involved, but in doing so they will hurt themselves more than they hurt us.

For example, if they acquire control over all the companies that produce burglar alarms abroad, they will drive down the foreign price and drive up the domestic price. Since they will not be maximizing profits, they will lose the value of some of their investment. Other companies will start producing burglar alarms for the domestic market and will make extra profits because prices will be high. On balance, U.S. residents gain at the expense of foreigners.

Only where an industry is vital to our defense does there seem to be reason to restrict foreign investments. There are no obvious economic reasons for restricting the extent of foreign investments in most sectors.

2
Principles of International Portfolio Selection*

Donald R. Lessard

The logic of diversifying a portfolio across countries is no different than that of diversifying along any other dimension—whenever returns on different assets are not subject to exactly the same risks, the risks of a diversified portfolio can be less than the risks of the typical individual security. However, international diversification is of special interest for two reasons. First, empirical evidence suggests that it may represent one of the most powerful dimensions for risk reduction through diversification. Second, it is subject to a number of obstacles, including currency and political risks, additional taxes and transaction costs, less efficient markets, and, in some cases, outright barriers. Thus, international portfolio selection involves complex tradeoffs between the potential for reducing investment risk through diversification and the costs and risks unique to international investment. As a result, the ideal internationally diversified portfolio is likely to differ for investors with different preferences, different tax situations, and different beliefs about their ability to "beat the market" on one or another dimension.

This section reviews the logical evidence regarding international diversification, then explores the actual or perceived obstacles to cross-border investment and their implications for portfolio selection. A discussion of passive and active international investment strategies concludes. The emphasis is on equities, where diversification gains have been shown to be greatest, but discussion also encompasses international diversification of bonds and money market holdings.

GAINS FROM INTERNATIONAL DIVERSIFICATION

The Logic of Diversification

It is generally accepted that investors should and can expect higher rates of return on risky investments than they can earn on less risky investments. Thus the required *expected rate of return* on a particular investment will consist of the interest rate, reflecting time preference as well as a premium for inflation, and a risk premium.

$$R_j = r + \text{risk premium}$$

where R_j is the required rate of return on security j (a project, firm, or security issued by a firm) and r is the nominal interest rate on a riskless security.

As long as returns from different assets are not subject to exactly the same risks, the risk of a portfolio of these assets will be less than the risk of a typical security in the portfolio. This implies that the risk of an asset in the context of a well-diversified portfolio, termed its "systematic risk," will be less than its total risk. Recognizing this, risk-averse investors

---

*This article is reprinted, with permission, from Giddy and George, (eds) *International Finance Handbook,* New York: John Wiley & Sons, 1983.

EXHIBIT 1

Risk Reduction Through Diversification: The Domestic Case

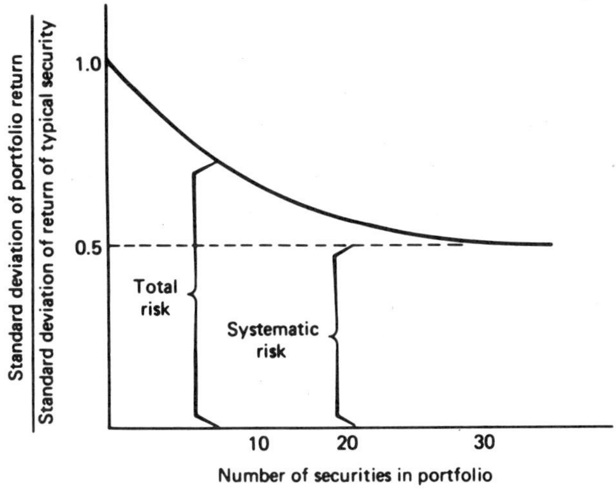

will hold diversified portfolios of assets. As a result, in equilibrium (when all investors have the same information and can adjust their portfolios without cost) the premiums that individuals demand for bearing risks will reflect only systematic risk, that portion of a risk that cannot be diversified away within an economy. The relationship between total risk, non-diversifiable risk and diversifiable risk, and the extent of risk reduction possible diversification is illustrated in Exhibit 1.

The Magnitude of Risk Reduction Through Diversification

The proportion of total risk that is systematic depends on the degree of correlation among the outcomes of the various securities. For the United States, the degree of *correlation* between returns on shares of individual firms and the completely diversified portfolio, the market aggregate of all risky securities, typically is around .5. This means that on average, the systematic risk of a security is 50% of its total risk. Figures for a variety of other countries are presented in Exhibit 2.

In general, the proportion of risk of securities that is systematic in other countries is higher than in the United States. This reflects the fact that these countries typically have a less diverse industrial base than the United States and, in some cases, a more volatile political environment. This is particularly true for less-developed countries where there is little room for risk reduction through domestic diversification.

When *diversification* is extended across national boundaries, a substantial proportion of the risk that is systematic within each country can be averaged out. Exhibit 3 illustrates this, comparing the risk reduction through diversification within the United States to that obtainable through international diversification. In the international case, portfolio risk drops to 33% of that of the typical stock, one third less than the U.S. figure.

The reason for this additional diversification is that returns on diversified single-country portfolios display considerable independence. This can be seen by examining the correlations between returns on the stock markets of seven major countries and the United States for different periods of time, reported in Exhibit 4. In interpreting these correla-

EXHIBIT 2

Risk Reduction Through Domestic Diversification

Country	Standard Deviation of Market Portfolio Divided by Standard Deviation of Typical Stock		
	Solnik (1967–73)	Lessard (1969–73)	Lessard (1958–68)
Argentina	—	—	.81
Brazil	—	—	.69
Chile	—	—	.71
Colombia	—	—	.69
France	.57	.68	—
Japan	—	.52	—
Switzerland	.66	.71	—
The Netherlands	.49	.63	—
United Kingdom	.59	.61	—
United States	.52	—	—
West Germany	.66	.66	—

Source B. H. Solnik, "Why Not Diversify Internationally?" *Financial Analysis Journal*, July–August (1974); D. R. Lessard, "World, National, and Industry Factors through International Diversification," *Financial Analysis Journal*, January–February (1976); and D. R. Lessard, "International Portfolio Diversification: A Multivariate Analysis for a Group of Latin American Countries," *Journal of Finance*, June (1973).

tions, it should be kept in mind that each of these single-market portfolios is completely diversified within the country, reflecting only 50% to 70% of the risk of the individual securities that it includes. As a result, a useful benchmark for comparison is the typical correlation between well-diversified portfolios such as mutual funds in the United States and the overall U.S. market portfolio. These correlations average around .9.

EXHIBIT 3

Risk Reduction Through National and International Diversification

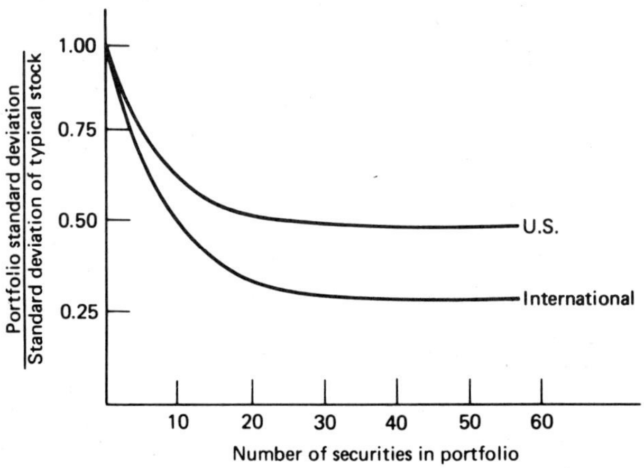

EXHIBIT 4

Correlations of Major World Equity Markets with the United States*

Country	1959–63	1964–68	1969–73	1973–74	1975–79
France	.45	.02	.20	.37	.32
Japan	.02	.07	.42	.39	.36
Switzerland	.52	.35	.49	.49	.45
The Netherlands	.67	.60	.54	.37	.50
United Kingdom	.29	.19	.41	.08	.34
West Germany	.48	.12	.41	.52	.38

*All returns measured in U.S. dollars, based on stock market data reported by *Capital International Perspective*, Capital International S.A., Geneva, Switzerland.

Expected Returns, the Other Part of the Equation

Risk reduction is nice, but it is only part of what an investor seeks by diversifying across national boundaries. The investor is interested in enhanced *risk-adjusted returns*, not in risk reduction per se. In an idealized, perfectly integrated, efficient world capital market, there would be no question that a world portfolio would dominate all single-country portfolios. In such a market, all securities would be priced to yield future total returns in line with their contribution to the risk of the world portfolio and any subportfolio not perfectly correlated with the world portfolio would be inferior in terms of the ratio of expected return to risk. In such a setting, the relation of the U.S. portfolio to the world portfolio would be much like that of a portfolio of, for example, Texas-based firms or firms in a single industry, such as utilities, to the U.S. market. No investor would hold such a portfolio unless they expected overwhelming returns on it relative to the overall market.

Of course, the world capital market does not match the ideal. There are barriers to cross-border investment and there is no proof that various national markets are always priced properly in relation to each other. Thus, investors must consider the returns they are likely to earn in each market in relation to the risk that these investments contribute to their portfolios.

Logue and Rogalski (1979) distinguish between two types of gains from international diversification—*beta gains* and *alpha gains*. Beta gains are those outlined in the previous sections—gains due to the fact that a significant fraction of those risks that cannot be diversified within a single country are diversifiable internationally. These gains exist whether or not shares in various countries are properly priced. Alpha gains, in contrast, arise when securities in one market are mispriced relative to others and are likely to provide unusually high returns. Of course, an alpha gain to, for example, a U.S. investor in European securities is an alpha loss to a European investor in U.S. securities. In order to identify potential alpha gains, investors can turn to two types of data: (1) returns that have been earned in the past, and (2) expectations for future returns based on fundamental analysis.

Historical returns over the last two decades generally are favorable to international diversification from a U.S. perspective. Solnik and Noetzlin (1982) show that realized returns on equities in all major countries but Italy and Spain exceeded those for the United States from 1970 to 1980. The Capital International EAFE (Europe, Australia, Far East) Index for example, which is capitalization weighted within and across countries and hence a good proxy for the non-U.S. equity market, posted an annualized 13.4% U.S. dollar return over this period compared to 6.8% for the United States. Hanna (1980) and Solnik and Noetzlin (1982) obtain similar results for bonds. From 1970 to 1980, total bond returns for all countries with well-developed bond markets except Canada exceeded those of the United States, typically at least doubling the 5.7% U.S. returns.

These high realized returns on foreign securities, though, do not represent a sound basis for estimating future returns for two reasons. First, in the case of equities, they cover a period of major opening of the international economy, which most benefited trading nations such as Japan and West Germany, as well as of the integration of the European economy, which certainly benefited those economies relative to others in the world system. While structural changes are likely over the next 10 years, they are unlikely to reoccur in the same pattern. In the case of bond returns, a large part of the higher foreign returns is attributable to the drop in the dollar. This event is unlikely to be repeated since this period covers the major transition from the dollar as a currency whose value was actively supported by such devices as the interest equalization tax, the temporary import surcharges, and constraints on capital movements, to one whose value is determined primarily by market forces. Second, and probably more important, if all investors believed that these situations would persist, everyone would try to tilt their portfolios toward non-U.S. securities. This, of course, would bid up these share and bond prices (lower bond interest rates) relative to U.S. securities, until the expected returns fell into line with the relative riskiness of each market.

Given the low likelihood that realized returns will provide reliable estimates of future returns, many analysts favor examining various fundamental indicators in order to estimate growth rates for various economies. The track record of such forecasting, however, is spotty. Further, even if reliable growth estimates can be obtained, it does not follow that the fast-growing countries represent more attractive investment options. The key question is whether or not the growth prospects for a country are properly reflected in the price of the shares of stocks from these countries. Thus, fundamental projections regarding economic performance will be relevant only to the extent that they are substantially different from the consensus projections regarding individual economies. Projections in line with the consensus will be fully discounted in securities' prices.

Other analysts focus on comparative *price earnings ratios* or apply dividend discount models to determine if shares in different markets are appropriately priced relative to each other. Since earnings typically are not comparable across countries due to differences in accounting practices and in rates of inflation, those comparisons are complex. While some analysts might be able to use them to identify alpha gains, there are no credible statistical demonstrations of this ability to date.

For these reasons, most economists prefer to emphasize beta gains as the basis for international investment. In so doing, they focus on the returns that investors could logically expect to earn if they all were to agree on future prospects and select portfolios accordingly. Under the simplifying assumptions that there are no barriers to cross-border investment in the form of additional costs or risks and that no investors have special forecasting skills, all investors would choose to hold the (world) market portfolio. Given that there are some barriers to international investment, though, the equilibrium structure of returns will not necessarily imply that all investors should hold the world market portfolio. With this more complex situation, different investors would choose to hold different portfolios. This point is also covered below when the effects of various obstacles to international investment are discussed.

Is the Home Bias of U.S. Investors Justified?

If the logic of capital market equilibrium is accepted, it is very hard to explain why U.S. investors have diversified so little overseas. In a recent study of U.S. pension funds, Ehrlich (1981) found that less than 2% of all U.S. assets were invested abroad—a far cry from the roughly 50% of world capitalization represented by non-U.S. markets. Investors of other countries also display strong home biases in their portfolio holdings. This implies that investors in aggregate bear much more risk than is necessary. In an example developed to illustrate required returns from a U.S. perspective, Lessard (1976) suggests that the expected annualized returns on U.S. holdings would have to exceed expectations on foreign securities by more than 3% to justify this extreme degree of home bias.

While some investors might forecast such a divergence based on their own estimates of future returns, there is no evidence that a significant proportion of investors possess this degree of forecasting skill. Incremental costs or risks, of course, might justify a home bias, but it is unlikely that they add up to 3% annually if investments are made over anything other than the shortest time periods.

An examination follows of the various incremental costs and risks associated with cross-border investments, costs and risks that are perceived by investors as obstacles to international diversification and that might explain some of the home bias.

OBSTACLES TO INTERNATIONAL INVESTMENT

Currency Risk

The prime motivation for diversifying a portfolio internationally is to improve the reward-to-risk tradeoff by taking advantage of the relatively low correlation among returns on assets of different countries. However, since international investment implies investing in assets that provide returns in a variety of currencies whose relative values can fluctuate, it involves taking *foreign exchange risks*. A key question facing the investor, then, is whether these exchange risks are so large as to offset the benefits of international diversification. A related question is, what—if any—special strategies should be followed to reduce the impact of foreign exchange risk?

There is no question that the volatility of currency movements has increased in recent years and that it is significant relative to the volatility of equity markets. Exhibit 5 shows the volatility of equity returns in local currency, the volatility of exchange rate changes, and the volatility of returns in dollars (standard deviation) for the major equity markets from 1970 to 1980.

In all cases, the dollar returns are more volatile than the local currency returns, although often by a very small margin relative to the volatility of the exchange rate. The reason for this is that the volatility of dollar returns depends not only on the volatility of local currency returns and exchange rate changes, but on the correlation between the two

EXHIBIT 5

Equity and Currency Volatility, 1970–80

Country	Return Volatility in Local Currency	Volatility of Exchange Rate	Return Volatility in US$
Australia	24.6	9.2	27.2
Belgium	13.3	11.0	18.8
Canada	18.9	4.2	20.3
France	22.0	10.2	25.8
Hong Kong	48.0	5.6	45.8
Italy	24.2	8.6	26.2
Japan	16.4	10.4	19.6
Singapore	35.8	6.5	36.0
Spain	16.7	9.1	20.3
Switzerland	16.8	14.7	21.4
The Netherlands	16.4	11.0	18.9
United Kingdom	28.9	8.9	31.6
United States	16.0	—	16.0
West Germany	13.9	11.9	18.4

Source B. H. Solnik, and B. Noetzlin, "Optimal International Asset Allocation: Lessons from the Past," *Journal of Portfolio Management*, 1981.

as well.* If local currency returns are independent of the exchange rate—in which case the share could be characterized as an instrument "denominated" in the local currency—the volatility of dollar returns would be substantially less than the sum of the underlying volatilities.† For West Germany, it would be 18.3, for Japan 19.4, for The Netherlands 19.8, for Switzerland 22.3, and for the United Kingdom 30.2. Most of the actual dollar volatilities are slightly lower than these figures, showing that local currency returns are slightly negatively related to movements in the currency. In the case of Hong Kong, though, dollar volatility is less than volatility in local terms, suggesting that returns on local shares can be more aptly characterized as "dollar-denominated" than as "denominated" in the local currency. (For the 1973–77 period, Lessard, 1979, identified several cases where the dollar volatility of share returns was less than the volatility measured in the local currency.)

This result has important implications. To the extent that local currency share prices are negatively correlated with the exchange rate, the exchange risk faced by the foreign investor is reduced. By the same token, the local investor is exposed to some exchange risk.

There are two other aspects of currency risk that must be taken into account. One is that currency risk as measured above is a valid concept only if investors judge risk and return in nominal terms in their local currency. Given the substantial volatility of inflation in most economies, this is unrealistic. A pension fund, for example, should judge

*Formally, $\sigma^2(R_\$) = \sigma^2(R_L) + \sigma^2(R_s) + 2\rho(R_L, R_s)\,\sigma(R_L)\,\sigma(R_s)$, where $R_\$$ is the dollar return, R_L the local currency equity return, and R_s the change in the exchange rate.

†From the above formula, $\sigma^2(R_\$) = \sigma^2(R_L) + \sigma^2(R_s)$ when R_L and R_s are uncorrelated.

returns after adjustment for inflation. If this adjustment is made, exchange risk typically will be reduced and domestic securities will be viewed as having significant inflation risk. The choice of perspectives, however, does not make too much difference in the estimation of gains from diversification across equity markets, since the variance of stock prices is largely unrelated to changes in exchange rates or inflation. With bonds or money market instruments, though, which are less volatile in nominal terms but which bear a closer relationship to changes in purchasing power of the local currency, the choice of the appropriate perspective is critical.

Another consideration is that currency risks can be hedged by borrowing in the local currency or selling it forward. Thus, the benefits of international equity investment can be obtained without any significant currency exposure. (Here reference is made solely to the risk of fluctuations in exchange rates, not to the possibility of foreign exchange controls. The latter are discussed under "Political or Sovereign Risk," this section.)

This expected *cost of hedging* in the case of borrowing is the difference between the interest differential of the two currencies and the expected percentage change in the exchange rate. The cost of hedging through forward contracts is the difference between the forward discount or premium and the expected percentage change in the exchange rate. Barring controls on capital flows or on access to forward markets, these two costs will be identical through the interest rate parity relationship.

The cost of hedging is often incorrectly defined as the interest differential itself or the forward discount or premium, with no consideration of the expected change in exchange rates. This incorrect definition often leads to statements that hedging is prohibitively expensive and rests on the implicit assumption that foreign exchange markets are inefficient and do not reflect anticipations regarding a currency's future.

The incorrect definition of the cost of hedging is often accompanied by a view that shares in countries with strong currencies are good investments, while those in countries with weak currencies are poor ones. If the strength of weakness of a currency is generally recognized, it will be reflected in interest rates and forward rates as well as in equity prices and hence will have no bearing on the attractiveness of the investment.

In summary, *currency risk* is not a significant obstacle to international investment (see Lessard and Stulz, 1984, for a more extensive discussion). First, shares are not denominated in the local currency and hence are not necessarily more risky in a foreign reference currency than in the local currency. Second, currency risk should be considered in light of its effect on real (i.e., constant purchasing power) returns to the investor. From this perspective, currency risk typically is smaller than when returns are viewed in nominal terms. Third, regardless of the first two points, currency risk can be isolated through hedging and the risk-reducing benefits of international equity diversification can be obtained without significant currency exposure. (Since the local currency value of shares is volatile, currency exposure cannot be completely hedged. However, with frequent revisions in hedge positions, most of this volatility can be eliminated.) Finally, expected currency movements that are reflected in interest rates and forward rates have no bearing on investment decisions. The same arguments apply to bond and money market investment. However, when hedged, foreign money market investments become dollar money market instruments and bonds become much less volatile. Thus, when viewed properly, currency risks can reduce the attractiveness of money market and bond diversification much more than is the case for equities.

Political or Sovereign Risk

Political or sovereign risk is viewed by many as a major obstacle to international investment. Clearly, *political factors* are a major determinant of the attractiveness for investment in any country. Countries viewed as likely candidates for internal political upheaval or with a pronounced trend toward elimination of the private sector will be unattractive to all investors, foreign and domestic alike. As a result, securities of these countries should be priced accordingly, and little new private real investment will take place. The general question of the impact of political risk on international investment strategies can be broken down into three specific questions: (1) Are political risks properly reflected in securities' prices? (2) Do they differ from the perspectives of foreign and domestic investors? (3) If so, what does this imply about international investment strategies? There is little research relating to any of these questions. Most research on sovereign risk focuses on the conflict between host governments and firms with direct investment; little has been directed at portfolio investment. Further, what little has been done relates primarily to bank loans to developing countries.

In judging whether political risks are properly reflected in prices, the only available evidence is that relating to the overall efficiency of markets. This evidence suggests that information is reflected rapidly in major markets, and that realized returns, in general, bear a reasonable relationship to the risks taken.

The key consideration is that local investors as well as foreign investors typically are affected by these risks. There is no reason to believe that local investors will be systematically optimistic regarding their country's future. When political risks increase significantly, such investors will attempt to diversify from the home market as rapidly as will foreigners. As a result, prices will fall until someone will be satisfied to hold the securities of a risky country. One case where this will not be true, and where foreign investors might be able to shift political losses to local investors, is when domestic investors are prevented from liquidating their domestic holdings or from purchasing foreign assets by national regulations or moral suasion. In such cases, the market prices may not reflect generally shared views of the political situation. Of course, if foreign investors are constrained by the same regulations, then all investors lose. A careful evaluation of the relative flexibility of domestic and foreign investment, therefore, is a key element in determining whether political risks jeopardize cross-border holdings. The risk of currency controls is one of the few political risks that is borne primarily by foreign investors.

In some cases, political risks might even favor foreign investors relative to domestic investors. This is because risks are domestic phenomena that can be diversified away internationally. As a result they will have a greater impact on the risk of a domestic investor whose portfolio is concentrated in home assets than an internationally diversified investor. Accordingly, domestic shares might well be more attractive to foreign than domestic investors in periods of perceived high political risk.

Limited Size and Depth of Foreign Markets

A recurrent objection to international diversification is that the practical scope for foreign investing is limited. Many markets are perceived to be small, less liquid, and less efficient than those of the United States. Some investors question whether foreign markets are large enough and active enough to allow them to accumulate meaningful positions and realize profits from them. The fact is that foreign markets have come of age. Exhibits 6

EXHIBIT 6

Percentage Breakdown of World Stock Market Capitalization

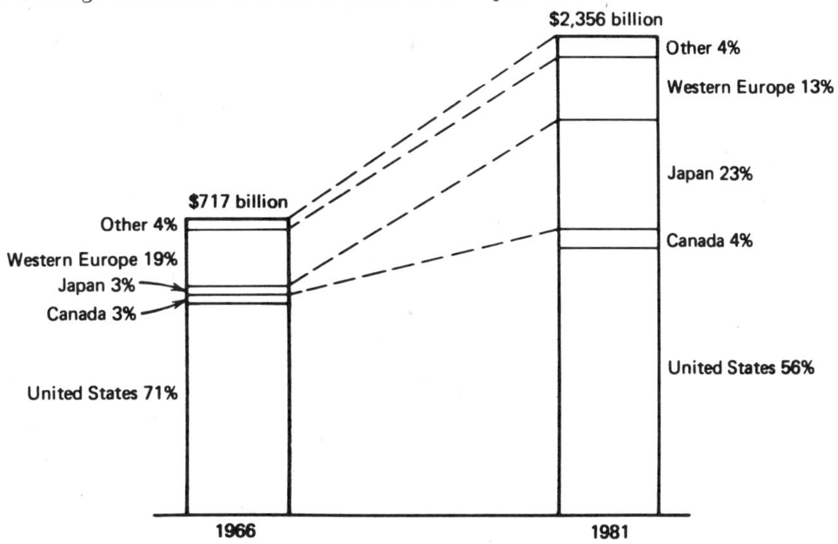

Source *Capital International Perspective*, March 1976 and March 1981.

and 7 illustrate the growth of these markets since 1966 in terms of capitalization and turnover. The growth of turnover in foreign markets is especially striking—increasing from 24% of the world total in 1966 to 46% in 1980. This view is further reinforced by an examination of the number of companies with market capitalizations in excess of $2

EXHIBIT 7

Percentage Breakdown of World Share Turnover

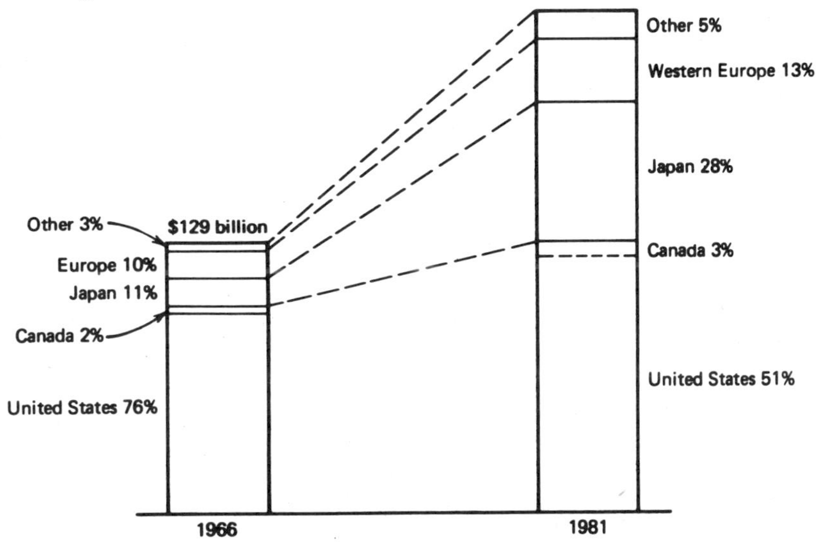

Source *Capital International Perspective*, March 1976 and March 1981.

EXHIBIT 8

Nationality of Firms with Capitalization in Excess of $2 Billion

United States	93
Japan	35
United Kingdom	9
Canada	9
West Germany	9
Switzerland	5
South Africa	3
Hong Kong	2
Australia	1
France	1
Italy	1
The Netherlands	1

Source *Capital International Perspective*, Geneva, Switzerland, 1981.

billion, as shown in Exhibit 8. There are 65 such firms outside of North America, compared with 93 in the United States and nine in Canada (*Capital International Perspective*, 1981).

Undoubtedly, there are many foreign stocks whose total capitalization and turnover are too limited for them to be of interest to most U.S. institutional investors. Further, in many markets—particularly the Japanese and West German—market capitalizations are often misleading indicators of an issue's marketability because a large proportion of the shares might be owned by banks, holding companies, or other concerns. However, these considerations do not necessarily imply that these markets are less attractive to foreign institutional investors than to local investors. In fact, just the opposite might be the case. Domestic investors who depend primarily on their own market for liquidity and diversification are likely to be more constrained by these limitations than international investors who, through diversification, can virtually eliminate the nonmarket risk unique to individual companies even if they hold only a small number of shares in each market. International investors also do not have to rely on any single market for liquidity and, as a result, can take a longer view in regard to each market and security, even though they will wish to realize profits within a reasonable period in each market and currency.

The constraints on diversification within a single market become apparent when one considers the degree of concentration within various markets. In many markets, such as Belgium, The Netherlands, and Switzerland, as well as in West Germany, a small number of shares account for a major portion of the value of all shares in most smaller markets. Considering that 30 or more issues in about equal proportions are necessary to diversity away most of the specific (nonmarket) risk within a single national market, even a moderate-sized domestic fund will find it difficult to achieve a high degree of diversification in such markets. This fact implies that domestic investors in such markets will want to hold foreign assets and that a substantial proportion of the shares of the dominant countries should be held by foreigners even if the systematic risk component of returns in the local economy is closely related to the world market index.

Relative Efficiency of Foreign Markets

A closely related concern is that of *market efficiency*. Although less efficiency can be desirable from an active investment manager's perspective because it implies that superior performance is possible, it also puts the international investor at a disadvantage relative to the domestic investor, who has greater knowledge and better information.

An efficient market is one where new information is quickly reflected in securities' prices and hence it is unlikely that any single investor will beat the market. Various types of tests can be performed to judge the degree of efficiency of a market. Three degrees of efficiency have typically been distinguished by researchers: (1) weak-form efficiency, where no useful information can be defined from the past sequence of stock prices, (2) semistrong efficiency, where it is impossible to exploit publicly available information to beat the market, and (3) strong-form efficiency, where all information is fully reflected in prices and no one can beat the market.

Most empirical research has focused on testing for the weak form of efficiency—whether sequences of price changes are related. The usual criterion of efficiency is whether share prices follow a random walk or martingale process (random walk with a trend). If so, momentum models (a type of technical analysis) are of no value. Researchers have performed some tests of the major European markets, and recently these same tests have been extended to the major Asian markets. The studies find that price changes show greater serial correlation in foreign markets than in the U.S. market. However, the magnitude of these departures from randomness typically is not sufficient to yield gains from trading strategies based on past prices.

Tests of the semistrong form of efficiency are substantially more complex. Since most tests involve comparing the results of a particular strategy with some benchmark portfolio, they involve joint tests of a particular equilibrium risk return relationship and the ability to outperform the standard implied by that relationship. This is a difficult problem even within a single country and most tests for superior performance in the United States have been called into question by Roll (1977) and others. For internationally diversified portfolios, the problem is even more difficult. The benchmark is undefined and it is difficult to attribute the performance to various testable aspects, such as country selection, stock selection within countries, and currency selection, because of the interaction among the three. Since most managed European portfolios include some foreign securities, the problem applies to tests of efficiency in these markets as well.

In order to be valid, tests of performance must compare portfolio results with benchmark results for the same universe of securities. If a study shows that domestically managed funds outperform the market index, care must be taken to ensure that their performance does not reflect foreign holdings or domestic securities not included in the benchmark index. Taking this into account, there appear to be no credible studies that show consistently superior performance by managed funds in many foreign markets. Since many European funds contain shares listed outside the base country, foreign shares listed on the local exchange, and bonds, tests of efficiency for any single market are extremely difficult.

In summary, studies of foreign markets suggest that they generally can be considered to be efficient in the sense that prices adjust rapidly to new information and relationships between risk and return are consistent with those predicted by capital market theory.

Whether they are efficient to the extent that most professional managers are unable to consistently outperform appropriate market benchmarks remains an open question. However, the results available suggest that the ability to consistently outperform the market is, at best, uncommon.

Taxes, Restrictions on Ownership, and Other Institutional Obstacles

There are several *institutional obstacles* that can make international investing costly, undesirable, or, in some cases, impossible. They include formal barriers to international transactions, such as exchange controls that do not allow investors in one country to invest overseas or that limit overseas investment to a fixed pool (such as those applied in the United Kingdom through 1979),* double taxation of portfolio income for certain investors in particular countries,† and restrictions on ownership of securities according to the nationality of the investor. These obstacles also include informal barriers, such as the difficulty of obtaining information about a market, differences in reporting practices that make international comparisons difficult, and, perhaps most important, subtle impediments to foreign investment based on traditional practice.

Few research studies have been conducted on the impact of these institutional and governmental obstalces on either appropriate investment strategies or portfolio performance. One study of U.K. investment trusts found that they benefited little from international diversification and attributed this to the costs imposed by the U.S. foreign investment controls (Guy, 1978). Whether these costs were necessary or whether they reflected unnecessary trading remains an open question. The U.S. interest equalization tax clearly hindered overseas investment by U.S. individual and institutional investors and, undoubtedly, the difficulty of buying into the Japanese market in the mid-1960s meant that its subsequent performance was academic to most U.S. investors.

A major implication of the existence of such obstacles is that even if one assumes an integrated, efficient world capital market, investors with different *legal domiciles* or *tax situations* might want to hold different. However, it is difficult to determine by how much such optimal portfolios portfolios should differ from the world market portfolio. This would depend on the balancing of the effect of the obstacles against the gains from more complete diversification. This is an area of active research and at least two theoretical studies that have explicitly introduced barriers into models of world capital market equilibrium show that investors should not hold the world market portfolio (Black, 1974, and Stulz, 1981a). Instead, investors should hold relatively high proportions of their home market portfolios and should select foreign assets least like assets from their home market. More research, both in terms of quantifying specific obstacles and ascertaining their impact on capital market equilibrium, is required before optimum international portfolios can be specified for particular investors.

*Under this system, U.K. investors seeking to invest abroad were required to purchase currency from an investment currency pool. As a result, the pound/dollar exchange rate paid to invest abroad rose to an often substantial premium relative to the regular exchange rate. Further, on liquidation, a portion of the proceeds had to be converted at the regular, typically less favorable, exchange rate. See Brealey and Cooper (1981) for an insightful analysis.

†United States pension funds, for example, might have to pay a withholding tax on income from some foreign countries but have no U.S. tax against which it can be credited. This problem is exacerbated by the movement of European countries toward the imputation of corporate taxes, which results in a different tax on foreign investors.

Conclusions Regarding Obstacles to International Investment

When examined closely, many of the obstacles to international investment are less serious than commonly thought. This does not mean that there are no difficulties, but it does appear that the advantages of diversification, when properly pursued, outweigh the drawbacks.

Regarding the major specific areas of concern, currency risks do not appear to reduce significantly the gains from broadly based diversification. There is little reason to believe that political risks are systematically ignored by local investors or that they weigh more heavily on foreign investors. Finally, major foreign markets are not as narrow or inefficient as might generally be perceived.

CONCLUSIONS

Evidence suggests that the potential for risk reduction through international diversification is large, but that investors exploit it only to a limited extent. The examination of various potential obstacles to international investment explaining this home bias suggests that currency risk should not be a large factor, the size or efficiency of foreign markets should have little bearing, and political risks should matter only to the extent that foreign investors can be singled out effectively for discriminatory treatment. The primary remaining explanations are explicit barriers to international investment in the form of discriminatory taxation, controls on inward or outward foreign investments, local regulation of institutional investors, or simply tradition. While barriers undoubtedly do exist, theoretical models suggest that it is hard to attribute to them the full degree of homeward bias. Thus, investors who overcome the traditional resistance to international investment should be able to expect a significantly superior risk-adjusted performance than investors who restrict themselves to their home markets.

Because of barriers and currency considerations, investors pursuing *passive strategies*—strategies that do not depend on forecasting skills—will not necessarily want to invest in the world market portfolio or even in a portfolio such as that represented by Capital International's EAFE Index for their foreign holdings. In any market where they face higher costs or higher taxes than local investors, or where local investors are restricted from investing abroad, foreign investors should buy the securities least like those available in markets where they have relatively favorable access. For example, they should purchase shares of major multinationals at home and in other markets fully open to them and concentrate on domestically oriented firms in more restricted markets. To the extent that the foreign currency positions implicit in the resulting portfolio differ from their desired currency positions, they should adjust that dimension through borrowing or forward contracts.

Investors who believe that they can forecast along one or more dimensions will pursue *active strategies*. The key element in designing effective active strategies is to be sure that bets are actually placed on the dimension of returns for which the investor disagrees with the general expectations embedded in market prices. For example, if an investor believes that the Dutch economy will perform much better than generally expected, he or she should not simply add more Dutch shares to the portfolio. Many of these shares are of multinationals that depend only to a small extent on the state of the home economy and might even be negatively affected by a strong local economy. Similarly, if the investor wishes to place a currency bet, to do so by shifting equity holdings is both costly and inefficient. Equity market transition costs far exceed those in money markets and although equity returns do have an implicit currency component, they carry many other risks as well.

These considerations make it clear that both the theory and practice of international investing are in their infancy and that the rewards to developing more refined passive and active strategies should be substantial.

REFERENCES

Black, F., "International Capital Market Equilibrium with Investment Barriers," *Journal of Financial Economics* (1974).

Ehrlich, E. E., "International Diversification by United States Pension Funds," *Federal Reserve Bank of New York Quarterly*, Autumn (1981).

Guy, J. R. F., "The Performance of the British Investment Trust Industry," *Journal of Finance*, May (1978).

Hanna, J., "Why Americans Should Have Diversified," *Euromoney*, March (1980).

Lessard, D. R., "World, Country, and Industry Relationships in Equity Returns: Implications for Risk Reduction through International Diversification," *Financial Analysts Journal*, January–February (1976).

Lessard, D. R., and R. Stulz, "Currency Considerations in International Equity Investment," Unpublished working paper, Massachusetts Institute of Technology Sloan School (1984).

Logue, D. E., and R. J. Rogalski, "Offshore Alphas: Picking Countries Instead of Stocks," *Journal of Portfolio Management*, Winter (1979).

Roll, R., "A Critique of the Asset Pricing Theory Tests," *Journal of Financial Economics*. Vol. 4, (1977).

Stulz, R. M., "On the Effects of Barriers to International Investment," *Journal of Finance*, September (1981). (a)

3

International Equity and Bond Returns*

Roger C. Ibbotson, Richard C. Carr and Anthony W. Robinson

The opportunity set for United States investors includes equities and bonds in foreign countries as well as those in the United States. Non-U.S. equities and bonds make up a large and growing proportion of world wealth and have had high returns. We regard equities and bonds in all countries as part of a world market that is at least somewhat integrated, although the flow of capital between countries may be inhibited by taxes, regulations and political and exchange risk.

It is instructive to examine aggregate market values and returns in the world market because we want to know the dimensions of the market in which we invest and because we want to be able to compare the realized returns from a wide variety of alternative investments. Furthermore, the comparative behavior of securities in different countries tells us about the extent of integration in world capital markets—that is, the extent to which goods, capital and labor actually cross national boundaries in response to profit opportunities.

The development of a world market for equities and bonds raises some challenging issues in financial economics. If there are no barriers to international investment (i.e., if national and currency borders are irrelevant), then world capital market results should reflect the traditional proportionality and parity theorems expounded by Irving Fisher and others. The world market is integrated only to the extent that national and currency borders actually are irrelevant. The data on non-U.S. asset returns presented here, while not formally testing proportionality and parity theorems, will suggest conclusions as to the realism of the parity assumptions.

This article presents annual total returns on equities and bonds, along with correlations and regression results, exchange and inflation rates and some other macroeconomic data, for 18 countries for the period 1960 through 1980. It also compares long-term and short-term yields, exchange returns and inflation rates on a country-by-country basis, suggests interpretations of the data in the light of intranational and international parity theorems, and discusses the implications of international diversification and currency risk for the United States investor.

---

*This article is abridged and reprinted, with permission, from *Financial Analysts Journal,* July–August 1982. pp. 61–83. See original for more complete year-by-year data and description of data sources and methodology.

[1]Footnotes appear at end of article.

Equities: Returns and Aggregate Market Values

The composition of the world equity and bond market at the end of 1980 is depicted in Figure A. Bonds make up a slightly larger share than equities. The United States represents more than half of the equity market, but less than half of the bond market. It should be noted that, as U.S.-based researchers, we have access to more information on the United States than on foreign countries. Our estimate of U.S. equity aggregate market value includes the New York and American stock exchanges and nearly every stock of any size traded over-the-counter; the non-U.S. equity measures are not as broad. A further caveat is that some companies traded in both the United States and a foreign stock exchange may be double-counted.

Figure B shows the market values in U.S. dollars of the various equity markets as of the end of 1980. The U.S. equity market is by far the largest, comprising more than half the world market. Japan has the largest non-U.S. equity market, representing 15 per cent of the world equities and 34 per cent of the non-U.S. market. The United Kingdom has the

FIGURE A

Size of World Equity and Bond Markets at the End of 1980 in Billions of U.S. Dollars (World Total = $5,289.9 Billion)

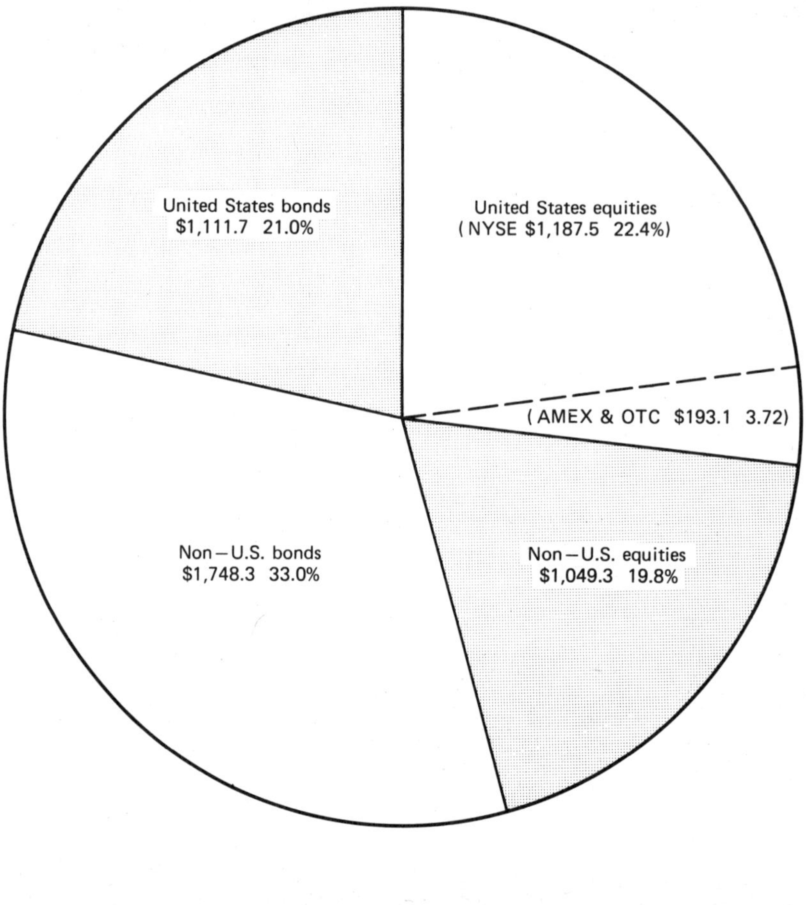

FIGURE B

Market Values of Non-U.S. Equities at the End of 1980 in Billions of U.S. Dollars (Non-U.S. Equity Total = $1,049.3 Billion)

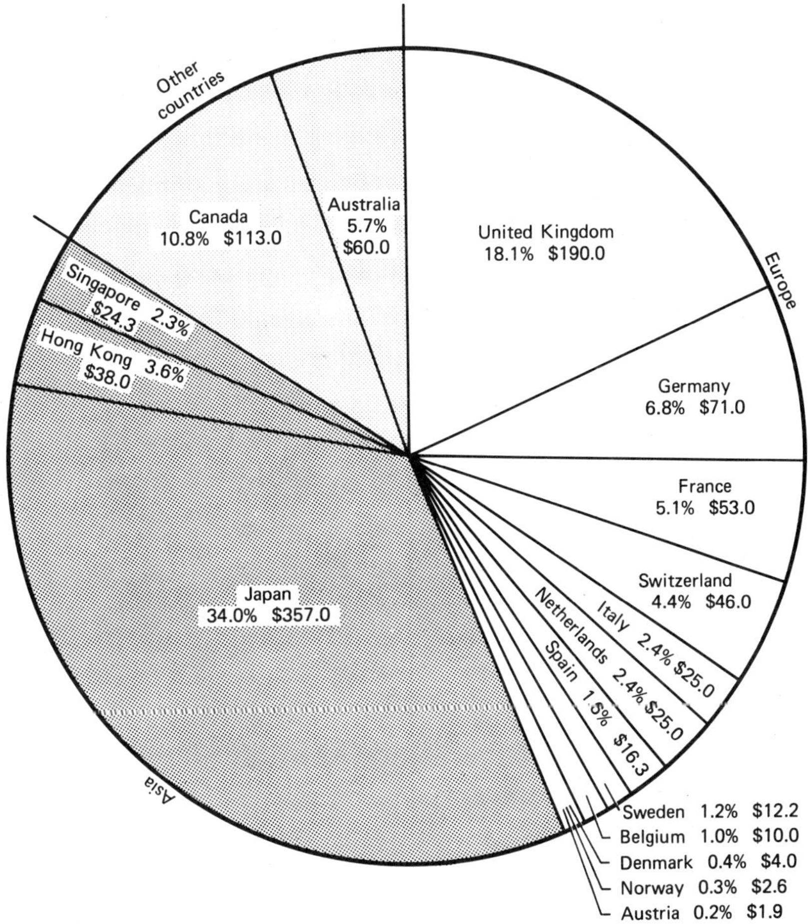

largest equity market in Europe. The world equity market had a value of approximately $2.4 trillion at the end of 1980.

Table 1 presents summary statistics for country-by-country and portfolio returns on equities. We formed market-value-weighted portfolios of various regions (Europe, Asia, etc.) and of the world, using as the weight of a country for a given year its aggregate market value at the end of the previous year. All returns are converted to U.S. dollars and include both capital appreciation and income.

In terms of the cumulative wealth index results, Asian equities were the best performers over the period, with $1.00 invested at the end of 1959 growing to $22.29 by the end of 1980. This extraodinary growth was not without substantial risk: The standard deviation of annual returns was 33.0 per cent for Asian equities, the highest of any equity portfolio. It should be noted that the return achieved by Asian equities—15.9 per cent per year compounded over the period—is not unprecedented in equity markets. The U.S. market,

TABLE 1

World Equities: Summary Statistics, 1960–1980

Asset	*Annual Returns in U.S. Dollars* Compound Return (%)	Arithmetic Mean (%)	Standard Deviation (%)	*Year-End Wealth Index 1959 = 1.00*	*1980 Year-End Value In Billions U.S. $*
Non-U.S. Equities:					
Europe					
Austria	9.1	10.3	16.9	6.23	1.9
Belgium	9.2	10.1	13.8	6.39	10.0
Denmark	9.5	11.4	24.2	6.72	4.0
France	6.2	8.1	21.4	3.56	53.0
Germany	8.3	10.1	19.9	5.32	71.0
Italy	2.4	5.6	27.2	1.63	25.0
Netherlands	9.3	10.7	17.8	6.45	25.0
Norway	10.3	17.4	49.0	7.81	2.6
Spain	8.4	10.4	19.8	5.49	16.3
Sweden	8.4	9.7	16.7	5.40	12.2
Switzerland	10.2	12.5	22.9	7.74	46.0
United Kingdom	10.0	14.7	33.6	7.39	190.0
Europe Total	8.4	9.6	16.2	5.47	457.0
Asia					
Hong Kong*	24.6	40.3	61.3	11.24	38.0
Japan	15.6	19.0	31.4	20.86	357.0
Singapore*	23.2	37.0	66.1	9.96	24.3
Asia Total	15.9	19.7	33.0	22.29	419.3
Other					
Australia	9.8	12.2	22.8	7.12	60.0
Canada	10.7	12.1	17.5	8.47	113.0
Other Total	10.6	11.9	17.1	8.24	173.0
Non-U.S. Total Equities	10.6	11.8	16.3	8.23	1049.3
U.S. Total Equities	8.7	10.2	17.7	5.78	1380.6
World Total Equities	9.3	10.5	15.8	6.47	2429.9

*1970–1980.

as measured by the Standard & Poor's index with dividends reinvested, returned 15.6 per cent per year over the 21-year period 1943–63. A similar return was earned in U.S. equities in 1908–28, but in that instance, the rise was followed by a crash.

European countries' compound annual returns ranged from a high of 10.3 per cent in Norway to a low of 2.4 per cent in Italy. The European portfolio had a relatively low compound annual return of 8.4 per cent. Returns in the United States, Canada and Australia were higher at 8.7, 10.7 and 9.8 per cent per year, respectively. The world equity portfolio returned 9.3 per cent per year, with $1.00 invested at the end of 1959 growing to $6.47 by the end of 1980.

Table 2 shows year-by-year total returns in per cent, for each country and for the various portfolios. Examination of the year-by-year data reveals some interesting market facts. One-year individual country returns ranged from a high of +211 per cent for Singapore in 1972 to a low of −60 per cent for Hong Kong in 1974. Italy's cumulative

TABLE 2

World Equities: Year-by-Year U.S.-Dollar-Adjusted Total Returns (in per cent)

	World Equities											
	Non-U.S.											
	Europe											
Year	*Austria*	*Belgium*	*Denmark*	*France*	*Germany*	*Italy*	*Netherlands*	*Norway*	*Spain*	*Sweden*	*Switzerland*	*United Kingdom*
1960	52.28	-7.99	3.77	6.72	42.32	46.18	3.24	12.24	10.14	5.51	43.82	0.13
1961	41.14	22.84	3.81	13.62	2.14	14.73	12.49	18.14	36.42	5.57	54.89	12.56
1962	-12.76	-1.99	8.12	11.38	-21.70	-10.44	-5.39	-15.43	19.65	12.47	-8.51	4.76
1963	-4.28	18.06	17.77	-14.77	14.87	-12.71	17.71	0.42	0.15	12.92	-14.49	22.80
1964	3.78	8.04	11.88	-1.17	4.70	-26.43	9.61	10.22	10.44	23.17	-7.16	-5.14
1965	-1.16	-2.65	11.93	-4.10	-12.63	30.16	-10.00	0.37	16.12	11.00	-11.74	12.66
1966	-4.88	-15.82	5.63	-8.18	-15.06	8.89	-14.54	-7.61	11.87	-23.93	-12.91	-2.07
1967	0.97	13.35	-11.88	0.46	51.80	-2.51	38.97	1.09	-8.48	7.69	52.39	16.57
1968	2.95	13.63	17.81	14.81	13.61	4.23	37.58	21.55	31.42	45.52	30.44	51.34
1969	6.90	7.18	3.36	18.39	23.42	15.19	-4.42	24.75	46.87	1.75	5.05	-12.52
1970	13.49	9.66	-6.47	-5.14	-23.76	-17.52	-6.50	39.53	-3.68	-18.92	-13.17	-5.72
1971	8.44	25.00	10.18	1.66	24.61	-12.34	1.76	14.13	26.26	36.12	27.41	47.99
1972	37.65	32.69	112.20	24.83	18.54	15.33	29.56	9.03	42.30	16.82	28.61	3.93
1973	25.09	18.16	5.44	3.83	-4.44	10.18	-4.74	128.52	24.03	2.86	-3.75	-23.44
1974	15.00	-11.74	-10.74	-22.43	17.20	-33.43	-15.56	-39.98	-8.49	11.72	-12.37	-50.33
1975	-2.90	17.45	23.96	45.08	30.09	-8.69	50.23	-15.14	0.05	21.00	41.18	115.06
1976	15.58	13.00	7.23	-20.03	6.57	-26.55	16.94	14.98	-36.00	6.37	10.42	-12.55
1977	-3.76	11.02	1.74	5.07	23.08	-18.92	14.65	-23.83	-19.66	-21.64	25.49	56.49
1978	15.68	33.27	9.47	73.19	26.96	46.37	20.83	6.81	7.86	23.96	21.82	14.63
1979	19.43	21.08	-2.18	28.90	-1.93	17.39	19.95	183.01	5.51	2.64	12.21	22.20
1980	-11.90	-11.40	15.80	-1.30	-8.20	78.40	11.90	-17.30	4.60	21.00	-7.10	38.80

	World Equities										
	Non-U.S.									U.S.	
	Europe	Asia				Other					
Year	*Europe Total*	*Hong Kong*	*Japan*	*Singapore*	*Asia Total*	*Canada*	*Australia*	*Other Total*	*Non-U.S. Total*	*U.S. Total*	*World Equities Total*
1960	13.65		38.50		38.50	-1.16	-0.07	-0.69	13.84	0.83	4.60
1961	15.11		-13.03		-13.03	39.03	14.86	26.49	14.08	27.52	22.91
1962	-2.35		4.68		4.68	-6.84	0.95	-3.43	-1.86	-9.29	-6.79
1963	7.08		8.78		8.78	14.39	24.92	19.19	9.18	21.04	17.04
1964	-2.13		10.93		10.93	24.36	5.17	16.12	2.25	16.71	12.11
1965	3.74		21.39		21.39	4.81	-9.75	-1.27	4.45	15.26	12.15
1966	-5.92		9.04		9.04	-9.24	4.87	-3.92	-4.17	-8.21	-7.18
1967	18.98		-4.85		-4.85	7.18	44.70	22.42	17.02	30.45	26.63
1968	35.05		26.43		26.43	26.61	28.62	27.46	32.76	14.95	19.63
1969	1.51		34.15		34.15	3.21	16.10	8.26	6.43	-9.86	-5.57
1970	-9.04	21.31	-6.35	-5.43	-4.09	15.81	-19.14	1.10	-6.40	-1.00	-2.59
1971	27.33	59.52	46.55	65.52	48.41	14.13	-1.59	7.59	26.68	18.16	20.77
1972	16.45	161.66	126.56	211.04	134.88	33.12	21.06	29.15	41.17	17.71	24.48
1973	-7.78	-39.01	-20.13	-34.58	-24.62	-3.11	-12.06	-5.72	-11.42	-18.68	-16.38
1974	-23.34	-60.33	-15.65	-46.69	-19.75	-26.52	-32.97	-28.54	-22.99	-27.77	-25.76
1975	44.78	99.56	19.84	63.57	23.84	15.07	50.71	27.61	35.86	37.49	36.78
1976	-7.56	40.55	25.80	13.83	26.17	9.71	-10.00	3.81	4.83	26.68	18.36
1977	21.26	-11.58	15.70	4.60	13.39	-1.37	11.25	2.89	15.50	-3.03	3.43
1978	25.51	18.61	53.33	45.31	51.13	20.55	22.24	21.06	34.62	8.53	18.25
1979	15.38	83.50	-11.69	28.58	-5.57	52.26	43.44	49.75	11.29	24.18	18.77
1980	14.53	69.90	29.70	61.20	34.09	22.00	52.20	30.95	24.27	33.22	29.25

TABLE 3

World Equities: Cross-Correlations of Annual U.S.-Dollar-Adjusted Total Returns, 1960–1980

Series	*Austria*	*Belgium*	*Denmark*	*France*	*Germany*	*Italy*	*Nether-lands*	*Norway*
Austria	1.000							
Belgium	0.308	1.000						
Denmark	0.224	0.387	1.000					
France	0.155	0.559	0.259	1.000				
Germany	0.258	0.303	0.058	0.273	1.000			
Italy	0.180	−0.104	0.156	0.398	−0.004	1.000		
Netherlands	−0.012	0.567	0.342	0.484	0.537	0.031	1.000	
Norway	0.343	0.359	−0.100	0.188	−0.212	0.119	0.010	1.000
Spain	0.260	0.208	0.413	0.326	−0.075	0.338	−0.102	0.171
Sweden	−0.038	0.311	0.281	0.277	0.285	0.131	0.429	−0.100
Switzerland	0.454	0.465	0.134	0.444	0.700	0.129	0.658	−0.021
United Kingdom	−0.349	0.284	0.152	0.432	0.258	0.104	0.675	−0.136
Europe Total	−0.039	0.493	0.266	0.643	0.505	0.289	0.783	−0.039
Hong Kong	0.127	0.447	0.743	0.387	0.131	0.324	0.729	0.046
Japan	0.216	0.331	0.831	0.361	0.302	0.307	0.284	−0.257
Singapore	0.260	0.510	0.921	0.404	0.311	0.353	0.614	−0.157
Asia Total	0.211	0.337	0.845	0.365	0.281	0.314	0.308	−0.228
Australia	−0.241	0.281	0.213	0.504	0.321	0.420	0.766	0.089
Canada	0.239	0.623	0.341	0.441	−0.037	0.269	0.554	0.469
Other Total	0.029	0.544	0.329	0.528	0.157	0.363	0.743	0.358
Non-U.S. Total Equities	0.062	0.559	0.557	0.646	0.470	0.390	0.774	−0.114
U. S. Total Equities	−0.076	0.389	0.243	0.214	0.210	0.208	0.730	0.009
World Total Equities	−0.042	0.483	0.358	0.384	0.322	0.281	0.804	−0.045

Series	*Spain*	*Sweden*	*Switzer-land*	*United Kingdom*	*Europe Total*	*Hong Kong*	*Japan*	*Singa-pore*
Spain	1.000							
Sweden	0.313	1.000						
Switzerland	0.127	0.233	1.000					
United Kingdom	−0.039	0.301	0.454	1.000				
Europe Total	0.178	0.471	0.712	0.882	1.000			
Hong Kong	0.418	0.376	0.563	0.487	0.598	1.000		
Japan	0.337	0.340	0.240	0.171	0.374	0.707	1.000	
Singapore	0.585	0.439	0.584	0.338	0.547	0.898	0.927	1.000
Asia Total	0.338	0.337	0.244	0.198	0.391	0.759	0.997	0.952
Australia	0.090	0.282	0.432	0.674	0.731	0.667	0.184	0.512
Canada	0.260	0.312	0.350	0.360	0.505	0.791	0.231	0.598
Other Total	0.195	0.340	0.432	0.550	0.676	0.800	0.247	0.609
Non-U.S. Total Equities	0.242	0.522	0.643	0.716	0.905	0.785	0.688	0.826
U.S. Total Equities	−0.115	0.398	0.454	0.617	0.627	0.814	0.216	0.579
World Total Equities	−0.015	0.470	0.557	0.703	0.774	0.848	0.385	0.700

Series	*Asia Total*	*Aus-tralia*	*Canada*	*Other Total*	*Non-U.S. Total Equities*	*U.S. Total Equities*	*World Total Equities*
Asia Total	1.000						
Australia	0.224	1.000					
Canada	0.280	0.577	1.000				
Other Total	0.296	0.863	0.907	1.000			
Non-U.S. Total Equities	0.704	0.704	0.586	0.717	1.000		
U.S. Total Equities	0.260	0.699	0.710	0.787	0.667	1.000	
World Total Equities	0.422	0.753	0.716	0.818	0.831	0.967	1.000

wealth index showed a loss over the period 1959–79; the 1980 bull market, however, pushed Italy to a gain for the entire period.

Cross-Correlations

Table 3 presents cross-correlations of the equity series. A *priori*, we might expect substantial equity comovement to be related to geographical proximity, institutional currency relationships, partnership in trade, cultural similarity or similarity of the economic bases of the countries.

The results show that European equities exhibit a good deal of comovement, with geographically adjacent Germany, Switzerland and the Netherlands forming a distinct "bloc." The United Kingdom, France, Belgium and the Netherlands, all of which face the trade routes of the English Channel and the North Sea, form a less distinct bloc. Countries that are culturally allied may have low equity correlations: Note in particular Norway and Sweden (−0.10), which have different economic bases (Norway is a resource economy, while Sweden is heavily industrial), and Germany and Austria (0.26). On the other hand, the three Asian countries exhibit very high cross-correlations. Finally, the United States, Canada and Australia form a bloc. This bloc of English-speaking countries also has high correlations with the United Kingdom, the present or former British colonies of Hong Kong and Singapore, and the Netherlands (a world trading center whose equity market is dominated by the multnational Royal Dutch/Shell Group).

BONDS: RETURNS AND AGGREGATE MARKET VALUES

The world bond market at the end of 1980 was dominated by non-U.S. bonds. Figure A shows the distribution of U.S. and non-U.S. bonds at that date. In Figure C, the non-U.S. bond market is broken down by country. The Japanese domestic bond market represents nearly one-third of the non-U.S. market and is half the size of the U.S. market. The vast majority (89.3 per cent) of the non-U.S. bond market consists of domestic bonds, with all "crossborder" categories comprising the balance.

Table 4 summarizes the country-by-country U.S.-dollar-adjusted total (coupon plus capital appreciation) returns on a market-value-weighted portfolio of corporate and government bonds plus cash equivalents in each country. (The U.S. series excludes cash equivalents.) The returns thus measure the fixed-income market in each country and are not strictly comparable, since maturities and default premiums differ from one country to another. With this in mind, the best performing domestic bond market was that of Japan. Most other domestic bond markets had returns clustering (in U.S.-dollar-adjusted terms) around five per cent per year.

Crossborder Bonds

We use the term "crossborder bond" to refer to any non-domestic bond. We consider a bond to be domestic if it meets both of the following criteria—(1) the currency of the bond is the currency of the borrower's home country and (2) the bond is primarily bought by nationals of the borrower's home country. The set of crossborder bonds subsumes the traditional designations of foreign bonds and Eurobonds. Every bond can thus be classified as domestic or crossborder.

This naming scheme corresponds to the way we believe risks are distributed in the world bond market. From the point of view of a U.S. investor, U.S. dollar crossborder bonds are exposed to political risk (sovereign risk, repatriation of funds risk, etc.) while

FIGURE C

Market Values of Non-U.S. Bonds at the End of 1980 in Billions of U.S. Dollars (Non-U.S. Bonds Total = $1,748.3 Billion)

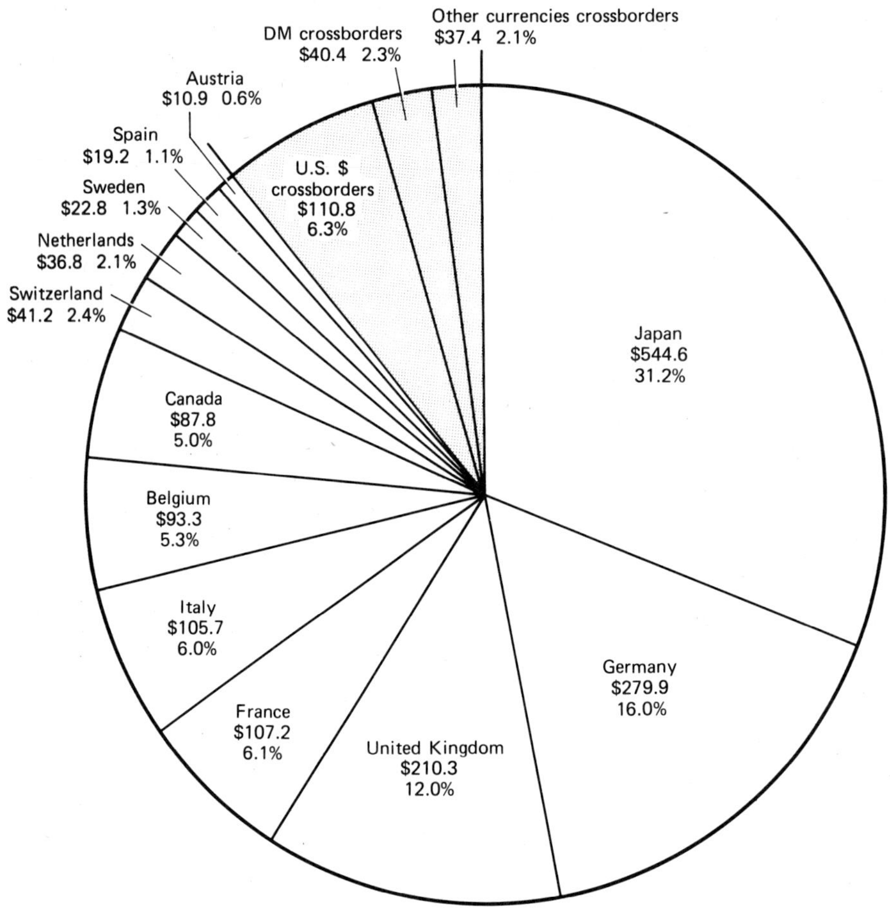

U.S. dollar domestic bonds are not. Likewise, the German investor finds Deutschemark crossborder (but not domestic) bonds exposed to political risk. Exchange risk, on the other hand, is determined by whether the bond currency matches the currency with which the bondholder intends to buy goods.

Crossborder markets are not new, but the development of a large crossborder sector can be traced to the imposition of the Interest Equalization Tax by the United States in 1963. The Eurobond market, which is the largest part of the crossborder sector today, enabled U.S. investors to avoid this tax. At first, the Eurobond market was thin and contained a large proportion of low-quality issues. In the 1970s, this market came of age and in fact continued to grow, rather than decline (as might have been expected), after the Interest Equalization Tax was removed in 1974.

Table 4 shows that over the 21-year period, U.S. dollar and Deutschemark crossborder bonds outperformed the domestic bond markets in those currencies by 1.7

TABLE 4

World Bonds: Summary Statistics, 1960–1980

Asset	Annual Returns in U.S. Dollars: Compound Return (%)	Annual Returns in U.S. Dollars: Arithmetic Mean (%)	Annual Returns in U.S. Dollars: Standard Deviation (%)	Year-End 1980 Wealth Index 1959 = 1.00
Domestic Bonds:				
Austria	8.1	8.6	9.9	5.15
Belgium	7.7	8.1	9.4	4.75
Canada	3.3	3.5	6.3	1.99
Denmark	6.3	7.0	12.8	3.58
France	5.3	6.0	12.3	2.95
Germany	10.3	10.6	9.2	7.77
Italy	2.4	3.4	13.4	1.66
Japan	10.6	11.2	11.9	8.26
Netherlands	7.6	7.9	8.1	4.66
Spain	4.6	5.2	11.2	2.56
Sweden	6.2	6.4	5.9	3.57
Switzerland	8.4	9.1	12.4	5.48
United Kingdom	5.9	6.8	14.9	3.32
United States	4.2	4.3	5.4	2.36
Crossborder Bonds:				
Deutschemarks	10.4	10.8	9.5	7.97
Dutch Guilders*	11.6	11.9	8.5	1.93
Japanese Yen*	18.0	19.8	19.2	2.71
Swiss Francs*	15.5	16.7	16.0	2.38
U.S. Dollars	5.9	6.0	4.4	3.34
Other Currencies**	5.7	5.8	2.5	1.25

*Returns measured over the period 1975–1980; wealth index 1974 = 1.00.

**Returns measured over the period 1977–1980; wealth index 1976 = 1.00.

and 0.1 percentage points per year, respectively. Since crossborder bonds expose the investor to political risk not faced by the typical (domestic) investor in domestic bonds of the same currency, we might expect that such a premium would be observed on crossborder bonds as a compensation for the extra risk. Arbitrage between domestic and crossborder sectors should, however, prevent the crossborder excess return from getting too high. The observed high excess return on U.S. dollar crossborder bonds may, then, be due to the probable greater default risk of the issues in that sector, particularly in the 1960s, rather than to a pure crossborder premium.

Table 5 presents year-by-year total returns for all the categories of bonds. (Portfolios were not formed since market weights were not available.) The Dutch guilder, Japanese yen, Swiss franc and other crossborder currency sectors (studied over a much shorter period) had high returns, but these were largely the results of exchange appreciation against the dollar in 1975–78.

Table 6 shows the cross-correlations of the bond categories. Crossborder and domestic bond returns for the same currency are very highly correlated because of the application of the same exchange adjustments to both series. Among domestic bond markets, most of the comovement is due to comovement in the currencies. The countries of Continental Europe (excluding Italy and Spain) are highly correlated, as are Canada and the United States.

TABLE 5

World Bonds: Year-by-Year U.S.-Dollar-Adjusted Total Returns (in per cent)

	World Bonds									
	Non-U.S. Domestic									
Year	*Austria*	*Belgium*	*Canada*	*Denmark*	*France*	*Germany*	*Italy*	*Japan*	*Nether-lands*	*Spain*
1960		-4.20	-0.72	-7.53	3.93	5.15	1.74	8.37	2.22	13.24
1961		7.31	2.75	-7.57	5.18	11.42	5.35	6.18	8.68	9.80
1962		9.61	-0.11	9.25	8.31	4.75	0.55	-0.02	3.16	8.10
1963		2.81	4.09	18.44	4.76	6.49	-1.94	19.24	1.07	1.30
1964		0.17	6.39	-7.74	4.87	3.83	1.33	8.45	1.08	2.89
1965	4.09	6.01	1.82	-5.17	-2.40	-0.08	12.74	12.24	0.43	0.54
1966	3.67	3.87	1.72	3.58	0.58	7.95	7.60	8.02	3.60	-0.35
1967	3.41	8.40	0.46	-4.58	8.15	10.20	5.96	6.25	7.25	-9.89
1968	8.89	5.13	2.38	18.96	0.59	8.64	6.94	7.84	4.48	4.44
1969	7.13	1.80	0.64	-7.75	-13.13	8.73	-0.80	6.65	0.10	4.04
1970	5.77	7.96	23.77	6.87	12.21	6.10	-6.79	7.26	8.70	-6.33
1971	18.68	23.51	10.11	21.42	14.61	21.93	25.58	23.30	19.12	20.29
1972	10.61	8.38	2.51	18.61	7.62	6.78	15.12	14.24	7.43	19.71
1973	15.30	10.57	2.37	7.01	10.00	22.95	2.92	6.43	13.27	13.35
1974	17.24	16.93	1.00	1.52	3.76	21.74	-30.72	-1.35	21.75	-6.88
1975	6.52	1.30	1.48	25.14	17.94	5.53	10.38	10.35	3.99	5.34
1976	27.05	16.47	16.30	4.05	-5.36	25.31	-24.53	14.56	18.45	-4.31
1977	17.99	17.64	-1.69	5.62	15.96	30.01	12.82	42.70	15.92	-12.10
1978	28.48	32.69	-2.82	42.27	43.56	16.84	23.00	30.26	25.32	28.73
1979	17.93	6.13	5.81	5.26	6.07	9.36	15.75	-17.72	7.17	24.28
1980	-13.39	-12.26	-4.40	-0.98	-21.46	-10.16	-11.72	22.25	-7.32	-7.62

	World Bonds									
	Non-U.S. Domestic			*U.S. Domestic*	*Crossborder*					
Year	*Sweden*	*Switzer-land*	*United Kingdom*	*United States*	*Deutsche-marks*	*Dutch Guilders*	*Japanese Yen*	*Swiss Francs*	*U.S. Dollars*	*Other Curren-cies*
1960	-0.76	3.52	-0.47	10.74	9.54				3.74	
1961	4.34	2.76	4.72	2.66	7.57				5.85	
1962	8.19	1.86	13.19	5.94	6.00				8.39	
1963	2.00	0.67	5.04	2.33	5.65				6.11	
1964	2.96	0.46	-1.18	4.15	4.30				6.22	
1965	3.50	4.30	4.80	-0.26	0.87				2.07	
1966	6.40	0.66	5.27	1.09	-0.62				0.69	
1967	4.10	4.36	-11.43	-4.29	11.22				2.29	
1968	9.91	5.98	1.55	2.21	7.81				5.97	
1969	0.34	-1.43	1.65	-4.63	4.10				-0.95	
1970	7.29	3.68	8.64	14.36	8.92				4.17	
1971	15.30	20.41	28.61	10.52	22.57				14.12	
1972	8.06	7.26	-12.53	5.81	13.93				10.94	
1973	9.92	16.18	-7.05	2.30	23.11				4.00	
1974	14.81	30.22	-2.63	0.17	21.90				1.87	
1975	-3.41	7.84	9.62	12.29	7.60	5.50	20.40	15.30	15.80	
1976	12.83	22.82	-9.06	15.58	26.30	18.77	15.95	23.76	14.16	
1977	-4.32	31.08	53.66	2.99	27.08	17.24	42.62	37.84	7.03	9.28
1978	17.84	37.74	6.64	1.17	21.37	23.01	32.65	29.74	4.10	6.39
1979	11.52	5.13	16.05	2.28	7.87	8.85	-18.67	2.35	2.31	2.33
1980	3.83	-14.23	28.01	3.05	-10.31	-1.68	25.98	-9.04	7.23	5.00

TABLE 6

World Bonds: Cross-Correlations of Annual U.S.-Dollar-Adjusted Total Returns, 1960–1980

Series	*Austria*	*Belgium*	*Canada*	*Denmark*	*France*	*Germany*	*Italy*
Austria	1.000						
Belgium	0.853	1.000					
Canada	0.244	0.159	1.000				
Denmark	0.481	0.548	-0.010	1.000			
France	0.544	0.716	0.010	0.693	1.000		
Germany	0.823	0.771	0.179	0.217	0.427	1.000	
Italy	0.141	0.248	-0.225	0.426	0.530	-0.009	1.000
Japan	0.154	0.318	-0.172	0.358	0.276	0.265	0.239
Netherlands	0.884	0.928	0.211	0.448	0.644	0.862	0.036
Spain	0.344	0.309	-0.102	0.488	0.472	0.044	0.612
Sweden	0.586	0.630	0.264	0.418	0.281	0.338	-0.039
Switzerland	0.882	0.895	0.037	0.475	0.662	0.854	0.075
United Kingdom	-0.005	0.095	-0.147	0.121	0.099	0.125	0.288
United States	0.150	0.049	0.632	0.228	0.146	0.098	-0.132
Deutschemark Crossborder	0.853	0.810	0.215	0.342	0.546	0.938	0.018
Dutch Guilder Crossborder	0.935	0.980	0.289	0.463	0.665	0.872	0.233
Japanese Yen Crossborder	-0.060	0.274	-0.478	0.262	0.251	0.249	0.005
Swiss Franc Crossborder	0.749	0.842	0.105	0.421	0.673	0.905	0.286
U.S. Dollar Crossborder	0.172	0.154	0.250	0.442	0.169	0.157	0.083
Other Crossborder	0.194	0.434	-0.619	0.173	0.341	0.634	0.114

Series	*Japan*	*Nether-lands*	*Spain*	*Sweden*	*Switzer-land*	*United Kingdom*	*United States*
Japan	1.000						
Netherlands	0.244	1.000					
Spain	-0.158	0.235	1.000				
Sweden	-0.183	0.631	0.440	1.000			
Switzerland	0.383	0.944	0.174	0.463	1.000		
United Kingdom	0.500	0.033	-0.128	-0.238	0.134	1.000	
United States	0.095	0.166	0.072	0.059	0.104	0.076	1.000
Deutschemark Crossborder	0.293	0.903	0.158	0.400	0.901	0.025	0.242
Dutch Guilder Crossborder	0.360	0.996	0.274	0.462	0.968	-0.198	0.025
Japanese Yen Crossborder	0.982	0.242	-0.481	-0.355	0.408	0.400	-0.061
Swiss Franc Crossborder	0.594	0.858	-0.047	-0.032	0.949	0.104	0.115
U.S. Dollar Crossborder	0.325	0.178	0.117	0.036	0.167	0.168	0.715
Other Crossborder	0.944	0.443	-0.553	-0.554	0.610	0.666	0.160

Series	*Deutsche-mark Cross-Border*	*Dutch Guilder Cross-Border*	*Japanese Yen Cross-Border*	*Swiss Franc Cross-Border*	*U.S. Dollar Cross-Border*	*Other Cross-Border*
Deutschemark Crossborder	1.000					
Dutch Guilder Crossborder	0.931	1.000				
Japanese Yen Crossborder	0.281	0.273	1.000			
Swiss Franc Crossborder	0.933	0.868	0.550	1.000		
U.S. Dollar Crossborder	0.288	-0.113	0.215	0.132	1.000	
Other Crossborder	0.624	0.500	0.917	0.786	0.683	1.000

Relationships Between Equities, Bonds, Inflation and Exchange

Table 7 presents summary data on equity and bond returns, yields, and inflation and exchange rates, along with 1980 population and gross domestic product (GDP) statistics.

Examination of the first two columns reveals that the United States and the Scandinavian and Germanic countries have the highest per capita GDP. (Consumer prices are generally higher in northern Europe than in the United States, lowering the estimate of the real prosperity of these European countries.) Comparing populations in Table 7 with equity market sizes in Figure B shows that Singapore and Hong Kong have the largest per capita equity markets, reflecting these locales' importance as financial centers. The United States and Switzerland, likewise, have large equity markets relative to their populations. European countries have generally lower equity market sizes per capita than the non-European countries studied; but the European equity markets are very large relative to those markets not studied (which include most of Asia, Latin America and Africa).

Yields and Inflation Rates within Countries

Economists, starting with Irving Fisher, have developed a self-consistent and elegant theory of prices and returns in a multisovereign world, based on the principles of economic equilibrium and rational expectations.[1] The intranational (within one country)

TABLE 7

Comparative Data on 18 Countries

				Compound Annual Rates of Return, 1960-1980				
					Local Currency		*Exchange-Rate-Adjusted*	
Country	*1980 Population (millions)*	*1980 GDP (billions of U.S. $)**	*Exchange Rate in US $/FCU (end of 1980)***	*Exchange Return (%)*	*Inflation Rate (%)*	*Short-Term Yields (%)*	*Equity Returns (%)*	*Bond Returns (%)*
Australia	14.6	140.0	1.1815	−3.0	6.4	N/A	9.8	N/A
Austria	7.5	76.3	0.0718	3.1	4.8	6.1	9.1	8.1
Belgium	9.9	110.9	0.0316	2.2	5.1	6.3	9.2	7.7
Canada	24.1	245.8	0.8386	−1.1	5.3	5.9	10.7	3.3
Denmark	5.1	66.4	0.1663	0.7	7.6	7.7	9.5	6.3
France	53.7	571.3	0.2208	0.4	6.7	6.6	6.2	5.3
Germany	61.6	824.6	0.5074	3.7	3.8	4.3	8.3	10.3
Hong Kong	4.9	20.8	0.1957	0.4***	N/A	N/A	24.6***	N/A
Italy	57.1	323.6	0.0011	−1.9	8.8	7.1	2.4	2.4
Japan	116.8	990.0	0.0049	2.8	7.2	5.6	15.6	10.6
Netherlands	14.1	161.4	0.4717	2.8	5.5	4.9	9.3	7.6
Norway	4.1	57.3	0.1935	1.6	6.2	N/A	10.3	N/A
Singapore	2.4	9.0	0.4819	1.8	N/A	N/A	23.2***	N/A
Spain	37.4	201.0	0.0126	−1.3	10.3	6.3	8.4	4.6
Sweden	8.3	101.5	0.2288	0.8	6.5	5.8	8.4	6.2
Switzerland	6.3	97.4	0.5618	4.4	4.1	3.4	10.2	8.4
United Kingdom	55.9	405.1	2.3950	−0.8	8.6	7.7	10.0	5.9
United States	226.5	2576.6	—	—	5.3	5.5	8.7	4.1

N/A = Not Available

*GDP = Gross Domestic Product

**FCU = Foreign Currency Unit.

***1970–1980.

components of this theory are the interest-inflation relationship, the expectations hypothesis for bond forward rates, and the capital asset pricing model (CAPM) for stocks.[2] Interest rates are postulated to consist of a relatively stable and relatively low real riskless rate of return plus the anticipated inflation rate over the life of the security, plus any interest rate risk (maturity) premiums that may exist. Thus we expect to observe a strong relationship between inflation rates and short-term yields in every country.

An examination of year-by-year data show that short-term securities markets have more or less predicted short-term inflation rates, although there have been some notable exceptions. Japan in 1974 had a short-term yield of 5.8 per cent and an inflation rate of 24.6 per cent; that high real rate, however, did not persist, and Japanese inflation quickly fell to the level of the short-term yield. In the United States in early 1982, real rates are at a post-World War II high; we expect that they too will move toward their long-term mean (near zero per cent), with either rising inflation or falling yields, or both.

Long-term yields tell a somewhat different story. Since they incorporate anticipated inflation over a long period, they are much less suceptible to rapid wide swings. As world inflation rates have risen over the 1960–80 period, long-term yields have risen in every country studied. But these yields do not (and theoretically should not) match year-to-year changes in the inflation rate. Countries that have had moderate inflation, such as Switzerland, have had modest increases in long-term yields, while most countries have exhibited dramatic increases in both numbers.

Inflation and International Exchange Rates

The international components of the equilibrium theory of prices and returns are based on the Law of One Price, which, in its simplest form, states that a good (physical or financial) cannot differ in price between two locales by more than the transport and transaction costs, or else arbitrage would take place to equalize the difference. Where there are governmental or other barriers to the flow of either goods or money, the Law of One Price breaks down. We can thus see to what extent the world capital market is integrated or segmented by observing the degree to which this law holds. A corollary of the Law of One Price is Purchasing Power Parity, which applies the law to market baskets of goods. Purchasing Power Parity asserts that, under ideal conditions, exchange rates instantaneously respond to local price level changes.

A number of applications of the Law of One Price to exchange rates, inflation rates and interest rates in an international setting can be expressed as parity theorems. First, expected changes in exchange rates are equal to expected differences in rates of inflation. (If, for example, U.S. expected inflation is 10 per cent and British expected inflation is 15 per cent, then the British pound is expected to decline by five per cent per year in U.S. dollar terms.) Second, the difference in interest rates between two countries (for any maturity) will reflect the differences in expected inflation. (Continuing the above example, yields on British bonds should be five percentage points higher, for a given maturity, than U.S. bond yields.) Third, as a consequence of the first two parity theorems, expected exchange rate changes are equal to the interest rate differential between two countries. Thus dollar-adjusted interest rates should be the same in every country.

The realism of these parity theorems over the long term can be assessed using the data in Table 7. The countries with the highest inflation rates over the 1960–80 period have generally had the poorest exchange returns, casually confirming the inflation-exchange hypothesis. Japan, with an above-average exchange rate despite high inflation, is the most notable exception. Austria, Germany and Switzerland, which have experienced modest inflation, have had excellent currency performance against the dollar. Local currency short-term yields match inflation rates to a recognizable degree, with real rates negative in most of the larger markets over the period.

Referring back to Table 7, we may examine the proposition that interest rates, converted to U.S. dollars, should be the same in every country. The 21-year compound annual dollar-adjusted bond returns in Table 7 range from 2.4 per cent for Italy to 10.6 per cent for Japan, suggesting that, at least over this turbulent period in the bond markets, there were substantial differences in (realized) returns among countries.

Equity Expectation Parity

To the existing list of international parity theorems presented here we add Equity Expectation Parity. This is the proposition that beta-adjusted expected returns on stocks will be the same in every country. (If stock prices are set in a world CAPM framework, rather than

TABLE 8

Dollar-Adjusted Equity Returns: Regressions on World Equities and Correlations with Bonds and Inflation

	*Excess Return Regressions of Country Equities on World Equity Portfolio**				*Correlation Coefficients of Equity Returns*	
Country or Region	*Alpha (%)*	*Alpha T-Statistic*	*Beta*	R^2	*With Dollar-Adjusted Bonds*	*With Local Inflation Rates*
Austria	4.86	1.15	0.01	0.000	0.224	0.048
Belgium	2.44	0.82	0.45	0.217	0.491	−0.113
Denmark	2.91	0.53	0.60	0.106	0.338	−0.199
France	0.17	0.04	0.50	0.099	0.606	0.106
Germany	2.41	0.53	0.45	0.079	0.277	−0.285
Italy	−1.92	−0.31	0.41	0.014	0.265	−0.076
Netherlands	0.65	0.25	0.90	0.636	−0.041	0.021
Norway	13.39	1.16	−0.27	0.000	N/A	−0.126
Spain	4.73	0.96	0.04	0.000	0.526	−0.662
Sweden	1.69	0.48	0.51	0.195	0.325	−0.168
Switzerland	2.66	0.58	0.87	0.312	0.143	−0.300
United Kingdom	1.76	0.31	1.47	0.466	0.515	0.348
Europe Total	0.14	0.06	0.80	0.590	—	—
Hong Kong**	20.58	1.88	2.81	0.702	N/A	N/A
Japan	9.49	1.36	0.81	0.123	0.410	−0.499
Singapore**	18.26	1.16	2.59	0.476	N/A	N/A
Asia Total	9.61	1.33	0.92	0.153	—	—
Australia	1.52	0.42	1.02	0.521	N/A	−0.119
Canada	2.75	0.95	0.77	0.488	0.170	−0.104
Other Total	2.17	0.93	0.85	0.648	—	—
Non-U.S. Total	1.97	0.90	0.86	0.685	—	—
United States Total	−0.69	−0.63	1.08	0.934	0.210	−0.130

*Returns are measured in excess of the U.S. Treasury bill return, which was 5.4 per cent compounded annually over 1960-1980 and 6.7 per cent compounded annually over 1970-80 (the period for which the Hong Kong and Singapore regressions were run). The dependent variable in each case is the country or region's dollar-adjusted equity market year-by-year return from Table III, less the contemporaneous one-year return on rolled-over 30-day U.S. Treasury bills. The independent variable in each case is the dollar-adjusted world equity market portfolio year-by-year return from Table III, less the same Treasury bill returns.

**1970-1980.

locally, this theorem will hold.) We regressed U.S.-dollar-adjusted equity (country and regional) returns on the U.S.-dollar-adjusted world equity market portfolio. (The regressions were performed in excess return form—i.e., in excess of U.S. Treasury bill returns.) Table 8 shows the results.

Alphas ranged from −1.92 for Italy to +20.58 for Hong Kong (in per cent per year). The alpha for the United States was −0.69, indicating below average beta-adjusted performance. Alphas approached significance for Hong Kong and Japan. Betas ranged from −0.27 for Norway to +2.81 for Hong Kong. The United States equity market had a world equity market beta of +1.08.

Table 8 also shows correlations of each country's U.S.-dollar-adjusted equity returns with its dollar-adjusted bond returns and local inflation rates. The generally high correlation within a country between equity and bond returns reflects the application of the same exchange rate adjustment to each return series. The generally negative correlations between equities and inflation show that inflation hurts the stock market not just in the United States, but in most of the world. Many theories have been propounded to explain this relationship, but the mystery has not yet been solved.

Do International Parity Theorems Hold?

The international parity theorems we have expounded here are the subject of intense debate. The work of Frenkel and others has generally supported the hypotheses.[3] Aliber found that the exchange-inflation relationship held more closely over the long term than in the short run.[4] (Officer has summarized the various views of this relationship in a review paper.[5]) Frenkel and Levich have detected greater deviations from the interest-exchange relationship in domestic markets than in crossborder markets, attributing the finding to the greater degree of regulation in domestic markets (making crossborder markets more efficient).[6]

The efficiency of exchange markets themselves has also been investigated: Levich presents evidence that foreign exchange markets do not fully reflect all the available information, while Cornell leans toward an affirmation of market efficiency in the forward exchange market.[7] On the equity side, Stehle has shown that equity pricing is somewhat better explained by a world-market CAPM line than by local (within each country) CAPM lines.[8]

Our own view is that the set of theorems makes logical sense, and that barriers to international capital, goods and labor flows are likely to produce most of the observed deviations from the postulated relationships. We thus would not expect efficient-market-affirming results in the present international context. Black has propounded a theory of international capital market equilibrium with investment barriers, and we might expect a theory of this kind to reflect reality better than any set of purely efficient market hypotheses.[9]

THE ADVANTAGES OF INTERNATIONAL DIVERSIFICATION

International diversification has the same advantages as diversification along any other dimension: If asset returns are imperfectly correlated, risk is reduced at a given level of expected return. Lessard and Solnik each have developed this idea in detail.[10] The cross-correlations of equities in Table 3 and bonds in Table 6, along with the intracountry stock-bond correlations in Table 8, are low enough in general to suggest substantial gains purely from diversification.

A second argument for diversifying internationally is that segmentation in the world market may produce bargains. If securities are priced according to their local systematic risk, some of that risk becomes unsystematic and therefore diversifiable in a global context. Further, low past levels of U.S. investment in foreign markets may have led to underpricing in those markets; an investor might thus capture excess returns in non-U.S. securities. Regulations producing barriers to investment in a country may produce excess returns for an investor able to overcome those barriers.

A final argument for international investigating in the sheer size of the non-U.S. market. It is desirable as a matter of general principle to maintain as wide a horizon as possible so as not to exclude opportunities. The non-U.S. market has developed into a mature set of institutions surpassing the U.S. market in combined size. We believe that the U.S. investor should regard all investments, U.S. or foreign, traditional or non-traditional, as part of his opportunity set (excepting, perhaps, securities rendered totally unsuitable by tax laws or other international capital barriers).

If international parity theorems hold strictly, then exchange risk is not an issue in international investment; exchange rates adjust instantaneously to reflect true value, and the U.S. dollar investor faces exactly the same risk as the local currency investor. We believe that sufficient doubt has been cast on the "instantaneous" version of parity that we admit the possibility of uncompensated exchange risk in a given non-U.S. security. Over the long term, however, we expect that exchange risk would dampen (i.e., that the Law of One Price would hold better over the long run than over the short run). Furthermore, investors can diversify away a portion of exchange risk by investing in different countries, or hedge against it completely in forward markets, incurring some transaction costs in the process.

We have not determined whether the world capital market is segmented or integrated. Since international investment occurs, markets cannot be totally segmented. But interest rates and equity returns (and, we might speculate, equity expectations) appear to differ substantially from country to country. We view the world market as partly segmented and partly integrated, moving in the direction of integration as investors expand their horizons and foreign markets grow.

NOTES

1. Irving Fisher, *The Theory of Interest* (New York: Macmillan, 1980).

2. The most comprehensive treatment of the three intranational theories taken as a unit is in Roger G. Ibbotson and Rex A. Sinquefield (foreword by Laurence B. Siegel), *Stocks, Bonds, Bills, and Inflation: The Past and The Future* (1982 Edition) (Charlottesville, Va.: Financial Analysts Research Foundation, 1982).

3. Jacob A. Frenkel and Harry G. Johnson, eds., *The Economics of Exchange Rates: Selected Readings* (Reading, Mass.: Addison-Wesley, 1978).

4. Robert Z. Aliber, *Exchange Risk and Corporate International Finance* (New York: John Wiley & Sons, 1978). See especially Chapters 5, 6 and 7 for tests of international parity theorems.

5. Lawrence H. Officer, "The Purchasing Power Parity Theory of Exchange Rates: A Review Article," *Staff Papers*, March 1976.

6. Jacob A. Frenkel and Richard M. Levich, "Transactions Costs and Interest Arbitrage: Tranquil Versus Turbulent Periods," *Journal of Political Economy*, November/December 1977, pp. 1209–1226.

7. Richard M. Levich, "The Efficiency of Markets for Foreign Exchange: A Review and Extension," in *International Financial Management*, Donald R. Lessard, ed. (Boston: Warren, Gorham & Lamont, 1979), pp. 243–276; Bradford Cornell, "Spot Rates, Forward Rates, and Market Efficiency," *Journal of Financial Economics*, August 1977, pp. 55–65.

8. Richard E. Stehle, "An Empirical Test of the Alternative Hypotheses of National and International Pricing of Risky Assets," *Journal of Finance*, May 1977, pp. 493–502.

9. Fischer Black, "International Capital Market Equilibrium with Investment Barriers," *Journal of Financial Economics*, December 1974, pp. 337–352.

10. Donald R. Lessard, "World, National, and Industry Factors in Equity Returns: Implications for Risk Reduction Through International Diversification," *Journal of Finance*, May 1974, pp. 379–391; Bruno H. Solnik, "Why Not Diversify Internationally?" *Financial Analysts Journal*, July/August 1974, pp. 48–54.

Direct Investment

4

The Product Cycle Hypothesis in a New International Environment*†

Raymond Vernon

The last decade has produced a flowering of hypotheses that purport to explain the international trade and direct investment activities of firms in terms of the so-called product cycle. My purpose in this paper is to suggest that the power of such hypotheses has been changing. Two reasons account for that change: one, an increase in the geographical reach of many of the enterprises that are involved in the introduction of new products, a consequence of their having established many overseas subsidiaries; the other, a change in the national markets of the advanced industrialized countries, which has reduced some of the differences that had previously existed between such markets.

A WORD ON THEORY

The fact that new products constantly appear, then mature, and eventually die has always fitted awkwardly into the mainstream theories of international trade and international investment. Hume, Ricardo, Marshall, Ohlin, Williams, and others have observed the phenomenon in passing, without attempting any rigorous formulation of its implications for international trade and investment theory. In the past decade or two, however, numerous efforts have been made to fill the gap. Some have dealt mainly with the trade aspects of the phenomenon.[1] But some have pushed beyond the immediate trade effects, tracing out a pattern that eventually culminated in foreign direct investments on the part of the innovating firm.[2]

***This article is reprinted, with permission, from *Oxford Bulletin of Economics and Statistics*, Vol. 41, November 1979, pp. 255–267.**

†David Felix, Seev Hirsch, Sanjava Lall, L. T. Wells, Jr. and L. H. Wortzel reacted critically to various points in an earlier draft, a fact that led to some significant revisions.

[1]For instance, M. V. Posner, 'International Trade and Technical Change', *Oxford Economic Papers*, October 1961, pp. 323–341; Gary Hufbauer, *Synthetic Materials and the Theory of International Trade* (Cambridge: Harvard University Press, 1966); Seev Hirsch, 'The Product Cycle Model of International Trade—A Multi-Country Cross Section Analysis', *Oxford Bulletin of Economics and Statistics*, November 1975, vol. 37, no. 4, pp. 305–317; W. B. Walker, 'Industrial Innovation and International Trading Performance', mimeo, Science Policy Research Unit, Sussex University, October 30, 1975; and M. P. Claudon, *International Trade and Technology: Models of Dynamic Comparative Advantages* (Washington, D.C.: University Press of America, 1977).

[2]S. H. Hymer, *The International Operations of National Firms* (Cambridge: MIT Press, 1976) based on the author's 1960 Ph.D. thesis; Raymond Vernon, 'International Investment and International Trade in the Product Cycle', *Quarterly Journal of Economics*, May 1966, pp. 190–207; W. H. Gruber and others, 'The R & D Factor in International Investment of US Industries', *Journal of Political Economy*, February 1967, pp. 20–37; Thomas Horst, 'The Firm and Industry Determinants of the Decision to Invest Abroad: An Empirical Study', *Review of Economics and Statistics*, vol. 54, August 1972, pp. 258–66; S. P. Magee, 'Multinational Corporations, The Industry Technology Cycle and Development', *Journal of World Trade Law*, vol. 11, no. 4, July–August 1977, pp. 297–321; P. J. Buckley and Mark Casson, *The Future of the Multinational Enterprise* (New York: Holmes and Meier, 1976); Paul Krugman, 'A Model of Innovation, Technology Transfer, and The World Distribution of Income', *Journal of Political Economy*, April 1979, pp. 253–266.

According to the product cycle hypothesis, firms that set up foreign producing facilities characteristically do so in reliance on some real or imagined monopolistic advantage. In the absence of such a perceived advantage, firms are loath to take on the special costs and uncertainties of operating a subsidiary in a foreign environment.[3] One such special strength is an innovational lead.

The product cycle hypothesis begins with the assumption that the stimulus to innovation is typically provided by some threat or promise in the market.[4] But according to the hypothesis, firms are acutely myopic; their managers tend to be stimulated by the needs and opportunities of the market closet at hand, the home market.

The home market in fact plays a dual role in the hypothesis. Not only is it the source of stimulus for the innovating firm; it is also the preferred location for the actual development of the innovation. The first factor that has pushed innovating firms to do their development work in the home market has been simply the need for engineers and scientists with the requisite skills. That requirement, when gauged through the eyes of the typical innovating form, has tended to rule out sites in most developing countries and has narrowed the choice to some site in the advanced industrialized world. As between such advanced country sites, the home market has generally prevailed.[5] Locating in the home market, engineers and scientists can interact easily with the prospective customers whose needs they hope to satisfy, and can check constantly with (or be checked by) the specialists at headquarters who are concerned with financial and production planning.

The propensity to cluster in the home market is fortified by the fact that there are some well-recognized economies to be captured by an innovating team that is brought together at a common location.[6] These include the usual advantages that go with subdividing any task among a number of specialists, and the added advantages of maintaining efficiency of communication among the research specialists.[7]

The upshot is that the innovations of firms headquartered in some given market tend to reflect the characteristics of that market. Historically, therefore, US firms have developed and produced products that were labour-saving or responded to high-income wants; continental European firms, products and processes that were material-saving and capital-

[3]That is a central proposition of the S. H. Hymer work, cited earlier. See also my 'The Location of Economic Activity', in J. H. Dunning, *Economic Analysis and the Multinational Enterprise* (London: George Allen and Unwin, 1970), pp. 83–114.

[4]Various empirical studies demonstrate that innovations which do not arise out of a market stimulus—innovations, for instance, that are dreamed up by the laboratory as a clever application of some new scientific capability—have a relatively low chance of industrial success. See for instance Summer Myers and Donald Marquis, *Successful Industrial Innovations*, National Science Foundation Report No. 69-17, G.P.O., Washington, 1969, p. 31.

[5]For econometric evidence of the tie between the choice of a productive location, skills and innovation, see Sanjaya Lall, 'Monopolistic Advantages and Foreign Involvement by U.S. Manufacturing Industry', *Oxford Economic Papers*, forthcoming, March 1980.

[6]For evidence of such clustering, see D. B. Creamer, *Overseas Research and Development by United States Multinationals, 1966–1975* (New York: The Conference Board, 1976); Robert Ronstadt, *Research and Development Abroad by U.S. Multnationals* (New York: Praeger Publishers, 1977); and Vernon, *Storm Over the Multinationals*, pp. 43–45.

[7]See especially T. J. Allen, *Managing the Flow of Technology* (Cambridge: MIT Press, 1978). An important exception is pharmaceuticals, a case in which US regulation has driven the innovation process abroad. See e.g. H. G. Grabowski and J. M. Vernon, 'Innovation and Invention: Consumer Protection Regulation in Ethical Drugs', *American Economic Review*, vol. 67, no. 1, 1977, pp. 359–364.

saving; and Japanese firms, products that conserved not only material and capital but also space.[8]

If innovating firms tend to scan their home markets with special intensity, the chances are greatly increased that their first production facilities will also be located in the home market. In many cases, the transitions from development work to pilot plant operation to first commercial production take place in imperceptible steps. But other factors also figure in the choice. One is the fact that if the firm perceives its principal market as being at home, it may prefer a home location to minimize transport costs. The second factor is that the specifications for new products and the optimal methods for manufacturing such products are typically in flux for some time; hence, fixing the optimal location of the first production site is bound to be an exercise based on guesswork. A final factor that may explain the tendency to produce at home is the characteristic inelasticity in the demand of the earliest users of many new products. That inelasticity is thought to make the innovator relatively indifferent to questions of production cost at the time of introduction of a new product.

Once the innovator has set up its first production unit in the home market, any demand that may develop in a foreign market would ordinarily be served from the existing production unit. Eventually, however, the firm may consider other alternatives, such as that of licensing a foreign producer or of setting up its own producing subsidiary abroad. For new products, the licensing alternative may prove an inferior choice because of inefficiencies in the international market for technology.[9] If licensing is not the preferred choice, then the firm makes the usual familiar comparison between the delivered cost of exports and the cost of overseas production. That is, the marginal costs of producing for export in the home unit plus international transport costs and duties are compared with the full cost of producing the required amount in a foreign subsidiary.

Although not essential to the product cycle hypothesis, it is commonly assumed that a triggering event is likely to be required before the producer will seriously make the calculations that could lead to the creation of a foreign producing facility. The triggering event ordinarily occurs when the innovator is threatened with losing its monopoly position. In the usual case, rival producers appear, prepared to manufacture the product from locations that could undersell the original innovator.

The obvious question is why the original innovator was not already aware that the costs of production might be lower abroad. Part of the answer may lie in the indeterminateness of the threat before it has actually materialized: the difficulty of deciding what is at stake in failing to find the least-cost location, what alternative sites need to be investigated, and what the costs of investigation are likely to be.

These conditions change, however, as the threat begins to crystalize. Eventually, it

[8]For evidence, see W. H. Davidson, 'Patterns of Factor-Saving Innovation in the Industrialized World', *European Economic Review*, No. 8, 1976, pp. 207–217.

[9]See Buckley and Casson, pp. 36–45, 68–69. Their observations are strengthened by data presented in Raymond Vernon and W. H. Davidson, 'Foreign Production of Technology-Intensive Products by U.S.-Based Multinational Enterprises', Working Paper 79–5, Harvard Business School, 1979, xeroxed, p. 66. These data show that in establishing a source of foreign production for 221 innovations, 32 large US-based multinational enterprises elected the subsidiary route far more frequently than licensing, but the degree of preference declined as the innovation aged. For similar conclusions relating to petrochemicals, see R. B. Stobaugh, 'The Product Life Cycle, U.S. Exports, and International Investment', unpublished D.B.A. thesis, Harvard Business School, 1968.

may be clear that the innovator is threatened with the loss of its business in a given foreign market. At that point, the areas to be investigated as possible production sites have been narrowed while the size of the risk has been more explicitly defined. Accordingly, the decision whether to invest in added information is more readily made. Once having felt compelled to focus on the issue, the innovator will decide in some cases to set up a local producing unit in order to prolong some of the advantages that were created by its original monopoly.

TWO CRITICAL CHANGES

The Networks' Spread

For the past three decades or so, the process of innovation, export, and investment has been progressing full tilt. One result has been a transformation in the industries in which innovations tend to be especially prominent, such as chemicals, electronics, machinery, and transportation equipment. In industries such as these, innovating firms that are limited to their own home markets no longer are very common. Instead, enterprises with highly developed multinational networks of producing units typically account for more than half the global output in their respective product lines.

In spreading their networks of subsidiaries around the world, multinational companies have followed some reasonably well-defined patterns. These patterns offer some strong clues regarding the changing perceptions of the enterprises and their likely lines of future behaviour.

First, a word on the extent of the spread itself. Table I compares the scope of the overseas subsidiary networks of a group of the world's largest firms in 1950 with the networks of those same firms in the 1970s. The dramatic increase in the overseas networks of such firms is apparent.

Detailed data have been developed for the 180 US firms in the group, indicating more exactly how the overseas spread took place.[10] According to these data, the overseas spread of the firms in our sample was consistent and stable throughout the three decades following World War II. Firms typically set up their subsidiaries, product lines, and new products in a sequence that began with the geographical areas with which they were most familiar, such as Canada and the United Kingdom, and eventually spread to those that had originally been least familiar, such as Asia and Africa. As time went on, however, the unfamiliar became less so, and the disposition to move first into the traditional areas visibly declined. To illustrate: For product lines introduced abroad by the 180 firms before 1946, the probability that a Canadian location would come earlier than an Asian location was 79 percent; but for product lines that were introduced abroad after 1960, the probability that Canada would take precedence over Asia had dropped to only 59 percent.

The consequences of this steady shift in preferences could be seen in a corresponding shift in the geographical distribution of the foreign subsidiaries of the 180 firms. Before 1946, about 23 percent of the subsidiaries had been located in Canada; but by 1975, the proportion was about 13 percent, with the offsetting gains being recorded principally in Asia, Africa, and the Middle East.[11]

[10] The data on which the next few paragraphs are based are presented in detail in Raymond Vernon and W. H. Davidson, 'Foreign Production of Technology-Intensive Products by U.S.-Based Multinational Enterprises', cited earlier.

[11] Some measures employed in the Vernon-Davidson study—counts based on 954 individual products rather than on subsidiaries or product lines—show Latin America also increasing its relative share. See Table 17, p. 52 of the report.

TABLE 1

Networks of Foreign Manufacturing Subsidiaries of 315 Multinational Companies 1950s and 1970s

Number of Enterprises with Networks Including	180 US-Based MNCs		135 MNCs Based in UK and Europe	
	1950	1975	1950	1970
Fewer than 6 countries	138	9	116	31
6 to 20 countries	43	128	16	75
More than 20 countries	0	44	3	29

Source Harvard Multinational Enterprise Project.

With numerous indications that US firms were feeling at ease over a wider portion of the earth's surface, it comes as no surprise that the interval of time between the introduction of any new product in the United States and its first production in a foreign location has been rapidly shrinking. Table 2 portrays the time lapse between the introduction of 954 products in the United States and their first overseas production via the manufacturing subsidiaries of the introducing firm.

The data also suggest in various ways that the trends just discussed have been strongly self-reinforcing. For instance, firms that had experienced a considerable number of prior transfers to their foreign producing subsidiaries were quite consistently quicker off the mark with any new product than were firms with fewer prior transfers. Besides, as firms introduced one product after another into a given country, the lapse of time between the introduction of successive products in that country steadily declined.

TABLE 2

Spread of Production of 954 New Products by 57 US-Based MNCs to Their Foreign Manufacturing Subsidiaries, Classified by Period When Initially Introduced in the United States

Period When Introduced in US	Number of Products	Percentage Transferred Abroad, by Number of Years between US Introduction and Initial Transfer	
		Within 1 Year After %	Within 2–3 Years After %
1945	56	10.7	8.9
1946–1950	149	8.1	10.1
1951–1955	147	7.5	10.2
1956–1960	180	13.3	17.8
1961–1965	165	22.4	17.0
1966–1970	158	29.7	15.8
1971–1975	99	35.4	16.2
Total	954	18.0	14.0

Source Vernon and Davidson, cited in text.

All told, therefore, the picture is one of an organic change in the overseas networks of large US-based firms. The rate of spread of these networks, whether measured by subsidiaries or by product lines, is slightly lower in the first half of the 1970's than in the latter half of the 1960's; but the spread persists at rates that are rapid by historical standards. Besides, the changes in the rate of spread, according to various econometric tests, seem quite impervious to changes in exchange rates or in price-adjusted exchange rates;[12] so it seems reasonable to assume that we confront a basic change in the institutional structure of the MNCs concerned.[13]

The Environmental Changes

In the period after World War II, the descriptive power of the product cycle hypothesis, at least as it applied to US-based enterprises, had been enhanced by some special factors. In the early part of the post-war period, the US economy was the repository of a storehouse of innovations not yet exploited abroad, innovations that responded to the labour-scarce high-income conditions of the US market. As the years went on, other countries eventually achieved the income levels and acquired the relative labour costs that had prevailed earlier in the United States. As these countries tracked the terrain already traversed by the US economy, they developed an increasing demand for the products that had previously been generated in response to US needs. That circumstance provided the consequences characteristically associated with the product cycle sequence: exports from the United States in mounting volume, followed eventually by the establishment of foreign producing subsidiaries on the part of the erstwhile US exporters.

But many of the advanced industrialized countries that were tracking over the US terrain were doing something more: They were closing in on the United States, narrowing or obliterating the income gap that had existed in the immediate postwar period. In 1949, for instance, the per capita income of Germany and of France was less than one-third that of the United States; but by the latter 1970's, the per capital income of all three countries was practically equal. In the same interval, Japan increased its per capita income from 6 percent of the US level to nearly 70 percent of that level. That shrinkage, of course, weakened a critical assumption of the product cycle hypothesis, namely, that the entrepreneurs of large enterprises confronted markedly different conditions in their respective home markets. As European and Japanese incomes approached those of the United States, these differences were reduced. And as the United States came to rely increasingly on imported raw materials, the differences in the factor costs of the various markets declined further still.

Not only have the differences in income levels among these major markets been shrinking; the differences in their overall dimensions also have declined. This has been due partly to the convergence of such income levels, but partly also to the development of the European Economic Community. As a result, entrepreneurs with their home base in these different markets confront conditions that are much more similar than they had been in the past.

Some of the starting assumptions of the product cycle hypothesis therefore are clearly in question. It is no longer easy to assume that innovating firms are uninformed about conditions in foreign markets, whether in other advanced countries or in the developing

[12]Vernon and Davidson, pp. 19–20.

[13]Although the data for testing the assumption are not at hand, I have assumed that parallel changes are occurring in European and Japanese firms.

world. Nor can it be assumed that US firms are exposed to a very different home environment from European and Japanese firms; although the gap between most of the developing countries and the advanced industrialized countries palpably remains, the differences among the advanced industrialized countries are reduced to trivial dimensions. With some key assumptions of the product cycle hypothesis in doubt, what organizing concepts are still available by which one can observe and assess the role of innovation in the operations of the multinational enterprises of different countries?

THE GLOBAL NETWORK IN OPERATION

To try to answer the question, I have classified multinational companies crudely into three ideal types, and have sought to explore their likely behaviour.

The first type is purely hypothetical, a result of armchair speculation. Picture an MNC with an innovating capability that has developed a powerful capacity for global scanning. Communication is virtually costless between any two points of the globe; information, once received, is digested and interpreted at little or no cost. Ignorance or uncertainty, therefore, is no longer a function of distance; markets, wherever located, have an equal opportunity to stimulate the firm to innovation and production; and factory sites, wherever located, have an equal chance to be weighed for their costs and risks. But some significant economies of scale continue to exist in the development activities as well as in the production activities of the firm.

An enterprise of this sort, we can presume, will from time to time develop an innovation in response to the promise or threat of one of the many markets to which it was exposed. The firm might launch the innovative process in the market that had produced the stimulus; or, if economies of scale were important and an appropriate facility existed elsewhere in the system, in a location well removed from the prospective market. In either case, once the innovation was developed, the global scanner would be in a position to serve any market in which it was aware that demand existed; and would be in a position to detect and serve new demands in other markets as they subsequently arose. Presumably such demands would grow in other countries as they attained the income levels or the factor cost configurations of the country whose needs had first stimulated the invention. For some products, such as consumer goods, the demand in different national markets could be expected to appear in a predictable pecking order, based largely on income levels and labour costs.

The global scanner, therefore, would be in an advantageous position as compared with those firms without such a scanning capability. Firms that were confined to a country which was down the ladder in the pecking order, including most firms headquartered in the developing countries, would be at a disadvantage in relation to the global scanner. As the incomes of their home countries grew, the nonglobal producers might well perceive the opportunity to fill a growing demand; but they would be handicapped by comparison with the enterprises that were already producing in the higher income countries, including the global scanners.

In a world composed of such firms, the product cycle hypothesis would play only a very little role. Although innovating firms might prefer locations in one of the advanced industrialized countries due to the supply of engineers and scientists, the preference for a location in the home market would be weaker. The exports generated by the innovations might come from the country in which the product had initially been introduced; but then again they might not. Whatever the original source of the exports might be, the hold of the exporting country would be tenuous, as the global scanner continuously recalculated the parameters that determined the optimal production location.

The hypothetical global scanner, of course, is not to be found in the real world. The acquisition of information is seldom altogether costless; and the digestion and interpretation of information always entails cost. The typical patterns of behaviour that one observes in the real world reflect that fact.

One typical pattern, which provides the basis for a second model, consists of firms that develop and produce a line of standardized products which they think responds to a homogeneous world demand rather than to the distinctive needs of individual markets. Some firms have been able to take this approach from the very first, because of the nature of their products; the oil, chemical, and crude metals industries, for instance, were always in a position to develop and purvey a standardized line of products to world markets. But the trend has been moving beyond such products to well-elaborated manufactures: to aircraft, computers, pharmaceuticals, and automobiles, for instance. The trends of the automobile industry in that direction are particularly striking.[14]

By standardizing their product on a world basis, firms can hope for two kinds of benefit: they can reduce or avoid the costs of processing and interpreting the information that bears on the distinctive needs of individual markets; and they can capture the scale economies of production and marketing on a global scale. Whether those advantages outweigh the disadvantages of being unresponsive to the needs of individual markets is an empirical question the answer to which may well vary by product lines and other factors; those firms that decide in the affirmative for some or all of their product lines cannot be said to be engaged in an irrational response.

Firms in this category, innovating for a global market, are obliged to play their innovational gambles for relatively heavy stakes. Accordingly, they can be expected to maintain the central core of their innovational activities close to headquarters, where complex face-to-face consultation among key personnel will be possible; in this respect, such firms are likely to perform consistently with the product cycle pattern. To be sure, with increased ease of communication and transportation, various routine aspects of the development work, not involving the most critical choices in the development process, can be spun off to more distant locations. To reduce their development costs and to respond to the pressures of various governments in whose territories they hope to do business, firms in this category are commonly prepared to establish some carefully selected development activities at distant points; but integration at the centre is still needed.[15]

Firms in this category also have a strong need to integrate their global production facilities. Seeking to exploit scale economies, they are likely to establish various component plants in both advanced industrialized countries and developing countries, and to crosshaul between plants for the assembly of final products. That pattern will be at variance with product cycle expectations.

[14]See A. J. Harman, 'Innovations, Technology, and the Pure Theory of International Trade', unpublished Ph.D. thesis, MIT, September 1968, pp. 131–134; J. M. Callahan, 'GM Adopting Worldwide Purchasing Coordination', *Chilton's Automative Industries*, July 1978, pp. 47–49; 'Ford's Fiesta Makes a Big Splash', *Business Week*, August 22, 1977, pp. 38–39; and 'SKF Reintegrates Internationally', *Multinational Business*, The Economist Intelligence Unit, No. 4, 1976, pp. 1–7.

[15]Compare the observations of Sanjaya Lall, 'The International Allocation of Research Activity by U.S. Multinationals', in this issue.

It need not be anticipated, however, that all firms with a capacity for global scanning will commit themselves unequivocally to the development of standard global products such as the IBM 370, the Boeing 757, or the GM world car. General Motors, after all, continues to respond to certain distinctive national characteristics in some of its product lines, in spite of its commitment to a world sourcing strategy. Other automobile firms, including Renault and Chrysler, seem prepared to respond to national factors for even a larger proportion of their output, foregoing the advantages of a world product and long production runs. In computers, a number of IBM's rivals survive by their willingness and ability to adapt to the requirements of local markets, including the requirements of national governments, to a degree that would be incompatible with the standardization of their products and the global rationalization of their facilities.[16] Many European and Japanese firms still find it useful to treat the US market as a distinctive entity, justifying distinctive products and strategies.[17]

Accordingly, we can picture firms that make different decisions on the benefits of global optimization, according to the characteristics of each product line. And we can picture markets in which different firms have settled on somewhat different strategies for closely competing products. If past history is any guide, such differences can persist in a given product market over extended periods of time.[18]

A third type of innovating MNC that merits some speculative consideration is the firm whose choices of innovations and production sites remain myopically oriented to the home market while leaving all analysis of foreign markets to its individual foreign producing subsidiaries. Firms in this category simply put out their home-based innovations for production by their foreign subsidiaries; or, perhaps even more commonly, such firms allow the initiative for such decisions to come from the subsidiaries themselves.[19] Drawing from a shopping list of products generated by the headquarters unit, subsidiaries choose those that seem appropriate for intensive exploitation in their local markets. As long as the proposed production in the subsidiary seems to have no considerable impact on the facilities of the firm located in other countries, the managers at headquarters are disposed to give the local managers their head.

Firms that pursue a policy of this sort can justify their approach readily enough: One possibility is that the firm perceives the cost of interpreting the information needed for pursuing a more centralized policy in production and marketing as exceeding the likely

[16]This point is being developed in detail by Yves Doz at the Harvard Business School.

[17]For evidence on Japanese firms in this category, see Terutomo Ozawa, *Japan's Technological Challenge to the West, 1950–1974* (Cambridge: MIT Press, 1974), pp. 97–98.

[18]This proposition is of course consistent with the theory of strategic groups; see R. E. Caves and M. E. Porter, 'From Entry Barriers to Mobility Barriers: Conjectural Decisions and Contrived Deterrence to New Competition', *Quarterly Journal of Economics*, vol. XCI, no. 2, 1977, pp. 241–261. It is consistent also with the long established observation that different geographical locations offer different combinations of benefits and costs such that widely separated locations applying different production techniques may be competitive for sustained periods. See Max Hall, *Made in New York* (Cambridge: Harvard University Press, 1959).

[19]For illustrations, see 'IBM World Trade Corporation' and 'YKK (Yoshida Kogyo KK)', both in Stanley M. David, *Managing and Organizing Multinational Corporations* (New York: Pergamon Press, 1979). Also, from Intercollegiate Case Clearing House, see *Corning Glass Works* (A), (B), and (C) (numbers 9-477-024, 9-477-073, and 9-477-074); *International Calculators (Australia) Pty. Limited* (9-572-641); *Veedol France* (ICH 10 M 31); *The International Harvester Company (B)* (9 512 009), *Princess Housewares Gmb H (A)* (ICH 13 M 117); *General Foods Corporation—International Division (D2)* (ICH 13 G 214); *AB Thorsten (A)* (9-414-035); and *Sanpix Industries* (9-278-673).

benefits. Another possibility is that the firm has found it impossible to fashion an organization that has the capability for absorbing and being influenced by signals that originate in the subsidiaries.[20]

Where this pattern of operation exists, the hypothesized behaviour of the product cycle may still be visible. But the phase of the product cycle in which the parent is responsible for serving foreign markets will be foreshortened and the oligopolistic strength of the innovating firm will be relatively weak, given the existence of firms in other markets that face similar demands and factor cost conditions.

Cases in this category will of course deviate from the pattern that a global scanner would generate. First, as long as the subsidiary is the initiator, the geographical spread of products will be affected by the risk-taking propensities and drives of individual subsidiary managers and by the resource slack of individual subsidiaries rather than by a consistent set of decision rules and allocations from the centre.[21] Second, in cases in which the initiative for transfer comes from the subsidiary rather than the parent, the possibility of producing in some third country where neither the parent nor the subsidiary is located is unlikely to be considered.

All this leads to a simple conclusion. As we search for a hypothesis that would replace the product cycle concept as an explicator of the trading and investing behaviour of the innovating multinational company, a simple variant such as that of the global scanner will not take us very far. Global scanning is not costless, even when a network of foreign subsidiaries is already in place; costs of collecting and interpreting the information, as the firm perceives those costs, may not be commensurate with its expected benefits. In assessing the benefits, flexibility may be a problem: either the flexibility that firms have lost from decisions in the past, or the flexibility they are fearful of losing in an uncertain future.

So the day of the global scanner as I defined it a few pages back is not yet here. Nevertheless, even if the global scanner is not yet the dominant model, nor perhaps ever will be, the power of the product cycle hypothesis is certainly weakened.

THE PRODUCT CYCLE RECONSIDERED

The evidence is fairly persuasive that the product cycle hypothesis had strong predictive power in the first two or three decades after World War II, especially in explaining the composition of US trade and in projecting the likely patterns of foreign direct investment by US firms. But certain conditions of that period are gone. For one thing, the leading MNCs have now developed global networks of subsidiaries; for another, the US market is no longer unique among national markets either in size or factor cost configuration. It seems plausible to assume that the product cycle will be less useful in explaining the relationship of the US economy to other advanced industrialized countries, and will lose

[20]For indications of the formidable difficulties associated with developing such an organizational capability, see Allen, *Managing the Flow of Technology*, *op. cit.*

[21]This, of course, is a familiar phenomenon, long observed by business historians and organizational behaviourists. More recently the concept has been elevated to the status of theory in Harvey Leibenstein's formulation of his X-inefficiency concept; see his *Beyond Economic Man: A New Foundation for Microeconomics* (Cambridge: Harvard University Press, 1976).

some of its power in explaining the relationship of advanced industrialized countries to developing countries. But strong traces of the sequence are likely to remain.[22]

One such trace is likely to be provided by the innovating activities of smaller firms, firms that have not yet acquired a capacity for global scanning through a network of foreign manufacturing subsidiaries already in place. The assumptions of the product cycle hypothesis may still apply to such firms, as they move from home-based innovation to the possibility of exports and ultimately of overseas investment.

Moreover, even firms with a well-developed scanning capability and a willingness to use it may be found behaving according to the expectations of the product cycle hypothesis. As noted earlier, the specifications of new products are usually in such a state of flux that it is infeasible for a time to fix on a least-cost location. Some firms therefore are unlikely to make intensive use of their scanning capability when siting their first production facility. To be sure, such innovators cannot expect to retain their innovational lead for very long, in view of the fact that the innovators of many countries now confront such similar home conditions. But a shadow of the hypothesized behaviour may well remain.

Moreover, the product cycle may gain some support as a predictive device from other developments.

One such development is the improved position of European and Japanese firms an innovators. As noted earlier, the innovations of these firms, when compared with those of US firms, have tended to place greater emphasis on material-saving and capital-saving objectives, while placing lesser relative emphasis on labour-saving measures and on new mass consumer wants. The costs of materials and capital have risen rapidly over the past few years, both in relative and absolute terms. Accordingly, it may be that the long-time emphasis of the Europeans and Japanese firms will generate an increasing demand for their innovations. The world's increased use of European and Japanese small-car technology and of Japanese steel technology are cases in point, fitting nicely within the structure of the product cycle hypothesis.

However, the product cycle hypothesis would also predict that the European-Japanese advantage on this front will only be temporary. As US firms confront factor-cost conditions in their home market that are similar to those of Europe and Japan, one would expect a stream of innovations from the Americans similar to those of their overseas competitors; General Motors, for instance, is now seen as a potential threat to European and Japanese car makers for the 1980's.

A less equivocal case for the continued usefulness of the product cycle concept is found in analysing the situation of the less-developed countries. Although income, market size, and factor cost patterns have converged among the more advanced industrialized countries, a wide gap still separates such countries from many developing areas. Accordingly, despite the fact that so many MNCs have created producing networks all over the globe, the subsidiaries of such firms located in the developing countries have yet to acquire all of the products that their parents and affiliates produce in richer and larger markets. Most of the developing countries, therefore, are still in process of absorbing the innovations of other countries introduced earlier, according to patterns that remain reasonably consistent with product cycle expectations.

The performance of firms in some developing countries, moreover, follows the expec-

[22]But see I. H. Giddy, 'The Demise of the Product Cycle Model in International Business Theory', *Columbia Journal of World Business*, vol. xiii, no. 1, Spring 1978, pp. 90–97.

tations of the product cycle in a very different sense. Firms operating in the more rapidly industrializing group—in countries such as Mexico, Brazil, India, and Korea—are demonstrating a considerable capability for producing innovations that respond to the special conditions of their own economies.[23] Once having responded to those special conditions with a new product or process or with a significant adaptation of an existing product or process, firms of that sort are in position to initiate their own cycle of exportation and eventual direct investment; their target, according to the hypothesis, would be the markets of the other developing countries that were lagging a bit behind them in the industrialized pecking order.

Indications that some such process was going on in a limited way in the developing countries were already being reported in the 1960's in occasional illustrations and anecdotal materials; but those early cases for the most part involved the subsidiaries of multinational enterprises, which were making modest adaptations of products and processes originally received from the foreign parents.[24] Innovations such as these sometimes gave the subsidiaries a basis for exporting more effectively to neighbouring countries that were lower on the development scale.

In the 1970's, however, the anecdotal materials began to involve firms that were headquartered in developing countries.[25] Firms were reported developing products and processes of special importance to other developing countries, to be followed eventually by the creation of producing subsidiaries in those countries.[26] Of course, the direct investments of the firms of developing countries in other developing countries have not all been of the product cycle variety. The foreign subsidiaries of firms headquartered in developing countries often maintain their position through oligopolistic strengths other than a technological lead.[27]

[23]See, for example, Julio Fidel, et al., 'The Argentine Cigarette Industry: Technological Profile and Behavior', IDB/ECLA Research Programme in Science and Technology, Buenos Aires, September 1978, pp. 92–94; C. J. Dahlman, 'From Technological Dependence to Technological Development: The Case of the USIMINAS Steel Plant in Brazil', IDB/ECLA Research Programme in Science and Technology, Buenos Aires, October 1978; and Jorge Katz *et al.*, 'Productivity, Technology and Domestic Efforts in Research and Development', IDB/ECLA Research Programme in Science and Technology, Buenos Aires, July 1978. For evidence of the increasing capacity of some developing countries to sell plants and engineering services, see Sanjaya Lall, 'Developing Countries as Exporters of Industrial Technology', *Research Policy*, forthcoming, vol. 9, no. 1, January 1980.

[24]W. A. Yeoman, 'Selection of Production Processes for the Manufacturing Subsidiares of U.S.-Based Multinational Corporations', D.B.A. thesis, Harvard University, April 1968, chap. 5; Jorge Katz and Eduardo Ablin, 'Technology and Industrial Exports: A Micro-Economic Analysis of Argentina's Recent Experience', IDB/ECLA Research Programme in Science and Technology, Buenos Aires, August 1978; and by the same authors, 'From Infant Industry to Technology Exports: The Argentine Experience in the International Sale of Industrial Plants and Engineering Works, IDB/ECLA Research Programme in Science and Technology, Buenos Aires, October 1978.

[25]See for instance L. T. Wells, Jr., 'The Internationalization of Firms from Developing Countries', in Tamir Agmon and C. P. Kindleberger, *Multinationals from Small Countries* (Cambridge: MIT Press, 1977), pp. 133–166; by the same author, 'Foreign Investment from the Third World: The Experience of Chinese Firms from Hong Kong', *Columbia Journal of World Business*, Spring 1978, pp. 39, 49; and A. J. Prasad, 'Export of Technology from India', unpublished Ph.D. thesis, Columbia University, 1978, pp. 123–156.

[26]Extensive data on this tendency are being developed by L. T. Wells, Jr., for eventual publication.

[27]Such firms also have been known, for instance, to develop special skills in the maintenance and repair of second hand machinery, and a supply of scarce spare parts for such machinery. See Wells, 'Hong Kong', and Prasad, 'India', p. 147.

Accordingly, the product cycle concept continues to explain and predict a certain category of foreign direct investments. Although it no longer can be relied on to provide as powerful an explanation of the behaviour of US firms as in decades past, it is likely to continue to provide a guide to the motivations and response of some enterprises in all countries of the world.

5

Foreign Direct Investment as a Sequential Process*

Bruce Kogut

The primary advantage of the multinational firm, as differentiated from a national corporation, lies in its flexibility to transfer resources across borders through a globally maximizing network. Recent models of direct foreign investment have tended to downplay these advantages of a coordinated multinational system; rather, they have stressed the motivational behavior arising out of essentially national factors and market imperfections, e.g., proprietary knowledge, domestic industrial structure, and product differentiation. The neglect of the advantages of multinationality obscures, though, an important distinction between the original motivations to establish plants in foreign countries and the subsequent investment decisions. There is, in short, a fallacy of explanation by genesis in failing to distinguish between the initial investment decision and the subsequent incremental investment flows.

This paper argues that current foreign direct investment (FDI) must be understood as laregly sequential flows stemming from the advantages of flexibility of a multinational system. The empirical foundation for this argument can be seen in the change over the past 30 years of the dominant channels of US FDI from new intercompany outflows to reinvested earnings. In 1970, the ratio of equity and intercompany account outflows to reinvested earnings was 1.39. By 1979, the ratio was 0.32. (The complete time series is given in table 1.) The predominant share of FDI flows are incremental investments in already established subsidiaries. In light of these trends, previous theories of FDI which stress the oligopolistic behavior of corporations in their home markets provide incomplete explanations for current FDI. What is required is a greater consideration of the systemic advantages inherent in a multinational network.

These trends carry implications also for the way data on FDI flows are categorized and used. Rather than collecting data according to entries and exits, information should be gathered concerning the conduit of flows as well as changes in the stock of FDI at the firm level. Data which reveals the industry and regional breakdown of both reinvested and new FDI flows would provide a critical platform by which the systemic advantages of the multinational corporation (MNC) can be appraised.

This is not to deny that the advantages of the MNC have been studied. The broader field of research on the MNC has been sensitive to these issues. Especially in the consideration of the political complexities posed by multinational corporations, the peculiar strengths attributed to the operation of a multinational network have been discussed.[1] Such issues as transfer pricing, tax arbitrage, bargaining or negotiating powers, and cost advantages have been analyzed in isolation or in group.[2] There has not been, however, a thorough integration of these issues and the theory of foreign direct investment in the literature, with the partial exception of Dunning (1979).

The purpose of this paper is to move toward such an integration. Section I reviews

*This article is reprinted, with permission, from Kindleberger and Audretsch (eds.), *The Multinational Corporation in the 1980s,* Cambridge, MA: The MIT Press, 1983.

TABLE 1

US Foreign Direct Investment (in Millions of Dollars)

Year	Total	Equity and Intercompany Account Outflows	Reinvested Earnings of Incorporated Affiliates	Ratio of Equity Outflows to Reinvested Earnings
1950	1,088	621	475	1.31
1955	1,766	823	962	0.86
1960	2,039	1,675	1,266	1.32
1965	4,994	3,468	1,542	2.25
1966	4,318	3,625	1,791	2.02
1967	4,768	3,050	1,757	1.74
1968	5,347	2,855	2,440	1.17
1969	6,186	3,130	2,830	1.11
1970	7,387	4,413	3,176	1.39
1971	7,280	4,441	3,176	1.40
1972	7,118	3,214	4,532	0.71
1973	11,435	3,195	8,158	0.39
1974	8,765	1,275	7,777	0.16
1975	13,971	6,196	8,048	0.77
1976	12,759	4,253	7,696	0.55
1977	13,039	5,612	7,286	0.77
1978	17,957	4,877	11,469	0.43
1979	24,844	5,904	18,414	0.32

Source *Survey of Current Business*, US Department of Commerce, vol. 61, no. 2 (February 1981).

briefly the recent FDI literature and introduces a more generalized model in the hope of elucidating the importance of the multinationality factor in FDI flows. The cutting edge of this model is the view of the MNC as a collection of valuable options which permits the discretionary choice of altering real economic activities or financial flows from one country to the next. Section II discusses the valuation of systemic advantages. Finally, section III discusses the importance of this expanded theory from the point of view of host and home countries and comments upon trends likely to persist into the 1980s.

I MULTINATIONALITY AND SEQUENTIAL INVESTMENT

Particular aspects of the contribution of multinationality to the value of the firm and to explaining its behavior have been examined. Kindleberger (1969) considers the conflict between the host country and a multinational firm who are maximizing conflicting objective functions. Agmon and Lessard (1977) and Lessard (1979) note the incremental value of being able to arbitrage tax regimes. Hirsch (1976) cites in a revealing analysis the effects of joint production and trade in intermediate goods in the context of subsequent investment decisions. Vernon (1979) stresses the information- and profit-scanning functions of a multinational network. Davidson (1980) demonstrates the significance of experience effects upon FDI flows.

A growing body of research concerns the combination of location and trade theory with that of internalization. Magee (1977) argues that FDI is motivated by the difficulties of appropriating rents from the trade and licensing in proprietary knowledge. Buckley and Casson (1976) argue similarly that plant location is determined by, one, locational advantages and, two, market failure in the trade of proprietary knowledge, especially that of research and development.

Dunning (1977, 1979) has more recently expanded upon these ideas in developing what he calls the "eclectic theory" of FDI. The theory combines usefully trade theory with transportation theory. Thus, a country's endowment and geographical position create certain "locational" advantages. Dunning then proceeds to consider the factors which determine entry barriers and sustainable oligopolies. These factors, e.g., patented information, brand names, technology, form what he calls "ownership" advantages. Ignoring the possibility of licensing, the various combinations of these advantages suggest a scheme such as shown in figure 1. In the upper right box, for example, the firm possesses a unique technology or some cost advantage. Its home domicile is, however, characterized by higher factor or transportation costs than foreign locations. As a result, it invests overseas. Thus investment occurs only when the home firm possesses a unique asset and the host country is relatively advantaged in location. Finally, the theory of internalization is introduced to explain why licensing is not a preferred mode to FDI.[3] Thus, trade and location theory is wedded to that of internalization in order to explain FDI flows as a response to market imperfections.

Nevertheless, the importance of a multinational network as an important contribution to the value of a firm and its economic opportunities and to the determination of the likely conduits of FDI have not been sufficiently analyzed. In the view of Buckley and Casson, for example, foreign direct investment is the by-product of the search for minimum cost production sites and the internalization of markets. The absence of uniquely international factors is starkly apparent in Hirsch's model, which is considered in more detail in the next section. While Hirsch discusses economies of scale and joint production in marketing at a single location, there is no variable that represents the revenue impact of the ownership of a globally operated system. Dunning (1981) as well does not analyze the precise systemic opportunities generated by multinationality, though he does list several types of advantages.

FIGURE 1

Trade and FDI Outcome for a Single Industry in the Home Country

		location	
		advantaged	disadvantaged
ownership	advantaged	export	FDI outward
	disadvantaged	FDI inward	import

But does the factor of multinationality add to our understanding of the determinants of FDI? One way to answer this question is to consider whether MNCs would still have cause to exist in the absence of the commonly listed market imperfections. Let us suppose, then, that the four of the five imperfections that Buckley and Casson list in the market for technology could be eliminated. These imperfections are (1) the absence of forward markets to hedge the risk of development, (2) the impossibility to arrange contracts that would permit discriminatory pricing, (3) the presence of monoponistic purchasers, and (4) informational assymetry. (The fifth imperfection is that of government intervention, which—along with such events as changes in exchange rates—can create unique arbitrage opportunities for the MNC.) If in some idealized state, these imperfections were altered to the requirements of perfect markets, would there still be the MNC?

The answer would be affirmative, due to three characteristics which enable the MNC to exploit uniquely international distortions in markets or production: one, the ability to arbitrage institutional restrictions; two, the informational externalities captured by the firm in the conduct of international business; three, the cost saving gained by joint production in marketing and in manufacturing. These imperfections, which are carefully considered in the studies on the political dilemmas posed by multinationals and on multinational planning and control, are curiously understated in the mainstream economic literature.

This neglect is derived largely from not considering international projects as incremental at a global level. Although conceiving international investment within a dynamic theory of the firm, the internationalization literature fails to consider the value of the *operational* flexibility and externalities of a multinational system. Rather, the stress is placed upon the *structural* elements of plant location and the elimination of transaction costs.

There is, in short, a tendency to view FDI as a decision made at a discrete point of time. This is the fallacy of genesis to which I previously alluded. The decision to transfer resources internationally is only one aspect of FDI. Given the structural outcome of this decision, the other aspect is the series of sequential decisions which determine the volume and direction of these transferred resources.

Contrary to the structural approach, consideration of the operational value of a global system places stress upon the unique ability of multinationals to reduce the costs of operating in an uncertain world.[4] This is best illustrated by considering explicitly the three factors that were claimed above to be uniquely international attributes. The first is the ability of the MNC to arbitrage institutional restrictions, e.g., tax codes, antitrust provisions, financial limitations, and even national security prohibitions on trade. In effect, the operation of an international system has provided the multinational with a string of options written on contingent outcomes. The difference between the inclusion of taxes, financial incentives, etc., as part of a theory of location and this approach is that the consideration of institutional arbitrage as an option emphasizes the unique ability of the MNC to exploit the conditions of uncertainty in institutional environments. The MNC can, in effect, exercise an option upon the occurrence of an event, e.g., its option to choose in which country to declare its profits. Boundaries do not represent only the costs of tariffs and transport; they also represent profit opportunities which can only be exploited by a multnational corporation.

The second factor concerns the capture of externalities in information, or what we call learning cost externalities. There is an information set required of international business that is separable from that required of domestic business. Corporations spend vast resources in their recruitment of internationally skilled personnel, in political analysis, in intercultural education programs, and in the development of monitoring and control mechanisms. They also invest in information scanning and processing in order locate markets and customers internationally. But most critically, there are important learning curves involved in these activities as well as "first mover advantages." Occidental Petroleum's knowledge and status as a long-standing supplier/customer of the Soviet Union is not easily duplicated.

Joint production economies can occur in both marketing and manufacturing on a global scale. Niehans (1977) has noted that, for example, economies of scale in marketing or servicing coupled with constant or decreasing scale economies in manufacturing can serve to explain the growth of the MNC. Similarly, joint production economies due to the creation of a multinational network reduce the physical capital or labor costs of production and marketing of incremental investments. For example, the multinational network permits the export of otherwise nonexportable goods. since the fixed costs of establishing sales offices, hiring personnel, and locating plant sites are already sunk. The incremental cost saving can permit, as Hirsch suggests, an increase in the export of intermediate products or in the market entry of new products sharing production economies. In addition, the multinational network can serve to export additional final goods or to service the export of other firms' goods in times of slack capacity; the Japanese trading companies are an example of the latter facility. Unquestionably, the formation of a multinational network poses significant barriers to entry. The implications of these barriers are analyzed in greater detail in the conclusions.

II A CAPITAL BUDGET FORMULATION

The value of international factors can be illustrated in a capital-budgeting formulation. In an instructive article, Hirsch (1976) suggests that the decision to service a market by exports or by foreign direct investment can be modeled as minimizing the present value of four cost variables discounted at some appropriate rate: production and tax transportation costs P, research and development costs K, marketing costs M, and control costs C. Demand is assumed as given. Marketing costs are argued to be higher for exports than host-manufactured goods, while control costs rise with the internalization of production. These assumptions are intuitively reasonable. Moreover, Hirsch argues that M and C are increasing functions of K. Implicitly, Magee argued the same in his claim that the opportunity loss of appropriability rises with information content at every stage of production. Hirsch's reasons rest in the costs of market exploration and organizational communication. Since neither argument is mutually exclusive, both can be subsumed in Hirsch's model.

Given this formulation of the model, Hirsch demonstrates convincingly that the failure of conventional trade theory is its consideration solely of the comparative costs of production. Expanding the model to include the production of several goods, Hirsch also shows that economies of joint production can change the investment decision when production for each good is maintained as an independent project. The model is also expanded to consider multistage production, whereby Hirsch shows that overseas investment production can increase the export of previously non-competitive intermediary goods.

While Hirsch discusses economies of joint production in marketing at a single location, there is no variable that represents the cost savings of the ownership of a global system. As suggested earlier, these cost savings arise from considering a global network as a sunk cost and sequential investments as incremental. (There is also the factor that in a world of imperfectly diffused information, the scanning advantages of a multinational widens its set of investment opportunities.) The impact of these cost factors is to reduce the incremental values of C, K, and M and to expand the firm's investment opportunities.

We can illustrate the value of systemic advantages by considering explicitly how a capital budget formulation might account for these benefits, particularly those of the first factor. The first factor, that of arbitraging institutional and national barriers, contributes directly to the enhancement of the discounted revenue stream. Such a contribution is the result of one, a possible reduction in the discount rate, and two, the addition of a string of real but usually nontradeable options. The advantages accrued by international diversification in financial markets and the role of MNCs in providing diversification have been commented upon by several authors, in particular by Solnik (1974), Lessard (1976), and Agmon and Lessard (1977). In a world of no barriers to portfolio flows and of purchasing power parity, the cost of capital at the margin is the same for all investors in a taxless world, regardless of nationality. Since changes in the exchange rates and nominal interest rates would reflect equally changes in prices, discounted cash flows before taxes are the same no matter what their currency denomination.[5] When capital markets are segmented by national barriers and policies, discount rates vary between countries. These variations reflect national differences in risk bearing and in time preferences. To the extent that barriers are imperfect, discount rates tend toward a world rate plus or minus the transaction costs of subventing these barriers. Considered in this light, the equilibrium discount rates can be viewed as prices for a single commodity adjusted for transportation costs, when all countries are equally distant from one another.

The argument for the advantages of the MNC in financial markets boils down to the following set of simple statements. Multinational firms are able to invest across national borders and thereby avoid costly barriers to portfolio flows. Because of its access to more diversified international financial markets, the MNC can, holding everything else equal, invest in marginal projects rejected by host firms. Since the MNC adjusts its risk according to a world portfolio and the domestic firm according to a more homeweighted portfolio (due to capital market imperfections and barriers), the risk-adjusted cost of capital is relatively lower for the MNC. Secondly, if the foreign project represents a unique asset in terms of the available portfolio investments on the world market, the home investor is willing to pay the MNC a premium for contributing an otherwise unattainable asset to his or her portfolio. In conclusion, then, in a world of imperfect international capital flows, MNCs receive a premium relative to their purely domestic home competitors—if their foreign investments are unique and nontraded assets—and invest at a lower capital cost relative to the purely domestic host country competitors.[6]

An aspect that has received less attention in the literature regarding the evaluation of a multinational network is the value of holding a string of options defined by institutional barriers. These barriers include limits on shifting real activities to profit from shifts in real exchange rates, taxes, sovereign risk, and legal prescriptions on equity ownership, form of remittance, etc. To illustrate the importance of these options, consider an MNC operating a series of plants in several countries which serve purely domestic markets. The future cash flows are uncertain. Upon realization of its cash flows, the MNC can through transfer pricing, financial packaging, and other methods alter to a nontrivial extent the structure and level of its obligations. The contingent events are the realization of taxable earnings in each of the various countries. The nature of the option is that the MNC can choose in which geographical jurisdiction to declare these profits so as to minimize the tax burden.

Consider, for a second example, the MNC with several export markets and a few manufacturing plants. By design, the plants operate on average at less than full capacity. In country X, it must renegotiate a set of extraction or labor contracts. In response to unacceptable (however subjectively defined) bargaining positions, the MNC can shift production to other plants to service its overseas markets, given that labor constraints are not binding. (This potential has secondary effects in terms of its bargaining strength, as discussed in section III.) Thus given the uncertainty over the outcomes of negotiations, the MNC has the real option of mitigating the costs of factor price increases or higher taxes in the short term, and the physical adjustment costs in the long term, through maintaining excess capacity in diverse national plants. A similar case is that of variable real exchange rates. The ability to shift exports from a country whose currency is appreciating to one where other plants are located is a valuable option.

What is important to note is that all the above-described options are valuable because the future state of the world is uncertain.[7] Moreover, the more variable the environment, the more valuable are these options. From the point of view of the MNC, the variance of its cash flows and of factor prices in the context of national restrictions presents a set of valuable options relative to the opportunity set of a purely domestic firm. Since these options are exercisable only by the MNC and cannot be traded and purchased by individual investors in any meaningful sense, the value of the firm is enhanced by the incremental value of these options.[8]

Based on the above discussion, the value of the firm can be described as

$$NPV = \sum_{0}^{t} \frac{(\text{cash flows} + \text{learning} + \text{joint production} + \text{options})_t}{(1 + R)^t}$$

The discount rate may be lower than that available on the world market and, as is more likely, lower than that available to host country firms when capital markets are segmented. (The appropriate discount rate for each term is likely to vary according to its systematic risk, but for simplicity, we assume one rate.) The first term represents simply the discounted cash flows from a series of independent projects that are owned by globally unintegrated firms. The next three terms capture the advantages arising out of the interdependence of the cash flows of projects undertaken by an MNC. We have indicated these advantages to be learning-cost and joint-production economies, and the possession of real nontradeable options.

How may these advantages be actually evaluated?[9] Once the initial investment is made, learning cost and joint production externalities are likely to be incorporated in the capital budget through an incremental analysis. A more complex analysis is to evaluate at the time of the initial investment the value of the option to expand into other products or into other markets. The option to arbitrage national barriers is similarly difficult to evaluate. Given the recent interest in evaluating financial options, it would appear that the analytical methods are already available to value real options numerically.[10] There are, however, serious obtacles to such an extension which are not always noted in the literature. In brief, a financial option can be valued because one assumes that there exists a shadow security whose price follows a particular type of stochastic process. In the absence of such a shadow security, we have no reason to believe that the price of the real asset will also follow such a path since there is no means to arbitrage the real option against its shadow security. Nevertheless, the options literature provides the appropriate framework for understanding the reasoning behind the claim that the option to exercise certain rights, e.g., where to declare taxes, where to shift production, is a valuable hedge against contingent events.

The inclusion of these three elements in addition to the normal cash flows generated by project illustrates the opportunities that stem from a multinational system. As a result of these opportunities, we expect that growth in FDI is more likely to be in the form of expansion of existing activities than in new entries. The consequences of this trend from the perspective of governments are discussed in the next section.

III IMPLICATIONS FOR FUTURE INVESTMENT TRENDS

From the firms' point of view, the flexibility to transfer resources across borders is a positive contribution to its earning stream. As discussed in an abundant literature, the viewpoints of governments are often less sanguine. Rather than consider the larger issues of government and MNC relations, we concentrate on a few specific issues, e.g., monetary stabilization, regulation, and negotiation. Through these examples, we illustrate that the well-established issues of contention between governments and MNCs are comprehensible only within the context of the systemic flexibility of the MNCs.

How is a government likely to view these systemic advantages of MNCs when pursuing domestic monetary stabilization objectives? If an MNC speculates on currencies, its behavior tends to give markets greater liquidity and thereby accelerates the speed of adjustments. Even if the MNC is not a speculator, it forecasts and hedges its contractual and noncontractual exposure. Whether it speculates or is able merely to shift currencies more easily from one country to the next or to write more inexpensive contractual hedges, these activities clearly tend to negate the ability of governments to pursue objectives such as the stabilization of its currency countervailing to the market trend. Thus the presence of MNCs limits further the ability of governments to pursue independent objectives in an international economy.

If governments are more constrained in their ability to pursue monetary objectives due to the existence of MNCs, are they more constrained in pursuing other objectives? Consider a government which desires to regulate a foreign-owned industry. Under closed borders, enterprises are essentially hostage to the partisan coalitions of its environment. Since exit except in the form of selling its holdings is impossible, the regulated enterprise consents to government regulation, while it may itself seek to join a political coalition.[11] For the MNC whose foreign assets are primarily in the form of proprietary knowledge, regulation is unlikely to be successful. It is especially unsuccessful in its most extreme form—that of nationalization, for as long as the ongoing value of the subsidiary is dependent on a sequential stream of innovations, nationalization results merely in the elimination of industry. The effects of less extreme interventions, e.g., an increase in taxation, invoke most likely less extreme reactions. Nevertheless, the implications are the same. To the extent that multinational corporations contribute more to the economy than that of the new policies, their partial or total withdrawal are a real loss to the host country. Moreover, if multinational corporations are truly global, then the argument applies to home countries in which governments attempt to regulate, for example, outward flows of capital.

When FDI is primarily transmitted in the form of fixed capital with known and stable technologies, the bargaining position of the MNC and host government is reversed. This situation, which is known as the obsolescent bargain, has been extensively analyzed.[12] Mining is a classic example. The original investment requires a large fixed capital component. Presumably the MNC chooses to internalize this transaction in order to gain access to guaranteed supplies, to speculate on future prices when futures markets do not exist or do not trade claims on contracts many years out, or to acquire oligopolistic advantages. At the time of the investment, the host government's bargaining position is constrained by competition from other countries. The host government can, however, capture part, if not all, of the rents ex post to the investment through a process of renegotiation. If, for example, the value of its mineral resources is higher than expected, the host government has the option of capturing part of the consequent excess returns. To the extent that this gaming behavior is expected and that equity claims and other financial contracts are difficult to enforce, it is likely that MNCs will be reluctant to invest in mineral extraction without adequate guarantees or insurance.

What does the above analysis imply for the growth and the role of the American MNC in the 1980s? There are three principal implications. First is that the entry of new firms in international markets is likely to slow, holding changes in investment opportunities constant. Evidence for this transition is suggested, as noted earlier, in the growth of reinvested earnings relative to new equity investment in total FDI flows. These figures have been given in table 1.

The benefits of institutional arbitrage, learning curve effects, and joint production economies create, then, substantial barriers to entry. The importance of these factors is underlined in light of the present proportion of intra-firm trade which accounted roughly for 50% of all US imports in 1977 (Helleiner, 1979). Discussions of antitrust implications have usually stressed the feedback of FDI on competition in the home market (Bergsten et al., 1978). Perhaps a more troubling aspect is the impact of these barriers on the entry of firms from LDCs or from developed countries which were slow to create international firms. While FDI between LDCs has been increasing, such investments appear to be characterized more by the capture by small firms of investment gaps ignored by the much larger MNCs. Thus, FDI by LDCs is likely to be explained by a theory of FDI by small firms than by entry openings unique to the skills of LDC enterprises.[13]

Another implication lies in the persisting role of research and development in explaining some, though perhaps a relatively decreasing amount, of flows of proprietary capital over international borders. For those end products that are oriented towards the home market, FDI is often in the form of overseas production of intermediary products. In this case, FDI is related to research and development only insofar as the end product embodies a large value of technological expenditure. The overseas production of intermediary goods can involve minimal research and development expenditures in terms of value added. Moreover, FDI is in this form partially trade enhancing.

What should be noted is that the production of technologically sophisticated products is of less importance—though still of indubitable significance—in future FDI flows. Instead, we can imagine the development of decentralized structures that permits the delegation of product selection and research and development to subsidiaries but leaves the strategic variables of financing, production, and tax arbitrage to the home office.

There is some indication that this devolution is already perceptible in the food industry (Katz, 1981).

Related to the above implications is the tendency of the MNCs to develop and expand their trading divisions. In part, this evolution is derived from the hazards of the obsolescent bargain as well as from the erosion of market advantages as the original technological edge in some products evaporates. Vernon (1977) has termed this latter trend "senescence." The difference between these two trends is simply that the obsolescent bargain refers to loss of property rights, senescence to loss of market shares. The underlying cause of both trends is, however, similar, i.e., the loss of some technological advantage specific to the firm which maintains its bargaining or market position. In the first case, the MNC can limit its exposure by financing extraction in the form of debt with payoffs denominated in a specified quantity of the underlying mineral or product, or by long-term contracts, or by providing managerial services and downstream marketing and relinquishing its ownership or contractual obligations. In the second case, the MNC is also induced toward eliminating its productive activities and in effect leasing the services of its global network. In both cases, the possession of a multinational network provides a stream of benefits and investment opportunities independent of the products being traded. Examples of this development are the oil industry, Japanese trading companies, and the diversification of large firms into trading third-party products, such as in the case of Thyssen.

Consequently, the MNC of the 1980s is likely to be engaged less in equity investments in primary extraction industries, but relatively more in the provision of marketing and consulting services. Trade in intermediate products is also likely to increase, because the MNC can optimize production and marketing within an already existing global system. These trends, of course, are a continuation of a pattern that has been visible for several years.

IV CONCLUSIONS

I have tried to detail the precise advantages arising from a multinational network and its implication for the identity of the agents and the type of investment flows in the future. By and large, policy implications have not been discussed. The reasons for this omission are simple. Having developed our model under the assumption of profit maximization, optimal policy recommendations which differ from a competitive profit-maximizing outcome can only be motivated if the national objective functions are specified. I have not attempted such a specification, although the dropping of the assumption of profit maximization would be an interesting exercise.

The question has been left open whether the profitability and growth of the MNC is a result of its market power or productive efficiency.[14] I have, however, implicitly suggested the importance of first-mover advantages that current MNCs possess relative to potential entrants. If we are concerned over the absence of bargaining power on behalf of many LDCs, then our analysis reinforces the recommendations for an international regulation of MNCs or the creation of countervailing institutions or enterprises to enhance the bargaining power of LDC countries. Such regional efforts as ASEAN's recent consideration of the formation of trading companies similar to those of the Japanese are illustrations of efforts to create potential countervailing enterprises. But hidden beneath such developments and recommendations is an irony often noted in the case of MNCs from developed countries. That is, though the rents from learning-curve and joint-production externalities accrue to the home MNC and hence potentially to the home countries, the creation of truly global enterprises poses challenges to the national sovereignty of governments through their maximization of global profits and through their arbitraging of institutional borders. In other words, is it reasonable to expect that an MNC originating in a developing country which maximizes its return from its global activities, should be more sensitive to the sovereignty and interests of its national government?

Consequently, the conflict of nation-states and international firms remains an issue in the 1980s. Countries face incentives not only to regulate the entry of firms, but also their exit. There has appeared the ironic evolution that LDCs have been concerned to establish strict rules of entry, whereas developed countries increasingly seek to control the exit of firms and the immediate loss of jobs and production. Whether the combined impact of these trends is to reduce the benefits of a global network remains to be seen; but, in any event, it represents the forefront of future discussions on the merits of FDI and the multinational corporation.

NOTES

I would like to thank Stephen Kobrin of New York University and Richard D. Robinson of the Massachusetts Institute of Technology for their comments on an earlier draft. I am especially grateful to Donald Lessard of the Massachusetts Institute of Technology for his comments on the first and subsequent drafts.

1. See, for example, Kindleberger (1969), Vernon (1971, 1977), or Stopford and Wells (1972).

2. Such issues as transfer pricing, tax arbitrage, bargaining or negotiating power, and regulation are discussed by Lessard (1979), Bergsten et al. (1978), and Robinson (1976).

3. For a review of the internalization literature, see Rugman (1981). It should be noted that the concept of internalization is already adumbrated, like so many ideas in the literature on FDI, in Kindleberger (1969), pp. 19–22.

4. Undoubtedly, it can be claimed that the theory of internalization accounts precisely for these operational facets. (See e.g., Buckley and Casson, 1976, p. 69.) But by placing stress upon the cost aspect of transactions, it fails to consider the profit opportunities generated by a global system.

5. This can be shown by considering whether to discount the overseas earnings by the home or foreign discount rate. If we assume purchasing power parity, changes of nominal interest rates are canceled by identical changes of nominal exchange rates.

6. In his contribution to this volume, Robert Aliber revives his earlier argument that FDI can be explained at the macroeconomic level, i.e., the arbitrage of international markets. Though such an approach appears weak in explaining such phenomena as cross-hauling, it has a tantalizing appeal in its attempts to link such anomalies as FDI waves to concepts as Tobin's *q*. There may be a macroeconomic story after all.

7. In the cases where uncertainty may appear as irrelevant, such as in tax arbitrage, governments are well-equipped to develop monitoring and enforcement services. It is the uncertainty of the realized profits that keeps the costs of these services relatively high to the benefits of reducing arbitrage behavior.

8. Some readers may be misled into inferring that the above argument suggests that total variance does matter after all to the investor. To the contrary, since these options are similar to monopoly or proprietary rents, the firms earn abnormally high rates of return but the stocks written on the firm, as long as they are traded in competitive capital markets, are priced in the expectation of a market rate of return adjusted for systematic risk.

9. See Lessard (1981) for a thorough discussion of the application of adjusted present value techniques for valuating international projects.

10. See the path-breaking article by Black and Scholes (1973) for the evaluation of financial options. Our concern with the shadow security is directed primarily at recent extensions of the Black-Scholes model into the evaluation of real assets. MacDonald and Segal (1981) are certainly aware of these difficulties, whereas Broyles and Cooper (1981) simply assume the existence of a shadow security without substantial comment.

11. See the interesting article by Magee in this volume which discusses the impact of political coalitions on FDI flows.

12. See the writings of Vernon (1971), Stopford and Wells (1972), and Bergsten et al., (1978).

13. We have not tried here to develop such a theory of FDI by small firms. Briefly, one relevant factor would seem to be trade in custom-designed products, i.e., small producers are more sensitive to the "voice" (in Hirschman's terminology) of smaller producers (Hirschman, 1971). Another factor is the trading by small firms of used capital equipment. Since used capital equipment is difficult to valuate, the seller may attempt to eliminate the costs of discounting incurred through the asymmetry in information by taking an equity position. Indeed, joint ventures between LDCs are relatively common. These factors, in addition to the ones discussed above, tend to explain some characteristics of FDI between LDCs, whose markets tend after all not to be dominated by large domestic enterprises as those in developed countries. For a discussion of FDI between LDCs, see Wells (1977).

14. A number of articles in this volume attempt to measure econometrically the relationship between the profitability of the MNC and barriers to entry. Though the factor of efficiency is not explicitly specified in these regressions, the results are nevertheless interesting in showing the significant correlation of these profits and barriers to entry.

REFERENCES

Agmon, Tamir, and Donald Lessard, 1977. "Financial Factors and the International Expansion of Small-Country Firms," in T. Agmon and C. P. Kindleberger (eds.), *Multinationals from Small Countries*. Cambridge, Mass.: MIT Press.

Bergsten, C. Fred, Thomas Horst, and Theodore Moran, 1978. *American Multinationals and American Interests*, Washington, D.C.: Brookings.

Broyles, J. E., and I. A. Cooper, 1981. "Growth Opportunities and Real Investment Decisions," in F. G. L. Derkinderen and R. L. Crum (eds.), *Risk, Capital Costs, and Project Financing Decisions*. The Hague: Nijhoff.

Buckley, Peter J. and Mark Casson, 1976. *The Future of the Multinational Enterprise*. London: Holmes and Meier.

Davidson, William, 1980. "The Location of Foreign Direct Investment Activity: Country Characteristics and Experience Effects," *Journal of International Business Studies*, pp. 9–22.

Dunning, John H., 1977. "Trade, Location of Economic Activity and the MNE: A Search for an Eclectic Approach," in Bertil Ohlin et al. (eds.), *The International Allocation of Economic Activity*. London: Holmes and Meier.

______, 1979. "Explaining Changing Patterns of International Production: In Defense of the Eclectic Theory," *Oxford Bulletin of Economics and Statistics* 41, pp. 269–96.

______, 1981. "Explaining Outward Direct Investments of Developing Countries: In support of the Eclectic Theory of International Production," in *Multinationals from Developing Countries*, Lexington, Mass.: Maxwell G. McLeod.

Helleiner, Gerald K., 1979. "Transnational Corporations and Trade Structure: The Role of Intra-firm Trade," in H. Giersch (ed.), *On the Economics of Intra-Industry Trade*. Tübingen: J. C. B. Mohr.

Hirsch, Seev, 1976. "An International Trade and Investment Theory of the Firm." *Oxford Economic Papers* 28, pp. 258–270.

Hirschman, Albert O., 1970. *Exit, Voice, and Loyalty. Responses to Decline in Firms, Organizations, and States*. Cambridge, Mass.: Harvard University Press.

Katz, Jan Hack, 1981. "Does Foreign Direct Investment Theory Reflect Reality: The

Case of the American Food Processors." Sloan School of Management Working Paper. Massachusetts Institute of Technology.

Kindleberger, Charles P., 1969. *American Business Abroad: Six Lectures on Direct Investment.* New Haven: Yale University Press.

Lessard, Donald, 1976. "World, Country, and Industry Relations in Equity Returns: Implications for Risk Reduction through International Diversification," *Financial Analysts' Journal*, January/February, pp. 2–8.

———, 1979. "Transfer Prices, Taxes and Financial Markets: Implications of Internal Financial Transfers Within the Multinational Firm," in R. G. Hawkins (ed.), *Economic Issues of Multinational Firms.* New York: JAI Press.

———, 1980. "Evaluating International Projects: An Adjusted Present Value Approach," in R. Crum and F. Derkinderen (eds.), *Capital Budgeting Under Conditions of Uncertainty.* The Hague: Nijhoff.

McDonald, Robert, and Daniel Segal, 1981. "Options and the Valuation of Risky Projects." (unpublished paper), August, presented at the Finance Research Seminar of Sloan School of Management, Massachusetts Institute of Technology.

Magee, Stephan P., 1977. "Information and the Multinational Corporation: An Appropriability Theory of Direct Foreign Investment," in J. Bhagwati (ed.), *The New Economic Order: The North-South Debate.* Cambridge, Mass.: MIT Press.

Niehans, Juerg, 1977. "Benefits of Multnational Firms for a Small Parent Economy: The Case of Switzerland," in T. Agmon and C. P. Kindleberger (eds.), *Multinationals from Small Countries.* Cambridge, Mass.: MIT Press.

Robinson, Richard D., 1976. *National Control of Foreign Business Entry.* New York: Praeger.

Rugman, Alan M., 1980. "Internalization as a General Theory of Foreign Direct Investment: A Re-Appraisal of the Literature," *Weltwirtschaftliches Archiv* 116, pp. 365–79.

Solnik, Bruno H., 1974. "Why Not Diversify Internationally?", *Financial Analysts' Journal*, July-August, pp. 48–54.

Stopford, John, and Louis Wells, 1972. *Managing the Multinational Enterprise. Organization of the Firm and Ownership of the Subsidiaries.* New York: Basic Books.

Vernon, Raymond, 1971. *Sovereignty at Bay: The Multinational Spread of US Enterprises.* New York: Basic Books.

———, 1977. *Storm over the Multinationals: The Real Issues.* Cambridge, Mass.: Harvard University Press.

———, 1979. "The Product Cycle Hypothesis in a New International Environment." *Oxford Bulletin of Economics and Statistics* 41, pp. 255–267.

Wells, Louis, 1977. "Firms from Developing Countries," in T. Agmon and C. P. Kindleberger (eds.), *Multinationals from Small Countries.* Cambridge, Mass.: MIT Press.

Capital Market Integration and Asset Valuation

6

Pricing Capital Assets in an International Setting: An Introduction*

Rene M. Stulz†

SECTION 1 INTRODUCTION

Capital asset pricing models play a central role in finance theory.[1] For instance, they provide the basis for finding appropriate discount rates in capital budgeting problems. However, when one tries to extend such models to an international setting, one is confronted with several important problems

1. Whereas most basic capital asset pricing models use the simplifying assumption that returns are denominated in a numeraire good whose price is fixed, such an assumption makes little sense when one has to choose a portfolio in a world in which inflation rates are stochastic and differ across countries.
2. In deriving capital asset pricing models, one generally assumes that investors have identical tastes with respect to commodities and consume identical baskets of goods. While this may be a reasonable approximation in a single country, it is not very useful in an international setting since investors based in different countries consume locally produced, nontraded goods and, probably, differing proportions of internationally traded goods. Since the relative prices of traded and nontraded goods fluctuate significantly, real returns on any particular asset depend upon which investor's perspective is taken.
3. Capital asset pricing models generally assume that all investors have the same investment opportunity set—i.e., that any distribution of returns feasible for one investor is feasible for all investors. In an international setting, taxes, transactions costs and holding costs differ across securities and across investors. Furthermore, some investors are restricted from buying some securities.

In this paper, we show how differences across countries of (1) inflation rates, (2) consumption baskets of investors and (3) investment opportunity sets of investors matter when one applies capital asset pricing models in an international setting. In particular, we show how the fact that countries differ affects the portfolios held by investors, the equilibrium expected returns and the financial policies of firms. Many results presented in this paper are already known. The main contribution of this paper is a systematic and unified examination of the implications of what we believe to be the three most important differences among countries for applications of capital asset pricing models in an interna-

---

*This article is reprinted, with permission, from *Journal of International Business Studies.*

†Associate Professor, Faculty of Finance, College of Administrative Sciences, Ohio State University. I am grateful to Don Lessard for useful conversations and extensive comments, and to Thierry Bollier, Jim Bodhurtha, and Steve Buser for useful comments. I also thank three anonymous referees for comments.

tional setting.[2] The purpose of this paper is to discuss problems one encounters when applying capital asset pricing models rather than to derive international asset pricing models under the most general assumptions. Throughout the paper, we provide references to more general derivations of the results we present, when such references are available, and otherwise provide directions for more general derivations of our results. It is hoped that the reader will find that the added clarity in our discussion, which results from its not being burdened by a lot of technical baggage, makes up for the lack of generality and sophistication of our approach.

Although we believe that all three differences among countries we explore affect asset prices in a significant way, we choose to introduce first in the discussion the difference among countries whose impact on capital asset pricing models is the easiest to understand. As we proceed, we relax our assumptions to obtain more realistic but also more complex models of capital asset pricing. The plan of the paper is as follows. In Section 2, we discuss differences in inflation rates. The effect of these differences on asset holdings and expected returns are further explored in Section 3. In Section 4, we introduce differences in consumption baskets. Differences in investment opportunity sets are discussed in Section 5. Section 6 offers some concluding remarks.

SECTION 2 DIFFERENCES IN PURCHASING POWER RISKS ACROSS CURRENCIES

In this section, we show how differences in purchasing power risks across currencies affect an investor's holdings of risky assets and the equilibrium expected returns of risky assets when there are no real differences among investors. By purchasing power risks we refer to the differing, uncertain purchasing power of individual currencies under the assumption that goods markets are in equilibrium. In other words, in this section all investors face the same real investment opportunity set and consume the same basket of commodities. While this may appear to be an unrealistic set of assumptions, it is one that has been used in much of the international asset pricing models. Further, it provides an excellent case to understand under which conditions internationalization of capital asset pricing models makes no difference. In Section 4 below, we deal with the more complex but realistic situation in which there are not only differing rates of inflation across currencies, but there also are relative price changes and investors have differing consumption preferences.

While earlier research has presented models that show how differences in purchasing power risks across currencies can be incorporated in a model of asset pricing, this section uses yet another model.[3] In the perspective of this paper, the model used here is attractive for at least two reasons. First, it is simpler than earlier models as it constitutes a straightforward extension of the Black (1972) capital asset pricing model without risk-free lending and borrowing. Second, throughout this paper, we derive equilibrium expected returns by perturbating an investor's portfolio at the optimum. The model used in this section is helpful to introduce this approach.

2.1 Some Assumptions

To focus the discussion on inflation rates, we assume that all investors consume the same commodity and that the price of the commodity in any particular currency is the same in all countries. In other words, there are no barriers to international trade and the law of one price as well as purchasing power parity hold all the time.+ Furthermore, we assume a one-period world in which investors maximize a utility function that is increasing in the expected value of end-of-period consumption and, because of risk aversion, decreasing in the variance of end-of-period consumption. End-of-period consumption, in a one-period world, is equal to end-of-period real wealth, i.e., nominal wealth divided by the price of the commodity consumed. With our assumptions, it follows that investors care only about the mean and variance of *real* returns. Finally, we assume that financial markets are perfect, i.e., all investors are price-takers, there are no transactions costs, no taxes and no restrictions on short sales.

Without loss of generality, we assume that there are only two countries, the domestic country and the foreign country. Prices and returns denominated in foreign currency are denoted by stars. As the law of one price holds, real returns are the same for all investors. To understand this, let P_{ij} (P^*_{ij}) be the price of security i in domestic (foreign) currency and P_j (P^*_j) be the domestic (foreign) price of the commodity at date j, $j = 0,1$. Notice that the price at home of security i in terms of the commodity at date j is P_{ij}/P_j whereas abroad it is P^*_{ij}/P^*_j. Let e_j be the price of one unit of foreign currency at date j. The law of one price implies that $P_j = e_jP^*_j$. It immediately follows that $P_j = P^*_{ij}/P^*_j = e_jP^*_{ij}/e_jP^*_j = P_{ij}/P_j$. As the price of a security in terms of the commodity is the same everywhere, real returns must be the same everywhere.

2.2. Equilibrium Expected Real Returns

To show the determinants of equilibrium expected returns, we assume that markets are in equilibrium and use the first-order conditions of the representative investor's portfolio optimization problem. The fact that real returns on securities are the same for all investors means that the country of residence of an investor is irrelevant. We can look at a representative investor and use only real returns. This investor chooses a portfolio that is mean-variance efficient, i.e., a portfolio such that, for a given variance of real return, no other portfolio has a higher real expected return. Random variables are denoted by tildes. Let $\tilde{r}_i$ be the real return of security i and σ_{ij} be the covariance of the real return of security i with the real return of security j.

Given our assumptions about the investor's expected utility function, the solution of the investor's portfolio choice problem is a portfolio, i.e., weights w_i, $i = 1, \ldots, n$, which maximizes his expected real wealth subject to the constraint that the variance of the real return of his portfolio equals some number K and that the w_i's sum to one. Consequently, to solve for the optimal w_i's, the investor maximizes the following Lagrangian function:

$$L = E\left(\sum_{i=1}^{n} w_i\tilde{r}_i\right) + \lambda\left(\sum_{i=1}^{n}\sum_{j=1}^{n} w_iw_j\sigma_{ij} - K\right) - \mu\left(\sum_{i=1}^{n} w_i - 1\right) \quad (1)$$

where $E(.)$ denotes the expectation operator. Let w^o_i be the optimal value of w_i, for all i's. By the fact that w^o_i and w^o_j are optimal, a small change in w^o_i and w^o_j, so that $w^{o\prime}_i = w^o_i + \Delta$ and $w^{o\prime}_j = w^o_j - \Delta$, leaves the optimized value of L unchanged. It follows that

$$\frac{\partial L}{\partial w^o_i} - \frac{\partial L}{\partial w^o_j} = E(\tilde{r}_i) - E(\tilde{r}_j) + \lambda\left[\sum_{k=1}^{n} w^o_i\sigma_k - \sum_{k=1}^{n} w^o_k\sigma_k\right] = 0 \quad (2)$$

The economy we are looking at has many investors who are not all the same. Suppose, however, that we could construct an artificial economy that would be exactly the same as the economy we are considering here, except for the fact that in that artificial economy all investors are the same. Our representative investor is equivalent to an investor in that artificial economy. Therefore, the representative investor must hold the market portfolio—otherwise the market portfolio would not be held in the artificial economy.[5] Let $\tilde{r}_m$ be the real return on the market portfolio and $\tilde{r}_z$ the real return on a portfolio uncorrelated with the return on the market portfolio. Equation (2) then implies that[6]

$$E(\tilde{r}_i) - E(\tilde{r}_z) = \beta_i[E(\tilde{r}_m) - E(\tilde{r}_z)] \tag{3}$$

where

$$\beta_i = \frac{\mathrm{Cov}(\tilde{r}_i, \tilde{r}_m)}{\mathrm{Var}(\tilde{r}_m)} \tag{4}$$

Equation (3) shows that the real expected return on a security is a linear function of the beta of the security. Furthermore, similarly to the Black (1972) model, the expected real return on a security in excess of the expected real return on the zero beta portfolio is an increasing function of the expected real return on the market portfolio in excess of the expected real return on the zero beta portfolio. Notice, however, that the market portfolio includes all securities in the world and not only domestic securities. Whereas it seems reasonable to argue that investors cannot borrow or lend at a real risk-free rate, note also that when such borrowing and lending opportunities are available, the real risk-free rate of return replaces $E(\tilde{r}_z)$ in equation (3).

SECTION 3 SOME IMPLICATIONS OF DIFFERENCES IN PURCHASING POWER RISKS ACROSS CURRENCIES

As the model presented in Section 2 is similar to the Black model of asset pricing without risk-free borrowing and lending, it is not surprising that its implications for holdings of risky assets by investors are the same as those of the Black model. In particular, in this model, investors hold portfolios that are mean-variance efficient in real terms. The representative investor holds the market portfolio, which is mean-variance efficient. An investor more (less) risk-tolerant than the average investor holds a portfolio more (less) risky than the market portfolio. As there is no good reason to expect the risk tolerance of investors to differ much across countries, the model implies that investors tend to hold similar portfolios everywhere in the world. As it is generally believed that investors hold very different portfolios across countries and that the portfolio held by an investor tends to be heavily weighted toward investments in his home country, the model developed so far offers an incomplete view of portfolio choice and, consequently, of asset pricing in open economies. It is, however, worthwhile to pursue the implications of this model for equilibrium expected returns, as this allows us to understand how differences in purchasing power risks across currencies affect equilibrium expected real returns. We conclude the section with a discussion of the concept of exchange rate risk.

3.1 Equilibrium Expected Returns of Common Stocks

The real return on security *i* is equal to the percentage change in the real price of secuirty *i*. The real price of security *i* is its price in a currency divided by the price in the same currency of the commodity consumed by investors. As the law of one price holds, one can use domestic currency prices without loss of generality. Consequently, the real return on security *i* is

$$\tilde{r}_i = \frac{\tilde{P}_{i1}}{\tilde{P}_1}\left(\frac{P_{i0}}{P_0}\right)^{-1} - 1 = \frac{\tilde{R}_i - \tilde{I}}{1 + \tilde{I}} \tag{5}$$

where $\tilde{I}$ is the domestic rate of inflation, i.e., $\tilde{P}_1/P_0 - 1$, and $\tilde{R}_i$ is the nominal rate of return on asset *i*, i.e., $\tilde{P}_{i1}/P_{i0} - 1$. Substituting for $\tilde{r}_i$ in equation (3) and using equation (5) we get

$$E\left(\frac{\tilde{R}_i - \tilde{I}}{1 + \tilde{I}}\right) - E\left(\frac{\tilde{R}_z - \tilde{I}}{1 + \tilde{I}}\right) = \beta_i\left[E\left(\frac{\tilde{R}_m - \tilde{I}}{1 + \tilde{I}}\right) - E\left(\frac{\tilde{R}_z - \tilde{I}}{1 + \tilde{I}}\right)\right] \tag{6}$$

where

$$\beta_i = \frac{\text{Cov}\left(\frac{\tilde{R}_i - \tilde{I}}{1 + I}, \frac{\tilde{R}_m - \tilde{I}}{1 + \tilde{I}}\right)}{\text{Var}\left(\frac{\tilde{R}_m - \tilde{I}}{1 + \tilde{I}}\right)} \tag{7}$$

Equation (6) shows that, in general, the model developed in this section yields different expected returns for securities than converting returns into domestic currency returns and using the Sharpe-Lintner capital asset pricing model.[7] With the model developed in this section, the expected real return of individual assets in excess of the expected real return on the zero beta portfolio is a linear function of the beta of these assets computed using real returns for the assets and for the market portfolio. In contrast, the Sharpe-Lintner model is generally interpreted as stating that the expected nominal return of individual assets in excess of the return of the riskless nominal asset is a linear function of the beta of these assets computed using nominal returns for these assets and for the market portfolio. To gain some insights into how the expected returns given in equation (6) differ from those given by the Sharpe-Lintner model, it is useful to pause briefly and look at the relation between nominal returns and inflation. The traditional view is that common stocks are good hedges against unanticipated inflation because common stocks are claims to real resources. However, in general, common stock returns can be positively or negatively correlated or negatively correlated with unexpected inflation depending on the activities of the corporation considered. For instance, one would expect that the higher the face value of the nominal debt of a firm, *ceteris paribus*, the higher the gain of that firm from unanticipated inflation. Nevertheless, the empirical evidence is that, on average, nominal common stock returns are uncorrelated or negatively correlated with unexpected inflation.[8]

To make the implications of equation (6) more explicit, we briefly discuss the special case in which the nominal rate of return on the market portfolio is uncorrelated with the rate of inflation. Consider a security whose nominal return is uncorrelated with the rate of inflation and with the nominal rate of return of the market portfolio. This security has a Sharpe-Lintner beta equal to zero. However, the real beta of this security, i.e., the beta computed according to equation (7), is positive, as both the real return of this security and the real return of the market portfolio are negatively correlated with the rate of inflation. Furthermore, the Sharpe-Lintner beta will underestimate (overestimate) the risk of assets whose real rate of return is negatively (positively) correlated with the rate of inflation.[9] To understand this, notice that an asset whose Sharpe-Lintner beta is equal to zero but whose real rate of return is negatively (positively) correlated with the rate of inflation has a positive (negative) real beta.

3.2 The Relation Between the Forward Exchange Rate and the Expected Future Spot Exchange Rate

The model derived in Section 2 can be used to show how the forward exchange rate is related to the expected future spot exchange rate. The payoff from holding a one-period foreign currency forward contract is $e_1 - F$, where e_1 is the spot exchange rate at date 1 and F is the forward exchange rate at date 0 for a contract that matures at date 1. This follows from the fact that the investor can sell at a price e_1 the currency he has to purchase at a price F. As a forward contract involves no initial outlay, the forward price F must be such that the present value of a payoff equal to $e_1 - F$ is equal to zero. Consequently, the forward exchange rate is a decreasing function of the systematic risk an investor must bear when he holds a forward contract. The difference between the expected future spot exchange rate and the forward exchange rate compensates investors for the systematic risk they bear while being long in the foreign currency. The extent to which the forward exchange rate underpredicts the future spot exchange rate is an increasing function of this systematic risk.

Using the model of Section 2, we have

$$E\left(\frac{\tilde{d} - f}{1 + \tilde{I}}\right) = \beta_d\left[E\left(\frac{\tilde{R}_m - \tilde{I}}{1 + \tilde{I}}\right) - E\left(\frac{\tilde{R}_z - \tilde{I}}{1 + \tilde{I}}\right)\right] \tag{8}$$

where

$$\beta_d = \frac{\mathrm{Cov}\left(\frac{\tilde{d} - f}{1 + \tilde{I}}, \frac{\tilde{R}_m - \tilde{I}}{1 + \tilde{I}}\right)}{\mathrm{Var}\left(\frac{\tilde{R}_m - \tilde{I}}{1 + \tilde{I}}\right)} \tag{9}$$

In equation (8), $\tilde{d}$ is the percentage rate of change of the exchange rate, i.e., $\tilde{e}_1/e_o - 1$, while f is the forward premium. Equation (8) gives a formal content to our discussion, as it shows that, for a given expected rate of change of the exchange rate, the forward exchange rate is a decreasing function of β_d, which is the beta of the payoff of a forward contract expressed as a fraction of the current spot exchange rate. Notice that β_d is almost equal to the beta of the rate of change of the exchange rate. If β_d is equal to zero, the forward exchange rate is roughly an unbiased predictor of the future spot exchange rate. This result is not surprising in the light of our discussion, as in this case a long position in the foreign currency has no systematic risk.[10]

3.3 Defining Exchange Rate Risk

The model derived in Section 2 is useful to characterize exchange rate risk in terms of its impact on the expected return of risky securities. One way to define exchange rate risk is by the standard deviation of the exchange rate. This definition is not very useful when investors can hold a portfolio of risky assets, as it is possible that holding an asset whose return is perfectly correlated with the exchange rate does not add risk to a portfolio. It is, therefore, more useful to use the concept of systematic exchange rate risk, i.e., that part of exchange rate risk which gives rise to a risk premium, and the concept of diversifiable exchange rate risk, i.e., that part of exchange rate risk that does not add to the risk of a well-diversified portfolio. It is important to notice that exchange rate risk is not necessarily a risk intrinsic to the exchange rate. In fact, one would not expect it to be. Under a regime of fixed exchange rates, exchange rates would not be risky, but this does not imply that, somehow, there would be less risk in the world. Furthermore, in the model developed in Section 2, the exchange rate risk is a function of each country's purchasing power risks only. Some authors, therefore, would argue that in our simplified model, with more than one currency but no departures from purchasing power parity, exchange rate risk does not exist, as in the absence of purchasing power risks there would be no exchange rate uncertainty.[11]

Some authors associate exchange rate risk with unanticipated deviations from purchasing power parity, i.e., with unanticipated deviations of P/eP^* from one, where P and P^* are price indices.[12] The rather subtle argument made by those who favor this definition of exchange rate risk is that an asset whose return is correlated with deviations from purchasing power parity may have an expected rate of return that differs from the expected rate of return predicted by the model of Section 2. We show in the next section that an asset whose return is correlated with deviations from purchasing power parity may earn a risk premium in addition to the risk premium explained by the covariance of the real return of the asset with the real return of the market portfolio. However, this additional risk premium is not explained by the fact that investors bear the risk of deviations from purchasing power parity that, somehow, are an exogenous factor in the economy. This additional risk premium is explained by the fact that deviations from purchasing power parity are correlated with changes in other variables that affect the investors' expected lifetime utility.

SECTION 4 DIFFERENCES IN CONSUMPTION ACROSS COUNTRIES

In Section 2, we assumed that all investors are alike except for their risk tolerance. The fact that investors use different numeraires was of no importance once it was recognized that investors cared only about real consumption. In this section, we assume that investors consume different baskets of goods across countries. As a result, the model of this section differs from the one developed in Section 2 because purchasing power risks differ across countries, rather than merely across currencies. This crucial difference between Section 2 and this section implies that in general an investor's portfolio depends on his country of residence and that the expected real return on a risky asset is a function of other characteristics of the real return of this asset than its covariance with the real return on the market portfolio only. We now show why this is the case.

4.1 Differences in Consumption Baskets and Asset Holdings

At each point in time, investors in different countries are likely to consume different baskets of goods.[13] These differences in consumption baskets arise for essentially two reasons. First, investors do not have the same tastes across countries. Second, relative prices of commodities differ across countries because of tariffs, transportation costs, taxes and so on. Furthermore, changes in relative prices differ across countries over time. A commodity can become relatively more expensive in one country while it becomes relatively less expensive in another country.

We assume that there exists a price index P that can be used to deflate the nominal expenditures of a domestic investor to obtain his real expenditures.[14] In other words, P is equivalent to the investor's CPI and, if there is only one commodity, as in Section 2, P is equal to the price of that commodity. If P^* is the price index for a foreign investor, there is no reason for purchasing power parity to hold when consumption baskets differ across countries. Consequently, P need not be equal to eP^*. For simplicity, we assume that all investors in a country use the same price index.

If P is not equal to eP^*, and all the other assumptions of Section 2 hold, it is still true that the investors care only about the distribution of real returns. (In particular, the optimization problem of investors is still the same as in Section 2). However, now the real return of a security is not the same for individuals in different countries because the price index used to compute real returns differs among investors. All investors of a given country choose their portfolio of risky assets among the same set of efficient portfolios as, by assumption, all investors of a given country consume the same basket of commodities. In contrast, investors in different countries choose their portfolio among different sets of efficient portfolios.

Consider now the portfolio choice problem of an individual investor. If this investor is highly risk-averse he is willing to sacrifice substantial return to reduce the variance of his real wealth. In the absence of purchasing power risks, this investor would invest a substantial proportion of his wealth in a bond that promises a safe nominal return as it would yield a safe consumption stream. However, in the presence of purchasing power risks, such a bond is not a safe asset in real terms. To reduce the purchasing power risks of his investment in the nominal bond, the investor hedges all or part of his holdings of the nominal bond against purchasing power risks. A perfect hedge portfolio, i.e., a portfolio that can be used to eliminate all purchasing power risks, is a portfolio whose real return is perfectly correlated with changes in the purchasing power of a currency. We assume, for simplicity, that such a perfect hedge portfolio exists and call it a domestic purchasing power risks hedge portfolio, as it can be used to eliminate the purchasing power risks of the domestic riskless nominal asset as well as of risky assets whose real return is negatively correlated with inflation. In the absence of purchasing power risks, the domestic investor invests his wealth in the domestic risk-free bond and in the tangency portfolio of risky assets, i.e., the portfolio that, for the domestic investor, is at the point of tangency of the capital market line and the mean-variance frontier. With purchasing power risks, the investor also invests in the purchasing power risks hedge portfolio.[15] By investing in the hedge portfolio, the investor can decrease the variance of the real return of his wealth for a given expected real return.

To understand the costs and benefits of investing in the hedge portfolio for the domestic investor, it is useful to focus first on the effect of such an investment on the variance of the return of his real wealth. If, prior to investing in the hedge portfolio, the real return of the investor's wealth is negatively correlated with the rate of inflation, an investment in the hedge portfolio decreases the variance of the investor's end-of-period real wealth. This follows from the fact that the real payoff of the hedge portfolio is, in this case, negatively correlated with the real payoff of the other investments of the investor and, therefore, an unexpectedly high real payoff of the hedge portfolio is expected to offset an unexpectedly low real payoff of the other investments of the investor. Consequently, if the investor's real wealth is exposed to unanticipated inflation before the increase in the investor's holdings of the hedge portfolio, it is less exposed to unanticipated inflation afterwards. As the risk-free bond, on theoretical grounds, and the tangency portfolio, on empirical grounds, are exposed to unanticipated inflation, in the sense that their real return is negatively correlated with the rate of inflation, one expects the change in the investor's portfolio to decrease the variance of the real return of that portfolio.

The effect of an increase in the investor's holdings of the hedge portfolio on the expected real rate of return of his wealth is more difficult to understand. For expositional purposes, it is useful to start by looking at the special case in which the expected nominal return of the domestic purchasing power risks hedge portfolio is equal to the nominal return of the domestic safe bond. Without loss of generality, we can choose the expected nominal payoff of both bonds to be one dollar. In this case, the real payoff of the safe asset must be $1/E(\tilde{P}_1)$, as the nominal payoff is then equal to $\tilde{P}_1/E(\tilde{P}_1)$ and its expected value is equal to $E(\tilde{P}_1/E(\tilde{P}_1)) = 1$. The expected real payoff of the nominal bond is, however, equal to $E(1/\tilde{P}_1)$. By Jensen's Inequality, $E(1/\tilde{P}_1) > 1/E(\tilde{P}_1)$ and, consequently, the expected real payoff of the nominal bond exceeds the real payoff of the safe real asset. The previous analysis shows that if it is costless to hedge a nominal bond against purchasing power risks in nominal terms, the expected real return of a portfolio hedged against purchasing power risks is lower than the expected real return of the same portfolio not hedged against purchasing power risks. It turns out that, in this setting, if the risk tolerance of the investor is large enough, he is even willing to go short in the hedge portfolio.[16] In a more general setting, the expected nominal return of the hedge portfolio in general differs from the nominal return on the safe nominal bond. As the expected real return of the hedge portfolio increases, *ceteris paribus*, one would, in general, expect investors to be more likely to have a long position in that portfolio. Furthermore, one would, in general, expect the value of the position in the hedge portfolio to increase as the expected real return of that portfolio increases.

4.2 Expected Returns with Differences in Consumption Baskets Across Countries

Empirical research has shown that changes in P are rarely equal to changes in eP^*.[17] In other words, the real exchange rate, eP^*/P, changes over time. Furthermore, the variation in eP^*/P is often large compared to the variation in P or P^*. While this does not mean that there exist arbitrage opportunities on commodity markets, it does imply that asset holdings may differ substantially across countries because investors in different countries face substantially different purchasing power risks and hence hold different hedge portfolios. However, for hedge portfolios to matter in the pricing of assets, it is required that across countries investors take positions in such portfolios. As shown in the earlier part of this section, this is not necessarily the case. Furthermore, for the investors' holdings of hedge portfolios to matter, the positions taken in these portfolios must not offset each other across countries.

To see how holdings of hedge portfolios affect expected returns, suppose that asset i has a nominal return that is positively correlated with changes in P. If the risk tolerance of domestic investors is low, they want to hedge against purchasing power risks. Suppose however that asset i is priced in line with the Sharpe-Lintner model. In this case, domestic investors want to take a long position in asset i in excess of their holdings of asset i in the tangency portfolio, as they want to hedge against purchasing power risks. For a given supply of asset i, the usefulness of asset i in hedging against domestic purchasing power risks decreases its expected return. However, whether asset i has a higher expected return than predicted by the Sharpe-Lintner model depends also on whether asset i is useful to hedge purchasing power risks for investors in other countries. If investors in some other country have to go short in asset i to hedge against unanticipated changes in their price index, it may turn out that the expected return of asset i is higher than predicted by the Sharpe-Lintner model.

With this analysis, the expected return of a security depends on how useful it is for investors to hedge against purchasing power risks and on how much they are willing to pay to do it. As the purchasing power risks differ across countries, it would seem that one has to find how useful a security is to hedge the purchasing power risks in each country and how much investors are willing to pay to hedge purchasing power risks in each country. Whereas some authors have constructed models along these lines,[18] it is doubtful that such models are very useful as they make the expected return of a security depend on the sum of a large number of risk premia whose value is difficult to compute in a reliable way.

It turns out, however, that it is possible to obtain a simple model to describe expected returns.[19] Notice first that the model of Section 2 still holds, except that the market portfolio in the equation for expected returns is replaced by the portfolio held by a domestic investor and that real returns are computed by using the price index of domestic investors. To understand this, notice that domestic investors still care only about the distribution of real returns and still choose to hold an efficient portfolio of risky assets. However, there is no reason for them to hold the market portfolio as they face purchasing power risks that differ from those faced by other investors and hence may hold a hedge portfolio in addition to their holdings of the tangency portfolio and of the nominal risk-free asset. The portfolio of risky assets held by a representative domestic investor is not directly observable, which makes the model of Section 2 not very useful in this context. However, as in Section 2, we can use the fact that at the optimum, a change in the investor's asset holdings cannot increase his expected utility, to derive a useful result on the pricing of risky assets when consumption baskets differ across countries.

We assume that the representative domestic investor's utility at date 1 is $U(c_1)$, where c_1 is his real consumption at date 1. The investor is assumed to be risk-averse and c_1 is a random variable as of date 0. Suppose that the investor is holding an optimal portfolio. If this investor, at the optimum, decreases his holdings of security i and increases his holdings of security j marginally, his expected lifetime utility should be unchanged. Clearly, the change in the investor's portfolio has no effect on his consumption at date zero, as the purchase of security j is financed by the sale of security i. Consequently, the change in the investor's portfolio should not affect his expected utility for date 1, as otherwise his current portfolio would not be optimal. This implies that

$$E(\tilde{U}_{c1}(\tilde{r}_i - \tilde{r}_j)) = 0 \tag{10}$$

where U_{c1} is the first derivative of the investor's utility of real consumption at date 1. Using the definition of a covariance, (10) can be rewritten as

$$-\text{Cov}(\tilde{U}_{c1}, r_i) + \text{Cov}(\tilde{U}_{c1}, r_j) = E(\tilde{U}_{c1})E(\tilde{r}_i) - E(\tilde{U}_{c1})E(\tilde{r}_j) \tag{11}$$

Let r_{zu} be the return on a portfolio whose return is uncorrelated with changes in marginal utility. One can choose asset j to be such that $r_{zu} = r_j$ and obtain from equation (11) that

$$-\frac{\text{Cov}(\tilde{U}_{c1}, \tilde{r}_i)}{E(\tilde{U}_{c1})} = E(\tilde{r}_i) - E(\tilde{r}_{zu}) \tag{12}$$

It follows from equation (12) that the expected return on security i is a decreasing function of the covariance of the security's return with the marginal utility of consumption. Furthermore, this function is linear with a slope equal to $-(1/E(\tilde{U}_{c1}))$ and an intercept equal to $E(\tilde{r}_{zu})$. To understand the relation between a security's expected return and its covariance with the marginal utility of real consumption, consider an investor who can choose between receiving a dollar if his marginal utility is high or if his marginal utility is low at date 1. The investor will choose to receive the dollar when his marginal utility is high, as this is when he values a dollar the most. By the same token, the individual prefers an asset that pays off when his marginal utility is high and hence requires a smaller risk premium to hold such an asset.

It is useful to notice that marginal utility is negatively correlated with consumption. This implies that an asset whose return is negatively correlated with c_1 has a lower expected return than an asset whose return is positively correlated with c_1. The relation between consumption and marginal utility is not linear and, consequently, the relation between the expected returns of risky assets and the covariance of their returns with consumption is not linear in general. However, under certain assumptions, the covariance of marginal utility with asset returns in equation (12) can be rewritten so that expected returns are a function of the covariance of asset returns with changes in consumption rather than with changes in marginal utility. The most innocuous of these assumptions is that trading takes place continuously so that one can take the limit in continuous time of the expression for expected returns. Alternatively, one can assume that the joint distribution of marginal utility and asset returns is multivariate normal.[20] Notice finally that if the utility function is quadratic (like $U = ac_1 - \frac{1}{2}bc_1^2$), then the marginal utility is linear in consumption ($U_{c1} = a - bc_1$) and the expected return of an asset is a linear function of the covariance of the real return of that asset with consumption.

When one rewrites expected returns as a function of $Cov(\tilde{c}_1, \tilde{r}_i)$, one obtains a relation in terms of observables which makes it possible to compute expected real returns for all assets on markets which are perfect for domestic investors. Notice that a first-order Taylor-series expansion of marginal utility around $E(\tilde{U}_{c1})$ makes it possible to write $Cov(\tilde{U}_{c1}, \tilde{r}_i)$ as $E(\tilde{U}_{c1c1})$ Cov $(\tilde{c}_1, \tilde{r}_i)$ plus a remainder term that, in the limit of continuous time, is negligible. Let w_i^p, i=1, . . . ,n, be known portfolio weights. One can use equation (12), after replacing $Cov(\tilde{U}_{c1}, r_i)$ with $E(\tilde{U}_{cc1c1})$ Cov $(\tilde{c}_1, \tilde{r}_i)$, to compute the real expected return $E(\tilde{r}^p)$ on the portfolio with weights w_i^p, i=1, . . . ,n:

$$E(\tilde{r}^P) - E(\tilde{r}_{zc}) = \frac{\text{Cov}(\tilde{c}_1, \tilde{r}_p)}{E(\tilde{c}_1)} \tag{13}$$

where $E(\tilde{r}_{zc})$ is the expected real return on a portfolio whose real return is uncorrelated with real consumption. Using equation (12) and (13), it follows that

$$E(\tilde{r}_i) - E(\tilde{r}_{zc}) = \beta_{ic}[E(\tilde{r}_p) - E(\tilde{r}_{zc})] \tag{14}$$

where

$$\beta_{ic} = \frac{\mathrm{Cov}(\tilde{r}_i, \tilde{c}_1)}{\mathrm{Cov}(\tilde{r}_p, \tilde{c}_1)} \tag{15}$$

Equation (14) implies that there is a linear relation between expected real returns and consumption betas. As c_1 is the real consumption of a representative domestic investor, one can use domestic real consumption per capita in equations (14) and (15). Notice that equation (14) can be used to compute the risk premium incorporated in the forward exchange rate in the same way as in Section 3.

4.3 A More General Interpretation

Equations (14) and (15), which make it possible to compute real expected returns for all assets traded on perfect markets for domestic investors, hold under assumptions that are much less restrictive than those made so far in this section. Indeed, equations (14) and (15) hold in a multiperiod world in which the distribution of the returns changes over time and in which the distribution of the rates of change of goods prices changes over time. Because the model of asset pricing developed in this section holds under very general assumptions about exchange rate dynamics, it is particularly well-suited to price assets in an international setting. In particular, this model holds even when the risk premium incorporated in the forward exchange rate changes over time.

To understand why the model developed in this section holds even when investment and consumption opportunity sets change over time, it is useful to notice that to obtain the equation for expected returns (i.e., equation 14), we use the fact that at the optimum the investor cannot be made better off by rearranging his portfolio. Thus we again obtain Equation (10)

$$E(\tilde{U}_c\,(\tilde{r}_i - \tilde{r}_j)) = 0 \tag{10}$$

However, this relation still holds in a multiperiod model in which investment and consumption opportunity sets change over time. To understand this, suppose that in a multiperiod world the investor has chosen an optimal investment policy that prescribes how he will invest his wealth over time. We assume that the investor has a von Neuman-Morgenstern time-additive expected utility function of lifetime real consumption. Consider now a hypothetical experiment in which the investor deviates from his optimal policy at date 0 by increasing his investment in asset i and decreasing his investment in asset j marginally for one period, i.e., at date 1 the investor goes back to his optimal policy. This change in the investor's portfolio does not affect his consumption at date 0. If the change in his investment policy makes it possible for the investor to increase his expected utility for date 1 and maintain the same expected utility for all other dates, the investor has not chosen an optimal investment policy. This implies that relation (11) must hold. However, we have not assumed that consumption and investment opportunity sets are constant through time.

Notice that if the investment opportunity set changes over time, investors in general want to hedge against unanticipated changes in the investment opportunity set, as these changes affect the investors' lifetime expected utility. Consequently, investors take positions in a variety of hedge portfolios in addition to taking a position in a purchasing power risks hedge portfolio. In this setting, when one wishes to compute the proper discount rate for a risky project, one can still compute the risk premium by looking at the covariance of the real cash flows of the project with changes in real consumption. However, as the investment opportunity changes over time, the covariance of changes of the real cash flows with changes in real consumption is a function of the state of the world. While the consumption-based capital asset pricing model offers a simple and intuitive explanation for the cross-sectional variation of the expected returns of risky assets, its empirical implementation is made difficult by the fact that consumption rates are endogenous variables that are solved for by investors when they maximize their lifetime expected utility.[21]

SECTION 5 THE IMPLICATIONS OF BARRIERS TO INTERNATIONAL INVESTMENT

The analysis of Section 4 makes it possible to understand why investors in a given country do not hold the world market portfolio and why there are some similarities in asset holdings among investors of a given country. It would not be reasonable to believe that the results of Section 4 alone can explain the asset holdings of investors. There exists a wide variety of barriers to international investment that play a significant role in how investors allocate their wealth among risky assets. Barriers to international investment can take the form, for instance, of exchange rate restrictions, explicit limits on capital flows, differential taxes, holding costs, risks of expropriation, and so on. Because barriers to international investment are so numerous and diverse, we can only discuss some general types of barriers to international investment. We first show that the model developed in Section 4 holds in the presence of barriers to international investment. It can be used to compute the expected real return of risky assets that are traded in perfect markets (i.e., not subject to taxes, transactions costs, holding costs and political risks) for investors of at least one country. Barriers to international investment that take the form of differential taxes and transactions costs are then explored. Finally after discussing political risks briefly, we show how barriers to international investment affect the financing policies of firms.

5.1 Consumption Betas and Barriers to International Investment

In Section 4, we showed how the equilibrium expected real rate of return on a risky asset can be computed for all assets that domestic investors can trade in perfect markets. Consequently, one can apply the model of Section 4 even when foreign or domestic investors cannot trade some assets in perfect markets. If foreign investors face restrictions on holding domestic assets but domestic investors face no restrictions on holding any assets, all assets are traded on perfect markets for domestic investors. Consequently, domestic consumption betas can be used to compute the real expected returns of all assets. If domestic investors face restrictions in holding some foreign securities but foreign investors face no restrictions on holding these assets, one can compute the expected real returns on these assets from the perspective of foreign investors, as foreign investors trade these assets on perfect markets and use foreign consumption betas.

5.2 Taxes, Transactions Costs and Barriers to International Investment

The model of Section 4 can be applied under a wide variety of circumstances when barriers to international investment exist. We show here how the model can be used to compute the expected return abroad of foreign assets which are subject to barriers to international investment for domestic investors.[22] To make this comparison, we assume for simplicity that there exists a safe real asset in the domestic country and that the reference portfolio p is chosen to be a portfolio of domestic assets only.

We consider a situation where the barriers to international investment take a form that is equivalent to a tax. This way of characterizing barriers to international investment is fairly general, as the tax rate can be a surrogate for the certainty-equivalent cost of expropriation, cross-border tax adjustments, holding costs, transactions costs, or for the shadow price of quantity constraints on foreign investment (like an upper limit imposed by the host country on the fraction of a firm that can be owned by foreign investors). For simplicity, we assume that the tax rate is the same for all foreign assets held long by domestic investors and that it applies to the end-of-period price of a share. To model barriers to international investment, it is more reasonable to apply the tax to the end-of-period value of an investor's position abroad than to tax positive returns on that position only because many costs associated with investing abroad must be paid even if returns are negative. If the tax rate on a long position is equal to τ, the after-tax real return for domestic investors on some foreign asset held long, say security i, is equal to

$$r_i^A = \left(\frac{e_{i1}P_{i1}}{e_{i0}P_{i0}^*}\right)\left(\frac{P_1}{P_0}\right)(1-\tau) - 1 = \frac{(1+d)(1+R_i)(1-\tau)}{(1+I)} \tag{17}$$

where d is the rate of change of the exchange rate and I is the rate of inflation in the domestic country. If foreign assets held long by domestic investors are subject to a tax, the model of Section 4 still applies, but now it applies to after-tax returns:

$$E(\tilde{r}_i^A) - r = \beta_{ic}^A[E(\tilde{r}_p) - r] \tag{18}$$

where

$$\beta_{ic}^A = \frac{\text{Cov}(\tilde{r}_i^A, \tilde{c})}{\text{Cov}(\tilde{r}_p, \tilde{c})} \tag{19}$$

It follows that assets that have the same before-tax beta can have different after-tax returns. As foreign assets held long have higher after-tax foreign currency expected returns for foreign investors than for domestic investors, one would expect that, in general, domestic investors have a smaller long position in foreign assets than foreign investors.

Domestic investors may hold some foreign assets short. Consequently, we have to investigate the effects of a tax on short holdings of foreign assets. Let γ be the tax rate on short holdings of foreign assets by domestic investors. If γ is positive, short sales benefit from a subsidy. For instance, in a situation in which only *net* holdings of foreign assets are subject to a tax, $\tau = \gamma$, and the Black (1974) model holds. As after-tax expected real returns on foreign assets held short by domestic investors are still given by the model of Section 4, it follows that

$$E(\tilde{r}_i) - \gamma - r = \beta_{ic}\,[E(\tilde{r}_p) - r] \tag{20}$$

If $\gamma \neq \tau$, some foreign assets may not be held at all by domestic investors. In other words, some assets may not be traded internationally. To understand this, suppose that $\gamma < 0$. We consider two risky assets, one domestic and the other foreign, whose returns in domestic currency are perfectly correlated. If foreign investors face no barriers to international investment, they can arbitrage between two assets so that their expected pretax returns in domestic currency are the same. In such a situation, domestic investors do not hold the foreign asset at all, as the domestic asset is a perfect substitute for the foreign asset and is not subject to a tax. If foreign asset j is not held by domestic investors, its expected real return is given by

$$E(\tilde{r}_j) - h - r = \beta_{jc}\,[E(\tilde{r}_p) - r] \tag{21}$$

where $\tau < h < \gamma$. Not surprisingly, in this setting, a domestic investor takes a position in a foreign asset only if the benefits from doing so are large enough to offset the tax he has to pay when he holds that asset. Not all foreign assets have expected benefits large enough to insure that domestic investors take a position in these assets.

5.3 Political Risks

One barrier to foreign investment often mentioned is the possibility that investments made abroad will be expropriated by the government of the country in which these investments are made.[23] The model developed in this paper makes it possible to compute the risk premium investors of one country, say country A, require to bear political risks when they invest in another country, say country B. Note that expropriation can be complete or partial. Governments often impose regulations that discriminate against foreign investors. The imposition of such a regulation in country B will decrease the value of investments made in that country by investors of country A and is called here a partial expropriation. Let x, $0 \leq x \leq 1$, be the fraction of the holdings of assets of country B by investors of country A that is expropriated at the end of the period. At the beginning of the period, x is a random variable and is written $\tilde{x}$. If $\tilde{x}$ is independent of the level of real consumption, the expected return on an asset subject to the risk of expropriation is the same as the expected return on an equivalent asset that is not subject to this risk. This implies, however, that the expected real return on an asset of country B is $E[(\tilde{r}_j+\tilde{x})/(1-\tilde{x})]$ where $\tilde{r}_j$ is the real return on an asset of country A with the same consumption beta as the asset of country B. It follows that the expected real return on an asset of country B exceeds the expected real return on an asset of country A if one does not take into account political risks. This discussion is relevant, however, only if investors of country A hold assets of country B, as otherwise a consumption beta from country A cannot be used to compute the expected real return of an asset in country B.

It is possible for x to be correlated with changes in real consumption in country A. To the extent that investors can share risks internationally, it is likely that real consumption is positively correlated across countries. If country B is a net borrower from country A and is more likely to declare unilaterally a moratorium on its interest payments to investors of country A, x is negatively correlated with changes in real consumption in country A, assuming that changes in real consumption are positively correlated across countries. As the real return for investors of country A on an investment in country B is negatively correlated with x, the lower the covariance of x and changes in the real consumption of investors of country A, the higher the expected rate of return required by investors of country A on investments in country B. This discussion shows that if the probability of expropriation increases when the rate of real consumption unexpectedly decreases, the investors of country A require a (positive) risk premium to bear the risk of expropriation when they invest in country B.

5.4 Barriers to International Investment and Financial Policies of Firms

In the earlier sections of this paper, the expected return on an asset in a given numeraire is the same for all investors, irrespective of where they are located. In such a situation, all the results of the theory of finance about capital budgeting and financial policies hold. That a firm's shareholders are located in different countries is of no relevance to the firm's managers. The usefulness of the results developed in the earlier sections of this paper for corporate policies is that they make it possible to assess more carefully the risk of the projects whose present value has to be computed. In particular, they make clear how to compute the present value of a project undertaken in country B by a firm of country A when the capital markets of countries A and B are fully integrated. The capital markets of two countries are fully integrated if investors in each country face no barriers to international investment when they invest in the other country.

When there are barriers to international investment, it matters where an asset is traded. In this case, investors in different countries are willing to pay different prices for the rights to the same stream of cash flows, which has wide-ranging implications for the financial and investment policies of firms. However, these implications can only be discussed briefly here.

In the presence of barriers to international investment, the same project may not have the same value for different firms. Such a situation may arise for a variety of situations. For instance, investors in country B may not have access to capital markets from other countries and investors from other countries may not have access to the capital market of country B. In such a situation, investors from country B, in general, use a different discount rate to evaluate projects than investors from other countries. In terms of the model of Section 2, risks that are diversifiable for most investors in the world may not be diversifiable for investors of country B. Also different firms may value the same project differently because these firms are exposed to different types of political risks or different tax structures. As a result, in the presence of barriers to international investment, a firm may undertake a project that some other firm would not undertake.[24]

With barriers to international investment, the domestic currency price of securities sold by a firm is likely to depend on the country in which securities are sold. In efficient markets, one would not expect to make profits by issuing securities in some countries and investing the proceeds in other countries. However, it is perfectly possible that selling securities in one country yields more income for the firm than selling securities in another country. Taxes which will be paid by investors who hold a security may depend on where the security is issued and traded. For instance, many countries impose withholding taxes on interest income paid by domestic corporations to non-resident investors when securities are issued in the domestic country. If a corporation wants to sell securities to non-resident investors, it will generally be able to sell securities at a higher price if it issues them on off-shore markets in such a way as to eliminate the requirement for non-resident investors to pay withholding taxes in the domestic country. Firms can take advantage of barriers to international investment in numerous ways through financial transactions. For instance, mergers with firms of foreign countries can provide diversification benefits for shareholders in the domestic country which they would not be able to obtain on their own when the firms face less stringent barriers to international investment than individual investors.[25] As another example, joint ventures can enable domestic firms to make it possible for investors in foreign countries to share some risks internationally.

SECTION 6 CONCLUSION

In this paper, we have discussed some problems that arise when one tries to use capital asset pricing models in an international setting. In such a setting, barriers to international investment and dynamics of commodity prices play a crucial role in the determination of expected returns on risky assets.

Not all assets are equally good hedges against unanticipated changes in the price of a consumption good. Therefore, one would not expect the expected return of risky assets to be a function of their Sharpe-Lintner beta, the expected rate of return of the market portfolio and the risk-free interest rate only. One would also believe that how good an asset is to hedge various risks (for instance, commodity price risks) that differ from stock market risk would affect the expected return of this asset.

In general, models that allow the expected return of a risky asset to be a function of the covariance of the return of that risky asset with variables other than the return on the market portfolio can be formulated in two different ways. First, one can obtain an equation for the expected return of risky assets, which makes each expected return equal to the expected return of a risk-free portfolio plus a sum of risk premia. Second, one can get an equation that yields expected returns as the sum of the expected return of a risk-free portfolio plus a positive constant times the covariance of the return of the risky assets with changes in consumption. Both approaches can be derived from the same assumptions and both approaches are difficult to implement empirically.

The consumption-based approach to asset pricing has, however, some distinct advantages. First, from a theoretical standpoint, it seems to provide a more intuitive understanding of the difference between the expected return of a risky asset and of the riskless portfolio. This difference is proportional to the covariance of the return of the risky asset with changes in consumption rather than being a function of a large number of covariances of the return of the risky asset with changes in state variables. Second, the consumption-based approach is a general equilibrium approach, while models that impose artificial constraints on price dynamics or on the number of state variables of interest cannot claim this distinction. Third, the consumption-based approach makes it easy to take into account barriers to international investment, which we believe play a significant role in the pricing of assets from some countries. Finally, while we believe that the consumption-based approach is more empirically tractable than other approaches—especially in the presence of barriers to international investment—there is currently no consensus on this issue among financial economists. However, given the current state of research in international asset pricing, it is safe to expect that the most exciting discoveries will come from empirical work.

NOTES

1. See Jensen (1972) for a review of these models.

2. This paper is not meant to be a review of the literature; see Adler and Dumas (1983) for additional references to the literature. Bodurtha (1983) provides empirical evidence that the three differences among countries studied in this paper affect expected returns significantly.

3. See especially Grauer, Litzenberger and Stehle (1976), Kouri (1977) and Fama and Farber (1979). These models are often contrasted with the model of Solnik (1974), which assumes that exchange rate changes are perfectly correlated with changes in the terms of trade. Solnik's (1974) model is a special case of the model we develop in Section 4. Throughout the paper, we use a discrete-time framework. Furthermore, the model developed in this section is a mean-variance model. While the assumptions one has to make for a mean-variance model to result from the solution of the investors' portfolio choice problem (see Dybvig and Ingersoll, 1982 and the references therein) are unpalatable, it turns out that the results of this section can be obtained in a continuous-time model that requires less stringent assumtpions.

4. The commodity may be viewed as a basket of goods. With this interpretation, all investors must have identical

and constant expenditure shares on the various goods. See Adler and Dumas (1983) for references to the law of one price and to purchasing power parity.

5. An alternative and more general derivation would aggregate asset demands across investors. Such a derivation would not require the nontrivial assumption that a representative investor exists, but it would still yield equations (3) and (4). See Constantinides (1982) and Rubinstein (1974) for conditions under which a representative investor exists.

6. To obtain (3), note that $\Sigma w_i \sigma_{ik}$ is the covariance of $\tilde{r}_i$ with $\tilde{r}_m$ if the w_i's are the weights of the market portfolio. Let Cov $(\tilde{r}_j, \tilde{r}_m) = 0$, so that j has the same expected return as the portfolio with return $\tilde{r}_z$. Finally, eliminate λ by noticing that $E(\tilde{r}_m) - E(\tilde{r}_z) = \gamma \text{Var}(\tilde{r}_m)$.

7. See Sharpe (1964) and Lintner (1965). If one is willing to assume that $E(I\tilde{r}_i)$ is negligible for all securities, (6) and (7) can be rewritten as

$$E(\tilde{R}_i) - E(\tilde{R}_f) = \beta_i[E(\tilde{R}_m) - E(\tilde{R}_f)] \tag{6'}$$

and

$$\beta_i = \frac{\text{Cov}(\tilde{R}_i - \tilde{I}_1, \tilde{R}_m - \tilde{I})}{\text{Var}(\tilde{R}_m - \tilde{I})} \tag{7'}$$

8. See Fama and Schwert (1977) and the references therein. See Solnik (1983) and Gultek;in (1983) for international evidence.

9. See Friend, Landskroner and Losq (1976) for a similar result.

10. For papers that obtain similar results, see the papers referenced in footnote 3 and Frankel (1980).

11. See Grauer, Litzenberger and Stehle (1976).

12. See, for instance, Solnik (1974).

13. For models that use this assumption in one form or another, see Solnik (1974), Sercu (1980), Stulz (1981b) and Adler and Dumas (1983). Stulz (1981b) allows explicitly for nontraded goods and changes in price levels as well as changes in relative prices.

14. A utility function that satisfies the assumption of constant expenditure shares satisfies our assumption. See Samuelson and Swamy (1974). The analysis in Stulz (1981b) does not require this assumption. Stulz (1983) discusses some implications of utility functions that do not have constant expenditure shares.

15. See Breeden (1983) for an analysis of hedging and references to the literature.

16. See Stulz (1983) for a proof of this statement in a continuous-time model and for references to the literature.

17. See Levich (1983) for references.

18. Adler and Dumas (1983) assume that price indices differ across countries but have a constant investment opportunity set and assume that the dynamics for price indices are constant. Hodrick (1981) assumes that purchasing power parity holds but lets the investment opportunity set change over time.

19. The following presents a discrete-time version of Stulz (1981a) assuming constant expenditure shares. See also Grossman and Schiller (1982) and, especially, Wheatley (1983).

20. For the continuous-time approach, see Breeden (1979). For an approach that assumes that the joint distribution of price relatives and consumption is lognormal, see Rubinstein (1976).

21. For a critical view of consumption-based asset pricing models, see Cornell (1981). For a discussion of some practical problems one encounters when using such models, see Hansen and Singleton (1982) and Wheatley (1983). Various measures of consumption expenditures are published regularly in the United States. It must be noted that the measure of consumption used in the model includes expenditures on nondurable goods plus the services consumed from the stock of durable goods, while published estimates of total consumption expenditures include purchases of durable goods.

22. This is especially useful in tests of whether asset markets are segmented internationally. For recent work that derives asset pricing equations when markets are segmented and then proceeds to test them, see Bodurtha (1973), Wheatley (1983) and Losq and Errunza (1983). The present discussion builds on Stulz (1981a) and, partly, Wheatley (1983), who derives the Stulz (1981a) model in a consumption-based capital asset pricing model.

23. For a review of the forms political risk can take and of the literature on political risk, see Lessard, Bollier, Eckaus and Kahn (1983). See also Shapiro (1982).

24. See, for instance, Adler (1974).

25. See, for instance, Adler and Dumas (1974).

REFERENCES

Adler, M. "The Cost of Capital and Valuation in a Two-Country-Firm." *Journal of Finance*, March 1974, 119–133.

Adler, M., and Dumas, B. "Optimal International Acquisitions." *Journal of Finance*, March 1975, 1–20.

Adler, M., and Dumas, B. "International Portfolio Choice and Corporation Finance: A Synthesis." *Journal of Finance*, June 1983, 925–984.

Black, F. "Capital Market Equilibrium with Investment Barriers." *Journal of Business*, July 1972, 444–454.

Black, F. "International Capital Market Equilibrium with Investment Barriers." *Journal of Financial Economics*, December 1974, 337–352.

Bodurtha, J. N. "Asset Pricing in International Markets: Theory and Evidence." Working Paper, College of Administrative Science, Ohio State University, June 1983.

Breeden, D. T. "An Intertemporal Asset Pricing Model with Stochastic Consumption and Investment Opportunity Sets." *Journal of Financial Economics*, September 1979, 265–96.

Constantinides, G. M. "Intertemporal Asset Pricing with Heterogenous Consumers and without Demand Aggregation." *The Journal of Business*, April 1982, 253–269.

Cornell, B. "The Consumption-Based Asset Pricing Model: A Note on Potential Tests and Applications." *Journal of Financial Economics*, March 1981, 103–108.

Dybvig, P. H., and Ingersoll, J. E. "Mean-Variance Theory in Complete Markets." *The Journal of Business*, April 1982, 233–252.

Errunza, V., and Losq, E. "International Asset Pricing Under Mild Segmentation: Theory and Test." *Journal of Finance* forthcoming.

Fama, E. F., and Farber, A. "Money, Bonds and Foreign Exchange." *American Economic Review*, September 1979, 639–649.

Fama, E. F., and Schwert, G. W. "Asset Returns and Inflation." *Journal of Financial Economics*, November 1977, 115–146.

Frankel, J. "The Diversifiability of Exchange Risk." *Journal of International Economics*, November 1979, 115–146.

Friend, I., Landskroner, Y. and Losq, E. "The Demand for Risky Assets and Uncertain Inflation." *Journal of Finance*, December 1976, 1287–1297.

Grauer, F. L. A., Litzenberger, R. H., and Stehle, R. "Sharing Rules and Equilibrium in an International Capital Market under Uncertainty." *Journal of Financial Economics*, June 1976, 233–256.

Grossman, S. J., and Shiller, R. J. "Consumption Correlatedness and Risk Measurement in Economics with Non-Traded Assets and Heterogenous Information." *Journal of Financial Economics*, June 1982, 195–210.

Gultekin, N. B. "Stock Market Returns and Inflation: Evidence From Other Countries." *Journal of Finance*, March 1983, 49–66.

Hansen, L. P., and Singleton, K. T. "Stochastic Consumption, Risk Aversion, and the Temporal Behavior of Stock Market Returns." *Journal of Political Economy*, April 1983, 249–265.

Hodrick, R. J. "International Asset Pricing With Time-Varying Risk Premia." *Journal of International Economics*, November 1981, 573–587.

Jensen, M. "Capital Markets: Theory and Evidence." *The Bell Journal of Economics and Management Science*, Autumn 1972, 357–398.

Kouri, P. K. J. "International Investment and Interest Rate Linkages under Flexible Exchange Rates." In R. Aliber (ed.), *The Political Economy of Monetary Reform*. London, MacMillan & Co., 1977.

Lessard, D., Bollier, T., Eckaus, R., and Kahn, R. "Country Risk, Capital Market Integration and Project Evaluation: A Canadian Perspective." Mimeographed, Sloan School of Management, MIT, 1983.

Levich, R. M. "Empirical Studies of Exchange Rates: Price Behavior, Rate Determination and Market Efficiency." Working Paper No. 112, National Bureau of Economic Research, 1983.

Lintner, J. "The Valuation of Risk Assets and the Selection of Risky Investments in Stock Portfolios and Capital Budgets." *Review of Economics and Statistics*, February 1965, 13–37.

Lucas, R. E., Jr. "Interest Rates and Currency Prices in A Two-Country World." *Journal of Monetary Economics*, November 1982, 335–359.

Rubinstein, M. "An Aggregation Theorem For Securities Markets." *Journal of Financial Economics*, Autumn 1974, 225–244.

Rubinstein, M. "The Valuation of Uncertain Income Streams and the Pricing of Options." *The Bell Journal of Economics*, Autumn 1976, 407–425.

Samuelson, P. A., and Swamy, S. "Invariant Index Numbers and Canonical Duality: Survey and Synthesis." *American Economic Review*, September 1974, 566–593.

Sercu, P. "A Generalization of the International Asset Pricing Model." *Revue del' Association Francaise de Finance*, June 1980, 91–135.

Shapiro, A. *Multinational Financial Management*. Boston, MA: Allyn & Bacon, 1982.

Sharpe, W. F. "Capital Asset Prices: A Theory of Market Equilibrium under Conditions of Risk." *Journal of Finance*, September 1964, 425–442.

Solnik, B. "Equilibrium in an International Capital Market under Uncertainty." *Journal of Economic Theory* 8, 1974, 500–524.

Solnik, B. "The Relation Between Stock Returns and Inflationary Expectations: The International Evidence." *Journal of Finance*, March 1983, 35–48.

Stulz, R. M. "On the Effects of Barriers to International Investment." *Journal of Finance*, September 1981a, 923–934.

Stulz, R. M. "A Model of International Asset Pricing." *Journal of Financial Economics*, December 1981b, 383–406.

Stulz, R. M. "The Demand for Foreign Bonds." *Journal of International Economics*, October 1983, 225–238.

Stulz, R. M. "Currency references, Purchasing Power Risks and the Determination of Exchange Rates in an Optimizing Model." *Journal of Money, Credit and Banking*, forthcoming, 1984.

Svennson, L. E. O. "Currency Prices, Terms of Trade and Interest Rates: A General Equilibrium Asset-Pricing Cash-in-Advance Approach." Institute of International Economic Studies, University of Stockholm, 1983.

Wheatley, S. "A Test of International Capital Markets Integration: Preliminary Results." Mimeographed, University of Rochester, 1983.

7

Overlapping National Investment Portfolios: Evidence and Implications of International Integration of Secondary Markets for Financial Assets*

Steven W. Kohlhagen

I. INTRODUCTION

This is a depressing paper. The reader should be fairly forwarned that he or she will have to provide his or her own antidote for the depression. The author found little help for his, despite a lengthy search. For various reasons, past work on secondary asset markets has provided little in the way of insight into the question of how well capital markets are integrated. Unfortunately, with the exception of pointing out the relevance of one well-known and not very elegant test and only a few hopeful suggestions, I have been forced to conclude that future work in this area is equally unlikely to generate any more useful empirical tests.

This paper critically reviews past work on secondary markets in the context of how it relates to the notion of capital market integration. We consider capital market integration in the economic sense that has been developed in the existing literature. We conclude that capital markets are perfectly integrated if investors can earn the same expected return on investments in each market (and, concomitantly, if borrowers pay the same rate for capital across markets) appropriately adjusted for risk. Thus, Los Angeles, San Francisco, Chicago, and New York are all (or are at least perceived to be) part of the same capital market, adjusting for transaction costs and information costs (especially for small borrowers in the case of information costs). San Diego and Mexico City (or, for that matter, Tijuana) are not. This notion is consistent with the definition of capital market integration outlined in Kenen (1976) (and described as the "law-of-one-price" version), Hawkins (1972), and Cooper (1971) and is related to how well assets or liabilities across markets are substitutes for each other. It is also then consistent with the notion that capital market integration is to be equated with interdependence (or, in the small-country case, dependence; see, especially Allen and Kenen, 1980). In this latter sense, the *process*, as well as the *evidence*, of integration are important to understanding the implications of integration (see Cooper, 1968; Allen and Kenen, 1980; and Kenen, 1976). This paper looks mostly at the evidence and only briefly at the implications, thus concentrating much less on the *process* than some of the other papers in this volume. It is also consistent with the efficient market views, wherein markets are well integrated to the extent that there are no unusual profit opportunities from arbitraging across the markets.

Underlying the usefulness of this (or any) definition of market integration is some

---

*This article is reprinted, with permission, from Hawkins and Levich (eds.), *Research in International Business and Finance,* vol. 3, JAI Press, 1983, pp. 113–137.

notion of risk. Assets will not be perfect substitutes if they contain inherently different risk characteristics, unless investors are compensated for bearing this risk. There is a distinction—especially important in the equity literature—between systematic risk that cannot be diversified away and that will be borne only for compensation, and nonsystematic or diversifiable risk for which there is no compensation. Thus, if there is evidence that market participants are bearing diversifiable risk, either willingly or unwillingly, i.e., when the risk-adjusted rate of return on such assets is lower than on assets with no such risk, the markets are segmented (i.e., not fully integrated).

On the other hand, the existence of systematic or nondiversifiable risk does not *necessarily* segment markets. It could presumably be over- or undercompensated for in the market, thus segmenting markets. But this would be difficult to test and, to my knowledge, nobody has tried to do so. If the systematic risk associated with each asset remained constant, then the observed differences in rates of return could be explained by the systematic risk. Over time, the rates of return in such a market would still be highly (or even perfectly) related. If, on the other hand, the systematic risks were changing over time, then rates of return across markets that were highly integrated might bear little relation to each other and might appear to be highly segmented, even though they were not. This could especially be a problem with foreign exchange risk that could segment markets when it is nonsystematic and that, when it is systematic—if highly variable—would be very difficult to identify empirically in a maner that would allow one to identify correctly integrated markets. But this is the specific subject of other papers in this volume (see Dornbusch, Kouri, Ross), and will not be dealt with in any detail in this paper. Suffice it to say that the empirical problems—of which this is only one—make capital market integration an operationally slippery concept.

In light of this view of integration, we analyze the insights available from the evidence on secondary markets. In the next section, we look at the literature on overlapping national equity markets. We then analyze existing evidence and extend the analysis on the national bond markets in the subsequent section.

II. THE INTERNATIONAL MARKET FOR COMMON STOCKS

The work on the international diversification of stock market portfolios, at both the theoretical and empirical levels, is an extension of the principle that investors can improve their return-to-risk ratio by diversifying their investment portfolio. The presumption is that these benefits are even greater if the analysis (or the investments, presumably) can be extended to the world portfolio. In the context of capital market integration, the extent to which analyses of stock market behavior indicate an integrated or segmented international stock market is potentially quite important.

The relevant underlying model of mean variance (MV) choice was developed by Markowitz (1959) and Tobin (1958) and then extended to yield insights into the equilibrium pricing of financial assets through the capital asset pricing model (CAPM) by Sharpe (1964) and Lintner (1965). The two major conclusions of this model are: (1) the return on an asset is the risk-free rate of return plus a risk premium that is a function of the asset's covariance with the market portfolio (i.e., the nondiversifiable or systematic risk); and (2) it is optimal for each investor to hold a linear combination of the riskless asset and the market portfolio.

Applications of this model to international finance were originally developed by Grubel (1968), Grubel and Fadner (1971), and Levy and Sarnat (1970). International extensions of the CAPM (ICAPM) were developed independently by Solnik (1974a) and by Grauer, Litzenberger, and Stehle (1976) (hereinafter GLS). Basically, these authors and those that followed tried to determine (a) if the special features characterizing international financial markets were sufficiently different from each domestic market individually so that, when analyzed, they yielded important results; and (b) if there were benefits from diversifying investments in common stocks across national boundaries (and thus across currency denominations).

The concept of capital market integration versus market segmentation was one of the keys to the motivation behind this international portfolio diversification literature (see especially McDonald, 1973; Cohn and Pringle, 1973; Lessard, 1974, 1976; and Adler and Dumas, 1975). The literature, however, has developed in the direction of merely showing whether or not there have in fact been benefits from international diversification and has not looked into the reasons for the existence or nonexistence of those benefits. The relationship of these studies to the original motivating notion of the degree of capital market integration has been largely ignored.

Consider, for example, that there are benefits from diversification with perfect capital market integration, with perfectly segmented markets, or with any conceivable market condition anywhere on the spectrum in between these two polar points (McDonald, 1973; and Lessard, 1974, 1976). The benefits to diversification with already fully integrated markets are only the benefits from the diversification of the nonsystematic risk in each security from a world perspective. The benefits from diversification of a previously segmented market include not only the elimination of that part of the domestically measured systematic risk that was systematic only in a domestic sense, but also a shift in the efficient frontier and a decrease in the rate of return to nondiversifiable risk, reflecting increased allocational efficiency.[1] Consider, also, that while the theoretical models stress a world of perfect integration[2] (e.g., GLS, 1976, who assume a world with no deviations whatsoever from perfect financial conditions, and Solnik, 1974a, who assumes no trade), the empirical work continues to struggle with a world of differential taxes, capital controls, exchange rate changes that deviate from that predicted by strictly financial factors or from Purchasing Power Parity (PPP), limited markets, different national preferences, political risks, etc. (see, especially, Guy, 1978a,b; Lessard, 1983; Levy and Sarnat, 1975; and Logue and Rogalski, 1979).

With few exceptions, this literature has found benefits to be derived from international diversification of common stock holdings whether the sample period has been during fixed or floating exchange rate periods, whether the markets have been developed or developing or both, whether the methodologies have been correct or incorrect, weak or strong. Grubel (1968), Levy and Sarnat (1970, 1975), and Grubel and Fadner (1971) used ex-post data to derive the MV efficient frontier.[3] Agmon (1972), Lessard (1974, 1976, 1983), Solnik (1974b,c), Stehle (1977), and Biger (1979) test the ICAPM to find evidence of national and international factors in determining asset prices. In general, they discover benefits from diversification and influences by both an international and a national factor, indicating some market integration. Critics of these tests have contended that the results are not very robust, as they are consistent with a large number of alternative hypotheses (see, especially, Bicksler, 1974; Wallingford, 1974; and Adler and Dumas, 1975). McDonald (1973) finds benefits from international diversification for French mutual funds, Lessard (1973, 1975) uses multivariate methods of factor and principle-component analysis to find that diversified portfolios from four Latin American exchanges dominate each of the national portfolios, and Jacquillat and Solnik (1978) find that investment in the stocks of U.S. MNCs directly is no substitute for international diversification.[+]

In opposition to the general result of diversification gains, Guy (1978a,b) finds that there have *not* been gains from diversification in the case of the British investment trusts. The results of this work are especially noteworthy in light of the fact that the paper itself presents the most careful treatment of capital market imperfections in the literature. Guy adjusts his empirical work so as to accurately reflect the effects of the U.K. capital controls and then finds, astonishingly, that the trusts were unable to take advantage of available selective strategies to benefit from holding diversified portfolios of U.K. and U.S. stocks. In fact, they did not even outperform the 1960–1979 London Stock Exchange.

There are, to say the least, serious methodological problems with most of the empirical work surveyed above. In addition to the fact that there is very little that any of this empirical work says specifically about capital market integration, there may be very little that any of it says in general about portfolio diversification. In the first place, all of the theory is ex ante, and all of the empirical work tests the theory using ex-post data. Thus, the tests are not only of the maintained hypothesis, but also of the existence of a risk premium and of the rational nature of expectations. This concern is most eloquently stated by Sharpe (1978, p. 918): "Unless one is prepared to reject the most rudimentary notions about risk aversion, it follows that at least some of the measured ex post values do not adequately reflect ex ante predictions. . . . Any test using ex post values is a joint test of a theory of asset pricing and a model of a return-generating process" (see, also, Lessard, 1980). We will return to this notion in the next section, when its importance becomes even more clear in evaluating the contributions of the empirical work in international bond markets. As we will see, in light of the recent growth in international financial markets, this problem throws doubt on any empirical work (including that presented above) that evaluates ex-post asset returns in the context of capital market integration.

In addition to this specific data concern, Roll (1977) has indicated that the problem is even deeper—namely, there is, in fact, little possibility of ever being able to generate a correct empirical test of the CAPM (see also Ross, 1978, and Sharpe, 1978, for discussions of the improbability of successfully testing the CAPM; Adler and Horesch, 1974, and Logue and Rogalski, 1979, for specific empirical criticisms along this line; and Solnik, 1977, and Dumas, 1977, for a similarly pessimistic discussion about the ICAPM.) Roll's basic, and so far irrefutable, facts are that: (1) the CAPM is not testable unless the exact composition of the true market portfolio is known and used empirically, and (2), more importantly, it cannot be proved or disproved empirically because of the tautological nature of the linear relationship between average security returns and the betas. If it is correct that the CAPM cannot be tested empirically, then it is unlikely that past tests that have accordingly been incorrectly designed will shed much light on the extent of international capital market integration.

Whereas Roll's concerns raise serious doubts about the possibility of obtaining significant empirical insights from this literature, Solnik's (1977) pessimism about tests for international capital market integration seems to be less serious (see, especially, Dumas, 1977). Solnik expresses two basic concerns. First—and here he is entirely correct—the ability to discriminate between an integrated and a segmented international capital market may not be possible merely by looking at relationships among asset prices. This observation was first stated by Lessard (1973, 1975) and Adler and Dumas (1975) and has even more serious implications for the bond market literature discussed and extended in the next section.

It is probably impossible to tell whether strong correlations in rates of returns imply that there are integrated capital markets or imply that there are segmented markets where the correlations are merely a result of common underlying economic factors or international shocks. The difference is crucial for understanding future behavior, as rates of return in segmented markets will behave quite differently once the underlying factors in each market are no longer highly correlated. Along this line, Kenen (1976) points out that correlations of rates of return only test for market integration *after* allowing for all possible correlations due to correlations of underlying factors. Zero correlation almost certainly implies segmented markets, but strong correlations cannot be used to distinguish between integrated and segmented markets. Rising or falling correlations imply nothing about the changing nature of capital market integration.

Second, Solnik (1977) contends that the existing empirical evidence implies that the GLS (1976) ICAPM model is indistinguishable from the Solnik (1974a) ICAPM model or from models of segmented capital markets. This claim may not be true. Dumas (1977) points out that the correct conclusion from Solnik's (1977) empirical work is that the GLS model is preferred to the Solnik model. Critical to this analysis is the conclusion from the GLS model that the valuation of an asset is independent of the currency of the investor's residence. That is, investors are intent on maximizing real wealth and do not suffer from exchange illusion. In a GLS world of perfect, integrated, capital markets with exchange rates that fluctuate only because of monetary factors, this is certainly true. But in a world of segmented capital markets, different investors will find it optimal to hold different portfolios.[5] Few would argue, for example, that Iranian investors had the same ranking of international investment opportunities as German and U.S. investors in January 1980! Their risk from holding dollar assets was unique to them and nondiversifiable. It thus could not be compensated for, and therefore the Iranian investors' optimal portfolios were clearly different from the rest of the world's. That is, the market was clearly segmented. As Black (1974) points out in a theoretical context, in a world with barriers to capital integration, investors would not hold the international market portfolio. Market imperfections quickly take us out of a GLS world and into an empirical world, where it may just be possible to distinguish between segmented and integrated capital markets.[6]

In this vein, two papers with opposite results give a glimmer of hope that it is possible to distinguish between relatively segmented and integrated capital markets. Levy and Sarnat (1975) find that the efficient investment sets are completely different for Israeli and U.S. investors, due almost certainly to market imperfections and discrete exchange rate changes during the period. This is clearly inconsistent with the GLS world outlined above. Biger (1979), on the other hand, finds for the major industrialized countries that the efficient sets are not all that different, almost certainly because of a closer approximation to a GLS world of simultaneous determination of yields in an equilibrium market.[7]

We cannot, of course, reject the notion that the results of one or both of these studies is merely wrong because of the empirical problems in testing the CAPM noted above. But if we can accept these results—or at least accept their potential—then it implies that there is a possibly fruitful area for future research. Namely, by testing for efficient international investment sets from the viewpoint of different national investors, when the composition of the sets is virtually the same across investors, then the home markets in which these investors reside have relatively integrated capital markets. Where the efficient sets differ significantly, we might be able to infer that markets are segmented. I am skeptical, however, about the potential for this test, as it is likely to be dominated by the empirical problems outlined earlier.

There are two other possible areas for research in this international common stock literature. First, Black (1974) proposed, as a way of measuring the barriers to integrated capital markets, actually analyzing known barriers and taking them at face value. Despite the difficulty of this approach, Guy (1978a,b) has shown the way toward developing tests that may yield significant insights and still avoid the distasteful task of employing casual empiricism. Second, nobody, to my knowledge, since Solnik (1974c) has looked at returns from holding stock portfolios covered against exchange risk.[8] This is an experiment that might be well worth pursuing, because it reduces at least one element in the ex-post returns to a true measure of ex-ante expected returns.

Friend, Westerfield, and Granito (1978) have presented results of preliminary tests utilizing ex-ante data on expected returns rather than expost data on realized returns. Hopefully, their early success will generate useful data series, greater effort, and eventually more advanced techniques that can be applied to international capital markets. In addition, they address themselves to an issue on which most researchers in this field have been strangely silent. Namely, that the international investment portfolio includes more than merely common stocks. It also includes fixed income assets. They extend tests of the domestic CAPM to include both common stocks and domestic bonds. This then brings us to the research on international bond markets. Before making the obvious observation that research on international common stocks and research on international bonds might be fruitfully integrated in the Friend, Westerfield, and Granito manner, I will review and extend the tests of international bond market integration.

III. THE INTERNATIONAL MARKET FOR FIXED INCOME ASSETS

Historically, researchers have treated the international bond markets differently than the international stock markets in testing for the extent of market integration. A thorough and excellent survey of the capital flow and bond market literature is provided in Logue, Salant, and Sweeney (1976) (referred to hereafter as LSS), and there is therefore no point in repeating their work in any detail here (see also Hodjera, 1973). Briefly, past studies have indicated a high level of integration, with little evidence of greater integration over time. There have been essentially three broad concepts of integration developed by past authors: (1) the sensitivity of international capital flows to covered or uncovered interest rate differentials; (2) the "capital reflow" approach that concentrates on interrelationships among domestic policies, domestic conditions, and foreign conditions; and (3) the relationship among interest rates across countries. This latter concept has been handled in three distinct ways: (a) examining the level of interest rates across countries, (b) examining the covariability of interest rates, and (c) testing for deviations from interest parity.

Neither the capital flow nor the capital reflow approaches are potentially fruitful areas for testing for the extent of capital market integration. They each entail difficulties with testing for causality, with reliably measuring many of the variables, with correctly treating the endogeneity of many of the often-used explanatory variables, with meaningfully generalizing from the limited two-country model, and with the difficulty of distinguishing between endogenous and exogenous policy variables (see LSS). The interest-rate approach, on the other hand, unlike the first two approaches above, is consistent with the notion of capital market integration developed in the Introduction—namely, to what extent are the costs of capital and the returns from investment opportunities (adjusted for returns to the bearing of nondiversifiable risk) the same across markets?

The first interest-rate approach—namely, whether there has or has not been convergence in the *level* of interest rates across countries, as examined by Cooper (1971), Hawkins (1972), and Minot (1974) (and extended and criticized by LSS), is not relevant to whether or not capital markets have become more or less integrated. Unless exchange rates are expected to remain fixed for the duration of the assets' maturities, we would not expect international interest rates to converge as capital markets became better integrated. In a floating-exchange-rate world (or, for that matter, in an adjustable-peg world), interest differentials reflect expected exchange rate changes and thus differences in monetary conditions, rather than only the extent of market segmentation. Clearly, the cost of capital and the return on investments across currencies can be the same, even with large deviations in interest differentials. In fact, ex-ante (ex-post) returns will be the same whenever the expected (actual) exchange rate change is the same as the interest differential. In the fixed-rate world of the 1950s, 1960s, and early 1970s, it may have made sense to look at the convergence of interest rate levels. This is no longer the case.

On the other hand, LSS attempt to show how significant insights into the extent of capital market integration can be obtained through the second interest rate approach—namely, the analysis of the covariability of interest rates (see also Tollison, and Willett, 1973). They develop a methodology directly from a capital asset pricing model that is consistent with the work on international stock markets surveyed in the previous section of this paper. Their resulting methodology is to use factor analysis of rates, of return on assets across international markets (see LSS, pp. 106–120, and their two appendices.) They then claim that the more closely rates of return across international investment opportunities are explained by an "international" factor, the better integrated are the markets. The more other factors link subcountries within the markets, the less integrated are international capital markets as a whole. In the limiting case of perfect market integration, rates of return across countries would be fully explained by an international factor. In perfectly segmented markets, a separate country factor would be required to explain each country's assets' rate of return.

The empirical work reported by LSS analyzed results for quarterly uncovered interest rates on medium- to long-term government bonds for many of the OECD countries for 1958–1973.[9] Their results indicate that, whereas there was significant capital market integration during the period, it was by no means complete integration. The international factor explained up to 40% of the variation in the first differences and percentage changes in the interest rates. In addition, they found evidence of a second factor, a diversifiable risk factor, which distinguished between the "Germanic" countries (Germany, the Netherlands, Sweden, and Switzerland) and the "Atlantic" countries (the United States, United Kingdom, and France).

Before rigorously dveloping the shortcomings of this approach, some obvious improvements and extensions of the LSS tests immediately suggest themselves as interesting. First, no allowance was made for exchange rate gains and losses.[10] Second, the correct analysis should be on the rate of return of holding the asset during the period, not merely on the differences or percentage changes in the yields.[11] Third, we now have had seven years' experience with floating rates, and it might be useful to test for capital market integration during the 1973–1979 period.

Tables 1 through 5 present the summaries of factor analysis on various rates of return from holding comparable 90-day and long-term government bonds during the 1973–1979 floating-rate period. Rates of return include capital gains and losses from selling assets before maturity, and either the cost of forward cover (when the investments were covered) or the realized exchange gains and losses (when they were not), as indicated.

Table 1 presents the results of factor analysis on the rates of return to a U.S. investor from buying a sequence of 90-day assets quarterly in each of the seven countries, holding them to maturity, and then converting the proceeds back to dollars.[12] The table also gives the correlations of returns of these investment opportunities from 1974:12 to 1979:06.[13] These results do not strongly imply the existence of an international factor. Factor 1 is more than likely a "European" factor, distinguishing between the rates of return on European assets, on the one hand, and then Japan, the United States, and Canada in increasing order of divergence from the European market. The second factor more

TABLE 1

Uncovered Short-Term Interest Rates Every Three Months: 1974:12–1979:06

	Canada	France	Germany	Japan	Switzerland	United Kingdom	United States
A. Correlation Matrix							
Canada	1.000						
France	−.450	1.000					
Germany	−.273	.657	1.000				
Japan	−.404	.258	.190	1.000			
Switzerland	−.375	.540	.693	.450	1.000		
United Kingdom	−.296	.489	.495	.071	.395	1.000	
United States	.288	.262	.148	−.440	−.020	.438	1.000

B. Cumulative Percentage of Variance Explained by Each Factor

Factor 1	44.1
Factor 2	69.3

C. Factor Loading (Correlation of Interest Rates with Factors) and Communality (Proportion of Variance Explained by Factors)

	Factor 1[a]	Factor 2[b]	Communality
Canada	−.507	.462	.372
France	.796	−.105	.646
Germany	.784	−.127	.623
Japan	.399	−.619	.442
Switzerland	.777	−.358	.628
United Kingdom	.607	.142	.469
United States	.152	.911	1.001

Notes: [a]Unrotated.

[b]Rotated.

TABLE 2

Uncovered Short-Term Interest Rates Every Month: 1974:12–1979:09

	Canada	France	Germany	Japan	Switzerland	United Kingdom	United States
A. Correlation Matrix							
Canada	1.000						
France	.021	1.000					
Germany	.110	.810	1.000				
Japan	−.095	.596	.530	1.000			
Switzerland	.022	.712	.839	.567	1.000		
United Kingdom	−.051	.537	.511	.445	.502	1.000	
United States	.134	.157	.126	−.192	.054	.257	1.000

B. Cumulative Percentage of Variance Explained by Each Factor

Factor 1	49.5
Factor 2	67.4
Factor 3	81.1

C. Factor Loadings (Correlation of Interest Rates with Factors) and Communality (Proportion of Variance Explained by Factors)

	Factor 1[a]	Factor 2[b]	Factor 3[b]	Communality
Canada	.019	.066	.290	.089
France	.855	.175	−.018	.733
Germany	.943	.062	.288	1.003
Japan	.687	−.143	−.418	.690
Switzerland	.846	.039	.043	.731
United Kingdom	.642	.436	−.256	.582
United States	.124	.693	.248	.513

Notes: [a]Unrotated.

[b]Rotated.

sharply delineates the United Kingdom, Canada, and the United States from the others, the so-called Atlantic factor (see LSS). The two factors together explain about 70% of the variance in the rates of return.

Table 2 analyzes a slightly different investment opportunity—namely, the purchase and sale every month (i.e., before maturity) of the comparable 90-day assets. The investor thus incurs both exchange-rate and interest-rate risk, as both the domestic-currency price and the exchange rate subject the investor to capital gains and losses. There is, again, no international factor. Factor 1 (explaining 50% of the variance) is clearly an Atlantic factor (i.e., the United States and Canada), and factors 2 and 3 do not lend themselves to any obvious interpretation.

We turn to an analysis of rates of return on long-term assets in Table 3, where we *do* see evidence of an international factor explaining about 40% of the variance (although the United Kingdom, perhaps because of its extensive capital controls, is an obvious outlier). Here, again, investors risk capital gains and losses from both interest rate and exchange rate changes (the rates of return are on purchasing long-term bonds and selling them three

TABLE 3

Uncovered Long-Term Interest Rates Every Three Months: 1973:03–1979:06

	Canada	France	Germany	Japan	Switzerland	United Kingdom	United States
A. Correlation Matrix							
Canada	1.000						
France	.155	1.000					
Germany	.334	.547	1.000				
Japan	−.083	.357	.411	1.000			
Switzerland	.125	.570	.633	.462	1.000		
United Kingdom	−.036	.154	.062	.083	−.071	1.000	
United States	.636	.248	.404	−.060	.194	−.153	1.000

B. Cumulative Percentage of Variance Explained by Each Factor

Factor 1	39.2
Factor 2	62.1
Factor 3	76.6

C. Factor Loadings (Correlation of Interest Rates with Factors) and Communality (Proportion of Variance Explained by Factors)

	Factor 1[a]	Factor 2[b]	Factor 3[b]	Communality
Canada	.431	.740	.006	.550
France	.663	.192	.171	.499
Germany	.820	.379	.070	.680
Japan	.430	−.145	.064	.374
Switzerland	.769	.095	−.151	.745
United Kingdom	.018	−.067	.692	.486
United States	.552	.857	−.135	.769

Notes: [a]Unrotated.

[b]Rotated.

months later[14]). Factor 2 separates out the effects of the Atlantic factor, distinguishing clearly between the United States and Canada and the rest. Factor 3 again separates the United Kingdom rate of return from the rest.

Table 4 presents results for the quarterly buying and selling of long-term bonds, covered against exchange risk. Except for Japanese investments, the results are not dramatically different from those presented in Table 3 for the first two factors. The Japanese investments are now separated out with those in the United States and Canada, as part of the Atlantic factor in factor 2. Germany and Japan are separated out from the rest by factor 3, when covered forward.

Whereas these results may provide some evidence about the extent of capital market integration across domestic capital markets, there are a number of caveats about the results of this type of analysis (see Kenen, 1976, and LSS, pp. 129–130). First, as was the case for equity markets, correlations of returns do not necessarily bear a strong relationship to the extent of capital market integration. As stated earlier, zero correlation implies a lack of integration, and perfect correlation may imply perfect integration, but higher correla-

TABLE 4

Covered Long-Term Interest Rates Every Three Months: 1974:03–1979:06

	Canada	France	Germany	Japan	Switzerland	United Kingdom	United States
A. Correlation Matrix							
Canada	1.000						
France	.477	1.000					
Germany	.434	.324	1.000				
Japan	.079	.206	.426	1.000			
Switzerland	.209	.420	.363	.140	1.000		
United Kingdom	−.016	.121	.222	.122	.297	1.000	
United States	.696	.334	.295	−.175	.095	−.244	1.000

B. Cumulative Percentage of Variance Explained by Each Factor

Factor 1	36.7
Factor 2	59.7
Factor 3	73.7

C. Factor Loadings (Correlation of Interest Rates with Factors) and Communality (Proportion of Variance Explained by Factors)

	Factor 1[a]	Factor 2[b]	Factor 3[b]	Communality
Canada	.773	.110	.133	.656
France	.603	.390	.173	.394
Germany	.627	.336	.473	.501
Japan	.271	.115	.824	.694
Switzerland	.476	.704	.076	.545
United Kingdom	.102	.475	.119	.257
United States	.722	−.157	−.143	.942

Notes: [a]Unrotated.

[b]Rotated.

tions do not necessarily imply higher integration otherwise. Strong positive correlations may merely reflect common shocks to each underlying economy and imply nothing about integration. Second, these tests say nothing explicit about the speed of adjustment across markets. Third, the analysis grants equal weights to each investment alternative, whereas, remembering Roll's (1977) concern about the ultimate testability of these capital asset pricing models, proper analysis of the optimally diversified international portfolio should contain assets in proportion to their relative importance in the true market portfolio.[15] Fourth, since LSS show that these tests are equivalent to tests of the ICAPM, they are subject to all of our criticisms of tests of that model developed above. And, fifth—and, as it turns out, most important—most of this analysis is performed over ex-post rate-of-return data, while our hypothesis is that ex-ante rates of return would be perfectly correlated in a fully integrated market. The hypothesis does not necessarily imply that ex-post rates of return will be perfectly correlated in such a market.

How important is this to our results and to our understanding of capital market integration? Unfortunately it is unavoidably critical! Imagine that in international financial markets there was a set of available investments across all currencies, each of which yielded the identical rate of return for an investor, in terms of whichever currency or mix of currencies his or her income or consumption was denominated. Also imagine that there was a set of borrowing sources across all currencies, each of which cost the identical amount for a given investor. Such markets would certainly be fully integrated.

It turns out that such markets *do* exist, at least for short-term assets and liabilities! This fact then brings us to our third interest-rate test—namely, tests of covered interest parity. In the short-term Eurocurrency markets, the evidence is overwhelming that covered interest parity holds.[16] That is, one cannot make significant profits by borrowing Eurodollars in London, converting them to Euromarks, and investing them covered in London or Zurich. The cost of borrowing Eurodollars is identical to the cost of borrowing covered Euromarks or covered Eurosterling, while the returns on deposits of Eurodollars are identical to returns on deposits of covered Euromarks or covered Eurosterling. These markets are perfectly integrated.

If we had had Euromarket data for our factor analysis, rates of return on covered deposits should have proven to be perfectly correlated (or at least nearly perfectly correlated, allowing for some measurement error and perhaps even transaction costs). One factor should have explained almost all—if, in fact, not all—of the variance in the rates of return. This factor could be called an "international factor," but, in fact, it is only a single-country factor, since a covered yen loan is really a dollar loan. As can be seen from Table 5, even using several domestic short-term bond markets, rather than Euromarkets, covered returns are in fact almost completely correlated.[17] The "international factor" explains 84% of the variance across the portfolio of returns.[18] Because it is possible to realize the identical short-term rate of return from any comparable investment in the Euromarkets and almost the same return in the domestic markets, invariant to the political, exchange, and default risks, these short-term covered markets are clearly well, if not perfectly, integrated. The lack of perfect integration reported in Table 5 is not confined to transactions across currencies. Rates of return on assets denominated in the same currency, but held in different money market centers, can also yield different returns (see Herring and Marston, 1976). A different rate of return on dollars in New York versus London could certainly be interpreted as strong evidence of a lack of perfect capital integration and could be a result of differences in political risk, tax regulations, or controls.[19]

What do we then conclude about the extent of integration in the markets when investments are uncovered? We know from the covered yields that the markets are integrated. As investors are not forced to take uncovered positions against their will, we must presume that the uncovered investment opportunities represent markets that are no less integrated than the covered opportunities.[20] What can we then conclude from the implied relatively low levels of international integration in the uncovered markets reflected in the results reported in Tables 1 and 2, compared to the results in Table 5? We are forced to conclude that analysis of our ex-post data reveals nothing about the extent of market integration. The fact that investors who *willingly* took open positions, with respect to foreign exchange risk, earn (or pay) a rate of return that is different from that available domestically or when forward cover is purchased implies nothing about market integration. The exchange risk was incurred in anticipation of profits. Presumably, the ex-ante expected exchange gain compensated the investor or borrower for the risk incurred. If not,

TABLE 5

Covered Short-Term Interest Rates Every Three Months: 1974:12–1979:09

	Canada	France	Germany	Japan	Switzerland	United Kingdom	United States
A. Correlation Matrix							
Canada	1.000						
France	.713	1.000					
Germany	.990	.721	1.000				
Japan	.707	.482	.709	1.000			
Switzerland	.995	.707	.993	.715	1.000		
United Kingdom	.803	.843	.833	.582	.809	1.000	
United States	.991	.717	.990	.693	.994	.810	1.000

B. Cumulative Percentage of Variance Explained by Each Factor

Factor 1 83.6

C. Factor Loadings (Correlation of Interest Rates with Factors) and Communality (Proportion of Variance Explained by Factors)

	Factor 1	Communality
Canada	.986	.972
France	.757	.572
Germany	.994	.987
Japan	.701	.491
Switzerland	.989	.978
United Kingdom	.858	.736
United States	.985	.970

then domestic markets or forward cover would have been used to guarantee that the rate of return or cost could have been the same as the domestic rate.[21]

The results in Tables 1 and 2 are then merely interesting—not important. They reveal certain patterns of ex-post returns in international investment alternatives, but they tell us nothing about capital market integration. Similarly with the results for long-term assets reported in Tables 3 and 4. We see patterns in ex-post international returns for investors willing to take risks due to interest-rate and exchange-rate changes in long-term investments that may or may not be interesting. But we cannot tell from this data if ex-ante returns (even risk-adjusted) are equalized across markets.

For markets where forward markets exist, then, we can test for the existence of covered interest parity and the correlation of covered ex-ante returns and thus determine the extent of capital market integration. When forward markets do not exist—say, for longer-term assets—we cannot make such a test. Presumably, risks are taken with some expected return. Unfortunately, this expected return is not empirically observable and, thus, as we have discussed, for these markets the extent of capital market integration is not determinable. Where does this leave us, then, with respect to such markets? Not very far, unfortunately.

Someone might pursue the obvious extension suggested by the Friend, Westerfield, and Granito (1978) work to look at both the equity and fixed-income markets to derive the optimal portfolio, then to see if it is the same across investors from different countries, in the manner suggested in the previous section. Once again, I am skeptical about the likelihood of meaningful results with ex post data. Black (1974) (and, similarly, Dooley, 1976) suggest that we look at specific capital controls and take them at face value. Guy (1978a,b) has done just that for U.K. trusts and the international equities markets.[22] It might be useful for someone to apply Guy's methodology to the international bond markets. A cursory knowledge of such controls indicates that, for the major industrialized countries, they have been relaxed—but not eliminated—during the current floating exchange rate experience and would seem to imply that capital market integration has been increasing.[23]

Certainly, one piece of evidence on capital market integration—although non-rigorous—has been the rate of increase of the Eurocurrency and Eurobond markets (see Hawkins, 1972, for a discussion of the integrating role of the Euromarkets with respect to the EEC). One obvious source of market segmentation has been government regulation and controls of domestic financial markets. The growth of the Euromarkets is testimony, on the one hand, to the markets' ability to become integrated despite these controls and, on the other hand, to the extent of controls that have segmented national markets and

TABLE 6

Size of the Eurocurrency Market (in Billions of Dollars, End of Period)

Year	Gross[a]	Net[b]
1964	20	14
1965	24	17
1966	29	21
1967	36	25
1968	50	34
1969	85	50
1970	111	65
1971	145	85
1972	200	110
1973	303	160
1974	370	215
1975	460	250
1976	565	310
1977	695	380
1978	895	485

Source *World Financial Markets* (Morgan Guaranty Trust Co.), various issues [1964–1969, as reported in Dufey and Giddy, *The International Money Market*, 1978].

Notes: [a]Includes interbank liabilities.

[b]Excludes interbank liabilities.

TABLE 7

Eurobond Issues, by Currency of Denomination (in Millions of Dollars)

Year	U.S. Dollar	German Mark	Dutch Guilder	Canadian Dollar	French Franc	European Unit of Account	Other	Total
1970	1,775	688	391	0	0	54	58	2,966
1971	2,221	786	298	0	20	166	151	3,642
1972	3,908	1,129	393	15	491	0	398	6,335
1973	2,447	1,025	194	0	166	99	262	4,193
1974	996	344	381	60	0	174	179	2,134
1975	3,738	2,278	719	558	293	371	610	8,567
1976	9,125	2,713	502	1,407	39	99	443	14,328
1977	11,627	4,131	452	655	0	28	878	17,771
1978	7,290	5,251	394	0	0	165	1,025	14,125
1979	12,565	3,626	531	425	0	253	1,326	18,726

Source *World Financial Markets* (Morgan Guaranty Trust Co.), various issues.

have made the Euromarkets a necessary phenomenon. In fact, the common textbook explanation for the development of Euromarkets has been this very avoidance by multinational banks of onshore controls (see, among others, Eiteman and Stonehill, 1979, and Dufey and Giddy, 1979).

As discussed above, the Eurocurrency markets, where interest parity holds instantaneously, are clearly perfectly integrated. Table 6 shows the growth in these markets over the past fifteen years. Domestic national short-term markets are somewhat less well integrated, but covered assets appear to be nearly perfect substitutes. The Eurobond markets offer long-term sources of capital and vehicles for investment that are free from official domestic restrictions that segment the various long-term national markets. Table 7 clearly shows the dramatic growth in the Eurobound markets across a number of currencies. This may be the best evidence available for longer-term assets that markets exist outside of national boundaries that are becoming increasingly integrated. It is certainly suggestive of that fact. Unfortunately, no rigorous test seems currently available. We have exhausted our search.

SUMMARY

This paper has shown that empirical tests of capital asset pricing models (in either equity or bond markets) do not shed much light on the extent of capital market integration. There are several reasons for this, the most important of which turns out to be that ex-post data simply are inappropriate for use in testing ex-ante models. Investors or borrowers take risks for which it is their *expectation* that they will be compensated (or they presumably would not take them). The fact that ex-post *observed* rates of return are different across investments implies nothing about the extent to which markets are integrated. Thus, tests, like the ones presented in this paper, may be interesting for determining the extent to which international factors, as opposed to regional or economically segmented factors, explain ex-post rates of return, but they do not answer any of our questions about capital market integration.

Only to the extent that covered interest parity holds do we know that capital markets are fully integrated, in that we can *observe* that ex-ante expected returns are identical across markets. Thus, it seems that shorter-term Eurocurrency markets are integrated, domestic short-term markets in the major industrialized countries are somewhat less so, and we can say little about longer-term markets. In this vein, the dramatic growth of the Eurocurrency and Eurobond markets over the past fifteen years is almost certainly evidence in and of itself that international capital markets outside of national domestic markets are becoming more fully integrated, while barriers to full integration still exist across the various domestic markets. Those barriers are the very segmentations that have induced the enormous growth in the Euromarkets in the first place.

DATA APPENDIX

DESCRIPTION AND SOURCES

Short-Term Rates (End of Month)

Canada	3-month prime finance company paper
France	3-month interbank money against private paper
Germany	3-month interbank deposits
Japan	Tokyo interbank call money, unconditional, lenders' rate
Switzerland	3-month interbank deposits (Dec. 1974–Dec. 1977)
United Kingdom	3-month interbank deposits
United States	3-month prime industrial paper

Sources For Canada, France, Germany, Japan, United Kingdom, and the United States, Morgan Guaranty Trust Company, *World Financial Markets*, various issues; for Switzerland (Jan. 1978–Oct. 1979), Federal Reserve Board.

Long-Term Rates (End of Month)

Canada	Bank of Canada yield on all direct government bonds due or callable in 10 years or more
France	Average of yields to maturity of Equipment Bonds, monthly yields based on last Friday prices (7 years' maturity)
Germany	7% public authority bond average (10 years' maturity)
Japan	Arithmetic average of yields on government bonds with 7 years' maturity
Switzerland	Weighted average of yields on government bonds with at least 5 years' maturity
United Kingdom	Actuaries 20-year government stock through December 1975; since December 1975, actuaries 25-year government stock
United States	Morgan Guaranty 20-year U.S. Government Bond Index

Sources For Canada, Germany, United Kingdom, and the United States, Morgan Guaranty Trust Company, *World Financial Markets*, various issues; for France, Japan, and Switzerland, International Monetary Fund.

Forward and Spot Exchange Rates (End of Month)

Sources Federal Reserve Board of Governors

NOTES

I would like to thank David Babbel, Jeff Frankel, Peter Kenen, Don Lessard, Dennis Logue, Terry Turner, and Clas Wihlborg for helpful discussions during the preparation of this paper; Robin Layton for her research assistance; Pat Decker of the Board of Governors of the Federal Reserve Board, Nick Sargen of Morgan Guaranty, and Esther Suss of the IMF for their help in obtaining the data; the Institute of Business and Economic Research of the University of California, Berkeley, for their support; and the members of the NYU Conference on the Internationalization of Financial Markets for their comments.

1. See Cohn and Pringle (1973) for a discussion of the financial implications of the lifting of conditions of market segmentation.

2. A notable exception is the work by Black (1974), which seems to be largely, and unjustifiably, ignored.

3. See Guy (1978a, pp. 1425–1426) for a brief discussion of the upward and downward biases in these studies.

4. Jacquillat and Solnik (1978) along with Levy and Sarnat (1978) oddly separate the variance (and covariance) of equity returns and exchange rate changes as though they were separable and could be analyzed in isolation from each other. Since they do not subsequently "rejoin" these effects, this mistake makes it essentially impossible to determine the importance or validity of their results.

5. This result is true regardless of whether there are deviations from purchasing power parity or segmentations in capital markets.

6. Possible that is, if we can ignore, or at least overcome (which is unlikely), the problems of using ex-post data to test an ex-ante theory and Roll's empirical concerns.

7. See Stehle (1977) for an *unsuccessful* attempt to test this type of hypothesis.

8. And Solnik's use of forward rates in this case is a mystery because he was using *weekly* changes in prices and his results were for the 1966–1971 fixed rate period.

9. Their tests thus only included the first quarter of the current floating rate experience and, as near as I can tell from the paper, did not adjust rates of return for actual exchange rate changes during the period.

10. Even though they analyzed essentially a fixed rate period, they should have adjusted for the discrete parity changes that did occur.

11. These calculations ignore or are at least only first approximations to the capital gains and losses from buying a long term asset at one point and then selling it before the maturity date.

12. In all the results, we report the unrotated first factor and rotated factors in all other cases, because the rotated factors better distinguish whatever patterns of segmentation exist. The first factor, on the other hand, *should* reveal to what extent an international factor exists. Only those factors that had eigenvalues exceeding 1.0 were reported. For a more complete discussion of factor analysis, see LSS (1976) and Morrison (1967).

13. Swiss 90-day asset yields are not available before 1974:12. Results without Swiss assets from 1973.3–1979:06 were not substantively different from those reported in Table 4.1.

14. Yield data were end of month and were already adjusted for coupon payments, where relevant.

15. For example, the worst problem may well be the exclusion of all those assets with the clearly improper weight of zero in our analysis.

16. See Aliber (1973), Goldstein (1965), Herring and Marston (1976), Marston (1976), Minot (1974), and Roll and Solnik (1977) for evidence that not only are covered rates of return and costs of financial capital identical in the short-term Euromarkets, but that market traders may actually *set* forward rates equal to their interest-parity levels *consciously* (see Kohlhagen (1978) for a discussion of the implications of this phenomenon). For an excellent discussion on the effects of capital controls on interest parity, see Dooley (1976). When political risk and default risk are *perceived* to be identical across currencies in the Euromarkets (at least, that is, until late 1979), covered rates of return for different currencies are relatively riskless vis-à-vis each other and thus are identical across major currencies. The freezing of Iranian dollar assets by the United States in November 1979, even those in non-U.S. banks, and the possible resulting court decisions could, of course, adversly affect these relationships in the Eurocurrency markets in the future.

17. See Aliber (1973) and Minot (1974) for discussions and empirical analyses of deviations in interest parity between national markets versus the Euromarkets.

18. Significantly, the only countries for which the rate of return does not explain at least 97% of the variance are those that are normally associated with capital controls: Japan, France, and the United Kingdon.

19. For example, conversations with bankers reveal that even without Regulation Q ceilings, dollar deposit rates usually have a 20 to 30 basis points difference between London and New York and can, at times, reach or even exceed 100 basis points, even on a reserve-adjusted basis.

20. Actually, I know of no rigorous data showing that all financial positions are not in fact covered against exchange risk. The impression, however, has been formed among the experts on these markets that the forward markets are not used by participants as much as they could be or as much as they might otherwise be expected to be used (see, for example, McKinnon, 1979, and Group of 30, 1980). Financial and nonfinancial firms might, of course, be using other techniques, or even the financial positions themselves, to take fully covered positions at all times. But there is little evidence of this in discussions with market participants or in material in the financial press, in the academic literature, or in international financial textbooks. Finally, whereas investors do not have perfect access to the wholesale forward markets from which our data are taken, transaction costs in the market are generally so low (see Kohlhagen (1982) and the references cited therein) that any international investor of any size is in a position to purchase forward cover without significantly reducing covered rates of return.

21. As discussed in the introduction, market participants should only be compensated for bearing undiversifiable exchange risk; there is no market return to bearing diversifiable risk. A full treatment of the subject of exchange risk, in the context of market integration, is the subject of the papers by Ross, Kouri, and Dornbusch in this volume, and this is not pursued any further here. I think it is important, however, to note that: (a) at least for short-term maturities, when forward markets are well developed, exchange risk is avoidable (i.e., diversifiable), and thus the return to bearing exchange risk (appropriately adjusted for risk) should be no greater than the average cost of forward cover, or the deviation between the forward rate and the spot rate at maturity; and (b) it will remain difficult, if not impossible, to measure ex-ante exchange risk with ex-post exchange rate data.

22. Herring and Willett (1972) analyzed the effect of U.S. capital controls on international capital flows. Such capital flow models, however, do not seem to be a productive avenue for research into capital market integration, as discussed above.

23. Germany and the United States dismantled their major controls in 1974, the U.K. in 1979. Controls still exist in Japan, Switzerland, and, to some extent, in France, as indicated by the results in Table 5 for all but Switzerland. In addition, differential tax treatment for different investors or for different kinds of earnings (e.g., foreign versus domestic, or long-term capital gains versus short-term capital gains versus ordinary income), and accounting standards for foreign exchange gains and losses that distort investment opportunities (see, for example, Aliber and Stickney, 1975), almost certainly segment markets so much that otherwise perfectly substitutable assets have significantly different rates of return. Actual capital controls are described in detail in the IMF's *Exchange Restrictions*, published annually.

REFERENCES

Adler, M. and B. Dumas (1975), "Optimal International Acquisitions." *Journal of Finance* (March).

Adler, M. and R. Horesh (1974), "The Relationship among Equity Markets: Comment." *Journal of Finace* (September).

Agmon, T. (1972), "The Relations among Equity Markets: A Study of Share Price Comovements in the United States, United Kingdom, Germany and Japan." *Journal of Finance* (September).

Aliber, R. Z., and C. P. Stickney (1975), "Accounting Measures of Foreign Exchange Exposure: The Long and Short of It." *The Accounting Review* (January).

Aliber, R. Z., and C. P. Stickney (1975), "Accounting Measures of Foreign Exchange Exposure: The Long and Short of It." *The Accounting Review* (January).

Allen, P. R., and P. B. Kenen (1980), *Asset Markets, Exchange Rates, and Economic Integration*. Cambridge University Press.

Bicksler, J. L. (1974), "Comment." *Journal of Finance* (May).

Biger, N. (1979), "Exchange Risk Implications of International Portfolio Diversification." *Journal of International Business Studies* (Fall).

Black, F. (1974), "International Capital Market Equilibrium with Investment Barriers." *Journal of Financial Economics* (May).

Cohn, R. A., and J. J. Pringle (1973), "Imperfections in International Financial Markets: Implications for Risk Premia and the Cost of Capital to Firms," *Journal of Finance* (March).

Cooper, R. N. (1968), *The Economics of Interdependence: Economic Policy in the Atlantic Community*. McGraw-Hill.

——— (1971), "Towards an International Capital Market." *In North American and Western European Economic Policies*. Edited by C. P. Kindleberger and A. Schonfield. St. Martin's Press.

Dooley, M. P. (1976), "Note on Interest Parity, Eurocurrencies, and Capital Controls." International Finance Discussion Paper No. 80. Washington: Board of Governors of the Federal Reserve System (February).

Dufey, G., and I. H. Giddy (1978), *The International Money Market*. Prentice-Hall.

Dumas, B. (1977), "Discussion." *Journal of Finance* (May).

Eiteman, D. K., and A. I. Stonehill (1979), *Multinational Business Finance*, 2nd ed. Addison-Wesley Publishing Co.

Friend, I. R. Westerfield, and M. Granito (1978), "New Evidence on the Capital Asset Pricing Model." *Journal of Finance* (June).

Goldstein, H. N. (1965), "The Elasticity of the Speculative Demand Curve for Forward Exchange: A Rejoinder." *National Banking Review* (December).

Grauer, F. A., R. A. Litzenberger, and R. E. Stehle (1976), "Sharing Rules and Equilibrium in an International Capital Market." *Journal of Financial Economics* (June).

Group of Thirty (1980), *The Foreign Exchange Markets under Floating Rates*. New York: Consultative Group on International Economic and Monetary Affairs, Inc.

Grubel, H. G. (1968), "Internationally Diversified Portfolios: Welfare Gains and Capital Flows." *American Economic Review* (December).

Grubel, H. G., and K. Fadner (1971), "The Interdependence of International Equity Markets." *Journal of Finance* (March).

Guy, J. R. F. (1978a), "An Examination of the Effects of International Diversification from the British Viewpoint on Both Hypothetical and Real Portfolios." *Journal of Finance* (December).

——— (1978b), "The Performance of the British Investment Trust Industry." *Journal of Finance* (May).

Hawkins, R. J. (1972), "Intra-EEC Capital Movements and Domestic Financial Markets." In F. Machlup, W. S. Salant, and L. Tarshis (eds.), *International Mobility and Movement of Capital*. Columbia University Press.

Herring, R. J., and R. C. Marston (1976), "The Forward Market and Interest Rates in the Eurocurrency and National Money Markets." In C. H. Stem, J. H. Makin, and D. E. Logue (eds.), *Eurocurrencies and the International Monetary System*. Washington: American Enterprise Institute.

Herring, R. J., and T. P. Willett (1972), "The Capital Control Program and U.S. Investment Activity Abroad." *Southern Economic Journal* (July).

Hodjera, Z. (1973), "International Short Term Capital Movements: A Survey of Theory and Empirical Analysis." *International Monetary Fund Staff Papers* (November).

International Monetary Fund (1979), *Exchange Restrictions*. Annual Report.

Jacquillat, B., and B. H. Solnik (1978), "Multinationals Are Poor Tools for Diversification." *Journal of Portfolio Management* (Winter).

Kenen, P. B. (1976), "Capital Mobility and Financial Integration: A Survey." Princeton Studies in International Finance, No. 39, Princeton University.

Kohlhagen, S. W. (1978). "The Behavior of Foreign Exchange Markets: A Critical Survey of the Empirical Literature." New York University Monograph Series in Finance and Economics.

_____ (1982), "The Behavior of Transaction Costs and the Accuracy of Forward Rate Predictions during the Current Float." In Studies in Exchange Rate Flexibility. Edited by R. J. Sweeney and T. D. Willett. Washington: American Enterprise Institute (forthcoming).

Lessard, D. R. (1973), "International Portfolio Diversification: A Multivariate Analysis for a Group of Latin American Countries." *Journal of Finance* (June).

_____ (1974), "World, National, and Industry Factors in Equity Returns." *Journal of Finance* (May).

_____ (1975), "The Structure of Returns and Gains from International Diversification." In E. J. Elton and M. J. Gruber (eds.), *International Capital Markets*. Amsterdam: North-Holland Publishing Co.

_____ (1976), "World, Country, and Industry Relationships in Equity Returns: Implications for Risk Reduction through International Diversification." Financial Analysts Journal (Jan.–Feb.).

_____ (1983), "Principles of International Portfolio Selection." In A. M. George and I. H. Giddy (eds), *The Investment Manager's Handbook* New York: John Wiley.

Levy, H., and M. Sarnat (1970), "International Diversification of Investment Portfolios." *American Economic Review* (September).

_____ (1975), "Devaluation Risk and the Portfolio Analysis of International Investment." In E. J. Elton and M. J. Gruber (eds.), *International Capital Markets*. Amsterdam: North-Holland Publishing Co.

Lintner, J. (1965), "The Valuation of Risk Assets and the Selection of Risky Investments in Stock Portfolios and Capital Budgets." *Review of Economics and Statistics* (February).

Logue, D. E., and R. J. Rogalski (1979), "Offshore Alphas: Should Diversification Begin at Home?" *Journal of Portfolio Management* (Winter).

Logue, D. E., M. Salant, and R. J. Sweeney (1976), "International Integration of Financial Markets: Survey, Synthesis, and Results." In C. H. Stem, J. H. Makin, and D. E. Logue (eds.), *Eurocurrencies and the International Monetary System*. Washington: American Enterprise Institute.

McDonald, J. G. (1973), "French Mutual Fund Performance: Evaluation of Internationally Diversified Portfolios." *Journal of Finance* (December).

McKinnon, R. I. (1979), *Money in International Exchange: The Convertible Currency System*. Oxford University Press.

Markowitz, H. (1959), Portfolio Selection: *Efficient Diversification of Investments*. New York: John Wiley.

Marston, R. C. (1976), "Interest Arbitrage in the Euro-currency Markets." *European Economic Review* (January).

Minot, W. G. (1974), "Tests for Integration between Major Western European Capital Markets." *Oxford Economic Papers* (November).

Morrison, D. F. (1967), *Multivariate Methods*. McGraw-Hill.

Roll, R. (1977), "A Critique of the Asset Pricing Theory's Test." *Journal of Financial Economics* (March).

Roll, R., and B. H. Solnik (1977), "A Pure Foreign Exchange Asset Pricing Model." *Journal of International Economics* (May).

Ross, S. A. (1978), "The Current Status of the Capital Asset Pricing Model (CAPM)." *Journal of Finance* (June).

Sharpe, W. F. (1964), "Capital Asset Prices: A Theory of Market Equilibrium under Conditions of Risk." *Journal of Finance* (September).

_____ (1978), "Comment." Journal of Finance (June).

Solnik, B. (1974a), "An Equilibrium Model of the International Capital Market." *Journal of Economic Theory* (August).

_____ (1974b), "The International Pricing of Risk: An Empirical Investigation of the World Capital Market Structure." *Journal of Finance* (May).

_____ (1974c), "Why Not Diversify Internationally Rather than Domestically?" *Financial Analysts Journal* (July–August).

_____ (1977), "Testing International Asset Pricing: Some Pessimistic Views." *Journal of Finance* (May).

Stehle, R. (1977), "An Empirical Test of the Alternative Hypotheses of National and International Pricing of Risky Assets." *Journal of Finance* (May).

Tobin, J. (1958), "Liquidity Preference as Behavior Towards Risk." *Review of Economic Studies*.

Tollison, R. O., and T. D. Willett (1973), "International Integration and the Interdependence of Economic Variables." *International Organization* (Fall).

Wallingford, B. A. (1974), "Comments." *Journal of Finance* (May).

Part II
The Currency Factor

INTRODUCTION

Of the three major factors that distinguish international corporate finance from its domestic counterpart—multiple currencies, differential taxation, and barriers to financial flows—the currency factor is given most attention both by managers and academics. This has been especially true in the recent period of volatile exchange rates and has been accentuated by the debate surrounding the accounting recognition of exchange gains or losses. Currency risk is perceived as a major obstacle to international business, and more substantial corporate resources are being devoted to the management of foreign exchange exposure.

Most normative statements regarding decisions involving foreign exchange are based on implicit assumptions regarding the behavior of exchange rates and their relationships to other economic phenomena, many of which are not founded in fact. The selections in Part II provide the positive background on exchange rate behavior and the linkages between exchange rates, interest rates, and prices that are needed to draw conclusions regarding the correct treatment of currency risks in specific management decisions.

The majority of the selections emphasize recent developments in the theory of exchange rate determination or evidence on the behavior of exchange rates and related financial variables that are only now being incorporated into textbook international macroeconomics. These new developments, which emphasize the role of markets for money and securities in the determination of exchange rates and, as a result, focus on the efficiency of markets for foreign exchange, are particularly relevant to international financial management. They point to certain subtleties in the relationship among exchange rates, interest rates, price levels, and relative prices that are critical to corporate operating and financial decisions.

OUTLINE OF PART II

Determinants of Exchange Rates

The two articles in this section provide broad syntheses of current views regarding the role of asset markets in the determination of exchange rates. They represent a major departure from mainstream views of only a few years ago in which spot exchange rates were seen as being determined primarily in the market for goods and hence closely linked to a country's current trade situation and in which speculative, financial considerations primarily played on forward exchange rates. Frenkel (Article 8) summarizes the behavior of exchange rates since return to floating in the early 1970s, focusing on their volatility and their large and often persistent deviations from purchasing power parity. In order to explain this behavior, he outlines a view of exchange rate determination where expectations regarding the future, which are constantly modified by the arrival of news, play a key role like that played by shifts in expectations in the valuation of any other financial claim. He shows that the extreme volatility of exchange rates does not imply that these markets are not efficient. In fact, he argues that given the magnitude of the underlying disturbances in that period, the volatility is to be expected. Similarly, since the exchange rates are seen as shifting in response to changes in expectations about the future, it should not be surprising that purchasing power parity does not hold in the short run. The bottom line of his discussion is that exchange rates should be thought of as relative prices of financial assets as opposed to the relative prices of national outputs.

Dornbusch (Article 9) links an asset market view of exchange rate determination to underlying models of macroeconomics. He briefly reviews the three basic views of the exchange rate: the relative price of monies, the relative price of goods, and the relative price of bonds (financial assets). He points out that each of these models should be viewed as partial, but stresses that sharply articulated partial models are likely to provide the best understanding of the phenomenon given our current state of knowledge. He also reintroduces the result of current account surprises and explicitly incorporates the impact of official interventions. At the policy level, Dornbusch concurs with Tobin's statement that we should "throw some sand in the wheels of our excessively efficient international money market," which reflects policymakers' frustration with the loss of control over exchange rates and interest rates due to the potential for international capital flows. Thus, the integration of capital markets clearly plays a key role in the modern view of exchange rate determination.

Financial Parity Relationships and Market Efficiency

Solnik (Article 10) opens this section with a concise review of the key equilibrium tendencies that link interest rates, prices, and forward and spot exchange rates—purchasing power parity, interest rate parity, forward parity, and by implication, the international Fisher effect—and illustrates the key interactions between them. He points out that since the forward parity relationship links present variables with risky future variables it need not be an unbiased one and probably is not. Thus, he links the traditional theory of financial parity relationships in exchange markets with more recent developments in financial economics which recognize that exchange rate risk is likely to be priced.

The following two articles provide empirical tests of the interest rate parity relationship, the only arbitrage relationship in the constellation and hence the most testable one. Dooley and Isard (Article 11) examine the effects of German capital controls on differences between Euromark rates and domestic Deutschemark rates. They find that political risk in the form of prospective capital controls can lead to deviations from interest rate parity and segment a national market from other markets. Otani and Tiwari (Article 12) examine a similar phenomenon for Japan in the late 1970s, comparing deviations from the interest rate parity condition in London and Tokyo. They find that the capital controls of 1978 and 1979 did segment financial markets and cause IRPT to break down. However, they find that by late 1980, the differences had largely vanished and in this sense at least, Japan could be seen as largely integrated into international financial markets.

Cumby and Obstfeld (Article 13) investigate the Fisher hypothesis, that the differences in interest rates across currencies will reflect anticipated exchange rate movements. They employ Eurocurrency rates to abstract from jurisdictional controls explored by the previous two articles. Their results reject simple Fisher parity, but with deviations that are small and autocorrelated. They attribute this to the existence of risk premia in line with recent developments in financial economics as outlined by Stulz (Article 6) and Solnik.

Levich (Article 14) concludes this section with an empirical examination of the performance of professional currency forecasters. The issue here is whether there are sufficient deviations from market efficiency that well informed individuals can "beat the market" on a sustained basis. Tests of this proposition are not simple and much of the paper is spent discussing how they should be undertaken. The results themselves are quite interesting, since depending upon the time period that is taken, forecasters either appear to have some information or have little. Thus, the conclusion appears to be that markets are close to efficient but forecasters may have some useful information from time to time.

Purchasing Power Parity and the Real Exchange Rate

Deviations from purchasing power parity and related shifts in the relative prices of goods and factors across national boundaries play a critical role in corporate finance since they give rise to shifts in the cash flows from operations facing different degrees of global competition. Shapiro (Article 15) examines the theoretical and empirical content of the purchasing power parity concept under the assumption that both asset and goods markets are efficient and analyzes the sources of deviations from strict versions focusing on the role played by uncertainty, relative price changes, inappropriate measurement, and government intervention. His conclusion is that although deviations from purchasing power parity appear to be fairly large and persistent, it is not clear that these deviations can be exploited for profit. Further, Shapiro argues that these deviations should not be viewed as a disequilibrium state of affairs, but as arising from equilibrium change factors including changes in relative prices within countries.

Williamson (Article 16) takes a more traditional macroeconomic approach, assuming that real exchange rules can and do vary. He attempts to define deviations from purchasing power parity by developing a model of fundamental equilibrium exchange rates and seeing how and why actual exchange rates have differed from these rates over time. While he does not address the question of whether or not his results could be used profitably in financial markets, they do appear to provide interesting insights regarding the impact of exchange rate and relative price shifts on cash flows of corporations operating across national markets.

Determinants of Exchange Rates

8

Flexible Exchange Rates, Prices, and the Role of "News": Lessons from the 1970s*

Jacob A. Frenkel†

Recent experience with flexible exchange rate systems has led to renewed interest in the operation of foreign exchange markets as reflected in many recent studies of the principal determinants of exchange rates. The 1970s witnessed dramatic alteration of the international monetary system from a regime of pegged exchange rates, which had prevailed for about a quarter of a century (since the Bretton Woods conference), into a regime of flexible (though managed) rates. As a consequence of the emergence of the new legal and economic system traders, national governments and international organizations were confronted with new economic problems, choices, and instruments. During the 1970s exchange rates fluctuated widely and inflation rates accelerated. The international monetary system had to accommodate extraordinarily large oil-related shocks that affected trade flows in goods and assets. Huge oil payments had to be recycled. Uncertainties concerning future developments in international politics reached new heights and the prospects for the world economy got gloomier. These developments placed unprecedented pressures on the markets for foreign exchange as well as on other asset markets. They were associated with a large slide in the value of the US dollar and resulted in speeding up the creation of new institutions like the European Monetary System, which provided the formal framework for the management of exchange rates among members. The increased interdependence among countries and the realization that exchange rate policies by one national government exert influence on other economies have also induced legal responses from international organizations. For example, in late April 1977 the Executive Board of the International Monetary Fund approved the details of the second amendment to article IV of the amended Articles of Agreement dealing with the principles and procedures for surveillance of exchange rate policies of member countries.

These developments provide the background for this article, which is intended to sum

---

*This article is reprinted, with permission, from Bhandari and Putnam (eds.), *Economic Interdependence and Flexible Exchange Rates,* Cambridge, MA: MIT Press, 1983, pp. 3–41 and is a somewhat abridged version of Frenkel (1981b).

†I am indebted to Lauren J. Feinstone for helpful suggestions and efficient research assistance and to the National Science Foundation grant SOC 78-14480 for financial support. I have benefited from useful comments by Andrew Abel, William Branson, Sebastian Edwards, Stanley Fischer, Craig S. Hakkio, Edi Karni, Paul Krugman, Leonardo Leiderman, Robert E. Lucas, Jr., Allan Meltzer, Michael L. Mussa, Sam Peltzman, Nasser Saidi, and Roland Vaubel as well as of participants in seminars held at the NBER, Columbia University, New York University, Harvard University, the University of Virginia, the University of Rochester, Oxford University, Tel Aviv University, and the International Monetary Fund. This research is part of the NBER's Program in International Studies. The views expressed are those of the author and not necessarily those of the NBER, Inc.

up the relevant evidence bearing on a set of related questions and to present a brief of key issues and lessons from the experience with floating rates during the 1970s. The main orientation of the paper is empirical and the analysis is based on the experience of three exchange rates involving the dollar/pound, the dollar/french franc, and the dollar/DM. Section 1.1 provides an analysis of the efficiency of foreign exchange markets by examining the relation between spot and forward exchange rates. The extent of exchange rate volatility is also examined. This analysis of the foreign exchange markets sheds light on several questions, including (i) whether exchange rates fluctuate "excessively," (ii) whether speculation in the foreign exchange markets is destabilizing, (iii) whether there is "insufficient" speculation in the foreign exchange markets, (iv) whether there is evidence for market failure in the sense that there are unexploited profit opportunities. These issues are significant in assessing the performance of floating rates as well as in evaluating the need for government intervention in the foreign exchange markets. The analytical framework that is used for interpreting the volatility of exchange rates and the association between spot and forward rates is the modern theory of exchange rate determination. Within this framework exchange rates are viewed as the prices of assets that are traded in organized markets and, like the prices of other assets, are strongly influenced by expectations about future events.

The relation between exchange rates and interest rates is analyzed in Section 1.2. One of the key issues that is raised in this section is the distinction between anticipated and unanticipated changes in rates of interest. As an analytical matter this distinction is important because the modern approach to exchange rate determination implies that exchange rates are strongly influenced by "news," which by definition is unpredictable. Therefore, it is unanticipated rather than anticipated changes in interest rates that should be closely associated with changes in exchange rates. This prediction is tested empirically.

Section 1.3 analyzes the relation between exchange rates and prices by examining the patterns of deviations from purchasing power parities. The main point that is being emphasized is that there is an important intrinsic difference between exchange rates and national price levels. Exchange rates are more sensitive to expectations concerning future events than national price levels. As a result, in periods which are dominated by "news" that alters expectations, exchange rates are likely to be more volatile and departures from purchasing power parities are likely to be the rule rather than the exception. The analysis of the relation between exchange rates and prices is relevant for assessing whether the flexible exchange rate system was successful in providing national economies with an added degree of insulation from foreign shocks, and whether it provided policymakers with an added instrument for the conduct of macroeconomic policy. The evidence regarding deviations from purchasing power parities is also relevant for determining whether there is a case for managed float. Section 1.4 contains concluding remarks.

1.1 THE EFFICIENCY OF THE FOREIGN EXCHANGE MARKET AND THE MOVEMENT OF EXCHANGE RATES

1.1.1 The Efficiency of the Foreign Exchange Market

One of the central insights of the monetary (or the asset market) approach to the exchange rate is the notion that the exchange rate, being a relative price of two assets, is determined in a manner similar to the determination of other asset prices and that expectations concerning the future course of events play a central role in affecting current exchange rates.[1]

If the foreign exchange market is efficient and if the exchange rate is determined in a fashion similar to the determination of other asset prices, we should expect current prices to reflect all currently available information. Expectations concerning future exchange rates should be incorporated and reflected in forward exchange rates. To examine the efficiency of the market, I first regress the logarithm of the current spot exchange rate, $\ln S_t$, on the logarithm of the one-month forward exchange rate prevailing at the previous month, $\ln F_{t-1}$, as in equation (1):[2]

$$\ln S_t = a + b\ln F_{t-1} + u_t. \tag{1}$$

If the market for foreign exchange is efficient, so that prices reflect all relevant available information, then the residuals in equation (1), u_t, should contain no information and therefore should be serially uncorrelated. Further, if the forward exchange rate is an unbiased forecast of the future spot exchange rate (as should be the case under an assumption of risk neutrality), then the constant term in equation (1) should not differ significantly from zero[3] and the slope coefficient should not differ significantly from unity. I examine three exchange rates: the dollar/pound, the dollar/franc, and the dollar/DM. Equation (1) was estimated using monthly data for the period June 1973–July 1979. (Data sources are listed in the appendix.) The beginning of the period was set so as to concentrate on the experience of the current exchange rate regime (following the initial post-Bretton Woods transition period). The resulting ordinary least squares estimates are reported in table 1.1. Also reported in table 1.1 are additional regressions, which will be analyzed shortly. As may be seen for the dollar/DM exchange rate, the hypotheses that (at the 95 percent confidence level) the constant term does not differ significantly from zero and that the slope coefficient does not differ significantly from unity cannot be rejected. These hypotheses are rejected for the dollar/franc exchange rate and are rejected (marginally) for the dollar/pound exchange rate. The joint hypotheses, however, that the constant is zero *and* that the slope coefficient is unity, cannot be rejected at the 95 percent level for the dollar/pound and the dollar/DM exchange rates and at the 99 percent level for the dollar/franc exchange rate. The test statistics for testing the joint hypotheses are reported in the column headed by F in table 1.1. These results are relevant for assessing whether the forward rate is an unbiased forecast of the future spot rate. We turn next to the question of efficiency.

It was argued above that in an efficient market, expectations concerning future exchange rates are reflected in forward rates and that spot exchange rates reflect all currently available information. If forward exchange rates prevailing at period $t - 1$ summarize all relevant information available at that period, they should also contain the information that is summarized in data corresponding to period $t - 2$. It thus follows that including additional lagged values of the forward rates in equation (1) should not greatly affect the coefficients of determination and should not yield coefficients that differ significantly from zero. The results reported in table 1.1 are consistent with this hypothesis; in all cases the coefficients of $\ln F_{t-2}$ do not differ significantly from zero and the inclusion of the additional lagged variables does not improve the fit. Most important, in all cases the Durbin-Watson statistics are consistent with the hypothesis of the absence of first-order autocorrelated residuals, and an examination of higher order correlations (up to 12 lags) shows that no correlation of any order is significant.[4]

To examine further the relation between the various exchange rates we note that one of

TABLE 1.1

Efficiency of Foreign Exchange Markets—Monthly Data: June 1973–July 1979 (Standard Errors in Parentheses)[a]

Dependent variable $\ln S_t$	Estimation method	Constant	$\ln F_{t-1}$	$\ln F_{t-2}$	R^2	s.e.	D.W.	F	m
Dollar/pound									
	OLS	0.033 (0.017)	0.956 (0.024)		0.96	0.027	1.72	1.86	
	OLS	0.031 (0.018)	1.047 (0.116)	−0.088 (0.113)	0.96	0.027	1.94		
	IV	0.030 (0.018)	0.961 (0.025)		0.95	0.027	1.74		2.01
Dollar/franc									
	OLS	−0.237 (0.078)	0.843 (0.051)		0.79	0.029	2.23	4.83	
	OLS	−0.225 (0.082)	0.706 (0.117)	0.146 (0.117)	0.79	0.029	1.90		
	IV	−0.236 (0.080)	0.844 (0.053)		0.78	0.030	2.24		2.26
Dollar/DM									
	OLS	−0.023 (0.027)	0.971 (0.032)		0.93	0.032	2.12	0.51	
	OLS	−0.019 (0.028)	0.913 (0.119)	0.063 (0.122)	0.93	0.032	1.96		
	IV	−0.021 (0.027)	0.973 (0.032)		0.93	0.032	2.10		0.91

[a]s.e. is the standard error of the equation and R^2 is the coefficient of determination; in the case of instrumental variables estimation the R^2 was computed as $1 - \text{var}(\hat{u}_t)/\text{var}(\ln S_t)$. The F-statistic tests the joint restriction that the constant equals zero and the slope equals unity. The test statistic is distributed as $F(2, 71)$. Critical values for $F(2, 71)$ are 3.13 (95 percent) and 4.92 (99 percent). The instrumental variable (IV) estimation method is used in order to allow for the possibility of errors in variables arising from using $\ln F_{t-1}$ as a proxy for the expected future spot rate: the instruments are a constant, time, time squared, and lagged values of the dependent and the independent variables. The m-statistic which tests for the absence of errors in variables is distributed χ^2 with 2 degrees of freedom. The critical value for χ^2 (2) is 5.99 (95 percent).

the assumptions underlying equation (1) was that the forward exchange rate measures the unobservable value of the *expected* future spot exchange rate. This assumption provided the justification for using equation (1) instead of the explicit specification of the rational expectations hypothesis that is embodied in equation (2):

$$\ln S_t = E_{t-1} \ln S_t + \epsilon_t, \tag{2}$$

where $E_{t-1} \ln S_t$ denotes the expected (logarithm of the) spot exchange rate for period t based on the information available at period $t - 1$. If, however, the forward exchange rate at $t - 1$ is a "noisy" proxy for the expected future value of the spot rate (i.e., it measures it with a random error), then we obtain

$$a + b \ln F_{t-1} = E_{t-1} \ln S_t + v_{t-1}, \qquad E(v_t) = 0, \tag{3}$$

and substituting equation (3) into equation (2) yields

$$\ln S_t = a + b \ln F_{t-1} + (\epsilon_t - v_{t-1}). \tag{4}$$

In this case the error term in equation (1) would be $u_t = \epsilon_t - v_{t-1}$, the assumption that the covariance between $\ln F_{t-1}$ and u_t is zero would entail a specification error, and the application of the ordinary least squares (OLS) procedure would yield biased estimates due to the classical errors in variables bias.

In order to examine the possibility that the OLS estimates may be subject to the errors in variables bias, one needs to test the hypothesis that cov $(u_t, \ln F_{t-1}) = 0$. This test follows the specification test outlined by Hausman (1978).[5] To perform the test, equation (1) was estimated by applying the OLS procedure as well as by using an instrumental variables (IV) estimation method. Under the null hypothesis of no misspecification, the OLS coefficients vector $\hat{b}_0$ is an efficient and an unbiased estimate of the true coefficient vector. Under the alternative hypothesis of misspecification, the vector $\hat{b}_0$ is biased and an unbiased coefficient vector $\hat{b}_1$ can be obtained by applying an instrumental variables estimation procedure. The test statistic relevant for testing the null hypothesis can be written as

$$m = (\hat{b}_1 - \hat{b}_0)'(\mathrm{var}\hat{b}_1 - \mathrm{van}\hat{b}_0)^{-1}(\hat{b}_1 - \hat{b}_0), \tag{5}$$

where var$(\hat{b}_1)$ and var$(\hat{b}_0)$ denote the variance-covariance matrices of $\hat{b}_1$ and $\hat{b}_0$, respectively. Under the null hypothesis m is distributed (in large samples) as χ^2 with two degrees of freedom. Table 1.1 reports the results of estimating equation (1) by applying the instrumental variables estimation method. As may be seen, for all exchange rates the two vectors of coefficients $\hat{b}_1$ and $\hat{b}_0$ are very close. For example, for the dollar/pound exchange rate the constants are 0.033 and 0.030 and the slopes are 0.956 and 0.961; consequently, the resulting m statistic is 2.01, which is well below 5.99—the critical value of $\chi^2(2)$ at the 95 percent confidence level. The m statistics corresponding to the other exchange rates are also below this critical value. It is concluded, therefore, that the use of the forward exchange rate as a proxy for expectations does not introduce a significant errors in variables bias, and thus the use of the OLS estimation procedure seems appropriate.[6]

The principal conclusions that may be drawn from the previous discussion are that the behavior of the foreign exchange market during the 1970s has been broadly consistent with the general implications of the efficient market hypothesis.

1.1.2 Exchange Rate Movement: Volatility and Predictability

As is well known, during the same period exchange rates have been very volatile. The standard errors of the monthly percentage changes of the three exchange rates have been about 3 percent per month. Further, the standard errors of the regressions in table 1.1 indicate that the forecasts of future spot exchange rates based on the forward rates are very imprecise; the standard errors of the equations are about 3 percent per month.

These characteristics of price changes (volatility and unpredictability) are typical of auction and organized asset markets. In such markets current prices reflect expectations concerning the future course of events, and new information which induces changes in expectations is immediately reflected in corresponding changes in prices, thus precluding unexploited profit opportunities from arbitrage. The strong dependence of current prices on expectations about the future is unique to the determination of durable asset prices: it is not a characteristic of price determination of nondurable commodities. The strong dependence of asset prices on expectations also implies that periods which are dominated by uncertainties, new information, rumors, announcements and "news," which induce frequent changes in expectations, are likely to be periods in which changes in expectations are the prime cause of fluctuations in asset prices. Further, since the information which alters expectations must be *new*, the resulting fluctuations in price cannot be predicted by lagged forward exchange rates which are based on past information.[7] Therefore, during such periods, one should expect exchange rates (and other asset prices) to exhibit large fluctuations. When the prime cause of fluctuations is new information, one may expect that lagged forward exchange rates (which are based on past information) are imprecise (even though possibly the best unbiased) forecasts of future spot rates.

To gain further insights into the implications of this perspective on the relation between predicted and realized changes in exchange rates, figure 1.1 presents plots of predicted and realized percentage changes in the dollar/DM exchange rate where the predicted change is measured by the lagged forward premium. Also presented in this figure are the differentials in national inflation rates, which are discussed in section III. The key fact which emerges from this figure is that predicted changes in exchange rates account for a very small fraction of actual changes.[8] This phenomenon is also reflected in the comparison between the variance of actual and predicted changes in exchange rates; the variance of monthly percentage changes in exchange rates exceeds the variance of monthly forward premia by a factor that is larger than twenty.[9] This fact suggests that the bulk of exchange rate changes seem to be due to "new information" which, by definition, could not have been anticipated and reflected in the forward premium or discount which prevailed in the previous period. A similar pattern also characterizes the dollar/french franc and the dollar/pound exchange rates.

This view of the foreign exchange market can be exposited in the following simple model.[10] Let the logarithm of the spot exchange rate on day t be determined by

$$\ln S_t = z_t + bE_t(\ln S_{t+1} - \ln S_t), \tag{6}$$

where $E_t(\ln S_{t+1} - \ln S_t)$ denotes the expected percentage change in the exchange rate between t and $t + 1$, based on the information available at t, and where z_t represents the ordinary factors of supply and demand that affect the exchange rate on day t. These factors may include domestic and foreign money supplies, incomes, levels of output, and so forth. Equation (6) represents a sufficiently general relation which may be viewed as a "reduced form" that can be derived from a variety of models of exchange rate determination. These models may differ in their emphasis of the determinants of $z(t)$, but they all are likely to share a similar reduced form.[11] Assuming that expectations are rational in that equation (6) applies to expectations of future exchange rates, it follows, by forward iteration, that

$$E_t \ln S_{t+j} = \frac{1}{1+b}\sum_{k=0}^{\infty}\left(\frac{b}{1+b}\right)^k E_t z_{t+j+k}. \tag{7}$$

Thus, the current exchange rate ($j = 0$) and current expectations of future exchange rates ($j > 0$) are linked because both depend on expectations concerning the future z. The strength of the link depends on the magnitude of b which characterizes the dependence of the current exchange rate on the expected percentage change thereof.[12] The presumption is that due to profit opportunities from arbitrage this link is strong at least for the exchange

FIGURE 1.1

Monthly Percentage Changes of the US/German Consumer Price Indices [Δ ln (COL_{US}/COL_G)] of the Dollar/DM Exchange Rate (Δ in S_1), and the Monthly Forward Premium [$\ln(F_{t-1}/S_{t-1})$]: July 1973–July 1979

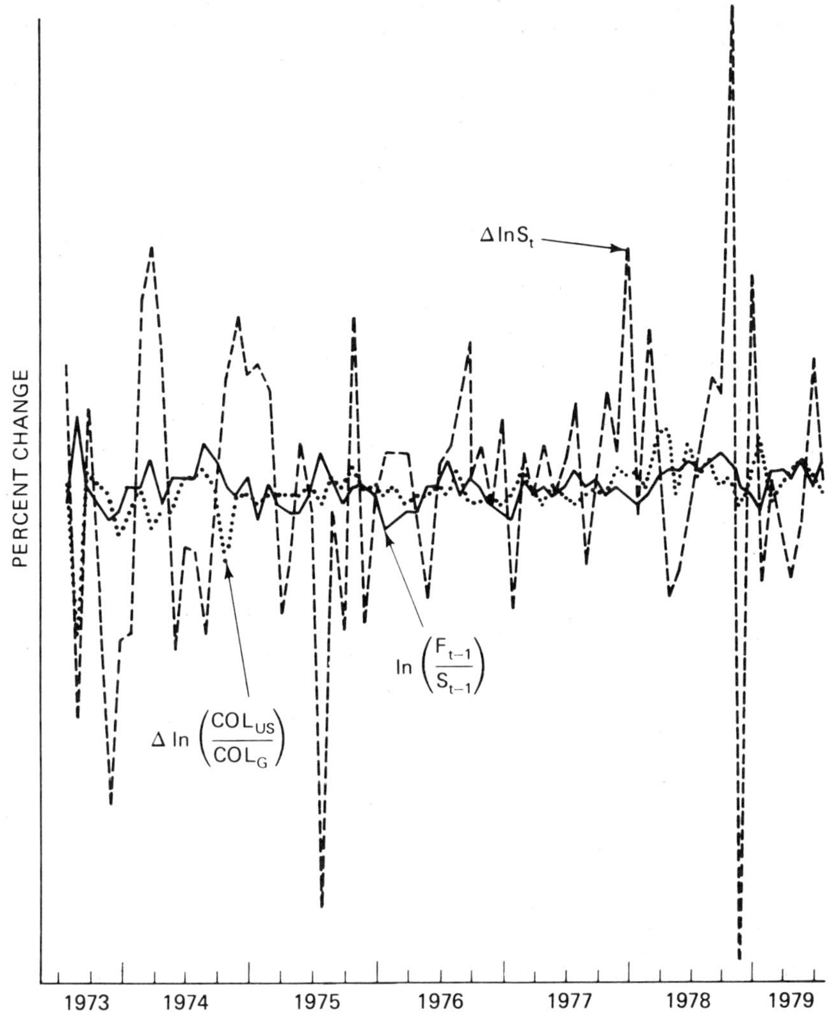

rates expected in the near future. Hence, the current exchange rate, $\ln S_t = E_t \ln S_t$, should be closely linked to the current expectation of the next period's exchange rate, $E_t \ln S_{t+1}$, which in turn should be closely linked to the exchange rate expected for the following period, $E_t \ln S_{t+2}$, and so on.

In order to examine this hypothesis, I present in figure 1.2 plots of spot and contemporaneous forward exchange rates for the dollar/DM, and a similar pattern characterizes the other two rates. Also presented is the ratio of national price levels discussed in section III. If the dominant factor underlying changes in rates is new information which alters views about current and expected future exchange rates by approximately the same amount,

FIGURE 1.2

Monthly Observations of the Dollar/DM Spot (ln S_t) and Forward (ln F_t) Exchange Rates and the Ratio of the US/German Cost of Living Indices [ln (COL_{US}/COL_G) (Scaled to Equal the Spot Exchange Rate at the Initial Month)]: June 1973–July 1979

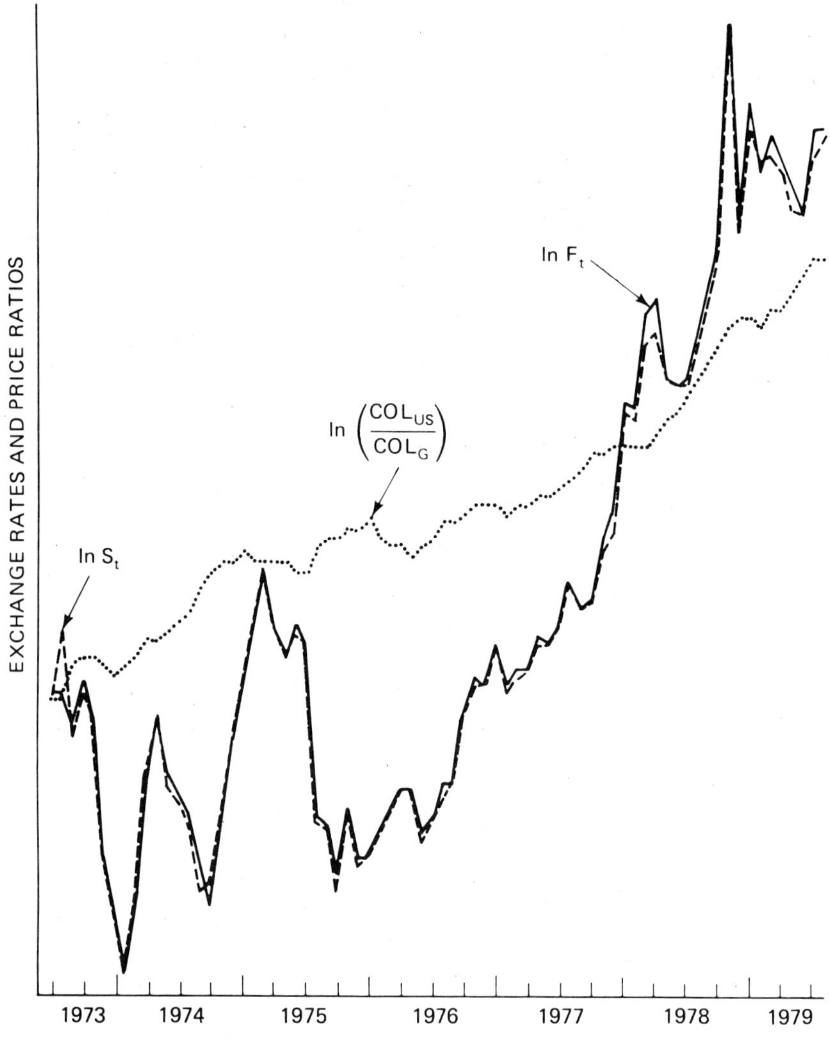

then one should expect a high correlation between movements of spot and forward rates. This fact is clearly demonstrated by figure 1.2, where it is seen that spot and forward exchange rates tend to move together and by approximately the same amount (the vertical difference between the two rates corresponds to the percentage forward premium or discount on foreign exchange). The correlations between the spot and the forward exchange rates for the three pairs of currencies exceed 0.99 and the correlations between the corresponding percentage changes of the spot and forward rates exceed 0.96. The high correlation between movements in spot and forward rates is expected since the two rates respond at the same time to the same flow of new information (which is presumed to affect the rate for more than one period). In general, the details of the relation between spot and forward exchange rates depend on the time series properties of the z in equation (7) and in particular on whether the new information is viewed as permanent or transitory.[13]

The comovement of spot and forward rates is evidence of the close link between current and expected future exchange rates which is illustrated by equation (7). This characteristic is typical of the foreign exchange market and is also shared by prices of many assets and commodities traded in organized markets. The recent pattern of gold prices provides a useful example of this general principle. Table 1.2 reports the spot and the futures prices of gold as recorded recently in the International Money Market (IMM) at the Chicago Mercantile Exchange on five consecutive days. The two key facts which are illustrated by this table are (i) the extent of day-to-day volatility in gold prices and (ii) the general uniformity by which these changes are reflected in the price of gold for immediate delivery as well as in the prices for the eight future delivery dates.

Another feature which is revealed by figure 1.2 is that the contemporaneous spot and forward exchange rates are approximately equal, thus indicating that the market's best forecast of the future spot rate is (approximately) the current spot rate. This phenomenon reflects the fact that, as an empirical matter, exchange rates have followed (approximately) a random walk process. For such a process current prices are indeed the best forecasts of future prices. (And to the extent that the exchange rate had some drift, the above statement should be interpreted in reference to that drift.) It is relevant to note, however, that while the random walk phenomenon seems to correspond to the actual paths of exchange rates, it does not reflect a theoretical necessity.

The final characteristic of the foreign exchange market is that generally (though not always) there is a positive correlation between the expected depreciation of the currency (as measured by the forward premium on foreign exchange) and the spot exchange rate.[14] This positive correlation may be rationalized by noting that currencies which are expected

TABLE 1.2
Futures Price of Gold on Consecutive Days—Daily Data: 1 May 1980–7 May 1980[a]

	Price (per ounce) and change from previous day									
Delivery date	1 May	Change	2 May	Change	5 May	Change	6 May	Change	7 May	Change
1980 May	516.0	14.4	511.0	−5.0	519.0	8.0	506.5	−12.5	512.0	5.5
June	517.0	10.5	575.5	−1.5	523.7	8.2	510.3	−13.4	516.0	5.7
September	536.0	10.5	533.5	−2.5	540.7	7.2	527.0	−13.7	531.5	4.5
December	554.0	9.5	551.0	−3.0	558.0	7.0	541.5	−16.5	547.0	5.5
1981 March	571.5	9.5	568.0	−3.5	574.7	6.7	557.0	−17.7	561.5	4.5
June	588.5	10.5	585.0	−3.5	591.0	6.0	571.5	−19.5	576.0	4.5
September	605.3	10.3	602.0	−3.3	607.0	5.0	585.5	−21.5	590.0	4.5
December	622.0	11.0	619.0	−3.0	623.0	4.0	599.5	−23.5	604.0	4.5
1982 March	638.5	11.5	636.0	−2.5	693.0	3.0	613.5	−25.5	618.0	4.5

[a]These prices are settlement prices at the International Money Market (IMM) at Chicago Mercantile Exchange as reported in the *Wall Street Journal* 2 May–8 May 1980.

to depreciate are traded at a discount in the forward market and, on average, these currencies also command a lower foreign exchange value in the spot market.[15] This relation is embodied in the specification of equation (6) and is interpreted further in the next section.

1.2. EXCHANGE RATES, INTEREST RATES, AND INNOVATIONS

1.2.1 Exchange Rates and Interest Rates: The Broad Facts

It is useful to recall the analysis which predicts a negative association between the rate of interest and the exchange rate. According to that analysis a higher rate of interest attracts foreign capital, which induces a surplus in the capital account of the balance of payments and thereby induces an appreciation of the domestic currency (i.e., a *lower* spot exchange rate). Another variant of this approach states that the higher rate of interest lowers spending and thus induces a surplus in the current account of the balance of payments, which results in a *lower* spot exchange rate. A third variant claims that the higher rate of interest implies (via the interest parity theory) a higher forward premium on foreign exchange: and to the extent that at a given point in time the forward exchange rate, which represents the expected future spot rate is predetermined by past history, as would be the case under the adaptive expectations hypothesis (which is clearly rejected by the evidence on the comovements of spot and forward rates), the required rise in the forward premium will be brought about by a *lower* spot rate (i.e., by an appreciation of the domestic currency). Whatever the route, by ignoring the distinction between nominal and real rates of interest, this approach predicts a *negative* relation between the rate of interest and the spot exchange rate (or, alternatively, a positive relation between the rate of interest and the foreign exchange value of the domestic currency).

While such a prediction might be appropriate for noninflationary environments, it might be entirely inappropriate for inflationary environments (like the one prevailing in the United States during the 1970s). In such periods variations in rates of interest are most likely to be dominated by variations in inflationary expectations rather than by liquidity effects associated with changes in the ratio of money to bonds. In such an environment the rate of interest is expected to be *positively* correlated with the exchange rate. The broad facts are consistent with this hypothesis. For most of the 1970s the rise in the rate of interest in the United States (relative to the foreign rate of interest) has been associated with a rise in the spot exchange rate (i.e., with a depreciation of the dollar) rather than with a fall in the spot rate. Figure 1.3 illustrates the point by plotting the foreign exchange value of the US dollar against the interest rate differential. As is evident, the higher (relative) rate of interest in the United States has been associated with a higher exchange rate (i.e., with a lower foreign exchange value of the dollar). It is relevant to note, however, that since mid-1979 this relation reversed itself.

The positive association between the rate of interest and the exchange rate in the context of the US dollar and the inflationary environment can be accounted for by the monetary (or the asset market) approach to the exchange rate, which puts a special emphasis on the influence of the expectations on current exchange rates.[16] For example, according to the monetary approach, a rise in the domestic (relative) rate of interest,

FIGURE 1.3

Weighted Average Foreign Currency Value of the US Dollar (top) and US-Foreign Interest Rate Differentials (Bottom)

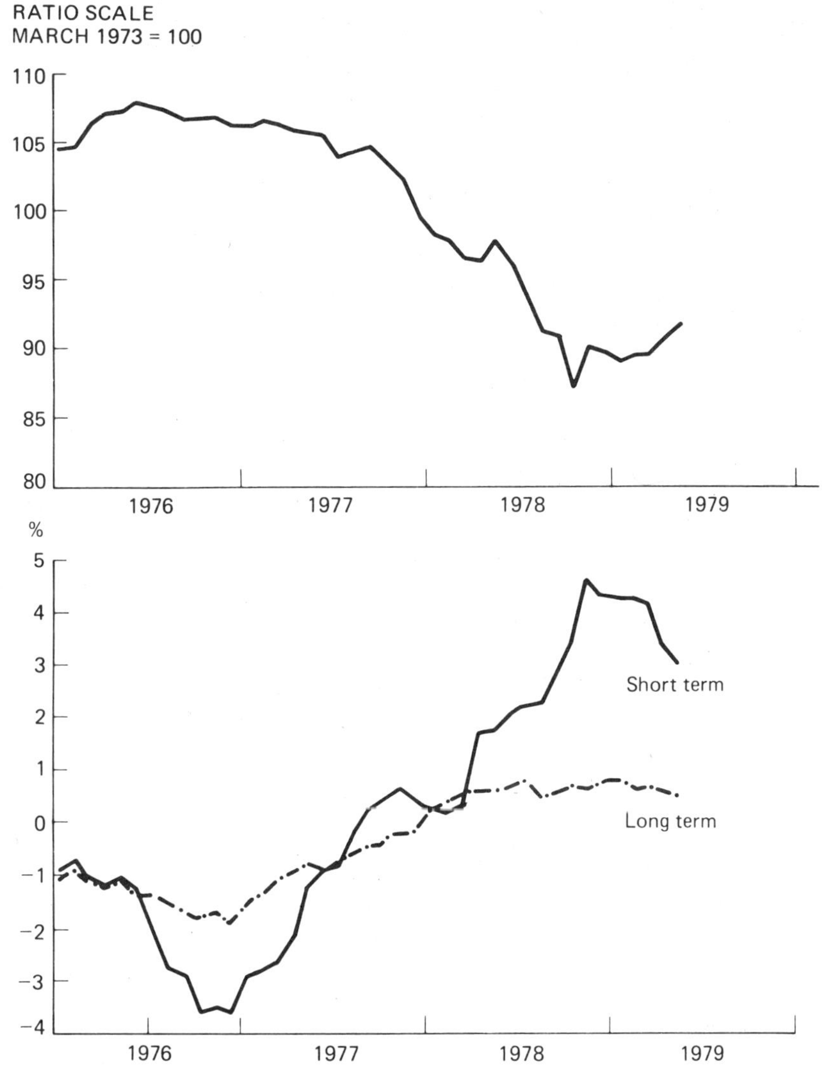

Source Mudd (1979).

which is dominated by a rise in the expected (relative) rate of inflation, induces a decline in the demand for real cash balances; for a given path of the nominal money supply asset market equilibrium requires a price level which is higher than the price which would have prevailed otherwise. When the domestic price level is linked to the foreign price through some form of purchasing power parity, and when the path of the foreign price is assumed to be given, the higher domestic price can only be achieved through a *rise* in the spot exchange rate (i.e., through a depreciation of the currency).[17]

This explanation of the positive association between interest rates and exchange rates has an intuitive appeal in that it implies that in an inflationary environment a relatively rapid rise in prices is associated with high *nominal* rates of interest as well as with a depreciation of the currency in terms of foreign exchange. This relation is embodied in equation (6), which states that an expected depreciation of the currency (which in our case is associated with inflationary expectations and high nominal rates of interest) results in an immediate depreciation.[18] The reversal of the relation between the U.S. interest and the external value of the dollar which has taken place since mid 1979, indicates that currently the prime cause for the fluctuations in U.S. interest rates is not variations in inflationary expectations but rather variations in the *real* rate of interest which are occasioned by the large U.S. budget deficit.

The foregoing analysis also provides the explanation for the observation (which was noted in section 1.1.2) that generally there is a positive correlation between the forward premium on foreign exchange and the level of the spot rate. Since during inflationary periods the spot rate is expected to be positively correlated with the interest rate differential and since, according to the interest parity theory, that differential must equal the forward premium on foreign exchange, it follows that during inflationary periods the forward premium is also expected to be positively correlated with the level of the spot rate.[19]

1.2.2 Exchange Rates and News

One of the central implications of the rational expectations hypothesis is that unanticipated events "news" play a predominant role in affecting real variables and asset yields. This implication is embodied in many expositions of modern macroeconomics and its empirical content has been the subject of numerous recent studies.[20] In the context of exchange rate determination the discussion in section 1 and in particular the contributions by Mussa (1977, 1979a) and Dornbusch (1978) emphasized that the predominant cause of exchange rate movements are "news" which could not have been anticipated.[21] Expressing the spot exchange rate at period t as the sum of factors which were anticipated from the past as well as factors which represent "news," Dornbusch (1978) decomposes the effects of "news" into those which alter the expected future spot rate between the last period and the present and those which lead to a reassessment of the one-period interest rate differential starting at the present, that is, "news" about the term structure. Both of these white noise serially uncorrelated components play a role in determining the spot exchange rate in Dornbusch's analysis.

The evidence presented in section 1 suggests that the forward rate summarizes the information that is available to the market when the forward rate is being set, and in equation (3) it was assumed that the expected exchange rate can be written as $a + b\ln F_{t-1}$ plus a serially uncorrelated error. We may therefore express the spot rate at period t as a function of factors which have been known in advance and are summarized by the lagged forward rate, as well as a function of the "news":

$$\ln S_t = a + b\ln F_{t-1} + \text{“news”} + w_t. \tag{8}$$

In what follows, this notion is applied to an empirical analysis of the role of "news" as a determinant of the exchange rate. The key difficulty lies in identifying the variable which measures the "news." Since quite frequently it is difficult to observe and quantify the "news," it is convenient to examine the relation between the exchange rate and a variable whose time series is likely to *manifest* the "news" promptly. Assuming that asset markets clear fast and that the "news" is immediately reflected in (unexpected) changes in the rates of interest, Equation (8) may be written as

$$\ln S_t = \underbrace{a + b\ln F_{t-1}}_{\text{"expected exchange rate"}} + \underbrace{\alpha[(i - i^*)_t - E_{t-1}(i - i^*)_t]}_{\text{"news"}} + w_t, \tag{9}$$

where the bracketed term denotes the innovation in the (one-month) interest differential and $E_{t-1}(i - i^*)_t$ denotes the interest differential which was expected to prevail in period t based on the information available at $t - 1$. The expected interest rate differential was computed from a regression of the interest differential on a constant, on two lagged values of the differential and on the lagged forward exchange rate in F_{t-1}.

As was argued, the association between exchange rates and interest rates is likely to be positive during periods in which most of the variations in nominal rates of interest are dominated by variations in inflationary expectations—a characteristic which seems to fit the inflationary environment of the 1970s. Under such circumstances, when the unexpected interest differential reflects "news" concerning inflationary expectations, the coefficient α in equation (9) is likely to be positive.[22] Table 1.3 reports the two-stage least squares estimates of equation (9) for the three exchange rates over the period June 1973–July 1979.[23] As may be seen, in all cases the coefficients of the expected interest differential are positive and in the case of the dollar/pound exchange rate the coefficient is statistically significant. In order to verify the importance of using the series of innovations in the interest differential, Table 1.3 also reports estimates of regressions which replace

TABLE 1.3

One-Month Interest Rate Differentials and Exchange Rates: Instrumental Variables—Monthly Data: June 1973–July 1979 (Standard Errors in Parentheses)[a]

Dependent variable $\ln S_t$	Constant	$\ln F_{t-1}$	$(i - i^*)_t$	$[(i - i^*)_t - E_{t-1}(i - i^*)_t]$	s.e.	R^2	D.W.
Dollar/pound	0.021	0.965	−0.152		0.028	0.95	1.69
	(0.020)	(0.026)	(0.118)				
	0.031	0.959		0.432	0.026	0.96	1.78
	(0.017)	(0.024)		(0.181)			
Dollar/franc	−0.024	0.992	−0.462		0.034	0.71	2.21
	(0.181)	(0.124)	(0.324)				
	−0.246	0.837		0.245	0.029	0.80	2.17
	(0.077)	(0.051)		(0.167)			
Dollar/DM	0.004	0.997	−0.180		0.033	0.93	2.12
	(0.064)	(0.064)	(0.394)				
	−0.022	0.972		0.413	0.031	0.93	2.05
	(0.026)	(0.031)		(0.347)			

[a]Interest rates are the one-month (annualized) Euromarket rates. The expected interest rate differential $E_{t-1}(i - i^*)_t$ was computed from a regression of the interest differential on a constant, two lagged values of the differential, and the logarithm of the lagged forward exchange rate. The two-stage least squares estimation method was used. The instruments for the interest differential were a constant, two lagged values of the differential, and the logarithm of the lagged forward exchange rate; the instruments for the unexpected differential were a constant, Durbin's rank variable, and the logarithm of the lagged forward exchange rate. $(i - i^*)_t$ denotes the actual interest rate differential, where i is the rate of interest on securities denominated in US dollars and i^* the rate of interest on securities denominated in foreign currency. $[(i - i^*)_t - E_{t-1}(i - i^*)_t]$ denotes the *unexpected* interest rate differential. s.e. is the standard error of the equation. A quasi-R^2 was computed as $1 - \text{var}(\hat{u}_t)/\text{var}(\ln S_t)$.

TABLE 1.4

One-Month Interest Rate Differentials and Exchange Rates: Instrumental Variables—Monthly Data: June 1973–July 1979 (Standard Errors in Parentheses)[a]

Dependent variable $\ln S_t$	Constant	$\ln F_{t-1}$	$(i - i^*)_t$	$[(i - i^*)_t - E_{t-1}(i - i^*)_t]$	s.e.	R^2	D.W.
Dollar/pound	0.018	0.969	−0.156	0.562	0.023	0.97	1.81
	(0.017)	(0.022)	(0.100)	(0.191)			
Dollar/franc	−0.136	0.915	−0.312	0.547	0.031	0.75	2.19
	(0.112)	(0.076)	(0.209)	(0.282)			
Dollar/DM	0.002	0.996	−0.173	0.599	0.032	0.93	2.07
	(0.044)	(0.045)	(0.286)	(0.457)			

[a]Interest rates are the one-month (annualized) Euromarket rates. The expected interest rate differential $E_{t-1}(i - i^*)_t$ was computed from a regression of the interest differential on a constant, two lagged values of the differential, and the logarithm of the lagged forward exchange rate. The two-stage least squares estimation method was used. The instruments were a constant, two lagged values of the interest differential, Durbin's rank variable of the unexpected differential, and the logarithm of the lagged forward exchange rate. $(i - i^*)_t$ denotes the actual interest rate differential, where i is the rate of interest on securities denominated in US dollars and i^* the rate of interest on securities denominated in foreign currency. $[(i - i^*)_t - E_{t-1}(i - i^*)_t]$ denotes the *unexpected* interest rate differential. s.e. is the standard error of the equation. A quasi-R^2 was computed as $1 - \text{var}(\hat{u}_t)/\text{var}(\ln S_t)$.

the innovations by the actual series of the interest differential. In all cases the coefficients of the actual interest differential do not differ significantly from zero. Table 1.4 describes analogous two-stage least squares estimates of regressions which include both the actual interest rate differential and the innovation in the differential.[24] Again, in all cases the coefficients on the actual differential do not differ significantly from zero, while the coefficients on the innovations are all positive and are significant for the dollar/pound and the dollar/franc exchange rates.

One possible interpretation of the positive coefficient on the (unexpected) interest differential may be given in terms of the prediction of the monetary approach to the exchange rate, in which case the estimate of the coefficient α in equation (9) might be interpreted as an estimate of a structural parameter. Under an alternative interpretation the innovations in the interest differential belong in equation (9) only as far as they *manifest* "news" which is relevant for exchange rate determination. If, for example, the dominant element of "news" was variations in inflationary expectations, then one could also use the innovations in other time series as long as they reflect this relevant "news." To examine this possibility the same regressions as in tables 1.3 and 1.4 were estimated using the 12-month interest differential and the results are reported in tables 1.5 and 1.6. As before, in all cases the coefficients on the actual differential do not differ significantly from zero, while in all cases the coefficients on the innovations in the differential are positive and significant for the dollar/pound and the dollar/franc exchange rates.[25]

On the whole the record shows that during the 1970s exchange rates and the interest rate differential have been associated positively, thus indicating that during that inflationary period the same factors which induced a rise in the interest differential also induced a rise in the spot exchange rates. Furthermore, consistent with the hypothesis that current changes in exchange rates are primarily a response to new information, the evidence shows the importance of the innovations in the interest differential.

The principle that current exchange rates already reflect expectations concerning the future course of events implies that unanticipated changes in exchange rates are primarily

TABLE 1.5

Twelve-Month Interest Rate Differentials and Exchange Rates: Instrumental Variables—Monthly Data: June 1973–July 1979 (Standard Errors in Parentheses)[a]

Dependent variable $\ln S_t$	Constant	$\ln F_{t-1}$	$(i - i^*)_t$	$[(i - i^*)_t - E_{t-1}(i - i^*)_t]$	s.e.	R^2	D.W.
Dollar/pound	0.027	0.960	−0.083		0.027	0.95	1.71
	(0.019)	(0.025)	(0.147)				
	0.031	0.959		0.887	0.025	0.96	1.81
	(0.017)	(0.024)		(0.291)			
Dollar/franc	−0.152	0.904	−0.230		0.030	0.77	2.32
	(0.155)	(0.107)	(0.320)				
	−0.246	0.837		0.729	0.029	0.80	2.10
	(0.077)	(0.051)		(0.342)			
Dollar/DM	−0.012	0.982	−0.074		0.032	0.93	2.11
	(0.063)	(0.063)	(0.395)				
	−0.022	0.972		0.979	0.031	0.94	2.07
	(0.026)	(0.031)		(0.663)			

[a]Interest rates are the twelve-month Euromarket rates. The exepcted interest rate differential $E_{t-1}(i - i^*)_t$ was computed from a regression of the interest differential on a constant, two lagged values of the differential, and the logarithm of the lagged forward exchange rate. The two-stage least squares estimation method was used. The instruments for the interest differential were a constant, two lagged values of the differential, and the logarithm of the lagged forward exchange rate; the instruments for the unexpected differential were a constant, Durbin's rank variable, and the logarithm of the lagged forward exchange rate. $(i - i^*)_t$ denotes the actual interest rate differential, where i is the rate of interest on securities denominated in US dollars and i^* the rate of interest on securities denominated in foreign currency. $[(i - i^*)_t - E_{t-1}(i - i^*)_t]$ denotes the *unexpected* interest rate differential. s.e. is the standard error of the equation. A quasi-R^2 was computed as $1 - \text{var}(\hat{u}_t)/\text{var}(\ln S_t)$.

due to innovations. Since the empirical work suggests that most of the actual changes in exchange rates are unanticipated, it follows that most of the actual changes in exchange rates are due to "news." In the present section this principle was applied to the analysis of the relation between exchange rates and interest rate differentials. The principle, however, is general. For example, it implies that the relation between a deficit in the balance of

TABLE 1.6

Twelve-Month Interest Rate Differentials and Exchange Rates: Instrumental Variables—Monthly Data: June 1973–July 1979 (Standard Errors in Parentheses)[a]

Dependent variable $\ln S_t$	Constant	$\ln F_{t-1}$	$(i - i^*)_t$	$[(i - i^*)_t - E_{t-1}(i - i^*)_t]$	s.e.	R^2	D.W.
Dollar/pound	0.024	0.965	−0.087	0.978	0.022	0.97	1.82
	(0.016)	(0.021)	(0.121)	(0.286)			
Dollar/franc	−0.180	0.884	−0.184	0.915	0.029	0.79	2.16
	(0.118)	(0.181)	(0.245)	(0.432)			
Dollar/DM	−0.013	0.981	−0.063	1.031	0.031	0.93	2.08
	(0.053)	(0.054)	(0.338)	(0.752)			

[a]Interest rates are the twelve-month Euromarket rates. The expected interest rate differential $E_{t-1}(i - i^*)_t$ was computed from a regression of the interest differential on a constant, two lagged values of the differential, and the logarithm of the lagged forward exchange rate. The two-stage least squares estimation method was used. The instruments were a constant, two lagged values of the interest differential, Durbin's rank variable of the unexpected differential, and the logarithm of the lagged forward exchange rate. $(i - i^*)_t$ denotes the actual interest rate differential, where i is the rate of interest on securities denominated in US dollars and i^* the rate of interest on securities denominated in foreign currency. $[(i - i^*)_t - E_{t-1}(i - i^*)_t]$ denotes the *unexpected* interest rate differential. s.e. is the standard error of the equation. A quasi-R^2 was computed as $1 - \text{var}(\hat{u}_t)/\text{var}(\ln S_t)$.

trade and the exchange rate depends crucially on whether the deficit was expected or not. A deficit that was expected may have no effect on the exchange rate since the latter already reflected these expectations. In contrast, an unexpected deficit in the balance of trade may contain significant new information that is likely to be accompanied by large changes in the exchange rate.[26] This distinction might be useful in interpreting the weak and unstable relation between the balance of trade and the exchange rate without having to rely on explanations like the J curve or on variable import and export elasticities.

1.3 EXCHANGE RATES AND PRICES

One of the striking facts concerning the relation between prices and exchanges rates during the 1970s has been the poor performance of the predictions of the simple versions of the purchasing power parity doctrine. The originators and proponents of the purchasing power parity doctrine (Wheatley and Ricardo during the first part of the nineteenth century and Cassel during the 1920s) have viewed the doctrine as an extension of the

TABLE 1.7

Purchasing Power Parities: Instrumental Variables—Monthly Data: June 1973–July 1979 (Standard Errors in Parentheses)[a]

Dependent variable $\ln S_t$	Constant	$\ln(P_W/P_W^*)$	$\ln(P_c/P_c^*)$	s.e.	D.W.	ρ
Dollar/pound	0.712	0.165		0.027	1.63	0.963
	(0.149)	(0.507)				
	2.982		1.070	0.029	1.66	0.998
	(2.978)		(0.897)			
Dollar/franc	−1.521	0.184		0.029	2.26	0.863
	(0.027)	(0.374)				
	−1.570		−1.070	0.029	2.30	0.901
	(0.047)		(0.817)			
Dollar/DM	−0.900	1.786		0.034	1.69	0.739
	(0.018)	(0.230)				
	−0.908		2.217	0.031	1.96	0.759
	(0.175)		(0.263)			
Pound/DM	−1.668	0.821		0.027	1.60	0.895
	(0.041)	(0.144)				
	−1.666		0.965	0.027	1.57	0.909
	(0.048)		(0.197)			
Franc/DM	0.863	−0.026		0.020	1.61	0.981
	(0.143)	(0.487)				
	0.602		1.180	0.019	1.48	0.929
	(0.048)		(0.327)			

[a] $\ln S_t$ denotes the logarithm of the spot exchange rate: $\ln(P_w/P_w^*)$ and $\ln(P_c/P_c^*)$ denote, respectively, the logarithms of the ratios of the wholesale price indices and the cost of living indices. The Cochrane-Orcutt iterative technique with two-stage least squares estimation method was used: the instruments are a constant, time, time squared, and lagged values of the dependent and independent variables. s.e. is the standard error of the equation.

quantity theory of money to the open economy. By now the consensus seems to be that, when applied to aggregate national price levels, purchasing power parties can be expected to hold in the long run if most of the shocks to the system are of a monetary origin which do not require changes in relative prices. To the extent that most of the shocks reflect "real" changes (like differential growth rates among sectors), the required changes in sectoral relative prices may result in a relatively loose connection between exchange rates and aggregate price levels. The experience during the 1970s illustrates the extent to which real shocks (oil embargo, supply shocks, commodity booms and shortages, shifts in the demand for money, differential productivity growth) result in systematic deviations from purchasing power parties. As illustrated in figure 1.1, short-run changes in exchange rates have not been closely linked to short-run differentials in the corresponding national inflation rates as measured by consumer price indices. Furthermore, this loose link seems to be cumulative. As illustrated in figure 1.2, divergences from purchasing power parities, measured in terms of the relation between exchange rates and the ratio of consumer price indices, seem to persist.

The link between prices and exchange rates is illustrated in table 1.7, which reports the results of regressions of the various exchange rates on the corresponding ratios of wholesale and of cost of living price indices. As may be seen, the results of the regressions which involve the US dollar are extremely poor. For the dollar/pound and the dollar/franc exchange rates the estimates of the coefficients of the price ratios are insignificant, and for the dollar/DM exchange rate the estimates differ significantly from unity. In contrast, the results of the regressions of exchange rates that do not involve the US dollar or the US price level (the pound/DM and the franc/DM exchange rates) are superior: except for the wholesale price indices in the franc/DM regression, all the coefficients are highly significent, and the elasticities of the exchange rates with respect to the various price indices do not differ significantly from unity.

The vast difference in the performance of the regressions for the various currencies can be explained by noting that first, due to transport cost, purchasing power parities are expected to hold better among the neighboring European countries than among each of these countries and the United States: second, changes in commercial policies and nontariff barriers to trade seem to have been more stable within Europe than between Europe and the United States: third, within Europe the snake agreement and later on the European Monetary System have resulted in a reduced degree of intra-European flexibility of exchange rates: and fourth, there seem to have been large changes in the equilibrium *real* exchange rate between the US dollar and the European currencies.[27] It should be noted, however, that to some extent the overall poor performance of the purchasing power parities doctrine is specific to the 1970s. During the floating rates period of the 1920s, the doctrine seems to have been much more reliable.[28]

The preceding discussion accounted for the persisting deviations from purchasing power parities in terms of changes in real factors which affect equilibrium relative price structure. It should be noted, however, that even in the absence of such changes there is a presumption that, at least in the short run, exchange rate fluctuations would not be matched by corresponding fluctuations of aggregate price levels. The discussion in section 1 emphasized that in periods which are dominated by "news" which alters expectations, exchange rates (and other asset prices which are traded in organized markets) are expected to be highly volatile. Aggregate price indices, on the other hand, are not expected to reveal such a degree of volatility since they reflect the prices of goods and services which are less durable and therefore are likely to be less sensitive to the news which alters

TABLE 1.8

Mean Absolute Percentage Changes in Prices and Exchange Rates—Monthly Data: June 1973–July 1979[a]

	Variable					
				Exchange rates against the dollar		
Country	WPI	COL	Stock market	Spot	Forward	COL/COL_{US}
United States	0.009	0.007	0.037	–	–	–
United Kingdom	0.014	0.012	0.066	0.021	0.021	0.007
France	0.011	0.009	0.054	0.020	0.021	0.003
Germany	0.004	0.004	0.030	0.024	0.024	0.004

[a]All variables represent the absolute values of monthly percentage changes in the data. WPI denotes the wholesale price index and COL the cost of living index. Data on prices and exchange rates are from the IMF tape (May 1979 version). The stock market indices are from *Capital International Perspective*, monthly issues.

expectations concerning the future course of events. It follows therefore that in periods during which there is ample "news" which causes large fluctuations in exchange rates there will also be large deviations from purchasing power parities.[29]

The difference between the characteristics of exchange rates and national price levels is also reflected in their time series properties and is fundamental for interpreting the deviations from purchasing power parities. The monthly changes in exchange rates exhibit little or no serial correlation, while national price levels do exhibit a degree of serial correlation. The "stickiness" exhibited by national price levels need not reflect any market imperfection, rather, it may reflect the costs of price adjustment which result in the existence of nominal contracts of finite length. Likewise, it may reflect the results of confusion between relative and absolute prices and confusion between permanent and transitory changes. This difference between the time series properties of exchange rates and prices is reflected in the low correlation between the practically random month-to-month exchange rate changes and the serially correlated differences between national rates of inflation.

The different degrees of volatility of prices and exchange rates are illustrated in table 1.8, which reports the average absolute monthly percentage changes in the various exchange rates and prices. As is evident, the mean absolute change in the various spot exchange rates has been about 2 percent per month (and even slightly higher for the changes in the forward rate). The magnitudes of these changes have been more than double the magnitudes of the changes in most of the various price indices as well as in the ratios of national price levels. For example, the mean monthly change in the cost of living price index was 0.4 percent in Germany, 0.7 percent in the United States, 0.9 percent in France, and 1.2 percent in the United Kingdom. These differences are even more striking for the detrended series.

The notion that exchange rates have been volatile is clearly illustrated by figure 1.1 and by table 1.8. The comparison of the magnitudes of the changes in the exchange rates with the magnitudes of the changes in the price indices and in the ratios of national price levels may suggest, according to a narrow interpretation of the purchasing power parity doctrine, that exchange rate fluctuations have been "excessive." The previous discussion, however, has emphasized that exchange rates, being the relative prices of assets, are fundamentally different from the price indices of goods and services and therefore are expected to exhibit a different degree of volatility, in particular during periods that are dominated by "news." An alternative yardstick for measuring the degree of exchange rate fluctuations would be a comparison with prices of other assets. Indeed, while exchange rate changes have been large relative to changes in national price levels, they have been considerably smaller than changes in the prices of other assets like gold, silver, many other commodities that are traded in organized markets, and common stocks. For example, table 1.8 also reports the mean absolute monthly percentage change in stock market indices. As may be seen, the

FIGURE 1.4

(*A*) The Dollar/DM: Deviations from PPP with Wholesale Price Indices. (*B*) The Dollar/DM: Deviations from PPP with Cost of Living Price Indices

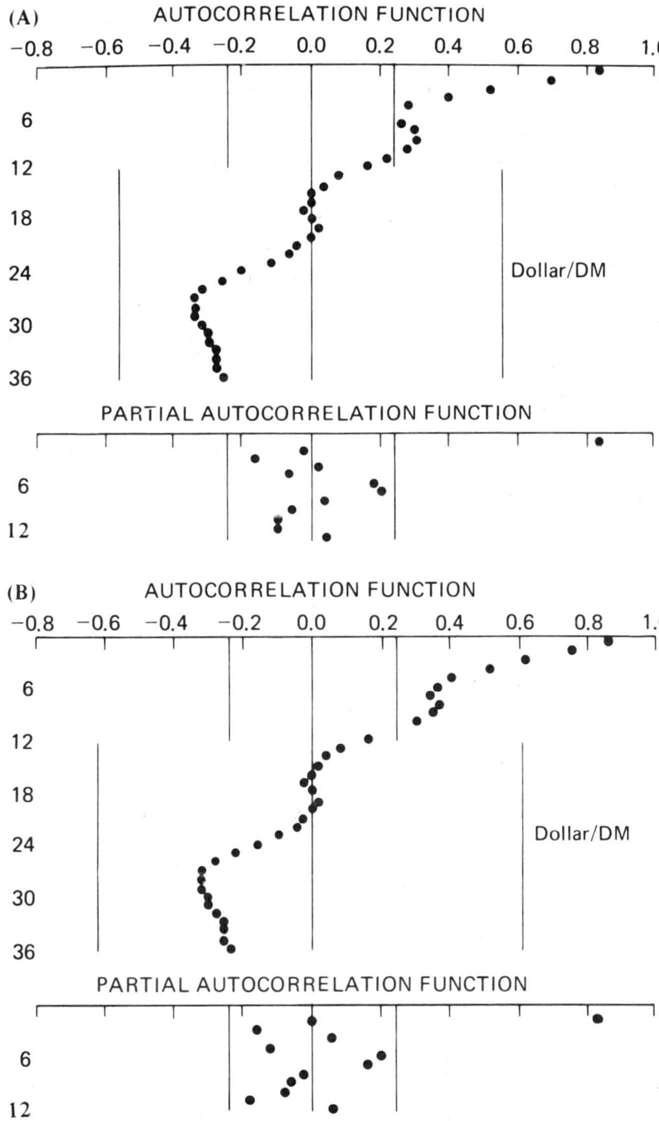

mean monthly change in these indices ranged from over 3 percent in Germany to over 6 percent in the United Kingdom. By these standards it is difficult to argue that exchange rates have been excessively volatile.

Given the short-run deviations from purchasing power parities, it is relevant to explore whether these deviations tend to diminish with time or tend to persist or even grow in size. In order to examine the patterns of the deviations, the autocorrelation functions and the partial autocorrelation functions of these deviations for the wholesale and the cost of living price indices have been computed. The deviation from purchasing power parities during month t is denoted by Δ and is defined as

$$\Delta_t = \ln S_t - \ln(P/P^*)_t. \tag{10}$$

Figure 1.4 illustrates the patterns of deviation for the dollar/DM exchange rate, and a similar pattern characterizes the deviations from purchasing power parities for the other two exchange rates. In all cases the autocorrelation function tails off at what seems to be an exponential rate and in all cases the partial autocorrelation function shows a spike at the first lag. This pattern seems to indicate (as might have been expected on the basis of the time series properties of exchange rates and price indices) that the deviations from purchasing power parities follow a first-order autoregressive process. It is noteworthy, however, that in all cases the value of the autoregression term is about 0.9, indicating the possibility that the series may not satisfy the stationarity requirement. To allow for this possibility the autocorrelation functions and the partial autocorrelation functions of $\Delta_t - \Delta_{t-1}$, that is, of the first difference of the deviations from purchasing power parities, have also been examined. The results indicate that these differences are serially uncorrelated and thus imply that the deviations Δ_t follow a random walk process. In view of this possibility it is concluded that the deviations from purchasing power parities seem to follow a first-order autoregressive process but that the data do not provide sufficient evidence to reject the alternative hypothesis of a random walk.[30]

1.4 CONCLUDING REMARKS

This article examined some aspects of the operation of flexible exchange rates. The analysis was based on the experience of the 1970s. The principle conclusions which may be drawn from the empirical work are

1. In spite of the extraordinary turbulence in the markets for foreign exchange, it seems that to a large extent the markets have operated efficiently. It should be emphasized, however, that the concept of "efficiency" that is being used in this context is somewhat narrow in that it only refers to the notion that the markets do not seem to entail unexploited profit opportunities. A broader perspective should deal with the special cost of volatility in terms of the interference with the efficiency of the price system in guiding resource allocation as well as with the cost of alternative outlets for the disturbances that are currently reflected in the volatility of exchange rates. As for the choice among alternative outlets for the disturbances, one may argue that since the foreign exchange market is a market in which risk can be bought and sold relatively easily, it may be reasonable to concentrate the disturbances in this market, rather than transfer them to other markets, such as labor markets, where they cannot be dealt with in as efficient a manner.
2. The high volatility of exchange rates (spot and forward) reflects an intrinsic charac-

teristic of the relative price of monies and other assets that are traded in organized exchange. The price of gold and the price of stocks, as well as exchange rates between national monies, depend critically on expectations concerning the future course of events and adjust rapidly in response to new information. In this perspective the exchange rate (in contrast with the relative price of national outputs) is being viewed as a financial variable which is determined in a macroeconomic setting.

3. During inflationary periods variations in nominal rates of interest are dominated by changes in inflationary expectations: as a result, high nominal rates of interest are associated with high exchange rates (a depreciated currency). This relation was supported by the empirical work. Since mid-1979 the relation between the rate of interest and the exchange rate reversed itself. This reversal indicates that since mid-1979 the main cause for fluctuations in the rate of interest was fluctuations in the real rate rather than in inflationary expectations.
4. The asset view of exchange rate determination implies that "news" is among the major factors which influence changes in exchange rates. In this context the key finding was the dependence of exchange rate changes on the unexpected changes in the rates of interest. This finding is in accord with the analytical prediction that current exchange rates already reflect current expectations about the future, while changes in the current exchange rates reflect primarily changes in these expectations which, by definition, arise from new information.
5. The experience of the 1970s does not support the predictions of the simple version of the purchasing power parity doctrine which relates the values of current measured prices to current exchange rates. The empirical work showed that deviations from purchasing power parities can be characterized by a first-order autoregressive process.
6. One of the key analytical insights that is provided by the monetary (or the asset market) approach to the exchange rate is that exchange rates reflect not only current circumstances but also those circumstances which are expected to prevail in the *future*. This anticipatory feature of the exchange rate (which is emphasized by Mussa, 1979b) does not characterize (at least to such a degree) the prices of national outputs, which reflect to a large extent *present* and *past* circumstances as they are embedded in existing contracts. Consequently, periods which are dominated by large and frequent changes in expectations are likely to be periods in which the future is expected to differ greatly from the present and the past. Under such circumstances one may expect to find frequent deviations from purchasing power parities when the latter is computed using current prices. These deviations reflect the intrinsic difference between asset prices and the national price indices.[31]
7. Since commodity prices do not adjust fully in response to exogenous shocks, it seems that intervention in the foreign exchange market which ensures that exchange rates conform with purchasing power parities would be a mistaken course of policy. When commodity prices are slow to adjust to current and expected economic conditions, it may be desirable to allow "excessive" adjustment in some other prices. Further, changes in real economic conditions requiring adjustment in the equilibrium *relative* prices of different national outputs occur continuously. An intervention rule which links changes in exchange rates rigidly to changes in domestic and foreign prices in accord with purchasing power parity ignores the occasional need for equilibrating changes in relative prices.

DATA APPENDIX

1. *Exchange rates* The spot exchange rates are end-of-month rates obtained from the IMF tape (May 1979 version, updated to July 1979 using the November 1979 issue of the *International Financial Statistics*) obtained from the International Monetary Fund.

   The forward exchange rates are end-of-month rates for one-month maturity. The forward rates for the UK pound and the DM for the period June 1973–June 1978 are bid prices obtained from the International Money Market (IMM). For the period July 1978–July 1979 they are sell prices obtained from the *Wall Street Journal*. The forward rates for the French franc for the period June 1973–July 1974 are bid prices calculated from the *Weekly Review* publication of the Harris Bank, which reports the spot rate and the forward premium: in each case the closest Friday to the end of the month was chosen. For the period August 1974–June 1978 the rates are bid rates obtained from the IMM, and for the period July 1978–July 1979 they are sell prices obtained from the *Wall Street Journal*.
2. *Prices* The wholesale and cost of living price indices are period averages obtained from the IMF tape, lines 63 and 64, respectively.
3. *Rates of Interest* All interest rates are 1-month Eurocurrency rates obtained from the *Weekly Review* of the Harris Bank. In all cases the figures used correspond to the last Friday of each month.
4. *Stock Markets* The stock market indices correspond to the last trading day of the month. The sources are *Capital International Perspective*, Geneva, Switzerland, monthly issues.

NOTES

1. For collections of articles summarizing this approach see the *Scandinavian Journal of Economics*, no. 2, 1976, and Frenkel and Johnson (1978).

2. For an application of the same methodology in analyzing the efficiency properties of the foreign exchange market during the German hyperinflation of 1921–1923 see Frenkel (1976, 1977, 1979). For an application to other exchange rates during the 1920s see Frenkel and Clements (1981): for an application to the 1920s and the 1970s see Krugman (1977); for an interesting analysis using time series and cross-section data see Bilson (1981); for an analysis of market efficiency using novel econometric techniques see Hakkio (1979) and Hansen and Hodrick (1980); and for surveys see Levich (1978, 1979).

3. More precisely, if (assuming risk neutrality) the forward rate measures the expected value of the future spot rate, then the constant term in the logarithmic equation (1) should be $-0.5\sigma_{\tilde{u}}^2$; see Frenkel (1979). The statement that under risk neutrality the forward rate equals the expected future spot rate neglects the effects of the stochastic elements in prices. As an empirical matter this neglect does not seem to be consequential; see Frenkel and Razin (1980).

4. Since $ln\ F_{t-1}$ is highly correlated with $ln\ S_{t-1}$ the Durbin-Watson statistic may not be appropriate since equation (1) is very similar to a regression of $ln\ S_t$ on its own lagged value. Durbin's h-statistic reveals however that the residuals are serially uncorrelated at conventional confidence levels.

5. This test was recently applied by Obstfeld (1978) to the analysis of the foreign exchange market during the 1970s and by Frenkel (1980a,b) to the analysis of the foreign exchange markets during the 1920s.

6. The efficiency of the foreign exchange market can also be analyzed from a different angle, as in Frenkel (1980b). Consider the equation

$$x_t = \alpha_0 + \alpha_1 l + \sum_{i=1}^{n} \beta_i x_{t-i} + \gamma\pi_{t-1} + w_t$$

where α_t denotes the percentage change of the spot exchange rate ($ln\ S_t - ln\ S_{t-1}$): π_{t-1}, the forward premium on foreign exchange ($ln\ F_{t-1} - ln\ S_{t-1}$): t, time: n, the number of lags: and w, an error term. If π_{t-1} summarizes all available information concerning the future evolution of the exchange rate, then *given* the value of the forward premium π_{t-1}, the past history of the percentage change of the exchange rate should not "help" the prediction (i.e., the past history should not be viewed as Granger-causing future changes), and the joint hypotheses that α_0, α_1, and β_i are zero and that γ is unity should not be rejected. The results of applying these tests to the three exchange rates for various numbers of lags as well as to the pooled data base of the three exchange rates show that the null hypothesis cannot be rejected at the 95 percent confidence level since the values of the various F-statistics fall well below the corresponding critical values. It is noteworthy, however, that the power of this test is low and that the joint hypothesis that α_0, α_1, β_i and γ are zero could also not be rejected. The difficulties in "explaining" the percentage change of the exchange rate in terms of past values of various variables reflect the fact that like the prices of other assets which are traded in organized markets, changes in exchange rates are dominated by "news" which by definition could not have been incorporated in past changes or in the lagged forward premium. For a further elaboration see the following section.

7. The analysis of the role of "news" in determining current exchange rates and in explaining forecast errors from the forward rate has been made forcefully by Mussa (1976a,b, 1977, 1979a) and Dornbusch (1978). The large degree of volatility is also analyzed by McKinnon (1976), who attributes it to insufficient speculation.

8. These and the following empirical regularities are analyzed in detail in Mussa (1979a). See also Frenkel and Mussa (1980).

9. For an analysis of the relation between the variances of series of predictions and series of realizations see Shiller (1979) and Singleton (1980).

10. The following paragraph draws on Frenkel and Mussa (1980).

11. See, for example, the comprehensive econometric model of Fair (1979).

12. A result of this general form is derived in Mussa (1976a). The unique role of expectations is also emphasized by Black (1973), Dornbusch (1976c, 1978), Kouri (1976), and Bilson (1978). In general the value of b may be viewed as the relevant parameter for determining whether a specific commodity [whose pricing rule is described in terms of equations like (6) and (7)] may be viewed as an asset. The higher is the value of b for a given commodity, the larger is its asset attribute.

13. New information must be "permanent" when the relevant horizon is a month, while it might be transitory when the relevant horizon is a year. In that case the correlation between the spot exchange rate and the contemporaneous 1-month forward rate is likely to be high, while the correlation between the spot rate and the 12-month forward rate is likely to be low. The perceived permanence of the new information can be inferred from the correlation between the spot and the various maturities of the forward rate. As expected it is generally found that this correlation diminishes with the maturity of the forward contract.

14. This correlation is exhibited in the fuller version of this paper in Frenkel (1981b).

15. It is noteworthy that since the forward premium (like the rate of interest) and the exchange rate are dimensionally incommensurate, their association raises questions that are familiar from the discussions of the Gibson paradox. In a separate paper I intend to examine the relation between exchange rates and the forward premium (or the interest differential) in light of the various explanations of the Gibson paradox.

16. For theoretical developments and applications of the approach see, for example, Dornbusch (1976a,b), Kouri (1976), Mussa (1976a), Frenkel (1976), Frenkel and Johnson (1978), Frenkel and Clements (1981), Clements and Frenkel (1980), Bilson (1978), Hodrick (1978), and Frenkel (1979).

17. It should be emphasized that this explanation of the positive association between the rate of interest and the exchange rate *does not* rely on a rigid form of the purchasing power parity theory. It only requires that domestic and foreign price levels, when expressed in terms of the same currency, are positively correlated. The evidence from the 1970s is consistent with this requirement: see Frenkel (1981a).

18. The traditional prediction of a negative relation between interest rates and the exchange rate could in principle be rationalized under the assumption that it concentrates on the short-run liquidity effects of monetary changes. It should be emphasized, however, that in an inflationary environment, like the one prevailing in the United States, the applicability of this rationalization is very limited. The short-run liquidity effect is emphasized in Dornbusch (1976b). The role of inflationary expectations in dominating exchange rate developments is emphasized in Frenkel (1976), Frenkel (1979) and Edwards (1979) attempt to integrate these two factors.

19. For evidence on the robustness of the interest parity relation see Frenkel and Levich (1977).

20. See, for example, Barro (1977) and Fischer (1980).

21. See also Bilson (1978), Frenkel and Mussa (1980), Isard (1980), and Longworth (1980).

22. In general, of course, the sign of the coefficient α depends on the source of the variation in the interest rate.

23. In all cases the lagged forward exchange rate was included as an instrument in order to obtain consistent estimates; see Nelson (1975). Adding lagged values of the percentage changes of the domestic and the foreign money supplies as determinants of the expected interest differential and adding the current values of the percentage change of the money supplies as instruments for the unexpected interest differential did not affect the results in any material way. In order to obtain consistent estimates the assumption that is being made in the regressions reported in tables 1.3–1.6 is that in forming expectations concerning the interest differential, individuals look only at the lagged forward premium and at past values of the differential. An alternative way to compute the expected differential would use data on the term structure of interest rates. Since data on the differential of two-month rates are not readily available, this computation would require interpolations.

24. The difficulties in obtaining instruments for data that are innovations are obvious since, by virtue of being "news," it is unlikely that variables which characterize the history can serve as good instruments. The difficulties are acute in cases in which a variable and its expected value appear in the same regression in which case consistent estimates require the use of an instrument that is contemporaneous with the innovation and is exogenous (see McCallum, 1979). Thus, in addition to a constant and the lagged forward exchange rate, Durbin's rank variable was used as an instrument for estimating the innovations in the interest rate differential.

25. To allow for the possibility that the exchange rate equation includes both the short- and the long-term interest rates, where, as suggested by Frankel (1979), the former captures liquidity effects and the latter captures expectations effects, equation (9) was also estimated using the innovations in both the 1-month and the 12-month interest differential on the right-hand side. Since the two sets of innovations are highly collinear, none of the coefficients differed significantly from zero. In this context it is also noteworthy that the 12-month interest rate contains elements of the 1-month rates due to the characteristics of the term structure of interest rates. As a result, coefficient estimates from regressions which use both rates, like those in Frankel (1979), must be interpreted with great care.

26. For a further elaboration on the relation between exchange rates and the current account see Kouri (1976), Branson (1977), Branson, Halttunen, and Masson (1977), Dornbusch and Fischer (1980), and Rodriguez (1980). For a special emphasis on the role of innovations in the trade balance see Mussa (1979c), and for empirical evidence see Hakkio (1980) and Dornbusch (1980). It should be noted that the empirical work on the association between exchange rates and current account innovations faces some difficulties since, in contrast with data on financial variables like interest rates, data on the current account are not available at short intervals. Furthermore, findings on the association between exchange rates and current account innovations should be interpreted with care since rather than reflecting the sensitivity of exchange rates to "news," they might just reflect invoicing practices according to which US exports are invoiced in terms of US dollars, while imports are invoiced in terms of foreign currencies.

27. The failure of the regression of the franc/DM exchange rate on the ratio of the wholesale price indices is explained in terms of the large changes in the French intersectoral relative prices; for an elaboration see Frenkel (1981a).

28. For evidence see Frenkel (1976, 1978, 1980a) and Krugman (1978).

29. On this see Mussa (1979a). It is noteworthy that the emphasis in the text has been on the words large *fluctuations*; this should be contrasted with periods during which there are large *secular* changes in the exchange rate (like the changes which occurred during the German hyperinflation). During such periods the secular changes do not stem necessarily from "news" and need not be associated with deviations from purchasing power parities.

30. If the deviations follow a random walk process, then they do not entail (ex ante) unexploited profit opportunities. For a study of the deviations from purchasing power parities see Roll (1979). For an analysis of equilibrium deviations from purchasing power parities see Saidi (1977). It may be noted that the main difference between accepting the AR(1) rather than the random walk hypothesis relates to the economic interpretation of the two alternative processes. The random walk process implies that deviations from purchasing power parities do not tend to diminish with the passage of time, while the stable AR(1) process implies that there are mechanisms which operate to ensure that in the long run purchasing power parities are satisfied. For the purpose

of forecasting the near future, however, there is very little difference between using the AR(1) process with an autoregressive coefficient of 0.9 and using the random walk process.

31. It is interesting to note that this phenomenon was recognized by Gustav Cassel—the most recognized proponent of the purchasing power parity doctrine—according to whom, "The international valuation of the currency will, then generally show a tendency to anticipate events, so to speak, and become more an expression of the internal value that the currency is expected to possess in a few months, or perhaps in a year's time" (Cassel, 1930, pp. 149–50).

REFERENCES

Barro, Robert J. (1977). "Unanticipated Money Growth and Unemployment in the United States." *American Economic Review* 67:101–15.

Bilson, John F. O. (1978). "Rational Expectations and the Exchange Rate." In *The Economics of Exchange Rates: Selected Studies*, edited by Jacob A. Frenkel and Harry G. Johnson. Reading, MA: Addison-Wesley.

Bilson, John F. O. (1981). "The 'Speculative Efficiency' Hypothesis." *Journal of Business* 54:435–51.

Black, Stanley W. (1973). "International Money Markets and Flexible Exchange Rates." Princeton Studies in International Finance, no. 32, Princeton University.

Branson, William H. (1977). "Asset Markets and Relative Prices in Exchange Rate Determination." *Sozialwissenschaftliche Annalen* 1:69–89.

Branson, William H., Halttunen, Hannu, and Masson, Paul (1977). "Exchange Rates in the Short Run: The Dollar-Deutschemark Rate." *European Economic Review* 10:303–24.

Cassel, Gustav (1930). *Money and Foreign Exchange After 1914*. London: Macmillan.

Clements, Kenneth W., and Frenkel, Jacob A. (1980). "Exchange Rates, Money and Relative Prices: The Dollar-Pound in the 1920's." *Journal of International Economics* 10:249–62.

Dornbusch, Rudiger (1976a). "Capital Mobility. Flexible Exchange Rates and Macroeconomic Equilibrium." In *Recent Issues in International Monetary Economics*, edited by Emil Claassen and Pascal Salin. Amsterdam: North-Holland.

Dornbusch, Rudiger (1976b). "The Theory of Flexible Exchange Rate Regimes and Macroeconomic Policy." *Scandinavian Journal of Economics* 78:255–75. Reprinted in *The Economics of Exchange Rates: Selected Studies*, edited by Jacob A. Frenkel and Harry G. Johnson. Reading, MA: Addison-Wesley, 1978.

Dornbusch, Rudiger (1976c). "Expectations and Exchange Rate Dynamics." *Journal of Political Economy* 84 (December 1976):1161–76.

Dornbusch, Rudiger (1978). "Monetary Policy under Exchange Rate Flexibility." In *Managed Exchange-Rate Flexibility: The Recent Experience*. Federal Reserve Bank of Boston Conference Series, no. 20.

Dornbusch, Rudiger (1980). "Exchange Rate Economics: Where Do We Stand?" *Brookings Papers on Economic Activity* 1:143–85.

Dornbusch, Rudiger, and Fischer, Stanley (1980). "Exchange Rates and the Current Account." *American Economic Review* 70:960–71.

Edwards, Sebastian (1979). "A Simple Monetary Model of Exchange Rate Determination in the Short Run—Some Preliminary Results for the Peruvian Experience 1950–1954." Unpublished manuscript, University of Chicago.

Fair, Ray C. (1979). "A Multicountry Econometric Model." National Bureau of Economic Research Working Paper Series, no. 414.

Fischer, Stanley (ed.) (1980). *Rational Expectations and Economic Policy*. Chicago: University of Chicago Press.

Frankel, Jeffrey A. (1979). "On the Mark: The Theory of Floating Exchange Rates Based on Real Interest Differentials." *American Economic Review* 69:610–22.

Frenkel, Jacob A. (1976). "A Monetary Approach to the Exchange Rate: Doctrinal Aspects and Empirical Evidence." *Scandinavian Journal of Economics* 78:200–24. Reprinted in *The Economics of Exchange Rates: Selected Studies*, edited by Jacob A. Frenkel and Harry G. Johnson. Reading, MA: Addison-Wesley, 1978.

Frenkel, Jacob A. (1977). "The Forward Exchange Rate. Expectations and the Demand for Money: The German Hyperinflation." *American Economic Review* 67:653–70.

Frenkel, Jacob A. (1978). "Purchasing Power Parity: Doctrinal Perspective and Evidence from the 1920's." *Journal of International Economics* 8:169–91.

Frenkel, Jacob A. (1979). "Further Evidence on Expectations and the Demand for Money During the German Hyperinflation." *Journal of Monetary Economics* 5:81–96.

Frenkel, Jacob A. (1980a). "Exchange Rates, Prices and Money: Lessons from the 1920's." *American Economic Review* 70:235–42.

Frenkel, Jacob A. (1980b). "The Forward Premium on Foreign Exchange and Currency Depreciation during the German Hyperinflation." *American Economic Review* 70:771–75.

Frenkel, Jacob A. (1981a). "The Collapse of Purchasing Power Parities During the 1970's." *European Economic Review* 16:145–65.

Frenkel, Jacob A. (1981b). "Flexible Exchange Rates, Prices and the Role of 'News': Lessons from the 1970's." *Journal of Political Economy* 89:665–705.

Frenkel, Jacob A., and Clements, Kenneth W. (1981): "Exchange Rates in the 1920's: A Monetary Approach." In *Development in an Inflationary World*, edited by M. June Flanders and Assaf Razin. New York: Academic Press.

Frenkel, Jacob A., and Johnson, Harry G. (eds.) (1978). *The Economics of Exchange Rates: Selected Studies*. Reading, MA: Addison-Wesley.

Frenkel, Jacob A., and Levich, Richard M. (1977). "Transaction Costs and Interest Arbitrage: Tranquil versus Turbulent Periods." *Journal of Political Economy* 85:1209–26.

Frenkel, Jacob A., and Mussa, Michael L. (1980). "The Efficiency of Foreign Exchange Markets and Measures of Turbulence." *American Economic Review* 70:374–81.

Frenkel, Jacob A., and Razin, Assaf (1980). "Stochastic Prices and Tests of Efficiency of Foreign Exchange Markets." *Economics Letters* 6:165–70.

Hakkio, Craig S. (1979). "Expectations and the Foreign Exchange Market." Unpublished Ph.D Dissertation. University of Chicago.

Hakkio, Craig S. (1980). "Exchange Rates and the Balance of Trade." Unpublished manuscript, Northwestern University.

Hansen, Lars P., and Hodrick, Robert J. (1980). "Forward Exchange Rates as Optimal Predictors of Future Spot Rates: An Econometric Analysis." *Journal of Political Economy* 88:829–53.

Hausman, Jerry A. (1978). "Specification Tests in Econometrics." *Econometrica* 46:1251–72.

Hodrick, Robert J. (1978). "An Empirical Analysis of the Monetary Approach to the Determination of the Exchange Rate." In *The Economics of Exchange Rates: Selected Studies*, edited by Jacob A. Frenkel and Harry G. Johnson. Reading, MA: Addison-Wesley.

Isard, Peter (1980). "Expected and Unexpected Changes in Exchange Rates: The Role of Relative Price Levels, Balance-of-Payments Factors, Interest Rates and Risk." Federal Reserve Board, International Finance Discussion Papers, no. 156.

Kouri, Pentti J. K. (1976). "The Exchange Rate and the Balance of Payments in the Short Run and in the Long Run: A Monetary Approach." *Scandinavian Journal of Economics* 78:280–304.

Krugman, Paul (1977). "The Efficiency of the Forward Exchange Market: Evidence from the Twenties and the Seventies." Unpublished manuscript. Yale University.

Krugman, Paul (1978). "Purchasing Power Parity and Exchange Rates: Another Look at the Evidence." *Journal of International Economics* 8:397–407.

Levich, Richard M. (1978). "Further Results on the Efficiency of Markets for Foreign Exchange." In *Managed Exchange Rate Flexibility: The Recent Experience*, Federal Reserve Bank of Boston, Conference Series, no. 20.

Levich, Richard M. (1979). "The Efficiency of Markets for Foreign Exchange." In *International Economic Policy: Theory and Evidence*, edited by Rudiger Dornbusch and Jacob A. Frenkel. Baltimore: Johns Hopkins University Press.

Longworth, David (1980). "An Empirical Efficient-Markets Model of Exchange Rate Determination." Unpublished manuscript, Bank of Canada.

McCallum, Bennett T. (1979). "Topics Concerning the Formulation. Estimation, and Use of Macroeconometric Models with Rational Expectations." Unpublished manuscript, University of Virginia.

McKinnon, Ronald I. (1976). "Floating Foreign Exchange Rates 1973–74: The Emperor's New Clothes." In *Institutional Arrangements and the Inflation Problem*, edited by Karl Brunner and Allan Meltzer. Vol. 3 of the Carnegie-Rochester Conference Series on Public Policy, a Supplementary Series to the *Journal of Monetary Economics*.

Mudd, Douglas R. (1979). "Do Rising U.S. Interest Rates Imply a Stronger Dollar?" *Federal Reserve Bank of St. Louis Review* 61:9–13.

Mussa, Michael (1976a). "The Exchange Rate, the Balance of Payments and Monetary and Fiscal Policy under a Regime of Controlled Floating." *Scandinavian Journal of Economics* 78:229–48. Reprinted in *The Economics of Exchange Rates: Selected Studies*, edited by Jacob A. Frenkel and Harry G. Johnson. Reading, MA: Addison-Wesley, 1978.

Mussa, Michael (1976b). "Our Recent Experience with Fixed and Flexible Exchange Rates: A Comment." In *Institutional Arrangements and the Inflation Problem*, edited by Karl Brunner and Allan Meltzer. Vol. 3 of the Carnegie-Rochester Conference Series on Public Policy, a Supplementary Series to the *Journal of Monetary Economics*.

Mussa, Michael (1977). "Exchange Rate Uncertainty: Causes, Consequences, and Policy Implications." Unpublished manuscript. University of Chicago.

Mussa, Michael (1979a). "Empirical Regularities in the Behavior of Exchange Rates and Theories of the Foreign Exchange Market." In *Policies for Employment, Prices, and Exchange Rates*, edited by Karl Brunner and Allan Meltzer. Vol. 11 of the Carnegie-Rochester Conference Series on Public Policy, a Supplementary Series to the *Journal of Monetary Economics*.

Mussa, Michael (1979b). "Anticipatory Adjustment of a Floating Exchange Rate." Unpublished manuscript, University of Chicago.

Mussa, Michael (1979c). "The Role of the Trade Balance in Exchange Rate Dynamics." Unpublished manuscript.

Nelson, Charles R. (1975). "Rational Expectations and the Estimation of Econometric Models." *International Economic Review* 16:555–61.

Obstfeld, Maurice (1978). "Expectations and Efficiency in the Foreign Exchange Market." Unpublished manuscript, MIT.

Rodriguez, Carlos A. (1980). "The Role of Trade Flows in Exchange Rate Determination: A Rational Expectations Approach." *Journal of Political Economy* 88:1148–58.

Roll, Richard (1979). "Violations of Purchasing Power Parity and Their Implications for Efficient International Commodity Markets." In *International Finance and Trade*, vol. 1, edited by Marshall Sarnat and Gikorgio P. Szego. Cambridge, MA: Ballinger.

Saidi, Nasser (1977). "Rational Expectations. Purchasing Power Parity and the Business Cycle." Unpublished manuscript, University of Chicago.

Shiller, Robert J. (1979). "Do Stock Prices Move Too Much to be Justified by Subsequent Changes in Dividends?" Unpublished manuscript, University of Pennsylvania.

Singleton, Kenneth J. (1980). "Expectations Models of the Term Structure and Implied Variance Bounds." *Journal of Political Economy* 88:1159–76.

9

Equilibrium and Disequilibrium Exchange Rates*

Rudiger Dornbusch†

Milton Freidman's 1950 essay "The Case for Flexible Exchange Rates" brought persuasive arguments against exchange control and fixed exchange rates and established firmly the profession's preference for flexible rates. The case rested on a triple advantage: no need for direct controls and inefficiency, the advantage of monetary sovereignity and the convenience of adjusting the exchange rate rather than the entire domestic price structure. The analogy with daylight savings time plainly made the case that "it is far simpler to allow one price to change, namely, the price of foreign exchange, than to rely upon changes in the multitude of prices that together constitute the internal price structure".[1] When the collapse of the Bretton Woods system led to flexible rates the profession accepted this as progress; that belief continues and predisposes us to see the experiment with flexible exchange rates as successful.

It is not always easy, however, to believe that the experiment has been an outright success. We do observe large, apparently self-reversing movements in exchange rates, both nominal and real. More importantly, we often have no good idea, either in theory or more informally, in what manner the current level of the exchange rate represents an equilibrium. It is at such times, of course, that we are reminded of the history of flexible exchange rates in the 1920s, especially the French episode, and the argument of the time that exchange rates were moved, under the influence of speculation, in ways incompatible with fundamentals and aggravating the problems of domestic stabilization. That view had been advanced by *Nurkse*:

> " *anticipations are apt to bring about their own realization. Anticipatory purchases of foreign exchange tend to produce or at any rate to hasten the anticipated fall in the exchange value of the national currency, and the actual fall may set up or strengthen expectations of a further fall. . . . Exchange rates in such circumstances are bound to become highly unstable, and the influence of psychological factors may at times be overwhelming. French economists were so much impressed by this experience that they developed a special 'psychological theory' of exchange fluctuations, stressing the indeterminant character of exchange rates when left to find their own level in a market swayed by speculative anticipations.*"[2]

---

*This article is reprinted with permission, from *Zeitschrift fur Wirtschafts und Sozialwissenschaften* 102, No. 6 573–599.

†I wish to acknowledge helpful discussions with Olivier Blanchard, Jeffrey Frankel, Alberto Giovannini, Dale Henderson, Maurice Obstfeld and Robert Shiller. Financial support was provided by a grant from The National Science Foundation.

[1]*Friedman* (1953), 173.

[2]*Nurkse* (1944), 118.

Nurkse's view was challenged by *Friedman*[3] who argued that no professional case had been made to the effect that speculation was destabilizing. On the contrary, speculation against the currency only anticipated a depreciation bound to come of its own. That criticism has been largely endorsed by the profession and ratified in exchange rate models where the current equilibrium exchange rate correctly reflects the anticipated path of future (exogeneous) money. The exchange rate then is merely a barometer of a government's inflationary intentions.

But such an interpretation misses an important point in Nurkse's view, namely, that there is an exchange rate indeterminancy because financial policies, which supposedly anchor the system, are in fact endogeneous and may be substantially caused by movements in the exchange rate. It is true that the exchange rate only reflects the possible paths the economy might take. But the likelihood of a particularly adverse path becomes higher once speculators' recognition of that possibility is reflected in the exchange rate and, from there, in prices and the requirements of monetary accommodation. This, of course, was very much the scenario that Nurkse was commenting on in pre-Poincare France.

The possibility that flexible rates may adversely affect the macroeconomy is certainly coming to be recognized. The idea of "virtuous and vicious circles" makes that point, as does the notion that flexible rates make the Phillips Curve steeper.[4] But while it is certainly recognized that flexible exchange rates may not do their work, this is not yet a commonly shared belief. Indeed, it is only controversy over sterling in 1979/80, the Yen in 1978–79 and the current controversy over the dollar that loudly suggest a fundamental problem with our exchange rate system.[5]

In fact there appear to be several separate problems. One emerges from international real interest differentials that arise in the course of monetary stabilization which lead to real appreciation and disruptive macroeconomic effects abroad. A second is associated with speculative bubbles that remove the exchange rate from a path dictated by fundamentals. In either event the exchange rate assumes a life of its own that may be seriously at odds with macroeconomic stability and that calls for remedies. This is also the case when extraneous beliefs join fundamentals in influencing the market rate.

There is certainly one thing the experience with flexible rates has done and that is to disillusion even the true believer on the subject of monetary sovereignity under flexible rates. That there is no sovereignity but rather sharp conflict of interest is brought out by the present dollar problem.

The Financial Times of January 26, 1982 in a commentary entitled "$ Rise undermines European Bid to cut interest rates" notes:

"The fresh wave of higher U.S. interest rates threatens to wreck the independent initiative launched last week by the Bank of England, the West German Bundesbank and other EEC central banks to lower the cost of credit in Europe and speed up economic recovery.

The sharp fall in sterling and other leading European currencies against the dollar yesterday may prolong the European recession just as an upturn had seemed likely.

[3]*Friedman* (1953), 176–177.

[4]See *Gray* and *Wallich* (1979) and *Dornbusch* and *Krugman* (1976).

[5]See Appendix 6 to the Treasury and Civil Service Report on Monetary Policy, U.K. House of Commons, London, 1981.

This is because EEC central banks may be forced to take action to prevent currency depreciation triggering off fresh inflation."

That these concerns go beyond technicalities of day-to-day money markets is represented in a follow-up article on January 28th: "Germans worried by U.S. deficit" which notes:

"However, despite the efforts of European central banks to coordinate a modest fall in interest rates last week, it is stressed here that Europe's scope to "uncouple" itself from U.S. developments remains very small. This is said to apply to West Germany despite its improved current account performance and relatively low inflation rate.

Bonn feels that the upshot may well be a further fall in investment, a rise in unemployment and more social unrest. "All elements of a depression are there", one official stressed.

This paper will take the perspective that exchange rates in the 1970s have not worked well. From that point of view, we attempt to establish in what ways the exchange rate system may have fallen short of what theory and policy beliefs suggest and what possible remedies there are. In the first section exchange rate theories and some empirical evidence are reviewed. The section concludes that theories have across the board failed to account for exchange rate behavior. The next section identifies four specific policy problems: bubbles, the peso-problem, extraneous beliefs and the dollar problem. Each deals with the possibility of disequilibrium exchange rates, although in different, possibly overlapping ways. The last section discusses (and dismisses) intervention as a policy tool and makes a case for real interest equalization taxes.

1. EXCHANGE RATE THEORIES

This section develops the main theoretical approaches to exchange rate determination and comments cursorily on their empirical success. The relevant theories are the monetary approach and the current account approaches in two variants emphasizing imperfect substitutability of assets and goods respectively.

The Monetary Approach

The monetary approach, no doubt, is the most popular model of exchange rate determination, anchored as it is in two outrageous simplifications of the economic scene: purchasing power parity and the quantity theory. The model assumes that national price levels are instantaneously flexible and determined by money supplies and real money demands. Moreover, with the "law of one price" prices are equalized internationally with exchange rate movements offsetting divergent national price trends.

The monetary approach gives rise to an exchange rate equation that includes relative nominal money supplies, relative velocities and relative levels of real income. In log form the exchange rate equation then becomes:

$$e = m - m^* + (v - v^*) - (y - y^*) \qquad (1)$$

where e is the dollar price of foreign exchange and m, v, y are nominal money, velocity and real income, an asterisk denoting the foreign country. Early endeavors with this equation were not unsuccessful, but by now there are, I believe, no more serious claims for the empirical relevance of this model.[6]

The Terms of Trade Model

The monetary model is highly restrictive in its assumption of the law of one price. This is apparent when we move to a transactions version of this model. Suppose q denotes the log of the expenditure deflator, a, is real spending and v now denotes the expenditure velocity. Home money market equilibrium can be stated in terms of the determinants of the expenditure deflator:

$$q = p + v - a \tag{2}$$

where q is a weighted average of home and import prices:

$$q \equiv xp + (1 - x)(e + p^*) \tag{3}$$

With a similar specification for the foreign country, and assuming foreign expenditure on domestic goods to have a share $x^* \leqslant x$, we derive an exchange rate equation of the form:

$$e = [(m - m^*) + (v - v^*) - (a - a^*)] + (x - x^*)\theta \tag{4}$$

where $\theta \equiv e + p^* - p$ denotes the terms of trade.

The extended model maintains the prediction of the monetary approach to the extent that changes in money or velocity are translated into equiproportionate depreciation, *given* the terms of trade. But now there is another source of exchange rate movement, namely, terms of trade changes. Changes in the equilibrium terms of trade affect the equilibrium exchange rate to an extent that depends among other factors, on the differential in expenditure shares, $x - x^*$.

The extended model is readily applied, in the manner of Fleming and Mundell, to the effects of a shift in demand toward domestic goods. Suppose capital is perfectly mobile and that the home country faces a given, unchanging foreign level of spending and interest rates. Assume also that product prices are given. Figure 1 shows the determination of the exchange rate at point A. The IS schedule is positively sloped because a real depreciation creates demand and raises output. The LM schedule is negatively sloped since an appreciation lowers the price level and raises the real money stock thus making room for a real expansion. Fig. 1 shows that a shift in demand toward domestic goods will raise income and lead to an appreciation. The expansion will be larger the larger the share of importables in the deflator. By contrast, a large import share in the expenditure deflator will tend to dampen the expansionary impact of a money expansion.

Even before we move to issues of imperfect asset substitution or expectations, exchange rate determination is already a macroeconomic problem involving the interaction of goods and asset markets. Consider now the extension to the case where output adjusts gradually to long-run excess demand and exchange rate expectations conform to perfect foresight. Under the assumption that capital mobility is perfect, home nominal interest rates equal those abroad plus the anticipated rate of depreciation:

$$i = i^* + \dot{e} \tag{5}$$

[6]For reference see, for example, *Dornbusch* (1980). See, however, the discussion in the Economic Report of the President, 1982.

FIGURE 1

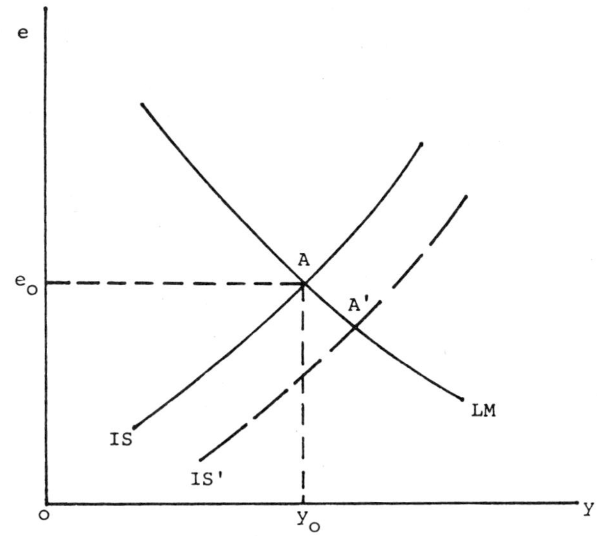

In Fig. 2, we show the phase diagram, noting that now the rate of depreciation $\dot{e}$, is a determinant of home velocity. From an initial equilibrium at A a monetary expansion leads to an immediate depreciation at point A′ on the saddlepath. The exchange rate in the short run must overshoot as output expansion is sluggish. At A′ the exchange rate has overdepreciated and thus anticipated appreciation lowers velocity relative to a static expectations world. Over time the economy converges to point A″ as output expands to meet the increase in demand. The economy proceeds from A′ to A″ along the perfect foresight path PP.

FIGURE 2

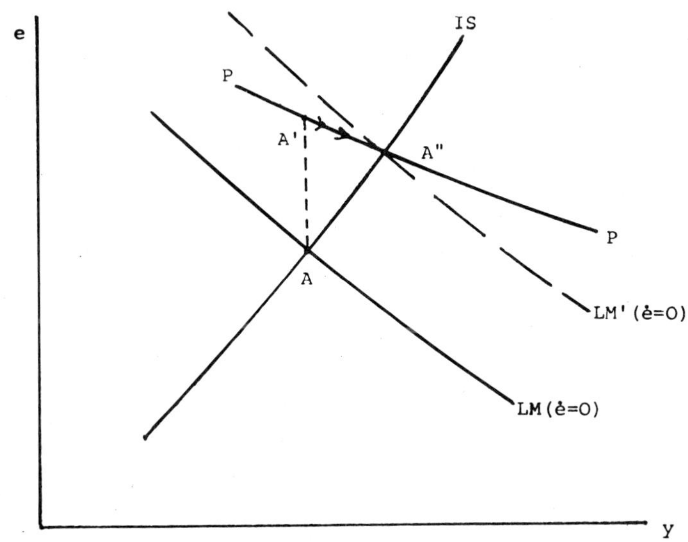

The analysis of expectations is readily extended in three directions. One is to add sluggish price adjustment and thus allow long run neutrality. The second extension is to consider the impact of anticipated future shocks. Third, and perhaps most important, we can introduce an explicit consideration of the current account as a source of dynamics. Current account imbalances, by redistributing net assets internationally, may affect demand to the extent that marginal spending patterns differ. If this is the case, current account imbalances lead to changes in equilibrium relative prices and thus to changes in the exchange rate.

We have reached the point where the *current* exchange rate is determined not only by current monetary factors—the relative supply and demand of money—but also by prospective monetary factors as well as the present and future demand for goods. An anticipated fiscal expansion, for example, will lead to immediate currency appreciation even though the demand expansion has, as yet, not materialized. But there is one important complication still left out, namely, the possibility of imperfect substitution among assets.

Imperfect Asset Substitutability

If asset holders are risk averse, and returns on securities denominated in different currencies are not perfectly correlated, risk premia may emerge that depend on relative asset supplies.

A risk premium modifies the relation between interest rates and expected depreciation in (5). The equation now becomes:

$$i = i^* + \dot{e} + \Phi\,(B/\bar{W},\ W/\bar{W});\ \Phi_1 > 0,\ \Phi_2 \leq 0 \tag{6}$$

where B denotes the supply of domestic outside nominal assets while W and $\bar{W}$ are home wealth and world wealth all measured in home currency. The extent to which the risk premium increases with a rise in the relative supply of domestic currency assets depends on the degree of risk aversion and the variance of relative asset returns. The exchange rate affects the variables $B/\bar{W}$ and $W/\bar{W}$ since it influences the domestic currency value of world wealth. A depreciation lowers the relative supply of domestic assets and domestic relative wealth.

The risk premium model of asset markets, in conjunction with money and goods markets, extends the range of exchange rate determinants which now include the current and prospective relative supplies of nominal outside assets and, possibly, the distribution of world wealth. It is interesting to note, in this context, that imperfect asset substitutability need, by no means, establish a link between current accounts and the exchange rate. *Frankel*[7] among others, has noted that what is at issue in the risk premium is the relative supply of nominal outside assets. Privately financed current account imbalances will not affect the world supplies of outside assets. Furthermore, even if the deficits were publicly financed there is no necessity that they be financed in terms of home currency denomination. More importantly, as has been noted, the relative supply of outside nominal assets is also affected by intervention and budget financing, thus obliterating any special role for the current account.

There remains the question whether current accounts, by redistributing world wealth, interact with a preferred domestic habitat in portfolios to change the risk premium and

[7]*Frankel* (1979).

therefore, affect exchange rates. As *Krugman*[8] has shown this possibility requires a coefficient of risk aversion larger than unity. Again it must be borne in mind that the relevant measure of wealth in the risk premium will also include real assets so that there is typically no direct relation between the current account alone and the distribution of world wealth. A stock market boom will have much larger effects on relative wealth than likely current account imbalances.

Empirical Evidence

Claims for empirically successful exchange rate equations are disappearing rapidly. Recently papers by *Frankel* (1982), *Isard* (1981), *Rogoff* and *Meese* (1981) and *Hacche* and *Townsend* (1981) all conclude that *simple* structural models of exchange rate determination all fail to account well for actual exchange rate behavior. This is the case whether a monetary approach is adopted, a Mundell-Fleming-Frankel model or models that include, in addition, current account or relative wealt variables.

Hacche and *Townsend* summarize their findings as follows:

"The predominant impresion left by our results is one of failure: we have not succeeded in finding empirical regularities in the data to help explain in any satisfactory way the fundamental determinants of sterling's effective exchange rate during the floating rate period. Our research has failed, often dramatically to yield support for any of the theories tested. . . ."[9]

The same conclusion is reached by *Meese* and *Rogoff* who conclude:

"Major bilateral exchange rates and the trade weighted dollar are all well approximated by a random walk. The representative structural models do not perform well out-of-sample; they predict poorly even when uncertainty about future values of the explanatory variables is removed."[10]

Isard (1981) and *Artus* (1982) similarly find that their tests are unsatisfactory except with the inclusion of a Reagan-dummy.

There are some reasons why tests may be faring poorly. First the models tend to give too much emphasis to money supply disturbances neglecting shifts in money demand, fiscal and demand disturbances which, of course, are as important as money supply changes. The neglect of demand and fiscal variables in empirical work is, in fact, quite complete.

The more important point is that exchange rate testing has given no room to the role of anticipated future events. But it should be clear that when major changes in the determinants of exchange rates are anticipated they must affect the level of the exchange rate, given current values of the exchange rate determinants. This point is readily made with the help of Fig. 3. The economy sits initially at point A and the expectation to a *future* increase in money and government spending, respectively, occur. The exchange rate will immediately jump in response to the news. In response to an anticipated future money increase it will depreciate to A′, in response to anticipated higher spending or tax cuts it

[8]*Krugman* (1980).

[9]*Hacche* and *Townsend* (1981), 253.

[10]*Meese* and *Rogoff* (1981), 23.

FIGURE 3

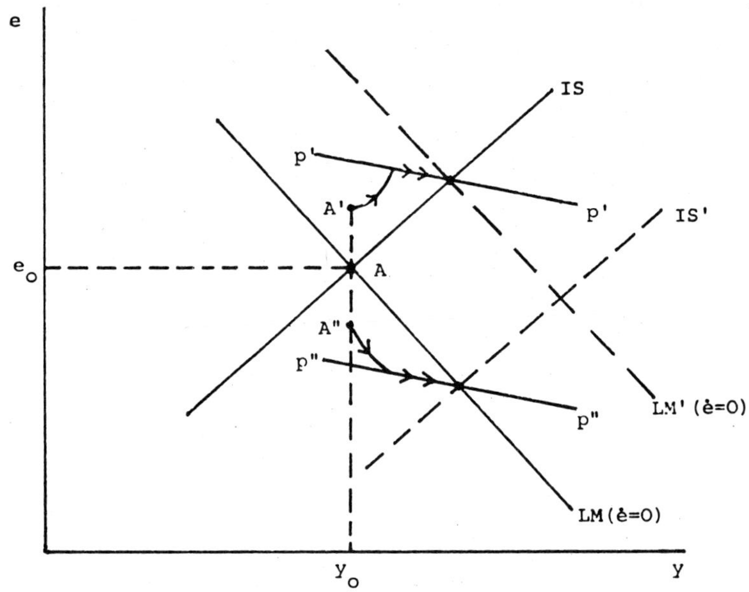

will appreciate to A″.[11] Thus given current money and fiscal policy, today's exchange rate may be any of three, A, A′, or A″ depending upon whether we anticipate easier money or easier fiscal policy or neither. Neglecting these "news" effects on exchange rates may thus eliminate most of the explanatory variables for the observed noise. This is more likely to be the case the more proximate and larger the anticipated changes.

The same point can be made, using the equation for the relationship between interest differentials, depreciation, and the risk premium. Noting that (6) $\dot{e}$ denotes the expected rate we can write:[12]

$$\dot{e}_{actual} = i - i^* + \Phi\,(B/\bar{W}, W/\bar{W}) + \text{"news"} \tag{7}$$

where we have used the fact that with rational expectations the actual depreciation rate is equal to the expected rate plus a white noise error or "news." Equation (7) singles out news as one of the determinants of movements in the exchange rate. Given current income, money and prices as well as the relative supplies of assets, the exchange rate may appreciate or depreciate because the expectation of a change in exchange rate determinants emerges. While that idea has been immediately accepted in the literature and indeed, reminds us of the 1920s discussion, it has received practically no empirical testing.[13]

[11] *Wilson* (1977) and *Rogoff* (1979) have studied the role of anticipated future disturbance in exchange rate dynamics.

[12] On this point see *Mussa* (1976), *Dornbusch* (1978, 1980) and *Isard* (1980).

[13] See, however, *Black* (1972), *Frenkel* (1981), *Dornbusch* (1980), *Engle* and *Frankel* (1982) and *Cornell* (1982b).

The literature differs sharply from the extensive and careful testing which expectations based macroeconomics has received in closed economy applications. Research here has particularly focussed on questions that run quite parallel: the effect of money, unanticipated versus anticipated, on unemployment and the real rate of interest.[14] It remains a question whether the very poor empirical performance of exchange rate models is due to a failure to distinguish news and anticipated realizations of the determinants of exchange rates. The work on anticipated future disturbances on the time path of exchange rates, for example, has amply shown that exchange rates may well lead anticipated money.

2. FOUR PROBLEMS

In this section, we sketch four problems that may have arisen under the flexible exchange rate regime of the 1970s. The first is the adverse side effect of inappropriate monetary-fiscal policy mixes. The second concerns the role of expectations about future policy changes that render current policy more difficult, a variant of the peso problem. The third concerns the possibility of speculative bubbles. The fourth involves extraneous beliefs.

Bubbles

Important research on the volatility of asset prices has forced the question whether asset prices move "too much" given the path of fundamentals such as interest rates or dividends.[15]

The same question arises in the context of exchange rates. Observing real exchange rates in Chart 1 where we show the Yen and DM rates, we might ask whether this large movement in real exchange rates is warranted by beliefs about the fundamental determinants of exchange rates.

Work by *Blanchard* (1979), *Blanchard* and *Watson* (1982) and *Tirole* (1980) among others discusses the conditions under which speculative bubbles or cumulative divergences from the path warranted by fundamentals may arise. An interesting model is that of *Blanchard* (1979) where risk neutral speculators are aware that a particular asset price is off the path of fundamentals. Indeed, they expect with probability α a crash and probability $1 - \alpha$ the continuation ot the bubble.

Suppose domestic and foreign assets are perfect substitutes. The interest rate differential must equal the expected rate of depreciation:

$$i - i^* = \tilde{e}_{t+1} - e_t \tag{8}$$

where $\tilde{e}_{t+1}$ is the expected future exchange rate. But given the probabilities α associated with a crash to the fundamental rate, $\bar{e}_t$ and $1 - \alpha$ of a continuing bubble, we have:

$$e_{t+1} - e_t = \frac{i - i^*}{1 - \alpha} + \frac{\alpha}{1 - \alpha}(e_t - \bar{e}_t) \tag{8a}$$

Equation (8a) describes a "rational" bubble. The exchange rate in the absence of a crash depreciates at a rate determined by three factors: the interest differential, the probability of a crash and the undervaluation, $e_t - \bar{e}_t$. The more undervalued the exchange rate and the higher the probability of a crash the more rapid the rate of depreciation. A positive interest differential implies depreciation, more so the higher the probability of a crash.

[14]For references see *Mishkin* (1982).

[15]See, for example, *Grossman* and *Shiller* (1980).

CHART 1
Real Effective Exchange Rates (1975 = 100)

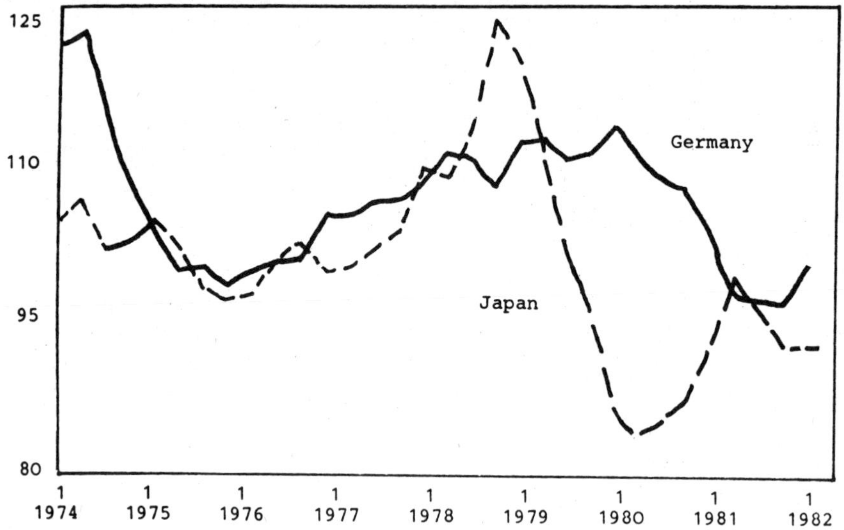

Source IMF.

Leaving aside interest differentials, the equation shows the fundamental problem of bubbles: the more *over*valued the exchange rate the more rapidly it is *ap*preciating, the more *under*valued the more rapidly the rate is *de*preciating. Bubbles are not self-correcting except by a crash. Bubbles, while they last, involve the possibility of temporary, cumulative deviations from fundamentals.

The presence of interest differentials introduces the possibility that the exchange rate can remain unchanged even though there is over or undervaluation. From (8a) we have the special case where the exchange rate remains constant:

$$\bar{e} - e_t = (i - i^*)/\alpha \tag{9}$$

Thus a positive interest differential in favor of the home country can sustain an overvaluation while a negative interest differential can sustain an undervaluation.[16] The bubble will be larger the larger the interest differential and the probability of a crash. For example, a 20% probability of a crash and a five percentage point interest differential sustain a 25% overvaluation!

The analysis has shown the possibility of temporary deviations of the exchange rate from the fundamental rate warranted by "the" model or fundamentals. Why should we be concerned about such deviations? The obvious reason is that given the path of policy variables an exchange rate bubble will have real effects on competiveness, inflation, and employment. It represents a macro-shock that, if possible, we would want to offset. The possibility of rational bubbles is important to recognize because is represents a fundamental departure from the view that markets do things right, all the time.

[16]In (8a) and (9) the fundamental rate $\bar{e}$ is constant. In a more complete model the question must be raised whether this is consistent with nominal interest differentials.

The Peso Problem

In the case of a bubble, all market participants are aware that the current exchange rate deviates from the fundamental rate, but the bubble may be sustained by new entrants and the belief that it may grow fast enough, thus providing existing asset holders with a commensurate return. A different kind of exchange rate problem emerges when expectations about the path of fundamentals affect the current level of the exchange rate. Such a possibility, particularly when it involves the consideration of a large change in policy regime, has an effect on the current exchange rate and, therefore, on the difficulty of macroeconomic management. Specifically, the expectation of expansionary policy (whether justified or not) will lead to current actual depreciation and thus to current inflationary pressures ahead of any expansion. Conversely, the belief in tightening will lead to appreciation and deflationary pressure.

This is the so-called "peso-problem."[17] *Salant* and *Henderson* (1976) have shown that it is a generic problem of asset markets where speculators have to recognize the possibility of a future change in regime that affects future asset prices. The point is illustrated with a simple log-linear monetary model of the exchange rate in the tradition of *Mussa* (1975). Suppose there is full purchasing power parity and price flexibility and that real money demand depends on expected inflation or depreciation:

$$m_t - e_t = -b(\tilde{e}_{t+1} - e_t) \tag{10}$$

Suppose also that next period and ever thereafter the money stock is with probability $(1 - \alpha)$ current m_t and with probability α equal to $m_t + x$. The forward solution to (10) yields a level of the current exchange rate:

$$e_t = m_t + \frac{b}{1+b}\alpha x \tag{11}$$

Thus the higher the probability of an increase in future money the higher is the current equilibrium exchange rate.

The problem raised here is very much like that of a bubble if the contingencies contemplated by the public are not in fact the intention of policymakers. The rate today is off the equilibrium path that policymakers have in mind for the economy. But there is, of course, the possibility that the fact of a depreciation, due to the beliefs about the possibility of an expansion, will force the actual expansion. Policies are rarely exogeneous and they may be largely or entirely endogeneous. If this were the case, then random variations in beliefs about future policies can shape actual policies and the economy is without anchor.

There is a sense in which the exchange rate, in this setting, behaves exactly right. Asset holders are concerned about the possibility of capital losses and in response to reassessments about the path of policies, they shift their portfolios and thus move the exchange rate. But there is also a sense in which this forward-looking, asset market-oriented adjustment of exchange rates works with an overkill. By adjusting to the whims and fears of the moment, the exchange rate moves, and possibly a lot, and it moves relative to other more stable or sticky prices. Thus the *real* exchange rate, which guides the international division of labor, is being moved in response to conjectures about the future course of monetary and fiscal policies.

[17]See *Lizondo* (1979) and *Krasker* (1980).

CHART 2
The French Franc, Effective Exchange Rate (1921 Jan. = 100)

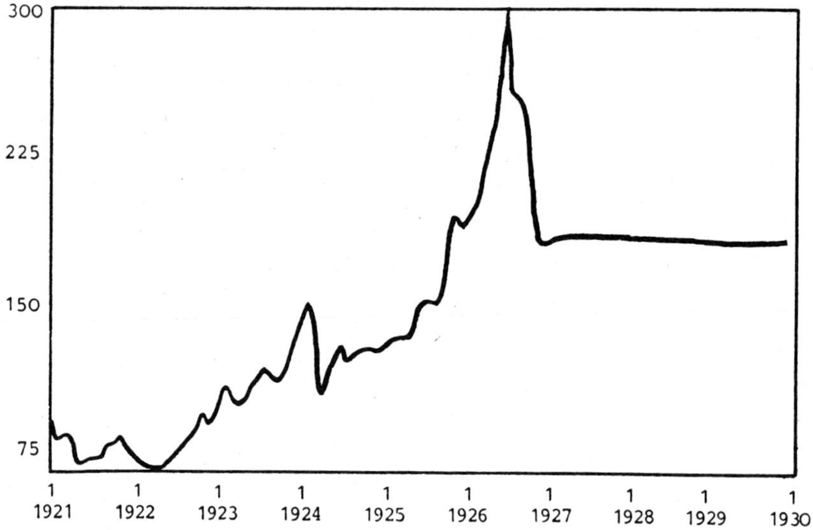

The importance of the Peso-problem is well-illustrated by the French experience in 1925–26. While the actual budget was in surplus and inflation was under control, the expectation that debt service should possibly be financed by money creation or capital taxation led to a flight out of the Franc. Chart 2 shows the Franc exchange rate collapsing in early 1926 and then, upon Poincare's assuming office with fiscal dictatorial powers, rapidly appreciating again.

The exchange rate links asset and goods market in a sticky price world. The double allegiance creates trouble because the exchange rate moves like an asset price and not as a real exchange rate should. But movements in the nominal exchange rate also affect the price level, through import prices, wages and competitive effects. Therefore movements in exchange rates, provoked by changing expectations about policy, have immediate effects on inflation. The moment the public comes to believe that a particular anti-inflation program is less likely to succeed, the ensuing exchange rate depreciation will make that a fact. Clearly here we face the unusual problem of a price that may be too flexible.

Extraneous Beliefs

There is another manner in which the public's perception of the world can lead the exchange rate to deviate from fundamentals. This arises when extraneous beliefs about the determinants of asset prices, via expectations, actually come to influence asset price. This point has been made by *Blanchard* (1976) in respect to the Phillips curve and by *Shiller* (1981) in the context of the stock market. If fads, fashions or misperceptions are highly autocorrelated asset prices can persistently and (in finite samples) undiscoverably deviate from fundamentals. The same point can be easily demonstrated in the context of exchange rates.

Suppose the model of the exchange rate is in fact (10) but that market participants believe the exchange rate is influenced by both the money supply and the current account, C_t:

$$\bar{e}_{t+1} = Em_{t+1} + \phi\, E(C_{t+1}) \tag{12}$$

where the actual current account follows a first-order autoregressive process and the money stock is a constant, m, plus white noise:

$$C_t = \theta\, C_{t-1} + u_t,\ m_{t+1} = m + v_{t+1};\ 0 < \theta < 1 \tag{13}$$

with u_t and v_t white noise. Using (12) and (13) we arrive at the equilibrium exchange rate:

$$e_t = m + kC_t + v'_t,\ k \equiv b\,\Phi\theta/(1 + b),\ v'_{t=1} = v_t/(1 + b) \tag{14}$$

Accordingly, the current account does affect the equilibrium exchange rate even though it is not part of the structural model. Note next that the forecast errors, $e_{t+1} - \bar{e}_{t+1}$ are given by:

$$e_{t+1} - \bar{e}_{t+1} = ku_{t+1} + v'_{t-1} - \theta(\Phi - k)\, C_t \tag{15}$$

If the autocorrelation of the current acount is high so that θ is close to unity and if the response of money demand to the alternative cost of holding money b, is high, $\theta\, b/(1 + b)$ is close to unity and the coefficient of C_t is close to zero. Regressions will not uncover that forecast errors are predictable on the basis of the current account. They cannot reject, except in extremely large samples, the hypothesis that the forecast errors are white noise.

The example is of interest because it suggests that extraneous beliefs about exchange rate determinants may introduce persistent and large deviations of the exchange rate from fundamentals and that these deviations are undetectable. The full rational expectations exchange rate (setting $\theta = 0$) would be $\bar{e}_t = v'_t + m$ and therefore the deviation from this "fundamentals rate," $\bar{e}_t$, is equal to kC_t. The variance of the fundamentals rate is $s^2_{\bar{e}} = s^2_{v'}$, whereas the asymptotic variance of the rate including current account beliefs is:

$$s^2_e = s^2_{v'} + k^2\, s^2_u/(1 - \theta^2) \tag{16}$$

It is immediatcly apparent that with θ close to unity extraneous current account beliefs introduce a potentially vast variability in the exchange rate.

The Dollar Problem

Since mid 1980, the US dollar has appreciated relative to other currencies and the real exchange rate today is substantially above the levels of 1973 or 1975. Chart 3 shows the movement of the real exchange rate (relative value added deflators) and also shows the level of US real interest rates. It is apparent that the real depreciation coincided with a move toward positive and higher average real rates.[18]

Theoretical models built around the idea of sticky prices or inflation rates suggest that a tightening in monetary growth, other things equal, will lead to an immediate appreciation of the real exchange rate in response to higher domestic interest rates and resulting portfolio shifts in favor of domestic assets. But unless there is an ongoing tightening, the move toward tighter money should rapidly translate into falling nominal interest rates and a reduction in inflation. In that adjustment process, the exchange rate would be *de*preciating (following the initial jump appreciation) at a rate that matches interest differentials

[18] This is the "Reagan-dummy" referred to above.

CHART 3

The US Real Exchange Rate and the Real Interest Rate

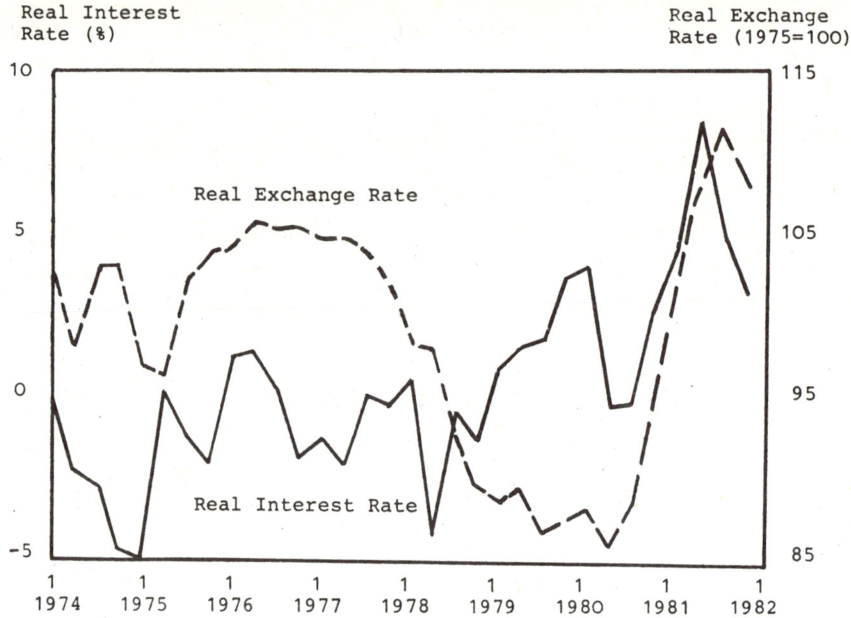

Source IMF and Morgan Guaranty.

adjusted for risk premia. Over the medium term there would be no appreciable change in the real interest rate.

Events, in a number of ways, do not fit the theoretical model. On one side there is an accompanying fiscal expansion which both in the short run and in the long run will tend to raise real interest rates. That increase in real interest rates in turn may have a long run effect on the equilibrium exchange rate while reinforcing the short run portfolio shifts. On the other hand, the experiment of monetary tightening is very much in the nature of the "peso problem" that was discussed above. Continuing nominal and real appreciation arises as the public re-evaluates its belief in tight money in the light of continuing Fed performance while the Fed itself assesses its course in the light of performance and approval. Thus monetary tightening is itself a medium-term exercise in which progressive tightening interacts with resolve to keep up the belief that this will be the case. The mix allows the possibility of continuing real appreciation over a two or three year period, the more so if inflation is sticky.

Monetary stabilization, certainly in combination with fiscal expansion, cannot fail to raise the real interest rate in the short run and therefore, to lead to international portfolio re-shuffling in favor of the dollar. The portfolio shifts, in turn, induce currency appreciation both in real and in nominal terms. That appreciation, which is an international side effect of our domestic stabilization policies, is a serious macroeconomic problem as the following evidence shows.

Table 1 shows estimates by the Federal Reserve, using their multicountry trade and

TABLE 1
Estimate of the Effects of a 20% Dollar Appreciation in 1980:3 to 1980:4

	Incremental Inflation			Incremental Growth		
	1981	1982	1983	1981	1982	1983
Germany	1.6	1.4	.7	.3	2.4	2.1
US	– 0.4	– 0.5	– 0.1	– .5	– 0.4	1.1

Source Hooper (1982).

payments model, of the 20% dollar appreciation on a trade weighted basis, on growth and inflation.

The OECD has also reported estimates of the effects of exchange rate changes in their multilateral model. Here the effects of a 10% dollar *de*preciation are studied, with the depreciation occurring at the outset.

The simulations of either model bring out clearly that exchange rates have a very strong impact on inflation and that they also affect real activity. A dollar *ap*preciation will reduce US inflation and raise inflation in Europe. Either model suggests that within a year, a 20% dollar appreciation would raise the European price level about 3% relative to what it would otherwise be. That *is* a very large inflation shock; it certainly is of the same order as the oil price shock. The inflationary shock is particularly large when there is comprehensive indexation that translates higher import prices into increased unit labor costs and thus speeds comprehensively through the economy.

The inflation shock is accompanied by a change in real GNP growth made up of two opposing tendencies. The terms of trade deterioration in Europe lowers real GNP directly. But there is an offset due to increased competitiveness that increases trade volume. Both sets of estimates show that ultimately the gain in competitiveness increases growth of real GNP, and quite strongly so in the Federal Reserve model. The OECD model, by contrast, shows both slower and smaller responses of growth.

Now it must be recognized that Europe can expand aggregate demand and raise growth, should she wish to do so. We can therefore *not* count the growth benefits of the dollar appreciation as an important offset against the imported inflation. In fact, what we must assume is that Europe in an attempt to contain inflation—after all, that is what

TABLE 2
OECD Estimate of the Effects of a 10% Dollar Depreciation (at Annual Percentage Rates)

	Incremental Inflation				Incremental Growth			
Half-Year	1st	2nd	3rd	4th	1st	2nd	3rd	4th
North America	0.4	0.7	0.3	0.1	– 0.2	0.1	0.4	0.3
Europe	– 0.5	– 0.1	– 0.6	– 0.3	0.0	– 0.2	– 0.4	– 0.3

Source OECD Economic Outlook, December 1981, 124–125.

every country is trying hard to do—must spend the gain in growth and quite a bit more to confine or offset the inflationary impact. This implies not only a reduction in growth but quite possibly too an environment less hospitable to investment. On balance then the dollar appreciation represents an *adverse supply shock* for Europe. There remains some scope for Europe to affect the composition of the shock between inflation and recession or reduced growth.

In the US, the exchange rate appreciation exerts a favorable effect on inflation, although the effect is small compared to those in Europe. The impact on growth is negative but small. It is apparent, therefore, that the US interests and those of other counties are sharply opposed. What to the US is a favorable side effect to tight money represents an adverse effect abroad. The question then must be whether these spillover effects are part and parcel of a well functioning exchange rate system or whether they represent an important shortcoming that needs serious consideration and remedy.

There is another respect in which US policies, and the changed policy environment, contribute to instability. *Engle* and *Frankel* (1982) report that money surprises—deviations of the Friday release of money data from forecasts—exert a significant effect on short term interest rates and on exchange rates. *Cornell* (1982) reports the astounding fact that these money news move not only the very short term rate, as might be expected when Fed correction of money is anticipated, but also the whole maturity structure up to 30 years bonds. The fact that the entire interest rate structure moves up in response to *weekly* money forecast errors reflects the fact that expectations about long term rates have become very diffuse and that now the short term rate is more nearly thought of as a random walk. In such a world volatility of interest rates may well bring about larger volatility of exchange rates.

3. WHAT IS TO BE DONE?

We have identified several problems that place in question the effective operation of the flexible exchange rate system. All issues arise because exchange rates are and behave like asset prices but do play an important role in goods markets as well. We now have to ask whether there are policy remedies to these problems and whether the possible remedies are cost effective. It is important to say at the outset that these issues are unresolved.

There are two possible avenues for influencing and controlling the behavior of exchange rates: one is (sterilized) intervention, the other is a real interest equalization tax (RIET). The case for intervention has been and is an uncomfortable one. The case for a RIET is, at first sight, more controversial, but is an avenue that in view of North Atlantic discord and disruption becomes increasingly realistic as an option.

Intervention

The case for intervention rests on the premise that domestic and foreign currency securities are imperfect substitutes and that, accordingly, changes in their relative supplies will induce portfolio disequilibria. At going interest rates there is a pressure for exchange rate adjustments and these adjustments in turn spread to other financial markets as well as to the goods markets. It is thus possible, on the premise of imperfect asset substitutability, to influence exchange rates by affecting the relative supplies of home and foreign currency outside securities or by management of the currency composition of world debt.

Henderson (1982) offers a definitive analysis of the case for intervention. He concludes that intervention is optimal (if feasible) in the case of portfolio shifts, which of course is

FIGURE 4

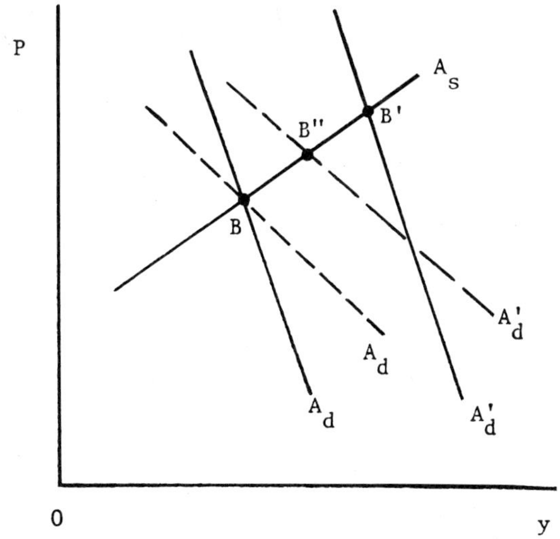

the traditional case for accommodating financial policies. For disturbances to aggregate demand, by contrast, a policy of maintaining non-intervention in money and exchange markets offers greater employment stability. The latter point is readily made with standard aggregate demand and supply schedules as shown in Fig. 4. The money wage is assumed fixed but prices are flexible. Thus there is an upward sloping aggregate supply A_s. The aggregate demand schedule A_d, embodies bond and money market equilibrium, given the alternative policy assumptions. Along the steeper schedule exchange and interest rates are held constant. Therefore, a decline in prices stimulates aggregate demand *only* through the effect on competitiveness. Along the dashed and flatter aggregate demand schedule money and debt are held constant. Therefore, a fall in prices lowers interest rates and expands demand while at the same time, for bond markets to clear, it induces a depreciation and thus reinforces the gain in competitiveness. Accordingly, a larger rise in output is required to restore balance.

A given autonomous increase in demand shifts the aggregate demand schedules out and to the right, the more so the more acommodating are policies. If interest rates and exchange rates are held constant, the demand expansion is not dampened by higher interest rates and appreciation. Accordingly, under such a "rates constant" policy as Henderson concludes, demand disturbances have a larger impact on employment and domestic prices (point B″) than is the case for an aggregate policy (point B′). There are significant complications to the model once we allow, as we should, supply side effects of exchange rate movements. Once these complications are introduced it becomes much less clearcut whether rates constant policies are preferred to policies that maintain aggregates. It also becomes more difficult to identify what is the disturbance that is affecting the economy. On both counts the case for an active intervention stance becomes less clear-cut, except for obvious portfolio shifts.

The ambiguity in the assessment of intervention is increased once we consider the imperfect substitution issue. There is, of course, no question that dollar and foreign currency assets are imperfect substitutes. This is the case because their returns are not perfectly correlated and in some cases are, in fact, negatively correlated. But there remains the question whether the variance of relative returns and the degree of risk aversion are sufficiently large to make imperfect substitutes an easy policy channel. Long and short bonds are imperfect substitutes but twisting the term structure through debt management never was a success. The same question arises in the exchange rate context: how large an intervention is required to move the $/DM rate 1%? To that question we have no serious answer.

If intervention does not look like a very reliable tool, are there any options? One option is a (moving) wide exchange rate band within which rates are flexible but at the margins of which rates would be defended. Such a band might be reasonable as a proposition to eliminate extreme risk. But in doing so we may also increase the mobility of capital and actually aggravate exchange rate instability within the band. The only sense of a band would be as a cooperative venture in forestalling disruptive policies that could spill over into excessive appreciation or depreciation. But it is also conceivable that such band setting may well assume protectionist overtones. On balance, there are serious doubts about such a policy.

The case for intervention is usually made as one of countering disorderly market conditions.[19] But there is no very good case why small noise in the market should be smoothed, and there is good reason that large noise cannot effectively be dealt with. A massive disturbance such as the dollar appreciation of 1980–82 probably cannot be dealt with by intervention, unless we allow the exchange authorities massive swings in the size and denomination of their assets. For such massive disturbances we need a more adequate tool.

Real Interest Equalization Taxes

History is aplenty with collapses and surges in exchange rates, whether we look at France in the 1920s, the US in the last years, or the laboratory experiments in Latin America. Invariably, the really vast changes in *real* exchange rates are associated not with changes in comparative advantage but rather with the medium-term adjustment to abandon of fiscal control or, on the other side, monetary stabilization. Taking the case of monetary tightening, real exchange rates easily move by 20 or 40 percentage points and therefore have, of course, vast effects on the economy over and above what tight money implies. In a small country, these effects are largely domestic, but when the policy is pursued in the US, unsynchronized with the rest of the world, then the policy spills over as an adverse disruptive supply shock abroad. In the trade field, market disruption is dealt with by quotas or *ad hoc* compensating duties. This is felt to be an effective policy dealing with a *transitory* disturbance. Much the same view should be adopted on capital account. Whenever unsynchronized policies open up disruptively large real interest differentials, we need ad hoc real interest equalization taxes that close the gaps and avoid a major impact on the real exchange rate.[20] There is no sensible argument that tightening of money should involve as a desirable side effect a loss of exports, an increase in imports, and international redistribution of real income and borrowing abroad. Because these side effects are undesirable, both here and abroad, we should attempt to the maximum possible extent to immunize the world economy against these spillovers.

[19] See Economic Report of the President, 1982, 189–191.

[20] *Tobin* (1978) has argued for a permanent tax on foreign currency transactions. *Liviatan* (1979) argues for transitory taxes associated with monetary stabilization.

Ad hoc duties to offset trade disruption are neither totally efficient nor totally effective. But nobody questions that they substantially accomplish their purpose of insulating an industry from some transitory foreign disturbance. The same applies to an RIET. There is little doubt that some inefficiency is involved and that certainly more than in the case of trade disruption duties, there is room for circumvention. But that is true for all forms of taxation and taxes, nevertheless, work. Similarly, a RIET is a highly desirable, second-best, instrument.

A real interest equalization tax is a second-best instrument in that at some efficiency costs, it avoids the even larger costs of adverse spillover of US policies abroad. The first-best world is one where transition to lower inflation has no real effects whatsoever, but proceeds with full employment and constant real interest harmony. The moment that scenario is disturbed because prices or inflation rates are sticky, there is a presumption that supplementary policies, both domestic and international, should accompany tight money. The relevant criterion by which to judge supplementary policies (tips, wage controls, investment tax credits, RIETs) is whether on balance they make the economy operate more efficiently without prejudicing the disinflation target. Surely, that must be the case for RIETs since they avoid, if effective, the adverse and totally unwarranted effects of US policies abroad. The argument against RIETs is that they are costly because they interfere with the free flow of capital. But that argument is empty since it fails to demonstrate that the costs of an RIET are larger than the benefits gained thereby in avoiding the spillover of US policy abroad. At present, we are spending a percent or more of GNP every year to try to reduce inflation. We cannot seriously argue that the allocational costs of RIETs are in any sense commensurate with the costs that are avoided by their preventing imported inflation in Europe.

On a cost benefit basis RIETs are assuredly a preferred policy option. The only serious question is how to design the system in a manner that makes coverage complete and administration automatic. One avenue that commends itself is a transitory withholding tax on interest bearing, dollar denominated assets. Because the tax is transitory, the offshore problems, while present, may not be overriding.

SUMMARY

It is shown that modern exchange rate theories have failed across the board to account for exchange rate behavior. Speculative bubbles, expectations about future policy changes and international side effects of inappropriate monetary-fiscal policy mixes are reasons for deviations of the exchange rate from the rate warranted by the fundamentals. As instruments to influence and control the behavior of the exchange rate, official exchange market intervention as well as a real interest equilization tax (RIET) are discussed. Exchange market intervention is rejected because large noise can not effectively be dealt with this tool. The RIET is a preferred policy option on a cost benefit basis.

REFERENCES

Artus, J. (1981), Effects of U.S. Monetary Restraint on the DM/$ Exchange Rate and the German Economy. Unpublished manuscript. International Monetary Fund.

Black, S. W. (1972), The Use of Rational Expectations in Models of Speculation, Review of Economics and Statistics. 161–165.

Blanchard, O. J. (1979), Speculative Bubbles, Crashes and Rational Expectation, Economic Letters. North-Holland Publishing Company. 387 to 389.

_____ (1976), Three Essays on Macroeconomic. Unpublished Ph.D. dissertation. M.I.T.

_____ and M. W. Watson (1982), Bubbles, Rational Expectations, and Financial Markets. Unpublished manuscript (January).

Buiter, W. H. and M. Miller (1981), Monetary Policy and International Competitiveness: The Problems of Adjustment, Oxford Economic Press 33, Oxford (supplement, July).

Cornell, B. (1982), Money Supply Announcements and Interest Rates: Another View. Unpublished manuscript. University of California, Los Angeles.

Dornbusch, R. (1980), Open Economy Macroeconomics. Basic Books.

_____ (1980), Exchange Rate Economics: Where Do We Stand? Brookings Papers on Economic Activity 1, 143–185.

_____ (1980), Exchange Risk and the Macroeconomics of Exchange Rate Determination. Unpublished manuscript. M.I.T.

_____ (1978), Monetary Policy under Exchange Rate Flexibility. Federal Reserve Bank of Boston, Conference Series, Managed Exchange Rate Flexibility.

_____ and S. Fischer (1980), Exchange Rates and the Current Account. The American Economic Review 70, 960–971.

_____ and P. Krugman (1976), Flexible Exchange Rates in the Short Term. Brookings Papers on Economic Activity 3.

Engle, C. and J. Frankel (1982), Why Money Announcements Move Interest Rates: An Answer from the Foreign Exchange Risk. Unpublished manuscript. University of California, Berkeley.

Flood, Robert (1982), Stochastic Process Switching and Inflation. Unpublished manuscript. Board of Governors of the Federal Reserve.

_____ and P. M. Garber (1981), Bubbles, Runs and Gold Monetization. Unpublished manuscript. University of Virginia (October).

_____ and N. P. Marion (1981), Exchange Rates Regimes in Transition: Italy 1974. International Financial Discussion Papers 193.

Frankel, J. (1979), On the Mark: A Theory of Floating Exchange Rates Based on Real Interest Differentials. The American Economic Review 69.

_____ (1979), The Diversifiability of Exchange Risk. Journal of International Economics.

_____ (1982), Tests of Monetary and Balance of Payments Models of Exchange Rates. University of California, Berkeley.

Frenkel, Jacob (1981), Flexible Exchange Rates in the 1970s. Journal of Political Economy 89.

Friedman, M. (1956), The Case for Flexible Exchange Rates. Essays in Positive Economics. University of Chicago Press.

Genberg, H. (1981), Effects of Central Bank Intervention in the Foreign Exchange Market. IMF Staff Papers.

Grossman, S. and R. Schiller (1981), The Determinants of the Variability of Stock Prices. The American Economic Review 71.

Hacche, G. and J. Townsend (1981), Exchange Rates and Monetary Policy Modelling Sterling's Effective Exchange Rate, 1972–80. Oxford Economic Papers 33.

Henderson, D. (1982), Exchange Market Intervention Operations: Their Effect and Their Role in Financial Policy. Unpublished manuscript. Board of Governors of the Federal Reserve System.

Hooper, P. (1982), Impact of the Recent Dollar Appreciation on GNP and Prices in Major Industrialized Countries: Simulations with the MCM. Unpublished memorandum. Board of Governors of the Federal Reserve.

Isard, P. (1980), Expected and Unexpected Exchange Rate Changes. Unpublished manuscript. Federal Reserve Board.

Krugman, P. (1980), Consumption Preferences, Asset Demands and Distribution Effect in International Financial Markets. Unpublished manuscript. M.I.T.

Liviatan, N. (1979), Neutral Monetary Policy and the Capital Import Tax. Unpublished manuscript. Hebrew University (October).

Lizondo, J. S. (1980), Foreign Exchange Futures Prices under Fixed Exchange Rates. Unpublished manuscript. ITAM (May).

Marris, S. (1981), Exchange Rates: Too Fixed or Too Flexible? Unpublished manuscript. Organization for Economic Cooperation and Development.

Meese, R. and K. Rogoff (1981), Empirical Exchange Rate Models of the Seventies: Are They Fit to Survive? International Finance Discussion Papers 184 (June).

Mishkin, F. (1982), Does Anticipated Monetary Policy Matter? An Econometric Investigation. Journal of Political Economy 90.

Mussa, M. (1979), The Empirical Regularities in the Behavior of Exchange Rates and Theories of the Foreign Exchange Market. Carnegie Rochester Conference Series 11.

______ (1976), The Exchange Rate and the Balance of Payments. Scandinavian Journal of Economics 2.

______ (1969), Three Times the Transfer Problem Plus David Hume. Unpublished manuscript. University of Chicago.

Nurkse, R. (1944), International Currency Experience: Lessons of the Inter-War Period. League of Nations. Princeton, New Jersey.

Obstfeld, M. (1982). Can We Sterilize? The American Economic Review (May).

Rogoff, K. (1979), Essays on Expectations and Exchange Rate Volatility. Unpublished manuscript. Ph.D. dissertation. M.I.T.

Salant, S. and D. Henderson (1978), Market Anticipations of Government Policies and the Price of Gold. Journal of Political Economy 86.

Shiller, R. (1981), The Use of Volatility Measures in Assessing Market Efficiency. Journal of Finance 36.

Tirole, J. (1982), On the Possibility of Speculation under Rational Expectations. Econometrica (September).

Tobin, J. (1978), A Proposal for International Monetary Reform. Cowles Foundation Discussion Paper 506, Yale University.

Wallich, H. and J. A. Gray (1980), Stabilization Policy and Vicious and Virtuous Circles, in: J. Chipman and Charles P. Kindleberger (eds.), Flexible Exchange Rates and the Balance of Payments. North Holland.

Williamson, J. The Open Economy and the World Economy. Basic Books, forthcoming.

Wilson, C. (1979). Anticipated Disturbances and Exchange Rate Dynamics. Journal of Political Economy 87.

Financial Parity Relationships and Market Efficiency

10
International Parity Conditions and Exchange Risk*

B. Solnik†

1. INTRODUCTION

The recent times of high and volatile inflation and its corresponding unstable exchange rates have taken people away from the basic lessons of international finance. Indeed many leaders of this world provide explanations for current exchange and interest rate behavior based on purely emotional, political and institutional reasons rather than on simple economic truths. The discrepancies between the two approaches might come from the poor understanding of economic phenomena by our political leaders but it is also caused by the over-simplification of the traditional theory of international finance developed originally some fifty years ago with a micro-economic basis. Indeed the usual assumptions of perfect markets for capital and goods, a single homogeneous consumption good and perfect certainty cannot be regarded as realistic nowadays. Judging from reality, deviations from these hypothetical situations seem to have a serious effect on exchange rate behavior.

The purpose of this paper is first to review what will be called here the traditional theory of international parity embodied in the writings of Keynes, Cassel and Irving Fisher. It will then present some of the recent equilibrium micro-economic works attempting to relax the original restricting assumptions regarding perfect markets. This part will focus more specifically on the definition of exchange risk and the determination of forward exchange rates which can be used to hedge against that risk.

2. THE TRADITIONAL THEORY OF INTERNATIONAL PARITY

In a recent article, Giddy (1976) claims to provide *An integrated theory of exchange rate equilibrium*. What looks like a very ambitious task is simply a restatement of 'theories' developed independently half a century ago by well-known authors.[1] Since some people still attempt 'de redécouvrir la roue', it might be worth starting by a brief summary of the traditional theory and insisting on the strict assumptions under which these conclusions have been *proven*.

A sufficient set of common assumptions to derive our traditional theory of international parity as suggested by the work of Cassel, Fisher and Keynes are:

(A.1) Financial markets are perfect. There are no controls, transaction costs, taxes, etc.

(A.2) Goods markets are perfect. International shipment of goods can take place freely, instantaneously and without cost or tariff.

---

*This article is reprinted with permission, from *Journal of Banking and Finance,* 2 (1978), pp. 281–293.

†I am grateful to CORDES for its financial support (Convention 76 96).

[1]Although Giddy claims to deal with theoretical issues in the title of his paper, he never specifies the assumptions of the model under which his conclusions are derived. Indeed, the only deviation from the traditional theory is to replace the future (but certain) exchange rate of the traditional theory by its expected value.

(A.3) There is a single consumption good common to everyone.

(A.4) The future is known with certainty.

Under some or all of these assumptions four parity conditions can be derived as building blocks of our theory, which will be briefly recalled.

2.1. Interest Rate Parity (IRPT)

For any pair of countries the interest rate differential must be equal to the forward exchange rate differential (or discount), otherwise riskless arbitrage will take place. Using the notations of table 1, we have:

$$\frac{1 + R_j}{1 + R_i} = \frac{F_{ij}^t}{S_{ij}^t}, \tag{1}$$

or with the linear approximation

$$R_j - R_i \simeq \frac{F_{ij}^t - S_{ij}^t}{S_{ij}^t} \tag{1'}$$

Note that this parity condition only requires assumption (A.1) to hold, otherwise it is a pure arbitrage condition. This relation originates in Keynes (1930).

2.2. Purchasing Power Parity (PPPT)

Assumptions (A.1) to (A.3) are sufficient to derive a simple version of the purchasing power parity theorem introduced by Cassel (1916). In these perfect markets, identical goods must have the same real price everywhere otherwise physical arbitrage will take place (Law of One Price). Since every country consumes the same good or basket this also applies to the national price indices and a unit of a given currency has the same purchasing power in every country.

In other words, the variation in exchange rate for two currencies is equal to the inflation differential in the two countries over a period of time:

$$\frac{S_{ij}^{t+1}}{S_{ij}^t} = \frac{1 + I_j^{t+1}}{1 + I_j^t} \times \frac{1 + I_i^t}{1 + I_i^{t+1}}, \tag{2}$$

with the linear approximation:

$$T_j - T_i \simeq \frac{S_{ij}^{t+1} - S_{ij}^t}{S_{ij}^t}. \tag{2'}$$

TABLE 1

List of Notations

R_j	interest rate of country j from period t to $t + 1$
r_j	real interest rate of country j
I_j^t	price level in country j from t to $t + 1$
T_j	inflation rate in country j during period t to $t + 1$
S_{ij}^t	spot exchange rate of currency i in units of currency j at time t
F_{ij}^t	forward exchange rate of currency i in units of currency j quoted at time t for delivery in $t + 1$

2.3. Fisherian Relation (FR)

Under assumptions (A.1), (A.3), and (A.4), the nominal interest rate in every country will be equal to the real rate of interest plus the expected future inflation rate [Fisher (1930)]:

$$(1 + R_j) = (1 + r_j)\left(\frac{1 + I_j^{t+1}}{1 + I_j^t}\right), \tag{3}$$

with the linear approximation:

$$R_j \simeq r_j + T_j. \tag{3'}$$

This is not a market arbitrage condition as (1) and (2) but a general equilibrium condition derived from first order optimality conditions from individuals' utility maximization.

The real rate of interest need not be constant from one period to the next (although it should not change much) nor equal in every country.

If we add the assumption of perfect goods market (A.2), purchasing power parity (2) combined with (3) implies that real rates of interest be equal everywhere. Since we know that the inflation differential is exactly offset by the currency appreciation, if real interest rates were different financial arbitrage would take place.

2.4. Forward Parity (FPT)

The combination of (A.1) and (A.4) implies that the forward exchange rate must be equal to the future (certain) spot exchange rate. Otherwise riskless arbitrage would take place:

$$S_{ij}^{t+1} = F_{ij}^t. \tag{4}$$

This relation might be considered as less important than the previous ones although it is implicit in the writings of many authors. It is a direct byproduct of the first three parity relations if we assume (A.1) through (A.4) but can be derived with (A.1) and (A.4) alone.

We will now see how these basic international conditions are affected if some of the idealized views of the world are incorrect. In other words we will review some of the conclusions derived from equilibrium micro-economic models relaxing some of the assumptions (A.1) to (A.4).

Our focus is on the recent developments dealing with uncertainty. Imperfections in the financial or goods markets are often hard to include in a formal model, usually leading to trivial equilibrium solutions or unsolvable mathematical atrocities. After a few words about market imperfections and multiconsumption problems in a world of certainty, the more realistic and interesting case of uncertainty will be considered.

3. DEVIATIONS FROM PERFECTION: THE CERTAINTY CASE

3.1. A Multigood World

Even with perfect markets and no uncertainty, differences in consumption tastes will affect the previous results [*relaxation of* (A.3)]. For example, countries might be characterized by their consumption baskets which would vary across nations.

The IRPT (1) and FPT (4) which are financial arbitrage conditions will still hold. A Fisherian relation will still be valid in each country if tastes are homogeneous within a country (3). However as shown by Samuelson, in the case of diverse tastes, a well behaved inflation index will only exist theoretically if individuals have homothetic utility functions. And even so the aggregation problem to arrive at a national (or international) consumer price index is not trivial.[2]

Strictly speaking, the Law of One Price (2) will still apply to individual commodities because of perfect goods markets but need not apply to national inflation indices based on consumption baskets of different composition (relative price variations). However many authors have gone beyond this micro-economic conclusion and stated that the purchasing power parity theorem would apply to general price level [Hawtrey (1919), Cassel (1930), etc.]. This requires a monetary equilibrium explanation which is beyond the scope of this paper. A discussion of this issue can be found in Frenkel (1976).

3.2. Market Imperfections

The introduction of market imperfections in a general equilibrium framework leads to complex models with few, if any, explicit solutions similar to the parity conditions described above. The easiest to accommodate, at least mathematically, are ad valorem transaction costs either in the financial markets or in the physical markets (i.e. instantaneous shipping of goods but proportional shipment costs or taxes).[3] Given the complexity of the task many authors have resorted to a more global macro-economic approach.

The usual belief is that financial markets are more perfect than goods markets, which for technical reasons adjust much more slowly to new information. Dornbusch (1976), for example, proposes an interesting deterministic monetarist model of international finance based on the idea that exchange rates are determined in a *financial* asset market. This switches the emphasis from trade markets theory to financial markets theory which is a favorite hunting ground for micro-economists. In this new monetarist approach,[4] investors are assumed to base their decisions on expectations which are in turn reflected in asset prices; in efficient financial markets current exchange rates or interest rates will therefore reflect all available information.

In Dornbusch's deterministic world with efficient financial markets, IRPT and FPT must hold. This implies that the interest differential will always be equal to the expected (certain) variation in exchange rate. However, the stickiness in goods prices implies that PPPT or FR will not necessarily hold in the *short run* while they should in the *long run* when full adjustment takes place. The length of the adjustment period depends on the degree of imperfection in the goods market.

The synergy between this 'new monetarist approach' and the micro-economic financial theory which takes risk into account, should be obvious.

[2]A micro-economic model of investment and the Fisherian relation in a closed economy with uncertainty and diverse homothetic tastes has been studied by Grauer-Litzenberger (1974) and Solnik (1975).

[3]With restrictive assumptions about production patterns. Grauer, Litzenberger and Stehle (1976) have shown that the impact of ad valorem taxes of international transfer of goods on market equilibrium conditions is quite limited even with price uncertainty. Black (1974) studied the case of proportional taxes on dividends and capital gains.

[4]For a more complete coverage of the monetary approach see Frenkel and Johnson.

4. THEORY OF FOREIGN EXCHANGE WITH UNCERTAINTY

The current economic unstability stresses the importance of uncertainty in economic theory. The literature on the theory of risk in domestic capital markets is very extensive; the application of its precepts to international finance is less developed.

Several sources of uncertainty might exist. Adler and Dumas (1976) studied the case where default risk could exist on loan contracts for which IRPT is supposed to apply; this would create deviations in IRPT. More generally, risk stems from uncertainty about future prices and rates of return and this will be the focus of this part of the paper since a better intuitive understanding of exchange risk is necessary.

4.1. Traditional Theory with Uncertainty

Assume that assumptions (A.1) to (A.3) hold but exchange rates are uncertain. Given physical goods arbitrage, PPPT must hold for the common consumption basket; fluctuations in exchange rate can only be caused by nominal variations of the price of the consumption good in various countries. In other words exchange rate variations are only caused by inflation i.e. monetary phenomena. Exchange risk, if any, is purely created by monetary or inflation uncertainty. In an almost perfect world with complete financial markets (existence of a real risk-free asset), perfect goods market and a single consumption basket, exchange rate fluctuations are some kind of 'white noise' which should not affect asset prices. Grauer, Litzenberger and Stehle (1976), G.L.S. hereafter,have studied such a world with free and costless international trade and identical tastes. The ratio of all goods prices expressed in two currencies will always equal the exchange rate between the two currencies. Fluctuations in exchange rates can only be caused by pure money inflation and real goods prices will be equal everywhere. In this model the fact that investors reside in a particular country is irrelevant. Since they have the same consumption tastes individuals face exactly the same investment and consumption opportunity set. The numeraire of residence, *by assumption of this simple model* cannot matter. One needs no elaborate proof to realize that there is as much difference (in this world) between Canadian, US and German residents, as there is between individuals whose first names are Frederick, Robert or Richard. The numeraire used does not count because residency is not defined in the model[5] and everyone is free to use any currency.

Of course, these conclusions would be changed if nationals of various countries differ in tastes, if (real) commodity prices were not identical everywhere because of transaction costs, or if the country of residence had a specific real influence (taxation, non-indexed wage income, etc.). Clearly a person is a person (almost) everywhere and the above differences exist within a country. Their magnitude is probably larger between countries because of geographical, historical, political, cultural and institutional reasons.[6] In G.L.S. everyone can buy his goods at the same (real) price and earn exactly the same

[5]Paying a bill systematically with \$1 or \$10 notes or drawing randomly from a wallet does not affect the real wealth of an individual. If the unit of account is one bank note, the exchange rate between the first 2 individuals is 10 and it is a random number with the third one. This is the kind of nominal exchange risk described here.

[6]Fluctuations in exchange rates in the past years clearly demonstrate that real prices of goods are not equal everywhere. Samuelson (1974) comments on this point.

return on each asset (with a real riskless asset). The so called 'international' contribution is only to add some new financial contracts (nominal riskless assets in various 'currencies'). The return on these assets depends on uncertain pure money inflation. They are just like lottery tickets. But again, these contracts are viewed identically by all investors: they provide to every one the same real return. In this world, exchange risk is, from the very construction of the model, pure monetary inflation uncertainty and money illusion.

4.2. A More General Theory of Foreign Exchange and Risk[7]

While the previous model (G.L.S.) focused on the monetary aspect of the international dimension, Solnik (1974) developed a model based on real differences between countries. The latter assumes marked differences in tastes but a free and perfect international capital market, and only studies the real impact of consumption differences by assuming away pure (neutral) money inflation [Solnik (1974, p. 505, footnote 9)]. The definitions of exchange risk are therefore fundamentally different since this theory only considers real exchange risk, not monetary risk: this real exchange risk stems from differences in tastes and/or different real prices and not from monetary inflation [Solnik (1974, p. 505, footnote 9)]. The definitions of exchange risk objectives are complementary, not competitive. It has been argued that the multi-taste problem is domestic as well as international but it seems that strong intercountry difference in tastes and real prices is a valid characterization of international equilibrium with real variables and that real exchange risk will generally exist.

In the 1974 paper, I mistakenly suggested that the model, in its simpler version, required a strict separation of consumption which was quite unrealistic as pointed out by G.L.S. However such an assumption[8] is not necessary. All that is required is that there exist differences in national tastes and every country could consume the same commodities but in different proportions[9] (different baskets). Let's consider a country to be defined by its tastes and therefore by its consumption good or basket. Following G.L.S. let's assume perfect trade markets with identical real prices for each commodity across the world. Further assume that the monetary authority of each country worries about his own citizens and inflation rate, attempting (and succeeding) to keep a constant domestic inflation rate; in other words the purchasing power of its currency in terms of the domestic consumption good is certain. Given relative price variations, exchange rates will fluctuate randomly with the relative value of national consumption baskets as long as they are different. This is the exact definition of exchange risk used in Solnik when there is no pure monetary inflation. All my previous results follow. A very simple example might be useful.

Let's assume a simple (and unrealistic) additive consumption basket for two countries:

[7]As suggested by Samuelson (1974), Roll and Solnik (1976) and others, another source of exchange risk could come from imperfect trade markets (transaction costs).

[8]Solnik (1974, p. 504, footnote 8), already stated: 'Because we are primarily interested in finding equilibrium conditions for the asset markets, the model assumes a single consumption good *Ck* for each country. The model could be generalized by making *Ck* a vector introducing the relative prices as state variables'.

[9]G.L.S. tend to forget that the fact that all Frenchmen have a utility function defined over the same consumption good or basket does not mean that they have a zero utility for the foreign consumption baskets but rather that theirs is optimal given their tastes. This 'consumption basket' formulation is easily derived with homothetic utility function [see G.L.S. or Solnik (1975)].

TABLE 2

	France		Japan	
	Price in Period (FF)		Price in Period (¥)	
	0	1	0	1
Wine (L)	1	1.111 = 30/27	1	1.500
Sake (L)	1	0.741 = 20/27	1	1.000
Value of the basket	10	10	10	10
Exchange rate FF · ¥				
Period 0	1			
Period 1	0.7441 = 20/27			

France and Japan. The French consumption basket consists of 9 liters of wine and 1 liter of sake while the Japanese basket is 9 liters of sake and 1 liter of wine. At the start of the period the relative price is one liter of sake per liter of wine and the exchange rate is 1 French Franc per Japanese Yen. Given the level of production, the relative price of sake and wine will change by the end of the period to 1.5 liter of sake per liter of wine. A reasonable change in consumption baskets induced by the relative price movement might be 8 liters of wine and 1½ liter of sake for the French and ⅓ liter of wine and 9½ liters of sake for the Japanese. The resulting equilibrium prices, assuming that the central banks keep a *zero inflation* rate on their domestic consumption basket, are given in table 2. The exchange rate has moved to 0.741 French Franc per Yen. In other words a French investor in Japan would have lost 35% on his Yen investment (in real terms) while the Japanese investor would not have lost anything in his domestic investment (e.g. a fixed interest bond). Note that despite the real influence of this exchange rate adjustment, the real value of each commodity is equal in both countries and there is no (monetary) inflation in France or Japan: of course PPP does *not* apply.

Given different tastes (uncertain) exchange rate movements will be created by (uncertain) changes in the real values of national consumption baskets.[10] This aspect of risk, is very important in the international setting. Of course, if governments do not keep a 'certain-inflation' policy, pure monetary risk could be added: but one should remember that the relevant measure of inflation is linked to the 'value' of the domestic consumption basket. While the first source of exchange risk (real) differs according to the citizenship, the second one (monetary) is global and identical for everyone.

4.3. The Parity Conditions and Exchange Risk

Recently Roll and Solnik (1976) considered the general case and the impact of uncertainty on the four parity conditions assuming perfect capital markets but placing no restrictions

[10]In fact the formulation is valid in the case where everyone consumes the same good but its price varies (randomly) in each country because of uncertain transaction costs, import or export taxes etc. All that is required is that Governments maintain a zero or certain inflation policy in their domestic currencies.

on utility functions or on the completeness of markets. Because of (A.1)—no default risk, no transaction costs—IRPT still holds in its usual form.

The empirical validity of interest rate parity is obvious to practitioners and has also been found by academicians as long as they used reliable data for similar instruments quoted at the same time [Aliber (1973), Frenkel and Levich (1976)]. Of course, if one considers exchange and interest rates quoted to the customers (as they often appear in newspapers) rather than interbank rates, the conclusions might be different.

The Fisherian relation (FR) will not hold in its traditional form since uncertainty will induce risk premia in equilibrium. Such a result should not be a surprise since the existence of liquidity or risk premia in interest rates has been recognized for a long time. Recent work by Fama (1976) provides empirical evidence of the existence of such risk premia in the U.S.A.

Similarly, the Law of One Price will still hold if assumption (A.2) is valid. Of course the comments made previously about PPPT with different compositions of national consumption baskets and inflation indices still apply. If the commodities markets are not perfect an uncertainty analogue of PPPT on expected prices can be derived as shown in Roll and Solnik (1976) with risk premia appended to the traditional form. Even more important is the fact that deviations from PPP, at least in the short run, are a prerequisite for the existence of real exchange risk. Roll (1977) studied the relative importance of inflation differentials and relative price changes in the determination of exchange rates. He found that, except for rapid inflation countries (such as Chile or Argentina), the relative price factor was, by far, dominant lending credence to the importance of exchange risk as a separate and important phenomenon rather than simply a monetary by-product.

Given exchange risk, the theory claims that a risk premium should be appended to the forward parity relation so that the forward rate (or interest differential) ought to be a biased predictor of spot rates. Since this result is relatively new and the center of much controversy regarding exchange risk, it is worth spending some time on it.

4.4. Foreign Exchange Efficiency and Risk Premia

Some authors [Aliber (1977), Frenkel (1976), Giddy (1976), Kohlagen (1974, 1976), Magee (1976)] interpret efficient market theory to mean that forward exchange rates should be unbiased predictors of future spot exchange rates. This ignores totally the notion of risk and attitudes towards risk. It is equivalent to saying that efficiency in the capital market requires that the forward interest rate implied in the long term interest rate be an unbiased predictor of the future interest rate (ruling out liquidity risk premia), or that efficiency in the commodities market require that the current future price of a commodity be an unbiased predictor of the spot price, or that efficiency in the stock market requires all expected returns on stocks to be equal to the risk free rate.

For example, Giddy (1976) chose to focus his discussion on what he calls a *forward rate theory of exchange rate expectations* which states that the forward rate should be exactly equal to the expected future spot rate (without any risk premium). Unfortunately Giddy's article is only theoretical in its title since there is no specification of the hypotheses under which such a conclusion could be demonstrated. Giddy's 'proof' is based on his personal belief that such a conclusion is erroneous without any theoretical discussion. On page 890, he says:

Indeed a number of researchers now believe that unhedged holders of forward contracts . . . must be 'compensated' for the risk they are taking. . . However it is difficult to see how such an argument could possibly hold symmetrically for both sides of the foreign exchange market: for if a French speculator in the French Franc/Sterling forward market is rewarded for taking risk, it follows that a British speculator holding the opposite side is penalized for taking risk!

At first glance, it might seem strange that a risk premium could exist in a 'symmetrical' market. In other words, if there is a positive risk premium on the Franc/dollar forward rate there must exist a negative risk premium on the dollar/franc forward rate. However, it all depends on relative risk aversion, consumption, tastes, net foreign investment and the composition of the investor's portfolio. . . The argument is not new to the traditional theory of commodities or exchange markets with its usual separation between 'speculators' who earn the risk premium and hedgers who willingly 'pay' the same risk premium.

Here let's take the example that Americans have a heavy *net* investment position in France (which seems the case) and that a French Franc devaluation is expected. As a result Americans might have a strong desire to hedge and would accept a forward rate (18 cents/FF) below the anticipated spot rate (19 cents/FF) to protect themselves against a larger than anticipated devaluation of the Franc (16 cents/FF). Indeed, typically, financial markets are symmetrical and most people would accept the idea of risk premia on these markets. There is one borrower for each lender, but there seems to be a positive risk premium (depending on maturity) paid by the borrower as mentioned earlier. Numerous examples could be found to run against Giddy's intuition.

The existence of a forward bias has found, so far, mixed empirical support. Aliber (1977), Bilson (1977), Cornell (1977), Kohlagen (1975) tend to reject such a bias while Kaserman (1973), McCallum (1976) and to some extent Frenkel (1976) and Levich (1976) find empirical evidence of the existence of a forward bias. The methodological problem of those tests is that the alternative to the null hypothesis of no bias is usually not specified (and therefore cannot be rejected). The forward bias is sometimes tested in the form of a constant additive one but the theory claims that it should be a more complex risk premium term.[11] The only direct test has been provided by Roll and Solnik (1977) with fairly positive although preliminary conclusions.

5. CONCLUSIONS

This review is not intended to be exhaustive but rather to survey the new efficient market approach to international finance. A fruitful development would be to extend these micro-economic models to a more global macro-economic approach. All recent empirical evidence and current experience indicate very strongly that exchange rates have a life of their own not fully explained by inflation differentials. This creates real exchange risk of great importance to corporations which affects their short and even longer run competitive positions in all countries. Given its magnitude, contribution to international

[11]Furthermore, forward rates seem to be poor predictors of future spot rates. In comparing forward premia to realized spot exchange rate movements, it is seldom that one could reject the hypothesis that there is no average difference between the two (no bias) or the hypothesis that there is a 5. or 10% average annual difference (positive bias) because of very large 'white noise'. Such studies which 'cannot reject the hypothesis of no bias' can hardly be considered as 'proving the non-existence of biases'.

unstability and real effect on government policies, exchange rate uncertainty cannot be ignored by theoreticians or treated as an unpleasant but minor imperfection. Further empirical and theoretical research in this area of international finance should prove very helpful for economic policy and corporate decision making.

REFERENCES

Adler, M., and B. Dumas, 1976, Portfolio choice and the demand for forward exchange. American Economic Review Proceedings. May.

Aliber, R. Z., 1973, The I.R.P.T.: A Reinterpretation. Journal of Political Economy. Nov.

Aliber, R. Z., 1977, A short guide to international finance.

Bilson, J. F. O., 1976, Rational expectations and the exchange rates: Theory and estimation, mimeo.

Black, F., 1974, International capital market equilibrium with investment barriers. Journal of Financial Economics. Dec.

Cassel, G., 1916, The present situation of foreign exchanges. Economic Journal 26.

Cassel, G., 1921, The world's monetary problems (Constable, London).

Cassel, G., 1928, Post war monetary stabilization (Columbia University Press, New York).

Cornell, B., 1977, Spot rates, forward rates and exchange market efficiency. Journal of Financial Economics. Aug.

Dornbusch, R., 1976, Expectations and exchange rate dynamics. Journal of Political Economy. Sept.

Fama, E. F., 1975, Short term interest rates as predictors of inflation. American Economic Review. June.

Fama, E. F., 1976, Inflation uncertainty and expected returns on treasury bills, Journal of Political Economy. June.

Fisher, I., 1907, The rate of interest. New York (Macmillan, London).

Frenkel, J. A., 1976, A monetary approach to the balance of payments: Doctrinal aspects and empirical evidence. Scandinavian Journal of Economics 78–2. May.

Frenkel, J. A., and H. G. Johnson, 1976, The monetary approach to the balance of payments (Allen and Unwin, London).

Frenkel, J. A., and R. M. Levich, 1975, Covered interest arbitrage: Unexploited profits? Journal of Political Economy. April.

Giddy, I., 1976, An integrated theory of foreign exchange equilibrium. Journal of Financial and Quantitative Analysis.

Grauer, F. L. A., and R. H. Litzenberger, 1974, A state preference model of the valuation of commodity futures contracts under uncertain commodity prices. Stanford Research Paper. 220. Aug.

Grauer, F. L. A., R. H., Litzenberger, and R. E. Stehle, 1976, Sharing rules and equilibrium in an international capital market under uncertainty. Journal of Financial Economics. June.

Hawtrey, R. G., 1919, Currency and credit (Longmand Green. London).

Kaserman, D. L., 1973, The forward exchange rate: Its determination and behavior as a predictor of the future spot rate. Proceedings of the American Statistical Association, 417–442.

Keynes, J. M., 1923. A tract on monetary reform (Macmillan. London).

Keynes, J. M., 1930, A treatise on money 1, (Macmillan. London).

Kohlagen, S. W., 1974, The forward rate as an unbiased predictor of future spot rates. University of California, mimeo.

Kohlagen, S. W., 1976. The foreign exchange markets: Models, tests and empirical evidence. Federal Reserve Bank, mimeo.

Levich, R. M., 1975, Tests of foreign exchange forecasting models and market efficiency. New York University Working Paper.

Magee, S. P., 1976, The empirical evidence on the monetary approach to the balance of payments and exchange rates. American Economic Review Proceedings. May.

Roll, R. W., 1977, Violations from the law of one price and their implications for differentially denominated assets. U.C.L.A. Working Paper.

Roll, R. W., and B. H. Solnik, 1976, On some parity conditions frequently encountered in international finance. U.C.L.A. Working Paper.

Roll, R. W., and B. H. Solnik, 1977. A pure foreign exchange asset pricing model. Journal of International Economics. May.

Samuelson, P. A., 1964, Theoretical notes on trade problems. Review of Economics and Statistics. May.

Solnik, B. H., 1974. An equilibrium model of the international capital market. Journal of Economic Theory. Aug.

Solnik, B. H., 1975, Multiconsumption, inflation and asset pricing: Some claufying comments. E.I.A.S.M. Working Paper.

11

Capital Controls, Political Risk, and Deviations from Interest-Rate Parity*

Michael P. Dooley and Peter Isard†

INTRODUCTION AND OVERVIEW

In his reinterpretation of the interest-rate parity theorem, Aliber (1973) distinguishes between exchange risk and political risk as determinants of deviations from interest-rate parity. Deviations from interest-rate parity reflect exchange risk when assets are denominated in different currencies and/or political risk when assets are issued in different countries (i.e., under different legal jurisdictions).

It is now well established (see Aliber 1973; Dooley 1974; Herring and Marston 1976) that assets differing essentially in only their currencies of denomination, such as Eurocurrency deposits issued by the same bank, exhibit interest differentials equal to the forward exchange premiums that must be paid to cover against exchange risk,[1] after adjusting for transactions costs.[2] In contrast, it is not well understood to what extent political risk has contributed to disparities between interest rates on assets denominated in the same currency but issued in different political jurisdictions. Aliber (1973, p. 1453) defines the concept of political risk as "the probability that the authority of the state will be interposed between investors in one country and investment opportunities in other countries"—that is, the probability that controls will be imposed on capital flows. By the nature of risk, this concept has nothing to do with existing capital controls per se but, rather, relates to the uncertainty of future capital controls. Thus interest differentials due to the political risk of future capital controls must be distinguished from disparities due to the effective tax that existing controls place on interest earnings.

---

*This article is reprinted, with permission, from *Journal of Political Economy,* 1980, vol. 88, no. 2, pp. 370–384.

†The views expressed herein are solely ours and do not necessarily represent the views of the Federal Reserve System. We have received helpful suggestions from Peter Clark, Jacob Frenkel, Frank McCormick, and two anonymous referees.

[1]It is also recognized that the interest-rate parity condition is an equilibrium relationship among four variables, any three of which can be independently influenced or pegged by policy authorities. Thus the forward premium is influenced fundamentals by the stance of policy.

[2]Branson (1969) and Frenkel and Levich (1975, 1977) have independently estimated that the round-trip cost of 90-day covered arbitrage transactions amounts to about 0.14 to 0.18 percent per annum; but see also McCormick (1979), who suggests that these numbers are overstatements, and the reply by Frenkel and Levich (1979). Prachowny (1970) has modeled the extent to which deviations from interest-rate parity can result from less-than-infinite elasticities of supply and demand for arbitrage funds, and maximal values of these elasticities have been estimated empirically by Frenkel (1973) and Frenkel and Levich (1975); but none of these studies has attempted to relate the esticities of funds to either political or exchange risk. Levi (1977) has modeled the extent to which deviations from interest-rate parity can result from international differences in the taxation of either interest earnings or gains from foreign exchange transactions.

The purpose of this paper is to establish that the interest differential due to political risk, given the prospect of future capital controls, depends essentially on the gross supplies of debt outstanding against different governments and the distribution of world wealth among residents of different political jurisdictions. This point is developed with a simple model of portfolio behavior, which is then used to explain the differential between the interest rate on Euromark deposits in Zurich (EDM) and the interest rate on interbank mark-denominated loans in Frankfurt (GDM) for 3-month maturities between January 1970 and December 1974. During that period Germany placed a series of controls on capital inflows (see the Appendix for a chronology), and the interest differential (GDM—EDM) fluctuated from near zero at the start of 1970 to an annual rate of more than 10 percent in April 1973, and then back to near zero after the controls were effectively removed in late 1973. Our reading of the empirical evidence suggests that most of the swing was due to shifts in the tax that controls effectively imposed on nonresident earnings from assets held in Germany. At its peak between February and October 1973, we estimate that this tax accounted for an interest differential of about 6 percent per annum. An additional differential of up to 2 percent was apparently required, in the context of political risk, to induce nonresidents to hold the excess supply of German outside debt.[3]

THEORETICAL UNDERPINNINGS

Under the modern theory of forward exchange—as developed by Spraos (1953), Tsiang (1959), and Sohmen (1961), who built on the important contribution by Keynes (1923)—the interest differential between mark deposits in Germany and Euromark deposits outside Germany can be attributed to intervention sales of marks by the German Bundesbank. Critical to this analysis is the assumption that private capital mobility was imperfect and, accordingly, that the Bundesbank succeeded in its objective of holding the spot value of the mark below the level to which private speculators would otherwise have pushed it. According to this view, speculative bids for forward marks, coupled with central bank sales of spot marks, opened a covered differential in favor of mark-denominated deposits at German banks. Arbitrageurs purchased marks spot (from the Bundesbank), invested the mark balances in German bank deposits (or other claims on German residents), and sold the marks forward (to private speculators). As the stock of these arbitrage positions grew, arbitrageurs became increasingly averse to increasing the share of their portfolios that was subject to political risk peculiar to nonresident claims on German residents. Individual arbitrageurs could have diversified and reduced their political risk by purchasing mark-denominated claims on non-German banks (i.e., Euromark deposits) instead of German bank deposits. But this would have forced Eurobanks either to hold uncovered mark liabilities subject to exchange risk or to pay a premium to purchase marks forward, or themselves to purchase claims on German residents and accept the associated political risk. Consequently, Eurobanks would have discouraged mark depositors by offering lower yields. Thus the difference between Euromark rates and the interest rates available on claims against German residents can be attributed to the reluctance of nonresident arbitrageurs, including Eurobanks, to acquire a larger stock of claims on German residents.

A graphic representation of this story would show markets equilibrating on the finitely elastic portion of the arbitrage schedule. There is an alternative story, however, which

[3]These estimates explain only four-fifths of the 10 percent peak in the interest-differential.

assumes that markets equilibrated on the infintely elastic (or risk-neutral) portion of the arbitrage schedule in the context of capital controls already in place. This alternative story attributes deviations from interest-rate parity to the effective tax that existing controls placed on nonresident interest earnings in Germany.

These conflicting stories suggest that estimation of the arbitrage schedule is the key to separating the interest differential due to capital controls already in place from the interest differential due to political risk associated with the prospect of additional controls. A major problem with such estimation, however, is that the arbitrage schedule traditionally has been viewed as describing the flow of arbitrage funds, which does not square well with the currently accepted stock-equilibrium model of portfolio behavior.[4] Our alternative approach is to consider the behavior of both the German private sector and nonresidents in choosing their portfolio stocks, implicitly taking account of arbitrage possibilities.

THE MODEL

Consider a world divided into the German private sector, the German government, and nonresidents. Let B denote the stock of mark-denominated claims against the German government, let B_{NR} denote the mark-denominated claims of nonresidents against the German government plus the net mark-denominated claims of nonresidents against the German private sector, and let B_G denote the mark-denominated claims of the German private sector against the German government plus the net mark-denominated claims of the German private sector on nonresidents. The market-clearing condition associated with these claims is

$$B_G + B_{NR} = B. \tag{1}$$

We let W_G and W_{NR} denote the "wealths" of the German private sector and of nonresidents, both valued in marks. The interest rates on mark-denominated claims against German residents and on Euromark and Eurodollar deposits held outside Germany are denoted by GDM, EDM, and EDOL, respectively. We interpret Eurodollar deposits as a composite of all assets not denominated in marks. Capital controls are assumed to apply only to nonresidents' claims against German residents.[5] The expected rate of appreciation of the mark against the dollar is denoted by $E\%X$.

Portfolio demands of the German private sector are viewed as depending on the difference between the yield on marks held in Germany (which exceeds the yield on Euromarks under the capital controls and political risk that we consider) and the expected mark-equivalent yield on Eurodollars, as well as on German wealth.

$$B_G = f(\text{GDM} - \text{EDOL} + E\%X, W_G); \tag{2}$$

Portfolio demands of nonresidents (valued for consistency in marks) are viewed as depending on the yield on mark-denominated claims on Germans relative to both the Euromark

[4]Early expositions of the stock-equilibrium model include McKinnon and Oates (1966), McKinnon (1969), and the two-country version by Girton and Henderson (1973).

[5]The analysis is not affected by the simplifying assumption that all claims against German residents are denominated in marks. More precisely, our regression specification would not be affected by extending the model to include dollar-denominated claims against German residents, paying an interest rate GDOL, provided the differential between GDOL and GDM was identical—as it should be—to the differential between EDOL and EDM.

rate and the expected mark-equivalent yield on Eurodollars and as depending also on both nonresident wealth (valued in marks) and the level of capital controls already in place (CC):

$$B_{NR} = g(\text{GDM} - \text{EDOL} + E\%X,\ \text{GDM} - \text{EDM},\ W_{NR},\ \text{CC}). \tag{3}$$

Our analysis treats as constant both the subjective probability distribution(s) of prospective controls on capital flows into Germany and the subjective probability distribution(s) about the size of future exchange-rate changes.[6] These constant subjective perceptions, which are implicitly embodied in the portfolio demand functions, affect the degrees of substitution between the different assets in the model.

Because of aversion toward exchange risk, the expected rate of appreciation of the mark can differ from the forward premium. The difference is referred to as the exchange risk premium, which we denote by φ. Since the forward premium is known to equal the excess of the Eurodollar rate over the Euromark rate, we can write

$$E\%X = \text{EDOL} - \text{EDM} + \varphi. \tag{4}$$

A positive value of φ reflects an unwillingness of portfolio managers to increase their uncovered holdings of mark-denominated assets unless they expect the mark to appreciate by more than the interest differential in favor of the dollar.

In order to avoid a nonlinear specification hypothesis, we assume that (2) and (3) have linear forms

$$B_G = a_0 + a_1(\text{GDM} - \text{EDOL} + E\%X) + a_2 W_G, \tag{2a}$$

$$B_{NR} = b_0 + b_1(\text{GDM} - \text{EDOL} + E\%X) + b_2(\text{GDM} - \text{EDM}) + b_3 W_{NR} + b_4\text{CC}, \tag{3a}$$

with a_1, b_1, b_2, and b_3 all positive in the normal case.[7] Substituting from (4) yields

$$B_G = a_0 + a_1(\text{GDM} - \text{EDM} + \varphi) + a_2 W_G, \tag{2b}$$

$$B_{NR} = b_0 + b_1(\text{GDM} - \text{EDM} + \varphi) + b_2(\text{GDM} - \text{EDM}) + b_3 W_{NR} + b_4\text{CC}. \tag{3b}$$

Together, conditions (1), (2b), and (3b) imply

$$\text{GDM} - \text{EDM} = c_0 + c_1 B - c_2 W_G - c_3 W_{NR} - c_4\varphi + c_5\text{CC}, \tag{5}$$

with c_1, c_2, c_3, and c_4 all positive in the normal case.

Condition (5) can be viewed as

$$\text{GDM} - \text{EDM} = \text{DIFF}_{PR} + \text{DIFF}_{CC}, \tag{5a}$$

where

$$\text{DIFF}_{PR} = c_0 + c_1 B - c_2 W_G - c_3 W_{NR} - c_4\varphi \tag{6}$$

represents the interest differential due to the political risk associated with prospective capital controls, and

$$\text{DIFF}_{CC} = c_5\text{CC} \tag{7}$$

[6] Thus we assume constant perceived variances of future exchange rates.

[7] Implicitly we assume that a_1, b_1, and b_2 are finite, reflecting risk aversion.

is the interest differential due to the effective tax imposed by capital controls already in place.[8]

Condition (6) reveals that the interest differential due to political risk is negatively related to the exchange risk premium. The latter is not an exogenous variable, and we have argued in Dooley and Isard (1979) that the exchange risk premium that portfolio managers must expect to earn on their uncovered holdings of mark-denominated assets is an increasing function of the stock of outside mark-denominated assets and a decreasing function of wealth variables, *ceteris paribus*. If we represent φ as a linear function of B, W_G, and W_{NR}, we can substitute into (6) to obtain

$$\mathrm{DIFF}_{PR} = d_0 + d_1 B + d_2 W_G + d_3 W_{NR}. \tag{6a}$$

By the arguments above we do not have prior information about the signs of the parameters in condition (6a). Note, however, that the interest differential due to political risk depends on the stock of gross claims against the German government and the distribution of world wealth between the German private sector and nonresidents.[9]

For the purposes of constructing measures of the independent variables and of interpreting the regression results, it is useful to note that B, W_G, and W_{NR} are each linear combinations of the cumulative German budget deficit (DEBT), official German holdings of foreign exchange reserves (RES), and the net stock of German claims on nonresidents that have been acquired through the accumulation of German current account surpluses (ΣCAS). In particular, claims against the German government are issued either to finance budget deficits or to acquire foreign exchange reserves; thus (if changes in the valuation of reserves are neglected)

$$B = \mathrm{DEBT} + \mathrm{RES}. \tag{8}$$

German private wealth is accumulated either as savings that are the counterpart of government deficits or as savings that are lent to nonresidents as the counterpart of current account surpluses; hence (again ignoring changes in valuation)

$$W_G = \mathrm{DEBT} + \Sigma\mathrm{CAS}. \tag{9}$$

Finally, the wealth concept on which we are focusing excludes claims on real assets, so global net worth must add to zero; and since $B - \mathrm{RES}$ represents the net debt of the German government, this implies

$$W_{NR} + W_G = B - \mathrm{RES}. \tag{10}$$

Thus, after substitution from (8) and (9),

$$W_{NR} = -\Sigma\mathrm{CAS}. \tag{11}$$

[8]This separation relies on our assumption that the probability of prospective capital controls was perceived to be constant throughout the sample period and was therefore uncorrelated with the level of existing capital controls. The assumption is strong and could be avoided by constructing a proxy variable to represent the probability of prospective capital controls. Allowing this probability to vary, however, would complicate the analysis by requiring us to separate the anticipatory encouragement to capital inflows from the discouragement that would ultimately result from an increase in the perceived probability of prospective controls.

[9]This conclusion is insensitive to the currency composition of gross claims against the German government, insofar as nonresidents perceive that prospective capital controls would apply equally to all nonresident claims against Germany, independent of their currency composition.

When it is recalled that nonresidents include official as well as private nonresidents, so that private nonresidents' claims on official nonresidents are netted out in W_{NR}, conditions (9) and (11) are seen to be symmetric.

DATA SOURCES AND THE REPRESENTATION OF CAPITAL CONTROLS

Our estimates are based on the following data. The 3-month Frankfurt interbank loan rate at or near the end of the month is GDM, as published by Morgan Guaranty Trust Company in *World Financial Markets*. The EDM is the 3-month Euro-DM deposit rate in Zurich, at or near the end of the month, from *London Financial Times* and international records of the Swiss Bank Corporation.[10] The DEBT is the cumulative sum, from an estimated end-of-1969 initial value, of the flow of German federal government indebtedness. The RES is measured as German official holdings of gold and external assets. The quantities DEBT, RES, and CAS are taken from various issues of the *Monthly Report* of the Bundesbank, tables VII.8, IX.6a, and IX.1, respectively. The variables B, W_G, and W_{NR} are constructed according to definitions (8), (9), and (11). The initial values of these variables are not important to the regression results, since errors in these initial values affect only the estimated intercept parameter and not the estimate of the interest differential due to political risk.

As described in the Appendix, controls on capital inflows were imposed or tightened in five major doses and a number of subsequent modifications.[11] For three of these doses it is impossible to compute from microeconomic principles the effective tax that controls imposed, and for the other two doses the computation is difficult. Accordingly, we have chosen to estimate the effects of capital controls from macroeconomic data under two somewhat arbitrary representations of the capital controls variable CC.

Our less sophisticated representation of CC is a step function constructed with five zero-one dummy variables, corresponding to the five major doses in which controls were imposed. Our other representation of CC assumes that the effective tax imposed by controls increased continuously between the first dose of controls in April 1970 and the last dose in February 1973. Here we follow Wilton's (1975) technique for representing structural shifts, as modified by Reid (1977), which allows us to specify CC as a polynomial of any degree m. We have chosen $m = 3$ as the mimimum value that allows for an inflection point. Given that the capital controls applied only to *increases* in nonresident claims on Germans, we assume in both representations that the effective tax imposed by controls dropped to zero when capital began to flow strongly out of Germany in the fourth quarter of 1973.[12]

[10]Because GDM—EDM is constructed as the difference between a loan rate and a deposit rate, our measure of the interest differential includes transactions costs (i.e., the natural spread between loan rates and deposit rates), and our estimates of the constant term (d_o) will be biased upward. This size of this bias, however, is fairly small relative to the estimated constant terms that we report in table 1. Accordingly, the empirical conclusions that we draw are not substantially affected when the bias is ignored.

[11]Not all of the doses were directed at bank deposits, but interest rates on bank deposits clearly responded to controls that directly affected interest rates payable on alternative assets.

[12]Official German tabulations of the overall balance of capital transactions (see the *Monthly Report* of the Bundesbank, table IX.1) show net inflows of DM 14.0, 0.6, and 4.2 billion during the first three quarters of 1973, followed by successive quarterly net outflows of DM 6.1, 10.4, 2.4, 7.4, and 5.2 billion.

EMPIRICAL RESULTS

Table 1 presents our regression results. The parameters were estimated by the ordinary least-squares technique using the Cochrane-Orcutt correction. The parameter estimates associated with each set of capital control variables are appropriate, with the exception of the equation (2) estimate that the effect of capital controls declined insignificantly in March 1972. Figure 1 compares the observed and fitted time paths of the dependent variable with the time paths of the interest differential that equations (1) and (2) attribute to existing capital controls. The two equations respectively attribute interest differentials of 5.6 (= 12.9 − 38.5 + 31.2) and 6.03 percent per annum to capital controls in place during their tightest interval between February and October 1973. These estimates represent 71 and 77 percent, respectively, of the average interest differential observed during this period and about the same percentages of the average interest differentials that the equations explain for this period.

The remainder of the explained interest differential can be attributed to political risk. The estimates presented in table 1 tell an interesting story about how the political risk premium responds to changes in wealth variables or asset stocks. Bearing in mind that asset stocks and wealth variables cannot shift in isolation but, rather, are constrained by condition (10), we can note the following.

First, when mark-denominated claims on the German government are increased without intervention and holding constant private German wealth, therefore implying an increase in nonresident wealth, the political risk premium is estimated to increase. Nonresidents will not allocate the entire increment in their portfolios to additional claims on German residents unless the premium for bearing political risk is increased.

Second, even when the increase in mark-denominated claims on the German government is matched entirely by an increase in private German wealth, with no change in nonresident wealth and no intervention, the political risk premium will increase to accommodate the desires of private Germans to diversify the increase in their wealth

TABLE 1

Regression Results*

1. $$GDM - EDM = \underset{(-.904)}{-14.0} + \underset{(1.23)}{.0235}\,B + \underset{(.857)}{.123}\,W_G + \underset{(1.25)}{.258}\,W_{NR} + \underset{(2.07)}{12.9}\,Z - \underset{(-2.62)}{38.5}\,Z^2 + \underset{(3.43)}{31.2}\,Z^3, \quad \bar{R}^2 = .895 \quad \rho = \underset{(3.65)}{.43} \quad \text{D-W} = 1.90$$

where Z increases linearly from zero in March 1970 to one in February 1973, remains at one between February and October 1973, and is zero prior to March 1970 and after October 1973.†

2. $$GDM - EDM = \underset{(-1.78)}{-21.3} - \underset{(-.132)}{.00214}\,B + \underset{(2.04)}{.228}\,W_G + \underset{(2.44)}{.399}\,W_{NR} + \begin{cases} \underset{(.111)}{.0725} \text{ from April 1970 through April 1971} \\ \underset{(1.40)}{.904} \text{ from May 1971 through February 1972} \\ \underset{(.528)}{.395} \text{ from March 1972 through May 1972} \\ \underset{(3.01)}{2.02} \text{ from June 1972 through January 1973} \\ \underset{(9.18)}{6.03} \text{ from February 1973 through October 1973} \end{cases}$$

$\bar{R}^2 = .919 \qquad \rho = \underset{(2.58)}{.318}$

D-W = 1.95

*The dependent variable is measured in percent per annum. B, W_G, and W_{NR} are in billions of DM. The Cochrane-Orcutt procedure was used to correct for first-order serial correlation. Numbers in parentheses are t-values. The sample period consists of 60 monthly observations from January 1970 through December 1974.

†The specification of Z conforms with the Wilton-Reid technique for allowing the estimated interest differential due to capital controls to shift continuously (along a third-degree polynomial path) between March 1970 and February 1973.

FIGURE 1

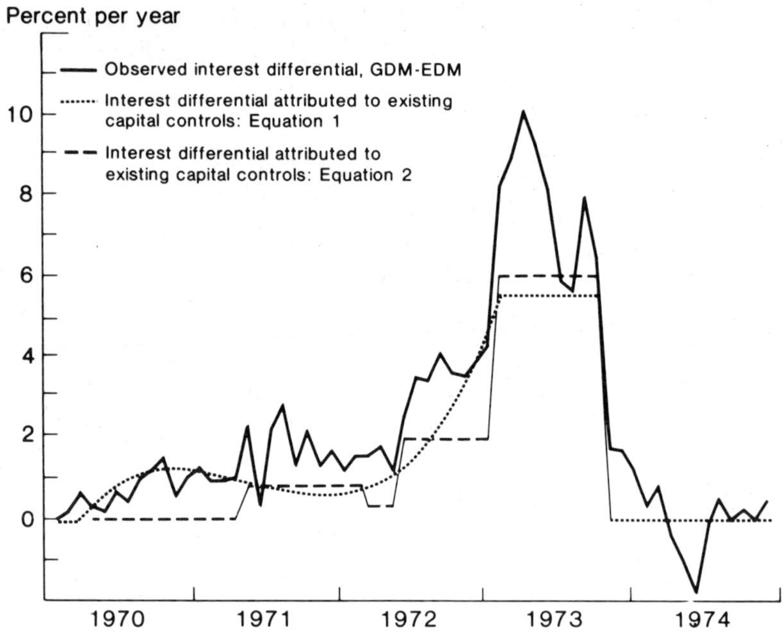

between mark-denominated and dollar-denominated assets. Such diversification can be accomplished only by inducing nonresidents to increase their mark-denominated claims on Germany and their dollar-denominated liabilities to Germans.

Third, for the general case in which the stock of mark-denominated claims on the German government is increased without intervention, the estimated increase in the political risk premium depends positively on the extent to which nonresident wealth increases relative to private German wealth as the counterpart of the increase in official German debt.

The coefficient on B is insignificant in both regressions, suggesting that the political risk premium does not increase in response to an intervention purchase of exchange reserves (dollars) that increases the stock of mark-denominated claims on the German government. Net claims on the German government are not changed by the intervention. But the increased political risk that nonresidents bear by holding an increased stock of gross claims on Germany cannot be presumed to be offset by the increased political risk that Germans assume by holding an increased stock of reserves, since during the sample period there was virtually no prospect that these reserve holdings would be discouraged by imposing capital controls (through either isolated or retaliatory policy actions).

The failure of the regression results to show a change in the political risk premium in response to exchange market intervention can be explained, however, by recalling from condition (6) that the political risk premium is negatively related to the exchange risk premium. The increase in the gross stock of mark-denominated claims on the German government not only pushes up the political risk premium directly by increasing the stock of claims subject to political risk but also pushes down the political risk premium indirectly by raising the exchange risk premium that portfolio managers can expect to earn on

FIGURE 2

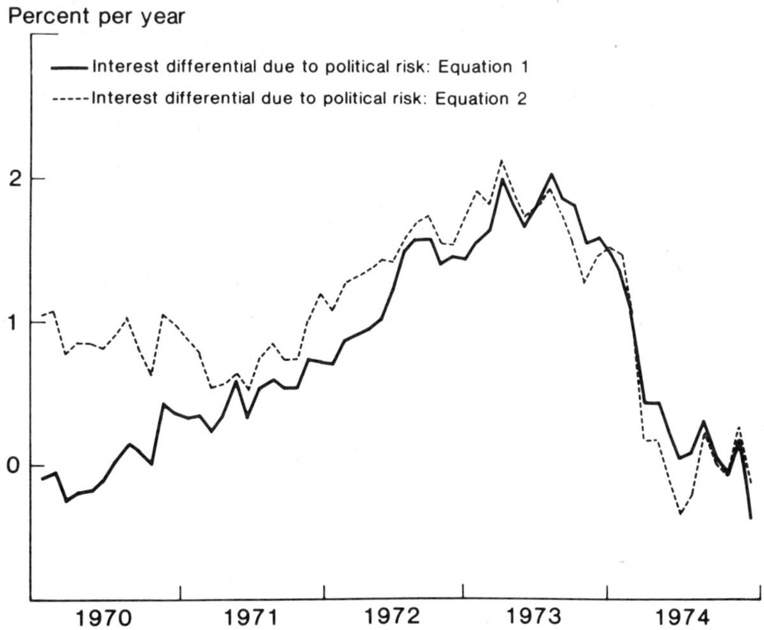

their increased stock of mark-denominated assets. The regression results suggest that these opposite effects on the political risk premium are largely offsetting.

Finally, as shown in figure 2, both regressions estimate that the political risk premium peaked at roughly 2 percent per annum. Equation (1) puts the peak at 2.0 percent at the end of July 1973; equation (2) puts the peak at 2.1 percent at the end of March 1973. The interest differential peaked at more than 10 percent at the end of April 1973.

SUMMARY AND CONCLUSIONS

This paper has explored Aliber's (1973) notion that political risk associated with prospective capital controls can lead to deviations from interest-rate parity. Using a simple model of portfolio behavior, we have established the theoretical point that, given the prospect of controls on capital flows into a particular country, the interest differential due to political risk depends essentially on the gross stock of outside claims against residents of that country and on the distribution of world wealth between residents and nonresidents.

Our empirical focus is on the differential between Euromark rates and interest rates on mark-denominated loans in Germany during the early 1970s, when Germany imposed a series of controls on capital inflows. The empirical problem is to separate the interest differential due to the political risk associated with prospective controls from the differential due to the effective tax imposed by existing controls. This effective tax cannot be computed from microeconomic principles in the German case, so we are forced to be somewhat arbitrary in modeling and estimating it.

Our reading of the empirical evidence suggests that most of the swing in the interest differential during the 1970–74 period was due to changes in the effective tax imposed by the series of capital controls that were put in place. At times, however, an estimated differential of as much as 2 percent per annum was required, in the context of political risk, to induce nonresidents to hold the excess supply of German outside debt, given the distribution of wealth between the German private sector and nonresidents.

APPENDIX

A CHRONOLOGY OF GERMAN CAPITAL CONTROLS[13]

I. On April 1, 1970, the Bundesbank reintroduced a special reserve ratio on the growth of banks' liabilities to nonresidents. With the exception of the 4-month period from September through December 1971, when liabilities of both residents and nonresidents carried equal special reserve ratios, bank liabilities to nonresidents were subject to higher reserve requirements than bank liabilities to residents. This program served two purposes. First, it induced German banks to pay lower deposit rates to nonresidents than to residents. (This effect of the program probably was less important after May 1971, when controls were tightened to make payment of interest on deposits held by nonresidents subject to prior approval by the Bundesbank.) Second, it absorbed reserves and thereby "sterilized" the increase in the monetary base resulting from bank-reported capital inflows.

II. On May 10, 1971, interest payments on nonresident bank deposits exceeding DM 50,000 were made subject to the prior approval of the Bundesbank, which was not normally granted.

III. On March 1, 1972, the federal government introduced a cash deposit requirement (*Bardepot*) of 40 percent on most types of new credits by nonresidents to German nonbanks that exceeded DM 2 million per individual. The cash deposit, held by the Bundesbank, did not bear interest. The deposit was increased to 50 percent effective on July 1, 1972, and the exempt amount was simultaneously reduced to DM 0.5 million. The exemption was further reduced to DM 0.05 million on January 1, 1973. On January 30, 1974, the cash deposit requirement was reduced to 20 percent and the exemption raised to DM 0.1 million. In mid-September 1974 the cash requirement was eliminated retroactively from August 1, 1974.

IV. On June 29, 1972, the federal government decreed that purchases of fixed-interest securities by nonresidents would require prior authorization. Fixed-interest securities included all maturities of bonds: for example, all bank bonds, mortgage bonds, communal bonds, industrial bonds, and public authority bonds. In practice, the authorization requirement was equivalent to the prohibition of such purchases. The authorization requirement for all but short-term securities (with fewer than 4 years to maturity) was terminated on January 30, 1974.

V. On February 5, 1973, the federal governmment extended its prior authorization requirement to the acquisition of domestic shares and mutual funds by nonresidents and to the raising of loans abroad by residents, including trade credits.

[13]Based on various issues of the *Monthly Report* of the German Bundesbank.

Controls now applied to almost all capital transactions with nonresidents and no longer just to transactions in fixed-interest securities. These additional measures were terminated on January 30, 1974.

REFERENCES

Aliber, Robert Z. "The Interest Rate Parity Theorem: A Reinterpretation." *J.P.E.* 81, no. 6 (November/December 1973):1451–59.

Branson, William H. "The Minimum Covered Interest Differential Needed for International Arbitrage Activity." *J.P.E.* 77, no. 6 (November/December 1969):1028–35.

Dooley, Michael P. "A Model of Arbitrage and Short-Term Capital Flows." International Finance Discussion Paper no. 40, Federal Reserve Board, Washington, 1974.

Dooley, Michael P., and Isard, Peter. "The Portfolio-Balance Model of Exchange Rates." International Finance Discussion Paper no. 141, Federal Reserve Board, Washington, 1979.

Frenkel, Jacob A. "Elasticities and the Interest Parity Theory." *J.P.E.* 81, no. 3 (May/June 1973):741–47.

Frenkel, Jacob A., and Levich, Richard M. "Covered Interest Arbitrage: Unexploited Profits?" *J.P.E.* 83, no. 2 (April 1975):325–38.

______. "Transaction Costs and Interest Arbitrage: Tranquil versus Turbulent Periods." *J.P.E.* 85, no. 6 (December 1977):1209–26.

______. "Covered Interest Arbitrage and Unexploited Profits? Reply." *J.P.E.* 87, no. 2 (April 1979):418–22.

Girton, Lance, and Henderson, Dale W. "A Two-Country Model of Financial Capital Movements as Stock Adjustments with Emphasis on the Effects of Central Bank Policy." International Finance Discussion Paper no. 24, Federal Reserve Board, Washington, 1973.

Herring, Richard J., and Marston, Richard C. "The Forward Market and Interest Rates in the Eurocurrency and National Money Markets." In *Eurocurrencies and the International Monetary System*, edited by Carl H. Stem, John H. Makin, and Dennis E. Logue. Washington: American Enterprise Inst. Public Policy Res., 1976.

Keynes, John Maynard. *A Tract on Monetary Reform*. London: Macmillan, 1923.

Levi, Maurice D. "Taxation and 'Abnormal' International Capital Flows." *J.P.E.* 85, no. 3 (June 1977):635–46.

McCormick, Frank. "Covered Interest Arbitrage: Unexploited Profits? Comment." *J.P.E.* 87, no. 2 (April 1979):411–17.

McKinnon, Ronald I. "Portfolio Balance and International Payments Adjustment." In *Monetary Problems of the International Economy*, edited by Robert A. Mundell and Alexander K. Swoboda. Chicago: Univ. Chicago Press, 1969.

McKinnon, Ronald I., and Oates, Wallace E. "The Implications of International Economic Integration for Monetary, Fiscal, and Exchange-Rate Policy." Studies in International Finance no. 16, Princeton Univ., Internal Finance Section, 1966.

Prachowny, Martin F. J. "A Note on Interest Parity and the Supply of Arbitrage Funds." *J.P.E.* 78, no. 3 (May/June 1970):540–45.

Reid, Frank. "Dummy Variables with a Transitional Phase." *Canadian J. Econ* 10 (May 1977):326–29.

Sohmen, Egon. *Flexible Exchange Rates: Theory and Controversy*. Chicago: Univ. Chicago Press, 1961.

Spraos, John. "The Theory of Forward Exchange and Recent Practice." *Manchester School Econ. and Soc. Studies* 21 (May 1953):87–117.

Tsiang, Sho-Chieh. "The Theory of Forward Exchange and Effects of Government Intervention on the Forward Exchange Market." *Internat. Monetary Fund Staff Papers* 7 (April 1959):75–106.

Wilton, David A. "Structural Shift with an Interstructural Transition Function." *Canadian J. Econ.* 8 (August 1975):423–32.

12

Capital Controls and Interest Rate Parity: The Japanese Experience, 1978–81*

Ichiro Otani and Siddharth Tiwari†

Over the past several years, the exchange rate for the Japanese yen has fluctuated widely, as has the intensity of capital controls. At times when the yen rate was believed to have "overshot" some unspecified appropriate level, the Japanese Government introduced measures to influence capital flows in an attempt to narrow the amplitude of exchange rate fluctuations. For example, in early 1978, when an appreciation of the yen was widely expected, the Government introduced capital controls to reduce net inflows and to moderate the yen appreciation; in 1979 and early 1980, when the Government thought that the yen had weakened too rapidly, measures aimed at inducing net inflows were introduced. However, since December 1980, when the Government implemented a law embodying the principle that all transactions in foreign currency may be carried out freely unless expressly restricted, capital movements have, in principle, been virtually free of controls. These policy changes are frequently credited with having had an important impact on (a) measured deviations from interest rate parity, (b) the exchange rate, and (c) the efficiency of the foreign exchange market.

The main purpose of this paper is to examine the extent to which these capital controls or the absence of them have influenced deviations from interest rate parity during the period 1978–81. An attempt is also made to measure the impact of such capital controls on distortions in the foreign exchange-cum-securities market during that period. Questions regarding the effectiveness of capital controls on influencing the exchange rate and the impact of these controls on the market efficiency will not be dealt with in this paper.

The approach adopted builds upon work by Frenkel and Levich (1975, 1977).[1] Utilizing basic price theory, it can be shown that the introduction of transaction costs into the Marshallian demand and supply apparatus has the effect of creating a band around the demand curve. Even though the realized price may deviate from the equilibrium price (which would prevail without transaction costs), the market would still be in equilibrium in the sense that there would be no unexploited profits.[2] Similarly, the introduction of

---

*This article is reprinted, with permission, from *International Monetary Fund Staff Papers,* vol. 28, 1981 pp. 793–815.

†The authors have benefited from discussions with Prabhat Goyal and Michael Mussa of the University of Chicago, John Makin of the University of Washington, and colleagues in the Fund.

[1]Dooley and Isard (1980) constructed a model of portfolio behavior to study effects of German capital controls on deviations from interest rate parity.

[2]Throughout this paper, the term "equilibrium" will be interpreted as a state where all profits have been exploited.

transaction costs into the foreign exchange and securities markets will create a band (neutral band in the Frenkel-Levich terminology) around the interest rate parity line. It can be shown that all covered interest differentials falling within this band are equilibrium points.[3] The introduction of capital controls will increase the cost of transactions to market participants and consequently increase the width of the "neutral band." The comparison of two such bands, where one reflects transactions in a market with free movements of capital while the other reflects controls on such movements, will provide a quantitative indicator of the effect of capital controls.

The imposition of controls may also have the effect of changing the expectations of market participants regarding possible capital controls in the future. This will determine, in part, whether the burden of adjustment of the forward premium (if any) owing to the imposition of controls falls on the spot exchange rate or the forward exchange rate or both. A comparison of the changes in the width of the band (owing to capital controls) with changes in the width of the band (owing to capital controls) with changes in interest rates (on domestic and foreign assets) and the forward premium shows the extent to which capital controls have been successful in affecting the exchange rates. This issue, although important, is not pursued in this paper.

The remainder of this paper is organized as follows. Section I presents an overview of the issues involved in discussing the relationships between capital controls and measured deviations from interest rate parity. Section II briefly describes the methodology that is to be used to quantify the influences exerted by capital controls in foreign exchange markets. Section III presents empirical results obtained from daily observation of exchange rates and interest rates in the Tokyo and London foreign exchange markets for the period 1978–81. Section IV summarizes the major findings and presents concluding remarks. Appendix I in the original paper provides a technical note on selecting an appropriate data set of observations necessary for the estimation of the neutral band. Appendix II in the original paper contains data descriptions, sources, and definitions.

I. AN OVERVIEW OF THE ISSUES

Consider two worlds, A and B. In each world, assets may be denominated in different currencies. The distinguishing characteristics of World A are that all assets are traded freely, and there are no institutional controls, taxes, tariffs, or quotas on transactions by residents of different regions. In contrast, in World B, the government of one region imposes controls on transactions between its residents and those of other regions. The exchange markets that we observe today are characterized by elements of both Worlds A and B. In addition, in each country, there is a unique combination of the taxes, tariffs, and quotas employed, and within each country, the tax/tariff/quota structure is applied differently to goods, factors, and securities.

Suppose that the portfolio of the economic agent is initially invested in domestic securities. The agent can either continue to hold assets denominated in domestic currency and earn income at the domestic interest rate (r_d) or transfer funds abroad to hold assets denominated in foreign currency and earn a return at the foreign rate of interest (r_f). Given an interest rate differential, if the forward exchange rate (F) (number of domestic

[3]If assets are not denominated in the currency of the same political jurisdiction, this ban will reflect both transaction costs and political risk (see Aliber (1973)).

currency units per unit of foreign currency) is high relative to the spot rate (S)—that is, if there is a covered interest rate differential in favor of foreign assets—agents will purchase foreign exchange at the spot rate, invest in foreign securities, earn income at the foreign interest rate, and buy a forward contract to convert back to domestic currency at the forward rate. Since all agents possess the same information set, arbitrage implies that if one agent can make profits then all can. However, if all attempt to make profits simultaneously, then no one can. Something in the system must change. Either the forward premium will adjust or the foreign interest rate differential will change to bring the system into equilibrium.

Much of the theoretical literature formalizing the relationship between the asset and exchange markets under perfect competition has come under the heading of interest rate parity theory and posits that in World A the current money market interest differential on assets denominated in different currencies is uniquely related to differentials between spot and forward exchange rates. Formally, in the absence of any distortions, this relationship is expressed as

$$\frac{(1 + r_d)}{(1 + r_f)} = \frac{F}{S} \tag{1}$$

or

$$\frac{(1 + r_d)S}{(1 + r_f)F} = 1 \tag{2}$$

where

S = number of units of domestic currency per unit of foreign currency for immediate delivery (say, at time t_0)

F = number of units of domestic currency per unit of foreign currency for delivery at some time (t_1) in the future ($t_0 < t_1$)

r_f = foreign interest rate that can be secured for the period from t_0 to t_1

r_d = domestic interest rate that can be secured for the period from t_0 to t_1

Thus, in World A, where no distortions exist (i.e., free capital mobility and flexible exchange rates in the context here), the interest rate differential between interest-bearing domestic and foreign assets will identically determine the differential between the forward and the spot exchange rates. Put differently, the forward premium or discount is completely determined by the current interest rate differential.

As will be evident to the reader, it is not surprising that conditions for interest rate parity may be found not to hold with strict equality in any empirical exercise designed to verify that proposition. In an illuminating survey, Officer and Willett (1970) identified two causes for deviations from interest rate parity. One is transaction costs and the other is a positively sloped (i.e., a less than perfectly elastic) "medium"-run or "long"-run supply curve of funds for arbitrage. Transaction costs depend on the differential costs of trading across different currencies and include not only brokerage costs but also information and time costs. One would expect the brokerage cost to vary with the volume of transactions, while the information cost would depend on the number of outlets searched and the marginal benefit from searching. The time cost will vary with the wage/shadow-wage rate or the marginal disutility of work.

Another significant contribution pertaining to the empirical verification of the interest rate parity theory was made by Aliber (1973). He argued that assets denominated in different currencies and issued in different countries carry with them two additional risks. First, different currencies imply that an economic agent, when formulating his portfolio, will have to incorporate the possibility of a change in the exchange rate. Second, assets issued in different countries carry with them different political risks. Differences in political risk can be thought of as arising out of different tax/tariff structures or capital controls. Political risk will not only reflect the existing structure of controls but also the markets' perception of future government actions based on past and current information. Aliber concluded that, for noncomparable assets (i.e., assets issued in different political jurisdictions), political risk accounts for much of the observed differential.

The above discussion suggests that the relationship presented by equation (1) would not hold exactly in a world where transaction costs exist. Typically, for every transaction, there is a positive transaction cost associated with it, whether it is a transaction between securities in the same currency or across different currencies. Furthermore, the presence of controls will increase transaction costs.[4]

The role of transaction costs in the foreign exchange and securities markets can be illustrated by the following simple example. Let us examine the sequence of transactions that an individual in Japan will need to consider in order to determine the portfolio that he should hold. Suppose the individual borrows yen-denominated funds amounting to x at the rate of interest r_d. Let the per unit transaction cost associated with borrowing the funds be t_d. For this individual, the total cost of borrowing the yen-denominated funds, including the transaction costs, is $x(1 + r_d)(1 + t_d)$.[5] This individual now sells yen at the prevailing spot exchange rate, S, and pays in yen the per unit transaction cost, t_s, for the sale in the spot market. Through such an exchange, the total amount of foreign currency (U. S. dollars) that the individual can obtain is $x/S(1 + t_s)$, which is equal to, say, y. These y dollars will now be invested in the dollar-denominated assets, which will yield a return of r_f. Investment in the dollar-denominated assets carries with it the per unit transaction cost of t_f, which must be paid in dollars. At the time of investing in the dollar-denominated assets, the individual also makes a forward contract to exchange $y(1 + r_f)/(1 + t_f)$ dollars at the prevailing forward exchange rate, F, and pays the associated transaction cost of t_F in dollars.[6] Thus, the amount of yen the individual expects to get by investing in the dollar-denominated securities is $y(1 + r_f)F/(1 + t_f)(1 + t_F)$, or $x.F(1 + r_f)/S(1 + t_s)(1 + t_f)(1 + t_F)$.[7] The individual will continue to borrow the yen-denominated funds and go through the sequence of the transactions outlined above as long as equation (3) is satisfied.

[4]Transaction costs defined in this paper include not only brokerage fees but also costs in terms of taxes, search time, political risks, and ways in which market participants need to maneuver around any capital controls.

[5]It is assumed that transaction costs are paid to lenders at the time of loan maturity.

[6]It is assumed that the total transaction costs associated with buying and selling securities are paid at the time of selling the securities.

[7]Given the nature of previous work in this area (e.g., Frenkel and Levich (1975, 1977)), there is need to briefly elaborate on the particular specification used here. Frenkel and Levich assumed that costs were paid in the currency bought and thus the effect of the introduction of transaction costs was a lower realized rate of return.

$$x(1 + r_d)(1 + t_d) < xF(1 + r_f)/S(1 + t_S)(1 + t_f)(1 + t_F) \tag{3}$$

or

$$\frac{(1 + r_d)S}{(1 + r_f)F} < \frac{1}{(1 + t_d)(1 + t_f)(1 + t_S)(1 + t_F)} \tag{4}$$

Under the circumstances governed by equation (4), capital moves out of the home country and into the foreign country.

Analogously, capital moves into the home country from abroad if equation (5) is satisfied.

$$(1 + t_d)(1 + t_f)(1 + t_S)(1 + t_F) < \frac{S(1 + r_d)}{F(1 + r_f)} \tag{5}$$

Since each expression for costs associated with transactions in the foreign exchange and securities markets is a very small fraction, total costs (TC) can be approximated by $(t_d + t_f + t_s + t_F)$. The expression for capital flows seeking unexploited profits can be rewritten as

$$(1 + TC) < \frac{S(1 + r_d)}{F(1 + r_f)} \tag{6}$$

and

$$\frac{1}{(1 + TC)} > \frac{S(1 + r_d)}{F(1 + r_f)} \tag{7}$$

If no unexploited profits exist, the following condition must be satisfied:

$$1 - TC < \frac{S(1 + r_d)}{F(1 + r_f)} < 1 + TC \tag{8}$$

where

$$1 - TC \simeq \frac{1}{1 + TC}$$

or

$$\left| \frac{S(1 + r_d)}{F(1 + r_f)} - 1 \right| < TC \tag{9}$$

Actual deviations from interest rate parity, therefore, are expected to be scattered around zero within a "neutral band" limited by the total transaction costs (TC), if no unexploited profits exist.

II. METHODOLOGY

To empirically study the effect of capital controls on transaction costs, or the deviations from the interest rate parity line, two empirical counterparts to World A and World B have been chosen.

However, the mirror image of this specification has been adopted here. Following Deardorff (1979), it has been assumed that costs are paid in the currency that is being sold. This specification shifts the focus from a lower realized rate of return to an increased cost (in current value terms) of undertaking the specified transaction. It is useful to note that for small transaction costs the two specifications are virtually the same.

World A is represented by London (Euro-currency market), where transactions are free of controls, taxes, and quotas so that capital is perfectly mobile. Two assets have been chosen: one denominated in Japanese yen (Euro-yen deposits) and another denominated in U. S. dollars (Euro-dollar deposits).[8] It can be hypothesized that any observed deviation from the theoretical (and deterministic) relationship in equation (1), defined as the "gap in London" (G_{LON}), is randomly distributed[9] and has the expected value of zero; that is

$$G_{LON} \sim R(0, \sigma^2_{LON}) \tag{10}$$

where

$$G_{LON} \equiv \frac{(1 + r_{ey})S_{LON}}{(1 + r_{ed})F_{LON}} - 1$$

r_{ey} = interest rate on three-month Euro-yen deposits

r_{ed} = interest rate on three-month Euro-dollar deposits

S_{LON} = Japanese yen/U.S. dollar spot exchange rate in London

F_{LON} = Japanese yen/U.S. dollar three-month forward exchange rate in London

World B is perceived as consisting of two locations—Tokyo and London. Since there has been a variety of controls on capital movements between the two cities, any observed deviation from equation (1), defined as the "gap in Tokyo" (G_{TKY}) will not be randomly distributed around a mean of zero; that is,

$$G_{TKY} \nsim R(\phi, \sigma^2_{TKY}) \qquad \phi \neq 0 \tag{11}$$

where

$$G_{TKY} = \frac{(1 + r_{gk})S_{TKY}}{(1 + r_{ed})F_{TKY}} - 1$$

r_{gk} = interest rate on three-month Gensaki[10] bonds

S_{TKY} = Japanese yen/U.S. dollar spot exchange rate in Tokyo

F_{TKY} = Japanese yen/U.S. dollar three-month forward exchange rate in Tokyo

[8]The interest rates on these assets are freely determined by market forces; in other words, they are not institutionally fixed.

[9]Randomness of the variables is due mainly to measurement problems—that is, "white noise"—which can be caused by recorded data that may not strictly correspond to the market rate. The differences between the recorded and the true market rate may be attributable to, say, rounding errors, differences in timing of sampling, or pure mistakes.

[10]Bonds sold with the repurchase agreement. Interest rates on the Gensaki bonds are determined essentially by market forces but may be subject to distortions owing to imperfections in the market.

To investigate the effect of controls, it is important to distinguish between (a) disparities owing to pure transaction costs and those owing to controls and (b) changes in disparity owing to the effect of a specific control promulgated by the government as opposed to a change in disparity reflecting a change in international economic conditions. Fortunately, G_{LON} is, in the aggregate, a joint indicator of both pure transaction costs and the effects of the world economic situation. Thus, the difference between G_{TKY} and G_{LON} captures the net effect of capital controls. If the hypotheses advanced by equations (10) and (11) are supported by empirical data, then the following relationship can be used to quantify the effect of controls on covered interest rate differentials between Tokyo and London.

$$C_{TL} = E(|G_{TKY}| - |G_{LON}|) \tag{12}$$

where

C_{TL} = measure of the effect of controls on transactions between Tokyo and London

E = expectations operator

Since most of the deviations from interest rate parity can be explained by "transaction costs," as defined earlier, C_{TL} represents opportunity costs that market participants have to incur if they are to evade capital controls in order to make a profit from covered interest rate differentials.

III. EMPIRICAL RESULTS

This section presents the empirical results of testing the hypotheses represented in equations (10) and (11) and quantifies the extent of capital controls represented by equation (12). The period under study runs from January 1978 to March 1981. Daily observations are used. The statistical results are followed by a brief summary of changes in capital controls that can explain the value of C_{TL}.

Hypotheses Testing

That the gap in London, as represented by equation (10), is randomly distributed narrowly around a mean of zero implies that there are negligible transaction costs in the London market and that if market participants were to trade on every non-zero value of the gap in London they would, on the average, make zero profits. Similarly, the hypothesis that the gap in Tokyo, as represented by equation (11), is not randomly distributed around a non-zero mean implies that if market participants were to trade on every non-zero value of the gap in Tokyo they may end up with non-zero profits. The hypothesis also implies that transaction costs (which account for the gap) are not negligible. However, the persistence of a significant non-zero gap would, a priori, indicate that the market is not free of controls. Thus, a reliable check of government intervention would be to examine basic statistics on gaps to determine whether or not they are randomly dispersed around a mean of zero.

Table 1 summarizes the means and t-statistics of the measured deviations from interest rate parity in the London and Tokyo markets. The results clearly support the hypothesis that the measured disparities are, by and large, randomly distributed around the mean of

TABLE 1

Japan: Mean, Standard Deviation, and *t*-Statistics of Deviations from Interest Rate Parity[1]

Period	Deviations in London			Deviations in Tokyo		
	Mean[2]	Standard deviation[2]	*t*-statistics	Mean[2]	Standard deviation[2]	*t*-statistics
1978						
First quarter	−0.094	0.179	−3.85[3]	0.837	0.256	23.05[3]
Second quarter	0.013	0.139	0.68	0.574	0.216	19.54[3]
Third quarter	−0.005	0.208	−0.17	0.641	0.124	38.68[3]
Fourth quarter	0.002	0.209	0.08	0.615	0.224	19.76[3]
1979						
First quarter	−0.029	0.185	−1.19	0.356	0.293	8.59[3]
Second quarter	0.056	0.201	2.03	−0.074	0.073	−7.40[3]
Third quarter	0.006	0.155	0.28	−0.060	0.109	−4.09[3]
Fourth quarter	0.067	0.179	2.77	−0.184	0.093	−14.19[3]
1980						
First quarter	−0.015	0.148	−0.78	−0.268	0.271	−6.92[3]
Second quarter	0.015	0.222	0.50	−0.136	0.185	−5.40[3]
Third quarter	−0.040	0.124	−2.37	−0.286	0.113	−18.28[3]
Fourth quarter	0.046	0.160	2.11	−0.082	0.097	−5.94[3]
1981						
First quarter	0.054	0.153	2.61	−0.005	0.094	−0.40

[1]Based on a set of uniformly distributed observations comprising 87 per cent of the samples. The definitions of the deviations from interest rate parity are given in equations (10) and (11).

[2]Expressed in per cent.

[3]Mean is signficantly different from zero at a 95 per cent confidence level.

zero in London for the entire sample period as well as for most of the subperiods.[11] The means in Tokyo were positive during the first five three-month periods ended March 1979, while they were negative during the following three-month periods ended March 1981. All of the estimated values of the means for Tokyo were significantly different from zero, except for the first quarter of 1981 (Charts 1 and 2).

Quantification of Capital Controls

In the previous section, it was established that deviations from the interest rate parity in the London market are, for all practical purposes, randomly distributed around the mean of zero. Thus, it can be said that, for the period 1978–81, the London market closely resembled World A, as described earlier. As mentioned above, by comparing the expected absolute value of the covered interest rate differentials in the two markets, one should be able to capture distortions present in the Tokyo market relative to those in the London market.

A reasonable estimate of the expected absolute value of the covered interest rate differentials, as represented by equation (9), can be obtained in two steps. First, one must obtain a data set of uniformly distributed observations.[12] This is necessitated by the strong possibility that some of the observed deviations from the interest rate parities seem to have

[11]However, the mean was significantly differnt from zero in the first quarter of 1978.

[12]The uniformly distributed observations are defined as those that have values increasing evenly when these values are arranged in ascending order. Therefore, these observations are linearly distributed with respect to their values. For a detailed discussion, see Appendix I in the original.

CHART 1

Japan: Deviations from Interest Rate Parity in London, 1978–81[1] (In per cent)

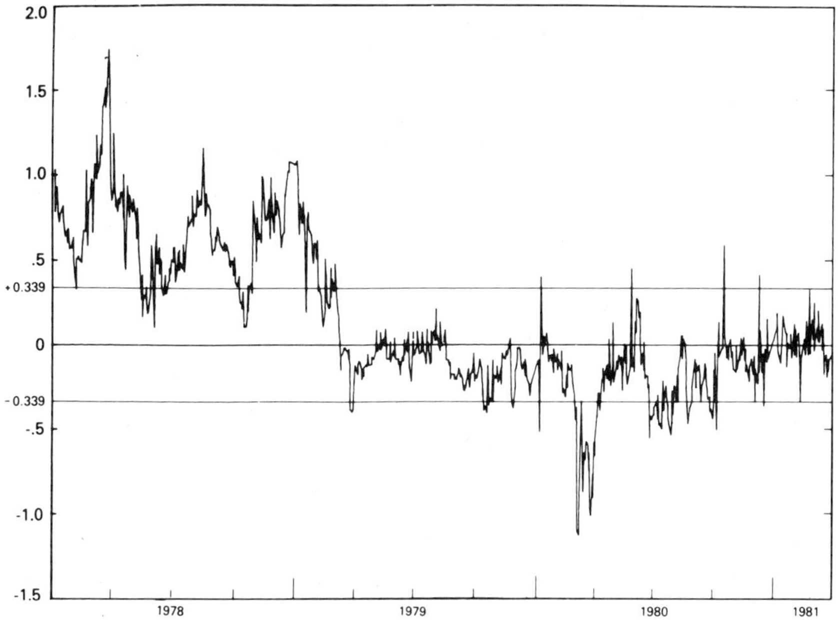

[1]Daily data; 100 G_{LON} (defined as the "gap in London").

The zone bounded by ± 0.146 represents the average width of the neutral band for the sample period as a whole.

extremely large or small values relative to most observations and to reflect measurement errors of large magnitudes. The empirical analysis suggests that the data set mentioned above can be obtained by eliminating the observations in any given quarter that belong to the set of the extreme 13 per cent of their absolute values when they are arranged in ascending order. Second, one must obtain the mean absolute value of the uniformly distributed sample in the data set for each market. The results are summarized in Table 2; these means are the estimated values of the transaction costs (or opportunity costs) defined earlier and represent the outer bound of the neutral band.

Charts 1, 2, and 3 and Tables 1 and 2 point to several interesting observations.

1. The movements in the deviations show no trends in the London market but definite trends in the Tokyo market.
2. The deviations in the Tokyo market were the largest in the first quarter of 1978, and their excess over the deviations in the London market was also the largest during that quarter. The difference in the mean value of absolute deviations is estimated to be about 0.7 percentage point in that quarter.[13]
3. The deviations in the Tokyo market were significantly lower in the last three quarters

[13]In other words, the capital control measures had an impact of raising the transaction costs in Tokyo to 0.7 percentage point above those in London.

CHART 2

Japan: Deviations from Interest Rate Parity in Tokyo, 1978–81[1] (In percent)

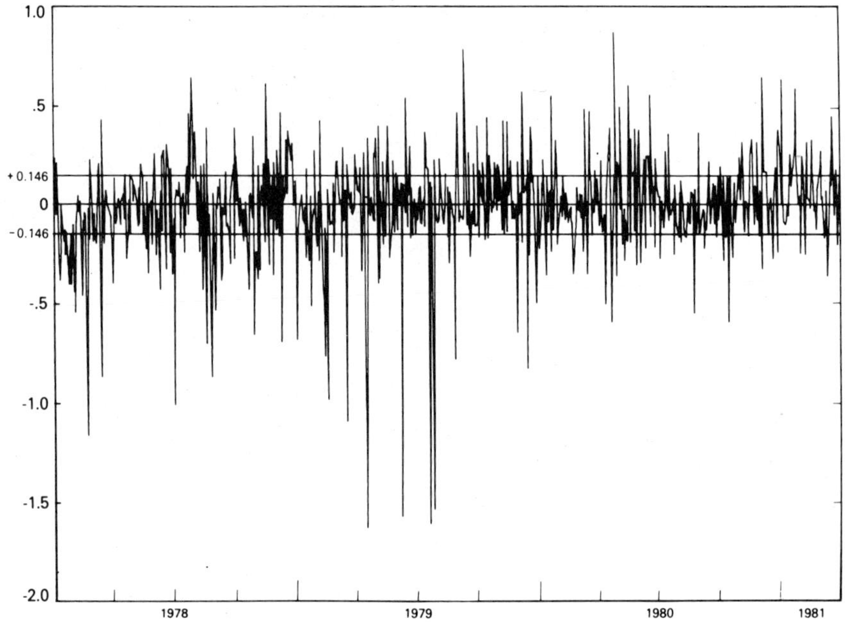

[1]Daily data; 100 G_{TKY} (defined as the "gap in Tokyo").

The zone bounded by ± 0.339 represents the average width of the neutral band for the sample period as a whole.

of 1979 than during 1978 and the first quarter of 1979, and the gap between the London market and the Tokyo market is virtually nonexistent in that later period. This indicates that the Tokyo market was as free from capital controls in the April-December period of 1979 as was the London market.

4. In the first quarter of 1980, the mean value of the deviation from the interest rate parity in Tokyo increased sharply from the level reached during the fourth quarter of 1979, suggesting a significant increase in distortion created by capital controls. (Note that the deviations in the London market remained virtually unchanged in the first quarter of 1980 compared with the previous quarter.)
5. During the second quarter of 1980, the deviations in the London market increased considerably. This may have been due to increased uncertainty in the capital market following a change in U.S. monetary policy late in the first quarter, that is, the introduction of controls over credit extended to consumers and businesses. On the other hand, the deviations in the Tokyo market declined sharply in that quarter, implying that distortions were reduced significantly, even though both the Tokyo market and the London market were subject to the same uncertainty owing to the shift in U.S. monetary policy.
6. In the third quarter of 1980, the mean value of the deviation from interest rate parity again increased considerably in Tokyo, indicating an increase in transaction costs. The increase reflected partly an introduction of capital controls; that is, deposit

TABLE 2

Japan: Estimated Transaction Costs—Means of Absolute Deviations from Interest Rate Parity, 1978–81 (in per cent)

Period	Transaction Costs London (A)	Transaction Costs Tokyo (B)	Effects of Capital Controls on Transaction Costs in Tokyo (B − A)
1978			
First quarter	0.161	0.837	0.676
Second quarter	0.114	0.574	0.460
Third quarter	0.164	0.641	0.477
Fourth quarter	0.171	0.615	0.444
1979			
First quarter	0.144	0.394	0.250
Second quarter	0.171	0.093	0.078
Third quarter	0.124	0.103	0.021
Fourth quarter	0.155	0.185	0.030
1980			
First quarter	0.120	0.289	0.169
Second quarter	0.186	0.199	0.013
Third quarter	0.113	0.286	0.173
Fourth quarter	0.137	0.107	−0.030
1981			
First quarter	0.135	0.081	−0.054
Average	0.146	0.339	0.208

institutions were asked to exercise restraint in accepting foreign currency deposits resulting from sales of foreign currency assets.

7. The month of December 1980 marks the implementation of the new Foreign Exchange and Foreign Trade Control Law. The new law provided that transactions in both the current and the capital account could be made freely unless expressly prohibited. Partly because of both the expectation that the new law would come into effect on December 1, 1980 and the actual implementation of the law, transaction costs in the Tokyo capital market declined significantly in the fourth quarter of 1980. These declined further in the first quarter of 1981. In both of these quarters, transaction costs were estimated to be lower in Tokyo than in London.

In short, it can be inferred that significant distortions were present in the Tokyo market for the five-quarter period ended March 1979 (Phase I). During the period April–December 1979 (Phase II), distortions were reduced considerably. During the first 11 months of 1980, temporary increases and decreases in distortions were observed. Distortions increased in the first and third quarters but declined in the subsequent quarters (Phase III). Since December 1980, distortions have remained low in Tokyo (Phase IV).

The implications drawn from this analysis closely correspond to changes in capital controls during the period under study.

Phase I (First Quarter 1978—First Quarter 1979)

During this period, expectations of a yen appreciation were very strong, and a large amount of incipient capital was induced into the Tokyo market. Mindful of a further appreciation of the yen, the authorities introduced various measures to reduce capital inflows and to encourage outflows, particularly in the first quarter of 1978. As a result, the

CHART 3

Japan: Measure of Distortions in Tokyo Market, 1978–81[1] (In per cent)

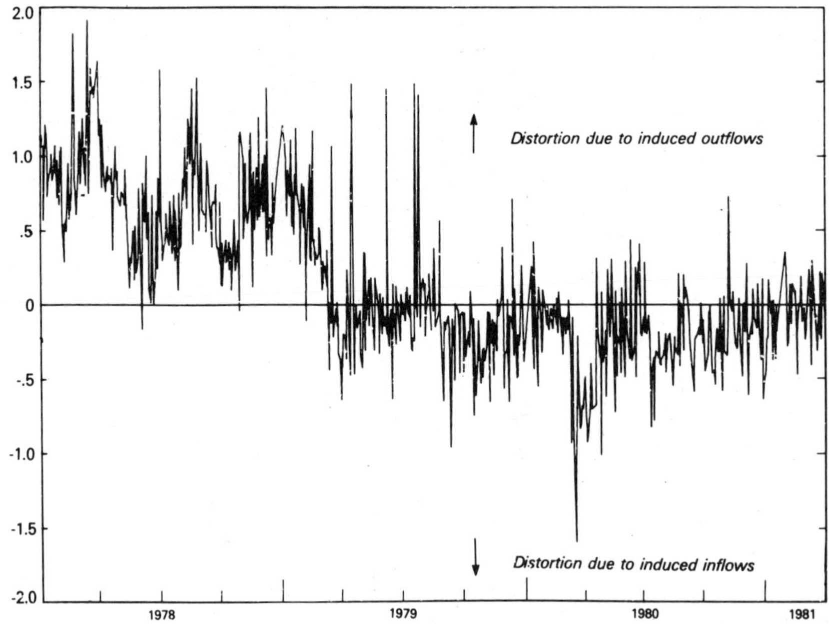

[1]Daily data. These observations are constructed by the expression $(G_{TKY} - G_{LON})100$.

market condition for internationally traded yen-denominated assets became *tight in Tokyo relative to London*. Reflecting these market conditions, the Gensaki rate continued to be above the Euro-yen rate in London (Chart 4), even though there was a gradual easing of the restrictive measures on capital inflows from the second quarter of 1978.

Since early November 1978, when the U.S. Government introduced a package of dollar defense measures, the yen started to depreciate rapidly in both the spot and forward exchange markets.

Phase II (Second Quarter—Fourth Quarter 1979)

The measures in effect in Phase I that attempted to reduce capital inflows were removed and certain types of outflows were discouraged. As a result, capital moved more freely than before, and the interest rates on yen-denominated assets in Tokyo and London moved very closely. A deterioration in the external current account balance and increased uncertainty following the second oil shock caused a continued depreciation of the yen.

Phase III (First Quarter—November 1980)

A package of yen defense measures was introduced in early March 1980. These measures included a provision that allowed Japanese banks abroad to raise funds in London and transfer them to their head offices in Tokyo. In addition, the ceiling on the interest rate on the nonresident free yen account was removed. Owing to the effect of these measures, capital flowed into Japan. The interest rate on the Euro-yen deposits increased signifi-

CHART 4

Japan: Interest Rates on Yen-Denominated Assets, 1978–81[1] (In per cent per annum)

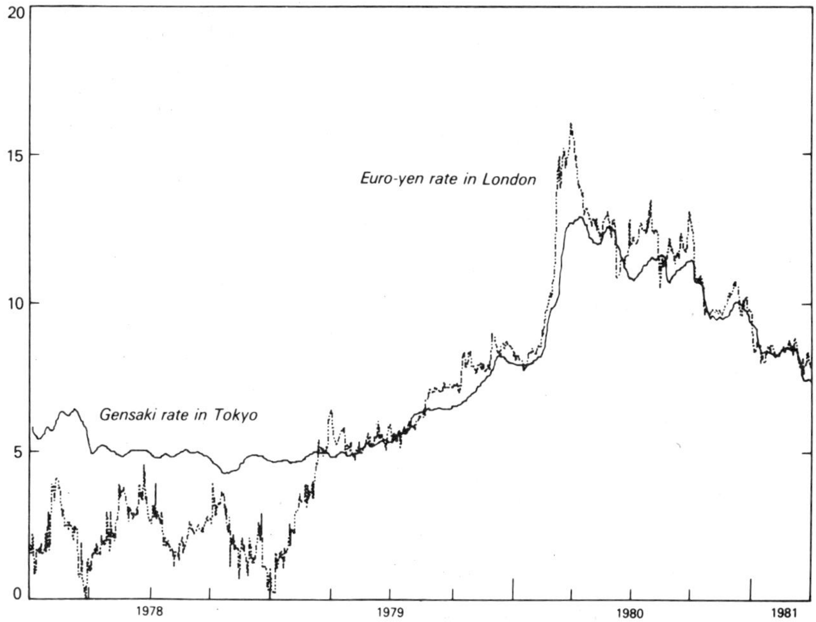

[1]Daily data.

cantly beyond the Gensaki rate,[14] reflecting capital inflows induced in part by the moral suasion exercised by the authorities in Tokyo. At the same time, the cost of transactions increased significantly, as mentioned earlier, owing mainly to increased uncertainty caused by changes in capital controls.

Phase IV (December 1980-First Quarter 1981)

In December 1980, the Government implemented the new Foreign Exchange and Foreign Trade Control Law. This law provided that many types of capital transaction would be free under normal circumstances; others would require prior notice. For a few types of transaction, advance approval is still required. On balance, capital controls have been reduced considerably, and the reduction in these controls has in turn reduced the transaction costs of short-term securities.

IV. CONCLUDING REMARKS

The main purpose of this paper has been to examine how capital controls affected deviations from interest rate parity during the period 1978–81. An attempt was also made

[14]Despite the substantial covered interest differential in favor of London, short-term capital flows increased sharply, particularly in April, when they amounted to $4.4 billion, compared with $0.2 billion in March. This trend continued in May and June.

to devise a quantitative indicator that can measure the extent to which capital controls create distortions in the foreign exchange market.

The indicator of distortions caused by capital controls shows that, since the beginning of the period under study (the first quarter of 1978), distortions in the market were on a generally declining trend. By mid-1979, the Tokyo market was as free from distortions as was the London market. However, in the first quarter of 1980, the distortions increased significantly, reflecting the moral suasion exercised by the authorities to encourage Japanese residents to bring in funds from abroad. However, the distortions declined considerably thereafter, possibly because moral suasion ceased to be applied, and has remained low since then, except for a brief period in the third quarter of 1980. Data also indicate that, in recent months, deviations from interest rate parity have been reduced to levels observed in the second half of 1979. The relaxation of capital controls following the implementation of the new Foreign Exchange and Foreign Trade Control Law in December 1980 contributed further to reducing transaction costs in the short-term securities market in Tokyo.

REFERENCES

Aliber, Robert Z., "The Interest Rate Parity Theorem: A Reinterpretation," *Journal of Political Economy*, Vol. 81 (November/December 1973), pp. 1451–59.

Deardorff, Alan V., "One-Way Arbitrage and Its Implications for the Foreign Exchange Markets," *Journal of Political Economy*, Vol. 87 (April 1979), pp. 351–64.

Dooley, Michael, and Peter Isard, "Capital Controls, Political Risk, and Deviations from Interest-Rate Parity," *Journal of Political Economy*, Vol. 88 (April 1980), pp. 370–84.

Frenkel, Jacob A., and Richard M. Levich, "Covered Interest Arbitrage: Unexploited Profits?" *Journal of Political Economy*, Vol. 83 (April 1975), pp. 325–38.

——, "Transaction Costs and Interest Arbitrage: Tranquil versus Turbulent Periods," *Journal of Political Economy*, Vol. 85 (December 1977), pp. 1209–26.

McCormick, Frank, "Covered Interest Arbitrage: Unexploited Profits?—Comment," *Journal of Political Economy*, Vol. 87 (April 1979), pp. 411–17.

Officer, Lawrence H., and Thomas D. Willett, "The Covered-Arbitrage Schedule: A Critical Survey of Recent Developments," *Journal of Money, Credit and Banking*, Vol. 2 (May 1970), pp. 247–57.

13

A Note on Exchange-Rate Expectations and Nominal Interest Differentials: A Test of the Fisher Hypothesis*

Robert E. Cumby and Maurice Obstfeld

This note tests the hypothesis that nominal interest differentials between similar assets denominated in different currencies can be explained entirely by the expected change in the exchange rate over the holding period. This proposition, often called the "Fisher open" hypothesis or the hypothesis of perfect asset substitutability, has been a major component of recent theories of exchange-rate determination, and has important implications for monetary policy.[1]

The Fisher hypothesis differs from the covered interest parity theorem enunciated by Keynes [11]. While covered interest parity equates the nominal interest differential between financial centers to a known premium or discount on forward foreign exchange, and is thus in principle riskless, Fisher parity involves risk in an essential way. The two conditions are equivalent only when forward exchange rates equal expected future spot rates. Recent theoretical work, for example that of Grauer, Litzenberger, and Stehle [8], Kouri [12], and Frankel [6], shows that this need not be the case when market participants are risk averse. Thus, while covered interest parity must always hold exactly in an informationally efficient asset market with no transactions costs, Fisher parity need not. Nominal interest differentials may reflect risk premia in addition to expected exchange-rate movements.[2]

It should be emphasized at the outset that the tests conducted in this paper are really joint tests of the Fisher hypothesis and a weak form of foreign exchange market informational efficiency. Levich [14] has argued that tests of market efficiency are always joint tests involving some hypothesized structure of "normal" equilibrium returns. Below, we assume informational efficiency and instead test Fisher's hypothesized arbitrage condition that nominal interest differentials equal expected percentage changes in exchange rates.

I. THE FISHER HYPOTHESIS

The Fisher hypothesis states that when two bonds are similar in all respects except currency of denomination, asset-market equilibrium requires that any nominal rate-of-return differential between them be offset by an expected exchange rate change over the

---

*This article is reprinted, with permission, from *The Journal of Finance,* vol. 36, no. 3, June 1981, pp. 697–703.

[1]The hypothesis is discussed in Fisher [5].

[2]If covered interest parity holds exactly, the extensive empirical literature on the relationship between forward exchange rates and subsequently-observed spot rates has implications for the validity of the Fisher parity. Recent contributions to this area include work of Hakkio [9], Hansen and Hodrick [10], and Meese and Singleton [16]. The findings of these authors are consistent with those reported below.

holding period. More formally, let s_t be the logarithm of the spot exchange rate, defined as the domestic-currency price of foreign exchange; let ${}_t s_{t+1}$ be the expected value of the logarithm of next period's exchange rate, conditional on information available at time t; and let r_t and r_t^* be the one-period nominal yields (between t and $t + 1$) on the domestic and foreign bonds, respectively. The Fisher parity condition may then be written as:

$$ {}_t s_{t+1} - s_t = ln(1 + r_t) - ln(1 + r_t) \simeq r_t - r_t^* \qquad (1) $$

To obtain an empirical test of condition (1), we require two assumptions. The first assumption is that ${}_t s_{t+1}$ is a mathematical conditional expectation, based on the true probability distribution underlying the events impinging on financial markets. The second is that the foreign exchange market is weakly efficient, in the sense that market expectations of future spot rates are always conditioned on an information set that includes past forecast errors.

The first assumption allows us to write the realized spot exchange rate as its expected value plus a forecast error having zero mean:

$$ s_{t+1} = {}_t s_{t+1} + \epsilon_t, \qquad E(\epsilon_t) = 0 \qquad (2) $$

The second assumption, taken in conjunction with the first, allows us to assert further that the stochastic process $\{\epsilon_t\}$ is a white noise process, so that the forecast errors are mutually uncorrelated at all lags.

Combining Equations (1) and (2), we obtain

$$ s_{t+1} - s_t - r_t + r_t^* = \epsilon_t \qquad (3) $$

Since all variables on the left-hand side of (3) are observable ex post, we may test the Fisher hypothesis by testing whether the process $\{\epsilon_t\}$ is white noise.[3]

Under a mean-variance theory of capital-asset pricing with risk-averse investors, ϵ_t is the sum of an expectational error *and* a risk premium that accounts for a divergence between the interest differential and the expected rate of depreciation over the holding period.[4] In such a setting, domestic and foreign bonds will not be perfect substitutes. If covered interest parity holds identically, this risk premium may be expressed as the difference between the logarithm of the one-period forward rate and the expected logarithm of the exchange rate one period hence,

$$ f_t - {}_t s_{t+1} = \text{risk premium} $$

where f_t denotes the logarithm of the forward rate.[5] Although the risk premium is not explicitly modeled here, we interpret serial correlation in $\{\epsilon_t\}$ as providing indirect evi-

[3]Levich [13] suggests a similar procedure. It is equivalent to testing the whiteness of forward-rate forecast errors when covered interest parity holds. A refree has pointed out that Equation (3) may also be obtained, under certainty, by assuming that real interest rates are equal across countries, that purchasing-power parity holds, and that nominal interest rates differ from real interest rates one-for-one with the inflation rate. Roll [20] derives an equation similar to (3) in this manner and interprets the test for whiteness of his series as a test of purchasing-power parity.

[4]Porter [18] examines the Fisher hypothesis using evidence on the Canadian-U.S. dollar exchange rate. He uses the estimated standard deviation of the previous year's exchange rate around its mean as a measure of exchange risk. This measure is inadequate, for it does not distinguish between diversifiable and nondiversifiable risk. Only the latter gives rise to a risk premium.

[5]See Cornell [3].

dence of the existence of such a premium. Of course, the risk premium may be positive or negative and does not have to be stable over time. Thus, a failure to detect serial correlation in $\{\epsilon_t\}$ is consistent with the existence of a risk premium that is itself serially uncorrelated.

This test differs in an important way from tests for the randomness of exchange rate movements which have been carried out periodically since the original work of Poole [17].[6] The random-walk model of exchange rate behavior is usually justified on the grounds that "new information arrives randomly and independently of information received in the past" and speculators use this information to "bid the current price to a level equal to the expected future spot price."[7] But as (3) shows, this statement is true in a world of perfect asset substitutability only when interest rates are equal across countries so that *any* exchange rate changes are unanticipated. In a world where central banks pursue independent inflation targets, the random-walk test says nothing about market efficiency or asset substitutability, for it fails to account properly for the opportunity cost of holding wealth in the form of one currency rather than another.[8]

II. DATA AND METHODS

The test of the Fisher hypothesis proposed above involves the sequence of random variables $\{\epsilon_t\}$ defined in (3), which, under the null hypothesis of Fisher parity, is just the sequence of unanticipated movements of the log of the exchange rate. To carry out this test, we use weekly observations on exchange rates and interest rates, so that ϵ_t is a one-week ahead forecast error when Fisher parity holds.[9] s_t is taken to be the national logarithm of the U.S. dollar price of foreign currency, r_t the one-week yield on seven-day London Eurodollar deposits, and r_t^* the one-week yield on seven-day London Euro-deposits denominated in the foreign currency. Eurocurrency rates are employed because of the similar political risk characteristics of Eurocurrency deposits.

We test for Fisher parity between U.S. dollar deposits and deposits denominated in Canadian dollars, French francs, Deutsche marks, Netherlands guilders, Swiss francs, and pounds sterling. Exchange rates are Friday closing bid rates, as reported by the Harris Bank (Chicago) in its *Weekly Review*.[10] Data on seven-day interest rates in the London Eurocurrency market come from the *Financial Times*, and are Friday closing bid rates as

[6]See Upson [22], Burt, Kaen, and Booth [2], Cornell [3], and Cornell and Dietrich [4].

[7]Poole [17], p. 468.

[8]The random-walk theory of exchange-rate behavior has been stated both as a proposition concerning percentage changes in exchange rates (or, approximately, first differences of the *logarithms* of exchange rates) and as one concerning first differences of the *levels* of exchange rates. The model seems to originate in a misunderstanding of Samuelson's [21] martingale theorem, which concerns the sequence of expected values of a *single* future price, rather than the sequence of expected values of a sequence of future prices. Upson [22] provides an example of the confusion surrounding the empirical application of Samuelson's result. Rogoff [19] applies it correctly to the market for foreign-exchange futures.

[9]The advantage of using weekly rather than monthly data is that more observations are available. A disadvantage is that percentage transactions costs on one-week deposits may be large when considered on an annual basis. However, McCormick [15] provides evidence that transactions costs are much smaller than has been widely believed.

[10]The series of Canadian exchange rates, however, is taken from the International Monetary Fund's *International Financial Statistics*.

well.[11] The data run from 5 July, 1974 to 27 June, 1980, giving 312 nonoverlapping observations for each currency.

The first statistical test we perform on the series $\{\epsilon_t\}$ is the standard Q test for whiteness. The Q-statistic is defined as

$$Q(k) = n \sum_{i=1}^{k} \hat{c}_i^2$$

where $\hat{c}_i = \Sigma\, \epsilon_t \epsilon_{t-1} / \Sigma\, \epsilon_t^2$, n is the sample size and k is an increasing function of n. $Q(k)$ is asymptotically distributed as χ^2 and k degrees of freedom under the null hypothesis that the ϵ_t are serially uncorrelated.[12]

Geweke [7] has suggested a likelihood ratio test having greater asymptotic power against some types of serial correlation than does the Q test. For this second test, we assume that the disturbances ϵ_t are normal with mean zero under either hypothesis and are generated by the autoregressive model

$$\Lambda(L)\epsilon_t = \xi_t \tag{4}$$

where $\Lambda(L) = \sum_{i=1}^{\infty} \rho_i L^i$ is a polynomial in the lag operator, $\rho_0 = 1$ and $\{\xi_t\}$ is a white noise process. The null hypothesis is just the hypothesis that $\Lambda(L) = 1$.

To test this hypothesis, we assume that we may truncate the autoregressive process (4) at lag length k, where k is increasing in n, and test whether $\rho_1 = \rho_2 = \ldots = \rho_k = 0$ in the autoregression

$$\epsilon_t = \sum_{i=1}^{k} - \rho_t \epsilon_{t-i} + \xi_t \tag{5}$$

The appropriate test statistic is $n \cdot ln(\hat{\sigma}_\epsilon^2/\hat{\sigma}_\xi^2)$, which is minus twice the logarithm of the likelihood ratio and is asymptotically distributed $\chi^2(k)$. $\hat{\sigma}_\epsilon^2$ is the estimated variance of the process $\{\epsilon_t\}$, while $\hat{\sigma}_\xi^2$ is the sample variance of the residuals obtained from estimating (5) by ordinary least squares. The likelihood ratio is large when past values of ϵ_t provide significant help in predicting future values; this leads to rejection of the null hypothesis.

If the null hypothesis is not rejected for an autoregression of order k, we test the hypothesis $\rho_k = 0$ using the standard normal test, and if this is not rejected, we again perform the likelihood-ratio test for an autoregression of order $k - 1$. We continue in this manner until the log likelihood ratio exceeds the critical value we have chosen. It is important to realize that this procedure results in a nested sequence of tests, and that the probability of committing a Type I error at each stage must be calculated accordingly. If the critical value for each normal test on individual coefficients is chosen so that its significance level would be α if that test were performed in isolation, and if the critical value for the likelihood ratio tests is chosen so that the probability of Type I error is β, then, under the null hypothesis, the probability of Type I error when one rejects as the jth stage is $1 - (1 - \beta)(1 - \alpha)^{j-1}$. In practice, we take $\alpha = .001$ and $\beta = .025$.

[11] One-months rates were used in the few instances when one-week rates were not reported. The fact that interest rates and exchange rates, while observed on the same day of the week, are observed in different financial centers, gives rise to an alignment problem that may bias the tests.

[12] See Box and Pierce [1].

TABLE 1

Results of the *Q* Test

Test Statistic	U.S./ Canada	U.S./ France	U.S./ Germany	U.S./ Netherlands	U.S./ Switzerland	U.S./ U.K.
$\chi^2(16)$	38.87	33.77	28.10	40.75	27.28	25.97[a]

[a]Not significant at the 5 percent significance level. The critical value for tests at the 5 percent level is 26.3; the critical value for tests at the 1 percent level is 32.0.

III. EMPIRICAL RESULTS

Table I reports the results of the *Q* test for serial correlation. The statistics are computed for 16 lags, and therefore are distributed asymptotically as $\chi^2(16)$.

Fisher parity was rejected at the 5 percent level in all cases save that of the pound sterling. In the cases of Canada, France, and the Netherlands, rejection at the 1 percent level was possible. The high serial correlation in the series of ex post nominal return differentials suggests that they are not simply series of forecast errors, as they would be under conditions of perfect asset substitutability.

The outcomes of the maximum likelihood tests appear in Table II. For all countries, the nested sequence of tests began with a 16-week autoregression. In all cases except that of the United Kingdom, rejection of the Fisher hypothesis at the 2.5 percent level occurred at once. Since no nesting of hypotheses took place, the probability of Type I error for the test procedure as a whole was also .025 for these currencies.

Immediate rejection at the 2.5 percent level was not possible for the United Kingdom, but occurred only after the imposition of zero contraints on the original sixteenth-order autoregression. Although the Fisher hypothesis was eventually rejected for the pound, the probability of Type I error was .035, somewhat higher than for the other currencies.

As indicated by the earlier *Q* test, the evidence against the hypothesis of perfect asset substitutability is weakest in the case of the United Kingdom. But even so, the significance level of 3.5 percent is quite low by conventional standards.

To summarize, the two statistical procedures we have employed yield essentially the same conclusions. Both suggest that the Fisher-parity relationship does not hold. Deviations from Fisher parity appear to be highly autocorrelated and so do not behave like

TABLE 2

Results of the Likelihood-Ratio Test

	U.S./ Canada	U.S./ France	U.S./ Germany	U.S./ Netherlands	U.S./ Switzerland	U.S./ U.K.
Order of χ^2 statistic	16	16	16	16	16	6
Value of χ^2 statistic	29.18	31.97	29.36	37.78	30.26	15.02
Critical value	28.8	28.8	28.8	28.8	28.8	14.4
Significance level of test	.025	.025	.025	.025	.025	.035

expectational errors. The observed behavior of the series of deviations may be interpreted as evidence favoring the existence of a foreign exchange risk premium for most major currencies. These findings lend support to recent theories suggesting that foreign exchange market efficiency is consistent with the existence of risk premia at equilibrium.

REFERENCES

1. G. E. P. Box and D. A. Pierce. "Distribution of Residual Autocorrelation in Autoregressive-Integrated Moving Average Time Series Models." *Journal of the American Statistical Association* (December 1970).
2. J. Burt, F. Kaen, and G. Booth. "Foreign Exchange Market Efficiency under Flexible Exchange Rates." *Journal of Finance* (September 1977).
3. B. Cornell. "Spot Rates, Forward Rates and Exchange Market Efficiency." *Journal of Financial Economics* (August 1977).
4. W. B. Cornell and J. K. Dietrich. "The Efficiency of Foreign Exchange Markets under Floating Exchange Rates." *Review of Economics and Statistics* (February 1978).
5. I. Fisher. *The Theory of Interest*. New York: Macmillan, 1930.
6. J. Frankel. "The Diversifiability of Exchange Risk." *Journal of International Economics* (August 1979).
7. J. Geweke. "The Relative Asymptotic Strengths of Some Tests Used in Time Series Analysis." Mimeo: University of Wisconsin, 1979.
8. F. Grauer, R. Litzenberger, and R. Stehle. "Sharing Rules and Equilibrium in an International Capital Market Under Uncertainty." *Journal of Financial Economics* (June 1976).
9. C. Hakkio. "Expectations and the Foreign Exchange Market." Doctoral dissertation, University of Chicago, 1979.
10. L. P. Hansen and R. J. Hodrick. "Forward Exchange Rates as Optimal Predictors of Future Spot Rates: An Econometric Analysis." *Journal of Political Economy* (October 1980).
11. J. M. Keynes. A *Tract on Monetary Reform*. London: Macmillan, 1923.
12. P. J. K. Kouri. "International Investment and Interest Rate Linkages." In *The Political Economy of Monetary Reform*, ed. R. Z. Aliber. London: Macmillan, 1977.
13. R. M. Levich. "Tests of Forecasting Models and Market Efficiency in the International Money Market." In *The Economics of Exchange Rates*, eds. J. A. Frenkel and H. G. Johnson. Reading, Mass.: Addison Wesley, 1978.
14. ______. "On the Efficiency of Markets for Foreign Exchange." In *International Economic Policy: Theory and Evidence*, eds. R. Dornbusch and J. A. Frenkel. Baltimore: Johns Hopkins Press, 1979.
15. F. McCormick. "Covered Interest Arbitrage: Unexploited Profits? Comment." *Journal of Political Economy* (April 1979).
16. R. A. Meese and K. J. Singleton. "Rational Expectations, Risk Premia, and the Market for Spot and Forward Exchange." Mimeo: Federal Reserve Board, 1980.

17. W. Poole. "Speculative Prices as Random Walks: An Analysis of Ten Time Series of Flexible Exchange Rates." *Southern Economic Journal* (April 1967).

18. M. G. Porter. "A Theoretical and Empirical Framework for Analyzing the Term Structure of Exchange-Rate Expectations." *IMF Staff Papers* (November 1971).

19. K. Rogoff. "An Empirical Analysis of Efficiency in Foreign Exchange Futures Markets." Mimeo: Massachusetts Institute of Technology, 1978.

20. R. Roll. "Violations of Purchasing Power Parity and their Implications for Efficient International Capital Markets." In *International Trade and Finance*, eds. M. Sarnat and G. Szego. Cambridge: Ballinger, 1979.

21. P. A. Samuelson. "Proof that Properly Anticipated Prices Fluctuate Randomly." *Industrial Management Review* (Spring 1965).

22. R. B. Upson. "Random Walks and Forward Exchange Rates: A Spectral Analysis." *Journal of Financial and Quantitative Analysis* (September 1972).

14

Evaluating the Performance of the Forecasters*

Richard M. Levich

The growing volume of international transactions helps to intensify the demand for foreign exchange forecasts and financial advice. With over eight years of floating exchange rates, many advisory services have accumulated a lengthy history of forecasts. It is therefore appropriate to pose some basic questions—Have exchange rate forecasts been very accurate? Could exchange rate forecasts have been used to improve currency exposure management? In the broadest sense, is there evidence that professional advisory services have demonstrated forecasting expertise?

The purpose of this section is to present a study of professional foreign exchange forecasters that addresses these questions. The study includes 12 services, nine currencies, four horizons and as many as 48 separate monthly forecasts, generating over 11,000 individual forecasts for analysis.

What we really want to know is: Do the foreign exchange rate forecasters beat the market? This is a difficult question to answer because there is not a universally accepted measure of the market's consensus forecast of the future spot exchange rate. Therefore, in this study, our focus is on a related question: Do the foreign exchange rate forecasters beat the forward rate? Under certain assumptions that are fairly plausible, it is theoretically correct to use the forward rate as the best representation of exchange rate expectations. We will argue this case shortly. Our objective—to check if forecasters beat the market—implies performance evaluation. This is always a tricky subject and the evaluation of forecasters is no exception. Several alternative performance measures will be proposed and computed.

Based on the evidence in hand, the simple answers to our questions are: No, exchange rate forecasts have not been as accurate as the forward rate prediction. Even so: Yes, exchange rate forecasts were very often on the correct side of the forward rate, therefore offering correct hedging or speculative advice. In this sense, the record of several forecasters is too good to be the result of guessing. This leads us to conclude that the industry has demonstrated forecasting expertise.

Some of the most impressive performances from our study are summarized in Exhibit 1. The first point worth noting is that 10 of our 13 sample advisory services appear in the Exhibit; most of the services have had at least one moment of glory. Second, it appears that more forecasters have been successful with the DM than with other currencies. But the most tantalizing question is: Who is best? The data do not permit a clean answer to this question (see Exhibit 1 for the explanation). Even though comparisons across services are difficult and require further sticky assumptions, our evidence clearly shows that several forecasters have performed remarkably well. In alphabetical order: Business International, Conti Currency, Predex Forecast and Wharton achieved statistically significant results for several individual currencies and significant overall performance for at least one horizon.

---

*This article is reprinted, with permission, from Richard Ensor (ed.), *The Management of Foreign Exchange Risk,* Second Edition, Euromoney Publications, 1982, pp. 121–134.

EXHIBIT 1

Leading Track Records Among Advisory Services (Percentage Correct Forecasts)

Horizon	Deutschemark		Canadian dollar		Pound sterling		Japanese yen		All currencies	
One-month	Predex	65–B	C.M.B.	69–A	Conti	65–B	Phillips	71	Conti	61·24–C
	BI	65–B	Conti	63–B	D.R.I.	61	Conti	63–B	BI	58·82–C
	Conti	63–B							Predex	57·64–B
	D.R.I.	61							Wharton	57·58
	M.C.M.	60								
Three-month	Wharton	82	Wharton	82	Wharton	64	Phillips	100	Wharton	71·72–B
	M.C.M.	73	C.M.B.	81–A	C.M.B.	63			Predex	61·11–B
	Phillips	71			Predex, ST	60				
	Predex	65								
Six-month	Wharton	90	Wharton	70	Predex, ST	69	Phillips	86	Predex	63·12–A
	M.C.M.	79	BI	67	Predex	60	Murenbeeld	66	Wharton	62·22
	Predex	77–A							M.C.M.	61·11
	Phillips	71							Predex, ST	60·15
12-month	M.C.M.	88	Wharton	75	Predex, ST	83	Phillips	100	Predex	68·83–A
	Wharton	75			M.C.M.	75	Murenbeeld	67	M.C.M.	65·28
	Predex	71			Predex	71	D.R.I.	65	Wharton	63·39
	Predex, ST	65							Predex, ST	60·87

Note. The data do not permit clean comparisons between services for two reasons.

1. All forecasters have not been monitored over the same time period. Take, for example, Wharton's 57·58% overall track record versus Conti Currency's 61·24% at the one-month horizon. The Wharton sample reflects 11 forecasts (on nine currencies) from 1980 while the Conti Currency record is based on 43 forecasts (also on nine currencies) from the period 1977–80. Conti Currency's record is statistically significant which might lead us to conclude that it is superior. But the two sample periods are so different, this would be comparing apples and oranges.

Even more dramatic are the 12-month Japanese yen results. The record for Phillips and Drew reflects two observations while the Murenbeeld record is based on 36 observations. Readers should refer to Exhibit 3.3.2 for an indication of the maximum sample sizes for each advisory service.

2. The probability of correct advice by a forecaster is estimated subject to error. Take the overall track records of Predex (63%), Wharton (62%), Multinational Computer Models (61%) and Predex Short-Term (60%) at the six-month horizon. These results are so close together that statistically, we could not reject the hypothesis that they are identical.

Entries are included in this table if the percentage correct track record exceeds 60% or if the track record is statistically significant at the 10% level. Entries are marked A, B, or C to indicate statistical significance at the 10%, 5% or 1% levels, respectively. If an entry is not footnoted, there is at least a 10% probability that the track record is the result of chance.

Multinational Computer Models also recorded many high percentage correct track records; however, most were not statistically significant because of small sample sizes.

We have presented answers to several questions, but so far we have glossed over many of the loaded phrases in our questions. How should we measure accuracy? What is a fair way to measure a track record? How impressive must a track record be before we conclude that the track record is the result of expertise? The remainder of this article explores these theoretical and methodological issues, and then presents the results of our empirical tests.

THE BIG ISSUES

How we structure an empirical test of forecasting expertise and how we interpret the results depends on a few key issues:

- What is the market's estimate of the future spot exchange rate?
- Does the foreign exchange market efficiently reflect available information?
- What is a reliable indicator of forecasting performance?

WHAT EXCHANGE RATE IS THE MARKET EXPECTING?

We often hear statements such as: "the market's belief that the dollar will remain strong . . .", "the market's view that the central bank will intervene if sterling reaches $1·60 . . ." or "the market's expectation that the Mexican peso will have a substantial devaluation soon. . .". Where do we observe the market's exchange rate expectations, and how do we quantify them?

One of the most commonly expressed beliefs about the foreign exchange market is that the forward rate does not reflect exchange rate expectations; rather it is felt that the forward rate simply reflects the interest differential between Eurocurrency interest rates. This is easy to understand. To verify this belief, we need only observe the forward premium (say, $/DM) and two interest rates (Euro-$ and Euro-DM) at the same moment. Casual observation and formal research concludes that the forward premium is nearly always established to eliminate covered arbitrage profits (i.e. the Interest Rate Parity Theorem).[1] To test whether the forward rate reflects exchange rate expectations, we would have to compare today's three-month forward rate with the spot rate three months hence. This establishes one datum. We would require many similar observations before we could begin to observe any empirical regularities between today's forward rate and the future spot exchange rate (i.e., unbiased forward rate prediction). It is unlikely that very many foreign exchange traders have made these calculations.[2]

In theory, the Interest Rate Parity Theorem and unbiased forward rate prediction are not incompatible. Under restrictive but not implausible assumptions, both relationships hold simultaneously.[3] Therefore, it is correct to assume that the forward exchange rate reflects exchange rate expectations. Unfortunately, the relationship may not be perfect. The forward rate may reflect several factors including:

1. Exchange rate expectations, $E(S_{t+n})$
2. Risk premium for exchange rate risk, RP_t
3. Role of transaction costs, TC_t
4. Role of government intervention, GI_t
5. Random error term, U_t

so that

$$F_{t,3} = E(S_{t+3}) + RP_t + TC_t + GI_t + U_t \qquad (1)$$

Equation (1) indeed illustrates that today's three-month forward rate reflects exchange rate expectations, but the forward rate also may capture other effects. Only if these other

[1]Jacob A. Frenkel and Richard M. Levich, "Transaction Costs and Interest Arbitrage: Tranquil Versus Turbulent Periods," *Journal of Political Economy* 86, No. 6 (November/December 1977); pp. 1209–26.

[2]The academic studies on this issue have led to mixed results. The forward rate appears to be an unbiased predictor of the future spot rate but the relationship between the forward premium and the future exchange rate change is very weak. See Richard M. Levich, "Are Forward Exchange Rates Unbiased Predictors of Future Spot Rates?" *Columbia Journal of World Business* 14, No. 4 (Winter 1979), pp. 49–61.

[3]Under certainty, both IRPT and unbiased forward rate prediction hold if exchange rates are determined so that purchasing power parity holds and interest rates reflect anticipated inflation (the Fisher effect). With uncertainty, both relationships will hold if forward speculators are risk-neutral. For details, see Ian H. Giddy, "An Integrated Theory of Exchange Rate Equilibrium," *Journal of Financial and Quantitative Analysis* (December 1976), pp. 883–92, and John F. O. Bilson, "Rational Expectations and the Exchange Rate," in J. Frenkel and H. Johnson (eds.). *The Economics of Exchange Rates*, Addison-Wesley, 1978.

variables offer zero contribution will there be an exact correspondence between the forward rate and exchange rate expectations.

The role of a risk premium may be illustrated easily using an analogy based on the term structure of interest rates. If we consider only interest rate expectations, an upward-sloping term structure signals that the market expects short-term interest rates to rise in the future. Suppose, however, that investors require a liquidity premium before they are willing to hold a longer-term bond. In this case, the upward-sloping yield curve reflects positive liquidity premiums rather than rising interest rate expectations. To deduce the market's interest rate expectations, analysts must adjust the implied forward interest rate for the liquidity premium.

Liquidity premia are, of course, prefectly consistent with a well-functioning, efficient bond market. There are logical reasons why investors might demand and be paid liquidity premia. The example serves to illustrate that even though the term structure of interest rates reflects interest rate expectations, liquidity premia make it more difficult to isolate the implied market interest rate expectations.

Similarly, market exchange rate expectations are not directly observable. Open foreign exchange positions involve risk and the market may pay a premium to people who maintain these positions. Consider the following example.[4] Suppose all market participants expect the \$/DM rate will be \$0·50 in three months. Suppose that all of today's transactions (i.e. both demand and supply) for three-month forward contracts have cleared the market, except for a DM 10 million remittance by a German subsidiary to its U.S. parent. In order to complete its sale of DM, the German subsidiary must induce someone who is happy with their \$, DM portfolio mix to part with dollars and accept DM 10 million. How can they provide this inducement? Simple—if the German subsidiary is willing to accept only \$0·49/DM they may induce someone to supply dollars (\$4,900,000 in this case). Even though the forward rate is \$0·49/DM, the market still maintains its expectation that the spot rate will be \$0·50 in three months. The German subsidiary has simply paid a \$0·01/DM premium to reduce its risks. Foreign exchange analysts must now adjust the observed forward rate (\$0·49/DM) by the risk premium in order to deduce the market's exchange rate expectations.

Paying a premium to reduce foreign exchange risks and demanding a premium to hold them are, of course, perfectly consistent with (but not required for) rational investor behaviour and market efficiency. In practice, the risk premium term in equation (1) may be zero if there is little net foreign exchange risk to be held or if the marginal foreign exchange participant is risk neutral.

What are the implications of this issue? Indeed the implications are major.

I. If the forward rate reflects a risk-premium, or terms in equation (1) other than exchange rate expectations, then we expect an advisory service forecast to outperform the forward rate.

II. If the forward rate reflects a risk-premium, then profits earned by following advisory

[4]Solnik refers to the impact of this imbalance of private capital flows as "hedging pressure" (Bruno H. Solnik, *European Capital Markets*, D. C. Heath, 1973). A foreign exchange risk premium can also be modelled around the excess supply of official government debt. See, Jeffrey A. Frankel, "The Diversifiability of Exchange Risk," *Journal of International Economics* 9, No. 3 (August 1979), pp. 379–93, and Michael P. Dooley and Peter Isard, "Capital Controls, Political Risk and Deviations from Interest-Rate Parity," *Journal of Political Economy* 88, No. 2 (April 1980), pp. 370–84.

service forecasts may represent only the fair return for taking on exchange risk, rather than an excess return for exploiting unusual forecasting expertise.

Empirical evidence on the existence and stability of an exchange risk premium remains sketchy.[5] Therefore, our tests of advisory service forecasts *vis-à-vis* the forward rate admit the possibility that the forecasters ought to beat the forward rate, because the forward rate is not a pure reflection of exchange rate expectations. Evidence that a professional forecast beats the forward rate will be inconclusive with respect to the market efficiency hypothesis, and it may not be very surprising to people who believe that the forward rate has proved, on occasion, to be a very bad forecaster.

IS THE FOREIGN EXCHANGE MARKET EFFICIENT?

Suppose for the moment that the forward rate is the pure reflection of exchange rate expectations, i.e. the terms RP, TC, and GI in equation (1) are zero. Does it follow that the forward rate will be a good forecaster, i.e. one with errors that are serially uncorrelated and average to zero? The answer depends on the efficiency of the foreign exchange market. If the market is efficient so that the forward rate quickly and fully reflects available information (and remember, we have assumed that risk premium terms are zero) then the forward rate will be a good forecaster.[6]

Market efficiency is an empirical question. The evidence from the stock market suggests a high degree of efficiency. However, research on the stock market confirms that market insiders earn excess return and investors who purchase information may expect an extra (fair) return for their expenditure on information.

Tests of the foreign exchange market have generally failed to reject the efficient market hypothesis, but these tests are difficult to formulate and interpret.[7] Interestingly, departures from market efficiency have been blamed on both too much and too little speculation. Journalists often portray foreign exchange rates as too volatile. Excessive speculation, it is argued, leads to exchange rate overshooting, and so forward rates will be poor predictors of future spot rates.[8] Ronald McKinnon argued that the move from Bretton Woods to managed floating in 1973 left the foreign exchange market with too little speculative capital. As a consequence, exchange speculators did not have the risk capital to stabilize rates and push forward rates toward the expected future spot rate.[9] Michael

[5]For an empirical test that rejects the risk premium hypothesis, see Jeffrey A. Frankel, "A Test of the Existence of the Risk Premium in the Foreign Exchange Market vs. the Hypothesis of Perfect Substitutability," *International Finance Discussion Papers*, No. 149, Federal Reserve System, August 1979.

[6]The forward rate may not be the "best" predictor because the available information has been combined according to "dollar votes" in the market place, rather than a formula that makes the best use of the information. This view is elaborated in Stephen Figlewski, "Market 'Efficiency' in a Market with Heterogeneous Expectations," *Journal of Political Economy* 86, No. 4 (August 1978), pp. 581–97.

[7]The literature of foreign exchange market efficiency is reviewed in Richard M. Levich, "Further Results on the Efficiency of Markets for Foreign Exchange," in *Managed Exchange-Rate Flexibility: The Recent Experience*, Federal Reserve Bank of Boston, Conference Series No. 20, 1978.

[8]A discussion of exchange rate overshooting appears in Richard M. Levich, "Overshooting in the Foreign Exchange Market," Group of Thirty Occasional Papers No. 5, New York, 1981.

[9]See Ronald I. McKinnon, *Money in International Exchange*, Oxford University Press, New York, 1979, pp. 155–62.

Rosenberg has argued that technical forecast rules often generate profits for the same reason—the speculative capital of banks and multinational corporations is relatively small and not sufficient to eliminate expected profits from open positions.[10]

What are the implications of this issue?

I. If the foreign exchange market is efficient and the forward rate does not contain a risk premium, then the forward rate represents the consensus market forecast, and it is the appropriate standard for comparisons against advisory service forecasts.

The forward rate will be an appealing forecaster in this case because it reflects the collective wisdom of thousands of well-informed, profit-seeking investors, it is updated continuously to reflect new information and it is free.

II. If the foreign exchange market is not efficient, then we expect advisory service forecasts to outperform the forward rate. Investors should earn a profit for their superior information. The profit may or may not compensate them for the cost of the advisory service.

HOW SHOULD WE MEASURE FORECASTING PERFORMANCE?

The analysis of forecasting performance is clearly an important issue. But unfortunately, two seemingly straightforward statistical tests can easily lead to misleading conclusions.[11]

The first approach concentrates on the forecast error defined as

$$\text{Forecast error} = \text{Predicted exchange rate} - \text{Actual exchange rate} \quad (2)$$

One desirable property of a forecast is that its forecasts errors be small. However, even this simple criterion needs qualification. For example, assume that today's forward rate is \$2·00 and two alternative forecasts of the future spot rate are \$1 = \$1·99 and \$2 = \$2·08. If the actual spot rate turns out to be \$2·02, the forecast error associated with \$1 (−\$0·03) is smaller than the forecast error associated with \$2 (+\$0·06). However, forecast \$2 is superior because it leads investors to take long and profitable positions in sterling—i.e. forecast \$2 leads to a correct decision.

As a further qualification, suppose that a third forecast, S3 = \$2·14, also exists. Even though its forecast error is +\$0·12, it does not follow that this forecast is twice as bad as forecast S2. If, for example, the firm is remitting a dividend to its U.S. parent and the firm is considering an all-or-nothing hedging decision, it will make the same decision using either S2 or S3 as a guide, and so there is no additional cost associated with S3's larger forecast error. On the other hand, forecast S3 may be more than twice as bad as forecast S2. If the firm is considering investing a variable amount in U.K. bonds, based on the substantial appreciation predicted by S3, the firm may invest 10 times as much in the U.K. as it would based on forecast S2. As a consequence, the firm foregoes other profitable investments. These opportunity costs of using S3 may exceed twice the costs of using S2.

[10]Michael R. Rosenberg, Chapter 2, section 5, in R. Ensor (ed.), *The Management of Foreign Exchange Risk*, Second Edition, London: Euromoney Publications, 1982.

[11]This section is based on Richard M. Levich, "Analyzing the Accuracy of Foreign Exchange Advisory Services: Theory and Evidence," in R. Levich and C. Wihlborg (eds.), *Exchange Risk and Exposure*, D. C. Heath, 1980.

Therefore, we conclude that there is no simple and unique relationship between the magnitude of forecast errors and the cost of forecast errors for investors. The implication of this statement is that there is no unique statistic for evaluating or ranking forecasters that will be correct for all investors. An all-or-nothing hedger will only be concerned that the forecast tells the correct direction, regardless of the magnitude of the forecast error. Investors who feel that exchange gains and losses are proportional to the forecast error will rank forecasters on the basis of mean absolute errors. Investors who feel that exchange gains and losses are proportional to the squared forecast error will rank forecasters on the basis of mean squared error. It is an empirical question whether these criteria will rank forecasters in similar order.

The second common approach for evaluating forecasting performance is to calculate the stream of returns that an investor could earn by following the forecast. We would conclude that the advisory service has expertise and that the forecasts are useful if the stream of investment returns (adjusting for risk) is high relative to alternative investments. Again, this straightforward evaluation procedure raises several difficult questions.

First, how does an investor translate a set of forecasts into a set of investment decisions? The investor recognizes that forecasts are seldom perfect. If the forward rate stands at \$2·00, the investor may not be willing to buy forward contracts unless the forecast is \$2·02, \$2·06 or perhaps higher. Furthermore, the investor is free to increase the number of forward contracts he purchases as his expected profits, and the confidence in those profits, increases. These issues are often handled by assuming that the investor uses the forecast to determine a lump-sum investment rather than an investment which increases with the expected returns predicted by the forecast or which decreases with the expected variance of returns.

The second difficult question is how we should measure the risk associated with currency investment. This calculation is necessary so that we can determine if the return on currency investment is high relative to the risk incurred. As we noted earlier, the measurement of the risk factor in forward contracts is somewhat controversial.

Examining the stream of speculative returns is prone to one further difficulty. Most extreme speculative returns result from large unanticipated exchange rate movements that were not predicted accurately by the advisory service and cannot be expected to recur in the future. For example, a 10% annual return following one service could be the result of a big move in one currency (15%) and losses in most other currencies. This situation would not suggest general forecasting expertise and furthermore, we could not be confident of a large exchange rate move to produce similar profits in the next period.

Instead of these two techniques, we propose a method that ignores the magnitude of forecast errors and calculates the fraction of periods in which the forecast correctly predicts only the direction of exchange rate movement. In our earlier example, S2 and S3 were correct relative to the forward rate while S1 was incorrect. If the fraction of correct forecasts is unusually high, then we can conclude that the advisory service has forecasting expertise.

A numerical example will help to illustrate the above procedure. In a sample of 100 observations (n), suppose there are 60 correct forecasts (r), or a 60% track record. Is this an unusually good track record or is it simply the result of a sequence of lucky guesses? The question is analogous to another basic statistics problem: If a fair coin is tossed 100 times, what is the probability that it will land on heads 60 or more times. The answer is, this event would occur with roughly 2·3% probability.[12] In this case, we would probably reject the notion that a fairly rare event happened, i.e. the forecaster guessed correctly on 60 of 100 trials. Instead, we would lean towards the view that the forecaster has some special expertise and that his probability of a correct forecast in the future is closer to 60%.

To summarize, we have drawn a distinction between correct forecasts (those that correctly predict the direction of change relative to the forward rate), and accurate forecasts. We have noted earlier that many exchange rate changes are very large and most are unanticipated by the market. Therefore, including these as large forecast errors may bias (upwards) our estimate of forecasting inaccuracy and our estimate of the potential for profits. In this sense, calculating the 'percentage correct forecast' may offer us a more useful and robust measure of forecasting expertise.

DATA DESCRIPTION AND GENERAL METHODOLOGY

Early in 1981, *Euromoney* invited more than 30 advisory services to participate in an analysis of their foreign exchange forecasts from the period 1977–80.[13] We received data from 13 advisory services. This represents 12 companies including Predex, which supplied two separate forecast series. The foreign exchange consulting services of all of the major banks were invited to participate but none accepted. Summary information on the sample services is presented in Exhibit 2. Six services forecast using econometric techniques, five services follow a judgmental approach and one service combines a basic purchasing power parity model with judgment. Predex's short-term forecasts are generated from a technical model.

Each advisory service supplied a copy of their forecasts for nine major currencies. These currencies were chosen because data on forward rates is available for comparison. Since the formats of these forecasts are not similar, several adjustments were required. For example, several services produce a quarterly average forecast. These figures were recorded as a point forecast for the mid-point of the quarter. Several services provide an end-of-quarter or end-of-period forecast. In this case we simply recorded the origin date and horizon date for each forecast. (The origin date is the date on which a subscriber could receive and act on a forecast. The services are trying to predict the exchange rate to be realized on the horizon date.) Wharton reports a sequence of end-of-month forecasts for the next 24 months. Our procedure was to record only the one-, three-, six- and 12-month ahead forecasts.

The final database includes a record of the origin date and the horizon date for every forecast. With this information, we construct a set of implied one-, three-, six- and 12-month ahead forecasts at each origin date for each advisory service. We do this so that the forecasts are compatible with available forward rate quotations. Our procedure to construct these forecasts uses linear interpolation.

In summary, our procedure is to compute the one-, three-, six- and 12-month ahead

[12]To make the calculation we compute $Z = (r/n - 0{\cdot}5)/\sqrt{0.25/n}$ which equals 2·0 in this example. The area under the standard normal curve to the right of 2·0 equals 0·023.

[13]We did not actively solicit technical or momentum services. For an analysis of these forecasting techniques, see Stephen H. Goodman, next section.

EXHIBIT 2

Summary Information on the Advisory Services

Name	Sample dates	Number of observations	Frequency	Type of forecast	Horizons	Methodology	Price (dollars)
1. Business International	Mar. 1978–Dec. 1980	34	12/year	Quarterly average	6 quarters	Econometric	980
2. Chase Econometrics	Jan. 1977–Dec. 1980	48	12/year	Quarterly average	8 quarters	Econometric	12,000
3. Chase Manhattan Bank Economics Department	Nov. 1977–Nov. 1979	16	sporadic	End-of-period	1, 3, 6, 12 months	Judgmental	Free
4. Citibank — Economics Department	Jan. 1977–Dec. 1980	35	9–10/year	Quarterly average	4 quarters	Judgmental	Free
5. Conti Currency	Jan. 1977–Dec. 1980	43	11/year	End-of-quarter	4 quarters	Judgmental	12,500–25,000
6. Data Resources	Aug. 1977–Nov. 1980	28	9–11/year	Quarterly average	6 quarters	Econometric	4,100–23,700
7. Exchange Rate Outlook	Nov. 1978–Dec. 1980	26	12/year	End-of-period	1 year ahead	Judgmental	350
8. Multinational Computer Models, Inc.	Oct. 1979–Dec. 1980	15	12/year	End-of-period	3, 6, 9, 12 months ahead	Real 'PPP' model plus judgment	1,000+
9. M. Murenbeeld and Associates	Jan. 1977–Dec. 1980	43	12/year	End-of-period	3, 12 months ahead	Econometric with judgment added	2,000
10. Phillips and Drew	Mar. 1980–Sept. 1980	7	12/year	End-of-period	Mid-year and year end	Judgmental	n.a.
11. Predex — Forecast	Jan. 1977–Dec. 1980	48	12/year	Quarterly average	6 quarters	Econometric	12,000+
12. Predex — Short Term Forecast	July 1978–Dec. 1980	30	12/year	Monthly average	1, 2, 3, months ahead	Technical	5,000 + 6,000 for trading signals
13. Wharton Econometric Forecasting Associates	Jan. 1980–Dec. 1980	11	11/year	Monthly average	24 months ahead	Econometric	25,000

forecasts on each origin date for each advisory service. In many cases these data transformations do not alter the original information provided by the service. But in at least two cases (Exchange Rate Outlook which reports only a one-year-ahead forecast, and Predex whose short-term forecasts extend to only three months) it is not clear that the forecasts were intended for use at other horizons.[14] One could argue that these techniques for transforming the various forecasts into a common format may violate a forecaster's exchange rate predictions. But a customer who received an advisor's forecast and had to apply it immediately to a one-, three-, six- or 12-month decision might make very similar calculations.

Five services (Chase Econometrics, Citibank-Economics Department, Conti Currency, M. Murenbeeld and Predex Forecast) produced forecasts throughout the entire sample period. Track record comparisons among these five services are therefore appropriate. The remaining services began their careers at various times after January 1977, and so their results are based on different time periods. How this will effect the results is unclear. For example, the percentage of correct forecasts by Wharton is generally greater than 50% but their service began only in 1980. On the one hand, it would be correct to argue that Wharton's track record is, statistically speaking, less significant because it is based on relatively few observations. On the other hand, one might also argue that Wharton's track

[14]Multinational Computer Models, Inc. markets a short-term forecast which would be intended for the one-month horizon, but we were not aware of this until our statistical analysis was completed.

record is enhanced in economic significance because their forecasts are concentrated in 1980, a year with extremely high exchange rate volatility.

Once we have recorded the forward rates ($F_{t,n}$) and the forecasts ($\hat{S}_{t,n}$) for each origin date and the future spot exchange rate (S_{t+n}), our methodology follows easily.[15] For each currency and advisory service, we calculate the percentage forecast error as:

$$E_{t,n} = (S_{t+n} - \hat{S}_{t,n})/S_{t+n} \tag{3}$$

where n may equal one, three, six or 12 months. The speculative return on an open position is

$$P_{t,n} = W_t(S_{t+n} - F_{t,n})/F_{t,n} \tag{4}$$

where

$$W_t = \begin{cases} +1 \text{ if } \hat{S}_{t,n} > F_{t,n} \text{ and we buy forward contracts} \\ -1 \text{ if } \hat{S}_{t,n} < F_{t,n} \text{ and we sell forward contracts.} \end{cases}$$

A variation on this calculation would set $W_t = +1$ or -1 only if $\hat{S}_{t,n}$ were greater (less) than $F_{t,n}$ by some predetermined amount, say 0·5%. Forecasts within the 0.·5% bound might be indicating no exchange rate change and so no action is required. The calculated returns in (4) can be added across time periods and currencies.

A forecast is correct if both $\hat{S}_{t,n}$ and S_{t+n} are on the same side of the forward rate. The fraction

$$p = r \text{ (correct forecasts)}/n \text{ (total forecasts)}$$

estimates the probability of correct advice in any period. We want to infer whether this probability is greater than one-half. Formally, we are testing the null hypothesis

$$H_0{:}p = 0.5 \text{ (advisory service has no expertise)}$$

versus an alternative hypothesis

$$H_1{:}p > 0.5 \text{ (there is forecasting expertise)}$$

Using the normal probability curve, we can calculate p1, a measure of our confidence that p is greater than 0·5. Small values of p1 suggest that it is unlikely that the track record was achieved by chance alone.

EMPIRICAL RESULTS

We first present a statistic that measures forecasting accuracy relative to the forward rate. For each currency and advisory service, we computed the mean absolute forecast error divided by the mean absolute forecast error of the forward rate. Values of this ratio less than 1·0 suggest that the advisory service is more accurate than the forward rate forecast. Exhibit 3 summarizes this ratio of the mean absolute forecast errors for the entire sample period. Overall, the data suggest that these 13 advisory services have not forecast as accurately as the forward rate.

At the 12-month horizon, only 33% of the entries are less than 1·0. This figure falls to 24% at the three-month horizon. Wharton is an exception to this result with 75% of their

[15]Our source for forward rate and spot rates is the Harris Bank *Weekly Review*.

EXHIBIT 3

Mean Absolute Error/Mean Absolute Forward Error

One-month horizon

Currency	Services 1	2	3	4	5	6	7	8	9	10	11	12	13	Percentage <1·0
Can $	1·20	1·03	1·03	1·32	0·90	1·06	n.a.	1·06	1·07	1·05	1·16	1·66	1·14	
£	1·01	1·11	1·15	1·44	0·89	0·95	1·03	1·05	1·09	1·30	0·99	1·11	1·13	
Bfr	1·20	1·0	n.a.	1·19	0·99	n.a.	n.a.	0·96	1·07	n.a.	1·09	1·05	0·87	
Ffr	0·89	0·96	1·18	1·31	1·06	n.a.	0·99	0·97	1·03	1·13	1·00	1·20	0·84	
DM	0·95	1·02	1·24	1·11	0·99	1·08	1·02	0·96	1·09	1·12	1·07	1·10	0·80	$\frac{30}{104}$ = 28·8%
Lit	0·96	0·94	1·20	1·20	0·90	n.a.	1·02	1·00	0·95	1·03	1·35	1·24	0·96	
Dfl	1·16	1·01	n.a.	1·19	0·93	n.a.	n.a.	1·02	1·07	1·28	1·04	1·06	0·82	
Swfr	0·92	n.a.	1·07	1.16	0·99	n.a.	n.a.	0·95	1·11	1·10	0·98	1·05	0·87	
¥	1·39	0·98	1·20	1·26	0·94	1·38	1·07	1·09	1·01	0·86	1·27	1·32	1·27	

Three-month horizon

Currency	1	2	3	4	5	6	7	8	9	10	11	12	13	Percentage <1·0
Can $	1·29	1·13	1·00	1·59	0·99	1·08	n.a.	1·47	1·17	1·03	1·47	1·74	0·80	
£	1·11	1·24	0·91	1·44	1·09	0·98	1·05	1·09	1·27	1·69	1·03	1·22	1·01	
Bfr	0·95	1·07	n.a.	1·33	1·17	n.a.	n.a.	0·99	1·21	n.a.	1·06	1·01	0·77	
Ffr	0·91	0·98	1·02	1·43	1·27	n.a.	0·98	0·92	1·00	0·96	1·03	1·16	0·70	
DM	1·08	1·13	1·07	1·28	1·19	1·35	1·06	0·83	1·19	1·07	1·13	1·04	0·76	$\frac{25}{104}$ = 24·0%
Lit	1·07	0·91	1·09	1·45	1·14	n.a.	1·12	1·12	1·00	1·17	1·64	1·54	0·93	
Dfl	0·80	1·10	n.a.	1·41	1·06	n.a.	n.a.	0·91	1·26	1·26	1·10	1·01	0·81	
Swfr	1·01	n.a.	1·08	1·21	1·32	n.a.	n.a.	0·86	1·06	1·04	1·04	0·94	0·63	
¥	1·42	1·05	1·02	1·23	1·08	1·45	1·09	1·24	0·94	0·47	1·31	1·30	1·79	

Six-month horizon

Currency	1	2	3	4	5	6	7	8	9	10	11	12	13	Percentage <1·0
Can $	1·40	1·34	1·05	2·06	1·20	1·24	n.a.	2·21	1·48	1·82	1·48	2·65	0·63	
£	1·38	1·33	1·28	1·56	1·02	1·04	1·20	0·99	1·36	1·28	1·02	1·39	0·97	
Bfr	1·22	1·13	n.a.	1·32	1·14	n.a.	n.a.	1·05	1·24	n.a.	0·86	1·05	0·93	
Ffr	1·10	1·02	1·21	1·35	1·23	n.a.	0·98	1·03	0·91	0·78	1·00	1·19	0·94	
DM	1·30	1·14	1·28	1·22	1·17	1·45	1·08	0·79	1·12	0·94	0·85	0·93	0·83	$\frac{30}{104}$ = 28·8%
Lit	1·24	0·99	1·39	1·61	1·09	n.a.	1·14	1·21	0·93	1·15	1·52	2·00	0·93	
Dfl	1·06	1·12	n.a.	1·39	1·09	n.a.	n.a.	0·94	1·18	0·85	0·93	0·98	0·92	
Swfr	1·12	n.a.	1·20	1·16	1·14	n.a.	n.a.	0·78	1·11	0·91	0·87	0·81	0·65	
¥	1·33	1·01	0·97	1·03	1·14	1·05	1·02	1·49	0·87	0·39	1·13	1·29	1·57	

12-month horizon

Currency	1	2	3	4	5	6	7	8	9	10	11	12	13	Percentage <1·0
Can $	2·35	1·16	1·44	2·16	1·32	1·53	n.a.	3·40	1·95	3·63	1·48	5·47	0·61	
£	1·59	1·27	1·28	1·62	1·23	1·16	1·40	0·89	1·31	1·05	0·85	1·03	1·44	
Bfr	1·47	1·03	n.a.	1·37	1·33	n.a.	n.a.	0·80	1·23	n.a.	0·78	1·40	0·90	
Ffr	1·41	0·92	1·29	1·51	1·19	n.a.	0·88	0·91	0·80	0·91	0·98	1·77	0·88	
DM	1·54	1·11	2·16	1·38	1·43	1·26	1·03	0·82	1·17	1·09	0·76	1·16	0·91	$\frac{34}{104}$ = 32·7%
Lit	1·30	0·94	1·28	1·58	1·12	n.a.	0·97	0·99	0·65	1·12	1·13	2·41	1·04	
Dfl	1·24	1·06	n.a.	1·37	1·35	n.a.	n.a.	0·77	1·13	0·89	0·80	1·31	0·91	
Swfr	1·32	n.a.	1·39	0·99	1·17	n.a.	n.a.	0·66	0·96	1·17	0·79	0·94	0·85	
¥	1·48	1·01	1·13	0·97	1·08	0·70	1·17	1·60	0·77	0·77	1·22	1·42	1·75	

n.a. = Data not available or not applicable.

entries less than 1·0. Other concentrations of forecasts that were more accurate than the forward rate are Conti Currency at the one-month horizon, Multinational Computer Models at horizons greater than three months, and Predex Forecast at the 12-month horizon. Even these services had difficulty making consistently accurate forecasts for the Japanese yen. But Phillips and Drew was more accurate than the yen forward rates, albeit for a small number of forecasts.

To keep perspective, it should be noted that 70% of the entries in Exhibit 3 are between 0·75 and 1·25. If the forward rate's average absolute forecast error is 4%, our data suggest that most average absolute errors are in the 3–5% range. For many purposes, this may not be a substantial difference.

Earlier we stressed the distinction between accurate forecasts and correct forecasts. Data on the percentage of correct forecasts over the entire sample period are summarized in Exhibit 4. One way to analyse the Exhibit is to count the number of track records greater than 70% (there are 67 or roughly 16%) or greater than 60% (there are 129 or 31%). Intuitively, this number seems like a high concentration of respectable track records. It certainly imparts an opposite impression of forecasting ability than we had from Exhibit 3. We can also observe that most of the high track records among our sample are concentrated in the econometric services. For econometric services, 47 of 212 track records (or 22%) are greater than 70%, and 91 of 212 (or 43%) exceed 60%. In this sample it also appears that services based on more complex econometric models (Chase Econometrics, D.R.I. and Wharton) did not consistently outperform other econometric models.

The track records alone do not tell the whole story of Exhibit 4. We must account for the number of independent observations in each track record to measure its statistical significance. For example, Phillips and Drew's 100% track record on 12-month yen is based on only two forecasts that could be followed to completion. When there is no forecasting expertise, the probability of two correct forecasts out of two attempts is 25%, the same as the probability of tossing heads two times in a row with a fair coin. After this calculation, we would probably not feel that the 100% track record demonstrates significant evidence for expertise; the track record could have happened easily by chance.

On the other hand, consider Business International's track record for the one-month Belgian franc, 73·5% correct. This is based on 34 observations. The chance that they might achieve 25 or more correct forecasts (73·5% of 34) by simply guessing is less than 1%—highly significant evidence favouring expertise in this case. The entries in Exhibit 4 are marked with the letters (A), (B), and (C) to indicate the statistical significance of each track record—10%, 5% and 1% respectively. All of the marked entries could be considered statistically significant. The entries marked (C) are the most unusual and significant.

Taken as a whole, do the entries in Exhibit 4 show statistically significant results in favour of forecasting expertise? Return for a moment to a coin-tossing experiment. The probability of three successive heads (or three successive tails) is 1/8 when tossing a fair coin. Chances are good that if we had eight monkeys, each tossing a fair coin three times, then one of the monkeys would toss three straight heads. The message is that, with many monkeys, the chances of observing an extreme outcome improve, even though everyone plays with a fair coin. In our case, Exhibit 4 represents many forecasters who predicted many currencies. Of the 416 live cells in the Exhibit we expect that 10% (or 42) will be significant at the 10% level, even though none of the forecasters had expertise. Similarly, we expect to find 21 entries that are significant at the 5% level and four entries that are significant at the 1% level, even if the forecasters have no special expertise to make correct

EXHIBIT 4

Percentage Correct Forecasts

One-month horizon

	Services												
Currency	**1**	**2**	**3**	**4**	**5**	**6**	**7**	**8**	**9**	**10**	**11**	**12**	**13**
Can $	56	44	69 (A)	54	63 (B)	57	n.a.	53	33	29	46	43	64
£	59	44	31	20	65 (B)	61	35	33	44	29	48	53	45
Bfr	74 (C)	42	n.a.	49	60 (A)	n.a.	n.a.	60	40	n.a.	63 (B)	47	55
Ffr	59	56	56	37	53	n.a.	58	60	56	43	69 (C)	47	64
DM	65 (B)	42	31	37	63 (B)	61	50	60	40	29	65 (B)	57	55
Lit	50	54	31	46	65 (B)	n.a.	54	47	56	57	71 (C)	57	73 (A)
Dfl	62 (A)	44	n.a.	37	60 (A)	n.a.	n.a.	53	44	29	67 (B)	50	64
Swr	56	n.a.	38	34	58	n.a.	n.a.	60	47	43	54	43	64
¥	50	56	44	49	63 (B)	43	38	53	49	71	38	53	36

Three-month horizon

Currency	**1**	**2**	**3**	**4**	**5**	**6**	**7**	**8**	**9**	**10**	**11**	**12**	**13**
Can $	56	46	81 (A)	34	58	54	n.a.	27	42	43	48	37	82
£	44	33	63	23	44	50	31	53	44	43	54	60	64
Bfr	62	48	n.a.	31	37	n.a.	n.a.	60	40	n.a.	65	47	82
Ffr	59	52	38	31	44	n.a.	54	67	65	57	81 (C)	63	91 (A)
DM	59	44	44	34	42	43	46	73	47	71	65	57	82
Lit	50	60	31	34	58	n.a.	50	33	56	29	77 (B)	50	55
Dfl	65	50	n.a.	34	49	n.a.	n.a.	67	47	43	65	53	91 (A)
Swfr	59	n.a.	25	43	42	n.a.	n.a.	93 (B)	53	71	65	73 (B)	82
¥	41	46	25	34	53	50	35	40	51	100	31	40	18

Six-month horizon

Currency	**1**	**2**	**3**	**4**	**5**	**6**	**7**	**8**	**9**	**10**	**11**	**12**	**13**
Can $	67	35	50	32	56	57	n.a.	21	32	14	34	48	70
£	30	20	31	15	51	43	16	36	32	29	60	69	50
Bfr	55	35	n.a.	41	37	n.a.	n.a.	79	41	n.a.	66	62	50
Ffr	55	52	50	47	30	n.a.	72	86	73	86	83 (B)	76	70
DM	45	35	38	38	42	50	48	79	54	71	77 (A)	55	90
Lit	27	61	31	32	56	n.a.	48	64	49	43	66	55	50
Dfl	61	41	n.a.	47	35	n.a.	n.a.	71	61	71	62	59	60
Swfr	55	n.a.	31	44	47	n.a.	n.a.	86	63	71	70	76	100 (A)
¥	24	41	38	41	42	54	52	29	66	86	51	41	20

12-month horizon

Currency	**1**	**2**	**3**	**4**	**5**	**6**	**7**	**8**	**9**	**10**	**11**	**12**	**13**
Can $	56	46	31	30	51	52	n.a.	13	22	0	41	39	75
£	11	20	0	3	30	35	11	75	33	50	71	83	50
Bfr	41	49	n.a.	33	19	n.a.	n.a.	88	42	n.a.	73	61	75
Ffr	41	76	13	30	27	n.a.	74	88	61	100	88 (A)	78	75
DM	44	44	6	47	22	48	53	88	53	50	71	61	75
Lit	19	59	13	23	30	n.a.	58	38	64	0	71	61	50
Dfl	48	51	n.a.	40	16	n.a.	n.a.	100	61	100	73	61	75
Swfr	41	n.a.	31	53	46	n.a.	n.a.	100	72	0	78	78	100
¥	37	51	19	50	46	65	42	0	67	100	54	26	0

n.a. = Data not available or not applicable.

Summary:	**Significance level**	**Expected number of significant entries**	**Actual number of significant entries**
	10% (A)	42	28
	5% (B)	21	17
	1% (C)	4	4

forecasts. The actual number of entries that are significant at the 10%, 5% and 1% levels is 28, 17 and four respectively—within the range expected under the null hypothesis. Therefore, as a group, these forecasters did not display statistically significant expertise.

However, the significant track records appear to be concentrated among a few services—Predex Forecast (with 10 significant entries), Conti Currency (with seven), Wharton (with four), and Business International (with three). As we noted before, several advisory services (Multinational Computer Models, M. Murenbeeld, Phillips and Drew, and Predex Short-Term) have many high-percentage track records, but these are based on too few independent observations to be statistically significant. Only more independent observations will make clear whether these track records are the result of true expertise or random chance.

One way to increase the number of observations and, therefore, to increase the efficiency of our search for expertise, is to pool together the track records from several currencies by a single forecaster. However, we must be careful to pool only independent forecasts. Five currencies (Canadian dollar, British pound, Deutschemark, Swiss franc and Japanese yen) move relatively independently of each other over the sample period.

EXHIBIT 5

Percentage Correct Forecasts for each Advisory Service Pooled Across Currencies

One-month	**1**	**2**	**3**	**4**	**5**	**6**	**7**	**8**	**9**	**10**	**11**	**12**	**13**
Percent correct	58·82	47·66	42·86	40·32	61·24	55·35	46·92	53·33	45·22	41·07	57·64	50.00	57·58
Nobs (independent)	306	384	112	315	387	112	130	135	387	56	432	270	99
Significance level	0·10 (C)	n.a.	n.a.	n.a.	0·00 (C)	12·85	n.a.	21·94	n.a.	n.a.	0·07 (C)	n.a.	6·58 (A)
Nobs (half dep.)	153	192	56	158	194	56	65	68	194	28	216	135	50
Significance level	1·45 (B)	n.a.	n.a.	n.a.	0·09 (C)	21·14	n.a.	29·27	n.a.	n.a.	1·24 (B)	n.a.	14·44

Three-month	**1**	**2**	**3**	**4**	**5**	**6**	**7**	**8**	**9**	**10**	**11**	**12**	**13**
Percent correct	54·90	47·39	43·75	33·34	47·55	49·11	43·08	57·04	49·35	57·14	61·11	53·33	71·72
Nobs (independent)	306	384	112	315	387	112	130	135	387	56	432	270	99
Significance level	16·11	n.a.	n.a.	n.a.	n.a.	n.a.	n.a.	17·26	n.a.	27·22	0·38 (C)	26·35	0·63 (C)
Nobs (half dep.)	153	192	56	154	194	56	65	68	194	28	216	135	50
Significance level	24·20	n.a.	n.a.	n.a.	n.a.	n.a.	n.a.	25·46	n.a.	33·41	2·07 (B)	32·74	4·11 (B)

Six-month	**1**	**2**	**3**	**4**	**5**	**6**	**7**	**8**	**9**	**10**	**11**	**12**	**13**
Percent correct	46·47	39·94	38·39	37·58	43·93	50·89	47·20	61·11	52·30	58·93	63·12	60·15	62·22
Nobs (independent)	297	368	112	306	387	112	125	126	369	56	423	261	90
Significance level	n.a.	n.a.	n.a.	n.a.	n.a.	46·98	n.a.	15·43	35·95	29·61	1·41 (B)	9·15 (A)	17·19
Nobs (half dep.)	148	184	56	153	194	56	62	63	184	28	212	130	45
Significance level	n.a.	n.a.	n.a.	n.a.	n.a.	47·86	n.a.	24·11	40·04	36·05	6·03 (A)	17·60	25·89

12-month	**1**	**2**	**3**	**4**	**5**	**6**	**7**	**8**	**9**	**10**	**11**	**12**	**13**
Percent correct	37·45	49·39	16·07	34·44	31·83	50·00	47·37	65·28	52·78	50·00	68·83	60·87	63·89
Nobs (independent)	243	328	112	270	333	92	95	72	324	16	369	207	36
Significance level	n.a.	n.a.	n.a.	n.a.	n.a.	50·00	n.a.	22·71	38·64	50·00	1·96 (B)	18·50	31·52
Nobs (half dep.)	122	164	56	135	166	46	48	36	162	8	184	103	18
Significance level	n.a.	n.a.	n.a.	n.a.	n.a.	50·00	n.a.	29·83	42·06	50·00	7·23 (A)	26·93	39·06

n.a. = not applicable. Percent correct is below 50%.

Summary:	**Significance level**	**Expected number of significant entries**	**Actual number (independent)**	**Actual number (half-dependent)**
	10% (A)	5·2	9	7
	5% (B)	2·6	7	5
	1% (C)	0·5	5	1

Four other currencies (Belgian franc, French franc, Italian lira and Dutch guilder) are linked to the DM via the European Monetary System, but these linkages (especially for the French franc and the Italian lira) have been relatively weak recently. Therefore, even though an advisor forecasts nine currencies, it is conservative to assume that only one-half of these forecasts are independent. The significance levels reported in Exhibit 5 incorporate this assumption.

Exhibit 5 reports the percentage of correct forecasts for each advisory service pooling across all currencies. Conti Currency recorded the best overall track record at the one-month horizon, 61·24%. Based on 387 total forecasts (43 forecasts on nine currencies) or only one-half that number (assuming some degree of dependence between currency forecasts), this result is highly significant and unusual. Several other overall one-month track records are high and statistically significant—Business International (58·82%), Predex Forecast (57·64%) and Wharton (57·58%). Our adjustment for dependent forecasts, as expected, reduces the significance level of each track record, but the results for Conti Currency, Business International and Predex Forecast remain statistically significant.

At the three-month horizon, Wharton records the best overall track record, 71·72%, and it is statistically significant even though it is based on a shorter time period. Predex Forecast's 61·11% three-month overall track record is also highly significant. Several other track records exceed 50%, but they are drawn from too few observations to indicate statistical significance.

At the six-month and 12-month horizon, Predex Forecast, Wharton, Multinational Computer Models and Predex Short-Term achieved overall track records in excess of 60%. However, the results for Predex Forecast are statistically significant because they are based on a larger sample of observations.

SOME ANTICIPATED QUESTIONS AND CONCLUSIONS

1. Do these results prove that the foreign exchange market is inefficient?

No, they do not. The reason is because the forward rate may contain a risk premium. If so, exchange rate forecasters ought to be able to forecast better than the forward rate. The profits earned by speculators who follow these forecasts may represent only a fair return for the extra foreign exchange risk incurred.

2. Do the results prove that the forecasters beat the forward rate?

The results clearly show that many services have a record of percentage correct forecasts that is not easily explained by chance. For users who face hedge everything/hedge nothing decisions and who can tolerate the risk associated with open positions, our results suggest that forecasts can help to improve exposure management performance.

3. The testing procedures are unfair to the advisory services. The forecasts of the different services are by nature different and not comparable. Clients realize that forecasts are not always up-to-date and they always phone for current advice. It is unrealistic to assume that clients always follow all advice and hold positions until maturity. Some positions will be liquidated early.

A user is forced to compare diverse forecasts. He is forced to extract information from a quarterly average forecast or an end-of-year forecast and make a decision today concerning his foreign exchange positions. The methods we have used do not introduce any obvious bias into the results.

We assume that the forecasts we have analysed constitute a representative sample of the forecasters advice on any day. The advice which is printed should be as good as the advice that is given over the phone. It may be the case that speculators follow a forecaster's advice on a three-month position and then reverse the position with one month remaining. The advice to reverse a position must be correct and timely (i.e. ahead of forward rate adjustments) if the reversal is to be profitable.

4. Advisory services hire and fire people and change their forecasting equations. Will an advisor's past track record be a helpful guide for the future?

We cannot know for sure. In the monkey example, the fact that one monkey tosses three straight heads does not improve the chances for tossing three more heads the next time out; the monkey still holds a fair coin. The foreign exchange forecasters in this study have compiled many good track records—for individual currencies (Exhibit 4), about the same number to be expected by chance, but when pooled across currencies for each service (Exhibit 5), too many high track records to be expected by chance.

One interpretation of the latter result is that forecasting expertise is an attribute of the advisory service—and therefore it should persist over time. The past may not be a good predictor of the future, but historic forecasts are all that we have available for concrete analysis. The efficient market hypothesis suggests that if forecasts convey useful information, speculators will purchase forecasts and use them until the information in the forecast is reflected in market prices, rendering the forecasts worthless. While these events may have been in process over the last several years, the data suggest that a significant number of forecasters were able to provide useful information concerning the position of the future spot exchange rate relative to today's forward rate.

Purchasing Power Parity and the Real Exchange Rate

15

What Does Purchasing Power Parity Mean?*

Alan C. Shapiro†

One of the most widely studied and debated empirical propositions in economics is purchasing power parity (PPP). In its absolute version, PPP states that the equilibrium exchange rate between domestic and foreign currencies equals the ratio between domestic and foreign price levels. In other words, a unit of currency should have the same purchasing power around the world. The relative version of PPP modifies this doctrine by stating that proportionate changes in the ratio of domestic and foreign prices will equal proportionate changes in the equilibrium exchange rate between domestic and foreign currencies.

In a world of perfect certainty, with uniform price changes, identical consumption preferences, all goods tradable, and no transportation costs or barriers to trade, the meaning of purchasing power parity is unambiguous. It is much less clear what the theoretical and empirical content of PPP is in a multicommodity world with relative price changes, differing consumption preferences across countries, nontraded goods, transaction costs, and uncertainty. The variety of tests performed and the differing conclusions reached concerning the validity of PPP, using similar data sets, all point to a good deal of confusion as to what PPP really involves. For example, suggestions as to the appropriate price index to use in testing for PPP have ranged from the price of the least traded commodity—labor (e.g., Hawtrey, 1919)—to an index of nontraded goods only (Graham, 1930) to the broadest domestic index available (e.g., Cassel, 1928) to an index comprised only of traded goods (e.g., Angell, 1922) to individual prices of traded commodities (Ohlin, 1933).

In large part, this confusion reflects the lack of a decision-theoretic framework. To select the appropriate version of purchasing power parity to test and then to compare and evaluate the test results properly requires an explicit loss function associated with the hypothesis of PPP. This, in turn, requires answers to the following questions. Why are economists interested in PPP? What decisions and/or policy recommendations are dependent on the presence (or absence) of PPP? What costs are associated with the incorrect decisions that result from mistakenly accepting (or rejecting) the hypothesis of purchasing power parity? It is conceivable that different decision problems require the testing of different versions of PPP; they are also likely to involve different loss functions. Thus the

---

*This article is reprinted, with permission, from *Journal of International Money and Finance,* 1983, 2, 295–318.

†I would like to thank Fischer Black and especially Richard Roll for their helpful comments without holding them responsible in any way for the final product. In addition, I appreciate the critical remarks of an anonymous reviewer for this journal. This paper was written under a research grant from the School of Business Administration, University of Southern California, which is gratefully acknowledged.

accept/reject decision for the PPP hypothesis is not independent of the purpose(s) for testing it.

The objective of this paper is to take stock of the issues having to do with the meaning and empirical testing of purchasing power parity. Although the paper references most of the important works in this area, it goes beyond being just a survey. In contrast to much of what has been written about PPP, this paper relies on the perhaps controversial assumption that goods and asset markets are continually in equilibrium; that is, it assumes that opportunities for profitable arbitrage are eliminated almost as soon as they are recognized. It is organized as follows: Section I presents some of the questions whose resolution depends on whether purchasing power parity exists. Section II examines the meaning of PPP from an efficient markets perspective while Section III seeks to adaress some of the issues raised in Section I. The final section summarizes and concludes the paper.

I. ISSUES INVOLVING PURCHASING POWER PARITY

Most research on purchasing power parity has focused on it as a theory of exchange-rate determination. More recent research efforts have emphasized the implications of PPP, and deviations from it, for macroeconomic behavior, specifically the degree to which national economies are linked by the mechanism of commodity arbitrage, and for international financial theory, particularly whether investors in different countries measure real investment risks and returns identically. From all three perspectives, the existence or absence of purchasing power parity is of more than just academic interest. It has an important bearing on the answers to a number of key questions.

IA. PPP and Exchange Rate Determination

Purchasing power parity was first stated in a rigorous manner by Cassel (1918), who used it as the basis for recommending a new set of official exchange rates at the end of World War I that would allow for the resumption of normal trade relations. Since then, PPP has been widely used by central banks as a guide to establishing new par values for their currencies when the old ones were clearly in disequilibrium.

In recent years, perhaps the most important policy role of purchasing power parity in its guise as a theory of exchange-rate determination has been to provide a benchmark against which to judge whether floating exchange rates exhibit excessive swings, causing unpredictably large changes in the relative table competitiveness of nations. This is the notion of 'overshooting', that relative to some standard (usually PPP), exchange rate movements are excessive. If floating rates do overshoot their equilibrium values, then the market may be inefficient, possibly justifying government intervention to stabilize these rates. On the other hand, if the foreign exchange market is operating efficiently, then overshooting may be due to the slow adjustment of goods prices relative to currency rates. In either case, overshooting would involve short-run deviations from purchasing power parity. The various theories that explain overshooting provide few clues as to the length of this short run.

From a management standpoint, purchasing power parity is often used to forecast future exchange rates, for purposes ranging from deciding on the currency denomination(s) of long-term debt issues to determining in which countries to build plants. As pointed out by Rogalski and Vinso (1977), the effectiveness of using PPP in this manner depends crucially on the extent to which PPP (or deviations from it) can signal profitable international arbitrage opportunities.

IB. PPP AND LINKAGES BETWEEN NATIONAL ECONOMIES

National economies are linked by trade in financial assets and commodities. The speed and efficiency with which these arbitrage mechanisms work determine the extent to which national economies are open or closed. The issue is whether domestic prices are primarily determined by domestic supply and demand (a closed economy) or by worldwide supply and demand (an open economy). In other words, the question is whether PPP holds in the short run, as well as in the long run.

Most macroeconomic models, at least for the United States, assume that national economies are closed rather than open. The international economy, if included at all, is treated as just one more economic sector, with minimal linkages with the domestic economy. This is the Martian model described by McCloskey and Zecher (1981), where each national economy is treated like a separate planet in the solar system having few interactions with the other planets or economies.

According to this model, governments can run independent monetary policies, thereby changing domestic prices relative to foreign prices converted into the home currency. Moreover, devaluation of the home currency can work to stimulate exports and reduce imports. This viewpoint, implicitly if not explicitly, rejects the existence of purchasing power parity, except possibly in the long run (at least one year and usually more like five years).

If, however, purchasing power parity does hold in the short run, as well as the long run, then governments cannot run independent monetary policies, devaluation will not work to improve a nation's trade competitiveness, and all macroeconomic models that rely for their validity on the assumption of a closed economy can be rejected.[1]

IC. PPP and International Financial Theory

According to modern capital market theory, investors allocate their funds globally in line with the real risks and rewards they anticipate. The existence of PPP insures that in the absence of taxes of other barriers to international investment investors from different countries will measure these real risks and returns identically and consequently will hold identical portfolios. Then, as shown by Grauer, Litzenberger and Stehle (1976), assets will be priced in a common context and an International Asset Pricing Model (IAPM) will exist. Conversely, deviations from PPP cause real returns to differ according to the investor's nationality and produce differing portfolio compositions by nation. As Adler and Dumas (1981) point out, these deviations also imply that the real gains from international diversification will be different for everyone and hence indeterminate. The existence of barriers to international investment will have qualitatively similar results (see, for example, Black, 1974; Stapleton and Subrahmanyam, 1977).

II. PURCHASING POWER PARITY AND MARKET EQUILIBRIUM

In order to address the questions raised in Section I, it is helpful to first establish, under certain simplifying assumptions, the equilibrium conditions that can be expected to hold between product prices and price levels in different countries and spot exchange rates. The basic premise underlying the development of these conditions is that prices and exchange rates adjust so as to eliminate all profitable arbitrage opportunities; i.e., goods and asset markets are efficient. This hypothesis, that agents behave optimally in seeking to maximize their own well-being, is untestable yet is the metaphysical basis for the theory of international trade, the modern theory of finance, and indeed, all of economics.[2] The alternative, which is to assume irrational agent behavior, would present great difficulties in modeling economic behavior.

IIA. The Classic View

Until recently, however, published works on PPP failed to explicitly link the utility-maximizing behavior of individuals with the hypothesized cross-country relationships between exchange-adjusted prices and price changes. Instead, most research in this area concentrated on the role of international factor and product mobility, nontraded goods, and measurement problems in short- and long-run PPP. (See Officer (1976) for a good survey of this literature.) Observed discrepancies in PPP not due to measurement error were attributed to disequilibrium in either the goods market or the foreign exchange market. These studies appeared not to recognize (or ignored) the fact that disequilibrium in a market possibly implies the existence of profitable arbitrage opportunities. In addition, Lucas and Sargent (1979, p. 7) point out that 'simply to look at any economic time series and conclude that it is a disequilibrium situation is a meaningless observation.' Moreover, work by Sonnenschein (1973) implies that the hypothesis of competitive equilibrium is untestable using economic time series.

IIB. Purchasing Power Parity and Market Efficiency

A new perspective was provided by Rogalski and Vinso (1977), who pointed out the inherent conflict between the efficient markets concept and any lagged adjustment to purchasing power parity. In a parallel but independent study, Roll (1979) developed a dynamic intertemporal theory of purchasing power parity from an efficient markets perspective.[3] Most recently, McCloskey and Zecher (1981) argued that PPP is the inevitable consequence of arbitragers seeking to exploit profitable opportunities on a global, rather than a purely domestic, basis and explored its implications for macroeconomic analysis.

Despite its grounding in fundamental economic reasoning, this viewpoint is a controversial one. Nevertheless, the analysis here takes it for granted that market efficiency prevails and examines its significance for the meaning of PPP under both certainty and uncertainty. It begins by assuming a two-country world and n different goods, with goods l through k being tradable and goods $k + l$ through n nontradable. Preferences within countries are assumed to be identical and homothetic with respect to consumption, but preferences between countries can differ. Hence, as shown by Samuelson and Swamy (1974), a unique own price index can be constructed for each country, giving each country a unique rate of inflation. Let

$$P_j(t) = \sum_{i=1}^{n} p_{ij}(t)x_{ij}$$

be the price level for country $j (j = 1,2)$ at time t as measured by a resident of j, where $p_{ij}(t)$ is the period t price of commodity i in country j and x_{ij} is the weight of commodity i in country j's own price index. With instantaneous and costless arbitrage, the law of one price must hold for all traded goods. That is $p_{i1}(t)=e(t)p_{i2}(t)$ for $i = 1, \ldots, k$, where $e(t)$ is the time t spot exchange rate (currency 1 price of currency 2). In general, with perfect foresight or instantaneous shipping, exchange-adjusted prices of identical tradable goods must be within transaction costs of equality worldwide.

Relatively unappreciated in most empirical studies of PPP (Roll, 1979, is a notable exception) is the fact that even if the law of one price held for all goods, traded and nontraded, $P_1(t)$ would not, in general, equal $e(t)P_2(t)$ unless $x_i = x_{i2}, i = 1, \ldots, n$.[+] An alternative version of absolute PPP that avoids this index number problem and is based on the law of one price will hold, however. Let $R_j(t)$ be the price level for country j using the other country's price index, i.e.,

$$R_1(t) = \sum_{i=1}^{n} p_{i1}(t)x_{i2} \text{ and } R_2(t) = \sum_{i=1}^{n} p_{i2}(t)x_{i1}$$

Then if the law of one price holds for all goods,

$$P_1(t) = e(t)R_2(t) \text{ and } R_1(t) = e(t)P_2(t)$$

The relevance of this commodity arbitrage version of PPP is reinforced by the careful empirical work of Kravis *et al.* (1975) which demonstrates that deviations from PPP are far smaller when using the same (US) weights than when using different (own) weights in calculating the US and foreign price indexes. In other words, differences in national consumption preferences are important in explaining PPP deviations measured using national price indexes. These PPP deviations, however, are not relevant for economic theory or policy, except insofar as either is based on these misleading statistics. Alternatively, the commodity arbitrage version of PPP can be written as

$$P_1(t)a(t) = e(t)P_2(t)$$

where $a(t)$ is the relative price in currency 1 of country 2's index per country 1's index during t, i.e.,

$$a(t) = R_1(t)/P_1(t)$$

The dynamic analog is

$$e(t)/e(t-1) = b(t)[1 + \pi_1(t)]\ [1 + \pi_2(t)]$$

where

$$\pi_j(t) = [P_j(t) - P_j(t-1)]/P_j(t-1)$$

is the rate of inflation in country j's own price index and

$$b(t) = a(t)/a(t-1)$$

is the intertemporal change in country 2's price index relative to country 1's index, all expressed in currency 1. As Stockman (1980) and others have shown, this means that a change in relative prices that increases (decreases) country 2's price index relative to country 1's index will cause a decrease (increase) in the value of currency 1 relative to currency 2. The net result can be a change in the equilibrium exchange rate even though each country's own price level remains the same.

With the law of one price holding for only the subset of goods being traded, the above equations must be modified. Let $F_1(t)$ be the price index of freely traded goods in country 1 and currency i during period t, with

$$F_1(t)d(t) = e(t)F_2(t)$$

where $d(t)$ is the relative price in currency 1 of country 2's traded goods index per country 1's index during period t. In addition, let

$$F_1(t) = g_i(t)P_i(t)$$

where $g_i(t)$ is the relative price in currency i during t of country i's traded goods index per country i's broad-based domestic index containing both traded and nontraded goods. Substitution yields an absolute version of PPP,

$$P_1(t)h(t) = e(t)P_2(t)$$

and a new relative version,

$$e(t)/e(t-1) = k(t)[1 + \pi_1(t)]/[1 + \pi_2(t)]$$

where

$$h(t) = g_1(t)d(t)/g_2(t) \text{ and } k(t) = h(t)/h(t-1)$$

In the latter version of relative PPP, it can be seen that exchange rate changes relative to measured own inflation rates in each country are a complex function of both changes in the relative prices of traded goods indexes in each country (relative to prices of nontraded goods) and between countries. As before, relative price changes can lead to exchange rate changes even if price levels remain constant in each country.

Critics of PPP have made much of the fact that arbitrage is neither instantaneous nor costless and that the law of one price need not hold for nontraded goods (e.g., Samuelson, 1964) or even for traded goods (e.g., Isard, 1977). Samuelson (1974) has gone further and argued that the conditions necessary for PPP to hold are so restrictive as to vitiate its empirical content. In attempting to sidestep some of these difficulties, others (e.g., Angell, 1922) have argued that PPP should pertain only to traded goods prices, although Keynes (1930) asserted that PPP calculated from traded goods prices only is close to a truism.[5]

Responding to the confusion caused by (and causing) the multiplicity of theories, tests, and conclusions concerning the validity of PPP, Roll (1979) proposed and developed a dynamic intertemporal theory of the law of one price and of PPP based on the anticipated returns in an efficient market to spatial and intertemporal speculation. The speculator/arbitrager is assumed to buy commodity (or index) i for sale in the next period. In the case of spatial arbitrage, the continuously compounded real rate of return to an individual from country 1 who purchases commodity i in period $t-1$ in country 1 and sells it the following period in country 2 is

$$\log_e[p_{i1}(t)e(t)/P_1(t)] - \log_e[p_{i1}(t-1)/P_1(t-1)]$$

An analogous expression can be fashioned for the speculator who engages in foreign intertemporal arbitrage, buying goods in a foreign country for future sale in that same country. The continuously compounded real return to a resident of country 1 who buys commodity i in country 2 for sale in 2 the following period is

$$\log_e[p_{i2}(t)e(t)/P_1(t)] - \log_e[p_{i2}(t-1)e(t-1)/P_1(t-1)]$$

Roll notes that there must be many goods for which the exchange-adjusted price differential between pairs of countries is consistently positive or negative and large enough to compensate for the risks and costs of shipping including the required return on the capital tied up during transit. Otherwise, no normal trade patterns could develop.[6] Thus, the law of one price should fail for those goods that consistently trade in one direction. The average real return taken over all goods that travel in both directions, however, should be zero or

$$J_2(t)e(t)/P_1(t) = J_1(t-1)/P_1(t-1)$$

where $J_i(t)$ is the period t value of a traded goods price index in country and currency i for goods trading in both directions. With certainty, there will be no relative price changes or

$$J_1(t-1)/P_1(t-1) = J_1(t)/P_1(t)$$

implying that the above expression can be rewritten as

$$J_2(t)e(t) = J_1(t)$$

This is the commodity arbitrage version of PPP. If the weights in the two traded goods indexes are not identical, this relationship will be $J_2(t)e(t) = J_1(t)c(t)$, where $c(t)$ is the relative price in currency 1 of country 2's index per country 1's index during period t.

Similarly, the average real return to intertemporal arbitrage should be zero or

$$e(t)/e(t-1) = [1 + \pi_1(t)]/[1 + \pi_2(t)]$$

based on a resident who buys (goods weighted according to) country 2's index in country 2 for sale the following period in 2. This is the relative version of PPP as originally stated by Cassel (1928, p. 33): "[T]he whole theory of purchasing power parity essentially refers to the internal value of the currencies concerned, and variations in this value can be measured only by general index figures representing as far as possible the whole mass of commodities marketed in the country.'

This view of PPP has come to be identified with the monetary position, which looks on money as an asset and emphasizes the role of equilibrium in asset markets in relating price levels and exchange rates. In particular, the monetary position is that 'the role of exchange rates is to clear asset markets by equating the purchasing power of the various currencies' (Frenkel, 1978, p. 173). This requires using the broadest domestic price index available in measuring PPP.[7]

There are two potential (though not necessarily serious) problems with Roll's argument, however. First, arbitragers will be hard put to inventory services and other nonstorable goods for sale in subsequent periods. Second, it is difficult, if not impossible, to arbitrage profitably storable goods whose real price is expected to decline, e.g., semiconductor chips or wheat when a bumper harvest is expected. Thus, it will be virtually impossible to profitably engage in intertemporal arbitrage with these two categories of commodities. An alternative approach suggested by Roll (1979, pp. 140–141) and developed and tested by Adler and Lehmann (1982), which is based on financial arbitrage, overcomes these potential difficulties with Roll's results. According to Adler and Lehmann, expected nominal and real returns on domestic and foreign bonds are related for domestic and foreign investors via the following generalized Fisher relationships:[8]

Domestic investors

$$1 + i_1(t) = [1 + r_1(t)][1 + \pi_1(t)] \tag{1}$$

$$1 + i_2(t) = [1 + r_1(t)][1 + \pi_1(t)]e(t-1)/e(t) \tag{2}$$

Foreign investors

$$1 + i_1(t) = [1 + r_2(t)][1 + \pi_2(t)]e(t)/e(t-1) \tag{3}$$

$$1 + i_2(t) = [1 + r_2(t)][1 + \pi_2(t)] \tag{4}$$

where $i_j(t)$ and $r_j(t)$ are the nominal and real interest rates, respectively, on country j bonds from time $t - 1$ to time t.

These relationships assume that investors in both countries have access to both bonds. Then, equation (1) and (3) [or (2) and (4)], yields:

$$e(t)/e(t-1) = q(t)[1 + \pi_1(t)]/[1 + \pi_2(t)] \tag{5}$$

where $q(t) = [1 + r_1(t)]/[1 + r_2(t)]$ is the ratio of real required returns in countries 1 and 2.[9] It is evident from (5) that the classical version of relative PPP requires only that the ratio of real required returns be constant. As long as $q(t)$ is a constant it cannot affect the variance or serial correlation properties of equation (5). As will be shown later, though, the existence of different consumption preferences and changing relative prices will introduce a bias when conducting empirical tests of (5) in its current form.

Under uncertainty, however, costless shipping is not sufficient to guarantee that relative PPP or the commodity arbitrage version of absolute PPP will hold. With a lag between the time of purchase and the time of sale, speculators (shippers) face uncertainty as to the prices at which they will be able to sell their goods. Thus, it would be unrealistic to expect the law of one price to always hold or for the actual real return from spatial or intertemporal arbitrage to be zero in all periods. Instead, Roll (1979) argues that in an efficient market the expected return from these speculative activities should be zero, or

$$E[p_{i2}(t)e(t)/P_1(t)] = p_{i1}(t-1)/P_1(t-1)$$

where E is the expectations operator for goods trading in both directions. For an index of two-way traded goods, this becomes

$$E[J_2(t)e(t)/P_1 t)] = E[J_1(t)/P_1(t)]$$

($E[J_1(t)/P_1(t)] = J_1(t-1)/P_1(t-1)$ because relative price changes are not forecastable in an efficient market). This is the efficient markets version of the law of one price, namely that exchanged-adjusted prices should be equal on an expected value basis and any deviations should be uncorrelated over time. In other words, while violations of the law of one price can be expected, they should not be consistently positive or negative (except for those violations due to transaction costs).

Similarly, the efficient markets version of relative PPP under uncertainty, as developed by Roll (1979) on the basis that what holds for individual prices must also hold for collections of prices,[10] is:

$$E[e(t)(1 + \pi_1(t))/(1 + \pi_2(t))] = e(t - 1) \tag{6}$$

This version does not claim that relative costs of living must equal the exchange rate (which is what absolute PPP says). Instead, equation (6) just says that the best prediction of next period's cost of living-adjusted exchange rate is the current spot rate. In other words, all information relevant for predicting next period's inflation-adjusted (or real) exchange rate should already be impounded in the current spot rate. No other variable should improve the predictive performance of the current spot rate. Adler and Lehmann (1982) develop an identical version of (6) using their equation (5) and converting all parameters to their expected values.

Strictly speaking, there is no necessary connection between market efficiency and the martingale property of prices and exchanges rates posited by Roll and Adler and Lehmann (see Lucas, 1978; LeRoy, 1982, for discussions of this issue). Only under risk neutrality or fairly stringent joint restrictions on preferences and the probability distributions of prices and exchange rates will the expected returns from arbitrage be zero. Absent these conditions, expected returns from speculation can be either positive or negative in an efficient market, depending on the sign of the risk premium associated with these speculative activities. However, judging by results from other asset markets (e.g., Fama's (1965) analysis of price movements on the New York Stock Exchange), the bias caused by risk aversion will probably not be significant in conducting empirical tests.[11]

What is likely to be significant is the bias due to testing PPP using its classical version instead of the efficient markets version. The classical version of PPP,

$$e(t)/e(t - 1) = [1 + \pi_1(t)]/[1 + \pi_2(t)]$$

is usually tested using the regression

$$\pi_1(t) - \pi_2(t) = \alpha_0 + \alpha_1 e(t)/e(t - 1) + \epsilon_t$$

with the hypothesis being $\alpha_1 = 0$ and $\alpha_1 = 1$. Roll (1979) points out that in an unconstrained regression of this form, the estimated slope coefficient $\hat{a}_1$ will converge in large samples to

$$\hat{a}_1 = 1 - \text{cov}\,[e(t)/e/(t - 1), \epsilon_t]$$

The error term, which largely reflects the intertemporal change in relative prices of the traded goods components of the two price indexes, as measured by the term $k(t)$ defined previously, will be positively correlated with changes in the exchange rate, causing $\hat{a}_1$ to be less than unity, even if $\alpha_1 = 1$. Thus, the classical form of PPP is subject to econometric problems caused by relative price changes and hence will be valid only when disturbances are due to monetary as opposed to real factors. On the other hand, random changes in transportation costs and other impediments to trade will lower the explanatory power of $e(t)/e(t - 1)$ and reduce the significance level of α_1, but should not significantly bias the coefficient estimates.

Roll's (1979) test of the efficient markets version of PPP involves running the regression

$$s(t) = \alpha_0 + \alpha_1 e(t - 1) + \sum_{i=1}^{k} \alpha_{t+1} s(t - i) + \epsilon_t$$

where

$$s(t) = e(t)[1 + \pi_1(t)]/[1 + \pi_2(t)]$$

is the inflation-adjusted or real exchange rate and k is an arbitrary number of lagged values of $s(t)$. If commodity markets are efficient, it is hypothesized that $\alpha_0 = 0$, $\alpha_1 = 1$, and $\alpha_1 = 0$ for $i > 1$. The estimated value of α_1, based on this regression should be unbiased because $e(t - 1)$ and ϵ_t should be uncorrelated.

An equivalent version of the efficent markets hypothesis, formulated by Roll (1979) and tested by Adler and Lehmann (1982), is that $s(t)$ should follow a random walk or, more precisely, a martingale process.[12] In other words, if

$$y(t) = s(t) - s(t - 1)$$

is the innovation in the real exchange rate, then the sequence $\{y(t)\}$ should be conditionally independently distributed. Thus, for $n > 1$, the best forecast of $s(t + n)$, conditional on all information available at t, is $s(t)$. Moreover, the best conditional forecast of future deviations from absolute PPP,

$$[e(t + n)\ P_2(t + n)/P_1(t + n)] - 1$$

is the current deviation from absolute PPP,

$$[e(t)P_2(t)/P_1(t)] - 1$$

By contrast, most theories of balance of payments adjustment assume that violations of PPP are persistent and predictable. It is taken for granted that if a nation experiences a higher rate of inflation than its trading partners, its exports will become less competitive overseas while imports will be more price competitive with domestic products. The resulting deficit in the nation's balance of trade will put downward pressure on its spot exchange rate. This downward pressure will disappear when the nation's currency has depreciated relative to its foreign competitors' currencies by the inflation differential. Only then will goods arbitrage cease to be profitable.

Empirically, this means that the predictive error for PPP should not follow a random walk but, rather, would exhibit negative serial correlation as traded goods arbitrage acts to eliminate the discrepancy. Thus, if the classical interpretation of PPP is correct,

$$\text{cov}\ [y(t), y(t + 1)] < 0$$

whereas the efficient markets version of PPP predicts that this covariance is zero, providing a straightforward way in which to discriminate between the two hypotheses.

The empirical results of Roll (1979), Darby (1982), Pippenger (1981), Adler and Lehmann (1982) and others, using different data sets and methodologies, all support the efficient markets hypothesis.[13] In the words of Roll (1979, p. 174),

With a few significant exceptions, there is little evidence of disequilibria nor of slow adjustment of prices to a long-run parity. Indeed, the general impression for most countries, and for all of the largest trading nations, is a very rapid adjustment of less than one month's duration.

On the other hand, results from the usual PPP test vehicle,

$$\pi_1(t) - \pi_2(t) = \alpha_0 + \alpha_1 e(t)/e(t - 1) + \epsilon(t)$$

provide only marginal support for short-term PPP because 'on average, . . . relative price change effects on exchange rates dominate the observed differences in inflation rates' (Roll, 1979, p. 148). Despite this relative price problem, discussed earlier, it should not be surprising that most tests of relative PPP as a long-run theory seem to confirm its validity. The reason is that over long periods of time with a moderate inflation differential, the general trend in the price level ratio will tend to dominate the effects of relative price changes. Similarly, during periods of hyperinflation, changes in the general level of prices will swamp the effects of relative price changes.

The above analysis demonstrates, and the empirical evidence supports the contention, that neither the law of one price nor identically constructed price indexes are necessary for relative PPP to hold on an expected value basis; either intertemporal or financial arbitrage is sufficient. In addition, relative PPP based on either of these arbitrage conditions is not affected by the usual difficulties associated with traded goods arbitrage: changes in the height of trade restrictions and the level of transportation costs, changes in national income and tastes, and structural changes leading to relative price changes. All that is necessary is that international capital flows be unimpeded.

III. ADDRESSING THE ISSUES

Armed with the theoretical and empirical evidence on purchasing power parity, it is now possible to address certain of the key issues whose resolution depended on the existence of PPP.

IIIA. PPP and Exchange Rate Determination

In order for purchasing power parity to provide the foundation for a theory of exchange-rate determination, it must be expected to hold *ex post* as well as *ex ante*. In other words, if exchange-adjusted prices or price levels deviate or threaten to deviate from their PPP-predicted values, there must be an arbitrage mechanism at work to rapidly eliminate these actual or potential deviations. This condition is met, at least in theory, by absolute PPP which relies on international trade and the law of one price for its validity. The classical basis of relative PPP is also traded goods arbitrage, although it permits a systematic difference to exist between exchange-adjusted prices, due, for example, to transportation costs, tariffs, and other barriers to trade.

The thrust thus far in this paper, however, has been to view PPP not as a theory of the determination of exchange rates *per se*, but, rather, as the result of a set of equilibrium conditions that must hold in efficient markets. The theoretical basis for relative PPP, as presented in the previous section, relies on financial arbitrage rather than goods arbitrage (foreign intertemporal arbitrage for Roll (1979); international interest arbitrage for Adler and Lehmann (1982)). Hence, if expectations are not realized (i.e., currency changes differ from those predicted by the actual relative rates of inflation), there is no arbitrage mechanism posited to realign the exchange rates so that relative PPP holds *ex post* as well as *ex ante*. All we can say is that, as in any efficient asset market, expectations of future foreign currency prices will not be systematically wrong. But these expectations do not cause future exchange rates to be what they are; rather we would expect that the same real factors that determine exchange rates also determine expectations of these rates. Therefore, the only systematic relationship in the foreign exchange market should be between expected exchange rate changes and expected inflation rates. To the extent that financial arbitrage serves as the basis for relative PPP, changes in the inflation-adjusted exchange rate will be unpredictable. Thus financial arbitrage alone cannot provide a complete theoretical foundation for an explanation of actual exchange rates; trade in goods must be modeled explicitly.

The central role played by the speed and efficiency of international commodity arbitrage in any PPP-based theory of exchange-rate determination has led to a good deal of empirical research on the law of one price. Although these studies generally agree that the law of one price does not hold exactly for all commodities at all times, their other conclusions are mixed. For example, Isard (1977) states that 'the law of one price is flagrantly and systematically violated by empirical data' while Kravis and Lipsey (1978), with the concurrence of Protopapadakis and Stoll (1982), 'think it highly unlikely that a high degree of national and international commodity arbitrage . . . is typical of the real world.' On the other hand, Crouhy-Veyrac *et al.* (1980) conclude that 'All in all, the law of one price emerges as a much less precarious, although a more qualified statement, than has been heretofore implied.' The extent to which the law of one price must hold in order for national economies to be linked (and for PPP to help determine exchange rates) will be discussed in the following section.

Alternatively, Magee (1978) argues that the presence of large and persistent deviations from the law of one price (and, hence, absolute PPP) could be just statistical flukes. According to Magee, even if exchange-adjusted prices are identical at the time contracts are signed, the existence of multiperiod contracting combined with the use of actual transaction prices rather than spot prices could result in spuriously autocorrelated deviations from PPP. Thus, empirical studies indicating the presence of unexploited arbitrage opportunities may just be evidence of inappropriate price data, instead of demonstrating that international goods markets are inefficient.

From the perspective of PPP being a theory that only relates expected rates of inflation to expected exchange rate changes, without assigning causality, price level changes may be as much a result of exchange rates changes as a cause, i.e., it is difficult to distinguish between cause and effect. The failure by various central bankers to understand the distinction between correlation and causation in PPP theory has led to some major errors in the quest for a measure of the equilibrium exchange rate.

The concept of an equilibrium exchange rate is itself the subject of some debate. A distinction is usually made between the short-run and the long-run equilibrium rate. The short-run equilibrium exchange rate is defined as the rate that would prevail in a freely floating exchange rate system. The long-run equilibrium rate is defined as the rate that would yield balance of payments equilibrium over a time period long enough to incorporate any cyclical fluctuations in the balance of payments due, for example, to domestic or world business cycles. The latter concept, that of a long-run equilibrium exchange rate, is controversial and rightly so since it lacks operational meaning.[14] There is controversy concerning the short-run equilibrium exchange rate as well, primarily based on the argument by some that freely floating exchange rates are subject to over- or undershooting because of the differential adjustment speed of goods and asset markets. Hence, it is argued, the market clearing spot rate may not be a truly equilibrium exchange rate. These issues are discussed later on in this section.

For now, it is assumed that freely floating exchange rates are equilibrium rates. The equilibrium exchange rate is itself affected by the level and direction of capital flows, foreign aid, dividend and interest payments, fees and royalties, unilateral transfers, and service income, as well as traded goods flows. Changes in these nonmerchandise flows will lead to relative price changes between domestic traded and nontraded goods and between domestic traded and foreign traded goods.

As indicated earlier, with relative price changes but no price level changes, the law of one price could still hold for traded goods while the equilibrium exchange rate will change. Using relative PPP to determine the equilibrium exchange rate will be effective, therefore, only if the disequilibrium in the current exchange rate is due to a monetary expansion which caused all prices in one country to increase uniformly relative to prices in the other country, i.e., there are no relative price changes in either country. If this is the case, which is unlikely, then regardless of differing consumption preferences or the existence of nontraded goods, the value of the first country's currency should decrease proportionately. In other words, PPP will only hold to the extent that it is a monetary phenomenon.

An important point often overlooked in estimating the equilibrium exchange rate while under a fixed rate system is that government-financed (sterilized) balance of payments deficits (surpluses) will cause relative price changes between imported and exported goods and between domestic traded and nontraded goods. In particular, in a two-country world, if X denotes a nation's exports, M its imports, and e the home currency value of the foreign currency, then the balance of payments deficit D is

$$eM - X = D \tag{7}$$

where home and foreign currency unit prices are set as 1 (if need be, the physical units of imports and exports can be redefined so that unit prices are 1).[15] Then e is also the price of imports relative to exports. To see the impact on e of a change in the amount of balance of payments deficit the government will fund, it is necessary to differentiate both sides of (7) to get[16]

$$e\frac{\partial M}{\partial D} + M\frac{\partial e}{\partial D} - \frac{\partial X}{\partial D} = 1 \tag{8}$$

or

$$\frac{\partial e}{\partial D} = \frac{1 + \dfrac{\partial X}{\partial D} - e\dfrac{\partial M}{\partial D}}{M} \tag{9}$$

The additional purchasing power provided to country 1's citizens by the government-funded balance of payments deficit will presumably be split between additional consumption of the country's exports and its imports; i.e., the income effect of a change in D should cause $(\partial X)/(\partial D) < 0$ and $(\partial M)/(\partial D) > 0$. Since the equilibrium quantities of exports and imports are also a function of the supply elasticities, so too will the magnitudes of $(\partial X)/(\partial D)$ and $(\partial M)/(\partial D)$ be affected by these supply elasticities. Although the sign of $(\partial e)/(\partial D)$ is ordinarily considered to be negative (i.e., the larger the deficit, the more overvalued a nation's currency will be), (9) indicates that the sign could be either positive or negative depending on the income and supply elasticities of exports and imports. In other words, a change in the balance of payments deficit could either increase or decrease the price of imports relative to exports.[17] The result is that a balance of payments deficit (or surplus) will bias price indexes and provide misleading information as to those relative price level changes that would have occurred in the absence of the deficit.

This bias will vary directly with the size of the deficit. Thus, switching from a fixed exchange rate with a government-financed balance of payments deficit to a freely floating exchange rate with a zero deficit will lead to a variety of relative price and price level changes whose direction and magnitude depend on relative supply and demand elasticities for exports and imports.[18] These relative price changes will in turn lead to changes in the assumed (and actual) price levels.

To the extent that a government-financed deficit in the balance of payments helps maintain an overvalued exchange rate for the domestic currency (i.e., $(\partial e)/(\partial d) < 0$, which is the most likely case), this will hold down the prices of traded goods, resulting in a downwards biased domestic price index. In effect, a government-financed payments deficit provides a price subsidy for imported goods, lowering costs to domestic consumers but also reducing returns to domestic traded goods producers. Upon removal of this subsidy, the domestic price level will exhibit a once-and-for-all increase, based largely on the rise in both the relative and absolute prices of traded goods. In effect, elimination of the subsidy reduces the quantity of goods available for domestic consumption relative to the supply of money, thereby reducing the domestic currency's purchasing power.

The fact that a particular fixed exchange rate is in disequilibrium does not necessarily mean that there are unexploited profit opportunities. Infra-marginal profits will exist from traded goods arbitrage but at the margin costs and returns from trade should be equalized, the assumption here being that marginal costs are rising more (or declining less) rapidly than marginal revenues. This implies that the law of one price could hold for all traded goods (within the limits posed by transaction costs and uncertainty) and yet the spot rate might not be a market-clearing exchange rate (with respect to private transactions). To the extent that traded goods prices obey the law of one price, this means that the use of a price index heavily weighted with traded goods (such as the wholesale price index) to measure the PPP-determined equilibrium exchange rate will tend to validate the existing exchange rate, even if it is in disequilibrium. Thus, the commodity arbitrage version of PPP appears to be an inappropriate choice for use in selecting a new equilibrium exchange rate when the existing rate is clearly in disequilibrium.

An oft-cited example of the high cost associated with employing the wrong version of PPP to calculate an equilibrium exchange rate involves England's 1925 return to the gold standard at the prewar mint parity with the dollar. Prior anticipation of a return to parity had led to a speculative appreciation of the pound from 10% below parity to less than 2% below it. The PPP-based equilibrium rate, computed using wholesale price indexes subsequent to the pound's appreciation, indicated an overvaluation of the pound of only 2–3% relative to its appreciated value. By contrast, Keynes (1932) pointed out that other price indexes less heavily weighted with traded goods revealed that the pound was actually overvalued by 10–12%. Despite Keynes' warning, the prewar parity rate was selected. The result, according to Officer (1976) and, as Keynes predicted, was deflation and unemployment for the United Kingdom.

To summarize, using price indexes containing traded goods prices in PPP calculations will bias the estimated equilibrium exchange rate in the direction of the current spot rate. This implies that when estimating equilibrium exchange rates in disequilibrium situations, purchasing power parities based on price indexes of nontraded goods only should be used. In other words,

$$\bar{e} = \sum_{i=k+1}^{n} p_{i1} z_i \Big/ \sum_{i=k+1}^{n} p_{i2} z_i$$

where $\bar{e}$ is the estimated equilibrium exchange rate and z_i is the appropriate weight for good i, and where nontradables such as housing, land, and services are matched as closely as possible. This measure still suffers from the problem that relative price changes will change the equilibrium exchange rate. Thus, it is only an exact procedure when the necessary exchange rate change is due to purely monetary causes.

In the limit, it has been argued that only the price of the least traded commodity—labor—should be used in these calculations (e.g., Hawtrey, 1919). While attractive because of its apparent simplicity, this suggestion has serious defects. For one thing, the cost of labor must be adjusted by its productivity to make cross-country comparisons legitimate, introducing measurement problems. Not the least of these problems is how to compute the value of production. Should these comparisons be based on productivity in the traded goods sector only, the nontraded goods (primarily service) sector only, or some combination of the two? In addition, the various types and qualities of labor make cross-country comparisons of unit labor costs difficult. An alternative approach is to use unit factor costs as a better measure of a country's ability to compete in the world market (Brisman, 1933). The overwhelming importance of labor relative to other factors of production, as well as the fact that exchange-adjusted energy, raw materials, and capital costs are generally the same worldwide, means that production cost parity will usually be approximated by labor cost parity with its attendant problems. Using a bundle of non-traded goods to conduct PPP calculations will probably reduce measurement errors relative to the case where only one commodity is being used to measure PPP. A more complete discussion of cost parity is provided in Officer (1976). It must be mentioned again, however, that regardless of how one measures the cost or price parity exchange rate, the actual equilibrium rate will be affected by capital and nonmerchandise flows.

Contrary to the previously stated assumption that freely floating exchange rates are continually in equilibrium, Dornbusch (1976) has used the notion of price stickiness to hypothesize that while PPP (and the law of one price) hold in the long run, the slow speed of adjustment in goods markets relative to asset and exchange markets will likely lead to exchange rate overshooting. According to Dornbusch, price stickiness will cause a domestic monetary expansion to become an increase in the real quantity of money, leading to a decline in domestic interest rates and to the anticipation of a depreciating exchange rate. Both factors will induce an incipient capital outflow, resulting in a depreciation of the spot rate. Since investors can engage in almost instantaneous and costless currency arbitrage, they will hold domestic currency assets only if the domestic currency is expected to appreciate at a rate just sufficient to offset the reduced domestic interest rate. In order for this expectation to be rational, the initial depreciation must 'overshoot' the long-run depreciation necessary to maintain purchasing power parity.

An alternative theory of exchange rate overshooting is provided by the portfolio-balance approach. As developed by Kouri (1976) and Branson (1979), this approach assumes that an increase in the domestic money supply will lower interest rates on domestic bonds, leading investors to purchase higher-yielding foreign bonds. The domestic currency will also depreciate initially, making exports more competitive overseas and providing the current account surplus necessary to accumulate the foreign assets. In order to reestablish portfolio balance (defined as a zero capital account balance), the domestic currency must then appreciate sufficiently to generate a trade deficit that just offsets the added interest earned on the newly acquired foreign bonds.

The attractive feature of both the Dornbusch and Kouri-Branson models is that they permit exchange rate disequilibrium (relative to the rate at which all markets clear) to coexist with the absence of profitable financial arbitrage, thereby countering Friedman's (1953a) argument that excessive swings in freely floating exchange rates must imply the existence of profitable opportunities for currency speculators. On the other hand, these models do allow for the existence of deviations from the law of one price that exceed transaction costs, providing profitable opportunities for commodity arbitrage. The Kouri-Branson model explicitly assumes these deviations persist long enough to be exploited whereas the Dornbusch model implicitly assumes that the reaction times of commodity arbitragers exceed their 'window of opportunity.'

Despite these differences, both models of currency overshooting predict a situation where rising domestic prices are accompanied by an appreciating exchange rate. This implies that an initial decline in the real or inflation-adjusted exchange rate will be followed by a period in which the real exchange rate is increasing. In order for these and other models of adjustment to balance of payments disequilibria to be correct, therefore, violations of PPP must have, in the words of Roll (1979), 'a persistent and predictable pattern' throughout the period of adjustment. The more rapid is the adjustment of prices to monetary expansion, the more responsive is output to an increase in aggregate demand, and the greater the possibilities of currency substitution, the lower the likelihood that this pattern of exchange rate overshooting will actually occur. Moreover, a recent extension by Mussa (1982) of Dornbusch's analysis demonstrates that if overshooting occurs, it is only in response to unanticipated monetary disturbances and not to expected monetary changes.

According to the empirical evidence presented in Section II, violations of PPP appear to follow a random walk, instead of exhibiting the positive or negative serial correlation predicted by the various disequilibrium theories. Apparently prices do adjust rapidly to changes in the money supply, possibly because of the high degree of currency substitution at the margin (see McKinnon, 1982). One implication of the available evidence is that rather than use PPP to determine whether freely floating exchange rates are in disequilibrium, equilibrium should be taken for granted and models that rely on or purport to demonstrate disequilibrium should be replaced by ones that are consistent with market efficiency in the spirit of Roll's (1979) work. Deviations from purchasing power parity would be dealt with by exploring their causes . . . assuming rational behavior on the part of agents. These causes might be measurement problems, government intervention in the market-place, transaction costs, or the use of an inappropriate model (e.g., one based on certainty instead of uncertainty).

The efficiency of foreign exchange markets has important implications with regard to management concerns as well. If real exchange rates follow a random walk, then the best forecast of the exchange-adjusted differential inflation rate at any future date t, $s(t)$ (defined previously), is the current spot rate $e(0)$. Thus, differences in exchange-adjusted costs of production can be expected to persist, an important consideration when deciding where to locate plants. However, a deviation in PPP *per se* is not the signal for profitable arbitrage opportunities. What is important are deviations from the law of one price for the specific factors of production, such as labor, that are used in the manufacturing process.[19] These deviations are less likely to exist than those determined using broad price indexes with their associated measurement problems. With regard to forecasting of nominal exchange rates, important when entering into nominal foreign currency contracts such as debt and forward contracts, the above discussion suggests these rates are no more or less forecastable than are future inflation rates.

IIIB. PPP and Linkages Between National Economies

The theoretical and empirical evidence presented in Section II indicates the strong likelihood that relative PPP holds on an expected value basis. The quality of expected exchange-adjusted price level changes, however, does not necessarily mean that prices of individual commodities and price levels are related *ex post*. This latter form of linkage will only be brought about by international trade. By the same token, absolute PPP and the law of one price can be systematically violated because of transportation costs or trade barriers, for example, and yet exchange-adjusted prices can still be related across countries. This is brought out most clearly by McCloskey and Zecher (1982, pp. 12, 13):

Imagine that some standardized piece of electrical equipment sells for 20% more in the United States than in Germany, after translating the prices at the exchange rate. Imagine further that deviations as little as plus or minus 1 percentage point from the 20% differential would create opportunities for profitable arbitrage, exploited instantly. . . . The economist stumbling into such data, were he ill-disposed toward purchasing power parity, would conclude that parity fails . . . yet . . . the prices in Germany and in the United States are mutually linked (plus or minus 1 percentage point). A monetary policy in the United States that had as one intended result a rise in electrical equipment prices in the United States relative to (exchange-adjusted) German prices would fail.

Similarly, a change in the equilibrium differential to 30%—due, for example, to a reduction in German value-added taxes—will apear to indicate a low correlation in prices between Germany and the United States, even though prices in the two countries could be just as strongly linked at a 30% differential as at a 20% one.

In addition, relative prices in an economy are set on the basis of tastes, technology, and resource endowments. If these real factors do not change with trade, then within each economy the relative prices of traded and nontraded goods must remain fixed. Hence, traded-goods arbitrage can be expected to relate not only the exchange-adjusted prices of tradables but also those of nontradables across economies. 'At the extreme, then, if Mars were connected to Earth by the market in chewing gum alone, the two price levels would nonetheless be fixed in relation to each other' (McCloskey and Zecher, 1981, pp. 15–16). This does not mean that the law of one price must hold for nontradables, just that the relative exchange-adjusted prices of nontradables are not free to wander independently of each other.

At issue is whether the world is essentially a unified market or a series of relatively autonomous national markets. Tests of the law of one price or of the correlation between exchange-adjusted price levels, however, cannot fully address this issue. While evidence of the law of one price or of high correlation between price levels would provide strong support for the integrated market hypothesis, contrary evidence does not imply its rejection. To the extent that all opportunities for profitable arbitrage are fully exploited (in the sense that the marginal risk-adjusted returns of the resources employed in arbitrage just equal their risk-adjusted returns employed elsewhere), the price level in one country could be fully determined by prices in the rest of the world, even if the law of one price is consistently violated. Similarly, as pointed out previously, exchange-adjusted prices could be tightly linked from an economic standpoint even while relative price changes and changing barriers to trade result in a low degree of statistical correlation between domestic and foreign price levels.

Although a number of studies have tried to examine whether the international price structure is tightly integrated, such as the studies cited previously by Isard (1977) and Kravis and Lipsey (1978), there has been little attempt to set a standard against which to measure the degree of tightness. One standard, proposed by Genberg (1976), is the correlation of prices between regions of the same country. If *international* price correlations are as high as *intranational* correlations, then the various countries can be said to comprise a unified market. Genberg's (1976, p. 302) conclusion is that this is indeed the case:

> *[T]he differences between OECD countries are no greater on the average than those between cities within the United States. Thus, if we believe that the whole of the US can be treated as a single market in a macroeconomic context, then the area composed of the above countries can be treated likewise.*

We would, of course, expect international price changes to be greater than domestic changes if goods are very different between countries (thus implying the likelihood of greater relative price changes) or if taxes and exchange controls change a lot.[20]

Another standard is the degree of variation in the domestic price level explained by the exchange-adjusted price levels of foreign countries. Using Canadian and British price levels converted into dollars, McCloskey and Zecher (1982) found that this data explained, respectively, 87 and 94% of the variation in the US GNP deflator. The slope coefficient differed from unity (at conventional levels of statistical significance) in both cases, however, which would lead to rejection of PPP and the integrated market hypothesis by the usual standards (but not to rejection of *ex ante* PPP with risk aversion). This appears to be further evidence of the important distinction that must be drawn between statistical and economic significance. Even without estimating the relevant costs of Type I and Type II errors, it would appear that when price movements in one country account for about 90% of the variation in a second country's price level, the two countries are closely linked economically.

From a policymaking standpoint, perhaps the most important reason for studying the integrated market hypothesis is to determine the degree to which a nation's monetary policy can alter its domestic prices relative to exchange-adjusted foreign prices and consequently its trade and payments balance.[21] The results of a regression by McCloskey and Zecher (1982) relating excess money growth to deviations from absolute PPP provide little support for the hypothesis that domestic monetary conditions can affect the exchange-adjusted price level differential. Moreover, those deviations from absolute PPP that do exist, whether or not the result of changes in monetary policy, appear not to represent arbitrage opportunities that give rise to trade flows as in the traditional balance of payments theory. According to McCloskey and Zecher (1982), statistics for the United States provide no evidence that the commodity trade balance responds to differences in exchange-adjusted prices, indicating that these deviations are more likely to be statistical artifacts (due, for example, to relative price changes) than unexploited profit opportunities.

Further evidence that the price structures of different national economies are closely linked through arbitrage is provided by Protopapadakis and Stoll (1982). If, as Kravis and Lipsey (1978, p. 243) believe, 'the links are loose rather than tight,' then exchange rate changes should lead to systematic deviations from the law of one price across commodities. Isard (1977, p. 942), in fact, asserts that 'exchange rate changes substantially alter the relative dollar-equivalent prices of the most narrowly defined domestic and foreign manufactured goods.' However, what Isard really shows is that deviations from the law of one price for specific commodities are correlated with currency movements; he does not demonstrate causation. In addition, apropos of Magee's (1978) argument, the observed serially correlated deviations from the law of one price could be entirely spurious, depending on whether the researchers used contract prices instead of the correct spot market prices.

If exchange rate changes can systematically alter a nation's terms of trade, then the contemporaneous cross-correlation of deviations from the law of one price should be significantly positive. However,

The evidence suggests that movements in exchange rates do not systematically change the terms of trade across commodities. The evidence also suggests that there is not a common macroeconomic adjustment mechanism that involves these commodities, that comes into play when prices deviate from the LOP (law of one price). While deviations from the LOP appear to persist over time because of arbitrage costs, there is no clear evidence of common behavior of different commodities within the arbitrage bands.

Interestingly, this conclusion by Protopapadakis and Stoll (1982, p. 23) indicates that they agree with McCloskey and Zecher (1982) rather than with Kravis and Lipsey (1978), despite their assertion to the contrary. One implication of the study by Protopapadakis and Stoll is that, contrary to Isard (1977) and Kravis and Lipsey (1978), a government cannot systematically change the exchange-adjusted prices of all commodities by changing its exchange rate. Deviations from the law of one price that do exist appear to be random, having little to do with exchange rate changes. The cause of these deviations is more likely to be changes in commodity-specific transportation costs or tariffs or the arbitrage incentive necessary to move goods in one direction (Roll, 1979).

Governments can, of course, change their terms of trade (and hence their trade balances) through tariffs, freight regulations, taxes, quotas, and policies that act on real prices. In addition, as pointed out above, a government can overvalue (undervalue) its currency (though not necessarily change its terms of trade) provided it is willing to sustain a balance of payments deficit (surplus) by borrowing (lending) overseas or running down (up) its reserves. This ability of a nation to change its international competitiveness is also dependent on the willingness of its trading partners to continue running balance of payments surpluses or deficits.

An examination of the terms of trade, however, should not reveal this changed competitive position because, as indicated by the work of Protopapadakis and Stoll (1982), the law of one price is independent of government monetary policy. According to equation (9), the evidence of a change in relative competitiveness will be provided in two ways. First, there should be a change in the volume and balance of trade. Second, there should be a change in the price of traded goods relative to that of nontraded goods within the country. As discussed in the previous subsection, this means that the law of one price for all traded goods can coexist with a disequilibrium exchange rate.

IIIC. PPP and International Financial Theory

Ross and Walsh (1983) show that as long as the law of one price holds, there is a single (world market) portfolio that is efficient in all price indexes. This result forms the basis for the key theorem that all investors (should) hold a linear combination of the world market portfolio, the weighted world bond portfolio, and the riskless bond in their price index. Thus, it is possible to derive an International Asset-Pricing Model in the presence of deviations from PPP caused by individuals measuring wealth using different price indexes.

Failure of the law of one price to hold, however, invalidates the Ross-Walsh results. As Wihlborg (1982) points out, deviations from the law of one price will lead to assets being priced, at least partially, in a domestic context, instead of in a common, world context. As shown earlier in this section, there are a variety of factors—including transportation costs and other barriers to trade, changes in capital and service flows, and changes in the government-financed balance of payments deficit—that can result in such deviations. The widespread existence of these factors would therefore, appear to obviate any attempt to develop an International Asset-Pricing Model (IAPM).

From a theoretical standpoint, of course, such a conclusion appears fully warranted. Empirically, however, it may not be. The law of one price is as essential for the development of the domestic CAPM as it is for the development of an IAPM, and is as likely to be violated domestically as internationally (though the magnitude of the domestic deviations are probably smaller). The real criterion, as Friedman (1953b) has forcefully argued, is not the realism of the assumptions underlying the development of a model, but the empirical validity of the conclusions derived from such a model. This test has yet to be met for any domestic asset pricing model (except arguably for the arbitrage pricing theory; see Roll and Ross, 1980), much less for an IAPM.

IV. SUMMARY AND CONCLUSIONS

Purchasing power parity is primarily of interest not for its own sake but because it holds the key to correctly analyzing a variety of macroeconomic policies, more appropriately modeling the pricing of international-traded assets, and developing better corporate strategies. The strictest version of purchasing power parity—that all assets, goods, and factors of production obey the law of one price—is demonstrably false. Governments can—and have—erected barriers to international trade and capital flows that are sufficiently high as to cause exchange-adjusted prices to systematically differ between countries. In addition, the presence of uncertainty combined with shipment lags, could result in deviations from the law of one price.

The real issue is whether those deviations from PPP that occur are sufficiently large, persistent, and predictable as to enable individuals or governments to successfully exploit them. Put this way, purchasing power parity becomes a metaphysical statement, the untestable (in the absence of a demonstrable pure arbitrage opportunity) economic hypothesis that markets are continually in equilibrium. From this perspective, rejecting PPP is equivalent to rejecting economic rationality. On the other hand, economic rationality is impossible to prove. Numerous empirical tests of purchasing power parity, however, have demonstrated that deviations from purchasing power parity appear to follow a random walk, providing support (but not proof) for the market efficiency hypothesis.

Perhaps the major and controversial conclusion of this paper is that rather than using purchasing power parity to determine whether goods or asset (including currency) markets are in disequilibrium, equilibrium (here meaning the absence of any unexploited profitable arbitrage opportunities), should be assumed to hold. The focus, instead, should be on analyzing the nature of this equilibirum, with observed deviations from PPP or the law of one price dealt with by exploring their causes—which might be measurement problems, the use of an unrealistic model, or inappropriate price data, transaction costs, or government intervention. The fruitfulness of this approach is evidenced by the recent spate of papers attempting, with a good deal of success, to do just that.

NOTES

1. Even though with PPP monetary policy can have no real effects, it can, of course, still have price level effects. A devaluation in conjunction with a change in the size of the government subsidized balance of payments deficit can change PPP (see Section III).

2. This hypothesis is potentially testable only in the sense that it would be rejected if one could demonstrate a pure arbitrage opportunity.

3. Strictly speaking, the key concept underlying PPP is that markets are continually in competitive equilibrium. This must be taken as given or else rejected because it is based on two untestable assumptions: markets clear and agents act in their own self-interest.

4. The problem with measuring PPP using differently constructed index numbers has, however, been pointed out in a number of theoretical studies of PPP, e.g., Keynes (1930), Viner (1937), and Samuelson (1964).

5. Keynes is correct only if the law of one price holds continually for traded goods.

6. This does not mean that speculation is the primary basis for international trade, only that in deciding whether to sell incremental output in the domestic market or overseas, the producer (or a middleman) will compare returns in the two markets. Specialization, which lies behind trade flows, provides the opportunity for a shipper to earn a real return.

7. Roll's derivation of relative PPP on the basis of intertemporal commodity arbitrage and a similar derivation by Adler and Lehmann (1982) using financial arbitrage (discussed in the next paragraph), correct the basic flaw in the monetary position, the lack of an arbitrage mechanism to bring about the equality of currency purchasing powers. Since these arbitrage arguments only establish relative PPP, however, the monetary approach really explains only changes in, rather than the absolute value of, the exchange rate.

8. This analysis was also given in a more general form (including the derivation of PPP under uncertainty) in Roll and Solnik (1979).

9. Roll (1979, p. 141) points out in a footnote that his version of relative PPP should also contain the parameter $q(t)$.

10. Strictly speaking, this statement only holds for identically weighted collections of prices. As shown by Roll, however, (6) will hold even with differently constructed indexes because relative price changes are unpredictable in general.

11. If the risk premium is constant, tests of *ex ante* PPP will still find that no 'nuisance' variables have explanatory power.

12. Rogalski and Vinso (1977) also had this basic insight although their test procedure failed to cope with the problem of changing relative prices.

13. An alternative explanation, which is untestable, is that PPP deviations do persist but there are so many random shocks that these deviations appear to follow a random walk.

14. See Officer (1976, p. 3) for a discussion of this controversy and references.

15. This simple model assumes that there are no service or capital flows. Thus, the balance of trade deficit also equals the balance of payments deficit.

16. Although Equation (9) is reminiscent of the familiar Marshall-Lerner stability condition for normal balance-of-payments adjustment, its orientation differs significantly. Instead of taking for granted the existence of a

balance-of-payments deficit and seeking to determine the conditions under which a domestic currency depreciation will restore equilibrium in the foreign exchange market, this approach seeks to explain the deficit's origins and its implications for the price of imports relative to exports.

17. Laffer's (1976) proof that a change in a nation's exchange rate cannot affect the relative price of foreign and domestic traded goods is valid only if the government-financed payments deficit remains constant. Once this deficit is allowed to change, however, Laffer's conclusions no longer hold.

18. In general, D equals net capital and service flows. A change in D due to market forces will have the same results as those depicted above for government intervention.

19. When wage rates are set by monopolistic labor unions, adjustments in the labor market will occur primarily through quantity changes rather than wage changes.

20. Cornell (1981) also concludes that *ex post* PPP is as violated among the states of the US as among foreign countries.

21. It should be noted that Darby (1983) and Laskar (1982) report evidence that nonreserve countries could and did influence their money supplies under the Bretton Woods System at least over a quarter year. This is inconsistent with goods being perfectly substitutable internationally.

REFERENCES

Adler, M. and B. Dumas, 'International Portfolio Choice and Corporation Finance: A Survey', *J. Finance* 38, 925–84.

Adler, M. and B. Lehmann, 'Deviations from PPP in the Long Run: A Random Walk?, Columbia University Working Paper, 1982.

Angell, J. W., 'International Table Under Inconvertible Paper', *Q. J. Econ.*, 1922, 36:309–412.

Black, F. (1974), 'International Capital Market Equilibrium With Investment Barriers', *J. Financial Econ.*, December 1974, 1:337–352.

Branson, W. H., 'Exchange Rate Dynamics and Monetary Policy', in Assar Lindbeck, ed., *Inflation and Employment in Open Economics*, Amsterdam: North Holland Publishing Co., 1979.

Brisman, S. 'Some Reflections on the Theory of Foreign Exchange' in *Economic Essays in Honour of Gustar Cassel*, London, 1933.

Cassel, G., 'Abnormal Deviations in International Exchanges', *Econ J.*, December 1918, 28:413–415.

Cassel, G., *Post-War Monetary Stabilization*, New York: Columbia University Press, 1982.

Cornell, B., 'A Note on Domestic Purchasing Power Parity', UCLA Working Paper, February 1981.

Crouhy-Veyrac, L., M. Crouhy and J. Melitz, 'More About the Law of One Price', CESA Working Paper, 1980.

Darby, M. R., 'Does Purchasing Power Parity Work?', *Proceedings of Fifth West Coast Academic/Federal Reserve Economic Research Seminar, December 1981*, San Francisco: Federal Reserve Bank of San Francisco, 1982.

Darby, M. R., 'Sterlization and Monetary Control: Concepts, Issues, and a Reduced-Form Test', in M. R. Darby, *et al.*, *The International Transmission of Inflation*, Chicago: University of Chicago Press, 1983.

Dornbusch, R., 'Expectations and Exchange Rate Dynamics', *J. Pol. Econ.*, December 1976, **84**:1161–1176.

Fama, E. F., 'The Behavior of Stock Market Prices', *J. Business*, January 1965, **38**:34–105.

Frenkel, J. A., Purchasing Power Parity: Doctrinal Perspective and Evidence from the 1920's, *J. Int. Econ.*, May 1978, **8**: 169–191.

Friedman, M., 'The Case for Flexible Exchange Rates', in his *Essays in Positive Economics*, Chicago: University of Chicago Press 1953 (1953a).

Friedman, M., 'The Methodology of Positive Economics', in his *Essays in Positive Economics*, Chicago: University of Chicago Press, 1953 (1953b).

Genberg, A. H., 'Aspects of the Monetary Approach to Balance-of-Payments Theory: An Empirical Study of Sweden', in J. A. Frenkel and H. G. Johnson, eds., *The Monetary Approach to the Balance of Payments*, London: Allen and Unwin, 1976.

Graham, F., *Exchange Prices and Production in Hyperinflation Germany, 1920–23*, Princeton: Princeton University Press, 1930.

Grauer, F. L. A., R. H. Litzenberger and R. E. Stehle, 'Sharing Rules and Equilibrium in an International Capital Market', *J. Financial Econ.*, June 1976, **3**:233–256.

Hawtrey, R. G., *Currency and Credit*, London: Longmans, Green and Co., 1919.

Isard, P., 'How Far Can We Push the Law of One Price?' *Am. Econ. Rev.*, December 1977, **67**: 942–948.

Keynes, J. M., *A Treatise on Money*, Vol. I, London: 1930.

Keynes, J. M., *Essays in Persuasion*, New York: 1932.

Kouri, P. J. K. (1976), 'The Exchange Rate and the Balance of Payments in the Short Run and in the Long Run: A Monetary Approach', *Scand. J. Econ.*, May 1976, **78**:280–304.

Kravis, I. B., Z. Kennessey, A. W. Heston and R. Summers, *A System of International Comparisons of Gross Product and Purchasing Power*, Baltimore: Johns Hopkins University Press, 1975.

Kravis, I. B. and R. E. Lipsey, 'Price Behavior in the Light of Balance of Payments Theories', *J. Int. Econ.*, May 1978, **8**: 193–246.

Laffer, A. B., 'Exchange Rates, The Terms of Trade, and the Trade Balance', in P. B. Clark, D. E. Logue and R. J. Sweeney, eds., *Effects of Exchange Rate Adjustments*, Washington, D.C.: Treasury Department, OASIA Research, 1976.

Laskar, D. M., 'Short-run Independence of Monetary Policy under a Pegged-Exchange-Rates System: An Econometric Approach', *J. Int. Money and Finance*, April 1982, **1**: 57–79.

LeRoy, S. F., 'Expectations Models of Asset Prices: A Survey of Theory', *J. Finance*, March 1982, **37**: 185–218.

Lucas, R. E., Jr., 'Asset Prices in an Exchange Economy', *Econometrica*, November 1978, **46**: 1429–1446.

Lucas, R. E. and T. J. Sargent, 'After Keynesian Macroeconomics', *Federal Reserve Bank of Minneapolis Quarterly Review*, Spring 1979, pp. 1–16.

Magee, S. P., 'Contracting and Spurious Deviations from Purchasing Power Parity', in J. A. Frenkel and H. G. Johnson, eds. *The Economics of Exchange Rates*, Reading, Mass.: Addison-Wesley Co, 1978.

McCloskey, D. N. and R. J. Zecher, 'The Success of Purchasing Power Parity: Historical Evidence and Its Implications for Macroeconomics', University of Iowa Working Paper, November 1981.

McKinnon, R. I., 'Currency Substitution and Instability in the World Dollar Standard', *Am. Econ. Rev.*, June 1982, **72**: 320–333.

Mussa, M., 'A Model of Exchange Rate Dynamics', *J. Pol. Econ.*, February 1982, **90**: 74–104.

Officer, L. H., 'The Purchasing-Power-Parity Theory of Exchange Rates: A Review Article', *IMF Staff Papers*, March 1976, **23**: 1–60.

Ohlin, B., *Interregional and International Trade*, Revised edition, Cambridge, Mass.: Harvard University Press. First edition 1933.

Pippenger, J., 'Purchasing Power Parity: An Analysis of Predictive Error', University of California, Santa Barbara Working Paper, July 1981.

Protopadakis, A. and H. R. Stoll, 'Spot and Futures Prices and the Law of One Price', Federal Reserve Bank of Philadelphia Working Paper No. 82–4, April 1982.

Rogalski, R. J. and J. D. Vinso, 'Price Level Variations as Predictors of Flexible Exchange Rates', *J. Int. Business Stud.*, Summer 1977, **8**: 71–81.

Roll, R., 'Violations of Purchasing Power Parity and Their Implications for Efficient International Commodity Markets', in M. Sarnat and G. P. Szego, eds, *International Finance and Trade*, Vol. 1, Cambridge, Mass.: Ballinger Publishing Co, 1979.

Roll, R. and S. A. Ross, 'An Empirical Investigation of the Arbitrage Pricing Theory', *J. Finance*, December 1980, **35**: 1073–1103.

Roll, R. and B. Solnik, 'On Some Parity Conditions Encountered Frequently in International Economics', *J. Macroecon.*, Summer 1979, **1**: 267–283.

Ross, S. A. and M. Walsh, 'A Simple Approach to the Pricing of Risky Assets with Uncertain Exchange Rates' in R. G. Hawkins, R. M. Levich and C. Wihlborg, eds, *The Internationalization of Financial Markets and National Economic Policy*, Greenwich, Conn.: JAI Press, 1983.

Samuelson, P. A., 'Theoretical Notes on Trade Problems', *R. Econ. and Stat.*, May 1964, **46**: 145–154.

Samuelson, P. A., 'Analytical Notes on International Real Income Measures', *Econ. J.*, September 1974, **84**: 595–608.

Samuelson, P. A. and S. Swamy, 'Invariant Economic Index Numbers and Canonical Duality: Survey and Synthesis', *Am. Econ. Rev.*, September 1974, **65**: 566–593.

Sonnenschein, H., '"Do Walras" Identity and Continuity Characterize the Class of Community Excess Demand Functions?' *J. Econ. Theory*, August 1973, **5**: 345–354.

Stapleton, R. C. and M. G. Subrahmanyam, 'Market Imperfections, Capital Market Equilibrium, and Corporate Finance', *J. Finance*, May 1977, **32**: 307–319.

Stockman, A. C., 'A Theory of Exchange Rate Determination', *J. Pol. Econ.*, August 1980, 88: 673–698.

Viner, J., *Studies in the Theory of International Trade*, New York: 1937.

Wihlborg, C., 'The Role of Risk in International Macroeconomies', New York University Working Paper. July 1982.

16

Measures of Exchange Rate Variability*

John Williamson

1 INTRODUCTION

Exchange rates among the world's principle currencies have now floated for over a decade. That is sufficient time to have established beyond doubt that floating rates display a great deal of variability and that the adoption of floating does not resolve all balance of payments problems. Whether it would be possible to do better than the present system of "unstructured floating," neither free nor managed according to systematic principles, is the key question addressed in this study.

The move to floating rates in 1973 was welcomed, with varying degrees of enthusiasm, by most economists. Many had been arguing the desirability of greater flexibility for years, and even those who would have preferred limited flexibility—a combination of a wide band and a crawling peg—breathed a sigh of relief when the attempt to prop up the adjustable peg[1] was abandoned. The dire predictions of the consequences of floating that were voiced by defenders of the *status quo ante* before the event, regarding a prospective seize-up of the foreign exchange markets and major disruptions to trade, failed to materialize.

But the demonstration that floating is *viable* has not been matched by a consensus that it is *desirable*. Instead, more and more observers have been alarmed by the violent swings in exchange rates among the floating currencies—swings dramatically bigger than anything experienced by the Canadian dollar in the 1950s, which provided the experiment with floating that nurtured support in the 1960s.

In assessing the implications of the observed variability in floating exchange rates, it is important to distinguish between *short-term volatility* and persistent *misalignments*. By volatility is meant the amount of short-run variability in the exchange rate from hour to hour, day to day, week to week, or month to month. By misalignment is meant a persistent departure of the exchange rate from its long-run equilibrium level. These two dimensions of variability are distinct, for rates can be volatile around an equilibrium level of competitiveness or stable over long periods while misaligned. This study seeks to provide measures of both these dimensions of variability. Measuring misalignments is difficult and the measures are inherently imprecise, since they require estimation of what is termed the "*fundamental equilibrium exchange rate*" (abbreviated, with apologies, to FEER). Estimates are presented for recent misalignments of the five major currencies that compose the SDR.

---

[1]The "adjustable peg" is the most apt term for the Bretton Woods exchange rate system, under which exchange rates were normally maintained within a narrow band around a fixed par value—but that par value or "peg" might occasionally be discretely adjusted, in a devaluation or revaluation.

2 MEASURES OF EXCHANGE RATE VARIABILITY

As argued above, it is important to distinguish the two dimensions of variability, which are now often referred to as volatility and misalignments.

Volatility

One can conceive of two alternative approaches to measuring volatility. The first would be to seek the typical change in the rate from one period (hour, day, week, or month) to the next. This approach has traditionally been employed by the IMF. Summarizing recent findings, the Fund states (IMF, 1983, p. 9n):

The increased flexibility of members' exchange arrangements in the 1970s as compared with the Bretton Woods system is evident from a comparison of the average magnitudes of exchange rate changes in the period January 1948–August 1971, and in the subsequent period through the end of 1981. For the Fund membership as a whole, the average monthly change (without regard to sign) rose fourfold, from 0.3 percent in the former period to 1.4 percent in the latter. . . . The increase in flexibility was more marked for the group of industrial countries, for which average monthly changes increased almost tenfold, from 0.2 percent to 1.9 percent.

The other approach is to seek the typical deviation of the rate from its short-run moving average. The natural measure of volatility under this approach is the *coefficient of variation (standard deviation divided by mean)* of exchange rates quoted at frequent intervals around a moving average. Rates quoted at frequent intervals cannot meaningfully be corrected for inflation, since price indices are published relatively infrequently, so the calculation is done in terms of *nominal exchange rates*. Similarly, what matter in the short-run decisions on which volatility impinges are *bilateral* rates against a particular currency, and especially against the major vehicle currency, the US dollar, rather than average—i.e., *effective*—exchange rates. Table 1 therefore compares the coefficient of variation of the other major currencies around a six-month moving average in the final years of the Bretton Woods system,[2] in the first year of floating for which data are available, and in 1982.

It can be seen that exchange rate volatility in the Bretton Woods period was very sensitive to par value changes. In 1969 the French franc was devalued and the DM was revalued, and in consequence volatility was substantial. Similarly, the measure of sterling volatility in 1968 reflects the sterling devaluation of late 1967. In years when there was no par value change, volatility was small, an average of 0.2 percent. Under floating, volatility is regularly as large as it used to be in the years of par value changes under the Bretton Woods system, an average of close to 2 percent. Since par value changes were infrequent occurrences, it is clear that volatility on this measure has increased greatly since the advent of floating, by a factor of between 5 and 10, just as on the IMF measure. Moreover, volatility has, if anything, increased since the early years of floating, rather than diminishing as the markets gained experience. The conclusions that the increase in volatility is not sensitive to the particular measures chosen, and that volatility has in-

[2]Data were not available for 1970.

TABLE 1

Exchange Rate Volatility Under Pegged and Floating Exchange Rates

	1968	1969	1975	1982
Deutschemark	0.3	1.2[a]	1.7	1.6
French franc	0.1	2.3[a]	1.6	2.2
Japanese yen	n.a.	n.a.	0.7	2.5
Pound sterling	0.7[a]	0.2	1.0	1.1

Source IMF *International Financial Statistics.*

[a]Figure was influenced by a par value change.

n.a. Not available.

Note Coefficient of variation of daily nominal exchange rate against dollar around six-month moving average, expressed as percentage.

creased since the mid-1970s, are consistent with the findings of Kenen and Rodrik (1983) and Shafer and Loopesko (1983).

It must be recognized, however, that other things besides the exchange rate regime changed between the late 1960s and the early 1980s. In particular, technological advances in telecommunications led to far closer links between the main markets, which enabled news to have an instantaneous worldwide impact on *financial markets.* Those advances occurred virtually simultaneously with the breakdown of the Bretton Woods system, so there is no easy test of the extent to which technological progress rather than floating may have been responsible for the increase in volatility that is shown by the data. In addition there has been a marked increase in capital mobility, resulting in part from the liberalization of capital controls in the United States in 1974, in Britain in 1979, and in Japan in 1980.

Misalignment

A misalignment was defined above as a "persistent departure of the exchange rate from its long-run equilibrium level." It is necessary to justify this definition and to explain why one may usefully regard a rate as being misaligned even though it may clear the market (i.e., equate demand and supply). The most convenient way of doing that is to distinguish three concepts of equilibrium.[3]

Market Equilibrium This is simply the exchange rate that balances demand and supply in the absence of official intervention. This concept refers to the *nominal* rather than the real exchange rate, and tends to change rapidly whenever some relevant "news" changes. It is relatively easy to identify the presence of equilibrium in this sense, since the

[3]The following discussion draws on Bergsten and Williamson (forthcoming 1983). The three-way classification suggested there has subsequently been extended to a five-level classification by Armington and Wolford (1983), who add "current underlying equilibrium" and "underlying equilibrium," but these concepts are not relevant for present purposes.

objective fact of nonintervention[4] implies that the rate is in equilibrium. Conversely, absence of equilibrium is signified by heavy intervention and perhaps reserve borrowing intended to sustain the rate. This concept of equilibrium is sometimes taken to be the only relevant concept by those of a monetarist persuasion.

Fundamental Equilibrium This term is intended to connote the obverse of "fundamental disequilibrium," the criterion for an exchange rate change under the Bretton Woods system. Although the term was never formally defined, the IMF's (1970) report on the exchange-rate system implied that fundamental disequilibrium was a situation in which a country could not expect to generate a current account balance to match its underlying capital flow over the cycle as a whole without, on the one hand, depressing its income below "internal balance" or imposing trade controls for payments purposes or, on the other hand, importing inflation. Conversely, therefore, the fundamental equilibrium exchange rate is that which is expected to generate a current account surplus or deficit equal to the underlying capital flow over the cycle,[5] given that the country is pursuing "internal balance" as best it can and not restricting trade for balance of payments reasons. This second concept is what is often meant by "the rate justified by fundamentals." It is also what people usually have in mind when they describe rates as "overvalued" or "undervalued"—and it is used in that sense in this study.

The fact that a rate can become overvalued when a country inflates faster than its partners makes it obvious that this concept of an equilibrium rate relates not to the nominal exchange rate but rather to the *real* rate—i.e., the exchange rate adjusted for inflation at home and in competitor countries. Another term sometimes used to describe the FEER is the "purchasing power parity" or "PPP rate"—an expression that has been resisted here because of its unjustifiable suggestion that relative price levels *alone* are sufficient to pin down the long-run equilibrium level of the exchange rate. *Other things being equal,* however, one expects the nominal exchange rate consistent with long-run or fundamental equilibrium to change in accord with differential inflation, as posited by PPP theory.

The fundamental equilibrium exchange rate may change either because the underlying capital flow changes or because of changes in the pattern of demand for, or conditions of supply of, traded goods. Changes in underlying capital flows can on occasion be important: for example, when a country like Brazil gains access to the international capital market (in the early 1970s) or loses its creditworthiness (in the early 1980s). Whether one should also adjust the FEER to reflect the changes in capital flows that result from such fiscal developments as the emergence of a structural budget deficit in the United States is a difficult question, discussed later in this section.

Changes in demand and supply which affect long-run real equilibrium exchange rates

[4]An element of ambiguity does, however, enter through the existence of government transactions. The usual resort is to define nonintervention as a situation where the government does not seek to alter the timing of its transactions with a view to influencing the exchange rate.

[5]Adoption of this definition for the FEER is in no way inconsistent with the fact that the vast bulk (probably over 90 percent) of the value of all exchange market transactions is on capital rather than current account, or with a belief that the *market* rate is determined by the views of wealth owners as postulated in the "asset market approach" to the explanation of exchange rates. (See Williamson, 1983, ch. 10 for an exposition of the asset market approach and references to the literature.)

go on all the time, but those large enough to have a perceptible macroeconomic impact seem to fall into three categories. First, differential productivity growth in different countries means that a fast-growing country like Japan will need some real appreciation over time.[6] Such changes are, however, gradual. Second, exploitation of important new resource discoveries—like North Sea oil—may permit a real appreciation. Such changes are easy to diagnose and relatively infrequent.

Third, *permanent* exogenous changes in the terms of trade may call for changes in competitiveness.[7] Terms of trade changes are again easy to observe, although judgment is certainly required to distinguish transitory from permanent changes. Even where changes are essentially permanent, as with the oil price increase of 1973, it does not necessarily follow that the real exchange rate should change greatly. Real exchange rate changes were called for to the extent that it was necessary to redistribute deficits among the oil importers, but they could not adjust away the surplus of the Organization of Petroleum Exporting Countries (OPEC), which depended only on the value of oil exports and the quantity of imports that OPEC chose to buy. In this instance the OPEC surplus changes underlying capital flows in a way that went a long way toward neutralizing the effect of changes in demand and supply.

This discussion suggests that, while fundamental equilibrium exchange rates are not immutable, they are not likely to change frequently and drastically. Moreover, it is possible to identify the factors that are likely to have a perceptible impact on (real) FEERs, and it is easy to trace the changes in nominal rates required to maintain real rates constant in the presence of differential inflation. Nevertheless, unlike the market equilibrium rate, there is no simple objective test of whether or not a rate is in fundamental equilibrium. At best, estimates of the FEER require judgments that in practice contain subjective elements regarding cyclical adjustment, the underlying capital flow, and trade elasticities. At worst, skeptics deny any hope of identifying the fundamental equilibrium rate. It is certainly true that the concept has a normative element, inasmuch as what constitute the "underlying capital flow" and "internal balance" depend on the macroeconomic policy regarded as appropriate. But the scope for differences to arise from pure divergencies in value judgments should not be exaggerated: one can sensibly debate the size (and sometimes the sign) of the capital flows needed to maximize welfare, and how much scope there is for expanding demand without rekindling inflation. Views on these topics *are* modified in the light of new evidence, even though one never expects to achieve unanimity.

Current Equilibrium This term is intended to indicate the rate that would obtain if markets had full knowledge of all relevant facts and reacted rationally to that knowledge. The current equilibrium rate will depend upon such temporary factors as the path of

[6]This is true, at least, when real exchange rates are measured by a broadly based price index like the CPI or GDP deflator. See the classic analysis of Balassa (1964).

[7]The terms of trade is defined as the price of exports *divided* by the price of imports, while competitiveness or the real exchange rate is measured by the price of home-produced tradable goods *divided* by the price of competing foreign products. The two concepts reduce to the same thing in the simple exportables-importables model of trade theory, but they are very different in the real world. Thus an oil price rise worsens the terms of trade of an oil-importing country, but need not influence its competitiveness. In general a large country's terms of trade are influenced *both* by exogenous factors like the real price of oil *and* by endogenous factors like its level of income and competitiveness.

interest rates, which in turn depends on the stance of macroeconomic policy and the state of the business cycle, and, given risk aversion, on net asset positions vis-à-vis the rest of the world. The current equilibrium rate will deviate from fundamental equilibrium when policy variables are set at levels which drive the exchange rate away from its FEER. For example, a high interest rate relative to other countries will appreciate the currency involved, so as to create expectations of a yield-equalizing depreciation over the period that the high interest rate is expected to persist, as in the classic Dornbusch (1976) analysis.

This is the concept of equilibrium that most economists have in mind when they model the behavior of exchange rates, and hence further understanding of the properties of the current equilibrium rate can be obtained by studying the voluminous professional literature on exchange rate determination. It is apparently also sometimes what is meant by "the rate justified by fundamentals"; clarity would be served if individuals who use this phrase would specify whether they are referring to the fundamental equilibrium rate or to the current equilibrium rate.

Given that knowledge is not perfect, one has to interpret the concept of the current equilibrium rate in a rational expectations sense, as the rate expected to equalize yields on comparable assets (in the simple case of risk neutrality) on the basis of currently available information. Like the market equilibrium rate, the current equilibrium rate adjusts in response to relevant news. It also refers to a nominal rather than a real rate. However, unlike the market equilibrium rate, identification of the current equilibrium rate requires subjective judgment.

The Size of Misalignments

Since a misalignment has been defined as a deviation of the market rate from fundamental equilibrium, measurement of the misalignment existing at any particular time requires an estimate of fundamental equilibrium. Such estimates are sought below. But before moving on to that task, one may observe that there is a second way of gaining a general idea of the size that misalignments have reached that does not depend on the credibility of any particular estimates of FEERs, but solely on the hypothesis that *changes* in those fundamental equilibrium rates have not been large.

Table 2 therefore shows the maximum swings in the real effective exchange rates[8] of the five major currencies for the decade since floating started in 1973 to the end of 1982. For comparability, figures are also provided for a similar 10-year period immediately prior to the abandonment of the adjustable peg and covering the breakdown of the Bretton Woods system. It is natural to present such estimates in terms of "real"—i.e., inflation-adjusted—exchange rates when seeking to measure misalignments, since differential inflation changes the equilibrium position measured in nominal terms. Similarly, it is natural to use "effective"—i.e., average (trade-weighted)—exchange rates, so as to avoid the equilibrium position's varying with changes in exchange rates among other currencies. There are various different measures of real effective exchange rates, which differ in the price indices they employ to adjust for inflation (wholesale prices in manufacturing, unit labor costs, consumer prices, etc.) and in the weight they use to compare different competitors (bilateral trade weights, bilateral weights modified to account for competition

[8]As measured by the IMF index of relative wholesale prices. The behavior of this index for the three major countries can be compared with that of 9 other indices of real effective exchange rates in appendix figures A1–A3 in the original.

TABLE 2

Maximum Swings in Real Effective Exchange Rates of Five Major Currencies, 1963–72 and 1973–82 (Percentages)

	1963–72	1973–82
Deutschemark	13	22
French franc	27	19
Japanese yen	14	35
Pound sterling	17	60
US dollar	14	32
Average	17	34

Source IMF statistics for relative wholesale prices vis-à-vis other industrial countries.

Note The results presented in the table cannot be dismissed as a reflection of wild swings in the first couple of years after floating was adopted, when the market was still undergoing a learning process. Elimination of the period 1973–75 would alter the figures only for the DM and French franc, reducing them marginally to 18 percent and 17 percent, respectively. (Deletion of the years 1963–65 would have a rather similar effect, reducing the figures for the French franc and yen to 24 percent and 10 percent, respectively.)

in third markets, multilateral weights based on comparative GNP or on the competitive relations implied by the IMF's multilateral exchange rate model, etc.). The different indices generally tell much the same story, although divergences can be sufficiently large to preclude attributing significance to movements less than 5 percent or so. (Different measures can drift apart over time by considerably more than this, but a change of 5 percent is rarely accompanied by an *opposite* movement of another index in the short run.) For purposes of the exercises reported below, six of the leading indices were combined into a composite index.[9]

Table 2 reveals that for four of the five currencies the maximum swings in real effective exchange rates (REERs) have been greater in the decade of floating than they were in the previous decade. Indeed, on average swings were twice as large under floating. There was, however, one currency (the French franc) for which the swing was actually less, and another (the DM) for which the swing much less than doubled. It is worth noting that those two currencies are the two that participated in the European Monetary System (and its predecessor, the snake), which has meant that a large part of the trade of Germany and, for much of the period, of France, has been conducted across pegged exchanges. Moreover, those pegs were periodically changed, in a way that roughly offset differential inflation.

[9]The composite indices are geometric means of the following series: Bank for International Settlements (BIS), Morgan Guaranty, IMF (63 110); BIS, IMF (65 um 110), IMF (65 umc 110). The French computation excludes the BIS-WPI series, which inexplicably moves far out of line with all others.

The swings in the real effective exchange rates of the three independently floating currencies have, however, been enormous: in every case they have exceeded 30 percent. Moreover the nominal exchange rate swings have often exaggerated rather than offset the changes in competitiveness resulting from differential inflation.

If the fundamental equilibrium exchange rate were constant over time, then one could infer that the US dollar (for example) *must* have been misaligned at some time since 1973 by *at least* 16 percent (one-half of 32 percent). If the FEER were not exactly half way between the highest and lowest values that the dollar touched, then misalignment must at some time have been even *greater* than 16 percent. Misalignments may admittedly have been smaller, to the extent that exchange rate changes were reflecting changes in fundamental equilibrium rates. But this analysis leaves a presumption that misalignments have been very substantial under floating, contrary to the expectation that was prevalent when floating rates were first accepted in 1973.

The Identification of Fundamental Equilibrium Rates

The traditional approach to estimating fundamental equilibrium exchange rates involves seeking a period during which exchange rates appear to have been at appropriate levels, and then making a "purchasing power parity" (PPP) comparison to identify the nominal exchange rate that would reproduce the real exchange rate of the base period *given* intervening inflation. For example, if the domestic country has suffered on average 10 percent more inflation than its trading partners since the base date, then one concludes that its currency should have depreciated by 10 percent compared to that base level. If instead the currency had appreciated by 5 percent in effective terms, then one would judge that the currency was 15 percent overvalued (in terms of the real effective exchange rate) compared to its fundamental equilibrium level.

An important technical issue concerns the choice of a price index for use in making PPP comparisons. Ideally one wants a measure that is able to diverge—as wholesale prices of primary products are not, under conditions; but that diverges only as the competitive position of the tradable sector changes—and not because (for example) consumer prices rise relative to the prices of tradables as a result of rapid productivity growth in the latter sector. The first criterion rules out export prices and argues for the use of wholesale prices of manufacturing output rather than inputs. The second criterion argues against the use of consumer prices.[10] Another choice relates to the use of an index of prices, which runs the danger that it may fail to reveal a deterioration in competitive position when suppliers shave their profit margins to defend their market share, versus an index of costs, which has the disadvantage that its coverage is usually only partial (specifically, that it is normally restricted to labor costs and excludes capital costs—though the IMF does publish a series based on value-added deflators which attempts to remedy this problem). There does not seem any convincing reason for preferring one type of index to the other, which is why the composite index used in this study (see footnote 9) combines indices using both wholesale prices and unit labor costs.

Table 3 shows some existing estimates of real effective exchange rates of the five major currencies based on the traditional PPP approach. The first three rows show the figures that Morgan Guaranty was using until July 1983, which employed March 1973 as a base when exchange rates were supposedly in equilibrium. The next three rows present the figures that Morgan Guaranty now uses, which have been rebased to take 1980–82 as a

TABLE 3

Real Effective Exchange Rates Relative to "Equilibrium" Base (Index Numbers, Base Period = 100)

Source	Base Period	Date	US Dollar	Japanese Yen	Deutschemark	French franc	Pound Sterling
Morgan Guaranty[a]	March 1973	1977	102.5	101.6	96.1	93.5	100.0
Morgan Guaranty[a]	March 1973	1982	96.4	135.2	95.6	82.8	116.9
Morgan Guaranty[a]	March 1973	1983 QI	97.7	124.3	95.7	88.8	117.0
Morgan Guaranty[b]	1980–82	1977	105.4	73.8	99.8	103.7	93.9
Morgan Guaranty[b]	1980–82	1982	99.1	98.8	97.7	92.3	109.8
Morgan Guaranty[b]	1980–82	1983 QI	100.6	90.6	97.9	96.9	110.2
CEA	1973–80	1977	101.4				
CEA	1973–80	1982	121.7				

Sources Morgan Guaranty, *World Financial Markets*, July and August 1983; Council of Economic Advisers' *Annual Report*, 1983, ch. 3 and table B-100.

[a]Old series.

[b]New series.

CEA Council of Economic Advisers.

Note A number greater than 100 signifies a currency appreciated above its base value.

base. This naturally has the effect of cutting the measured overvaluation of those currencies that experienced a large real appreciation between March 1973 and 1980–82, namely the US dollar and even more so the pound sterling. The final rows present the effective real overvaluation of the US dollar implicit in the choice of 1973–80 as a base and the use of the Federal Reserve Board's index of real effective exchange rates, as was done by the US Council of Economic Advisers in its 1983 *Annual Report*.

There are two obvious deficiencies in the procedure whose results are shown in table 3. The first is that any base date chosen is bound to be somewhat arbitrary: there never was a golden age to which one can look back when the world economy was in general equilibrium. This criticism can be met to some extent, though not totally, by taking as the base the average real effective exchange rate over some lengthy period, rather than its value on a specific date. The second deficiency is that the procedure makes no allowance for any change in the FEER that may have occurred since the base period in order to accommodate to changed circumstances. There *are* events which call for changes in the real effective exchange rate in order to promote adjustment: for example, permanent shifts in the terms of trade which have to be offset, and changes in the balance between thrift and productivity which make it rational to accept a larger or smaller surplus or deficit on the current account of the balance of payments. These deficiencies are glaringly apparent in the large changes in measured competitive positions that have resulted from Morgan Guaranty's recent decision to rebase its series: one may enthusiastically agree that a March

[10]An additional argument against the use of consumer prices applies where the price index is to be employed as the basis of a PPP rule for adjusting the exchange rate. This stems from the fact that what could be a purely transitory rise in consumer prices—for example, as a result of a bad harvest—would get built into the inflationary process if it were allowed to result in a depreciation.

1973 base is outmoded (because of the second deficiency), while remaining utterly unconvinced that the choice of a 1980–82 base addresses the first deficiency.

The present treatment seeks to remedy both those deficiencies in the traditional approach. Rather than search for a specific date or period when it may plausibly be argued that exchange rates were in equilibrium, it asks: what set of exchange rates would have been needed in a specific period, for which 1976–77 was chosen, to induce a set of current account balances that matched "underlying capital flows"? And in addition to extrapolating the exchange rates calculated to have represented "fundamental equilibrium" for 1976–77 forward by a mechanistic application of PPP, it asks what real changes in the interim have been sufficiently large to have had a macroeconomic impact, and seeks to make appropriate allowances. The assumptions needed to carry out such an exercise are undoubtedly heroic. The justification for nonetheless undertaking the exercise is that it is much less arbitrary than crude PPP extrapolations.

Underlying Capital Flows

A first step in estimating the FEERs for 1976–77 is to derive estimates for what have been called the "underlying capital flows" reflecting "thrift and productivity." It is easy enough to accept such a notion in concept. One expects that during any short time period the actual inflow or outflow of capital recorded by a country will reflect many short-term factors of a volatile nature: confidence, monetary policies relative to those abroad, speculation, timing accidents, and so on. At one time it was assumed that most such volatile movements would involve transactions in short-term assets, and conversely that the underlying capital flow could be approximated by transactions in assets with a long term to maturity. Unfortunately for analytical simplicity, neither assumption seems a reasonable approximation any more: many volatile flows involve switching into or out of long-term assets, while accumulation of working balances placed in short-term assets can be rather stable in aggregate. But this statistical difficulty in distinguishing volatile from underlying capital movements does not render the distinction unnecessary, for over a longer time horizon the short-term factors will tend to balance out, and what remains will be a reflection of the savings-investment balance in the economy. A country with a high rate of investment (in reflection of a high productivity of capital) relative to the level of domestically generated savings will find it advantageous to import capital (although the extent to which it is able to do so may be constrained by creditworthiness considerations). Conversely, a country with a high net savings rate and relatively few current investment opportunities can benefit by using a part of its savings to acquire investments abroad.

Unless public policy is distorting the level of saving (or conceivably investment) in a major way, the inflow or outflow of capital that results from such considerations will normally be socially beneficial, whether by augmenting domestic savings to permit a higher level of investment to be sustained, or by allowing savings to be invested in a more productive way (abroad). But realization of that potential gain requires that the capital flow be matched by a corresponding transfer of real resources. That is, it requires a matching current account surplus or deficit, so that the overall balance of payments is in equilibrium. Thus current account targets are the mirror image of underlying capital flows.

Problems arise when trying to translate these uncontroversial general principles into hard figures, given that the term to maturity is a poor indicator of volatility so that basic balance equilibrium is not a satisfactory target. We do not have the data on time preferences and marginal efficiencies of investment that might in principle allow welfare-maximizing capital flows to be estimated. But it would also be silly to pretend that we cannot develop any estimates as to the order of magnitude of desirable capital flows.

When I lived in Brazil in the late 1970s, I used to argue that an appropriate current-account target for Brazil would be a deficit of about $5 billion a year. Critics objected to the propriety of discussing such targets, and then proceeded to debate whether the figure should not have been $4 billion or $6 billion, but no one ever told me that a country with such promising prospects as Brazil should *not* have been importing capital on a substantial scale to accelerate its development nor that the proper target would have been over $9 billion a year (the actual average level of foreign borrowing from 1977 to 1981, which led to disaster).

Getting a reasonable idea of the "underlying" or desirable capital flow is even more difficult for the five major countries than for Brazil. A natural starting point is to consider the actual average current account outcome over a reasonably lengthy period: the average balance over the 1974–78 cycle is shown in the first row of table 4. It can be seen that the United States was in balance, that Germany and Japan were in large surplus, while France and the United Kingdom were in substantial deficit. Another approach is to look at long-term capital outflows, despite their inadequacies as noted above. The second row of table 4 reveals that for the four countries other than the United States the capital flows were broadly consistent with the state of their current balances. The United States, however, had a vast capital outflow without a corresponding current account surplus. The question therefore arises as to whether the capital outflow was a reflection of thrift and productivity which did not lead to a real transfer because of flawed adjustment policies, or whether the current account outcome was more consistent with the investment-savings balance while the capital outflow reflected lax monetary policies permitted by the dollar's reserve role.

Some data relevant to answering that question are shown in table 5. What stands out from this table is the low savings rate in the United States. Although the United States probably still has the highest capital-labor ratio in the world, it would seem impossible to argue that the discrepancy is so great that the United States would be justified in transferring a significant proportion of its limited savings overseas. A balanced current account seems a more reasonable objective. France was at that time the fastest growing economy of the five apart from high-savings Japan, so its role as a capital importer was appropriate.

TABLE 4

Data Relevant to Assessing Underlying Capital Flows (Billion Dollars, 1977 Prices)

	United States	Japan	Germany	France	United Kingdom	Total
Actual current account balance, 1974–78 average	0.1	4.8	5.8	−2.7	−3.0	5.0
Long-term net capital outflow, 1974–78 average	13.7	4.2	3.6	−0.7	−3.2	17.6

Sources OECD *Economic Outlook*, IMF *International Financial Statistics*.

Note Figures adjusted to 1977 prices by US wholesale price index.

TABLE 5

Savings and Investment in Five Major Countries, 1976–77 (Percentage of GDP, Average of 1976 and 1977)

	United States	Japan	Germany	France	United Kingdom
Savings					
Household	4.2	16.2	8.4	9.5	4.6
Corporate	1.6	1.0	1.4	−0.4	2.6
Government	−1.0	2.2	1.8	2.2	−0.7
Total	4.7	19.4	11.5	11.3	6.5
Net investment					
Household	2.7	6.5	8.0	5.4	0.9
Corporate	1.5	7.2		4.8	5.1
Government	1.5	4.9	2.7	2.2	2.6
Total	5.6	18.6	10.7	12.4	8.6
Current account	−0.5	1.2	0.9	−1.1	−1.1
Statistical discrepancy	−0.4	−0.4	0.0	0.0	−1.1

Source OECD National Accounts.

Note Totals may not add due to rounding.

The United Kingdom was in the mid-1970s investing heavily in capital-intensive North Sea oil development, so it was again quite rational to be importing capital. The position of Japan and Germany as capital exporters seems perfectly consistent with their savings-investment balances.

The remaining question is how large the capital imports by France and the United Kingdom and the capital exports by Japan and Germany should ideally have been. In order to apply the IMF's multilateral exchange rate model (MERM) and to limit the specification of current account objectives to the big five, the sum of the objectives must equal the sum of the actual outcomes of the five.[11] That sum averaged $1.4 billion in 1976–77. In view of the difficulties that both the United Kingdom and France experienced in financing their current account deficits at times in the mid-1970s, it seems clear that their actual deficits of around $3 billion a year were too large. A figure of around half that would represent my best judgment of what a reasonable target would have been. If one assumes that Japan and Germany should have had equal targets, arithmetic dictates that those targets would have been something over $2 billion a year.

The current account targets (or underlying capital outflows) suggested as reasonable by the preceding discussion are shown in the second column of table 6. As with the Brazilian target mentioned above, it would be silly to argue about their last billion dollars, but, at least to the writer, there seem to be quite strong arguments against figures drastically different from those in the table.

[11]One reason this exercise has been performed on a past period rather than on current data is to exploit this knowledge. In working out such targets for future application, it would be important that the interests of the rest of the world be introduced into the decision making of the five.

TABLE 6

Current Account Balances, Targets, and Desired Changes, 1976–77 (Billion Dollars, 1977 Prices)

	Actual Current Balance	Target Current Balance	Desirable Change in Current Account Balance
United States	−4.7	0	+4.7
Japan	7.4	2.2	−5.2
Germany	4.2	2.2	−2.0
France	−4.6	−1.5	+3.1
United Kingdom	−0.9	−1.5	−0.6
Total	1.4	1.4	0.0

Source OECD *Economic Outlook* and reasoning described in text.

Estimates of FEERs in 1976–77

Apart from nonprice competitiveness, which is nonquantifiable and in any event is unlikely to change rapidly, there are three factors that have a major systematic impact on the current account. The first is the terms of trade (see footnote 7). The second is the relative pressure of demand at home as against that in foreign markets. The third is price competitiveness, measured by the real effective exchange rate. Algebraically, one may write:

$$\text{Current balance} = f\left\{\begin{matrix}\text{terms of}\\ \text{trade}\end{matrix};\ \begin{matrix}\text{relative pressure}\\ \text{of demand}\end{matrix};\ \text{REER}\right\}$$

Since the terms of trade are partly influenced by factors exogenous to individual countries (like the real price of oil) and partly by relative demand pressures and REERs, as explained in footnote 7, this equation can in principle be solved for that value of the REER needed to produce a given current balance when relative demand pressures are cyclically normal. It is this value of the REER that has been defined as the FEER—a concept that is, as argued above, itself defined in terms of the REER. (It might have been more accurate to speak of a fundamental equilibrium real effective exchange rate, or FEREER, but there are limits to the extent to which authors can abuse their readers with inelegant acronyms!)

The question therefore arises as to whether relative demand pressures were cyclically normal in the period 1976–77 chosen as the base for this exercise. Unfortunately there do not now seem to be any published estimates of GNP gaps on an internationally comparable basis. The best figures to assess relative demand pressures would therefore seem to be the unemployment statistics, standardized for international comparability, published by the Organization for Economic Cooperation and Development (OECD). Unemployment is, however, a lagging indicator of the pressure of demand, so that demand pressures in 1976–77 are best measured by the unemployment levels of 1977, as shown in table 7. Column 4 then shows the excess of 1977 unemployment over the country's average for the 1974–79 cycle. The final column compares that excess with the excess for the OECD as a whole, to get an indicator of whether demand in each country was cyclically more or less slack than abroad.

It appears that most countries were fairly close to the cyclical average at that time. (The suspicion that this would be so in fact led to the choice of 1976–77 as the base period for

TABLE 7

Unemployment as a Measure of 1976–77 Demand Pressure in Five Major Countries (Percentages)

	Average 1974–79	1976	1977	Excess of 1977 over Cyclical Average	Excess of Country Excess over OECD
United States	6.6	7.5	6.9	0.3	−0.1
Japan	1.9	2.0	2.0	0.1	−0.3
Germany	3.2	3.7	3.7	0.5	0.1
France	4.5	4.4	4.7	0.2	−0.2
United Kingdom	5.1	5.5	6.2	1.1	0.7
OECD	4.9	5.2	5.3	0.4	0.0

Source OECD *Main Economic Indicators.*

these calculations.) The United Kingdom is an exception, which, according to this measure, had slacker demand than the other countries. In view of the United Kingdom's failure to master inflation in this period, however, it would seem difficult to argue that Britain was suffering from an abnormally high level of unnecessary slack in 1976–77. There is also some question as to whether an adjustment might be in order for the United States, where unemployment was falling rapidly, in contrast to the other countries. Such an adjustment would reduce the underlying US deficit below the measured deficit, and would therefore appreciate the estimated dollar FEER, somewhat. In the end, however, no adjustments were made for abnormal cyclical positions.

This means that the desired changes in current account balances (shown in the last column of table 6) can be found simply by subtracting the actual current balance (column 1) from the target (in column 2). How much would exchange rates have had to adjust in order to produce those changes in current balances, after lag effects had worked themselves out? There is one model, the IMF's multilateral exchange rate model (MERM), that was built with the precise object of answering that type of question. The version presented in Artus and McGuirk (1981) is based on 1977 data and can therefore be applied directly. It yields answers in the form of changes in bilateral nominal exchange rates against the dollar, which are shown in the first column of table 8. These numbers then

TABLE 8

Exchange Rate Changes Needed to Achieve Fundamental Equilibrium, 1976–77 (Percentages)

	Bilateral Dollar Exchange Rate	EER	REER
United States	n.a.	−4.9	−4.2
Japan	11.9	10.2	8.8
Germany	6.5	3.9	3.0
France	−2.9	−7.1	−5.5
United Kingdom	6.9	3.4	2.1
Other industrial countries	2.9	−0.8	−0.6

Sources Table 6 and the MERM (Artus and McGuirk, 1981).

n.a. Not applicable.

have to be transformed into effective exchange rates, which can be done by applying the MERM weights. Since the MERM allows for the partial neutralization of exchange rate changes through induced internal inflation, the implicit changes in *real* effective exchange rates are smaller than the needed changes in effective exchange rates calculated by the MERM. How much smaller they are can be estimated from the MERM's predictions of the effect of a 10 percent depreciation of a country's own currency on its GDP deflator. For example, the version of the MERM used for the present simulation, the version with "low-feedback parameters," implies that a 10 percent nominal depreciation of the French franc would raise French prices by 2.3 percent (Artus and McGuirk, 1981, table 2, p. 296), which—abstracting from any difference between the GDP deflator and the price indices used to measure real exchange rates—implies a real depreciation of 7.7 percent. Applying such "offset coefficients" to the effective exchange rate (EER) changes in the second column of table 8 yields the REER changes shown in the final column.

The MERM calculates only the change in exchange rates needed to achieve a specified change in current balances. To derive from this the *level* of the FEER, one needs to know the actual level of the exchange rate. Unfortunately the appropriate rate to take as the "actual" is not unambiguous, due to the well-established fact that exchange rate changes affect trade flows with lengthy distributed lags. For example, the MERM is supposed to show the changes that would occur after a lag of two to three years. Clearly the *average* lag is less than that, perhaps of the order of six months to a year. Hence one should calculate the FEERs for 1976–77 by applying the adjustments shown in the last column of table 8 to the average REERs for 1975–76, as is done in the last two columns of table 9. However, earlier columns show data on REERs for individual years in the period 1974–77, to allow those who would prefer a different base to see how much difference it would make.

Extrapolating FEERs to 1983

In order to assess the size of present misalignments, it is necessary to consider how much FEERs may have changed since 1976–77. There would seem to have been three new developments in that period potentially important enough to have exerted a perceptible impact on the FEERs of one or more of the major powers: the second oil price increase, the coming on stream of North Sea oil (for the United Kingdom), and the emergence of the United States as a large net capital importer.

TABLE 9

Actual REERs and Estimated FEERs for 1976–77 (Index Numbers, 1975 = 100)

	REERs					FEERs
	1974	1975	1976	1977	1975–76 Av.	1976–77
United States	103.0	100	103.5	101.5	101.8	98
Japan	108.7	100	101.1	106.2	100.6	109
Germany	105.6	100	100.1	103.4	100.1	103
France	89.9	100	97.9	94.4	98.9	96
United Kingdom	94.9	100	93.0	94.5	96.5	99

Source Composite data on REERs from appendix and table 8.

TABLE 10

Changes in REERs Needed to Neutralize Trade Balance Effects of Oil Price Increases (Percentages)

	Change in Oil Price from			
	1972–78	1972–80	1978–80	1978–83
United States	0	4	4	2
Japan	−11	−28	−15	−8
Germany	0	−3	−3	−2
France	−1	−3	−2	−1
United Kingdom	12	23	10	6

Source McGuirk (1983, table 12).

If the 1979–80 oil price increase is judged to be permanent, it implies a need for (real) exchange rate adjustments to the extent that there is a differential payments impact on different industrial countries that should be adjusted away rather than absorbed by offsetting changes in savings or investment. It is convenient to assume that adjustments to the oil price increase will be complete by 1985, so that by then OPEC will be spending all its additional income while energy demand and supply in the industrial countries will have adjusted to the new oil price level. (In 1983 OPEC is in fact in current account deficit, but it is questionable whether this will be sustained in the medium term with a constant oil price: creditworthiness constraints will limit the deficits that the "high absorbers" can afford, while the "low absorbers" will surely move back into surplus, to an extent that makes the assumption of overall OPEC balance reasonable.) Assuming that changes in OPEC import demand are distributed proportionately among the industrial countries, this permits calculation of incipient current account imbalances. McGuirk (1983) used the MERM to calculate the changes in REERs needed to restore current balance. Table 10 shows her estimates in the first two columns: the third is derived as the difference between the first two. The fourth reflects the erosion in the real price of oil from 1980 to 1983.

It is evident that the needed changes are quite modest, except in the two extreme cases of Japan (which is exceptionally dependent on oil imports) and the United Kingdom (which is a net oil exporter). They would be even more modest if a judgment were made that the oil price was likely to fall further. Another possible offsetting factor of relevance to the United Kingdom is the limited life of the oil fields whose current production is responsible for the sterling appreciation shown in table 10: if one takes the view that a part of the increased real income resulting from North Sea oil should be saved in the form of an increased current surplus, the justified appreciation would be smaller than calculated by McGuirk.

The second relevant development since 1977 is the change in the status of the United Kingdom from major oil importer to significant oil exporter. (The United Kingdom is currently the world's fifth largest oil producer, and oil exports account for over a fifth of total exports.) It has been calculated that, given the limited expected production lifetime of the North Sea oil fields, rational utilization of the income from North Sea oil would require saving about one-half of the oil revenue (Forsyth and Kay, 1980). Since investment in a country like the United Kingdom is primarily constrained by interest rates and expected real wages adjusted for productivity rather than by the availability of savings, that additional saving should be reflected largely in an increased surplus in the current account of the balance of payments. Anne McGuirk's estimate in column 2 of table 10, adjusted downward to allow for the erosion in the real oil price since 1980, would suggest that a real sterling appreciation of about 17 percent would have been needed to adjust away the whole of the oil surplus. If one takes the view that a half of the oil bonanza should have been saved, the desirable appreciation is halved to, say, 9 percent. This is *inclusive* of the sterling appreciation shown in the last column of table 10, not additional.

The most difficult question is whether the emergence of a structural budget deficit in the United States should lead to a revision of the dollar's FEER. Given the large tax cuts and the increases in defense spending not matched by equivalent reductions in other forms of government spending, it looks as if the United States will be running massive budget deficits in the next few years. This will reduce aggregate net US savings, by a similar order of magnitude that the first oil price increase raised world savings in the mid-1970s.[12] Feldstein (1983a) has argued that, while the deficit itself should be regretted, the second-best response to the deficit involves high real interest rates, capital imports, a high value of the dollar, and a current account deficit. If one accepts the US budget deficit as exogenous, one can scarcely reject the "Feldstein doctrine," and that would imply adjusting the FEER to reflect the fall in US thrift so as to allow the United States to borrow from the rest of the world.

But two further questions must be asked before one accepts the logic of the Feldstein doctrine. The first is whether the economic strategy of budget deficit, high real interest rates, foreign borrowing, overvalued currency, and current account deficit is *sustainable*. This is, after all, qualitatively similar to the policy package that evolved under President Lopez Portillo in Mexico (although the scale of the borrowing relative to GNP is perhaps only a third as large). Until 1982 the market was happily financing what everyone now recognizes to have been an unsustainable policy course in Mexico. The mere fact that the market is equally happily bidding the dollar up to new highs as this is written does not prove that current US policy is on a sustainable course: if confidence collapses, the result may be very unpleasant indeed.

While such a collapse seems likely (at some date) on present policies, it would be rash to assert that it is inevitable: a gradual return to fiscal responsibility might permit a "soft landing." But even if one is optimistic on that score, one has a second question to consider: whether large-scale net borrowing by the most capital-rich country on earth to enable it temporarily to lower its savings rate is really economically rational? With all due respect to the desirability of economists' exhibiting a decent humility, we surely have a rather strong hunch on the answer to that question.

One has to conclude that it would be quite wrong to accept macroeconomic follies like the US budget deficit as exogenous, and accommodate them without further question (by adjusting the FEER). On the contrary, a principal purpose of seeking a more structured exchange rate system is precisely to expose such examples of myopic and internationally inconsistent national decision making. If the administration had to explain that its budget-

[12]The tax cuts are estimated to have reduced revenue by about 4 percent of US GNP or $120 billion, and thus to have reduced total US savings by the order of $100 billion. OPEC ran a current surplus on the order of $40 billion per annum in the mid-1970s, equivalent to a rise in savings *ex ante* of perhaps $50 billion per annum. US prices have increased about 75 percent since 1975.

ary policy required approval of an appreciation of the dollar's FEER, which Congress could recognize would threaten a large number of tradable goods industries, it is surely likely that political forces to restore fiscal discipline would be strengthened. To rationalize recent exchange rates and argue for automatic adjustment of the FEER to reflect the budget deficit would gut this potentially important political force, as well as imply agreement that policy is on a sustainable and satisfactory course. Accordingly, no adjustment to the dollar's FEER has been made on this score.

There is, however, a second recent development that might justify some change in the underlying capital inflow of the United States: namely, the swing of direct investment from a normal net outflow of around $8 billion a year to an average inflow in the last two years of over $12 billion. Even if the recent figures prove erratically high, it seems reasonable to allow for a swing of say $12 billion. Using the customary rule of thumb that each 1 percent dollar depreciation improves the current account balance by about $3 billion a year, this suggests that a real appreciation of 4 percent might be justified on this score.

In addition to the discrete events considered above, continuing differences in productivity trends may call for changes in measured real exchange rates to maintain competitiveness constant. This would certainly be true if the indices underlying the composite included CPIs. With indices based on WPIs and unit labor costs, the only country for which such an adjustment seems called for is Japan. If the behavior of the index of export prices relative to that of wholesale prices from 1976 to 1982 in Japan is compared with that in Germany (the only other major country that publishes an export price index), one finds that export prices fell 15 percent relative to wholesale prices in Japan and only 6 percent in Germany. Thus it seems that technical advances continue to be made with particular rapidity in Japan's tradable goods industries. To compensate for this, it was assumed that Japan's FEER as measured by the composite index appreciates at a rate of 1 percent a year. Accordingly the net depreciation of the yen's FEER was reduced, from the 8 percent shown in table 10, to 2 percent.

TABLE 11

Estimates of Misalignments, 1983 QI

	Actual REER (1976–77 FEER = 100)	Changes in FEERs 1977–1983 (Percentage)	Actual REER (Current FEER = 100)	Fundamental Equilibrium Rate Against US Dollar	Nominal Appreciation Against US Dollar (Percentage)
US dollar	124.2	+6	118	n.a.	n.a.
Japanese yen	92.3	−2	94	¥ 205	15
Deutschemark	93.8	−2	96	DM 2.04	18
French franc	95.5	−1	97	FF 5.88	17
Pound sterling	120.5	+9	111	$ 1.58	3
Other industrial-country currencies	n.a.	n.a.	90[a]	n.a.	21[a]

Source Appendix table 10 in the original article, and calculations described in text.

[a]Residual.

n.a. Not applicable.

Current Misalignments

The real effective exchange rates of the five major currencies in the first quarter of 1983, the most recent period for which full data on REERs were available, are shown in the first column of table 11, using the estimated 1976–77 FEERs as a base. It can be seen, for example, that the dollar had appreciated in real effective terms by some 24 percent above the level that was previously calculated to have represented a fundamental equilibrium in the earlier period. The next column shows the real effective appreciation (+) or depreciation (−) that the previous section suggests would have been merited on the basis of changes in FEERs. For example, the oil price rise would have justified a real dollar appreciation of about 2 percent and the swing in direct investment a further 4 percent. Thus the estimate of dollar overvaluation is reduced somewhat, to 18 percent, as shown in column 3. That column also shows the pound to have been overvalued, while the yen, DM, and French franc were somewhat undervalued.

One can compare the misalignments estimated in this study with the results of Morgan Guaranty's calculations shown in table 3. On the March 1973 base that Morgan Guaranty has employed until recently, the pattern of overvaluation and undervaluation is similar to that found above and shown in table 11, though Morgan showed the pound as substantially more overvalued and the yen as somewhat more undervalued. The differences are more marked when comparison is made with Morgan Guaranty's new base of 1980–82. This reduces the dollar overvaluation and yen undervaluation, puts the DM in equilibrium, and transforms the pound into an *undervalued* currency. This occurs because the new base period includes the years 1980–81 when, by almost unanimous consent, the pound was grossly overvalued. The United Kingdom's current account surplus has already virtually disappeared despite Britain's having easily the highest unemployment rate of the five major countries and despite the strong case for Britain's aiming to run large current account surpluses during the present brief interlude of oil abundance: the explanation for this failure unquestionably lies in a continuing sterling overvaluation. There could scarcely be a more compelling example of the inadequacy of the conventional procedure of plucking rates from some base period and treating them as equilibria, and of the need instead to engage in the type of exercise presented above.

This is not to claim that those calculations are at all precise: on the contrary, the approach requires a belief that it is better to be roughly right than to be precise but irrelevant. The procedures employed are uncomfortably *ad hoc*.[13] Numerous heroic assumptions are needed. There is no way of calculating formal confidence intervals indicating the range beyond which FEERs are unlikely to lie: it is quite easy to change the base periods and other necessary inputs in ways that can alter the results by 5 percent to 10 percent. Indeed, it would be disingenuous to deny that some selection of the inputs in order to produce results that reflect one's presuppositions about FEERs is bound to take place when undertaking this type of exercise. The need to tell a consistent and credible story nevertheless limits the possibility of simply rationalizing one's preconceptions. Furthermore, undertaking such exercises provides the opportunity of engaging in serious

[13] An attempt was made to run simulations on two of the large multicountry econometric models to ask what constant real effective exchange rates would have been needed over the period 1974–77 to generate the desired pattern of current account surpluses and deficits in 1976–77 while achieving target levels of income in each country. It proved surprisingly difficult to change the variables that such models treat as exogenous in order to produce simulations that satisfied the desired constraints, and so in the end only the MERM was employed in the calculations.

debate out of which differences in view about FEERs may be narrowed. It remains open to anyone to provide a counterexample, but it is my impression that, without making major changes in the substantive assumptions, one would be unlikely to generate estimates that are more than 10 percent or so different from those presented in table 11.

The crucial point is that even a margin of error of 10 percent implies that exchange rates have been (and continue to be) misaligned. All three of the independently floating currencies have moved outside zones ±10 percent on either side on the implicit FEER line, two of them on both sides. Even the DM and French franc have come close to the edge of these rather wide zones. There is no indication that misalignments are subsiding over time as experience with floating accumulates; if anything, the reverse is true.

The final step is to convert the estimates of current FEERs in real effective terms back into a set of dollar exchange rates consistent with fundamental equilibrium. This was done using the MERM weights and treating the collective FEER of the smaller industrial countries as a residual. The results are shown in the fourth column of table 11. They suggest that a correct alignment in the first quarter of 1982 would have valued a dollar at about DM 2.04, ¥ 205, and FF 5.88, while the pound would have been worth some $1.58 and the smaller currencies would on average have needed to appreciate some 11 percent in real effective terms. There is little doubt that at present (in strong contrast to the situation in the late 1970s) the currencies of most of the smaller industrial countries are undervalued, although an average 10 percent undervaluation, larger than for the DM and yen, seems on the high side. However, as shown in the final column of table 11, the average implied nominal appreciation required of the smaller industrial countries would not be that much larger that those required of the DM and franc. Skeptics about this type of exercise may be interested to learn that the results finally presented here at best estimates of fundamental equilibrium rates do not match the author's preconceptions as well as did preliminary findings (which turned out to present severe consistency problems). The analysis has in fact led to some revision in my preconceptions.

Conclusions

This study has argued that the great failing of floating rates is the large misalignments they have allowed to emerge. Misalignments, defined as deviations of the real exchange rate from the level of competitiveness needed in the medium term, jeopardize central dimensions of economic performance: they can result in a roller coaster of boom followed by austerity, unnessary adjustment costs, unemployment in the tradable goods industries, deindustrialization, increased inflationary pressure, and protectionism. These misalignments may emerge either from market failure (inefficiencies in the foreign exchange market), or from policy failures (policy mixes chosen with no concern for their exchange rate consequences).

Misalignments can be identified, though admittedly not with any great precision. Misalignments are currently large, as they have been for much of the period of floating rates. It would therefore be highly desirable for governments, in consultation with the IMF, to set about seeking to identify the set of fundamental equilibrium exchange rates that would be appropriate from the standpoint of long-run competitive considerations. Ideally those FEERs might then become the central rates in a set of mutually consistent and publicly declared crawling target zones with soft margins, which countries would support by concerted intervention and, more important, by orienting their monetary policies in part to encouraging rates that stray outside the target zones to return toward them. Intervention policy would abandon its misconceived focus on "leaning against the wind" and concentrate instead on limiting misalignments.

REFERENCES

Ardito-Barletta, Nicolas, et al. 1983. *Economic Liberalization and Stabilization Policies in Argentina, Chile and Uruguay: The Monetary Approach to the Balance of Payments.* Washington: World Bank.

Armington, Paul S. 1981. "Closed, Multilateral Model of the International Adjustment Process, With No Sectoral Disaggregation." Paper presented to the International Workshop on Exchange Rates in Multicountry Econometric Models, University of Leuven, Belgium. Processed.

Armington, Paul S., and Catherine Wolford. 1983. "A Model-Based Analysis of Dollar Fluctuations." Paper presented to the Third International Symposium on Forecasting, June, Philadelphia. Processed.

Artus, Jacques R., and Anne Kenny McGuirk. 1981. "A Revised Version of the Multilateral Exchange Rate Model." IMF *Staff Papers.* June.

Atlantic Council of the United States. 1983. *The International Monetary System: Exchange Rates and International Indebtedness.* Policy study of the Working Group on International Monetary Affairs. Washington.

Balassa, Bela. 1964. "The Purchasing Power Parity Doctrine: A Reappraisal." *Journal of Political Economy,* vol. 72, no. 6 (December).

Begg, David K. H. 1982. *The Rational Expectations Revolution in Macroeconomics: Theories and Evidence.* Deddington, Oxon: Philip Allan.

Bergsten, C. Fred. 1982. "What To Do About the US-Japan Economic Problem." *Foreign Affairs,* vol. 60, no. 5 (Summer).

Bergsten, C. Fred, and John Williamson. Forthcoming 1983. "Exchange Rates and Trade Policy." In *Trade Policy in the 1980s,* ed. William R. Cline. Washington: Institute for International Economics.

Business Week. 1983. 27 June.

Clark, Peter B., and C. Haulk. 1972. "Flexible Exchange Rates and the Level of Trade: A Preliminary Analysis from Canadian Experience." Board of Governors of the Federal Reserve System, Washington. Processed.

Coes, Donald V. 1981. "The Crawling Peg and Exchange Rate Uncertainty." In *Exchange Rate Rules,* ed. John Williamson. London: Macmillan, and New York: St. Martin's Press.

Commonwealth Study Group. *Towards a New Bretton Woods: Challenges for the World Financial and Trading System.* London: Commonwealth Secretariat.

Cushman, David O. "The Effects of Real Exchange Rate Risk on International Trade." *Journal of International Economics.* Forthcoming.

Diaz-Alejandro, Carlos. 1976. *Foreign Trade Regimes and Economic Development: Colombia.* New York: NBER.

Dornbusch, Rudiger. 1976. "Expectations and Exchange Rate Dynamics." *Journal of Political Economy*, vol. 84, no. 6 (December).

______. "Flexible Exchange Rates and Interdependence." 1983. IMF *Staff Papers*. May.

Emminger, Otmar. 1982. *Exchange Rate Policy Reconsidered*. Group of Thirty Occasional Paper, no. 10. New York.

Ethier, Wilfred, and Arthur I. Bloomfield. 1975. *Managing the Managed Float*. Essays in International Finance, no. 112. Princeton, NJ: Princeton University.

Feldstein, Martin. 1983a. "Is the Dollar Overvalued?" Speech Before the Council on Foreign Relations, April, New York. Processed.

______. "The World Economy Today." 1983b. *The Economist*, vol. 287, no. 7293 (June 11).

Forsyth, P. J., and John A. Kay. 1980. "The Economic Implications of North Sea Oil." *Fiscal Studies*, no. 1.

Goldstein, Morris. 1980. *Have Flexible Exchange Rates Handicapped Macroeconomic Policy?* Princeton Special Papers in International Economics, no. 14. Princeton, NJ.

Haberler, Gottfried. Forthcoming 1983. "The International Monetary System in the World Recession." In *Contemporary Economic Problems, 1983–84*, ed. William J. Fellner. Washington: American Enterprise Institute.

Hause, J. D. 1966. "The Welfare Costs of Disequilibrium Exchange Rates." *Journal of Political Economy*, vol. 74, no. 4 (August)

Hooper, Peter, and Kohlhagen, S. W. 1978. "The Effects of Exchange Rate Uncertainty on the Prices and Volume of International Trade." *Journal of International Economics*, vol. 8, no. 4.

House of Commons Select Committee on the Treasury and Civil Service. 1983. *International Monetary Arrangements*. London: Her Majesty's Stationery Office.

IMF. 1970. *The Role of Exchange Rates in the Adjustment of International Payments: A Report by the Executive Directors*. Washington.

______. 1979. *Summary Proceedings of the Thirty-fourth Annual Meeting of the Board of Governors*. Washington.

______. 1983. *Annual Report on Exchange Arrangements and Exchange Restrictions*. Washington.

Johnson, Harry G. 1966. "The Welfare Costs of Exchange Rate Stabilization." *Journal of Political Economy*, vol. 74, no. 5.

______. 1969. "The Case for Flexible Exchange Rates, 1969." In H. G. Johnson and J. Nash, *UK and Floating Exchanges*. London: Institute for Economic Affairs.

Jurgensen Report. 1983. *Report of the Working Group on Exchange Market Intervention*. Washington: US Treasury.

Kenen, Peter B., and Clare Pack. 1983. *Exchange Rates, Domestic Prices, and the Adjustment Process*. Group of Thirty Occasional Paper, no. 1. New York.

Kenen, Peter B., and Dani Rodrik. 1983. "Measuring and Analyzing the Effects of Short-term Volatility in Real Exchange Rates." Princeton, NJ: Princeton University. Processed.

Keynes, John Maynard. 1936. *The General Theory of Employment, Interest and Money.* London: Macmillan.

Kohlhagen, Steven W. 1982. In C. Fred Bergsten et al. *From Rambouillet to Versailles: A Symposium.* Essays in International Finance, no. 149. Princeton, NJ: Princeton University.

Kuran, Timur. 1983. "Asymmetric Price Rigidity and Inflationary Bias." *American Economic Review,* vol. 73, no. 3 (June).

Lamfalussy, Alexandre. 1981. "A Plea for an International Commitment to Exchange Rate Stability." Paper presented at the 20th Anniversary Meeting of the Atlantic Institute for International Affairs, Brussels. Processed.

______. 1983. "Some General Policy Considerations for Tempering the Excesses of Floating." Paper presented to a *Financial Times* conference, February 16, London. Processed.

Magee, Stephen P. 1972. "The Welfare Effects of Restrictions on US Trade." *Brookings Papers on Economic Activity,* no. 3.

Makin, John. 1976. "Eurocurrencies and the Evolution of the International Monetary System." In *Eurocurrencies and the International Monetary System,* ed. Carl H. Stem, John H. Makin, and Dennis E. Logue. Washington: American Enterprise Institute.

Mayer, Helmut, and Hiroo Taguchi. 1983. *Official Intervention in the Exchange Markets: Stabilising or Destabilising?* Basle: Bank for International Settlements.

McKinnon, Ronald I. Forthcoming 1983. *A New International Standard for Monetary Stabilization.* Policy Analyses in International Economics. Washington: Institute for International Economics.

McGuirk, Anne Kenny. 1983. "Oil Price Changes and Real Exchange Rate Movements among Industrial Countries." Washington: IMF. Processed.

Mundell, Robert A. 1962. "The Appropriate Use of Monetary and Fiscal Policy under Fixed Exchange Rates." IMF *Staff Papers.* March.

Mussa, Michael. 1981. *The Role of Official Intervention.* Group of Thirty Occasional Paper, no. 6. New York.

Nurkse, Rgnar. 1944. *International Currency Experience.* Geneva: League of Nations.

Richardson, J. David. 1982. "The New Nexus Among Trade, Industrial, and Exchange Rate Policies." Paper prepared for presentation at a conference on the Future of the International Monetary System, cosponsored by New York University, the University of Southern California, and Tel-Aviv University, October 7–8, New York. Processed.

Roosa, Robert V. 1983. "How to Create Exchange Rate Target Zones." *Journal of Commerce,* 3 June.

Schulmeister, Stephan. 1983. "Exchange Rates, Prices and Interest Rates." New York: New York University. Processed.

Shafer, Jefffrey R., and Bonnie E. Loopesko,, 1983. "Floating Exchange Rates After Ten Years." *Brookings Papers on Economic Activity.* Washington: Brookings Institution.

Solomon, Anthony M. 1983. "Toward Realistic Cooperation." In G. de Menil and A. M. Solomon, *Economic Summitry.* New York: Council on Foreign Relations.

Taylor, Dean. 1982. "Official Intervention in the Foreign Exchange Market, or Bet Against the Central Bank." *Journal of Political Economy*, vol. 90, no. 2 (April).

Twenty-six Economists. 1982. *Promoting World Recovery: A Statement on Global Economc Strategy*. Washington: Institute for International Economics.

Williamson, John. 1982. "A Survey of the Literature on the Optimal Peg." *Journal of Development Economics*, vol. 11, (September)

______. 1983. *The Open Economy and the World Economy*. New York: Basic Books.

Part III
Financial Management of International Operations

INTRODUCTION

THE ENVIRONMENT OF FMIO

Financial management of international operations (FMIO) takes place in an environment characterized by volatile exchange rates, differences in national tax systems, and, on occasion, barriers to capital flows and restrictions on access to money and capital markets.

Foreign exchange considerations play an especially important role. Although exchange and money markets display a high degree of efficiency, barriers and restrictions do result in distortions. Furthermore, of the key equilibrium concepts discussed in Part II, only interest rate parity (IRP) and purchasing power parity (PPP) in the strict sense of goods market arbitrage are defined in terms of known, current values of variables. The others, forward parity (FP), the international Fisher effect (IFE), and PPP in terms of expectations are *ex ante* relationships; as a result, even if the markets are efficient, they need not hold among realized outcomes. In addition, because of complex interactions between markets for financial assets and real goods and because of imperfections in real goods markets, including oligopolistic pricing and production processes that are fixed in the short run, exchange rates often diverge from purchasing power parity. Finally, even if all equilibrium relationships hold, firms are not automatically protected against exchange rate effects but must incorporate market anticipations in their pricing and production decisions.

Tax factors also play an important role, since they often dictate the form if not the substance of a firm's financial transactions. They give rise to differences in the costs of internal transfers of cash and/or profits via different channels, and hence motivate a variety of interaffiliate transactions that would be irrelevant in a single-country setting. Exchange and credit restrictions play a similar role, again calling for a variety of internal ploys to take advantage of them or at a minimum reduce their costs to the firm.

RELEVANT DECISIONS IN FMIO

Given the complexity of the international environment, it is unlikely that operating managers will have a full awareness and understanding of many financial factors critical to appropriate operating decisions. Thus the international financial manager has the dual role of providing relevant information to operating managers and of making financial decisions.

The range of relevant management decision depends on the time frame. In the long run, all decisions regarding the firm's real operations and financial structure are open. However, not all decisions are relevant since some, such as day-to-day money management, are reversible in a very short period of time and, as a result, need not be locked-in over a longer period. In the medium run, some variables which are controls in the long run are parameters. For example, basic market positioning and plant locations are given and, as a result, decisions regarding production and marketing mixes are constrained. In the short run, most variables are given and the range of relevant decisions is quite narrow.

Figure 1.
Real and Financial Decisions in the Long, Medium, and Short Run

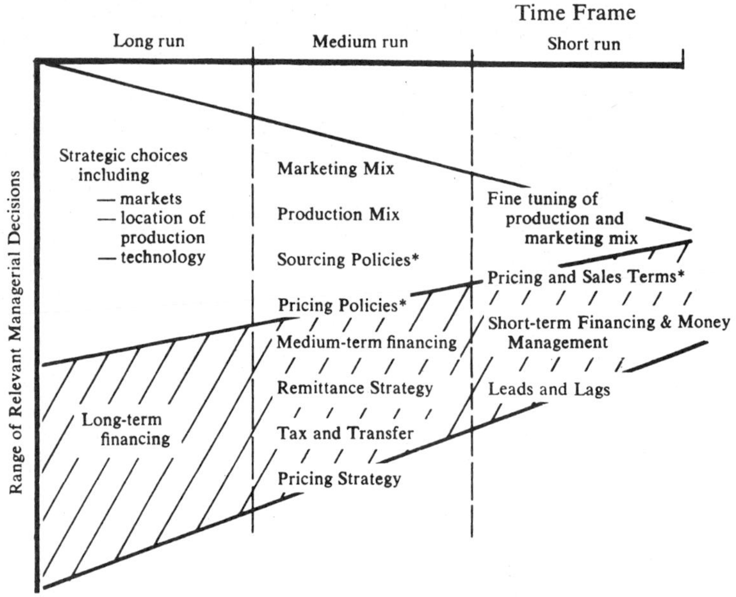

Unshaded area = real decisions
Shaded area = financial decisions

The rate at which the range narrows over time differs for real and financial decisions. The latter typically are reversible over a much shorter time span. Therefore, a relatively large proportion of financial decisions remain open in the short run. This narrowing down of relevant decisions is illustrated in Figure 1. In the short run, there are few degrees of freedom for real decisions but quite a few in terms of financial decisions. Even these, however, are constrained by longer term decisions. In the medium run, a substantially wider array of both financial and real decisions are open to the firm.

Short-run operating decisions that require financial inputs, and hence are part of FMIO, include pricing and fine-tuning of production and marketing plans. These decisions depend on (1) current and predicted deviations from purchasing power parity, which change the relative prices of the firm's inputs and products, and (2) anticipated changes in absolute exchange rates, since many operating decisions involve monetary contracts that will give rise to future foreign currency cash flows.

These decisions, together with the longer run decisions already made, will determine the firm's expected cash flow as well as its exposure to exchange rate fluctuations.

Financing decisions within FMIO depend on three sets of factors:

1. Financial market distortions, i.e., opportunities for arbitrage or speculation due to violations of interest rate parity, forward parity, and the international Fisher effect.
2. The firm's exposure to shifts in nominal and real exchange rates.
3. Tax factors.

To resolve these questions simultaneously is a difficult theoretical problem and one that is nearly impossible to solve in practice. Fortunately, FMIO often can be broken down into subparts in ways that do not lead to suboptimal decisions.

Most of the papers in Part III deal with subsets of the financial management of international operations, some of which are extremely narrow and others quite broad. Often they do not state clearly the linkage of the subproblem discussed with other parts of FMIO. Nevertheless, taken as a whole they provide quite a complete picture of the critical issues of FMIO. In order to integrate the various parts, brief overviews of three key issues are presented here before the individual papers are introduced. The issues are:

1. Objectives of the financial management of international operations.
2. Contractual and noncontractual aspects of exchange exposures.
3. Conditions for separating subproblems of FMIO.

OBJECTIVES OF FMIO

A major issue in FMIO is the choice of objective, in terms of both the relevant target variable and the treatment of risk. Mainstream corporate finance theory holds that firms should maximize share price or, more operationally, maximize the net present value of expected future cash flows discounted at a rate that reflects the systematic risk of these flows without regard to diversifiable risk. Management practice, in contrast, often appears to focus on current reported earnings, or even on a subset of total earnings identified explicitly as gains or losses from foreign exchange, and seeks to reduce the variance of earnings resulting from exchange fluctuations regardless of whether or not the fluctuations are diversifiable across firms.

These differences involve two separate questions: (1) Which measure of performance is relevant and (2) what trade-off should be made between the risk and expected level of this variable. Possible performance measures include the net present value of cash flows, total earnings, or the component of earnings identified as gains or losses on foreign exchange.

Risk-return trade-offs include (1) the maximization of expected value without regard to risk; (2) the minimization of risk without regard to expected values; (3) the trade-off between expected return and total risk (σ); and (4) the trade-off between expected return and systematic risk (β).

Differences between the cash flow and earnings perspectives are discussed in the section on economic and accounting aspects of exchange exposure, which follows. Differences between the alternative risk-return views are discussed below.

The first approach, maximizing expected value regardless of risk, implies risk neutrality on the part of the firm. Although some firms might contend that this is how they approach foreign exchange questions, it is unlikely that any follow it completely, since it would imply taking extremely large speculative positions in response to small return differentials. The second approach, that of avoiding risk at all cost, is even more unrealistic. Even firms that generally hedge exchange exposures would not do so if they felt costs were extreme. This leads to the more realistic, but less easily defined, views that involve some trade-off between return (cost) and risk. The two extremes identified are return versus total risk (σ) using some measure of corporate or managerial risk aversion, and return versus systematic risk (β) using a capital market measure of risk aversion.

The σ view holds that the overall risk-return profile of the firm is relevant to its managers, employees, lenders, and perhaps even its shareholders. The β view holds that since the firm's risky prospects are valued directly in capital markets, it makes no difference to the valuation of either the total market portfolio or the individual firm whether exchange rate risks (or commodity price risks, for that matter) are passed through to the capital market as part of the risk of the firm's shares or "laid off" and transferred directly to the market through forward exchange or foreign currency debt contracts.

The firm concerned with total risk (hereafter called the σ firm) will "lay off" foreign exchange risks as long as the cost in terms of expected cash flows or earnings is not "too great." It also, of course, will seek to exploit distortions (departures from IRP, FP, and IFE), but only to a limited extent because of the risks incurred.

For the firm concerned only with the capital market risk-return trade-off (hereafter called the β firm), the *only* relevant financial decisions in the short run and medium run are those that seek to exploit market distortions, since any "properly priced" alternatives will already reflect their systematic risk and hence will only move the firm along the security market line with no impact on the firm's value.

Most theoretical models of exposure management, and virtually all of management practice, implicitly or explicitly assume that the firm is concerned with total risk. This places exposure management in an uncomfortable grey area with respect to current capital market theory, but no more so than insurance or banking, which also do not fit comfortably with the "only β matters" view. The conflict, however, is more apparent than real, since the evidence presented in Part II on exchange market efficiency and the pricing of foreign exchange risk suggests that although laying off foreign exchange positions at "proper prices" should not add to the value of the firm, it also should not reduce it significantly.

Often compounding the apparent divergence between the two approaches are implicit assumptions regarding the degree of market efficiency. Writers working from the perspective of capital market theory typically assume market efficiency, often in extremely strong forms, while managerial writers often emphasize departures from efficiency. As a result, one must recognize which assumptions underlie the advice given. Selective hedging, for example, which is practiced by many firms, is motivated by perceived market distortions in the form of opportunities for excess returns through arbitrage or speculation rather than by a σ as opposed to a β view of the world.

If a σ view is adopted, insurance is an appropriate analogy to foreign exchange risk management. Firms typically self-insure a large proportion of the risks that average out within the firm and lay off the risks that are sufficiently large to affect net worth materially. Similar procedures should be applicable in the case of foreign exchange, although their use is clouded by the fact that foreign exchange management, rightly or wrongly, includes a significant amount of "bargain seeking" as well as risk management.

A major implication of accepting a σ view, often ignored in the literature, is that σ must be defined as the variability of the firm's total cash flows, not as the variability of some subset of them. This is in contrast to the β perspective, where individual risky prospects are valued directly on a capital market basis and hence independently of other components in a firm's portfolio. Thus great care must be taken in using mean-variance approaches for subsets of the FMIO problem. "Optimal" borrowing choices made independently of the distribution of operating cash flows conditional on exchange rates, for example, are likely to be suboptimal.

ECONOMIC VERSUS ACCOUNTING ASPECTS OF EXCHANGE EXPOSURE

Most managerial treatments of exchange exposure and its implications for the financial management of ongoing operations are based on accounting treatment of exchange effects. As a result, classes of exposure are identified in terms of where and when they affect reported earnings. Translation exposures are those which result from the conversion from one currency to another of balance sheets at the close of an accounting period. Transaction exposures, in contrast, are the potential for gains and losses on transactions that are closed out within an accounting period at home currency values different from those that they were entered into. Finally, operating exposures are the impacts on operating earnings not directly attributable to exchange rate effects that occur because of the impact of exchange rate shifts and related relative prices on the earnings potential of the firm's assets in place.

From an economic perspective, in contrast, exposures can be classified in terms of their nature or origin. Contractual exposures are exposures to gains and losses resulting from the impact of exchange rate changes on assets and liabilities whose nominal values are fixed by contract. Noncontractual exposures, in contrast, reflect the impact of relative price changes associated with real movements in exchange rates on the profit margins associated with sales for which no binding contractual commitments have yet been made.

Much of the discussion of foreign exchange exposure treats accounting and economic exposures as they were mutually exclusive categories. Actually, they are two different dimensions along which exposures may be characterized as illustrated in Figure 2. All economic exposures will have accounting counterparts at some point in time, and most accounting exposures will have economic counterparts, although not necessarily of the same magnitude. A few, such as the translation exposure of fixed assets, are fictitious from an economic perspective.

FIGURE 2

Economic Versus Accounting Exposures

Accounting Exposures	Contractual	Noncontractual	Fictitious
Transaction	Accounts rec., payable, and debt closed out during period		
Translation	Accounts rec., payable, and debt on books at end of period		Fixed assets
Operating	Booked orders & other off-balance sheet contracts	Profits from future sales for which no contractual commitments exist	
			Economic Exposures

As noted above, the effects of exchange rate changes on the firm can be viewed in terms of impacts on (1) the net present value of cash flows, (2) total earnings, and (3) those earnings effects identified as gains or losses on foreign exchange.

The net present value of cash flows captures the full range of exchange rate effects and is most in keeping with the objective of shareholder wealth maximization if investors are assumed to be sophisticated and rational. The total earnings effect is narrower since it focuses on short run impacts, ignoring medium or longer term effects on the firm of exchange rate changes. Finally, the fraction of the earnings effect identified explicitly as a gain or loss on foreign currency translation is the narrowest of all, since it excludes the impact of exchange rates on operating profits and captures only changes in the value of balance sheet items deemed to be exposed.

Current accounting rules for recognizing exchange rate impacts, outlined in Statement No. 52 of the Financial Accounting Standards Board (FASB 52), appear to be as controversial as the previous FASB 8 rule. They call for translation at current rates of all balance sheet items. However, when the dollar is the functional currency, they are similar to FASB 8 and include only monetary items that are recorded on corporate books and, therefore, provide a partial and potentially misleading measure of exchange rate effects.

From a present value perspective, *any* future cash flow whose dollar value will be altered by exchange rate changes is exposed. Foreign monetary items, by definition, are exposed since their values will fluctuate directly with exchange rate movements. In contrast, operating flows that are not contractually denominated are exposed only to

FIGURE 3

Types of Cash Flows

Cash Flow to Occur Months in Future	1–3	3–6	6–12	13–24	25–36	37–60	61–120
Contractual Monetary Items							
Accounts receivable[a]	x						
Accounts payable[a]	x						
Accepted orders for future delivery		x	→				
Labor contracts	x	→	→	→			
Sourcing contracts	x	→	→	→	→		
Securities and debt[a]	x	→	→	→	→	→	→
Depreciation tax shields	x	→	→	→	→	→	→
Implicit Monetary Items							
Prices announced or fixed by standard procedures	x	→					
Projected labor settlements					x	→	
Real Items[b]							
Revenue items							
Expense items				x	→	→	→

[a]Items covered by FASB 8 or 52 definitions of exposure.

[b]Real items are all cash flows not "locked-in" in money terms.

changes in exchange rates that cause relative prices to change, that is, to deviations from purchasing power parity.

In order to understand a firm's overall economic exposure, it is useful to view the firm as a portfolio of monetary (contractual) and real (noncontractual) cash flows. Monetary flows may be either contractual or implicitly contractual, while real cash flows may be linked to irreversible real decisions or to decisions that can be altered. Both monetary and real cash flows are illustrated in Figure 3.

Monetary items represent a substantial portion of cash flows that will occur in the near future and a much smaller proportion of total cash flows in later years when only long-term debt less depreciation tax shields remain. Non-contractual items pick up where monetary items taper off, but they also eventually taper off as the firm's production and marketing decisions become open to change. This time profile is illustrated in Figure 4.

The exposure of a firm to any particular currency can be expressed in terms of the percent responsiveness (β) of its net present value with respect to percent changes in that currency. If the firm's entire net present value were comprised of monetary items in the currency in question, its β with respect to that currency would be one. The responsiveness of real items is more difficult to determine. In the case of an exporter selling in a foreign market where local firms are dominant, total foreign sales revenues will be exposed. Thus, the responsiveness of operating profits to movements in real exchange rates will be one. To the extent that the effect of exchange rate changes is ameliorated by pricing or operating flexibility, the β will be reduced.

Since a firm is likely to have exposure in several different currencies, its total exchange risk will depend on the proportion exposed in each currency and the covariances of the various currencies. As a result, an attempt to simply add exposure across currencies is likely to be misleading. Further, the firm is likely to have exposures to both nominal and real exchange rate movements, and these may be less than perfectly correlated.

Figure 4.
Time Profile of Exposed Cash Flows

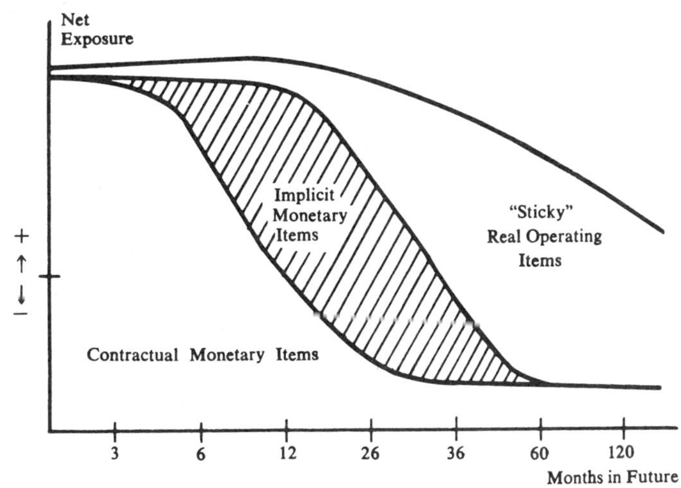

CONDITIONS FOR SEPARATING COMPONENTS OF FMIO

A major practical question in FMIO is the extent to which various issues can be treated separately yet correctly. Pricing and invoicing strategies, for example, do change the firm's contractual and noncontractual exposures; decisions to exploit perceived financial market distortions have exposure as well as tax implications; decisions to shift profits via interaffiliate transactions may constrain financing choices, and so on. This interdependency is exacerbated by the fact that if the firm is concerned with its total risk (σ), risk must be considered at the level of the complete corporate portfolio. Yet if each problem must be approached from a total system perspective, the formal solution often becomes extremely complex. Further, given that different issues are dealt with by different units or levels of units within the organization, simultaneous solutions will be impossible in practice.

In many cases, however, careful analysis will show that many subproblems are, in fact, independent. For example, in the case of currencies for which the firm has full access to forward markets and money markets in which IRPT and FP hold, it can do its pricing and invoicing with regard only to *expected* revenues and ignore the resulting contractual exposures since they can be treated separately. Similarly, if the same conditions hold, the firm can exploit distortions in segmented national markets without worrying about the exposure impact. Finally, if optimal interaffiliate tax structuring can be done regardless of external financing transactions, tax management can be separated from the other issues. Often, however, taxes and exposure management are so intertwined that the two must be considered simultaneously.

OUTLINE OF PART III

The papers in Part III deal with subsets of the overall FMIO problem: foreign exchange risk management, accounting for foreign exchange fluctuations and measuring performance, and taxation and financial logistics.

Foreign Exchange Risk Management

The section on foreign exchange management begins with a discussion of the relevance of foreign exchange exposure management, i.e., explicit operating and financial decisions aimed at reducing the variance of the firm's earnings or cash flows resulting from exchange rate fluctuations. Dufey and Srinivasulu (Article 17) outline the various arguments for and against the relevance of foreign exchange risk management at the level of the corporation. They acknowledge that from the perspective of investors, there is no reason for the firm to engage in hedging unless capital markets are incomplete, and thus limit investors' ability to modify their own currency positions, or unless investors, because they lack information about the firm's exposure, are not in a position to properly offset these exposures. However, they stress that there may be a number of organizational reasons to hedge. Managers, concerned about their jobs, promotions, and rewards, may behave more in line with shareholders' wishes if they can be insulated from large exchange rate fluctuations over which they have no control. Creditors, recognizing that exchange risk affects the risk of their claims, may want to limit a firm's exposure to exchange risk, and regulators, who often provide contingent backing to a firm or bank's operations, have a similar interest. Finally, shareholders will want the firm to hedge if it leads managers to behave more in line with their interests or if it makes lenders more willing to extend credit or suppliers or customers more willing to make long-term commitments to the firm. In all cases, reducing the variability of cash flows due to foreign exchange exposures can be seen as increasing the expected after-tax cash flows of the firm.

Adler and Dumas (Article 18) discuss the definition and measurement of foreign exchange exposure. They stress the distinction between currency risk—the uncertainty regarding the future purchasing power of a currency—and exposure—what a firm has at risk to such fluctuations. They then show that exposure should be thought of as a regression coefficient, that is the responsiveness of a firm's net worth or market value to exchange rate shifts. This view, in turn, lends itself to a clear definition of the appropriate hedge. Shapiro and Cornell (Article 19) describe the financial and operating sources of foreign exchange exposures and review the various types of measures that can be taken to offset these exposures. Their approach differs from most of the exposure management literature in stressing the importance of operating as well as financial steps that can be taken.

Giddy (Article 20) and Agmon and Eldor (Article 21) discuss a recent innovation, the foreign exchange option, and its relevance in foreign exchange risk management.

Accounting for Exchange Fluctuations and Measuring Performance

Ijiri (Article 22) provides an extensive historical and theoretical review of foreign currency accounting. He traces the four different sets of standards that have been in use over the last twenty years in the United States and discusses some of the key concerns with each. Most importantly, he shows how the various accounting perspectives relate to the key financial and purchasing power parity relationships. He also addresses the interaction of foreign exchange accounting with inflation accounting in terms of the restate/translate versus translate/restate controversy and the controversy over general price level adjusted accounting versus replacement cost accounting. He concludes by stating that the current approach, outlined in Financial Accounting Standards Board 52, opens a new avenue for price level adjustment in the sense that it is complete only when combined with price level adjusted accounting. Carsberg (Article 23) focuses more narrowly on FASB 52 and illustrates the various assumptions that lie behind it with numerical examples. He concurs with Ijiri's conclusion that the principal issue is the need to accompany the current approach with a realistic price level adjusted accounting in the various underlying currencies.

The next group of articles deal with the problem of measuring performance in a multinational firm. Lessard and Lorange (Article 24) focus narrowly on the currency component and suggest the creation of an "internal forward market" to allow an organizational separation of operating and financial aspects of FMIO. The purpose of their approach is to insulate operating managers from profit variances resulting from exchange exposures over which they have no effective control. Clearly, this will be the case for contractual items such as accounts receivable and payable, and it may be the case for certain noncontractual items associated with future operations that cannot be changed over the relevant planning horizon in response to shifts in the exchange rate.

Stewart (Article 25) provides an ambitious proposal for measuring the performance of foreign units, calling for the computation of income within each unit on a price level adjusted basis and then a conversion of this income into the parent currency at a purchasing power parity exchange rate. This approach removes much of the noise in translated income from operations in currencies with highly volatile inflation and real exchange rates, but only partially solves the problem of subsidiaries that should modify their pricing, output, or sourcing decisions in response to real exchange rate risks. Nevertheless, it provides an interesting glimpse of the types of performance measurement systems that are likely to evolve and provides concrete illustrations of the interaction between the accounting treatment of inflation and foreign exchange rate movements.

Taxation and Financial Logistics

Lessard (Article 26) analyzes the multinational firm as a financial system. He shows that the ability of the firm to choose the channels through which internal financial transfers are made and the timing of transactions within this controlled system may allow it to arbitrage across financial markets, tax systems, and regulatory systems. Thus, the multinational firm may be able to reap greater after-tax flows from a given set of operations than a group of single-country firms engaged in the same set of activities. Rutenberg (Article 28) develops a detailed total system model that shows how a firm should set up its internal transactions in order to cope with tax differences as well as barriers to financial transactions. While few firms have successfully implemented models of this nature, it illustrates very clearly the goals as well as mechanisms of FMIO.

Barrett (Article 27) describes some of the practical limitations to internal transactions designed to arbitrage tax and regulatory systems. Drawing on a composite of electronics firms operating in Europe, he provides a comic description of the internal and external havoc created by transfer pricing that seeks to minimize taxes and circumvent price controls.

Horst (Article 29) discusses U.S. tax treatment of domestically domiciled multinational firms and some of its implications for interaffiliate transaction. While his model is limited to a single period and to a firm with a single foreign subsidiary, it illustrates some of the intricacies of the interaction between a firm's home and foreign currency tax environments. Nobes (Article 30) discusses European systems for taxation of corporate income. Most European countries have made considerably more progress than the United States towards the integration of personal and corporate taxation, but this integration within countries often creates complications in cross-border taxation. Depending upon the degree of freedom that the firm has in the structure of its interaffiliate transactions, these complications can lead to further opportunities for tax arbitrage or may result in double taxation of some of its activities.

Foreign Exchange Risk Management

17

The Case for Corporate Management of Foreign Exchange Risk*

Gunter Dufey and S. L. Srinivasulu

The objective of this paper is to present the case for corporate management of foreign exchange risk. The arguments that oppose hedging at the level of the firm can be summed up as follows:

Foreign exchange risk does not exist; even if it exists, it need not be hedged; even if it is to be hedged, corporations need not hedge it.

In support of the above reasoning, one or more of the following arguments are advanced.

1. The Purchasing Power Parity (PPP) theorem implies compensating changes in price levels and exchange rates; hence, there is no exchange risk.
2. The Capital Asset pricing Model (CAPM) purportedly suggests that it makes no difference whether exchange risk is managed separately or passed along to the capital market; hence, even if exchange risk exists, it need not be hedged.
3. The Modigliani-Miller (MM) theorem implies that whatever the firm can do, investors can do; hence, even if exchange risk needs to be hedged, it need not be hedged by the firm.
4. The concept of self-insurance implies that—since the effects of exchange rate changes average out over time—no effort need be made to manage exchange risk. Similarly, if foreign exchange markets are efficient, forward contracts are appropriately priced and, as a consequence, nothing is gained by hedging.
5. Exchange-related gains and losses may be useful for hedging risks associated with the consumption bundle: thus, exchange-related fluctuations are desirable for investors, and corporations should not hedge them.
6. As both future forward rates and future spot rates are uncertain, hedging is of dubious value and does not reduce uncertainly.

While some of these themes (summarized in Exhibit 1) have been reviewed previously [17, pp. 8–10; 11, pp. 82–83; 9, pp. 2–4], they will be discussed in a logical sequence, and a case will be made for corporate management of foreign exchange risk.

*This article is reprinted, with permission, from *Financial Management* 12, No. 4, pp 54–62, 1984.

1. THE PURCHASING POWER PARITY (PPP) THEOREM AND SIMILAR PARITY CONDITIONS

There is a burgeoning volume of literature on Purchasing Power Parity and this is not the place to review this material (for a review refer to [18]). Instead, discussion shall be limited to the relationship between PPP and corporate management of foreign exchange risk.

According to PPP, exchange rate changes offset price level changes; hence, some argue, there is no exposure to exchange risk. For example, if the annual rate of inflation in France is 10 percent higher than that in the United States, the French franc will depreciate vis-à-vis the U.S. dollar by a corresponding percentage; as a result, there is no relative price risk. If one unit of American wheat exchanged for two units of French wine at the beginning of the year, that same exchange ratio will hold at the end of the year. The mere fact that the franc has depreciated need not cause concern. The effect on the American exporter of wheat or the French exporter of wine is nonexistent because the change in nominal prices in the respective national currencies has been compensated for by the exchange rate change.

Unfortunately, there are many "ifs" and "buts" that this highly simplified explanation of PPP does not take into account. First, all empirical tests have confirmed that the adjustment between changes in prices and exchange rates is not instantaneous and that there are lags in this relationship: the longer the time horizon, the greater the empirical validity of PPP. For shorter time periods, however, there are substantial deviations. So if a firm's planning horizon is shorter than that required for PPP to hold, the firm is exposed to exchange risk.

Second, even assuming that PPP holds in the aggregate with respect to the price level indexes (the weighted average prices) of two countries, it need not (and usually does not) hold for every commodity. Thus, the "law of one price" (LOP) does not hold. If the increases in the price levels of wheat in the U.S. and wine in France do not correspond to the increases in the inflation levels in their respective countries, there will be a relative price risk. Even if PPP and LOP hold, prices of a firm's *specific* inputs and outputs might change *relative* to each other, and thus expose the firm to risk, which—if caused by unexpected exchange rate changes—must be viewed as exchange risk. A clarifying analysis that separates inflation and exchange risk can be found in Cornell [4] and Shapiro [22].

The fact that there are deviations from PPP—at least for some periods—and that there are relative price risks for at least some goods implies the presence of exchange risk. Rather than present the numerical extimates of the extent of deviations from various empirical studies, we will quote below the conclusions of one major work in this field:

> *Students exposed to the pure theory of international trade have been seduced by visions of an imaginary world . . . . In reality, the law of one price is flagrantly and systematically violated by empirical data . . . . Exchange rate changes substantially alter the relative . . . prices of most . . . domestic and foreign manufactured goods . . . . Moreover, these relative price effects seem to persist for at least several years and cannot be shrugged off as transitory.* [10, *p.* 942]

To be sure, other studies draw somewhat different conclusions. But they all agree about one fact: there *are* deviations; they differ only in degree.

EXHIBIT 1

Arguments Against and for Corporate Management of Foreign Exchange Risk: Summary

Against	For
1. *Purchasing Power Parity Theorem:* PPP implies offsetting changes in price levels and exchange rates; hence, there is no exposure to exchange risk.	1. Deviations from PPP have been well documented; the shorter the time horizon, the greater the deviations. Even if PPP holds with respect to an index of tradeable goods, a particular firm may still be exposed to exchange risk, since the relative price of its inputs and outputs may change.
2. *Capital Asset Pricing Model (CAPM):* According to CAPM, what matters is only systematic risk; it does not matter whether exchange risk is managed separately in foreign exchange markets, or passed along to the capital market.	2. When default risk is important, hedging can reduce default risk and add to the debt capacity of the firm.
3. *Modigliani-Miller (MM) Theorem:* According to MM, what the firm does, an investor can do: hence, there is no need for corporate management of exchange risk.	3. There are several obstacles to individuals in coping better with exchange risk. A firm is in a position to obtain a low-cost hedge; also information on the firm's exposure is not symmetrically distributed between shareholders and managers.
4. *The Concept of Self-Insurance:* The forward market is a fair bet and does not provide bargains. The foreign exchange gains and losses average out over a period. *The Efficient Market Hypothesis:* Since the foreign exchange markets are efficient, forward contracts are priced properly and there are no excess returns from hedging.	4. This concept implies maximizing expected value without regard to variance, and thus assumes risk neutrality. However, economic agents are usually risk-averse. The objective of hedging is not to earn excess of returns, but to achieve a desired pattern of risk and return.
5. *Hedging of Consumption Bundle:* A firm's exchange-related gains and losses may be useful to hedge the consumption bundles of its shareholders.	5. As the consumption bundle is investor-specific, its management is better left to the shareholder. Firms should hedge exchange risk and the shareholder should hedge consumption bundle risk.
6. *The Uncertainty of Forward Rates and Spot Rates:* Since future forward rates are as uncertain as future spot rates, hedging is of dubious value.	6. Hedging makes available exact information regarding anticipated cash flows; such information can be useful for activities for which the planning and action horizon is the same as the maturity of the forward contract.

Implications for Corporate Policy

Can a corporation rely on the broad macroeconomic relationship of PPP and abdicate its responsibility to manage exposure? The experience of Rolls-Royce in 1979 confirms otherwise. As shown below, this firm relied on PPP in its planning and pricing decisions, and as a result suffered huge losses.

Rolls-Royce, the British jet-engine producer, relies on international markets for the sale of its products. In 1979, the value of its direct exports from the United Kingdom was on the order of £348 million, which constituted 41 percent of its total sales of £848 million. The proportion of its exports in earlier years had been about the same. In 1979, the firm had a loss of £58 million. Why? As its annual report poignantly records:

> *. . . the most important [influence] was the effect of the continued weakness of the U.S. dollar against sterling. The large civil engines which Rolls-Royce produces are supplied to American air frames. Because of U.S. dominance in civil aviation, both as producer and customer, these engines are usually priced in U.S. dollars and escalated according to American indices . . . . Inflation rates have risen at a higher pace than was expected and more sharply in the United Kingdom than in the U.S.A. Far from reflecting the differential rates of inflation the pound appreciated against the U.S. dollar. [20, p. 4]*

PPP would predict that, since the inflation rate in Britain was higher than that in the United States, sterling should depreciate. Instead, sterling appreciated, causing Rolls losses on both its dollar-denominated receivables and its expected sales revenues. But even if sterling had depreciated as predicted by PPP, there is no guarantee that the extent of depreciation would have been adequate to offset exactly the rate of inflation *relevant* for Rolls. The cost of producing jet engines in the United Kingdom might have risen at a rate different from that of British inflation in general.

Rather than relying on PPP, a firm should plan to cope with *deviations* from PPP. There are several actions a firm can take to cushion the impact of such deviations. To protect operating cashflow over the short term, forward sales of dollars or dollar debt can be used. As a long-term measure, appropriate operational strategies may be advisable [23]. Thus, Rolls-Royce may consider putting part of its operating expenses on a U.S. dollar basis through extensive sourcing of components or by moving production partially to the United States. The fine tuning of these policies requires further analysis, but our objective here is simply to show that belief in PPP is not an excuse for not managing foreign exchange risk.

2. THE CAPITAL ASSET PRICING MODEL (CAPM)

The implications of CAPM for corporate hedging decisions have been given extensive treatment by Logue and Oldfield [13] and Lessard [12, pp. 287–288]. According to CAPM, the essential factor that matters is the systematic risk. If exchange risk is unsystematic, it can be diversified away by the investors in the process of constructing their portfolios. On the other hand, if exchange risk is systematic and if forward exchange contracts are priced according to CAPM, all that a firm does by entering into these contracts is to move along the Security Market Line; that is, there is no addition to the value of the firm. As one author put it succinctly, "In the absence of imperfections like transactions costs and default risks, the value of a forward contract would be zero at the instant at which it was initiated" [1, p. 90].

However, among other objectives, the concern of corporate management about total variability is motivated by the need to avoid the cost of financial distress. Thus, greater variability of net cashflow implies a higher probability of bankruptcy and this, in turn, affects the firm's cost of funds and its ability to raise them. To quote some of the pertinent views from the literature:

. . . costs of capital in the short run can be influenced by the perceived riskiness of claims on multinationals and that perceived riskiness, relative *to other multinationals, could be altered in the short run by heavy exposure in foreign currencies. [14, p. 521]*

. . . creditors may be concerned with total variability of cash flows where default is possible. The realized yet unanticipated capital gains and losses that a firm experiences due to random currency fluctuations may influence valuation through the effect on debt capacity. Where total variability is important, hedging in the foreign exchange markets may add to the firm's debt capacity. [13, p. 21]

A third author argues that avoiding default seems to be the most justifiable of all the possible goals that a treasurer could have for hedging:

On the dimension of default risk, stockholders' and management's interests largely coincide. Stockholders are averse to bankruptcy risk on the grounds that the associated costs can permanently deplete their equity. When the market perceives a rise in default risk, share prices drop. Managers prefer to reduce the probability of default or of cash inadequacy so as to avoid abdicating control in favor of creditors. Jobs may then also be in jeopardy. Large exchange losses can affect the adequacy of reference currency cash flows. Consequently, bankruptcy-risk reduction can partly be achieved by a policy of hedging. [1, p. 91]

In summary, the desire to avoid default risk justifies minimizing variations in cash flows through hedging.

3. THE MODIGLIANI-MILLER (MM) THEOREM

By extending the original argument of the MM theorem to the international arena, it has been contended that corporate foreign exchange management is superfluous; what the firm does, an investor can do. In other words, every investor is a potential foreign exchange hedger.

In the domestic version of the MM theorem, a shareholder can obtain "homemade leverage" by borrowing for his own account: thus, the corporate borrowing decision is irrelevant. In the extended international version, it is argued that a shareholder can obtain "homemade hedging" by hedging for his own account: again, the corporate hedging decision is irrelevant. Indeed, Feger and Jacquillat [7] provide a formal proof of the MM theorem as applied to the forward currency positions of firms.

However, if for any reason hedging by investors is not as efficient as corporate hedging, then it will be in the interest of the shareholders to let the firm manage the exchange risk. Below, several obstacles to investor hedging will be examined.

a. Entry Barriers

There are two types of entry barriers: (1) size barriers and (2) structural barriers. Size barriers are caused by the fact that certain markets impose minimum size requirements for transactions of goods and services, whereas structural barriers are the result of the way different economic entities can structure their activities. These are described in turn below.

Size Barriers

The principal hedging instruments are forward markets, currency option markets. Eurocurency markets, and foreign money markets. The bank-based forward-, option-, and the Eurocurrency markets are wholesale in nature and deal in minimum amounts that tend to be too large for individual investors. Further, banks tend to limit access to forward and currency option markets to customers engaged in foreign trade or those who have foreign subsidiaries.

It is true that markets for currency futures, such as the IMM in Chicago, offer an alternative to the forward market that is readily accessible to individual investors. However, both the size of the contract and the delivery date are standardized in futures markets. Further, prices can fluctuate without limit in the forward market, but daily limits are imposed on exchanges in the futures market. Thus, the futures market is less flexible. In addition, a security deposit is required to operate in the futures market. In the forward market, banks may insist on compensating balances. But while such balances are typically maintained by firms in the course of their ongoing business activities, they represent an additional cost for the individual. It is true that markets for risk instruments are becoming better developed and more accessible. Since early 1983, for example, currency option contracts in major currencies have been traded at the Philadelphia exchange. However. some of the difficulties that apply to currency futures pertain also to option contracts—in addition to the problems posed by the "thinness" and uncertainties that characterize any immature market.

Hedging can be accomplished either by forward contracts or by foreign currency borrowing and lending. The former is known as a forward market hedge and the latter as a money market hedge. Hence, obstacles to individuals in foreign money markets are also, in essence, obstacles to investor hedging. In many foreign money markets, nonresidents are denied access to local borrowing facilities, or they may face discriminatory taxes. A local subsidiary of a multinational corporation, being a resident, may not face the same restrictions, or the restrictions it does face may be less severe. Thus, the firm is in a better position to obtain a low-cost hedge.

Structural Barriers

Some structural barriers have already been commented on above in connection with the discussion of size barriers.

The choice of currency for intercompany invoicing, leads and lags of intercompany or third-party payments, and judicious transfer pricing of both financial and real resources are some of the techniques for moving funds across borders and thus altering exposure. These techniques are available only to firms, not to individuals. In some cases, the firm is able to increase its level of local currency debt, which provides it with a desired hedge when operating cashflows are determined by the local currency, and this also arbitrages imperfections stemming from different tax systems and capital market regulations. To illustrate, many countries not only maintain exchange controls, but also ration credit resources in the domestic market, thus keeping interest rates artificially low. Therefore, for the multinational firm that obtains access to local sources of funds, arbitraging and hedging may turn out to be a joint decision (for details see [5, pp. 78–79]). In addition, from a regulatory point of view, the hedging aspect of such a financing activity may prevent the unfavorable attention from bovernment agencies or adverse public relations that a pure arbitrage decision would invite. This is due, of course, to the fact that hedging tends to have the connotation of being consistent with public policy, while financial arbitrage does not.

In addition, specific subsidies are available to hedgers in some countries. These take the form of special credit facilities, subsidized exchange risk insurance, or special forward rates ("swap facilities") offered by the Central Bank. Only firms can take advantage of these subsidies for hedging purposes: they are not available to individual shareholders.

b. Information Gaps

In order to plan and achieve efficient diversification, the individual investor needs to know the level and timing of foreign exchange exposure for all the companies in the portfolio. Such information is required not only for today but for every future date.

To calculate the exposure of the firm, investors need detailed information not only on the operations side (production, marketing sourcing, etc.) but also on the financial side (currency of denomination of monetary assets and liabilities). In the absence of this information the individual cannot make an optimal exposure decision.

Baron [3], in deriving his concept of "homemade covering" under which investors are indifferent to a firm's covering decision, assumes that output levels, production, and cost functions are deterministic and are known to all investors. With all this information, the investor can plan to cope with his residual exposure. This view assumes, in addition, zero transaction costs. It appears that this type of information is frequently unavailable to shareholders, and even under the most extensive disclosure rules, management will have a distinct edge over outside investors in forcasting more accurately future prices, sales volumes, and costs. Thus, hedging activity at the level of the firm seems preferable to that by an individual.

As a result of barriers and information gaps, the firm faces lower (or no) additional transaction costs for many decisions involving hedging. The information required to make hedging decisions may already have been collected by the firm for other purposes, such as planning for future sales, production, and financing. Thus, information gathering for hedging involves no additional oportunity cost. In contrast, an individual may have to incur considerable costs to obtain the same amount of information.

Given these advantages for firms, corporate hedging is preferable to investors' hedging, even though in an idealized world they are perfect substitites. This has clearly been recognized by Aliber in a somewhat different context: "The firm may have superior knowledge and may be able to protect against these risks at lower costs" [2, pp. 134–135].

4. THE CONCEPTS OF SELF-INSURANCE AND MARKET EFFICIENCY

The first argument based on the concept of self-insurance is that forward exchange markets do not provide bargains, but only fair gambles [7]. In other words, by leaving foreign exchange positions uncovered, a firm may experience gains and losses. These gains and losses tend to average out over a longer period, and hence an open position is essentially the same as a hedged position [2]. The implication is that one should maximize the expected value without undue concern for the variance of returns. Thus, this approach assumes risk neutrality on the part of the decision maker.

On a similar but more sophisticated level, it is argued that since foreign exchange markets are efficient in the sense that forward contracts are priced on the basis of all currently available information, one cannot earn any excess returns in those markets, and hedging is of no value. To quote, "unless capital market imperfections exist and persist, a treasurer . . . engaged in selective hedging . . . will not be able to earn consistent foreign exchange profits . . . in excess of those due to risk taking" [21, p. 51].

This argument rests implicitly on an extremely narrow concept of "hedging": the use of forward contracts to lower the effective cost of liabilities and/or to increase the return on financial assets. This, however, represents the perspective of a speculator in international financial markets.

This reasoning misses the whole point of corporate hedging. A treasurer wants to hedge not because of his desire for excess returns, but to achieve a level of risk/return with which his management feels comfortable. By means of hedging, the additional variability introduced by unexpected exchange rate changes is eliminated: the residual variance in a firm's returns will be due only to fluctuations in business activity, the management of which represents the essence of the firm's competitive advantage.

Several constituents of a firm are interested in reducing the variance of a firm's returns stemming from exchange rate changes. These include managers, bank regulators, stockholders, and creditors.

Managers

It has been argued that managers are concerned about their jobs, promotions, and rewards. Indeed, the largest proportion of managers' total portfolio tends to be invested in their careers; thus, they hold very undiversified portfolios. For that very reason managers have a strong interest in avoiding even questions as to the quality of their performance stimulated by an undue variability of results:

The managers may be concerned that occasional losses incurred from maintaining an exposed position would weigh more heavily against their long-term performance and career prospects. . . . [2, p. 131]

This is hardly surprising when consideration is given to the time horizon of a typical financial manager which is likely to be considerably shorter than the time period required for the impact of exchange market disturbances on a firm's portfolio to net to zero. [14, p. 521]

Evidence regarding managerial attitudes toward foreign exchange risks is provided by Rodriguez [19]. Managers certainly have a strong interest in reducing the variability of cash flows and, indeed, all manifestations of exchange risk.

Regulators

Another party interested in reducing the variability of earnings is bank regulators. Governments feel obliged to limit the risk of bank failure. Following some spectacular bank failures in the 1970s—most notably Herstatt Bank (June 1974) and Franklin National (October 1974)—governments around the world have stepped up their regulatory activity related to banks' foreign exchange exposure policies.

Stockholders

There are certain situations where higher variability can result in real losses. This can happen in the presence of progressive corporate taxation, discriminatory taxes, regulation that depends on the level of profits, and asymmetric laws regarding the carrying forward or backward of business losses.

Whenever there is progressive corporate taxation, a stable stream of earnings is better than a variable one. In some countries, profits in excess of a certain percentage of equity are subject to additional special taxes. In these cases, if a firm has highly variable earnings it may face a higher tax bill than if it had a stable stream of earnings with the same mean.

Also, the level of government regulation of corporations may be a function of the level of profits. Reporting higher profits in one year might mean inviting a greater degree of government control in fixing prices or in other matters. If there are limits to the carrying forward or backward of losses, a variable income stream might imply a higher tax bill. Under such circumstances, a stable stream of earnings is to be preferred to a variable one, even though both may have to hedge.

Creditors

As was shown earlier, reducing variability adds to debt capacity by reducing bankruptcy risk.

5. HEDGING OF CONSUMPTION BUNDLES

The ultimate purpose of wealth is consumption; therefore, changes in one's nominal wealth are irrelevant if those changes are offset by the price changes of one's consumption bundle. Consider the case of a firm that is owned by an individual, a U.S. resident, whose consumption bundle consists largely of Bordeaux wine. French brie, and baguettes. If the film has cash flows determined by the value of French francs, there will be exchange-related gains and losses whenever the dollar/franc rate changes. However, these losses and gains do not concern the shareholder, as his consumption is only of unique French goods, and therefore his preferred currency is the franc. A positive exposure in francs hedges his consumption risk: whenever the franc strengthens, his wealth in U.S. dollars will be greater, but he will need more dollars to buy his consumption goods. The reverse occurs when the direction of change is the opposite. These considerations form the basis for the argument that exchange-related gains and losses may be desirable [7, pp. 213–215].

Of course, this is true only if there is a perfect correspondence between the nature of the firm's exposure and the consumption bundle of its shareholders. The mere fact that shareholders consume imported goods does not imply that exchange-related gains and losses are desirable. In the example cited, if the firm had exposure only in Deutsche marks and its shareholder consumed only French goods, there obviously would be undesirable exchange risk. The hedging of the consumption bundle would require selling DM forward for francs.

At this point the question arises, who should hedge the consumption bundle? If a firm has only a few shareholders, it may be feasible for it to hedge the consumption bundle of its shareholders. But for a widely held firm with a diverse shareholder group, it would not be feasible to do so. Not only would the costs of collecting information about shareholders' consumption bundles as well as their investment positions be prohibitive, but for a group of heterogeneous consumers-investors an "optimal hedge" cannot be found.

As a practical alternative, the firm should hedge its cash flows in dollars, and individual shareholders, in turn, should hedge their consumption bundles. They may do so through forward exchange contracts, foreign currency debt, directly through commodity futures, or simply by taking positions in firms that are long in commodities consumed by them. According to the implicit separation axiom, then, firms should hedge foreign exchange risks and individuals should hedge consumption risks. To quote:

While the owners of the firm may view profits as a means to future consumption, and that consumption could take the form of goods imported from abroad, it still behooves the firm to maximize the certainty of its earnings in the form of the domestic currency only. *Then . . . the rather diverse shareholders . . . can adjust their portfolios to [fit] their own particular patterns of future consumption. . . . [16, p. 69]*

Discussing a paper by Eaker [6], Makin [15] reiterates the same position:

Since the optimal real bond differs for each investor with different expenditure paterns, which themselves change over time, management of real risks must be done at the investor level . . . information costs suggest that investors may find it easier to diversify real risks on their own while leaving management of foreign exchange risk to company managers. [p. 441]

Thus, two conclusions emerge: It is difficult for shareholders to hedge the foreign exchange exposure of their firms: and it is equally difficult for the firm to hedge the consumption bundle of its shareholders.

6. THE UNCERTAINTY OF FORWARD RATES AND SPOT RATES

The argument here is that both future forward rates and future spot rates are variable, and predicting future forward rates is as difficult as predicting future spot rates; hence, hedging is of dubious value [21, 8].

Consider an example, using the same notation as that used in Shapiro and Rutenberg [21]. For the next N years, a firm has yearly local currency (LC) earnings equal to C. The earnings, C, are fixed in LC, will not vary with the exchange rate, and accrue to the firm at the end of each year. In other words, the firm has an N year LC annuity of C. It has two alternatives for converting the LC proceeds to its home currency (HC), the dollar.

In the first alternative, it can wait each year for the receipt of LC and convert it to HC at the prevailing spot rate. Let e_i be the spot exchange rate ($ per LC) at the end of year i. In this method, the firm is not hedging. It has a variable stream of HC cash flow equal to e_i C in year i. Thus,

$$\text{Cash flow in year } i = e_iC;\ i = 1 \text{ to } N. \tag{1a}$$

$$\text{Its variance} = C^2\text{var}(e_i). \tag{1b}$$

In the second alternative, the firm can sell forward at the beginning of each year the C units of LC expected to be received at the end of the year. Let S_i be the one-year forward rate ($ per LC) at the beginning of year i. The firm would then receive S_iC units of HC at the end of year i. Its variance depends on the firm's planning horizon. Consider first the situation where the firm's planning horizon is longer than the maturity of the forward contract, *i.e.*, N > 1, say 10 years. In this situation, under the second alternative, the firm's cash flow and its variance are given by the following:

$$\text{HC cash flow in year } i = S_iC;\ i = 1 \text{ to } N. \quad (2a)$$

$$\text{Its variance} = C^2\text{var}(e_i). \quad (2b)$$

Whether var(e_i) is equal to var(S_i) is an empirical question, but e_i is as difficult to predict as S_i. In view of this, both Shapiro and Rutenberg [21] and Giddy [8] argue that both alternatives are equally uncertain and hedging provides no real benefit in reducing uncertainty. Giddy states the argument succinctly:

. . . exchanging currency via the forward market yields just as much uncertainty as would waiting until the payment date and exchanging currency in the spot market each time. [8, p. 100]

However, when the firm's planning horizon is the same as the maturity of the forward contract (*i.e.*, N = 1), there is one major difference between the two alternatives. Using the forward market, the firm knows at the beginning of each year what it is receiving at the end of that year. In the unhedged alternative, the firm does not know until the date of receipt the actual value of receipts. Thus, in the hedged alternative, the firm may be able to use the information for corporate cash planning and working capital decisions. In this case, for each year, the deviation of actual cash flow from that expected is zero. Thus, in general, for all activities for which the firm's planning and action horizon is equal to the maturity of the forward contract, hedging is useful. The question to ask is: What is the firm's planning and action horizon relative to the maturity of the forward contract? The crucial issue then is to distinguish between interperiod variance and intraperoid variance.

CONCLUSIONS

In an idealized world, without information and transactions costs, explicit or implicit contract periods, and other obstacles to instantaneous price adjustments, deviations from various equilibrium conditions such as purchasing power parity, the law of one price, and both the domestic and international Fisher effect would not occur; neither would firms be exposed to exchange risk, however, because real-world imperfections in markets for real goods and services as well as financial assets do exist, firms can be subject to exchange risk.

Even when one allows for the existence of corporate exchange risk, a legitimate question can be raised as to whether this risk should be managed at the level of the firm or by the ultimate beneficiaries, the firm's stockholders. In the spirit of the capital asset pricing model, for example, management of different risks in different markets is redundant and can always be bundled together and passed along to the capital market. Alternatively, in the idealized world assumed in the Modigliani-Miller theorem, corporate hedging and investor hedging are perfect substitues for each other. Also, various efficiency arguments applied to foreign exchange markets can be put forth to make the case against foreign exchange risk management at the corporate level.

The objective of this note was to identify comprehensively the various strands of thought that have been used to support the relevance of foreign exchange management at the corporate level. Obviously, some of these arguments are related by common factors. In making the case for considering foreign exchange management to be an appropriate concern of corporate management, a limited range of essentially empirical propositions was identified, all of which are based on market imperfections—incomplete securities markets, positive transactions and information costs, the dead weight costs of financial distress, and agency cost considerations. If one or more of those conditions exist, the case for foreign exchange risk management at the corporate level is made. The extent to which management can then cope with exchange risk completely is a different issue altogether.

REFERENCES

1. Michael Adler, "Translation Methods and Operational Foreign Exchange Risk Management." Chapter 6 in Göran Bergendahl (ed.). *International Financial Management*, Stockholm, Norstedts, 1982.
2. Robert Z. Aliber, *Exchange Risk and Corporate International Finance*, New York, John Wiley and Sons, 1979.
3. David P. Baron, "Flexible Exchange Rates, Forward Markets, and the Level of Trade," *American Economic Review* (June 1976), pp. 253–266.
4. Bradford Cornell, "Inflation, Relative Price Changes, and Exchange Risk." *Financial Management* (Autumn 1980), pp. 30–34.
5. Gunter Dufey and Ian Giddy, "International Financial Planning: The Use of Market Based Forecasts," *California Management Review* (Fall 1978), pp. 69–81.
6. Mark R. Eaker, "The Numeraire Problem and Foreign Exchange Risk," *Journal of Finance* (May 1981), pp. 419–427.
7. George Feiger and Bertrand Jacquillat, *International Finance: Text and Cases*, Boston, Allyn & Bacon, 1981.
8. Ian H. Giddy, "Why It Doesn't Pay to Make a Habit of Forward Hedging," *Euromoney* (December 1976), pp. 96–100.
9. James E. Hodder, "Hedging International Exposure: Capital Structure Under Flexible Exchange Rates and Expropriation Risk," unpublished working paper. Stanford University, November 1982.
10. Peter Isard, "How Far Can We Push the Law of One Price?" *American Economic Review* (December 1977), pp. 942–948.
11. Laurent L. Jacque, "Management of Foreign Exchange Risk: A Review Article," *Journal of International Business Studies* (Spring/Summer 1981), pp. 81–101.
12. Donald R. Lessard, *International Financial Management*. New York: John Wiley & Son, 1985.
13. Dennis E. Logue and George S. Oldfield, "Managing Foreign Assets When Foreign Exchange Markets Are Efficient," *Financial Management* (Summer 1977). pp. 16–22.
14. John H. Makin, "Portfolio Theory and the Problem of Foreign Exchange Risk," *Journal of Finance* (May 1978), pp. 517–534.
15. John Makin, "Discussion," *Journal of Finance* (May 1981), pp. 440–442.
16. Ronald McKinnon, *Money in International Exchange*, New York, Oxford University Press, 1979.
17. Ruediger Naumann-Etienne, "Exchange Risk in Foreign Operations of Multinational Corporations," doctoral dissertation, The University of Michigan, 1977.
18. Lawrence H. Officer, *Purchasing Power Parity and Exchange Rates: Theory Evidence and Relevance*, Greenwich, Conn., JAI Press, Inc., 1982.

19. Rita M. Rodriguez, "Corporate Exchange Risk Management: Theme and Aberrations," *Journal of Finance* (May 1981), pp. 427–439.
20. Rolls-Royce Annual Report, 1979.
21. Alan C. Shapiro and David P. Rutenberg, "Managing Exchange Risks in a Floating World," *Financial Management* (Summer 1976), pp. 48–58.
22. Alan C. Shapiro, "Currency Risk and Relative Price Risk," unpublished working paper, Los Angeles, University of Southern California, November 1982.
23. S. L. Srinivasulu, "Strategic Response to Foreign Exchange Risks," *Columbia Journal of World Business* (Spring 1981), pp. 13–23.

18

Exposure to Currency Risk: Definition and Measurement*

Michael Adler and Bernard Dumas

INTRODUCTION

U.S. corporations, including those with no foreign operations and no foreign currency assets, liabilities, or transactions, are generally exposed to foreign currency risk. Regional electrical utilities are a somewhat extreme case in point. With no foreign currency accounts on their books, they have no accounting exposure to exchange risk. From an economic perspective, however, the story is different. If their customer base is dominated by either importing or exporting firms whose activities and demand for electricity are affected by exchange rate changes, the electrical utilities' operations and stock prices themselves will also in principle be exposed to exchange risk.[1]

Accounting rules for foreign currency translation are largely powerless in this situation. Economic exposure to foreign currency risk must be defined and measured quite apart from the choice between current or historical exchange rates for translating particular foreign currency positions. What is needed, in short, is to replace the accounting approach with a technique for measuring the economic exposures of the market prices of financial and physical assets. This is done in the pages that follow which draw out the implications for practice of recent innovations on the theoretical front. The objective, it should be noted, is limited to definition and measurement; it is not the analysis of the determinants of exchange risk or exposure thereto. It is also not to analyze whether individuals or firms should hedge. These last are important problems which are best addressed once the exposure phenomenon itself has been precisely identified.

Section I distinguishes between currency risk and exposure. The latter is defined in Section II and measured in Section III. The practical implications of the approach are discussed in Sections IV and V.

I RISK VS. EXPOSURE

A currency is not risky because devaluation is likely. If the devaluation were certain as to magnitude and timing, there would be no risk at all. A weak currency can be less risky than a strong currency. A strong currency does not become risky because it has been used to denominate an individual's or a firm's debt. In short, expected exchange changes can

---

*This article is reprinted, with permission, from *Financial Management 13*, No. 2, 41–50.

[1]This point is not new. It has its origins in traditional trade theory and the notion that exchange rate changes can cause, or coincide with, fluctuations in domestic aggregate demand, employment and output and, therefore, also with the activities of non-trading domestic firms. See Laursen and Metzler [11].

be anticipated. Risk or uncertainty is a question of randomness, *i.e.*, unexpected exchange rate variations.[2]

Currency risk is not the exposure. Currency risk is to be identified with statistical quantities which summarize the probability that the actual domestic purchasing power of home or foreign currency on a given future date will differ from its originally anticipated value. Exposure, in contrast, should be defined in terms of what one has at risk.[3] The question at hand is how to measure it.

II CURRENCY-RISK EXPOSURE

For purposes of financial analysis, a reasonable measure of exposure to currency-risk should meet the following three criteria:

1. Its dimension should be an amount of currency, domestic for domestic currency risk and foreign for foreign currency risk.
2. It should be a characteristic of any asset or liability, physical or financial, that a given investor might own or owe, defined from that investor's viewpoint.
3. It should be implementable in the dual sense that, first, measurement can be accomplished with available techniques; and, second, exposure so measured can be hedged or covered with available financial instruments, such as forward exchange contracts.[4]

Assume a world with only two currencies, U.S. dollars and French francs, and that U.S. investors, who are all alike, perhaps improbably expect U.S. inflation, and therefore their domestic currency risk, to be zero. They expect, however, that the French inflation rate and therefore the exchange rate will be random. Forward contracts are available.

Consider next a representative U.S. investor who expects *with certainty* to receive exactly FF 1000 in three months from today. What will be his exposure on the target date three months away? The intuitive (and correct) answer is: precisely FF 1000. Why? The answer is apparent from Exhibit 1. FF 1000 represents exactly the sensitivity of the future *dollar* value of the franc balance to variations in the exchange rate. Furthermore, a hedge in the form of a forward contract to sell 1000 francs for three months at the forward rate F, which will pay off \$1000(F-S) at maturity, is exactly what is required to insulate the *dollar* value of the balance from unanticipated variations in the exchange rate. The dollar value of the hedged position remains constant, at \$1000F, across states of nature.

We can summarize these considerations in the following linked definitions of exposure and hedging, based on the theory set forth in the Appendix.

[2]The identification of exchange risk as randomness, distinct from expected currency strength or weakness, is a by-product of studies of exchange rates as random walks, beginning with Poole [13]. There is no need for present purposes to distinguish between nominal exchange risk, which may not matter under some assumptions, and relative price risk, which may. A critical review of the arcane debate on this point appears in Adler and Dumas ([4], section 6).

[3]Dumas [7] seems to have been the first to make this distinction in print. Though obvious, it bears repeating.

[4]The hedging scenarios to be considered are extremely simple by design. Useful insights can nonetheless be achieved. Futures contracts are excluded mainly because most large firms still prefer the forward to the futures markets. We also elide multiperiod or dynamic hedging strategies, restricting attention to a one-period setting. On both accounts, interest rate risk or reinvestment rate uncertainty remains outside our present purview. These exclusions indicate the direction that future extensions and modifications of the ideas should take.

EXHIBIT 1

Exposure of FF 1000, To Be Received in the Future, When There Are Three States of Nature

Future Quantities	State 1	State 2	State 3
FF Balance: P*	1000	1000	1000
Exchange Rate: S = $/FF	0.250	0.225	0.200
Dollar Value: SP*	$250	$225	$200
Proceeds of Forward Sale: $1000(F-S)	$1000(F-0.25)	$1000(F-0.225)	$1000(F-0.20)
Dollar Value of Hedged Position	$1000F	$1000F	$1000F

Exposures The amounts of foreign currencies which represent the sensitivity of the future, real domestic-currency (market) value of any physical or financial asset to random variations in the future domestic purchasing powers of these foreign currencies, at some specific future date.

Hedges The amounts of the foreign-currency financial transactions (*i.e.*, forward contracting or its equivalent) required to render the future, real, domestic-currency market value of an exposed position statistically independent of unanticipated, random variations in the future domestic purchasing powers of these foreign currencies.

There are several points to observe about these definitions. First, the concept of exposure has a definite target date. This is partly because the financial instruments used for hedging in practice have contractually fixed maturity dates. They can, therefore, protect exposures only within the period covered by the contract. In addition, exposures themselves may vary over time. They are future quantities which may be imagined as the equivalent of foreign currency deposits or debts which will exist or mature on some future date.[5] In most practical circumstances, exposure in any currency will not be a certain accounting quantity but will rather be a magnitude which must be projected and estimated by statistical means. Seen from the present, exposures six months ahead may be greater or smaller than exposures a year ahead.

A second point to be emphasized, and one that we shall investigate in detail below, is that the notion of exposure is not restricted to non-traded financial assets or liabilities with fixed, nominal, foreign-currency payoffs on the maturity date of the hedge. The exposure of such assets is easy to determine. They are 100% exposed in the specific sense that their exposure is exactly equal to their foreign-currency face value on that date, as the example

[5]This emphasis, that exposure depends on the covariance of *future* prices with *future* exchange rates, marks a radical departure from the current textbook wisdom. For example, Cornell and Shapiro [6] indicate that exposure should be measured in terms of the impact of unexpected exchange rate changes on the *present* value of the firm's future cash flows without reference to a target date. This apparently represents an attempt to collapse the dynamic evolution of exposure over time into a single measure. In our opinion, it is unsuccessful. When one thinks in terms of market prices, as one should, present-values are currently known. They are certain. The very idea of a covariance between the non-random current market price and random exchange rate variations over an indefinite horizon is, therefore, vacuous. The possibility of devising any other single-valued measure of association between a present value and exchange rates at every future date seems equally remote. In finance, notional changes in present values are used to evaluate the impact of current decisions that will affect future outcomes: but no financial decision is required for measuring exposure. The approach taken here enables financial decision analysis and exposure measurement to be kept apart: Exposure is a matter of the future, instantaneous covariation of contemporaneous prices and exchange rates either at discrete points of, or continuously over, time. It is the *value* of hedging that requires present value comparisons.

in Exhibit 1 demonstrates. However, the (real) domestic-currency price of *any* asset or liability, physical or financial, whose future foreign currency value is uncertain, may also be sensitive to, or correlated with, exchange rate fluctuations. To the extent of this sensitivity or correlation, such assets should indeed be considered exposed. This leads to the notion of exposure as a statistical property.

In the Appendix and in the next section we show that exposure is best measured with statistical regression techniques, as the coefficient(s) of the purchasing power variables(s), (*i.e.*, the exchange rates when domestic inflation is zero), in a multiple linear regression of an asset's future domestic-currency market price on (the set of) the contemporaneous foreign exchange rate(s).[6] Each such regression coefficient has the dimension of units of foreign currency. The idea behind defining exposure in this fashion is that it decomposes the probability distribution of a risky asset's domestic-currency price at a future instant into two parts: one that is correlated with the (set of) exchange rate(s) and a second that is independent of them. The first component may be considered exposed as its variability may be removed by financial hedging. It is the equivalent of the French franc deposit in the previous example. Residual variability remains, but it is not exposed as it cannot be further reduced by hedging. It should be clear that in this approach exposures can be positive, zero or even negative depending on the direction of the correlations between an asset's price and the exchange rates. If, furthermore, one thinks of long-term foreign bonds with nominally fixed redemption values but with maturities beyond the target date, the exposures of their *market* prices, translated into dollars, may be more or less than one-hundred percent.[7]

III EXPOSURE IS A REGRESSION COEFFICIENT

An asset may be simultaneously exposed to more than one currency. The reader should keep this in mind throughout what follows. It is only for simplicity of exposition that we construct the examples of this section using a single exchange rate. The intention of these examples is to demonstrate how exposure may be measured using well-known linear regression techniques. That it should be so measured is proved in the Appendix. When one wants to determine exposure to many currencies, the regressions in question simply become multiple linear regressions. This extension of the methodology will be mentioned again in Section IV.

For the purpose of the exercises that follow, we need no more than a simple setting with three possible future states of nature and two currencies, dollars and francs. We continue to assume that dollar inflation is nonrandom. The setting is fully described by

[6]The intellectual pedigree of this approach appears partly in the Appendix. It originated in Dumas [7] which followed several of his working papers beginning in 1976.

[7]See Adler and Dumas [2] for a two-period analysis of the determinants of exposure in this case. In the one-period framework of the present paper, a financial or physical asset is risky if its end-of-period, dollar market price is random. Financial assets include stocks and short and long-term bonds; physical assets are (manufactured) goods like plant and equipment and inventory. Financial and physical assets need not further be distinguished, as they must in multiperiod or continuous time models, according to the source of uncertainty: interest-rate risk in the case of long-term bonds; and cash flow or replacement-value risk, combined with interest-rate risk, in that of stocks and physical assets. Nominally riskless bonds and deposits are free of default risk in their respective currencies. Deposits are not traded prior to maturity and therefore are also free of interest rate risk. Nominally riskless foreign currency deposits are risky in dollar terms.

EXHIBIT 2

The Dollar Price of a Risky Foreign Asset in Three States of Nature

	French Franc Price: P_s^*	Exchange Rate: S_s	U.S. Dollar Price: $S_sP_s^* = P_s$
	P_1^*	S_1	$S_1P_1^* = P_1$
Time 0	P_2^*	S_2	$S_2P_2^* = P_2$
	P_3^*	S_3	$S_3P_3^* = P_3$

Exhibit 2. Looking ahead from now, time 0, to a future target date, the dollar value of a nominally riskless or risky French asset is uncertain. Uncertainty is captured by the fact that one out of three possible states of nature, subscripted by s, will occur. In each state the French asset will have a franc price denoted by P_s^*. P_s^* will have the same value in each state if the asset is nominally riskless, such as a bank deposit or a T-bill, and if it matures on the target date; and it will have different values across states if it is risky like a stock or a long-term bond which matures after the target date. Seen from now, the exchange rate, S_s, is also uncertain: it will take on different values within its possible range

EXHIBIT 3

Exposure and Hedging When There are Three States of Nature and a Fixed Amount, FF 1000, Due in the Future

(1) To Show: Exposure is the regression coefficient of the future dollar value of the FF position in a regression of that position on the exchange rate. In this case, exposure must also necessarily be FF 1000.

(2) Definitions:
P_s^* = FF 1000 in each state
P_s = Dollar value of FF 1000 in state s at time-t
= $\$S_sP_s^*$ = \$1000 S_s in this case.

(3) Regresion:
$P = a + bS + e$, where here, $a = \bar{P} - b\bar{S} = 0$;
$b = \text{cov}(P,S)/\text{Var}(S)$;
p_s = Probability of state s;
$\bar{P} = \Sigma_s p_s S_s P_s^* = \$1000\,\bar{S} = \$225$ below, since
$\bar{S} = \Sigma_s p_s S_s = 0.225$ \$/FF, from the data.
$\text{cov}(P,S) = \Sigma_s p_s (P_s - \bar{P})(S_s - \bar{S})$
$\text{var}(S) = \Sigma_s p_s (S_s - \bar{S})^2$

(4) Data:

States	p_s	S_s	P_s	$S_s - \bar{S}$	$P_s - \bar{P}$	$(S_s - \bar{S})^2$	$(P_s - \bar{P})(S_s - \bar{S})$
1	1/3	0.25	\$250	0.025	\$25	0.000625	0.625
2	1/3	0.225	\$225	0	0	0	0
3	1/3	0.20	\$200	−0.025	−\$25	0.000625	0.625

(5) Calculated Regression Coefficient:

$$b = \frac{\text{cov}(P,S)}{\text{var}(S)} = \frac{(2/3)(0.625)}{(2/3)(0.000625)} = \text{FF } 1000$$

of variation in each future state of nature. Consequently, whether or not P_s^* itself is constant, the dollar value of the French asset, $S_sP_s^* = P_s$, will be random.

In the Appendix we show that the exposure of the French asset, from the viewpoint of a U.S. investor who assumes that U.S. inflation is non-random and who has access to forward contracts, is properly measured by the coefficient, b, in a linear regression of P on S across the states of nature:

$$P = a + b \cdot S + e$$

where

a = regression constant

e = random error term such that $E(e) = 0 = cov(e,S)$

Note that the dimension of b is units of French francs: it therefore meets the first of our criteria for an exposure measure in the previous section.

We now demonstrate the application of this exposure measurement technique through two numerical examples. In each, the state probabilities are 1/3, that is, the states are equi-probable, a condition often associated with ignorance. The first, in Exhibit 3, which calculates the exposure of a French franc deposit, is included for comfort. It should be consoling to discover that the computed exposure is in fact equal to the deposit's face value as intuition demands. The second deals with a slightly more complex situation in which the French franc asset-price is also random. We defer discussion of the results till later.

Exhibit 3 provides the requisite consolation. In the situation where we know that the exposure is FF 1000, the regression technique produces exactly that result. This is also exactly the amount that can be hedged. Following the procedures of Exhibit 1 above, the outcome is that a hedge in the amount of FF 1000 will make the dollar value of the franc deposit *constant* across states of nature.

This constancy of the dollar value of the hedged position is possible *only* when the franc price of the French asset is itself constant across states of nature, that is, when the French asset is nominally riskless in franc terms and its maturity coincides with that of the forward contract. It is only such assets that are 100% exposed in the dual sense that their exposures equal their face values and they can be perfectly hedged.

When the underlying French franc price at the hedging horizon is *random*, the risky asset cannot be perfectly hedged. The Appendix teaches us that in such cases the best one can do is to hedge in the amount of the exposure. This will minimize the variance of the hedged asset and render the residual variability of the asset price in dollars, after hedging, *independent* of the exchange rate. The effect of determining exposure via regression, in other words, is to decompose the randomness of $P = SP^*$ into two components: one which is correlated with the exchange rate and is removed by hedging; and a second, that remains after hedging, whose variance is minimal and which is statistically unrelated to the exchange rate. This is demonstrated in Exhibits 4 and 5.

The top panel of Exhibit 4 provides the data for the dollar value of a risky French asset in each of three states of nature. In the middle panel we compute the regression coefficient, b, in the regression of P on S. This coefficient represents the exposure: it is FF 2000 in this example. The bottom panel reveals the results of a hedge in the amount of the exposure. Quite clearly, the dollar value of the hedged asset is not constant across states of nature. The hedge in this situation is obviously not perfect: the hedged asset is still risky.

EXHIBIT 4

Exposure Measurement When the French Franc Price is Random

1. Regression Equation $\tilde{P} = a + b\tilde{S} + \tilde{e}$, where $\tilde{P} = \tilde{S}\tilde{P}^*$
2. Data

States	P_s	P^*_s	S_s	P_s
1	1/3	1200	0.25	\$300
2	1/3	978	0.225	\$220
3	1/3	1000	0.200	\$200
Means			0.225	\$240

3. Calculation of the Parameters of the Regression of P on S.

States	$S_s - \bar{S}$	$(S_s - \bar{S})^2$	$(P_s - \bar{P})$	$(P_s - \bar{P})(S_s - \bar{S})$	$(P_s - \bar{P})^2$
1	0.025	0.000625	\$60	1.5	3600
2	0	0	−\$20	0	400
3	−0.025	0.000625	−\$40	1	1600
Means	0	(2/3)(0.000625)	0	(1/3)(1.5) + (1/3)(1)	1867

$$b = \frac{\text{cov}(P,S)}{\text{var}(S)} = \frac{[(1/3)(1.5) + (1/3)(1)]}{(2/3)(0.000625)} = \text{FF } 2000$$

$$a = \bar{P} - b\bar{S} = \$240 - \$(2000)(0.225) = -\$210$$

4. Hedge the Exposure: Sell FF 2000 Forward @ F: Proceeds = \$2000(F − S)

Results	State 1	State 2	State 3
Unhedged Dollar Value	\$300	\$220	\$200
Proceeds of Contract	\$2000(F-0.25)	\$2000(F-0.225)	\$2000(F-0.20)
Value of Hedged Asset	\$(2000F-200)	\$(2000F-230)	\$(2000F-200)

EXHIBIT 5

Demonstration That the Hedged French Asset Is Independent of the Exchange Rate

1. Dollar Value of Hedged Asset = $R_s = P_s + b(F - S_s)$
2. From Exhibit 4 calculate the following data:

States	P_s	R_s	$R_s - \bar{R}$	$S_s - \bar{S}$	$(R_s - \bar{R})(S_s - \bar{S})$	$(R_s - \bar{R})^2$
1	1/3	\$(2000F-200)	+\$10	0.025	0.25	100
2	1/3	\$(2000F-230)	−\$20	0	0	400
3	1/3	\$(2000F-200)	+\$10	−0.025	−0.25	100
Means		\$(2000F-210)	0	0	(1/3)(0.25) − (1/3)(0.25)	200

3. $\text{cov}(R,S) = E[(R_s - \bar{R})(S_s - \bar{S})] = (1/3)(0.25) - (1/3)(0.25) = 0$
4. Summary of Results of Hedging

Variance of Unhedged Asset	$= \text{Var}(P) = 1867\ (\$)^2$
Variance of Hedged Asset	$= \text{Var}(P - bS) = \text{Var}(R) = 200\ (\$)^2$
Variance Removed by Hedging	$= b^2\text{Var}(S) = (2000)^2(2/3)(0.000625) = 1667\ (\$)^2$

It is, however, the best that can be done in a very specific sense. As shown in Exhibit 5, the residual variability in the dollar value of the hedged asset, denoted by R, is statistically independent of the exchange rate: that is, as shown in the third panel, cov(R,S) = 0. What then has been accomplished by hedging? This is shown in the fourth panel of Exhibit 5. The variance of the unhedged position, computed in the rightmost column of panel 3 in Exhibit 4, is 1867 $(\$)^2$. The variance of the hedged but still risky asset, calculated in panel 2 of Exhibit 5, is 200 $(\$)^2$. Hedging has removed the part of the variance due to exchange rate variability, in the amount of 1667 $(\$)^2$. The remaining variability has been minimized and cannot further be reduced by forward exchange contracts or their equivalent. Other hedging instruments or methods such as diversification must be sought if it is to be avoided.

IV SUMMARY OBSERVATIONS ON THE MEANING OF EXPOSURE

It is perhaps worth reconsidering the concept of exposure in light of the measurement procedures described above. From the viewpoint of U.S. investors exposure, to be sure, is the regression coefficient or, if there are many currencies, the vector of partial regression coefficients, when an asset's dollar price is regressed on exchange rates. Seen in this way, it is clear that any asset, *regardless of its location*, may be exposed. U.S. stocks and real estate are exposed, for example, if their (future) market prices are correlated with one or more foreign exchange rates.[8] Nominally riskless U.S. deposits that are held to maturity, on the other hand, are not exposed to foreign currency risk on the maturity date. Their nominal dollar payoffs are constant, regardless of exchange rate changes.[9] They are, however, exposed to domestic currency risk if U.S. investors perceive the purchasing power of the dollar to be nonrandom. Nominally riskless foreign currency deposits whose maturities coincide with the hedging horizon are, in contrast, always exposed fully (*i.e.*, 100%) to their own exchange rate and to no other. Risky foreign assets whose market prices at the hedging horizon are uncertain are, in principle, no different from risky U.S.

[8]This point enables us to comment on the faulty claim, now enshrined in FAS 52, according to which local debt hedges fixed assets in foreign subsidiaries. In our approach, of course, this would not generally be true since the measured exposures of physical assets and foreign currency liabilities would not necessarily be equal or even offsetting for any given planning horizon. The exposures of physical assets like plant, equipment and inventories, wherever located, are simply the regression coefficients of their future dollar market values on exchange rates. These exposure coefficients, were one to analyze them further, would be seen to depend on the impact of exchange rates, via macro-economic and trade linkages, on the productivity of, and dollar cash flows from, the assets. Equally, the exposures of a firm's nominal short and long-term foreign currency liabilities are the coefficients from regressing their dollar market values on exchange rates. Following Adler and Dumas [2], these latter exposures will depend on the serial correlation of exchange rates, and their links, via their impact on inflationary expectations and default risks, with local borrowing rates. The determinants and, therefore, any potentially reasonable estimates of the exposures of physical assets and nominal liabilities are completely different. The latter may hedge the former to a greater or lesser extent, but this is an empirical matter. Finally, though parenthetically, physical asset exposures are independent of deviations from commodity or purchasing power parity; and the exposures of foreign bonds or deposits are independent of violations of interest-rate parity. For the reasons, see Adler and Dumas ([4], Sec. 8).

[9]Long-term U.S. bonds, on the other hand, are of course generally exposed at any hedging target date short of maturity. The main determinant of this exposure, which can be analyzed only in two-or-more-period models, is the correlation between interest rate risk and exchange risk. This, in turn, depends on the serial correlation properties of exchange rate and inflation rate expectations as these are embodied in the interest rate.

assets. Their exposures to one or more currency risks are an empirical matter, to be determined by the procedures already described.

Measuring an asset's exposure by its regression coefficient or coefficients essentially means splitting the random future dollar price into two components. One is the exposure. It is the equivalent of a foreign currency deposit (or a portfolio of foreign currency deposits if the regression is run over many exchange rates). This component can be perfectly hedged by an offsetting forward exchange transaction, just as foreign currency deposits themselves could be hedged. This equivalence of exposure to a (portfolio of) foreign currency deposit(s) is an idea to which we shall subsequently return. The second component is not exposed to exchange risk, in the specific sense that its randomness is not correlated with any exchange rate. It may, of course, be exposed to other identifiable risks: but these cannot be hedged with forward currency transactions.

Risky assets other than domestic and foreign currency deposits and long-term bonds, which promise payment of a specific amount of currency at maturity, have no intrinsic denomination in any currency. In other words, they are generally risky regardless of the choice of reference or measurement currency. An asset can be said to be denominated in a currency to the extent that its future dollar value, or some fraction thereof, behaves as if it were a riskless deposit in that currency.[10] Another way of looking at our concept of exposure is that it measures the extent to which any asset can be said to be denominated in one or more currencies. Common stocks, for example, regardless of where they are traded, and physical assets, regardless of where they are located, can therefore equally well be said to have no intrinsic currency denomination or to be denominated, to the extent of their exposures, in one or more currencies. In these cases, denomination like exposure cannot be identified in advance but instead is an empirical matter.

Finally, it is perhaps worthwhile emphasizing what hedging with forward exchange contracts can do and what it cannot. Hedging with forward exchange transactions does not in general remove currency risk.[11] It merely substitutes exposure to domestic purchasing power risk for exposure to foreign currency risk. When domestic purchasing power uncertainty is negligible, forward exchange transactions can remove the impact of exchange risk variability. They do so in effect by redenominating the exposed fraction of an asset's future domestic value, from foreign currency into domestic currency. When foreign asset prices are uncertain and/or when domestic inflation risk is present, the (real) dollar values of these assets cannot be fixed in advance merely with forward contracts. At most, one can hedge away that part of the nominal variation which is linearly correlated with exchange-rate randomness. The dollar prices of these assets will remain uncertain after hedging. The remaining uncertainty will be independent of the exchange rate. Only to this extent can the asset's total risk be said to have been hedged.

[10]The question of denomination, it should be clear, is quite different from the issue of the correct deflator for a firm's results discussed by Eaker [8]. His suggested numeraire is, in any event, problematic: one has few choices between the owners' CPI and separate indices for each of the firm's output and input goods. The latter, furthermore, will generally have different exposures. Exchange rate changes can indeed affect a firm's competitiveness even if CPP holds for every good and PPP holds at the level of the CPI, if the relative prices of inputs and outputs vary.

[11]Different limitations of hedging with forward contracts have been discussed by other authors. One key issue, which is largely outside the province of this paper, is whether hedging foreign exchange risk can add value to the firm. In informationally symmetric, quasi-complete markets, it cannot: see Adler and Dumas [1], Baron [5], Logue and Oldfield [12], and Dumas [7].

V CONCLUSION

Until now, corporate exposure to foreign exchange risk has largely been investigated in the literature from the viewpoint of the firm and its managers. Here we have looked at it in a way that conforms to the interests of stockholders and analysts. The notion that exposure can be measured as a regression coefficient should have immediate appeal to this group.

Stock analysts have long been accustomed to measuring the riskiness of a security or a portfolio by its beta in a regression of the portfolio's returns on the market index. Viewed slightly differently, beta represents a transformation of the *exposure* of the portfolio to the market. To hedge a portfolio with initial value V_t, one should short a quantity of index futures equal to (beta) (V_t).[12] Such a hedge, if interest rates remain constant, will render the future value of the portfolio largely independent of the index for the life of the contract.

Clearly, the idea of exposure to exchange risk is not intrinsically different from that of exposure to market risk. It is not, therefore, surprising that the two can be estimated in similar ways. Thus, for example, a portfolio's average exposure to exchange risk in the past can, in principle, be obtained by regressing its total dollar value on a vector of exchange rates: the partial regression coefficients will represent its exposure to each currency. If the future is like the past, portfolio managers could conceivably use the procedure usefully to strip the exchange risk component out of portfolio returns by hedging these exposures. The promise is there. Before it can be implemented, however, one must confront the usual but intricate problems of stationarity and multicollinearity. As exposures vary over time, it will be necessary further to attempt to derive multiperiod hedging rules. These are matters for future research.

In addition, several implications for corporate practice emerge from redefining exposure properly in terms of market rather than book values and measuring it as a regression coefficient. For one thing it may change or refine the way some treasurers think about exposure: that indeed is the paper's main aim. Exposure is a statistical quantity rather than a (projected) accounting number. Foreign currency liabilities and forward contracts have their own measurable exposures. They cannot therefore be expected to perfectly hedge fixed assets or foreign operating results, whose exposures are generally different, and in some circumstances may not do so at all. The firm as a whole is exposed. Its global exposure is not necessarily the sum of the exposures of the individual foreign operations or of specific foreign currency accounts, for this ignores the exposure of domestic operations. Nor is its global exposure some sum of its so-called "accounting" and "economic" exposures.[13] *Ex ante*, the two cannot be measured or hedged separately,

[12] More precisely, since the regression is run on rates of return, beta is the elasticity of the stock price with respect to the market. The elasticity is a dimensionless number while exposure is a dollar amount in this case. It is apparent from the Appendix that in this case: $\text{Exposure}_t = (\text{beta})(V_t)$, where V_t is the initial price of the stock. Naturally, if beta is stationary, exposure will change as V_t varies over time. This raises the issue of the specification of dynamic hedging strategies which is the object of much current research in connection with the use of index futures.

[13] The notion that economic exposure and accounting exposure are different is not new: the origin of the idea is obscure and the references too many to list. Most textbooks, *e.g.*, Eiteman and Stonehill [10] and Shapiro [16], rightly emphasize the distinction. However, they leave the impression that economic exposure is something which one somehow adds on to accounting exposure. Nor do they offer a summary measure of economic exposure.

in as much as future financial reports will reflect the impact of the economic environment and the firm's responses via current and future managerial decisions.

What the regression coefficient concept of exposure can provide is a single comprehensive measure that summarizes the sensitivity of the whole firm, as of a given future date, to all the various ways in which exchange rate changes can affect it. While problems of implementing this approach must be left to be treated elsewhere, it offers a further insight.[14] Once exposures are so measured they can, for purposes of managerial control, be decomposed into components, one for each kind of influence that exchange rates can have. If necessary, the decomposition can produce the counterparts of translation and transaction exposures as part of the total. Neither should necessarily be ignored, nor should they be hedged alone. When and if hedging is a desirable corporate decision, it is exposure as a whole, not some part of it, that should be protected. All this is at least conceptual progress in the direction of clarity.

We cannot end without a warning. Adapting firms' planning systems to the requirements of the proposed approach to exposure measurement may be expensive. Furthermore, financial theory suggests that hedging any exposure, however measured, might be useless to stockholders if they had the information to hedge for themselves. There is no empirical evidence to show that exchange risk exposure reduces, or that companies' hedging activities improve, stock values. The issues addressed here could conceivably be irrelevant from this viewpoint. There seem, however, to be two ways to justify costly exchange risk management in the name of the stockholders' interests. Once they are preliminarily identified, exposures can often be wholly or partly closed by shifting funds across borders through channels, other than forward contracts, that also reduce taxes. Identifying and hedging large exposures, furthermore, can lead to reduced perceptions of default risk, improved bond ratings and lower borrowing rates. When such savings are available, managers may balance the benefits against the costs.

REFERENCES

1. M. Adler and B. Dumas, "The Long-Term Financial Decisions of the Multinational Corporation." In E. J. Elton and M. J. Gruber (eds.), *International Capital Markets*, Amsterdam, North Holland, 1975.
2. M. Adler and B. Dumas, "The Exposure of Long-Term Foreign Currency Bonds," *Journal of Financial and Quantitative Analysis* (November 1980), pp. 973–995.
3. M. Adler and B. Dumas, "Foreign Exchange Risk Management." In B. Antl (ed.), *Currency Risk and the Corporation*, London: Euromoney Publications, 1980, pp. i45–158.
4. M. Adler and B. Dumas, "International Portfolio Choice and Corporation Finance: A Synthesis," *Journal of Finance* (June 1983), pp. 925–984.
5. D. P. Baron, "Flexible Exchange Rates, Forward Markets and the Level of Trade," *American Economic Review* (June 1976), pp. 253–266.

[14]An extended example which illustrates the requisite simulation analysis in a simple one-period setting with two states of nature appears in Adler and Dumas [2]. Adding states presents no particular difficulties. The multiperiod extension is more problematic. It could conceivably be structured as a (complex) dynamic program. Shapiro and Rutenberg [15] reveals the hazards of such efforts.

6. B. Cornell and A. C. Shapiro, "Managing Foreign Exchange Risks," *Midland Corporate Finance Journal* (Fall 1983), pp. 16–31.
7. B. Dumas, "The Theory of the Trading Firm Revisited," *Journal of Finance* (June 1978), pp. 1019–1029.
8. M. R. Eaker, "The Numeraire Problem and Foreign Exchange Risk," *Journal of Finance* (May 1981), pp. 419–426.
9. L. H. Ederington, "The Hedging Performance of the New Futures Markets," *Journal of Finance* (March 1979), pp. 157–170.
10. D. K. Eiteman and A. I. Stonehill, *Multinational Business Finance*, 3rd edition, Reading, Mass., Addison-Wesley, 1983.
11. S. Laursen and L. Metzler, "Flexible Exchange Rates and the Theory of Employment," *Review of Economics and Statistics* (November 1950), pp. 281–299.
12. D. E. Logue and G. S. Oldfield, "Managing Foreign Assets When Foreign Exchange Markets are Efficient, *Financial Management* (Summer 1977), pp. 16–22.
13. W. Poole, "Speculative Prices as Random Walks: An Analysis of Ten Time Series of Flexible Exchange Rates," *Southern Economic Journal* (1968).
14. M. E. Rubinstein, "The Valuation of Uncertain Income Streams and the Pricing of Options," *Bell Journal of Economics* (Autumn 1976), pp. 407–425.
15. A. C. Shapiro and D. P. Rutenberg, "When to Hedge Against Devaluation," *Management Science* (August 1974), pp. 1514–1530.
16. A. C. Shapiro, *Multinational Financial Management*, Boston, Allyn & Bacon, 1982.

APPENDIX

This Appendix offers a general and intuitively appealing definition of exposure and links it with hedging. Under specific assumptions exposure boils down to a (partial) regression coefficient. Hedging in the amount of the exposure minimizes the variance of the hedged position and leaves a residual rendomness that is independent of exchange rates.

Consider the random dollar price, P, of a risky asset on a given future date. The number of states of nature, K, is finite with known probabilities. In a given state, k, the outcome P_k is associated with a vector of state variables, $S_k = \{S_1, \ldots, S_n\}_k$, which may include exchange rates if these are called for by some underlying theory. Let S_i represent the ith state variable. Following Adler and Dumas [2], we may then define:

$$\text{Exposure of P to } S_i = E(\partial S_i)$$

This defines exposure as the current expectation, across future states of nature, of the partial sensitivity of P to S_i, the effects of all other variables held constant. The definition is intuitive and quite general. For the exposure to be hedgeable, side bets such as forward contracts on S_i must be possible and available.

When P and S are jointly normal, exposure as defined by (3) becomes the partial regression coefficient of S_i in a linear regression of P on S. This rests on two previous results. Rubinstein [14] considered the pricing of a contingent claim on P, g(P), in the presence of a single state variable S. When P and S are jointly normal, he obtained that:

$$\text{cov}[g(P),\ S] = E[g'(P)]\ \text{cov}(P,S)$$

Utilizing the same setting, Adler and Dumas [2] extended this result and showed that:

$$E\left\{\frac{\partial E[g(P)|S]}{\partial S}\right\} = \frac{\text{cov}[g(P),\ S]}{\text{var}\ (S)} = E[g'(P)]b_{p|s}$$

where $b_{p|s}$ is the regression coefficient of P on S, in the bivariate case.

The application of these relationships to present needs is immediate. First, note that in connection with exposure measurement, $g(P) = P$ so that $g'(P) = 1$ in all states of nature. Second, the definition of exposure can therefore be rewritten in the multivariate case as:

$$\begin{aligned} E(\partial P/\partial S_i) &= E\left\{\frac{\partial E[(P)|S]}{\partial S}\right\} \\ &= \text{cov}[S_i,\ P|S]/\text{var}(S_i) \\ &= b_{p\cdot s_i|s} \end{aligned}$$

where $b_{p\cdot s_i|s}$ is the partial regression coefficient on S_i in a regression of P on S. The extension to jointly lognormal random variables is equally immediate, with similar results.

The link between exposure and hedging can easily be inferred from the futures literature. The requisite insight emerges from a modification of Ederington [9].

Let P, as before, be the future price of a risky asset with current price P_o. Assume that there exists a costless forward sale contract on state variable S: the current forward price is F_o. At maturity the random gain or loss on the contract is $(F_o - S)$. Define the expected return and variance of a portfolio consisting of w_p units of P and w_s units of the forward contract:

$$\begin{aligned} E(R) &= w_p E(P - P_o) + w_s E(F_o - S) \\ \text{var}(R) &= w_n^2\ \text{var}(P) + w_s^2\ \text{var}(S) - 2\ w_p\ w_s \\ &\quad \text{cov}(P,S) \\ w_n &= a w_p \end{aligned}$$

Let

$$w_s = a w_p$$

In the futures literature, $a = w_s/w_p$ is called the hedge ratio or the proportion of the spot position that is hedged. In our terminology, the optimal value of a is the exposure. Substituting, we rewrite

$$\text{var}(R) = w_p^2\ \text{var}(P) + a^2\ w_p^2\ \text{var}(S) - 2\ w_p^2\ a\ \text{cov}(P,S)$$

The regression coefficient definition emerges from computing the minimum variance hedge, a^*:

$$\begin{aligned} \partial \text{var}\ (R)/\partial a &= 2w_p^2[a\ \text{var}(S) - \text{cov}(P,S)] = 0 \\ \Rightarrow a^* &= \text{cov}(P,S)/\text{var}(S) = b_{p|s} \end{aligned}$$

In short, when hedging so as to minimize the variance of the hedged position, one should hedge in the amount of the exposure.

We next show that, after hedging the exposure, the residual randomness of the hedged position is independent of S. First, we specify the regression to measure the exposure:

$$P = a + bS + e$$

where

a = regression constant;
b = regression coefficient, the exposure;
e = regression residual; where by construction,
$E(e) = 0 = \text{cov}(e,S)$; and
E = expectation, denoted by a superbar: $E(X) = \bar{X}$

The linear regression technique produces the following definitions:

$$a = \bar{P} - b\bar{S}$$

$$b = \text{cov}(P,S)/\text{var}(S), \text{ so that}$$

$$E(P|S) = a + b\bar{S}$$

$$\text{var}(P|S) = b^2 \text{ var}(S) + \text{var}(e), \text{ since } \text{cov}(e,S) = 0.$$

The random dollar value, R, of a position consisting of one dollar's worth of P hedged by the forward sale of b units of S at the forward rate F_o is:

$$R = P + b\,(F_o - S)$$

The variance of the hedged position is given by:

$$\begin{aligned} \text{var}(R) &= \text{var}(P - bS) \\ &= E(P - bS - \bar{P} + b\bar{S})^2 \\ &= E[(P - \bar{P}) - b(S - \bar{S})]^2 \\ &= E[(P - \bar{P})^2 - 2b(P - \bar{P})(S - \bar{S}) + b^2 (S - \bar{S})^2] \\ &= \text{var}(P) - 2b \text{ cov}(P,S) + b^2 \text{ var}(S) \end{aligned}$$

Recall from the definition of the regression parameters that:

$$\text{cov}(P,S) = b \text{ var}(S)$$

$$b^2 \text{ var}(S) = \text{var}(P) - \text{var}(e).$$

Hence, after substitution and rearrangement:

$$\text{var}(R) = \text{var}(e).$$

What we have shown is that the variance of the hedged position is equal to the variance of the regression error. Since this residual is *by construction* independent of S, so therefore is R. In other words,

$$\begin{aligned} \text{cov}(R,S) &= E[(P - bS - \bar{P} + b\bar{S})(S - \bar{S})] \\ &= \text{cov}(P,S) - b \text{ var}(S) \\ &= 0, \text{ by virtue of the definition of } b \end{aligned}$$

19

Managing Foreign Exchange Risk*

Bradford Cornell and Alan C. Shapiro

Since the introduction of the floating-exchange rate regime in 1973, foreign exchange risk has become of increasing concern to firms doing business internationally. With their integrated cross-border production and market operations, multinational corporations (MNCs) continually face devaluation or revaluation worries somewhere in the world. Hardly a day passes without a multinational announcing a foreign exchange gain or loss. And although the recent adoption of FAS #52 may do much to reduce the wild swings in the translated earnings of overseas subsidiaries, the problem of coping with volatile currencies remains essentially unchanged. Those MNCs which hedged FAS #8 earnings in the past will doubtless abandon their previous hedging strategies (which, as we shall argue, were misguided in the first place). But, fluctuations in exchange rates will nevertheless continue to have "real" effects on the cash profitability of foreign subsidiaries, complicating overseas selling, pricing, and buying decisions.

Many MNCs have responded to increased currency volatility, and the resulting greater uncertainty, by devoting more resources to the management of foreign exchange risk. Most existing corporate programs, however, lack a coherent and theoretically sound approach to the problem. The development of an effective strategy for managing currency risk should proceed in three distinct stages. First, management should determine what is at risk, and this requires an appropriate definition of foreign exchange risk. Second, it must clearly identify the objectives of its exchange risk management program. This step is important not only because success can only be measured relative to objectives, but because in practice the fundamental purpose of exchange risk management is often lost sight of or subordinated to other concerns: hedging specific transactions, reducing the variability of translated earnings, and even speculating on foreign currencies. Third, having determined the extent of its exposure to currency risk and defined its objectives, management can then design a set of company-wide policies to achieve its objectives.

This article attempts to guide management's thinking through each of these stages of development. The first section discusses the nature and origins of exchange risk. The second develops a theory of the "economic," as distinguished from the accounting, consequences of currency changes on a firm's value. The third evaluates current hedging practices and goals, concluding with a statement of our own view of the proper objective of multinational currency risk management. The fourth section offers suggestions for a comprehensive strategy for managing exchange risk—one designed to cope with both anticipated and unanticipated currency changes. Unlike the conventional recommendations of financial advisors, which generally focus exclusively on financial hedging, our proposed strategy for managing exchange risk calls for the integration of marketing and production decisions with more traditional financial responses.

---

*This article is reprinted, with permission, from *Midland Corporate Finance Journal,* vol. 1, no. 3, Fall 1983, published by Stern, Stewart, Putnam, and Macklis, Ltd., Corporate Financial Consultants.

FOREIGN EXCHANGE RISK AND EXPOSURE

As a result of its investment, production, and other operating decisions, a firm generates both a current structure of assets and liabilities, and a stream of expected future cash flows. A comprehensive program for managing exchange risk should attempt to incorporate expectations about changes in exchange rates into *all* basic corporate decisions affecting cash flow and financial structure. Once having assessed the effects of possible currency changes on the cash generation and financial structure of the firm, management is then in a position to decide whether to "self-insure" the risks of unanticipated (and largely diversifiable) currency fluctuations or to "lay them off" to financial markets.

Prior to making this decision, then, management must begin by determining what is at risk. Throughout this article, we will define exchange risk as the variability in the value of a firm—as measured by the present value of its expected future cash flows—caused by uncertain exchange rate changes. Thus, exchange risk is viewed as the possibility that currency fluctuations can alter the expected amounts or variability of the firm's future cash flows.

In choosing a definition of exchange risk based on market value, we are assuming that management's goal is to maximize the value of the firm. Whether management actually behaves in this fashion has been vigorously debated. Clearly, some managers will prefer to pursue other objectives. In fact, many, if not indeed most, multinational financial managers probably consider the reduction of the variability of translated earnings as the principal function of exchange risk management. Such a concern was clearly behind the earlier widespread practice of hedging FAS #8 earnings. Nevertheless, the assumption that management attempts to maximize (risk-adjusted) after-tax cash flow remains standard in much of the finance literature. Moreover, the principle of stockholder wealth maximization provides a rational guide to financial decision-making.

The companion to value maximization is market efficiency. If the capital market did not rationally price the firm's securities, managers would be hard pressed to design a foreign exchange strategy which could be expected to maximize firm value. Fortunately, there is strong evidence that capital markets are relatively sophisticated in responding to publicly available information. Most of the large body of research on financial markets suggests that when accounting numbers diverge significantly from cash flows, changes in security prices generally reflect changes in cash flows rather than reported earnings.

Our definition of exchange risk is very different from that employed by accountants, who rely on a balance sheet approach to measure exposure to exchange rate changes. Those who use an accounting definition—whether FAS #8, FAS #52, or some other method—divide the balance sheet's assets and liabilities into those accounts that will be affected by exchange rate changes and those that will not. The value of assets and liabilities are then translated back into the domestic currency.

The problem with this accounting approach is that book values and market values typically differ, so that the change in net worth produced by a movement in exchange rates often bears little relationship to the change in the value of the firm. And even if management focuses on the real instead of the accounting effects of currency changes, it still faces another problem. No matter how careful it is in measuring the true economic consequences of currency changes, management still has a fundamentally flawed picture of the firm's actual exposure unless it takes into account two key equilibrium relationships observed in international financial markets: Purchasing Power Parity and the International Fisher Effect.

The theory of purchasing power parity (PPP) maintains that changes in the ratio of domestic to foreign prices will cause offsetting changes in the exchange rate so as to maintain the relative purchasing powers of the currencies involved. Although purchasing power parity does not hold exactly, a large portion of exchange rate changes over the long run are explained by equal and opposite changes in national price levels.

The International Fisher Effect says that returns on assets held and the costs of liabilities incurred (should) implicitly incorporate anticipated currency changes. In other words, the difference in interest rates between countries (holding risk constant) should equal the expected change in the exchange rate during the term of the loan. For example, if the one-year U.S. interest rate is 10 percent while the equivalent English interest rate is 15 percent, the International Fisher Effect says that the pound is expected to decline by about 5 percent during the year. Of course, after the fact, interest rates adjusted for currency changes usually diverge from such expectations. This is because unexpected exchange rate changes occur. However, it is impossible, by definition, to expect to profit consistently from changes that are unexpected. All that the International Fisher Effect predicts is that, over time, exchange gains or losses on debt denominated in currencies likely to appreciate will be offset by lower interest rates and, on debt denominated in currencies likely to depreciate, by higher interest rates. This prediction appears to be borne out by the available empirical evidence.

Only by explicitly recognizing the implications of these equilibrium relationships for the estimation and valuation of future cash flows can we hope to come to grips with the problems of determining a firm's true economic exposure.

ACCOUNTING VERSUS ECONOMIC EXPOSURE

Accounting exposure arises from the need, for purposes of reporting and consolidation, to convert the results of foreign operations from local currencies (LCs) to the home currency (HC). When an exchange rate changes, this translation or restatement of the various accounts denominated in the foreign currency leads to a new accounting measurement of the dollar value of the firm's investment in the foreign subsidiary (or in the asset or liability itself). If translation gains and losses are recorded on the income statement, then this also results in a change in reported earnings. The possible size of this change in earnings is known as *translation exposure* to foreign exchange risk.

It has become clear, however, that retrospective accounting techniques, no matter how refined, cannot truly account for the economic effects of devaluation or revaluation on the value of a firm. The inevitable result of using an inappropriate definition of exposure is that the impact of exchange rate changes, as recorded on a firm's balance sheet and income statements, is so distorted as to make accounting results of little use to either investors or corporate managers. Because of this accounting distortion of economic reality, many multinational firms are now taking a longer-term look at their degree of exchange risk. This involves focusing on the firm's economic exposure.

Economic exposure to exchange risk, which we defined earlier as the extent to which the firm's value will be affected by changes in exchange rates, can in turn be separated into two components: transaction exposure and real operating exposure. *Transaction exposure* is the possibility of incurring exchange gains or losses, upon settlement at a future date, on transactions already entered into and denominated in a foreign currency. Some of these unsettled transactions, including foreign currency-denominated debt and accounts receivable, are already listed on the firm's balance sheet. But other obligations, such as contracts for future sales or purchases, are not. Although transaction exposure is often included under accounting exposure, it is more properly a cash flow exposure and, hence, part of economic exposure.

Real operating expousre is the possibility that currency fluctuations, together with price changes, can alter the expected amounts or variability of a company's future revenue and cost streams—in short, its operating cash flows. Measuring operating exposure requires a longer-term perspective, one which views the firm as an ongoing operation whose cost and price competitiveness will be affected by exchange rate changes.

The measurement of economic exposure is made especially difficult because it is impossible to assess the effects of an exchange rate change without simultaneously considering the impact on cash flows of the underlying relative rates of inflation in each currency. It is also necessary to consider the extent to which exchange rate changes cause *relative* price changes—that is, changes in the ratio of prices of individual goods, like oil, to the general level of prices. For example, in 1974 the price of gas fuels rose by 33.6 percent while the wholesale price index increased by only 8.0 percent. Thus, the year was characterized both by general inflation and by an increase in the relative price of oil. As you might expect, the press frequently confused the two events and attributed the effects of an increase in the relative price of oil to inflation.

The distinction between inflation and relative price changes is important because both affect exchange rates, but they have vastly different implications for exchange risk. As we shall show, a dramatic change in an exchange rate accompanied by an equal change in the price level will not alter real cash flows as long as relative prices remain constant.

Inflation and Exchange Rates

Let's begin by holding relative prices constant and looking only at the effects of general inflation. This means that if the inflation rate is 10 percent, the price of every good in the economy rises by 10 percent. In addition, we initially assume that all goods are traded in a competitive world market without transaction costs, tariffs, or taxes of any kind. Given these conditions, economic theory tells us that the law of one price must prevail; that is, the price of any good, measured in a common currency, must be equal in all countries.

If the law of one price holds, and if there is no variation in the relative prices of goods or services, then the rate of change in the exchange rate must equal the difference between the inflation rates in the two countries. Purchasing power parity does not imply that exchange rate changes will necessarily be small or easy to forecast. If a country has high and unpredictable inflation, like Argentina, then the country's exchange rate will also fluctuate randomly.

Nonetheless, without relative price changes, a multinational company faces no real operating exchange risk. As long as the firm avoids contracts fixed in foreign currency terms, its foreign cash flows will vary with the foreign rate of inflation. Because the exchange rate also depends on the difference between the foreign and the domestic rates of inflation, the movement of the exchange rate exactly cancels the change in the foreign price level, leaving dollar cash flows unaffected.

Of course, the above conclusion does not hold if the firm enters into contracts fixed in terms of the foreign currency. Examples of such contracts are fixed-rate debt, long-term leases, labor contracts and rent. However, the risk introduced by entering into fixed contracts is not exchange risk; it is inflation risk. For instance, an Argentine firm with fixed-rate debt in pesos faces the same risk as the subsidiary of an American firm with peso debt. If the rate of inflation in Argentina declines, the real interest cost of the debt rises and the real cash flow of both companies falls. The solution to the problem of inflation risk is to avoid writing contracts fixed in nominal terms in countries with unpredictable inflation. If the contracts are indexed, and if purchasing power parity holds, exchange risk is eliminated.

Relative Prices and Exchange Rates

In general, exchange rate changes occur in conjunction with relative price changes. But unless exchange rate changes are themselves the cause of relative price changes, what is usually termed "exchange risk" may be just the risk of relative price changes within and between countries. For example, the revaluations of the mark and the yen in the late 1970s are often blamed for shifting the export mix of West German and Japanese companies toward more technologically sophisticated and capital-intensive products. It is more likely, however, that these changes were dictated by technological advances in Germany and Japan which reduced capital costs relative to labor costs. By making German and Japanese goods more competitive, such advances were largely responsible both for the shift in exports and for the appreciation of the yen and mark.

The above example notwithstanding, changes in exchange rates can cause relative price changes. During the late 1970s worldwide demand for Swiss franc-denominated assets caused the Swiss franc to appreciate against the dollar by more than the inflation differential between the two countries. As a result, Swiss watchmakers were squeezed. Because of competition from Japanese companies, Swiss firms could not significantly raise the dollar price of watches sold in the United States. Yet, at the same time, the *dollar* cost of Swiss labor was rising because the franc wage rate remained unchanged, while the franc was appreciating against the dollar.

Real long-run exchange risk, then, is largely the risk associated with relative price changes that are brought about by currency changes. Such relative price changes are most likely to occur when a government intervenes to control prices and/or wages. For example, devaluations are generally accompanied by the imposition of price controls. These controls can benefit a multinational corporation that has a foreign subsidiary producing locally for export; the cost of wages and other local inputs remains largely unchanged while the devaluation makes exports more competitive, or even allows the subsidiary to raise prices abroad. By contrast, a subsidiary with extensive domestic sales will likely be hurt by price controls. For instance, following the recent floating of the peso, the Mexican government threatened "price gougers" with jail sentences. In this circumstance, price gougers were domestic and foreign businessmen raising prices to offset the effect of the devaluation on their cash flow.

To summarize, the economic impact of a currency change on a firm depends on whether the exchange rate is fully offset by the difference in inflation rates or whether, because of price controls, a shift in monetary policy, or some other reason, the exchange rate change results in relative price changes. It is these relative price changes that ultimately affect the value of the firm.

MEASURING ECONOMIC EXPOSURE

A hypothetical example illustrates our proposed procedure for measuring economic exposure to currency risk.[1] It also shows how the conventional accounting measure of translation exposure fails to represent real operating exposure.

Spectrum Manufacturing AB is the wholly-owned Swedish affiliate of a U.S. multinational industrial plastics firm. It manufacturers patented sheet plastic in Sweden. Sixty percent of its output is currently sold in Sweden and the remaining 40 percent is exported to other European countries. Spectrum uses only Swedish labor in its manufacturing process, but sources its raw material both locally and overseas. The effective Swedish tax rate on corporate profits is 40 percent. The annual depreciation charge on plant and equipment is Skr 9000,000. In addition, Spectrum AB has Skr 3 million in debt outstanding, with interest payable at 10 percent annually.

Based on the current exchange rate of Skr 4 = $1, Spectrum's projected sales, costs, after-tax income, and cash flow for the coming year are presented in Exhibit 1. All sales are invoiced in kronor.

Accounts receivable equal one-fourth of annual sales; i.e., the average collection period is ninety days. Inventory is carried at direct cost, valued on a last-in, first-out (LIFO) basis, and also equals 90 days' worth of sales. Accounts payable average 10 percent of sales while cash equaling 50 percent of sales is typically held. Spectrum's balance sheet (before any exchange rate change) is as shown in Exhibit 2.

Spectrum's Accounting Exposure

To contrast the economic and accounting approaches to measuring exposure, let's assume that the Swedish krona devaluates 20 percent, from Skr 4 = $1 to Skr 5 = $1. According to the current rate method of accounting for currency translation, as mandated by FAS # 52, Spectrum would have to recognize a loss of $935,000. (See Exhibit 3.)

Spectrum's Economic Exposure

On the basis of the information currently available, it is impossible to anticipate the economic impact of the krona devaluation. Therefore, two different scenarios have been constructed, and Spectrum's economic exposure has been calculated under each. These two scenarios are based on the following assumptions:

1. All variables remain the same.
2. Partial increases in prices, costs, and volume.

Scenario 1: All Variables Remain the Same

If all prices remain the same (in kronor) and sales volume does not change, then Spectrum's krona cash flow will stay at Skr 3,600,000. At the new exchange rate, this equals 3,600,000 × .2 dollars, or $720,000. Then the net loss in dollar operating cash flow the first year can be calculated as follows:

First-year cash flow (Skr 4 = $1)	$900,000
First-year cash flow (skr 5 = $1)	720,000
Net loss from devaluation	$180,000

[1]This example is based on a more extensive one presented in Alan C. Shapiro, *Multinational Financial Management* (Boston: Allyn & Bacon, 1982) pp. 132–140.

EXHIBIT 1

Summary of Projected Operations for Spectrum Manufacturing AB: Base Case

	Units (hundred thousand)	Unit Price (Skr)		Total (Skr)
Domestic sales	6	20		12,000,000
Export sales	4	20		8,000,000
Total revenue				**20,000,000**
Local labor (man-hours)	1.5	40		6,000,000
Local material	8	3		2,400,000
Imported material	6	4		2,400,000
Total operation expenditure				**10,800,000**
Net operating income			Skr	9,200,000
Overhead expenses				3,500,000
Interest on krona debt (@ 10%)				300,000
Depreciation				900,000
Total other expenses				**4,700,000**
Net profit before tax			Skr	4,500,000
Income tax @ 40%				1,800,000
Profit after tax			**Skr**	**2,700,000**
Add back depreciation				900,000
Net cash flow in kronor			Skr	3,600,000
Net cash flow in dollars (Skr 4 = $1)			**$**	**900,000**

EXHIBIT 2

Balance Sheet for Spectrum Manufacturing AB (Skr): Base Case

Assets		Liabilities	
Cash	1,000,000	Accounts payable	2,000,000
Accts Rec.	5,000,000	Long-term debt	3,000,000
Inventory	2,700,000	Total liabilities	5,000,000
Net fixed assets	10,000,000	Equity	13,700,000
Total assets	**18,700,000**	**Total liabilities & equity**	**18,700,000**

EXHIBIT 3

Impact of Krona Devaluation on Spectrum AB's Financial Statements

Assets and Liabilities		Kronor	U.S. dollars before krona devaluation (Skr 4 = $1)	U.S. dollars after krona devaluation (Skr 5 = $1)
Cash		1,000,000	250,000	200,000
Accounts		5,000,000	1,250,000	1,000,000
Inventory		2,700,000	675,000	540,000
Net fixed assets		10,000,000	2,500,000	2,000,000
Total assets	**Skr**	**18,700,000**	**$4,675,000**	**$3,740,000**
Accounts payable		2,000,000	500,000	400,000
Long-term debt		3,000,000	750,000	600,000
Equity		**13,700,000**	**3,425,000**	**2,740,000**
Total liabilities plus equity	Skr	18,700,000	$4,675,000	$3,740,000
Translation gain (loss)				**$(935,000)**

Moreover, this loss will continue until relative prices adjust. Part of this loss, however, will be offset by the $150,000 gain that will be realized at the end of year 3 when Skr 3 million loan is repaid (3 million × .05).[2] If a three-year adjustment process is assumed, then the present value of the economic loss from operations associated with the krona devaluation, using a 15 percent discount rate, equals $314,420 as follows:

Present Year	Postdevaluation Cash Flow		Predevaluation Cash Flow		Change in Cash Flow		15% Present Value Factor		Value
	(1)	−	(2)	=	(3)	×	(4)	=	(5)
1	$720,000		$900,000		−$180,000		.870		−$156,600
2	720,000		900,000		−180,000		.756		−136,080
3	870,000[a]		900,000		−30,000		.658		−19,740
Net loss									−$312,420

[a]Includes a gain of $150,000 on loan repayment.

This loss is primarily due to the inability of Spectrum to raise its sales price. The resulting constant krona profit margin tranlates into a 20 percent reduction in dollar

[2]For a systematic approach to calculating the after-tax costs of borrowing in foreign currencies, see Alan C. Shapiro (1975), "Evaluating Financing Costs for Multinational Subsidiaries," *Journal of International Business Studies*, Fall, pp. 24–32.

profits. Note, however, that the economic loss of $312,420 contrasts markedly with the accounting recognition of a $935,000 loss under FAS #52.

Scenario 2: Partial Increases in Prices, Costs, and Volumes

In reality, of course, prices, costs, volumes, and the input mix are likely to adjust somewhat. It is assumed here that the sales price at home rises by 10 percent to Skr 22 while the export price is raised to Skr 24, still providing a competitive advantage in dollar terms over foreign products. This results in a 20 percent increase in domestic sales and a 15 percent increase in export sales.

Total input prices are assumed to go up by 15 percent while the dollar price of imported material stays at its earlier level. This leads to some substitution of imported for domestic goods. Overhead expenses rise by only 10 percent because some components of this account, such as rent and local taxes, are fixed in value.

The net result of all these adjustments is an operating cash flow of $1,010,800, a *gain* of $110,800 over the predevaluation level of $900,000. (Exhibit 4.)

From this translated operating cash flow of $1,010,800 must be subtracted, in the first year, the $388,890 cash outflow associated with higher working capital requirements.

EXHIBIT 4

Summary of Projected Operations for Spectrum Manufacturing AB: Scenario 2

	Units (hundred thousand)	Unit Price (Skr)		Total (Skr)
Domestic sales	7.2	22		15,840,000
Export sales	4.6	24		11,040,000
Total revenue				**26,880,000**
Local labor (man-hours)	1.77	46		8,142,000
Local material	10.62	3.45		3,664,000
Imported material	6.2	5		3,100,000
Total operation expenditure				**14,906,000**
Net operating income			Skr	11,974,000
Overhead expenses				3,850,000
Interest on krona debt (@ 10%)				300,000
Depreciation				900,000
Total other expenses				**5,050,000**
Net profit before tax			Skr	6,924,000
Income tax @ 40%				2,769,000
Profit after tax			**Skr**	**4,154,000**
Add back depreciation				900,000
Net cash flow in kronor			Skr	5,054,000
Net cash flow in dollars (Skr 5 = $1)			**$**	**1,010,800**

EXHIBIT 5

Working Capital Requirements (Skr): Scenario 2

	Predevaluation	Postdevaluation	Net Change
Cash (5% of Sales)	1,000,000	1,344,000	344,000
Accounts receivable (25% of sales)	5,000,000	6,720,000	1,720,000
Inventory (25% of direct cost)	2,700,000	3,268,449[a]	568,449
Accounts payable	2,000,000	2,688,000	688,000
Net working capital	**Skr 6,700,000**	**Skr 8,644,449**	**Skr 1,944,449**
Increase in working capital, in dollars (Skr 5 = $1)			$388,890

[a] Sales volume rises by 180,000 units requiring an additional 45,000 units of inventory at a cost of Skr 568,449.

(The derivation of this figure is presented in Exhibit 5.) Inventory requirements increase to reflect the combination of an 18 percent higher unit sales volume and a 17 percent increase in unit costs, for an overall increase of 21 percent in krona terms (.18 × 1.17), or Skr 568,449.

Over the next three years, Spectrum's cash flows and its economic value will change as follows:

Year	Postdevaluation Cash Flow		Predevaluation Cash Flow		Change in Cash Flow		15% Present Value Factor		Present Value
	(1)	−	(2)	=	(3)	×	(4)	=	(5)
1	$ 621,910[a]		$900,000		−$278,090		.870		−$241,938
2	1,010,800		900,000		110,800		.756		83,765
3	1,160,800[b]		900,000		260,000		.658		171,080
Net loss									$12,907

[a] Includes $388,890 working capital outflow.

[b] Includes $150,000 gain on loan repayment.

Thus, under the latter scenario, the economic value of the firm actually *increases* by $12,907 as a result of the devaluation. The gain on loan repayment and on operating cash flows just manages to offset the additional investment required in working capital.

These two scenarios demonstrate the sensitivity of a firm's economic exposure to assumptions about its price elasticity of demand, its ability to adjust the input mix as relative costs change, its pricing flexibility, its use of local currency financing, and its ratio of net working capital to sales. Most important, though, this example makes clear the potentially large disparity between accounting-based measures of exchange gains or losses and the real impact of currency changes on a firm's value.

THE HEDGING DECISION

The preceding analysis implies that real economic exposure to exchange risk occurs under two general sets of circumstances:

1. Some cash flows are fixed in foreign currency terms.
2. Exchange rate changes cause relative price changes.

Of the two sources of risk, the second is the more significant. For one thing, in countries with high and variable inflation, fixed currency contracts are avoided as a matter of course; even taxes are indexed. Second, most of the month-to-month variation in exchange rates is unrelated to differential inflation rates. On the basis of a detailed study of 23 pairs of countries, Richard Roll reported that less than 10 percent of the monthly variation in any exchange rate is due to inflation. The 10 percent figure, furthermore, is for pairs of countries like the United States and Argentina, where the annual inflation differential is close to 100 percent. For pairs like the United States and Germany, where the inflation differential is small, inflation typically accounts for less than 2 percent of the monthly variation in exchange rates. In other words, there is a very strong relationship between exchange rate changes and relative price changes. Although Roll's work does not allow him to determine whether exchange rate changes cause relative price changes or vice versa, it seems clear that currency appreciations or depreciations are likely to affect relative prices—at least in the short run.[3]

To apply our theory of exchange risk to the individual firm requires a forecast of the relation between exchange rates, relative prices, and the company's real cash flow. Management should begin by considering possible future currency changes that would affect its business. For example, a U.S. firm selling products in West Germany might examine the possibility of a deutsche mark revaluation or a dollar devaluation. (Incidentally, such a firm might find that a devaluation of the French franc would affect its sales as strongly as would a change in the dollar-deutsche mark exchange rate, since France is West Germany's major trading partner.) Next, for each scenario, the projected effect of the devaluation or revaluation on relative prices and hence on the company's sales, costs, and capital requirements should be estimated, thus enabling management to derive an estimate of cash flow.

Then, by assigning probabilities to each of the scenarios, the expected level of cash flow and its variability can be estimated. Finally, the manager should evaluate how a foreign government is likely to respond to a devaluation or revaluation of its currency. Will price controls be imposed? If controls are introduced, will they be general or will certain goods be exempted? Will the local government act to prevent repatriation of profits, thereby reducing the parent's cash flow?

Obviously, the range of possible scenarios is infinite and the costs of gathering the required information can be substantial. Consequently, in selecting scenarios to evaluate, management should concentrate its efforts on those scenarios that have a high probability of occurrence and would also have a major impact on the firm.

The Value of Hedging

Given a forecast of the future relation between real cash flows and exchange rates, management must next decide whether to hedge or take other action to reduce exchange risk. As shown earlier, the real impact of nominal currency changes will probably be less severe than is generally supposed, primarily because of the offsetting effects of inflation.

[3]See Richard Roll, "Violations of the Law of One Price and Their Implications for Differentially Denominated Assets," in Marshall Sarnat and Georgio Szego, eds. *International Finance and Trade*, Vol. I, (Cambridge, Mass: Ballinger, 1979).

Even in cases where significant exchange risk exists, however, it may not be in shareholders' interest to hedge for several reasons. First, shareholders can reduce the risk of currency fluctuation by holding well-diversified portfolios. Second, shareholders may actually prefer that a portion of their returns be dominated in a foreign currency. If an investor purchases Japanese goods, his overall risk will be reduced by having yen inflows to match his yen outflows. Finally, hedging is expensive. Steven Kohlhagen estimates that a simple strategy of forward hedging in the major currencies costs about 0.65 percent per year.[4] And borrowing in local currency, when points and other fees are considered, is likely to be even more costly than forward cover. Of course, there is often no alternative to local borrowing because active forward markets exist in less than a dozen currencies.

It is also important to recognize that management cannot hedge against *anticipated* movements in exchange rates. Studies by Cornell and others show that the anticipated change in the exchange rate is reflected in the forward premium and the interest rate differential.[5] In the case of Mexico, for instance, the one year forward discount in the futures market was close to 100 percent just before the peso was floated.

Local borrowing and forward covering are not the only means of reducing exchange risk. Other standard techniques for hedging against possible devaluation are these:

- Reducing levels of local currency cash and marketable securities.
- Delaying payment of accounts payable.
- Invoicing exports in foreign currency and imports in local currency.
- Tightening trade credit in local currency.

Such techniques, however, are vastly overrated. If a devaluation is unlikely, they are costly and inefficient ways of doing business. If a devaluation is expected, as in the recent case of Mexico, then the cost of using the techniques, like the cost of local borrowing, rises to reflect the anticipated devaluation. Just prior to the Mexican devaluation, for example, every company in Mexico was trying to delay peso payments. Of course, this cannot produce a net gain because one company's payable is another company's receivable. As another example, if one company wants peso trade credit, another must offer it. Assuming that both the borrower and the lender are rational, a deal will not be struck until the interest cost rises to reflect the expected decline in the peso.

A company can benefit from the above strategies only to the extent that it can estimate the probability and timing of a devaluation with greater accuracy than the general market. Attempting to profit from foreign exchange forecasting, however, is speculating, not hedging. The hedger is well-advised to assume that the market knows as much as he does. Those who feel that they have superior information will choose to speculate, but this activity should not be confused with hedging.

Under some circumstances it is possible for a company to benefit at the expense of the local government without speculating. If exchange controls are not imposed to prevent capital outflows and if hard currency can be acquired at the official exchange rate, then money can be moved out of the country via intercompany payments. For instance, a

[4]See Steven W. Kohlhagen, "Evidence on the Cost of Forward Cover in a Floating System," *Euromoney* (September, 1975), pp. 138–141.

[5]See Bradford Cornell, "Spot Rates, Forward Rates and Market Efficiency," *Journal of Financial Economics* 5, (1977), pp. 55–65.

subsidiary can speed payment of intercompany accounts payable, make immediate purchases from other subsidiaries, or speed remittances to the parent. Unfortunately, governments are not unaware of these tactics. During a currency crisis, when hard currency is scarce, the local government can be expected to block such transfers, or at least make them more expensive.

Hedging Objectives

Management's decision about the specific financial hedging tactics and strategy to pursue will largely be determined by its objectives. These objectives, in turn, should reflect management's view of the world, particularly its beliefs about how markets work. Before setting its own hedging objectives, management should ask itself the key question posed by Gunter Dufey: "Could we profitably exist as a purely financial institution?"[6] Honest introspection would reveal that most companies earn their keep because of their superior marketing, production, organization, and technological skills.

There are two principal implications of this doctrine of "comparative advantage" for exchange risk management:

1. The principal exposure management goal of financial executives should be to arrange their firm's financial affairs in such a way as to minimize the real (as opposed to accounting) effects of exchange rate changes, subject to the costs of such rearrangements.
2. The major burden of exchange risk management must fall on the shoulders of marketing and production executives. They deal in imperfect product and factor markets where their specialized knowledge provides them with a real advantage; that is, they should be able consistently to outperform their competitors in the markets in which they operate because of their superior knowledge.

MANAGING EXCHANGE RISK

As we argued earlier, in order for a devaluation or revaluation to significantly affect a firm's value, it must lead to changes in the relative prices of either the firm's inputs, or the products bought or sold in various countries. To the extent that exchange rate changes do bring about relative price changes, the firm's competitive situation will be altered. As a result, management may wish to adjust its production process or its marketing mix to accommodate the new set of relative prices. Conceptually, this is no different than the adjustment to changing relative prices within a country—for example, the adjustment to higher energy costs.

By making the necessary marketing and production revisions, the firm can either counteract the harmful effects of, or capitalize on the opportunities presented by, a currency appreciation or depreciation. To show how, we introduce the concept of the real exchange rate. The *real* exchange rate is defined as the *nominal*, or actual, exchange rate adjusted for relative inflation rates. Thus, if changes in the nominal rate are fully offset by changes in the relative price levels between the two countries, the real exchange rate remains unchanged. Only deviations from PPP result in a change in the real rate.

This distinction between the nominal exchange rate and the real rate has important

[6] "Corporate Financial Policies and Floating Exchange Rates," a paper presented at the meeting of the International Fiscal Association in Rome, October 14, 1974.

implications for those marketing and production decisions that bear on exchange risk. As we saw, nominal currency changes that are fully offset by differential inflation (and thus do not lead to relative price changes between economic sectors) do not entail a material degree of real exchange risk for a firm, unless that firm has major contractual agreements in the foreign currency. A real devaluation or revaluation of a particular currency, however, can strongly affect the competitive positions of local firms and their foreign competitors.

The appropriate response to an anticipated or an actual change in a real exchange rate depends crucially on the length of time that real change is expected to persist. For example, following a real home currency revaluation, an exporter has to decide whether and how much to raise its foreign currenty prices. If the change were expected to be temporary, and if regaining market share would be expensive, the exporter would probably prefer to maintain its foreign currency prices at existing levels. While this would mean a temporary reduction in unit profitability, the alternative—raising prices now and reducing them later when the real exchange rate declined—could be even more costly. A longer-lasting change in the real exchange rate, however, would probably lead the firm to raise its foreign currency prices, at the expense of losing some export sales. Assuming a still more permanent shift, management might choose to build production facilities overseas.

In the absence of government intervention in the foreign exchange markets, most real exchange rate changes are likely to be transitory. Permanent changes in real exchange rates are usually due to the pegging activities of central banks. Hence, in selecting appropriate exchange risk management strategies, the focus must be on the present and anticipated objectives and policies of the central banks in question. Predicting a government's likely response requires an evaluation of the key political decision-makers, their often conflicting economic goals, the economic consequences of a currency change on these goals, the ruling party's ideology, and internal and external political pressures. A persistent problem for forecasters in a system of "managed floating" such as currently exists is that there is no certainty about the desired currency level. In fact, government officials often deliberately maintain confusion in order to increase the uncertainty facing currency traders and thereby prevent or defer speculative "attacks" on their currencies.

The lack of clear-cut exchange rate objectives is due primarily to conflicting economic goals. Devaluation may stimulate exports and temporarily increase employment, but it is also likely to fuel inflation. On the other hand, a revaluation, while reducing the competitiveness of exports, also helps to reduce inflation by lowering the home currency cost of imported goods and services.

In the remainder of this section, we offer a set of currency management policies for dealing with those changes in nominal exchange rates that lead to relative price changes within or between countries.

Marketing Management of Exchange Risk

One of the international marketing manager's tasks should be to identify the likely effects of an exchange rate change and then act on them by adjusting pricing, product, credit, and market selection policies. Unfortunately, multinational marketing executives have generally ignored exchange risk management. Marketing programs are almost always "adjusted" only *after* changes in exchange rates. Yet the design of a firm's marketing strategy under conditions of home currency (HC) fluctuation presents considerable opportunity for gaining competitive leverage.

Market Selection

Major strategic questions for an exporter are the markets in which to sell and the relative marketing support to devote to each market. From an exposure point of view, a key consideration is the impact of currency changes on the revenue to be gained from future sales in individual countries. Marketing management must take into account its economic exposure and selectively adjust the marketing support, on a nation-by-nation basis, to maximize long-term profit.

It is also necessary to consider the issue of market segmentation within individual countries. A firm that sells differentiated products to more affluent customers may not be harmed as much by a foreign currency devaluation as a mass marketer. On the other hand, following a currency devaluation, a firm that sells primarily to upper income groups may find it is now able to penetrate mass markets abroad.

Market selection and market segmentation provide the basic parameters within which a company may adjust its marketing mix over time. In the short term, however, neither of these two basic strategic choices can be altered in reaction to actual or anticipated currency changes. Instead, the firm must select certain tactical responses such as adjustments of pricing, promotional and credit policies. In the long run, if deviations from PPP persist, the firm will have to revise its marketing strategy.

Pricing Strategy

A firm selling overseas should follow the standard economic proposition of setting the price that maximizes dollar (HC) profits (by equating marginal revenues and marginal costs). In making this determination, however, profits should be translated using the forward exchange rate that reflects the true expected dollar (HC) value of the receipts upon collection.

In the wake of a foreign currency devaluation, a firm selling in that market should consider opportunities to increase the foreign currency prices of its products. The problem, of course, is that producers in the country whose currency has devalued will now have a competitive cost advantage. They can use that advantage to expand their market share by maintaining, or increasing only slightly, their local currency prices. In any event, the existence of local competitors will limit an exporter's ability to recoup dollar profits by raising foreign currency selling prices.

At best, therefore, an exporter can raise its product prices by the extent of the devaluation. At worst, in an extremely competitive situation, the exporter is forced to absorb a reduction in home currency revenues equal to the percentage decline in the exchange rate. In the most likely case, foreign currency prices can be raised somewhat and the exporter will make up the difference through a lower profit margin on its foreign sales.

Under conditions of a real home currency devaluation, it follows that exports will gain a competitive price advantage on the world market. However, a company does not have to reduce export prices by the full amount of the devaluation. Instead, it has the option of increasing unit profitability (price skimming) or expanding its market share (penetration pricing). The decision is influenced by such factors as whether this change is likely to persist, economies of scale, the cost structure of expanding output, consumer price sensitivity, and the likelihood of attracting competition if high unit profitability is obvious.

The greater the price elasticity of demand, the greater is the incentive to hold down prices and thereby expand sales and revenues. Similarly, if significant economies of scale exist, it is generally worthwhile to hold down price, expand demand, and thereby lower unit production costs. The reverse is true if economies of scale are nonexistent or if the price elasticity is low.

In the case of pricing after devaluation, a domestic firm facing strong import competition may have much greater latitude in pricing. It then has the choice of potentially raising prices consistent with import price increases, or of holding prices constant in order to improve market share. Again, the strategy depends on such variables as economies of scale and consumer price sensitivity.

In early 1978, for instance, General Motors and Ford took advantage of price increases on competitive foreign autos to raise prices on their Chevette and Pinto models. The prices of those small cars had previously been held down, and even reduced, in an attempt to combat the growing market share of West German and Japanese imports. However, the declining value of the U.S. dollar relative to the deutsche mark and yen led the West German and Japanese auto makers to raise their dollar prices. The price increases by the U.S. manufacturers, which were less than the sharp rise in import prices, were expected to improve profit margins while keeping U.S. cars competitive with their foreign rivals.

Of course, if a domestic firm is operating with weak or nonexistent import competition, then it will have little chance to adjust its prices after devaluation and its pricing latitude will be restricted. To improve its competitive position *vis-a-vis* other domestic producers, the firm would have to substitute local for imported materials and services.

Advance planning in pricing is particularly important if price controls are expected to follow a devaluation. Foreign firms are especially susceptible to such controls because they face subtle pressures to be "good corporate citizens."

Several options are available to a firm to counteract these expected controls. One possibility is to set prices at an artificially high level and accept the resulting loss of market share. If devaluation occurs and price controls are imposed, the firm is then in a better position to continue operating profitably.

An alternative approach is to raise list prices but continue selling at existing prices—in effect, to sell at a discount. This mitigates the problem of competing with higher prices before a devaluation or a similar change in the pricing environment (such as increased inflation). Price controls can be avoided by eliminating part or all of the discount.

Another common means of circumventing price controls is to develop new products that are only slightly altered versions of the firm's existing goods, and then sell them at higher prices. This method is particularly convenient for a multinational company already dealing in a range of different products with a continual stream of updated or new merchandise.

Such anticipatory or "preactive" planning is especially important for firms that are heavy users of imported materials. Companies unable to raise their prices when production costs increase will have the unpleasant choice of producing inferior merchandise, cutting back on service, sustaining considerable losses, or dropping unprofitable product lines.

Promotional Strategy

Promotional strategy should similarly take into account anticipated exchange rate changes. A key issue in any marketing program is the size of the promotional budget for advertising, personal selling, and merchandising. Promotional decisions should explicitly build in exchange risks, especially in allocating budgets among countries.

A firm exporting its products after a domestic devaluation may well find that the return per dollar expenditure on advertising or selling is increased as a function of the product's improved price positioning. The exporter may also find it has improved its ability to "push" the product based on the option of greater distribution margins or consumer dealing. Devaluation may well be the time to reevaluate the mix of advertising, personal selling, and merchandising because the firm has more market leverage. A foreign currency devaluation, on the other hand, is likely to reduce the return on marketing expenditures and requires a more fundamental shift in the firm's product policy.

Product Strategy

Exchange rate fluctuations may affect the timing of the introduction of new products. In periods of currency uncertainty, distributors may be reluctant to accept the risks associated with introducing new products, which involves up-front investment in marketing costs, especially for inventories and advertising. The firm must devise a strategy for new product introduction and market selection as a function of its relative exposure in different markets. Because of the competitive price advantage, the period after a home currency devaluation or foreign currency revaluation may be the ideal time to develop a brand franchise.

Similarly, decisions to eliminate products, as products become obsolete or fall into consumer disfavor, may be influenced by exchange risk considerations. Indeed, companies may continue manufacturing marginally profitable goods domestically if a home currency devaluation is expected. Conversely, they might stop producing those goods if a home currency revaluation or foreign currency devaluation is likely.

Exchange rate fluctuations also affect *product line decisions*. Related to the issue of market segmentation, a firm pursuing foreign markets after a home currency (HC) devaluation will potentially be able to expand its product line and cover a wider spectrum of consumers in the foreign market. Following devaluation, a domestic firm facing import competition in its local market may have the option to emphasize and place greater marketing support behind the top of its line (which generally has a higher margin) because it will be at a competitive price advantage.

Following a foreign currency devaluation or home currency revaluation, a firm may have to reorient its product line completely and target it to a higher-income, more quality-conscious, less price-sensitive constituency. Volkswagen, for example, achieved its export prominence on the basis of low-priced, stripped-down, low-maintenance cars. Its product line was essentially limited to one model: the relatively unchanging "Bug." The appreciation of the deutsche mark relative to the dollar in the early 70s, however, effectively ended Volkswagen's ability to compete primarily on the basis of price. The company lost over $310 million in 1974 alone attempting to maintain its market share by lowering deutsche mark prices.

To compete in the long run, Volkswagen was forced to revise its product line and sell relatively high-priced cars from an extended product line to middle-income consumers on the basis of quality and styling rather than cost.

Production Management of Exchange Risk

The adjustments discussed so far involve attempts to alter the dollar value of foreign currency revenues. Forward-looking exchange risk management should also consider the possibility of changing the firm's production and product sourcing strategies to reduce its dollar costs.

Input Mix

A primary reason for devaluation is to make domestically produced goods more competitive both at home and abroad. A well-managed firm should be searching for ways to substitute domestic for imported inputs, depending on the relative prices involved and the degree of substitution possible. In fact, plants can sometimes be designed to provide added flexibility in making substitutions among various sources of goods. Maxwell House, for instance, can blend the same coffee by using coffee beans from Brazil, the Ivory Coast, and other producers. The added design and construction costs must, of course, be weighed against the advantages of being able to respond to relative price differences among domestic and imported inputs.

Plant Location

A firm exporting to a competitive market whose currency has devalued may find that these short-term adjustments are not enough. Unit profitability could decrease so drastically that the firm would have to locate new plants abroad. In many cases, third-country plant locations are a viable alternative. Volkswagen, for example, began producing in Brazil before establishing U.S. production facilities.

Before making a major commitment of resources, however, management should attempt to assess the length of time a particular country will retain its cost advantage. If the local inflationary conditions that led to a nominal exchange rate change are expected to persist, a country's apparent cost advantage may soon reverse itself. In Mexico, for example, the wholesale price index rose 18 percent relative to U.S. prices between January 1969 and May 1976. This led to a 20 percent devaluation of the peso in September 1976. Within one month, though, the Mexican government allowed organized labor to raise its wages by 35 to 40 percent. As a result, the devaluation's effectiveness was nullified and the government was forced to devalue the peso again in less than two months.

Planning

Thus far, the marketing and production strategies advocated are based on knowledge of exchange rate changes. Even if exchange rate changes are unpredictable, however, contingency plans can be made. The first step is to take the currency scenarios described earlier and analyze the effect on the firm's competitive position under each set of conditions. Using the results of the analysis, the firm should set forth strategies to deal with each of the possibilities. Then, if a currency change actually occurs, the firm is able to quickly adjust its marketing and production strategies in line with the plan. It can immediately begin to redirect its marketing efforts toward those markets in which it has become more competitive. It can also begin to shift its production sourcing and input mix in the directions management has determined would be most cost-effective under the circumstances. If new plant locations are required, planning in advance reduces the lead time involved in site selection, labor recruitment, and contractor and supplier selection.

Financial Management of Exchange Risk

Even after the requisite marketing and production initiatives have been taken, there usually is some residual operating exposure. This cash flow exposure, if it seems large enough to warrant hedging, must be offset by forward contracts or other financial commitments. (In the case of the Spectrum AB subsidiary considered earlier, the residual exposure is probably small enough to call for a "passive" financial approach.) As mentioned earlier, the aim of financial hedging should be to structure the firm's balance sheet in such a way that a reduction in asset earnings due to exchange rate changes is matched by a decrease in the cost of servicing liabilities.

One possibility is to finance the portion of a firm's assets used to create export profits so that any shortfall in operating cash flows due to an exchange rate change is offset by a reduction in the debt service expenses. For example, a firm that has developed a sizable export market should hold a portion of its liabilities in the currency of that country. The portion to be held in the foreign currency depends on the size of the loss in profitability associated with a given exchange rate change. No more definite recommendations are possible because the currency effects will vary from one company to another.

As a case in point, Volkswagen, to hedge its operating exposure, should have used dollar financing in proportion to its net dollar cash flow from U.S. sales, or sold forward the present value of these future net dollar cash flows, or used some combination of the two methods. This strategy would have cushioned the impact of the deutsche mark revaluation which almost brought VW to its knees. But even this strategy would not have provided a perfect hedge. In VW's case, the shifting of some production facilities to a lower-cost country was probably the best solution.

The implementation of a hedging policy is likely to be quite difficult in practice, if only because the specific cash flow effects of a given currency change are hard to predict. Estimating these effects requires an intimate knowledge of the MNC's sales breakdown—domestic versus exports—and the import content of its inputs, along with an understanding of the firm's ability to choose between domestic and foreign input sources and its capacity to shift its market focus. Trained personnel are required to implement and monitor an active hedging program. Consequently, hedging should be undertaken only when the effects of anticipated exchange rate changes are expected to be significant.

SUMMARY AND CONCLUSIONS

The foregoing analysis leads to three principal conclusions. First, exchange risk cannot be measured in terms of accounting numbers. The proper way to measure exchange risk is to *forecast* the relation between changes in exchange rates and changes in the expected level and variability of real cash flow to the firm. Moreover, in measuring the degree of exchange risk, it is necessary to realize that currency risk and inflation risk are intertwined. For multinationals incurring costs and selling products in foreign countries, the net effect of worldwide devaluations and revaluations may be offset by price level changes in the long run.

Second, traditional hedging techniques are overrated as a means of reducing exchange risk. The cost of routine hedging is high, and last-second attempts to hedge are fruitless because prices will reflect anticipated changes in exchange rates. In addition, because investors can individually manage exchange risk by internationally diversifying their own portfolios, it may not be in the interest of shareholders to hedge.

The third, and perhaps most important, conclusion of this article is that currency risk affects all facets of a company's operations and, therefore, should not be the concern of financial managers alone. Operating managers, in particular, should develop marketing and production initiatives that help to ensure profitability over the long run. They should also devise anticipatory or "preactive" strategic alternatives in order to gain competitive leverage internationally.

The key to effective exposure management is to integrate currency considerations into the general management process. One approach used by a number of multinationals is to establish a committee concerned with managing foreign currency exposure. Besides financial executives, such committees should—and often do—include the senior officers of the company, such as the vice president-international, top marketing and production executives, the director of corporate planning, and the chief executive officer. The most desirable feature of this arrangement is that top executives are exposed to the problems of currency risk management. They can then incorporate exchange rate expectations into their own nonfinancial decisions.

Another way to encourage this process is to hold subsidiary and other operating managers responsible for net operating income targets expressed in the home currency. In this kind of integrated exchange risk program, the role of the financial executive would be threefold: to provide local operating management with forcasts of inflation and exchange rates, to structure evaluation criteria such that operating managers are not rewarded or penalized for the effects of unanticipated real currency changes, and to estimate and hedge whatever real operating exposure remains after the appropriate marketing and production strategies have been put in place.

REFERENCES

Cornell, Bradford., "Spot Rates, Forward Rates and Market Efficiency." *Journal of Financial Economics* 5, (1977).

Dufey, Gunter., "Corporate Financial Policies and Floating Exchange Rates," a paper presented at the meeting of the International Fiscal Association in Rome, October 14, 1974.

Kohlhagen, Steven W., "Evidence on the Cost of Forward Cover in a Floating System." *Euromoney* (September, 1975).

Roll, Richard., "Violations of the Law of One Price and Their Implications for Differentially Denominated Assets," in Marshall Sarnet and George Szego, eds. *International Finance and Trade*, Vol. I. Cambridge, Mass: Ballinger, 1979.

Shapiro, Alan C., *Multinational Financial Management*. Boston: Allyn & Bacon, 1982.

Shapiro, Alan C., "Evaluating Financing Costs for Multinational Subsidiaries," *Journal of International Business Studies*. Fall, 1975.

20

The Foreign Exchange Option as a Hedging Tool*

Ian H. Giddy

THE BASIC FUNCTION OF CURRENCY OPTIONS AS A HEDGING TOOL

Early this year a well-known U.S. electronics firm was asked to bid on a contract to supply the Swiss authority with switching systems. Bids were also to be submitted by French and Japanese firms, both of whose governments were keen on winning the contract. The result of the tender would be known some time during the following two months. Were its bid to be accepted the American firm would receive an initial payment of two million Swiss francs, with the remainder of the payments made in Swiss francs at fixed dates thereafter.

To submit a bid in Swiss francs, our firm could have assumed that the current Swiss franc/dollar exchange rate would remain unchanged and translated the bid at today's spot rate; this is the "no hedge" assumption. The danger, however, was that if the bid was accepted and the franc fell, the profit margin on the deal could easily have been wiped out. Alternatively, the firm could have sold the anticipated Swiss franc receipts in the forward market, as the then current forward exchange rate for two-month and later delivery dates. However, if its bid was *not* selected the firm would then have had a short position in Swiss francs and could have lost money.

A third and preferable strategy would have been to purchase an *option* to sell Swiss francs on the payment dates. This would have given the American firm the right to transfer the Swiss francs received at a prearranged exchange rate. If the contract was not won the firm could have allowed the option to expire (even sold the right to someone else) with no further obligation on its part. Note also that even if our firm's bid was accepted, it would have faced no compulsion to exchange any Swiss francs received at the prearranged rate; if the value of the Swiss currency rose, then the firm may have done better by selling the francs in the spot market.

Currency options of this kind can be an extraordinarily valuable addition to the international corporate treasurer's toolbox. All this flexibility, of course, does not come free. So, any company considering this technique must be prepared to evaluate whether the value received warrants the price paid. This article will set out some principles according to which international treasury managers can gauge the usefulness of currency options in hedging specific corporate currency risks.

A foreign exchange option is a rather simple concept: it is a contract conveying *the right to buy or sell a designated quantity of a foreign currency* at a specified price (exchange rate) during a stipulated period under stated conditions. The terminal date of the contract is called the *expiration date* (or maturity date). If the option may be exercised before the expiration date, it is called an *American option:* if only on the expiration date, a *European option*.

*This article is reprinted, with permission, from *Midland Corporate Finance Journal,* vol. 1, no. 3, Fall 1983, pp. 32–42, published by Stern, Stewart, Putnam and Macklis, Ltd., Corporate Financial Consultants.

The party retaining the option is the *option buyer*; the party giving the option is the *option seller* (or writer). The exchange rate at which the option can be exercised is called the *exercise price* (or strike price). The buyer of the option must pay the seller some amount, called the *option price* or the *premium*, for the rights involved.

A *call option in foreign exchange* is the right to *buy* a specified number of foreign currency units from the option seller at a specified exercise price (in dollars) up to and including the exercise date. A *put option* is the right to sell the foreign currency to the option seller at a specified dollar price, up to the expiration date. Since the right to buy German marks at a known exchange rate is also the right to sell dollars in exchange for German marks at the same exchange rate, it is evident that a foreign exchange put option is simply a call option seen from the other currency's viewpoint.

The key feature of a foreign exchange option is that it provides "asymmetric" risk protection. The purchase of either a put or a call option limits the buyer's loss to the price paid for the option contract (the premium). The option buyer's potential gain, however, is unlimited. It is this feature that differentiates options from forwards or futures, as we shall see below. The asymmetry of currency options has an important sidelight: if you think about it, the holder of a call on, say, one million Deutsche marks would *prefer* that the underlying currency be *more volatile!* The higher the variability of the mark, the more likely it is that the currency will rise substantially above the exercise price, producing a large profit. On the other hand his option risk from downward fluctuations is limited to the loss of the premium should he let the option expire. In essence, therefore, buying (or selling) an option represents a bet on the currency's volatility.

More on this aspect later. Let us now turn to a question asked by many corporate treasurers: when should foreign exchange options be used in preference to more conventional hedging techniques?

OPTIONS VERSUS FORWARD CONTRACTS FOR HEDGING

Few involved in tresury management of international corporations would want to forego the use of currency futures and forward contracts to hedge assets, liabilities, and future cash flows in foreign currencies. Yet it cannot have escaped the notice of these same treasury managers that forward and futures contracts are sometimes imperfect instruments for the hedging of certain common exchange risks faced by multinational firms. The reason is simply that a forward contract is a fixed and inviolable agreement to receive or deliver a currency at a specified price. Yet, in many practical instances, the hedger is uncertain whether the hedged foreign currency cash inflow or outflow will materialize. When an overseas deal falls through or when a bid on a foreign currency contract is accepted, or when a foreign subsidiary's dividend payments exceed (or fall short of) the expected amount, then the international corporate treasurer will find himself partially exposed. The most careful forward hedging cannot protect against such *quantity risk*.

In such cases what is needed is not the *obligation*, but the *right*, to buy or sell a designated quantity of a foreign currency at a specified price (exchange rate). This is precisely what a foreign exchange option provides.[1]

[1]For an analogous discussion of the different uses of interest rate futures and options, see Bluford Putnam's "Managing Interest Rate Risk: An Introduction to Financial Futures and Options," *Issues in Corporate Finance* (New York: Stern Stewart Putnam & Macklis, 1983).

Although options and forwards serve different purposes, they are linked in interesting ways. As may be seen in the box below the "profit picture" of a currency option is lopsided while that of a forward or futures contract is symmetric. Yet options can be made symmetric, by combining two of them in such a way as to mimic a forward contract, and this provides the fundamental link between options and forwards. A combination of *buying a call and selling a put* at the same exercise price is identical to *buying the currency*

Profit Profiles of Forward Options

"Profit Profiles" trace the relationship between the *exchange rate at expiration* of the contract and the *net gain* to the trader. These diagrams show how the profit profile of the *holder* and *seller* of a call or put option differs from the profit picture of a conventional forward contract at expiration.

1. Buy Sterling Forward

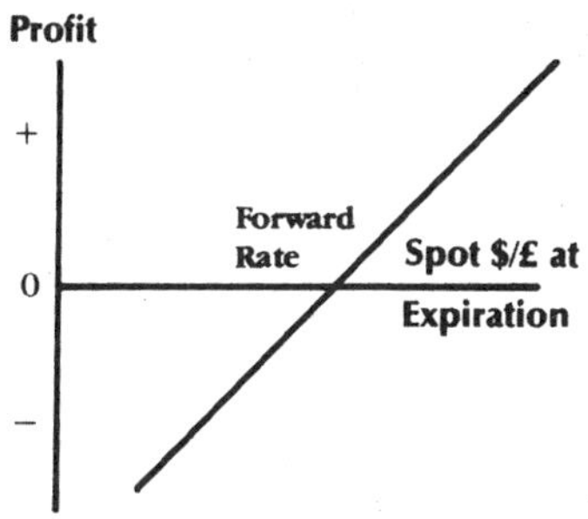

2. Sell Sterling Forward

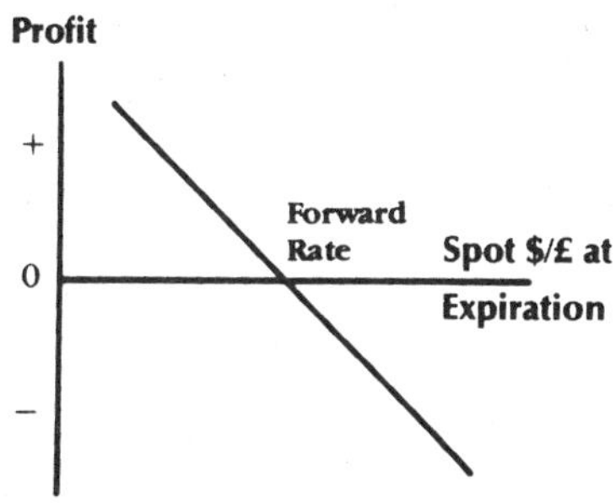

3. Buy a Sterling Call Option

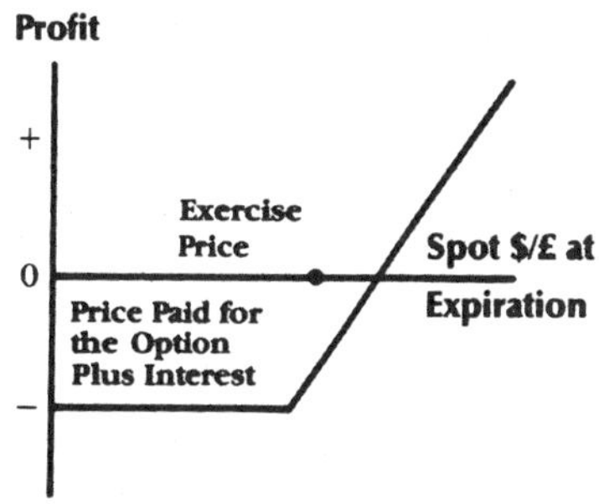

4. Buy a Sterling Put Option

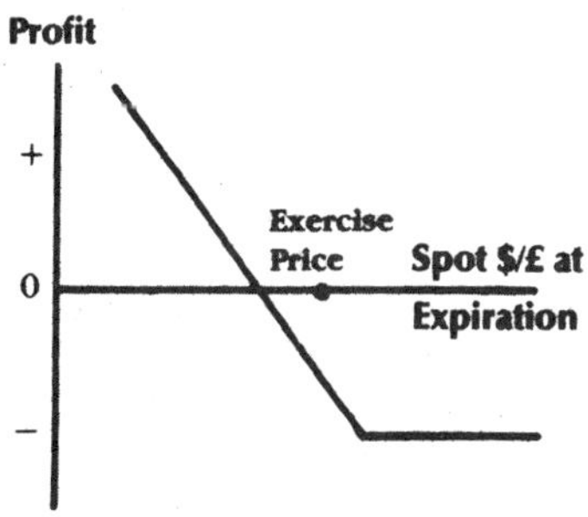

5. Sell a Sterling Call Option

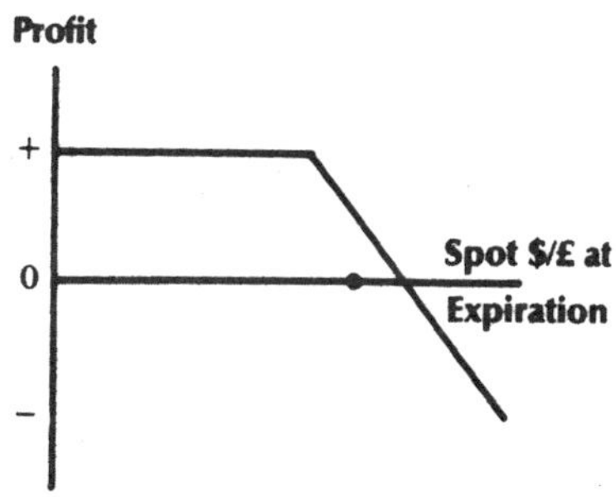

6. Sell a Sterling Put Option

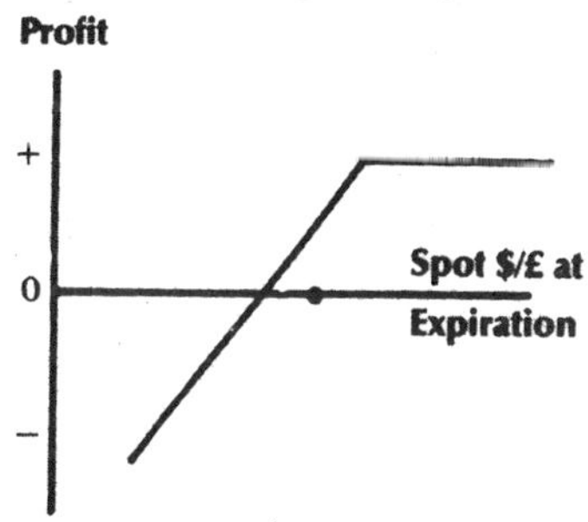

In a *forward contract*, diagrams 1 and 2 show, the long or short position produces a *one-to-one gain or loss* depending on whether the spot rate ends up relative to the contracted forward rate.

In an *options contract*, the gain or loss is *asymmetric*. Diagram 3 shows that, for a *call option* on pounds sterling, the loss is limited to the price originally paid for the option, plus interest foregone. As long as the spot rate exceeds the prearraged exercise price, some gain will be made, but the net profit will be positive only when the holder of the call has recouped the price of the option, plus interest. The holder of a *put option* will gain one-for-one only when sterling has fallen below the exercise price by more than the price of the put, plus interest. Again, downside loss is limited. The *seller* of puts or calls has a profit picture that is the upside-down mirror image of the buyer's: the most he can gain is the option price, plus accumulated interest; but the downside loss is unlimited.

forward: you gain if the currency rises above the forward rate and lose if it falls below. A similar link exists between buying a put plus selling a call and selling the currency forward. Arbitrage techniques called conversions and reversals ensure that options and forwards are linked in this fashion continuously. (See the author's article, "Foreign Exchange Options.")

The basic rules for distinguishing between the appropriate use of options and the use of forwards for *hedging* purposes can be summarized as follows. Other things being equal:

- When the quantity of a foreign currency cash outflow is known, buy the currency forward; when the quantity is unknown, buy a call option on the currency.
- When the quantity of a foreign currency cash inflow is known, sell the currency forward; when the quantity is unknown, buy a put option on the currency.
- When the quantity of a foreign currency cash flow is partially known and partially uncertain, use a forward contract to hedge the known portion and an option to hedge the maximum value of the uncertain remainder.

The above presupposes the use of both forwards and options as *pure hedging* tools, without regard to the treasurer's expectations about the direction or riskiness of the currency's possible fluctuation. It also presupposes that both forward and options contracts are priced fairly; that is, the prices reflect all available information about the expected value and variability of the exchange rate. These are in effect the "efficient market" criteria for the choice between options and forwards: they assume that the hedger should make no attempt to outguess the market.

When the corporation is selective about its hedging policies—i.e., when the firm tempers its decision to cover an exposure by assessing the extent to which its own currency forecasts agree with those of the market—the story changes. Such firms, indeed most firms, are prepared to take a risk in a currency when conditions are right. Consider three examples.

OPTIONS VERSUS FORWARDS: THREE CASES

Corporation X, a Swiss-based publishing company that distributes books printed in the United States, makes large monthly payments in dollars to its U.S. parent. During the early 1980s, the American Board of Directors became concerned about foreign exchange losses incurred on the Swiss franc revenues. These losses resulted from the sharp rise in the dollar during that period. In late 1982 the Board had a meeting with the Swiss treasurer, who persuaded them that the franc would rise significantly in the coming year and that to hedge then would be to lock in a disadvantageous exchange rate. The Board took his advice, warning him, however, to hedge should his forecast change.

This is the kind of situation to which forwards are better suited than options, because the top management of the firm is willing to take a position based purely on the expected value, or point forecast, of the Swiss franc's future value.

Corporation Y, a Chicago commodities firm with considerable experience in speculative trading, felt that signs were accumulating that the Japanese yen was entering a period of great instability—although it was not possible to predict which way the currency would go. Normally the firm's grain exports to Japan were fully hedged; all contractual yen receivables were sold in the Chicago futures market. But this time somebody suggested that the firm buy a put option on yen instead. Holding a put option would enable the firm to sell their yen receipts at the exercise price if the yen fell; and if the dollar/yen exchange rate ended up above the exercise price, the yen receipts could be sold at the higher market price.

Although the suggested strategy sounds appealing, it was not the optimal one for the simple reason that Corporation Y had a view on *volatility* but not on *direction*. A put option, when used alone, is not a bet solely on volatility; it is a combined bet on direction and volatility. To achieve a pure bet on volatility, Corporation Y should have (1) hedged against the unknown *direction* of the currency by selling yen futures as usual or using a forward contract, and (2) taken a bet on their *volatility* forecast—where they felt they had an edge on the market—by buying both a put and a call with a common exercise price equal to the forward exchange rate.

The latter combination is called a "straddle" and allows the firm to gain from increased volatility. If the currency rises above the exercise price, you exercise the call: if it falls below, you exercise the put. For this combination, of course, you have to pay both the put price and the call price; so a net gain is achieved only if the spot exchange rate moves away from the exercise price by more than the sum of the two premia. Since the premia themselves reflect the "market view" of volatility, buying a straddle is in effect a bet that your forcast of volatility exceeds that of the market. Whichever way the currency goes, you can profit, as long as it moves a lot!

Corporation Z is a New York-based advertising concern with considerable international operations. Like Corporation X, its foreign earnings had suffered from the dollar's strength in 1981 and early 1982. In June 1982 Z's management was wondering what to do about its German subsidiary's dividends that were to be paid at the end of the year. They felt that the German currency was due for a rise, which would of course benefit them. However, the company's management was also aware that the West German political situation was shaky, which might spell troubled times in the currency markets.

In short, they viewed the Deutsche mark as strong but potentially highly variable. They were therefore unwilling to leave the DM cash flow unhedged. On the other hand they wished to take advantage of a possible upturn in the currency's fortunes, "to recoup the past years' losses," as they put it.

A put option to sell DM in December was the instrument best suited to this firm's needs and views. Management had a view both on the direction and the volatility of the German mark. But was it worth paying the option's price? And what would they give up compared to a pure forward hedge?

Graph 1 provides some clue to the answers to these questions. Had Corporation Z bought a put option on June 17, 1982, it would have paid $12,320 for each $1 million of DM (at June rates) deliverable on December 15, 1982 at an exercise price of $0.4215 per mark, which is equal to the forward rate on June 17. As it turned out, the mark did not rise; it wobbled around a bit for two or three months, and in September began a downhill slide to as low as about $0.38 in early November. This made the right to sell DM at $0.42 rather valuable, and the put option's value accordingly climbed, as the graph shows, and later fell as the DM rose once more to a rate approaching $0.42.

Thus, the option evidently *did* provide downside protection, and would have been exercised on December 15. The value of the option is thus a measure of the downside protection it provides, as well as of the upside potential it allows. On the date of expiration, December 16, the option was worth precisely the difference between the exercise

GRAPH 1

Estimate of Weekly Changes in the Price of Hypothetical Deutsche Mark Put Option as it Nears Maturity During the Last 6 months of 1982.

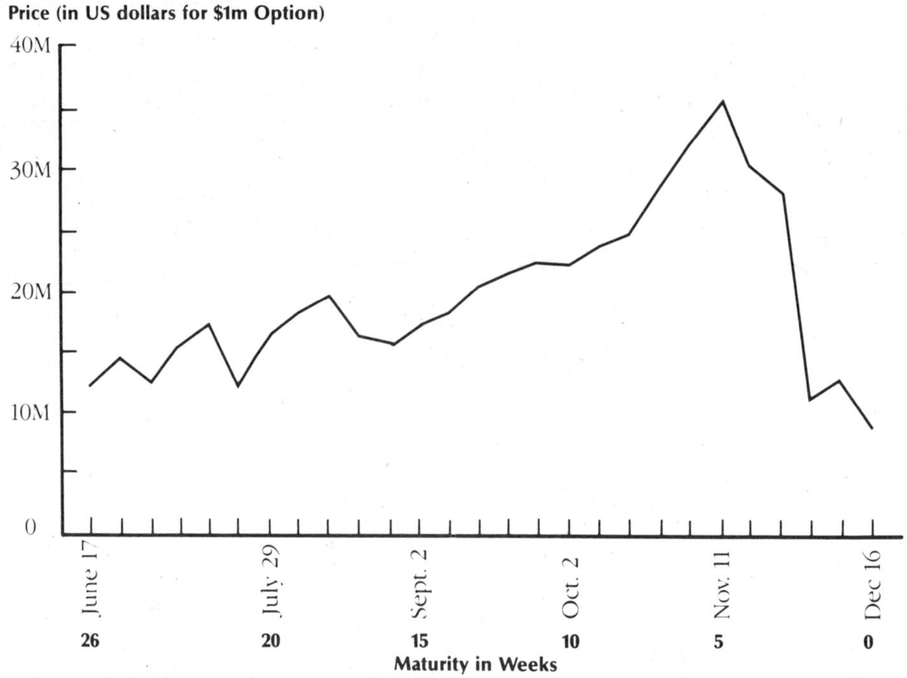

Note Option prices computed based on Garman-Kohlhagen method for a "European" call option with an annualized Standard Deviation of the percentage change of the exchange rate of 11.171%, as calculated from monthly changes over the four years 1979–1982. Futures prices for the December 1982 contract were used in place of forward rates; these and the Eurodollar interest rates were obtained from the International Monetary Market's Weekly Bulletin. Exercise price equals the futures price as of June 17, 1982, which was $0.4215 per DM.

price, $0.4215, and the spot rate on that day, $0.4128, i.e., $8,700 for a $1 million contract. In the end, however, the firm would have paid over $12,000 compared to a forward contract which would have locked in the same rate at no up-front cost. Thus, if Corporation Z had felt strongly about the direction the currency was heading, without regard to volatility, it would have paid to retain an open position or to hedge in the forward market.

APPLICATIONS OF CURRENCY OPTIONS IN CORPORATE EXCHANGE RISK MANAGEMENT

The previous section offered specific illustrations of corporate uses for currency options. To generalize from these cases, there are two basic conditions in which these instruments can be used effectively. Either is sufficient alone, but both are often present.

The first is whenever the firm already possesses a "natural option position," an uncertain foreign currency cash flow—that is, one where a third party has the right, but not the obligation, to buy or sell something in a foreign currency. The second is where the option buyer (or seller) has views about the direction and volatility of a currency's movements that differ from that of the market, i.e., where the option trader believes the option is under- or over-priced.

We have seen cases of companies that are willing to take a position on the direction and/or volatility of a currency. Suffice it to say that, for them, the options market opens up new opportunities for betting on expectations about volatility, bets that were not readily available in the forward or futures market.

Let us concentrate instead on the other situation—that is, on identifying the kinds of currency exposure for which options are particularly well-suited. We begin by stating the general rule:

A currency option is the appropriate hedging tool for any firm that has already granted an opposite currency option.

To put it differently, fight fire with fire, not with futures. Currency options can be employed to reduce exchange risk whenever a firm has given another party, such as a foreign customer, the right to buy or sell a product or service at a fixed foreign currency price. This brings us to the first application . . .

Fixing foreign currency prices? Buy a put on the foreign currency.

A firm that establishes a price list in, say, French francs as well as domestic currency (U.S. dollars) has in effect given away, for free, a put option on French francs.

Whenever any firm lists the price of the same good in two currencies, the firm has implicitly granted a currency put (or a currency call, depending on which currency you view it from—remember that a call option in one currency is a put option viewed from the other). What is the hedging implication? One cannot use a forward contract, for one never knows who's going to buy. Yet, because a foreign buyer will logically opt to purchase in the depreciated currency, the firm obviously faces a degree of exchange risk when its price lists are printed in two or more foreign currencies. If the customer opts to pay or buy in the weakened currency, the firm can protect itself by having the right to exchange the foreign currency for dollars at a prearranged rate. Buying an explicit call or put option in foreign currency thus offsets the exchange risk arising from the kind of international usiness that requires granting options in foreign currencies.

For example, an equipment firm may price a generator for European and Far Eastern customers in dollars, DM and yen. The firm then faces a combined "quantity" and "currency" risk: it faces uncertainty about both whether or not the equipment is bought, and the currency in which payment is made. Buying a put potion to sell DM or yen will protect the firm against both risks.

Bidding on a contract in foreign currency? Buy a put on that currency!

This application of the foreign exchange option is commonly used by those advocating options as a hedging device. If your costing is done in one currency (such as dollars) and bidding must be done in another, you face the risk of the foreign currency having depreciated by the time your bid is accepted. As the opening example illustrated, such currency risk can make a deal far less attractive, and cannot easily be hedged by means of forward contracts.

The reader will observe, however, that this situation is but a variation of the previous application: one is simply setting a price for a single service in a foreign currency. What this example does emphasize is that in making a bid that stands over some time period, the firm is giving away something valuable; the price of the option necessary to hedge this risk provides a basis for estimating how valuable.

There is some debate as to whether the cost of the option should be incorporated into business costing when bidding on foreign contracts (see, in particular, "Currency Options Cope with Uncertainty" by Agmon and Eldor). In my view, the options cost should not go into the specific costs for each bid, but rather into the overhead costs—such as the cost of drawing up proposals—that firms in the contracting business face.

Making an offer to buy a foreign firm? Buy a call on the foreign currency!

A Californian producer of pollution-control equipment recently sought to purchase a controlling share in a German firm manufacturing atmspheric gas-measurement devices. The U.S. firm's management regarded their offered price of DM 42 million as a reasonable one, but only at the present depreciated rate for DM. The German company insisted on 90 days to consider the offer. The Californians agreed to this reluctantly. In past months, they recalled, the German mark's value had fluctuated as much as 5 percent in a single week. The treasurer voiced concern that they could end up paying several

GRAPH 2

Estimate of Changes in the Price of Hypothetical Deutsche Mark 3 Month Call Options, 1980–1982

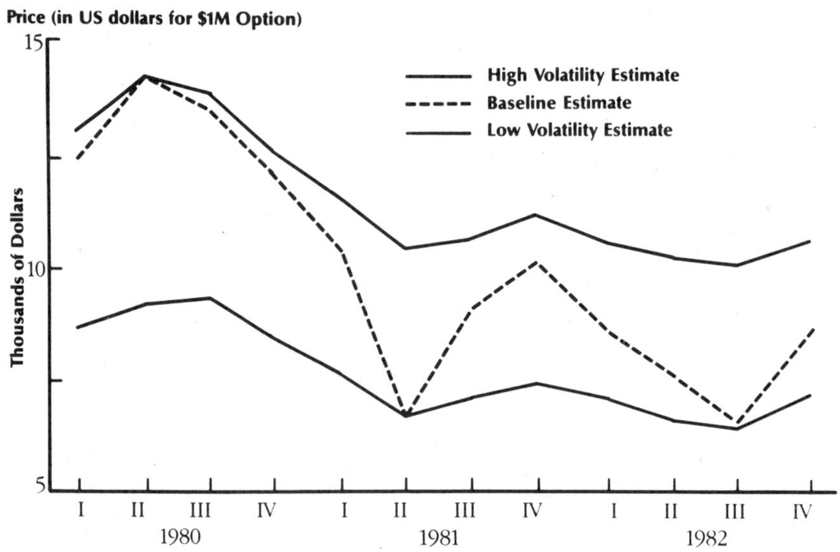

Note Option prices computed using Garman-Kohlhagen method for a "European" call option of 3 months maturity and an annualized standard deviation of the percentage change of the exchange rate calculated from the immediately preceding 12 months' rates. Forward rates and the Eurodollar interest rates are Friday rates at the end of each quarter, as provided by the Harris Bank. The solid bands above and below the broken line represent hypothetical prices assuming "maximum" and "minimum" estimates of the DM's volatility, based on the highest and lowest estimates of volatility calculated over the entire period.

million dollars more than intended if the mark rose significantly during the next 3 months. Consequently, he suggested buying a call option to give the firm the right to buy Deutsche marks at a known rate.

The treasurer was able to find a bank to accommodate his firm's need. The price was two percent of the contract's dollar value, which he thought was reasonable. But was it? To obtain an idea of what a similar 3-month DM call option for $1 million would have cost at theoretical fair prices during 1980, 1981, and 1982, see the quarterly estimates I have presented in Graph 2. The "baseline" graph shows that the option's cost would have varied from about 0.7 percent to 1.4 percent of face value. Because the most difficult part of estimating option prices is gauging volatility, I have drawn bands showing how "high" and "low" estimates of the currency's variance would have altered the price. Only a volatility much greater than that found historically could justify the two percent charged the Californian firm for a three-month option.

To conclude this section, let me summarize what we have learned about the answer to the question: are currency options worth the up-front cost? The answer must be twofold. If the option is fairly priced in a competitive market, the option is always worth purchasing for a firm that wishes to avoid the *contingent exchange risk* that arises from having granted implicit options in foreign currencies. But if the option is overpriced, or if the market is so thin that a suitable option cannot be found or existing options unwound, the option may not be worth the protection it provides.

Yet all is not lost. Mispriced options, as with any mispriced goods or services, create opportunities to make some money. If options are overpriced, sell options; if they're underpriced, buy them. And if you can't find the currency option you need for hedging purposes, you have an alternative: create a do-it-yourself option!

THE DO-IT-YOURSELF CURRENCY OPTION

The key feature of modern options pricing theory, as embodied most notably in the widely-used Black-Scholes model, is that the behavior of a call option's price is very similar to—and therefore can be mimicked by—a combination of holding the underlying security and investing (or borrowing) at the going risk-free interest rate.[2] The same is true of currency option pricing theory, except that instead of investing in securities and borrowing or lending, one simply holds long or short forward or futures contracts on the currency in some proportion to the amount to be hedged. This proportion, known as the "hedge ratio," changes continuously, and is a component of the option pricing model employed in this article: the Garman-Kohlhagen variation of the Black-Scholes model.

The do-it-yourself currency option replicating strategy relies on the fact that as the forward exchange rate for a currency changes, so does the price of an option to buy or sell that currency. Invariably, however, the option price changes by less than the change in the price of the forward exchange. Because the option price changes by less than the currency's value, in percentage terms, simulating an option by holding futures contracts implies holding less in futures than would be held in options. How much less depends on the sensitivity of the option price to the futures price.

[2]For a more thorough discussion of the intricacies of option pricing and the duplicating portfolio method, see the following article in this issue by Georges Courtadon and John Merrick, "The Option Pricing Model and the Valuation of Corporate Securities."

This sensitivity, this hedge ratio, depends on a number of things: the time to maturity, the underlying currencies' volatility, the prevailing interest rate and, most of all, where the futures price is relative to the exercise price of the option. For example, when the futures price is *equal* to the exercise price (the option is "at the money"), a one percent change in the futures price produces about a $\frac{1}{2}$ percent change in the call option price. Thus, to mimic a currency call option's hedging properties at this point, the hedger should hold about 50 percent (of the total amount being hedged) in futures contracts. But one cannot expect to construct a futures position to replicate a call or put option's behavior and then sit on one's ass. As the futures price and other conditions change, the proportion hedged must be revised.

There is not space here to go into more detail. Suffice it to say that if the technique described here can be used to *simulate* a currency option, it can also be used to hedge the risk incurred by anyone *selling* a currency option.

WHAT DETERMINES CURRENCY OPTION PRICES?

We have just seen that we can explain, and therefore mimic, the behavior of currency option prices using well-known instruments: futures or forward contracts. But if option price *behavior* can be explained in terms of the sensitivity of the option price to the forward or futures rate, can we not find the proper price *level* for an option in terms of the factors that influence this sensitivity?

Indeed we can, and this has been done in an elegant fashion in several recent papers (an incomplete selection of which is included at the back of this article). For our purposes it is important to know when a currency option is likely to be cheap, and when it is likely to be costly. The answers illustrated in 3, 4, and 5 turn out to be remarkably consistent with what common sense would tell us.

First and foremost, the value of a call option must always be positive (for no one would *pay* you to give you a right but not an obligation!). Further, it must at least equal the present value of the excess (if any) of the forward rate over the exercise price, in dollar terms. If it were less, you could buy the call option and sell the currency forward, and profit by eventually buying at the exercise price and selling at the higher forward price. The difference between the forward and the exercise price is thus called the *intrinsic value* of the call option.

But even if the forward rate is at or below the exercise price, a call option may still be valuable. The reason is that as long as the option has time before expiration there remains some chance that the forward will rise above the exercise price, and a profit can be locked in. This is shown in Graph 3. When the exercise price is equal to the forward rate, this hypothetical call option with a face value of \$1.00 is worth about \$0.02. When the exercise price is only 80¢ and the forward is \$1.00, the option is worth only its intrinsic value: about 20¢. When the exercise price exceeds the forward by 20 percent, the call option's value is negligible because there is little chance of the currency rising by 20 percent in three months.

This brings us to the second major influence on option prices: time to maturity. The longer the time to expiration, the greater the chance of a favorable movement to the holder, and so the more the seller will charge for the option. As may be seen in Graph 4, however, the value of a longer horizon diminishes beyond about two years for a typical currency option.

GRAPH 3

How the Price of a Currency Call Option Changes as the Exercise Price Changes in Relation to the Forward Rate

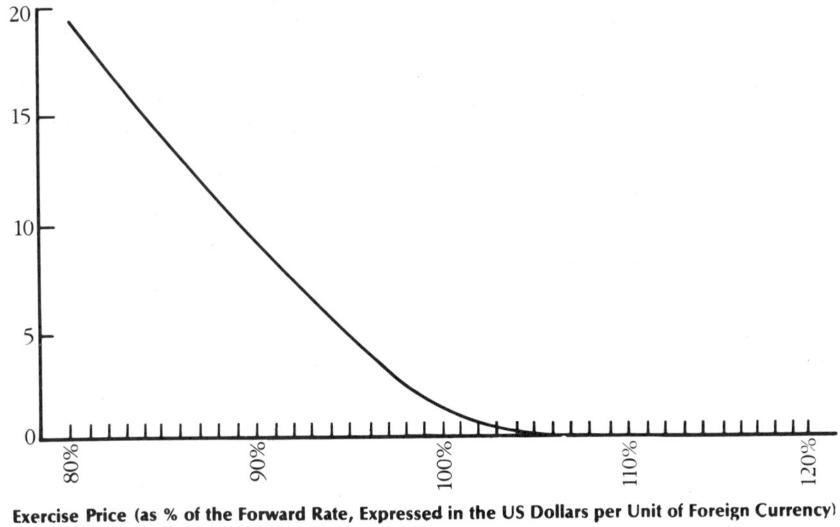

Note Option assumed to be a "European" call option with a Standard Deviation of the percentage change of the exchange rate of 10% and having three months to maturity. U.S. interest rate assumed to be 10%.

GRAPH 4

How the Price of a Currency Call Option Changes as Maturity Increases

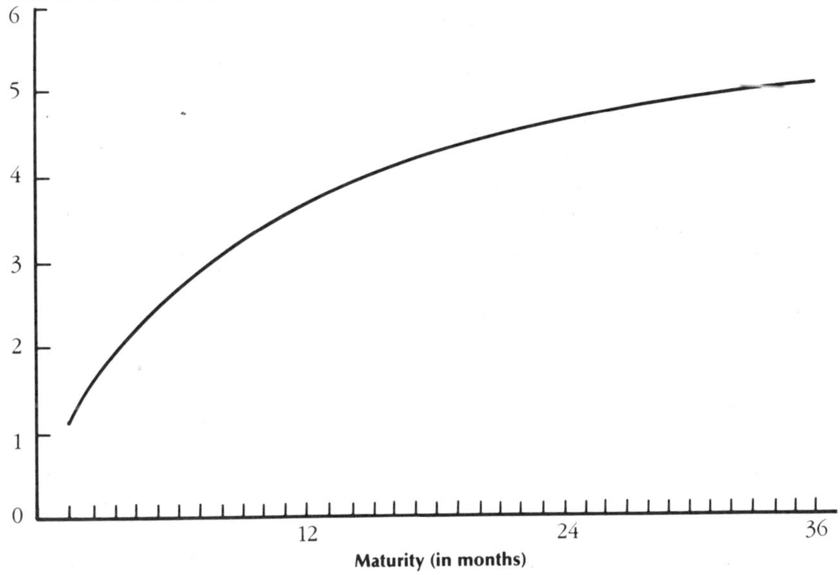

Note Option assumed to be a "European" call option with a Standard Deviation of the percentage change of the exchange rate of 10% and an exercise price equal to the forward exchange rate. U.S. interest rate assumed to be 10%.

GRAPH 5

How the Price of a Currency Call Option Changes as Volatility Increases

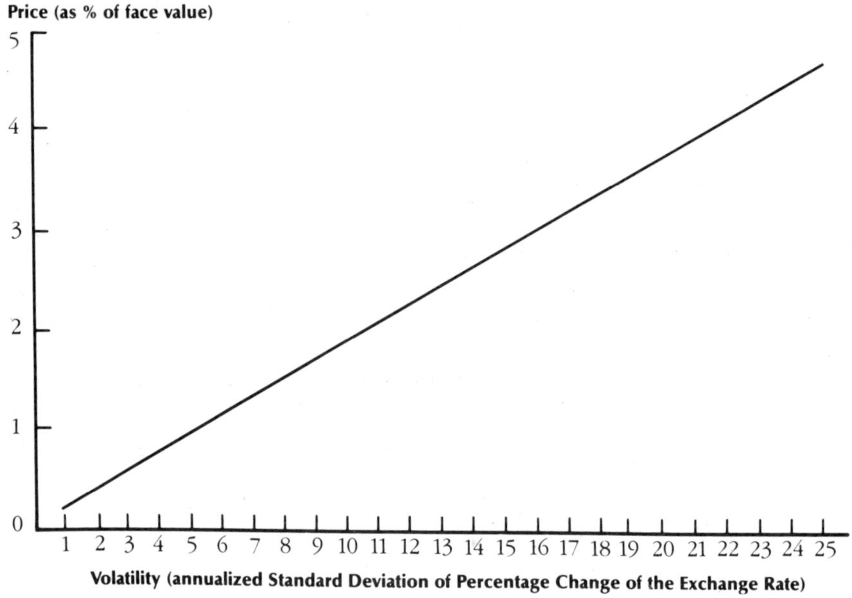

Note Option assumed to be a "European" call option with 3 months to maturity and an exercise price equal to the forward exchange rate. U.S. interest rate assumed to be 10%.

Last but not least, the greater is the volatility of the currency, the greater the chance that the option can be exercised at a profit, and so the higher the option price. Graph 5 shows that for an option whose exercise price equals the forward rate, the option price rises linearly with the standard deviation of the currency's fluctuations. This serves as a reminder that the price of any option incorporates the market's expectations about the future volatility of the currency. Thus one should speculate with options *only* if one's view of volatility differs from that implicit in the option's price. From the corporate viewpoint, the implication is that when option prices begin to rise may be just the right time to use options—for higher options prices may spell troubled waters in the currency markets.

CONCLUDING REMARKS

Foreign exchange options can be unequivocally endorsed as versatile and valuable tools for managing corporate exchange risk. They provide protection against, and information about, a currency's volatility as well as its trend. They provide the asymmetric protection necessary for multinational firms that incur asymmetric currency risk. They are simple in concept but their range of attributes and combinations is overwhelming. Consequently, many firms will hesitate to plunge in—and this is no doubt as it should be. But the acceptance currency options eventually gain will be a solid one.

Some firms will use options in inappropriate ways, where forwards would do the trick better. Those interested in the technique will therefore do well to recall the two basic criteria for the use of currency puts and calls:

- When you have a view on *volatility* that differs from that of the market, buy or sell options; when you only have a view on *direction*, use futures or forwards.
- When your firm has *given* an implicit option in a foreign currency, hedge the risk by *buying* the same kind of currency option.

REFERENCES

Agmon, Tamir and Rafael Eldor, (May 1983) "Currency Options Cope With Uncertainty," *Euromoney*, pp. 227–228.

Biger, Nahum and John Hull, (1982) "The Value of Currency Options," *Financial Management* 12, No. 4, pp. 24–28.

Black, Fischer and Myron Scholes, (1973) "The Pricing of Options and Corporate Liabilities," *Journal of Political Economy*, Vol. 81, (May/June), pp. 637–659.

Eldor, Rafael, (1982) "On the Valuation of Currency Options, Exchange Rate Insurance Policies and Quota Licenses," Unpublished working paper, Harvard University.

Feiger, George and Bertrand Jacquillat, (1979) "Currency Option Bonds, Puts and Calls on Spot Exchange and the Hedging of Contingent Foreign Earnings," *Journal of Finance*, Vol. 33, No. 5, (December) pp. 1129–1139.

Giddy, Ian H., (1983) "Foreign Exchange Options," *Journal of Futures Markets*, Vol. 3, No. 2, pp. 143–166.

Garman, Mark B. and Steven W. Kolhagen, (1982) "Foreign Currency Option Values," Unpublished working paper, University of California at Berkeley (December).

Grabbe, J. Orlin, (1983) "The Pricing of Call and Put Options on Foreign Exchange," Unpublished working paper, Wharton School, University of Pennsylvania.

Smith, Clifford W., (1976) "Option Pricing: A Review," *Journal of Financial Economics*, Vol. 3, (Jan/March) pp. 3–51.

21

Currency Options Cope with Uncertainty*

Tamir Agmon and Rafael Eldor

Trading in currency options on the Philadelphia Stock Exchange may provide perfect hedging-plus for corporations who submit bids with uncertain results. That is, in addition to perfect hedging, the firm takes part in an investment activity.

Assume that a US-based corporation has submitted a bid to install an electronic alarm system in a plant in the UK. The bid has to be submitted in domestic currency, in this case sterling. Bids are accepted up to January 30 1983. The British Company will notify those who have submitted bids by February 28, 1983. The alarm system manufacturer who has won will sign a contract on March 1 1983. The contract will specify that on June 1 1983 the system is installed. The supplier receives a promissory note for full payment in sterling by September 1 1983.

The US corporation has two currency problems: determining the price in sterling and handling the exchange risk.

Solving the second problem will help in solving the first. Once the system has been installed and the US corporation has received a promissory note for a given sum of sterling to be paid on a certain date, it can sell the sterling forward and thus transform a payment in foreign currency to a payment in domestic currency.

However, on January 30 1983 the US supplier does not know whether its bid will be accepted. Thus its claim on a certain sum in sterling, to be paid on September 1 1983, is contingent on the acceptance or the rejection of the bid submitted on January 30. The uncertainty will resolve itself by February 28 1983. A contingent claim calls for a contingent financial instrument. The currency option is such an instrument, as was explained in *Euromoney* (January 1983, pp 73–74).

Suppose the US supplier determines the sterling price of the bid at £1 million. Now the supplier has two alternatives. He may sell £1 million forward for September 1 1983, and buy a call option for £1 million with a striking price identical to the forward, with expiration date September 1 1983. If such an option does not exist, he may buy one with an expiration date as soon as possible after September 1. Or he may buy a put option with identical striking price for the forward rate on September 1 1983, with a similar expiration date. On January 30 1983, the US supplier faces two possible outcomes: the bid may be accepted or be rejected.

On the face of it the entire premium paid for the option, whether put or call, should be added to the price of the bid as an insurance premium (as suggested by Feiger and Jacquillat, *Journal of Finance*, December 1979, pp. 1129–1140). This is not correct. The hedging policy provided by the currency options allows the user an investment opportunity coupled with the hedging. This aspect of the currency options is described in the chart.

On January 30 the US firm has submitted a bid for £1 million. On the same date, the

---

*This article is reprinted, with permission, from *Euromoney*, May 1983, pp. 227–228.

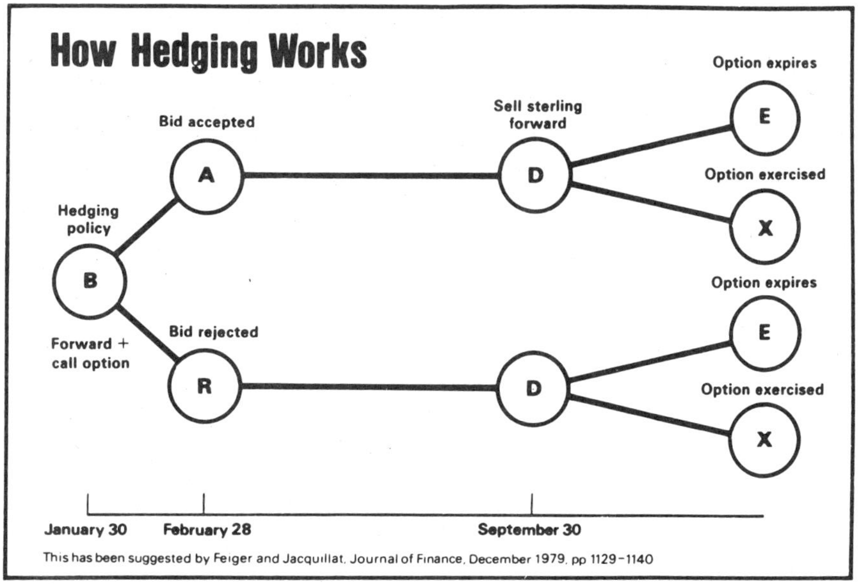

firm has sold £1 million forward for September 1 1983 at the rate F_t and bought a call option for £1 million at striking price F_t with expiration date September 1 1983. On February 18 1983, the US firm will find out whether its bid has been accepted or rejected. These are the possibilities:

1. *Bid Accepted* On September 1 the US firm will receive £1 million and will sell them according to its forward commitment for \$ ($F_t \times 1$ million). The US firm has now the option to buy £1 million for F_t. The option will be exercised if $S_t > F_t$ and will not be exercised if $S_t < F_t$, where S_t is the contemporaneous spot to the forward. In our case, S_t is the dollar/sterling rate on September 1. Hence, the additional financial profits due to the option will be ($S_t — F_t$) 1 million.
2. *Bid Rejected* On September 1, the US firm has to deliver £1 million for \$ ($F_t \times 1$ million). The firm also has the call option. If $S_t > F_t$ the firm is better off by exercising

TABLE 1

	Additional Financial Profits
Bid accepted and $S_t > F_t$	$(S_t - F_t) \times 1$ million
Bid accepted and $S_t < F_t$	0
Bid rejected and $S_t > F_t$	0
Bid rejected and $S_t < F_t$	$(F_t - S_t) \times 1$ million

TABLE 2

The Process of Transforming Domestic Currency Prices to Foreign Currency Prices

Stage one	Determine current price in domestic currency
Stage two	Ascertain the time profile of the bid and the resulting payment schedule.
Stage three	Convert the domestic currency price to foreign currency price by using the appropriate forward rate.
Stage four	Add the relevant part of the option premium to provide perfect hedging.

the option to meet its forward obligation. If however, $S_t<F_t$ it pays to let the option expire and buy sterling on the market; thus the firm will have the financial profit $(F_t—S_t)$ 1 million.

In both cases, there exists the prospect of financial profit. The various outcomes are presented in Table 1. The premium, or the price of the option, reflects the insurance component, the hedging and the investment component. In pricing a bid in foreign currency only the insurance component should be a part of the price.

Assume that the US firm has determined the price of the bid in dollars. The question is —how should the firm translate the domestic price to a foreign currency price. The forward market and the currency options market provide the firm with the necessary mechanism. The pricing process is described in Table 2.

The premium of the currency option is known at the time of the purchase. If we can determine the investment value of the option, the hedging value will be given by the identity.

$$\text{Option price (premium)} = \text{investment value} + \text{hedging value}$$

The investment value of using the currency options market is the present value of the financial profits presented in Table 1. The present value is a function of the joint probability of the acceptance of the $S_t>F_t$ and the joint probability of the rejection of the bid and $S_t<F_t$.

If the decision maker for the firm has been risk neutral it can be shown that the present value of the financial profits is exactly equal to the price of the option (the premium). In this case, the hedging is provided at no cost. If the decision maker is risk averse the present value of the financial profits of the option is less than its price. However, even in this case, the real cost of the hedging is less than the price paid for the option.

Accounting for Exchange Fluctuations and Measuring Performance

22
Foreign Currency Accounting and Its Transition*

Yuji Ijiri†

TRANSITION OF FOREIGN CURRENCY ACCOUNTING

1.1. FASB Statement 8

Foreign currency accounting is one of the most controversial areas in accounting. After years of debate, the Financial Accounting Standards Board (FASB), a private rule-making body authorized to prescribe accounting standards in the United States, issued in October 1975 Statement 8 on foreign currency translation (FASB 1975). Immediately after its issuance, pressure mounted on the Board to rescind it. The Board resisted the pressure but finally in 1979 it agreed to review Statement 8 as a part of an overall postenactment review of all pronouncements.

In August 1980, the Board issued an exposure draft adopting an entirely different approach to foreign currency translation from the one prescribed in Statement 8 (FASB 1980). This resulted in more controversies. The Board decided to withdraw the exposure draft, a highly unusual event, and replace it with a new one, which was published in June 1981 (FASB 1981). In December 1981, the Board adopted Statement of Financial Accounting Standards No. 52 (Statement 52), *Foreign Currency Translation*. This new statement will take effect for years beginning on or after December 15, 1982, that is, from calendar year 1983 for many companies. Earlier application is allowed and encouraged; some companies adopted the standard for 1981 financial statements.

Why is there so much controversy about foreign currency accounting? Attempts to answer this question reveal some fundamental dilemmas in establishing the standards by which the performance of foreign operations is to be measured. This chapter is aimed at providing a perspective on foreign currency accounting by reviewing its theories and practices with the aid of a simple network model of foreign currency transactions so that complex matters can be comprehended in the simplest manner.

1.2. Four Periods in History

To understand the significance of the change in practice to be brought about by the new pronouncement and to evaluate its potential economic consequences, a brief examination of the history of foreign currency accounting is provided.

It is perhaps reasonable to divide the history of foreign currency accounting in the United States into four periods. Their salient features in practice may be summarized as follows.

---

*This article is reprinted with permission, from *Managing Foreign Exchange Risk* by Richard J. Herring (ed.), Cambridge University Press, 1983, pp. 181–212.

†The author is indebted to Richard J. Herring for his valuable comments and suggestions on an earlier draft of this chapter. Helpful comments by James L. Murdy are also gratefully acknowledged.

1. *Pre-1963* Predominance of the current-noncurrent method; deferral of and reserves for unrealized exchange gains and losses accepted. Accounting Principles Board's (APB) Opinion 6 marked the end of this period (American Institute of CPAs 1965).
2. *1963–75* Coexistence of the current-noncurrent method and the monetary-nonmonetary method; deferral of and reserves for unrealized exchange gains and losses accepted. FASB's Statement 8 marked the end of this period.
3. *1975–82* Exclusive use of the temporal method, which is the monetary-nonmonetary method with a minor modification; deferral of and reserves for unrealized exchange gains and losses prohibited. FASB's Statement 52 marks the end of this period.
4. *1983–* A strict use of the current rate method coupled with a permanent deferment of translation gains and losses if they arise from the translation of the foreign entity's primary currency (called the "functional currency") into the reporting currency (the parent company's currency).

Briefly speaking, major controversies in foreign currency accounting are centered on two key issues:

Which exchange rate, historical or current, should be used in translating assets and liabilities of a foreign enterprise?

How should unrealized exchange gains and losses be recognized in income—immediately when a rate change occurs or deferred until the settlement?

Here, historical rate means the exchange rate that prevailed when the asset or liability in question was originally acquired. Current rate means the exchange rate that prevailed at the close of the accounting period for which financial statements are prepared. The rate may not be current by the time financial statements are published. Thus, "closing rate" is a more accurate term, but the term "current rate" has been widely used in the literature as well as in official pronouncements and will be used here also.

The current-noncurrent method applies the current rate to all current assets and current liabilities (i.e., those assets and liabilities expected to be converted into cash or settled in cash within one year) and the historical rate to all other assets and liabilities. This method has been supported by official pronouncements dating back to the 1930s (American Institute of CPAs 1931, 1934, 1939, 1953).

The monetary-nonmonetary method applies the current rate to monetary items (assets and liabilities denominated in fixed amounts of foreign currency) and the historical rate to all other items (nonmonetary items). Originally advanced by Hepworth (1956), its use gained acceptance among so many companies that the APB declared it as acceptable in a section of APB Opinion 6, which stated: "The Board is of the opinion that translation of long-term receivables and long-term liabilities at current exchange rates is appropriate in many circumstances." No specifications were provided, however, as to when such translations would be considered appropriate. Hence, the practice resulted in diverse uses of the current-noncurrent and the monetary-nonmonetary methods.

The temporal method is the same as the monetary-nonmonetary method except that nonmonetary items stated at current price in the foreign market are translated using the current exchange rate just like monetary items. The temporal method was originally advocated by Lorensen (1972) and adopted in FASB Statement 8.

The current rate method applies the current rate to all assets and liabilities regardless of whether they are current or noncurrent, monetary or nonmonetary. Many Euorpean countries have been using the current rate method. An approach similar to the one adopted in Statement 52 (i.e., the use of the current rate combined with a deferral of some exchange gains and losses) has been advocated by Parkinson (1972).

Exchange rate fluctuations create exchange gains and losses. Suppose that a U.S. company exports merchandise on November 30 for which the British customer agrees to pay 10 million pounds two months later. If the exchange rate is $2.10 to the pound on November 30, the receivable is valued at $21 million, setting aside the possible interest and collectibility issue. If the pound weakens to $1.80 by the time the receivables are paid and converted into dollars two months later, the company suffers a $3 million loss since 10 million pounds is worth only $18 million.

This $3 million loss is a realized loss since the deal has been closed and no more transactions are outstanding. No arguments have been raised against the view that such realized gains and losses should be taken into income. It is unrealized gains and losses that are at the focal point of controversy.

Suppose that as of December 31, while the receivable is still outstanding, the pound weakens from $2.10 to $2.00. Economically, the company has suffered a $1 million loss since the receivable is worth only $20 million. Yet the loss is "unrealized" since the transaction has not been completely settled yet. (Similarly, any gain and loss on a forward exchange contract are also unrealized until the contract is sold or closed, whether the contract is for hedging or for speculation, with a minor exception to be discussed later.)

Before FASB Statement 8 became effective in 1975, it was acceptable to defer such unrealized losses: Unrealized gains are normally deferred until realized for the sake of conservative accounting. It was also acceptable to make reserves for anticipated future losses. After Statement 8, all unrealized exchange gains and losses must be taken into income immediately upon the rate change, and no reserves are allowed for anticipated future losses (unless such losses meet the criteria stated in another FASB statement on contingencies).

Unlike earlier official pronouncements, Statement 8 distinguished, for the first time, between exchange gains and losses arising from a transaction such as already discussed and exchange gains and losses arising from a translation of foreign financial statements. If the sale of merchandise were carried out by a British subisidary instead of the U.S. parent, an unrealized loss of $1 million would arise from the translation of the 10-million-pound receivable recorded on the books of the British subsidiary, hence, a translation loss instead of a transaction loss.

Although the distinction was made, the temporal method resulted in the identical treatment of a transaction and a translation. This is because under the temporal method, a foreign enterprise is viewed as a shell and all of its transactions were translated as if they were conducted by the parent company. This, however, is no longer true under the approach in Statement 52.

1.3. Main Features of Statement 52

The main features of Statement 52 may be summarized as follows:

1. Use of current rate in translating all assets and liabilities.

2. Exclusion of certain unrealized exchange gains and losses from income using a newly introduced notion of "functional currency" as a basis of determining which gains and losses are to be excluded from income.

Here, functional currency is defined as the primary currency of the economic environment in which enterprise generates and expends cash. Generally, the functional currency is the currency of the country in which the enterprise is located. However, there may be many circumstances where this is not true, as spelled out in Statement 52. For example, if foreign operations are a direct and integral component or extension of the parent company's operations, the parent's currency would be the functional currency.

This statement requires that the financial statements of a foreign enterprise first be given in the functional currency using the generally accepted accounting principles of the United States. Any exchange gains and losses from transactions other than in the functional currency are taken into income of that foreign enterprise. There is no difference between this and the current practice under Statement 8. The crucial difference arises from the translation of foreign statements stated in the functional currency into the reporting currency, that is, the U.S. dollars. Currently all gains and losses arising from this translation are immediately recognized in income. Statement 52, on the other hand, requires that all gains and losses arising from the translation of foreign financial statements expressed in the functional currency into the reporting currency be accumulated in a "translation adjustment" account as a direct adjustment to the shareholders' equity of the U.S. corporation.

Such an accumulated translation adjustment remains in the shareholders' equity account until there is a sale or a liquidation of the foreign enterprise. When such a sale or a liquidation occurs, the corresponding portion of accumulated translation adjustment is eliminated from this account and recognized in income as an addition (gain) or as a deduction (loss).

Hence, in the previous example of a sale of merchandise for 10 million pounds, if the sale is carried out by the U.S. parent, the exchange loss is immediately taken into income, whereas if it is carried out by the British subisidary, the exchange loss is accumulated in the shareholders' equity of the consolidated entity until a sale or a liquidation of the subsidiary occurs.

Although exchange gains and losses from *transactions* in a foreign currency are recognized in income immediately, there are two exceptions to this, namely, gains and losses from intercompany foreign currency transactions that are of a long-term investment nature and from economic hedges of a net investment in a foreign entity. The former refers to intercompany foreign currency transactions between the parent and its subsidiary that are of a long-term financing or capital nature. The latter refers to foreign currency transactions that are intended to be and are effective as an economic hedge of a net investment in a foreign entity. Both exceptions are introduced for the sake of consistency with the treatment of translation adjustment so that if an exchange gain or loss goes to a translation adjustment account of shareholders' equity, a gain or loss from a related transaction (the parent side of the transaction or the hedging side of the transaction) will also go to the same account.

The introduction of the idea of functional currency and related deferment of recognition of exchange gains and losses created a whole new approach to the basic mechanism in foreign currency translation. Formerly, consolidated financial statements reflected the operations of the consolidated entity viewed uniformly from the standpoint of the U.S.

parent. This is no longer true under the new Statement. However, the financial relationships among elements of a balanced sheet of a foreign entity are preserved in the translation process since the entire statement is restated under one rate (the current rate), instead of applying different rates depending upon the nature of individual asset or liability.

2. A NETWORK OF FOREIGN CURRENCY TRANSACTIONS

2.1. Interest Rate Parity

Before various alternative methods in foreign currency accounting are examined, it will be useful to develop a basic network of foreign currency transactions that contains necessary ingredients for the discussion.

At a minimum, four types of cash concepts are needed. Let us denote by m' and M' a foreign currency and a domestic currency, respectively, at the beginning of a period and by m and M the same foreign and domestic currencies, respectively, at the end of the period. These symbols may be thought of as representing the indicated currency in a general sense or the amount of the currency held by an enterprise. In the latter case the unit of measurement will always be the unit of that currency; that is, m' and m are in marks if the foreign currency is German marks and M' and M are in dollars if the domestic currency is U.S. dollars. Exchange rates at beginning, r', and at end, r, are always expressed in price of a unit of foreign currency stated in domestic currency. Thus, foreign currency may be converted into its equivalent in domestic currency via $M' = r'm'$ and $M = rm$.

Depending upon the specific situation, r' may be referred to as current exchange rate and r, the future exchange rate or r, the current exchange rate and r', the past exchange rate. The same shift in time may be observed in m', m, M', and M, so as to look at these concepts and measures both from the standpoint of the beginning of the period and that of the end of the period.

Next, let s be 1 plus the interest rate prevailing in the foreign country and S be 1 plus the interest rate prevailing in the domestic country. To distinguish these from the interest rates, they will be referred to as *interest factors*. Then, foreign and domestic currencies may be expressed as a function of the same currency one period earlier, namely, $m = sm'$ and $M = SM'$, assuming there are no other transactions during the period.

Figure 1 depicts the relationship among the four currencies. In Figure 1, an arrow indicates the direction toward which the exchange rate or the interest factor is multiplied. Going the other way, the rate or the factor acts as a divisor. Normally, there is a spread between selling and buying rates as well as between borrowing and lending interest factors. However, for the sake of simplicity, such a spread is considered to be negligible.

The open interest parity relationship (sometimes referred to as the international Fisher Effect; see Aliber and Stickney 1975), states that investors operate in such a way that foreign investment, $M' \rightarrow m' \rightarrow m \rightarrow M$, will yield the same expected M as domestic investment. Hence, $M'S = M = M'(1/r')sr$. Therefore

$$r/r' = S/s \qquad (1)$$

2.2. Purchasing Power Parity

Another exchange rate relationship, purchasing power parity, was originally introduced by Cassel in 1916. It calls for an introduction of nonmonetary items into the picture. To

FIGURE 1

Foreign and Domestic Currencies

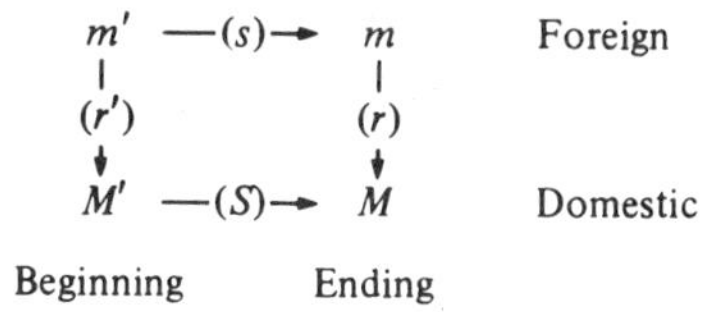

simplify, let us assume that there is one commodity that is commonly available both in foreign and domestic markets and that there are no other commodities existing in either market. The price of the commodity is p' at the beginning and p at the end of a period in foreign market, expressed in units of foreign currency. The price of the same commodity is P' at beginning and P at end of the period in domestic market, expressed in units of domestic currency.

Alternatively, it may be assumed that a bundle of commodities commonly exists in foreign and domestic markets and that they are always traded at the given commodity mix. Then, these prices indicate the price of a unit of a commodity basket. (When the mix is altered between foreign and domestic markets, a complex issue of international price indexing arises, but the issue is set aside here to focus on the basic elements in foreign currency transactions.)

Let n' and n be the physical units of the commodity in the foreign market at the beginning and end of a period, respectively, and N' and N be the same commodity in the domestic market at the beginning and end of the period, respectively.

In addition, it is necessary to define a factor analogous to the interest factors for the commodity to link n' to n and N' to N. Let us define h as the "holding" factor for the foreign commodity and H as the holding factor for the domestic commodity. Here, the holding factor may be less than 1, equal to 1, or greater than 1, depending upon whether the holding cost is positive, zero, or negative. The factor's being less than 1 means shrinkage of the commodity over time, whereas its being greater than 1 indicates natural or contractural growth of the commodity over time. Any holding cost or holding revenue is assumed to be stated as a percentage of the physical units of the commodity (negative for holding cost), and the holding factor is 1 plus such a rate.

Figure 2 depicts flows of money and commodity in foreign and domestic markets and across the international boundary. The purchasing power parity relationship may then be expressed as the equality of the yields of domestic and foreign commodity investments. Namely, domestic investment $M' \rightarrow N' \rightarrow N \rightarrow M$ yields the same M as in foreign investment $M' \rightarrow m' \rightarrow n' \rightarrow n \rightarrow m \rightarrow M$. Hence, $M'(1/P')HP = M = M'(1/r)(1/p')hpr$. For simplicity, if we assume that $h = H = 1$, then letting $f = p/p'$ and $F = P/P'$ be foreign and domestic inflation rates, respectively, we have,

$$r/r' = F/f \tag{2}$$

which expresses the purchasing power parity relationship. (This equation expresses the "absolute" purchasing power parity as against the "relative" purchasing parity; the latter results in an equality between the ratio of changes in the exchange rates and the ratio of changes in the inflation rates.) Like equation (1), equation (2) is an expression of an

FIGURE 2

Money and Commodity Flows

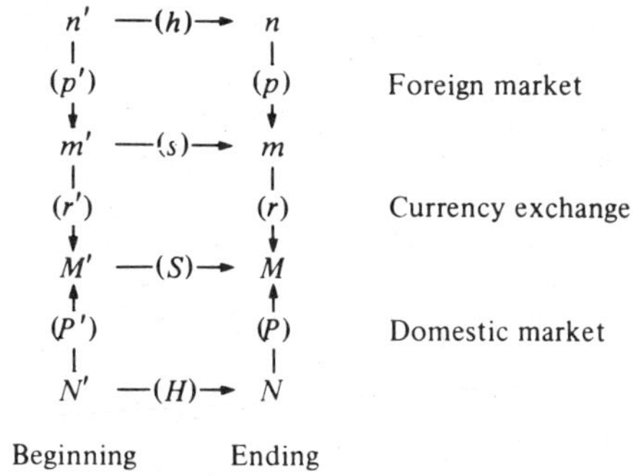

equilibrium condition. The purchasing power parity relationship has been frequently confirmed empirically (see e.g., Balassa 1964, Aliber and Stickney 1975). However, there are studies that cast doubt on its validity over the short run and especially for the markets in the 1970s (see Frenkel 1981a,b).

It is highly unlikely that all of these mechanisms will work efficiently so that the equilibrium relationships hold instantaneously. Part of the difficulties in foreign currency accounting comes from the fact that these factors and rates are frequently inconsistent, but accountants must choose one of them as a standard basis for translation. For an extension of this analysis to international commodity flows, see the Appendix.

3. A COMPARISON OF ALTERNATIVES

3.1. Current-Noncurrent Versus Monetary-Nonmonetary

Keeping in mind the transition of foreign currency accounting discussed in section 1 and the network of foreign currency transactions in section 2, let us now examine alternatives in foreign currency accounting. (See also the FASB Discussion Memorandum [1974], which summarizes some of the key issues in comparing alternatives in foreign currency accounting.)

First, let us compare the current-noncurrent method and the monetary-nonmonetary method. For this comparison, additional notations are necessary. Let c be net current items (current assets less current liabilities) and l be net noncurrent, or long-term, items (long-term assets less long-term liabilities). Both are expressed in units of foreign currency. Monetary items, m, are divided into the current portion, denoted by m_c, and the noncurrent portion, denoted by m_l. Likewise, nonmonetary items are divided into n_c and n_l. Although in reality current and noncurrent portions of nonmonetary items take considerably different forms, physically and economically, it is assumed here, for the sake of simplicity of illustration, that the same price p (current price) or p' (historical price) is applicable to both portions. This would make sense, for example, when a single commodity has a short-term use (consumption) and a long-term use (seeds for future crops).

Table 1 shows the difference between the two methods. The current-noncurrent

TABLE 1

Current–Noncurrent Versus Monetary–Nonmonetary Method

	Monetary items r	Nonmonetary items r'
Current items r	m_c	$n_c p'$
Noncurrent items r'	m_l	$n_l p'$

method applies the current rate r to m_c and $n_c p'$ and the historical rate r' to m_l and $n_l p'$, whereas the monetary-nonmonetary method applies the current rate r to m_c and m_l and the historical rate r' to $n_c p'$ and $n_l p'$. Here, p' is used to indicate that nonmonetary assets and liabilities are valued at the historical cost, the price at the beginning of a period at which the items were assumed to have been acquired. Although in some cases (as in an application of the lower-of-cost-or-market method) some nonmonetary items may be stated in the current price, such cases are exceptions rather than the principle. Hence it is assumed that all nonmonetary items are stated at the historical cost. More details on this will be discussed in the next section when the monetary-nonmonetary method is compared with the temporal method.

It is easy to understand what the translated figure means for current, monetary items, $m_c r$. It represents the amount in domestic currency that may be obtained now by disposing of the items or that may be required to replace the items now, if transactions cost can be set aside.

Virtually all monetary items are adjusted for interest. Thus, if there were a premium or discount in the acquisition cost, it is amortized over the remaining life of the items so that the book value can reflect realization of interest throughout the life. Of course, the market value of the monetary items may differ from the book value due to fluctuations in the interest rate and the collectibility of receivables, but the discrepancy tends to be minor in view of the fact that it is a short-term, current item.

It is also easy to understand what the translated figure means for noncurrent, nonmonetary items, $n_l p'r'$. It represents the amount in the domestic currency that would have been required if the items had been acquired in the domestic currency at the time they were actually acquired in the foreign currency. They are valued at the historical price p', that is, the foreign price at which the item was actually acquired and then translated at the exchange rate available at that time. Of course, depreciation may have changed the book value of the item from the actual acquisition cost, and the discrepancy may be accounted for as a reduction in the physical quantity n measured in units of service potential, just as depletion of oil and other natural resources is treated.

Controversies frequently occur with regard to the remaining two categories in Table 1. First, let us take current, nonmonetary items. Those who favor the monetary-nonmonetary method argue that $n_c p'r$ does not make sense since we are multiplying apples and oranges, that is, translating the historical price p' at the current exchange rate r. This price-rate mismatch has been one of the points of argument in foreign currency accounting.

Supporters of the current-noncurrent method argue that since current, nonmonetary items are relatively close to a point of realization where they are converted into monetary items, the discrepancy in rates r and r' is likely to be small and tolerable, except for LIFO (last in, first out) inventories for which the historical rate may be the exchange rate that was in effect decades ago.

More importantly, however, they question the logic of applying the current rate to noncurrent, monetary items, $m_l r$, the practice followed under the monetary-nonmonetary method. Long-term receivables and long-term debt may take years or decades before they mature. Why should income of a period be affected by frequent fluctuations of the exchange rates when the closing rate may have no relationship with what the rate ultimately might be at maturity? Why not fix the rate at the historical rate once and for all until maturity in a manner analogous to the historical cost principle that governs the price at which goods or services are valued?

Furthermore, these supporters point out a mismatch in a different sense. Quite often, foreign properties are acquired under a financing by foreign long-term debt, that is, $n_l = -m_l > 0$, focusing on this transaction only. Then, there is no net exposure to exchange rate fluctuation economically since assets and liabilities cancel out ($m_l + n_l = 0$), and this is the result obtained under the current-noncurrent method. Yet under the monetary-nonmonetary method, the liability side $i(m_l < 0)$ is exposed but not the asset side ($n_l > 0$) when in fact the two are an integral part of a foreign financing investment activity.

Although these arguments have merit, it seems difficult to overcome the argument for the price-rate consistency and the resulting simplicity in interpretation under the monetary-nonmonetary method. Furthermore, the monetary-nonmonetary method is given additional theoretical support by the purchasing power parity theory.

Those who support the purchasing power parity theory argue that $p'r'$ is also likely to reflect the "real" amount in the domestic currency that would have to be paid to acquire the item now in the domestic currency. If the purchasing power parity is observed accurately, then, as discussed in the previous section, $r/r' = F/f = F/(p/p')$. Hence, $p'r' = pr/F$, namely, the amount that must be paid now in the domestic currency, pr, adjusted for the domestic inflation factor F.

In particular, if the domestic inflation is negligible, that is, F is close to 1, $p'r' = pr$, which says that the translated amount using the historical rate reflects the current market value of goods in the foreign market translated by the current rate. This has been in fact approximately true in the case of hyperinflationary countries vis-à-vis the United States. Devaluation loss on inventories is normally recovered quickly a few months later by means of higher selling price of inventories.

Therefore, under the monetary-nonmonetary method, the translated amount maintains parity with the real cost of the item in the domestic market, and the principle of historical cost can be maintained in both markets. This balance will be disturbed if the current rate r is applied to the historical foreign price p'. More on this p[illegible] when the current rate method is examined.

3.2. Monetary-Nonmonetary Versus Temporal

The preceding analysis assumes that all nonmonetary items are carried at historical cost. This assumption was introduced to avoid an unnecessary complication that can occur when additional fine points are introduced at too early a stage.

Now it is time to be more precise. Note that the price-rate consistency attributed to the monetary-nonmonetary method is not exactly the consequence of the monetary-nonmonetary classification. Rather, the classification tied to the price-rate consistency is to divide items into current-price items and historical-price items, depending upon whether the item is priced under the current price or under the historical price in the foreign books of accounts. Then, the price-rate consistency is achieved by translating current-price items by the current rate and historical-price items by the historical rate.

This is the temporal method, aimed at achieving temporal consistency between the foreign price and the exchange rate. This consistency was also attributed to the monetary-nonmonetary method because monetary items are current-price items and most nonmonetary items are historical-price items, with the exception of current-price, nonmonetary items arising from an application of the lower-of-cost-or-market method or other minor exceptions to the prevailing historical cost principle.

The purchasing power parity relationship can still be applied to the temporal method since all historical-price items are nonmonetary, for which the purchasing power parity argument is applicable, and all current-price items do not require any restatement.

In fact, it is hard to support the translation of a current-price nonmonetary item using historical rate simply because it is nonmonetary. Therefore, the temporal method is an improvement over the monetary-nonmonetary method from a theoretical standpoint.

3.3. Temporal Versus Current Rate

The difference between the temporal method and the current rate method is that historical-price items are translated at the historical rate ($p'r'$) under the temporal method whereas they, as well as current-price items, are translated at the current rate ($p'r$) under the current rate method, which translates everything at the current rate.

Naturally, the supporters of the temporal method criticize the price-rate mismatch in the current rate method. What is a counter-argument by the supporters of the current rate method?

Supporters of the current rate method criticize those who view foreign operations strictly from the domestic standpoint as if the foreign entity were a shell, which is the basic premise underlying the emphasis on the price-rate consistency. They argue that foreign operations should be evaluated relative to their respective foreign environments in which the operations take place and not relative to the domestic environment. Functional currency is a way of establishing a standard of measurement in that foreign environment. Translation that occurs from the functional currency to the reporting currency is merely an incidental process for the sake of consolidation. Hence, the translated financial statements should not disturb the relationship among the figures in the foreign financial statements, and the only way of achieving this is to translate by a single rate. They then argue that the only rate meaningful for this single-rate method is the current (more precisely, closing) rate because all assets and liabilities are reported to reflect the status at the close of the period.

Although this argument is quite convincing in some respects, it has some serious weaknesses in its logic.

For most corporations operating in foreign countries, the ultimate objective of foreign investment is in recovery of investment in the domestic currency. If this is true, it seems that evaluation of foreign operations from the multi-environment viewpoint would not be useful except for local purposes. For example, a man climbing up a mast of the sinking Titanic may be commended if he climbs ten feet. But if the ship sinks thirty feet in the meantime, did he really gain ten feet or lose twenty feet? The loss of twenty feet seems to be the vital information for the investment-financing decision with respect to this foreign enterprise.

Second, what makes the matter worse is that the end result of translation is combined with statements of all other entities under a consolidated enterprise and reported in a single set of consolidated financial statements. A method meaningful for preparing stand-alone statements may not make sense when the statements are to be consolidated with other statements that may be prepared under entirely different methods. It is analogous to adding the distances climbed by men on different ships without adjusting for the changes in the ships' waterlines. In this regard, the domestic-environment view appears to be superior since it offers a unifying basis of consolidation. Under this view, regardless of how many different foreign environments the enterprise operations take place in, they are all viewed uniformly from the domestic standpoint.

The third problem with this multi-environment view is that even if its objective is accepted, that is, to view a multinational corporation from the multi-environment standpoint, the use of a single reporting currency defeats its entire objective. If the statements are reported in U.S. dollars, there is no way of avoiding the fact that financial figures on the statements are viewed from the U.S. standpoint.

This is because, when the reporting currency weakens, the financial statements of a multinational corporation look better (improved earnings and/or shareholders' equity) since its foreign investments are more valuable vis-à-vis the reporting currency. The converse is true when the reporting currency strengthens. It is normal for financial statements reported in one currency to show an entirely different trend compared with those reported in another currency.

A simple example here might be useful. Suppose an enterprise holds one unit of FC (foreign currency) and one unit of DC (domestic currency) from the beginning of a period to its end. At the beginning the exchange rate was 1FC = 1DC and at the end it is 2FC = 1DC. Did the enterprise gain or lose as a result of the rate change?

From the domestic standpoint, the enterprise lost 0.5DC since 1FC, which was worth 1DC at the beginning, is worth only 0.5DC at the end. But from the foreign standpoint, the enterprise gained 1FC, since 1DC, which was worth 1FC, is now worth 2FC. Which view is correct? In particular, how much did the enterprise gain or lose if it is truly a global company that does not distinguish between foreign and domestic countries. (For example, it has a 50% investment in country D and a 50% investment in country F at the beginning.)

To answer the question, a composite currency, such as the European Currency Unit (see a discussion in Rueschhoff 1976) must be brought in. But then, a difficult aggregation issue arises: Under what weights should different currencies be aggregated? A composite currency suitable for one corporation may not be suitable for another. And if a choice of composite currencies is allowed, intercorporate comparisons of financial data become very difficult.

The simplicity of the domestic-environment view seems to outweigh any benefit that may be achieved by introducing the multi-environment view. Although a full-scale implementation of the global view might be theoretically superior to the domestic view, it should be carried out only after careful studies on its impact on various parts of corporate financial reports.

4. INTERACTION WITH INFLATION ACCOUNTING

4.1. Restate-Translate Versus Translate-Restate

The single most important problem that the new approach in Statement 52 presents is the urgent need to consolidate issues in foreign currency accounting and price-level adjustment.

Although the current rate method in itself contains temporal inconsistency between price and exchange rate, this inconsistency can be eliminated if the translation is combined with general price-level adjustment. This idea was first introduced on a limited basis in the second exposure draft of the FASB (1981). However, the idea was rejected in Statement 52.

The exposure draft required a price-level adjustment, using the local inflation rate, before translating into the reporting currency, if the cumulative inflation rate of the country during the most recent three-year period is approximately 100 percent or more. Statement 52 elminated this provision and simply required use of the reporting currency as the functional currency for an enterprise in such a country.

Suppose a plot of land was acquired for 10FC ten years ago when 1FC = 1DC. If the inflation rate during the ten-year period is 1,900 percent in the foreign country and 100 percent in the domestic country, 10FC paid ten years ago is worth 200FC now in the foreign country, whereas 10DC (=10FC) paid ten years ago is worth 20DC now in the domestic country. If the purchasing power parity theory is actually observed, the current exchange rate will be 10FC = 1DC. Under the exposure draft, the cost of land is first adjusted to 200FC using the foreign inflation rate and then translated as 20DC using the current exchange rate. Under Statement 52, the DC is used as the functional currency, which means that 10FC is immediately translated as 10DC upon acquisition of the land and stays at that amount. No further adjustments are made since price-level adjustment is not allowed in U.S. financial statements, although a supplemental disclosure is required on some price-level-adjusted financial data.

If nonmonetary items are price-level adjusted, their translated price is changed from $p'r$ to $p'fr = p'(p/p')r = pr$, under the assumption of a single commodity (or a single mix of commodities). Because of multiple commodities with varying mixes, $p'f$ is not exactly equal to the current cost p. This is the aggregation issue that lies at the heart of the age-old debate between constant dollar accounting using general price-level adjustment and current cost accounting using specific price adjustment.

Although the choice between general price-level adjustment and specific price adjustment is an extremely important issue in accounting, it has been debated elsewhere independent of foreign exchange accounting, and the issues will not be repeated here other than to point out one conceptual note. That is, inflation is not merely fluctuations in individual commodity prices, which can occur without inflation. Inflation is an erosion of the purchasing power of money. Hence, it is most logical to use general price-level adjustment to adjust for the effect of inflation, though specific price adjustment may be introduced for some reasons other than inflation.

If the price-rate consistency in the current rate method can be attained only by coupling the translation process with a price-level adjustment, the domestic statements as well as foreign statements must all be adjusted for price-level changes in order to make consolidated statements meaningful. When this is done, then and only then can the entire set of financial statements acquire consistent meaning, showing the amounts of investment measured in the dollar equivalent of the purchasing power of current foreign currencies that were sacrificed in acquiring goods and services.

Currently, price-level-adjusted data are presented only partially and as supplemental information. A full-scale implementation of the price-level adjustment on a worldwide basis would not only make financial statements consistent under the current rate method, but would also be likely to stabilize exchange gains and losses reported in financial statements. This is because a significant part of the problems in the recognition of exchange gains and losses stems from the differential inflation rates among different countries that are often reflected in the exchange rate.

In the past, two basically different approaches have been proposed for the interaction of foreign currency translation and price-level restatement. One is the restate-translate method under which items in foreign statements are first restated using the inflation rate observed in the foreign country, and the restated amounts are then translated using the current exchange rate. The preceding discussion follows this method.

Using the notations introduced earlier, this means that a nonmonetary item n in a foreign country will be restated from the historical cost np' to the price-level adjusted historical cost using the foreign inflation rate $f = p/p'$, obtaining $np'f = np$, and then translated to npr using the current exchange rate r. Under the assumption of a single commodity or a constant commodity mix, the result of restate-translate, npr, shows the current amount of the domestic currency needed to acquire the nomonetary item in the foreign country.

The other approach, called the translate-restate method (see, e.g., Zenoff and Zwick 1969), means that a nonmonetary item n stated in historical cost np' is first translated into the domestic currency using the historical exchange rate r' to $np'r'$ and then restated using the domestic inflation rate $F = P/P'$, obtaining $np'r'F = nr'p'(P/P')$. Conceptually, the result of translate-restate shows the purchasing power in the domestic market that was sacrificed in order to obtain the foreign goods or services.

Although each method has its own logical support, it is clear that the adoption of the current rate method paved a way for the restate-translate method.

4.2. The Capital Charge

It has been pointed out (Ijiri 1976) that price-level-adjusted figures may be viewed in two different ways, one being the dual of the other. One is to consider them to have been prepared under the same accounting principles as figures in conventional statements but only expressed in a different unit of measurement, namely, in terms of the current purchasing power rather than in the nominal unit of money.

A dual viewpoint is to consider price-level-adjusted figures to have been prepared under the same nominal unit of money as in conventional statements but prepared under accounting principles different from conventional ones. The difference comes in the realization principle.

Price-level adjustment may be viewed as a way of relaxing the realization principle, which prohibits recognition of unrealized change in values of nonmonetary items so as to allow recognition of unrealized gains and losses of such items at a uniform rate specified by the rate of inflation. Thus, a plot of land costing \$1 million ten years ago is price-level adjusted to, say, \$2 million, not because it is now expressed in a different kind of dollars, but because appreciation in the land price is recognized to the extent of general price-level increase, which in this case amounted to \$1 million.

This view seems to support the current rate and the restate-translate methods, since viewed from this angle it seems to make sense to adjust the land price in a foreign country because of inflation in that country, not because of inflation in the domestic country.

An important part of the dual interpretation is not only to recognize appreciation in nonmonetary items based on general price-level increase but also to recognize appreciation in owners' equity that must be preserved in order to maintain the purchasing power of the owners' investment. An enterprise having m and n from the beginning to the end of a period with no changes in them gains from appreciation of nonmonetary items at the rate of inflation, $np'(f - 1) = np - np'$, recognized under this dual interpretation. But at the same time there is a "capital charge" to maintain the purchasing power of the owners' investment at the beginning of the period, w'; namely, $w'(f - 1) = (m + np')(f - 1)$. The difference between the two is the net effect of adjustment on income in this stationary example, which amounts to a gain of $np'(f - 1)$ less a loss of $(m + np')(f - 1)$ or $-m(f - 1)$. Under the primal interpretation, this is called a price-level gain (or loss, if negative) on monetary items, whereas under the dual interpretation the nonmonetary items and the capital charge on owners' equity caused the price-level gain.

4.3. Exchange Gains and Price-Level Gains

When foreign statements are price-level adjusted, their translated statements produce both price-level gains (or losses) and exchange gains (or losses). The two types of gains are related in a way that is commonly observed in analysis of variance between actual cost and standard cost.

Assuming no transactions during the period, the net worth w of a foreign enterprise changes from its beginning state $w' = m + np'$ to $w = m + np'f = m + np$ at the end of the period after price-level adjustment. Their translated version is

$$w'r = mr' + np'r' \tag{3}$$

at beginning and

$$wr = mr + npr \tag{4}$$

at end. Comparing the two, it may be noted that $mr - mr'$ is all exchange gain since monetary items are unchanged in the foreign statements. On the other hand, $npr - np'r'$ is a joint effect of the price-level change and the exchange rate change.

On the foreign statements, the price-level gain is shown as $np'f - np' = np - np'$; hence, the translated amount of price-level gain is $np'(f - 1)r' = npr' - np'r'$ using the exchange rate at beginning. (Using the current rate is another possible approach.) This leaves $npr - npr'$ as exchange gain, that is, the rate differential multiplied by the ending amount of nonmonetary items expressed in foreign currency.

Exchange gain of monetary items $mr - mr'$ and of nonmonetary items $npr - npr'$, combined with price-level gain of nonmonetary items $npr' - np'r'$, completely accounts

TABLE 2

Reconciliation of Exchange Gain and Price-Level Gain

	Exchange gain	Price-level gain	Total
Monetary	$mr - mr'$		$mr - mr'$
Nonmonetary	$npr - npr'$	$np'(f - 1)r'$	$npr - np'r'$
Net worth	$wr - wr'$	$np'(f - 1)r'$	$wr - w'r'$
Capital charge		$-w'(f - 1)r'$	$-w'fr' + w'r'$
Net income	$wr - wr'$	$-m(f - 1)r'$	$wr - w'fr'$

for the change in the translated amount of the net worth of the foreign enterprise from $mr' + np'r'$ to $mr + npr$, as shown in Table 5.2.

However, in price-level-adjusted statements, the increment of net worth is not all recognized as income but only the residual after a capital charge, the amount to be charged additionally in order to maintain the purchasing power of the owners' equity. The capital charge is computed in a manner analogous to nonmonetary items except that the sign must be reversed. Hence, the price-level component of the capital charge is $-w'(f-1)r'$.

There has been a proposal (see Shwayder 1972) to restate the shareholders' equity account of a foreign subsidiary not by the foreign inflation rate, but by the domestic inflation rate, which would result in a capital charge of $-w'(F-1)r'$. It is also useful for the purpose of evaluation to analyze the change in net worth of a subsidiary, taking into account the differences between the domestic and foreign inflation rates as discussed in Wyman (1976) for the translate-restate approach.

Basically, however, under the restate-translate approach adopted in the exposure draft for hyperinflationary countries, restated figures are inflation free as far as the foreign market is concerned. Since the underlying philosophy of Statement 52 is to respect the integrity of the foreign environment as the primary place where operations take place, mixing the domestic inflation rate in the analysis may go counter to this underlying view. Thus, if and when a price-level adjustment becomes a required process for U.S. financial statements, it will be the restate-translate approach, using the foreign inflation rates, that must be used in order to maintain the consistency between the adjustment and the translation.

4.4. Open Interest Rate Parity and Discounting

Before leaving the topic of interaction with inflation accounting, an issue related to this topic may be briefly mentioned.

Purchasing power parity has been introduced in accounting and its implications for accounting methods have been discussed quite widely. However, it is interesting to note that very little has been done in foreign currency accounting on the implications of the open interest parity relationship to accounting. To some extent, however, price-level adjustment and interest rate adjustment (discounting receivables and payables) present issues that are largely symmetrical—at least conceptually.

For example, instead of the restate-translate versus translate-restate issue, there is an issue of discount-translate versus translate-discount. To implement the interaction of discounting and translation, a future exchange rate at maturity is needed, since a foreign receivable is first translated in domestic currency using an exchange rate that is expected to be available upon maturity and then discounted using domestic interest rate.

Viewing Figure 1 from the standpoint of the beginning of the period, treating the end of the period as a future point in time, the discount-translate method means that a receivable or payable m is first discounted by the foreign interest factor s to arrive at m/s, which is then translated to domestic currency as $(m/s)r'$. The translate-discount method produces instead mr/S, using the future exchange rate and the domestic interest factor.

Pros and cons of these alternatives need to be explored in more detail in relation to the underlying accounting principles on discounting and amortization of premiums and discounts.

5. DISPOSITION OF EXCHANGE GAINS AND LOSSES

5.1. Income Volatility Under Statement 8

So far the discussions have been limited to the effect of a translation method on the balance sheet. As stated earlier, the other side of the issue in foreign currency accounting is how to dispose of exchange gains and losses.

Corporations complaining about Statement 8 frequently pointed out the volatile impact it had on income and the defensive hedging and other means they had to take to protect the integrity of reported income. Studies conducted to find out the economic consequences of Statement 8 (see, e.g., Peat, Marwick, Mitchell & Co. 1977, and Shank, Dillard, and Murdock 1979) consistently showed increasing hedging activities and various changes in the methods of foreign financing in order to reduce the volatile impact of Statement 8.

The primary reason for the income volatility is the requirement in Statement 8 that all exchange gains and losses be taken into income immediately in the period of the rate change and that no reserves be provided for anticipated losses (unless such losses meet the criteria in another FASB statement on contingencies). This eliminated a route for smoothing the impact of exchange rate fluctuation by deferring gains and losses or by setting reserves.

A secondary reason is that the use of the temporal method increased the net amount of exposure for many corporations, especially those with a large amount of foreign debt. Corporations using the current-noncurrent method prior to Statement 8 had a relatively small fraction, corresponding to the net working capital, of total assets exposed to the rate change as far as accounting exposure is concerned. This situation was drastically changed for many corporations after Statement 8 was introduced. If the corporation had a large amount of foreign debt with a relatively small amount of monetary assets, a switch to the temporal method could result in exposure to more than 50 percent of the total assets.

These two reasons, in conjunction with the volatile exchange markets in recent years, created significant fluctuations in reported income. Therefore, even when economic risk of operating in a foreign country is unchanged, "accounting risk" as measured by the volatility of the net income figure is worsened for many corporations as a result of Statement 8.

Although it is questionable whether such an accounting risk is a meaningful way to evaluate a corporation (see Shapiro 1977 on the definition and measurement of foreign exchange risks), the concern by corporations over the risk forced them to take hedging and other actions that they would not take under a different accounting method.

5.2. Income Smoothing

A key question that may have to be raised here with respect to the disposition of exchange gains and losses is whether income smoothing (by reserves for or deferment of exchange gains and losses) should be viewed as acceptable or even necessary for proper financial reporting.

An anti-smoothing view states that it is possible to take an accurate picture of an enterprise at the end of a period and, by comparing it with a picture taken at the beginning, it is possible to determine accurately the performance of an enterprise in a given period. Thus, the emphasis is on an accurate determination of the short-run income. Every factor that existed at the time such an assessment was made, whether it was ordinary or extraordinary, permanent or temporary, should be taken into account in the determination of income.

A pro-smoothing view starts with a fundamental premise that income of an entity can be determined only in the long run and that periodic income can be determined only by a collection of artificial rules. Therefore, under this view, emphasis is on the long-run profitability. Periodic income is viewed as important not in itself but in its ability to reflect the long-run profitability of the enterprise. Thus, it :s considered misleading and undesirable to incorporate factors that make income figures so volatile that their long-run trend is clouded.

Use of current rate suffers in this regard since it is subject to temporary fluctuations. Although volatility exists with historical rate, it should be remembered that historical rate is not a single rate but rather a collection of rates at different points in time at which various assets and liabilities were acquired; hence, their impact on income is gradual.

Unlike news media and other means of disseminating financial information that can provide information on a weekly or even daily basis, financial statements suffer from their basic timing limitations; that is, they are published only once a year (annual reports) or four times a year (quarterly reports) and at best a month or two after the close of the period. If they were published daily, like stock prices, the use of the current rate might be ideal since the task of sorting out the permanent and temporary factors could be passed on to the readers. Unfortunately, this is not the case in financial statements.

It is analogous to reporting stock prices only four times a year. Given this limitation, would it still be better to report the price at the close of each quarter because it is the most recent price available at that time, or would it be better to report, say, quarterly averages of daily prices because they are more likely to reflect the long-run trend of the stock price than four prices picked out of a fluctuating series? It is statistically obvious that a series of four prices a year can show quite a misleading trend whereas a series of quarterly changes has a much better chance of reflecting an underlying trend if there is any.

In addition to the misleading effect on trend, the use of current rate on all assets and liabilities in quarterly statements can also make foreign operations look riskier than they actually are because of volatile income figures when no reserves or deferments are allowed on exchange gains and losses.

5.3. Economic Reality and Accounting Information

All of these issues on income smoothing and related accounting "manipulations" may appear to be nonsense. After all, accounting information is useful only to the extent that it reflects the economic reality of the enterprise. Theoretically, managers should pursue their business in such a way that the "true" income of the enterprise is maximized. Their decisions should not be affected by how the consequences of their decisions might be reflected in the accounting income.

However, in reality few people can neglect the accounting consequences of their decisions. Only two kinds of managers can neglect accounting consequences completely: those who are extremely naive about the business world and those who are in a highly secure position (say, a son of the founder) in a highly secure enterprise (e.g., a monopolistic or a governmental enterprise).

Ordinary managers cannot neglect accounting information, which is only a surrogate for the economic reality, because no one can comprehend the economic reality with certainty. The greater the uncertainty, the more reliance people place on tangible surrogates. Those with more information and with more time and intelligence to absorb and analyze the information will be able to see through the accounting information and be less influenced by the manipulations of the accounting numbers that may have taken place. But most people must make decisions with only a limited amount of information, time, and intelligence. Oftentimes, they have no choice but to take whatever surrogates are available at their face value. That is when surrogates have a critical impact on decisions. Earnings per share, return on investment, or debt-equity ratio in an enterprise evaluation; degrees, certificates, or grade point average in a personnel evaluation—these are all examples of surrogates that can impact decisions.

The ultimate case of surrogates affecting decisions is when the interested parties agree to create a certain legal consequence based on the outcome that a surrogate has, for example:

1. An employee profit-sharing plan (incentive compensation plan) in which bonuses are determined by the accounting income.
2. A partnership agreement under which the distribution of proceeds is determined by the accounting income.
3. Income taxes, import duties, value-added taxes, and others that are levied at least in part based on accounting numbers.
4. Cost-plus contracts, mergers, and acquisitions, and other contracts in which, due to a high degree of uncertainty, a fixed-price contract is not possible and the parties decide to use accounting data to be generated in the future as a basis for determining the price.
5. Loan covenants that are based on accounting numbers such as net working capital, debt-equity ratio, and times interest earned.

In each of these situations, accounting information is not a surrogate for an economic reality; it *is* the economic reality in the sense that actual cash flows are legally determined by the information.

Considering these serious impacts on decisions (and hence on cash flows to and from the enterprise) that accounting numbers may have, it can be understood why foreign currency accounting is such a serious issue among multinational corporations. The severity of immediate recognition of all exchange gains and losses under Statement 8 may then be fully recognized. And the managers' desire to smooth income so as to minimize accounting risk arising out of foreign exchange activities may also be evaluated in the proper perspective.

The point elaborated in the foregoing discussion is critical not only in understanding foreign currency accounting of an enterprise, but also in understanding foreign exchange activities of the enterprise. This is precisely why an accounting article such as this appears in a volume on managing foreign exchange risk.

5.4. A Possible Solution

Although translation adjustment introduced in Statement 52 as a part of owners' equity has the effect of shielding a significant portion of exchange gains and losses from affecting current income immediately, it results in shielding some clearly permanent displacement of the exchange rate between functional and reporting currencies, along with its temporary fluctuations.

If the position taken by Statement 8, that is, immediate recognition in income of all exchange gains and losses, represents one extreme, the position taken by Statement 52 seems to represent another extreme, under which exchange gains and losses, at least a significant portion of them, are virtually permanently (until liquidation of the subsidiary) shielded from income determination.

One may wonder, however, whether there is not a theoretically meaningful way of disposing of exchange gains and losses between immediate recognition and permanent deferment.

Take long-term debt denominated in foreign currency, for example, and compare it with depreciation accounting on long-term assets. As soon as a long-term asset is installed, its resale value may be decreased substantially. However, the lower-of-cost-or-market method is not practiced in the case of a long-term asset, because under the assumption of going concern the asset is not expected to be sold in the near future but is expected to be put in service for a long period of time. Depreciation accounting thus neglects market value and concentrates on fair allocation of the asset's cost over its useful life.

The same approach may be taken with regard to long-term debt. Its dollar value may fluctuate due to the exchange rate fluctuation, as well as the fluctuation in the foreign bond market. But under the going-concern assumption, the debt is not supposed to be liquidated in the current market, but is to stay outstanding until the end of its term. In this case, the current exchange rate is used only as the best indicator of the exchange rate that will prevail when the debt is liquidated. If so, it would be most appropriate to amortize the gain or loss over the life of the debt. The amortized amount may be treated as a deduction from or addition to interest expense, which is certainly justifiable from a theoretical standpoint.

Undoubtedly, this is a domestic-environment view; the foreign debt of the subsidiary is viewed solely from the domestic standpoint. But the problems associated with the multi-environment view have already been pointed out. The simplicity of the domestic-environment view that underlies the temporal method is highly attractive. When the temporal method is coupled with the amortization of exchange gains and losses on long-term monetary assets and liabilities, the volatile impact on income from exchange rate fluctuation can be substantially mitigated. A major portion of complaints about Statement 8 could have been resolved without introducing the complex machinery of functional currency. (See the dissenting opinions in Statement 52.)

6. CONCLUDING REMARKS

Many controversies in foreign currency accounting bear striking resemblance to the dilemma observed in the aggregation theory.

The framework presented in Figure 1 may be compared with the one in the aggregation theory (see the framework of aggregation in Ijiri 1971) in the following manner. Instead of having foreign and domestic markets, there are micro- and macrophenomena. Instead of the beginning and end of a period, there are independent and dependent variables.

Thus, for example, m', which is now interpreted as a micro independent variable, may be first converted into a micro dependent variable m via $m = m's$ utilizing the functional relationship s observed in the microphoneomena, and then the resulting m may be "aggregated" using an aggregation function r on the dependent variable, obtaining msr. On the other hand, the same micro independent variable m may be first aggregated to a macro independent variable M via an aggregation function r' on the independent variable, and then their relation to the macro dependent variable may be determined by using the functional relationship S observed in the macrophenomena, obtaining $mr'S$.

The two outcomes, msr and $mr'S$, are not normally equal and this is the source of dilemma in the aggregation theory. Numerous articles have been written on such issues as how to select aggregation functions r and r' so that the microfunction s can be aggregated consistently with the macrofunction S, which is exactly the issue posed by the open interest rate parity relationship.

The dilemma in the aggregation theory essentially stems from *overidentification;* that is, there exists more than one legitimate way of determining a given variable M (i.e., msr and $mr'S$), yielding conflicting results. Yet in many cases it seems impossible to say one is right and the other is wrong.

The same is true with foreign currency accounting. It suffers from the same luxury of overidentification as plagued the aggregation theory.

The important point to be emphasized here is that a single method must somehow be selected and adhered to. Otherwise a vast number of legal relationships built upon accounting figures will be left unresolved.

The Financial Accounting Standards Board has made this important choice after years of studies. With so many alternatives on so many issues in foreign currency accounting, it is highly unlikely that what is prescribed in Statement 52 can satisfy anyone in every detail. Everyone is likely to have complaints on at least some aspects of the draft.

In particular, if the Board is going to allow (permanent) deferment of exchange gains and losses anyway, one may wonder whether the temporal method coupled with amortization of exchange gains and losses on long-term monetary items over their lives is not a simpler solution to the problems created by Statement 8.

The idea of functional currency has a theoretical justification in the assumption of multiple environments but will certainly make foreign currency accounting enormously complex. Given a rather considerable degree of latitude allowed the corporation in selecting the functional currency for each subsidiary, comparability among multinational corporations is likely to suffer even among those operating in a relatively similar mix of foreign environments.

However, the advantage of having a unified method for the sake of avoiding indefinite arguments seems to outweigh improvements that might be possible if the debates are to be continued.

The current rate method, combined with translation adjustments as pronounced in Statement 52, can do at least a satisfactory job in resolving many problems created by Statement 8, has theoretical justifications of its own, and most important, opens a new avenue for price-level adjustment in the sense that the proposed approach is complete only when it is combined with price-level adjustment. The last is perhaps the most important task that must be completed.

APPENDIX: MONEY AND COMMODITY FLOWS

A.1. REAL INTEREST RATE PARITY

This appendix extends the networks in Figures 1 and 2 to show that they are in fact only a part of the overall network of money and commodity flows in the three-dimensional space whose coordinates are characterized by foreign/domestic, money/commodity, and beginning/ending.

Let us first reverse the role of money and commodity depicted in Figure 2 and create another diagram, shown in Figure A.1. In this diagram, the international boundary is crossed by shipment of the commodity rather than remittance of money. Hence, instead of exchange rates r' and r, we have transportation factors t' and t, the factors at the beginning and end of a period, respectively.

Here, the transportation factor incorporates the cost of shipping the commodity from the foreign market to the domestic market. The cost is expressed in terms of physical units of commodity that must be given up to cover the transportation cost; thus, the transportation factor is normally a fraction representing 1 minus the transportation cost.

Although the exchange rates are not exactly reversible because of the discrepancy between the buying and selling rate, the discrepancy is relatively small and in this model the rates are treated as reversible. The transportation factor is in reality definitely irreversible, since the transportation cost must be paid in going one way or the other. However, for the sake of pursuing the symmetry between Figures 2 and A.1, let us assume for now that the transportation factor is reversible. That is, if one unit of commodity shipped from the foreign market reaches the domestic market in t units, the latter shipped back to the foreign market reaches there in the original one unit. Though unrealistic, the assumption helps highlight the reversible and irreversible roles of money and commodity in international markets.

Suppose that the holding factors h and H are both equal to 1. Now, an enterprise holding N' units of commodity in the domestic market considers two alternatives, namely, invest in domestic money or invest in foreign money, both of which appear to be better than just holding the commodity. The first investment means a path $N' \rightarrow M' \rightarrow M \rightarrow N$ and the second means a path $N' \rightarrow n' \rightarrow m' \rightarrow m \rightarrow n \rightarrow N$. Suppose that the outcomes of the two are equal due to arbitrage. This means that $N'P'S/P = N'(1/t')p's(1/p)t$. Using the inflation factors $F = P/P'$ and $f = p/p'$, we have $N'S/F = N'(s/f)t/t'$. If we define G and g to be real interest factor, namely $G = S/F$ and $g = s/f$, then we have

$$t/t' = G/g \tag{A.1}$$

Compared with equations (1) and (2), which represent the interest rate parity and purchasing power parity theories of exchange rate determination, equation (A.1) may be said to represent the real interest rate parity theory elaborated in Frankel [1979]. Here,

FIGURE A.1

Commodity and Money Flows

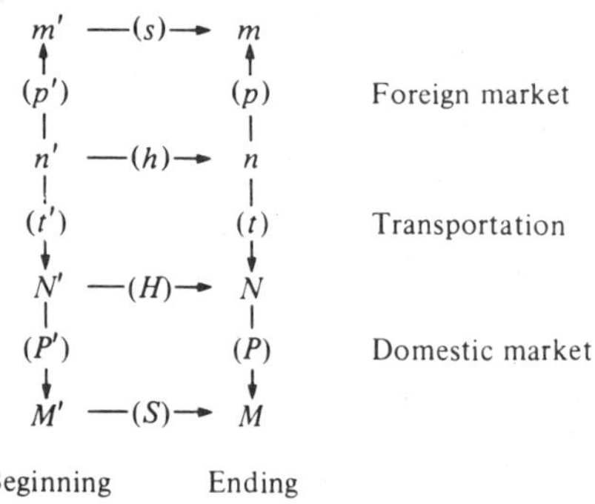

TABLE A.1

Arbitrage Possibilities

	Path of arbitrage	Consequence
International money market	$(M' \rightarrow m' \rightarrow m \rightarrow M \rightarrow M')$	$r/r' = S/s$
International commodity market	$(N' \rightarrow n' \rightarrow n \rightarrow N \rightarrow N')$	$t/t' = H/h$
International commodity shipment, current	$(M' \rightarrow m' \rightarrow n' \rightarrow N' \rightarrow M')$	$r'/t' = P'/p'$
International commodity shipment, future	$(M \rightarrow m \rightarrow n \rightarrow N \rightarrow M)$	$r/t = P/p$
Foreign market	$(m' \rightarrow n' \rightarrow n \rightarrow m \rightarrow m')$	$p/p' = s/h$
Domestic market	$(M' \rightarrow N' \rightarrow N \rightarrow M \rightarrow M')$	$P/P' = S/H$

however, what is related to the relative real interest is not the relative exchange rate of currencies but rather the relative transportation factor, such as the relative charter rates of tankers. The equation highlights the fact that what underlies the real interest rate parity concept is a notion of the rate of exchange of commodities across the international boundary. (See Giddy [1976] for other theories on exchange rate determination.)

It may also be noted here that Figure A.1 depicts the pressure on the exchange rate provided by the international shipment of gold (treated as commodity in the diagram) when the international gold standard was in effect.

A.2. MONEY AND COMMODITY FLOWS: A SUMMARY

Figure A.2 combines Figures 2 and A.1 to show all possible paths that connect money and commodity in foreign and domestic markets at two points in time. Looking at the diagram as a cube, each of its six faces represents an arbitrage or an equilibrium possibility. The six possibilities and their effects on various factors in the market are stated in Table A.1. The consequences stated in the table assume that the rates and factors are reversible. Since normally they are not reversible, rates or factors are determined only within a certain range rather than as a single value that the indicated equation implies.

FIGURE A.2

All Possible Paths of Money and Commodity

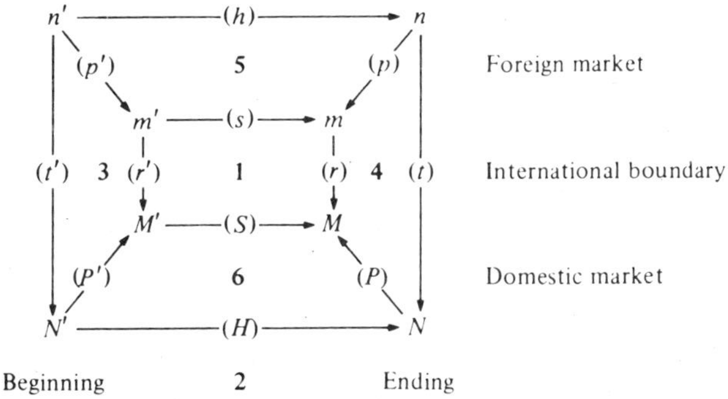

It is highly unlikely that all of these arbitrage or equilibrium possibilities work efficiently so as to have instantaneous and consistent adjustments of the exchange rate, transportation factor, interest factor, and holding factor, for current and future and for foreign and domestic markets. Part of the difficulties in foreign currency accounting comes from the fact that these factors and rates are frequently inconsistent, but accountants must choose one of them as a standard basis for translation.

REFERENCES

Aliber, Robert Z., and Stickney, Clyde P. "Accounting Measures of Foreign Exchange Exposure: The Long and Short of It." *Accounting Review* 50, 1 (January 1975), 44–57.

American Institute of CPAs. *Foreign Exchange Losses*. American Institute of CPAs, December 1931. (Bulletin of the AICPA No. 92)

American Institute of CPAs. *Memorandum on Accounting for Foreign Exchange Gains*. American Institute of CPAs, January 1934. (Bulletin of the AICPA No. 117)

American Institute of CPAs, Committee on Accounting Procedure. *Foreign Operations and Foreign Exchange*. American Institute of CPAs, 1939. (Accounting Research Bulletin No. 4)

American Institute of CPAs, Committee on Accounting Procedure, *Foreign Operations and Foreign Exchange*. American Institute of CPAs, 1953. (Accounting Research Bulletin No. 43, Chapter 12)

American Institute of CPAs, Accounting Principles Board, *Status of Accounting Research Bulletins*. American Institute of CPAs, 1965. (APB Opinion No. 6)

Balassa, Bela, "The Purchasing Power Parity Doctrine: A Reappraisal." *Journal of Political Economy* 72 (December 1964), 584–96.

Cassel, Gustav. "The Present Situation of the Foreign Exchanges." *Economic Journal* 31 (1916), 62–5, 319–23.

Financial Accounting Standards Board. *An Analysis of Issues Related to Accounting for Foreign Currency Translation*. Financial Accounting Standards Board, February 1974. (FASB Discussion Memorandum)

Financial Accounting Standards Board. *Accounting for the Translation of Foreign Currency Transactions and Foreign Currency Financial Statements*. Financial Accounting Standards Board, October 1975. (Statement of Financial Accounting Standards No. 8)

Financial Accounting Standards Board. *Foreign Currency Translation*. Financial Accounting Standards Board, August 1980 and June 1981. (Exposure Drafts)

Financial Accounting Standards Board. *Foreign Currency Translation*. Financial Accounting Standards Board, December 1981. (Statement of Financial Accounting Standards No. 52)

Frankel, Jeffrey A. "On the Mark: A Theory of Floating Exchange Rates Based on Real Interest Differentials." *American Economic Review* 69, 4 (September 1979), 610–22.

Frenkel, Jacob A. "The Collapse of Purchasing Power Parities During the 1970's." *European Economic Review* 16 1 (May 1981a), 145–65.

Frenkel, Jacob A. "Flexible Exchange Rates, Prices and the Role of 'News': Lessons from the 1970's." *Journal of Political Economy* 89, 4 (August 1981b), 665–705.

Giddy, Ian H. "An Integrated Theory of Exchange Rate Equilibrium." *Journal of Financial and Quantitative Analysis 11* (December 1976), 883–92.

Hepworth, Samuel. *Reporting Foreign Operations.* Ann Arbor: University of Michigan Press, 1956.

Ijiri, Yuji. "Fundamental Queries in Aggregation Theory." *Journal of the American Statistical Association* 66, 336 (December 1971), 766–82.

Ijiri, Yuji. "The Price Level Adjustment and Its Dual Interpretation." *Accounting Review* 51, 2 (April 1976), 227–43.

Lorensen, Leonard, *Reporting Foreign Operations of U. S. Companies in U.S. Dollars.* American Institute of CPAs, 1972. (Accounting Research Study No. 12)

Parkinson, R. MacDonald. *Translation of Foreign Currencies.* Toronto: Canadian Institute of Chartered Accountants, 1972.

Peat, Marwick, Mitchell & Co. *A Survey of the Economic Impacts of FASB Statement No. 8.* New York: Peat, Marwick, Mitchell & Co., December 1977.

Rueschhoff, Norlin G. *International Accounting and Financial Reporting.* New York: Praeger, 1976.

Shank, John K., Dillard, Jesse F., and Murdock, Richard J. *Assessing the Economic Impact of FASB No. 8.* New York: Financial Executives Research Foundation, 1979.

Shapiro, Alan C. "Defining Exchange Risk." *Journal of Business* 50 (January 1977), 37–9.

Shwayder, Keith R. "Accounting for Exchange Rate Fluctuations." *Accounting Review* 47, 4 (October 1972), 747–60.

Wyman, Harold E. "Analysis of Gains or Losses from Foreign Monetary Items: An Application of Purchasing Power Parity Concepts." *Accounting Review* 51, 3 (July 1976), 545–57.

Zenoff, David B., and Zwick, Jack. *International Financial Management.* Englewood Cliffs, N.J.: Prentice-Hall, 1969.

23

FAS #52—Measuring the Performance of Foreign Operations*

Bryan Carsberg

INTRODUCTION

During 1981, a British company purchased a business in the United States. The exchange rate was £1 = $2.50. The business made a low return during its first year—at least according to the dollar measurements. The value of the pound, however, fell to $2.00. Did the corresponding increase in the value of the dollar make the British company better off? Should the increase be reflected in the measurement of the income of the British company? How should the effect be measured and reported?

These questions seem to have been the most controversial considered in recent years by the bodies that set accounting standards in the United States and the United Kingdom. Other current issues such as accounting for the effects of changing prices, for leases, and for pension costs all present significant challenges. But none of them has provoked a level of concern in business comparable to that kindled by foreign currency translation.

No doubt this concern is attributable partly to the difficulty of the issues. Two methods of foreign currency translation have emerged as rivals, and neither has been acknowledged to have clear-cut superiority. A more important reason for corporate concern, however, is the magnitude of what is at stake. Many businesses now have large overseas operations; and exchange rates between different currencies can fluctuate with extreme volatility. Consequently, the choice of translation method can have a big impact on reported results.

Foreign currency translation also has an importance beyond its impact on financial statements published for shareholders and others. It is essential to the management functions of performance evaluation and control within the multinational company. Managers need to decide where changes should be made in their operations, where investment should be increased and where it should be cut back. And, in evaluating the success of such investment, multinationals need to be able to distinguish the performance of managers of overseas operations from the performance of the company as a whole.

The performance of overseas managers should be assessed mainly by comparing their performance with standards that reflect conditions in the local operating environment (i.e., local rates of interest and inflation). Finally, however, the success of a multinational's overseas investment policy must be evaluated according to the returns it generates for shareholders in the home country. Reported results should be consistent with investment policy in the sense that if the policy serves the interests of shareholders, and if actual results are as expected, then the reports should signal success.

Perhaps this aim of consistency is the most important consideration in formulating an approach to the translation of foreign currency. After translation, the reported results should reflect "economic reality"—insofar as this is possible, given the fallibility of

---

*This article is reprinted, with permission, from *Midland Corporate Finance Review,* vol. 1, Summer 1983, pp. 48–55, published by Stern, Stewart, Putnam and Macklis, Ltd., Corporate Financial Consultants.

accounting conventions—as perceived by everyone concerned. *The ultimate goal of overseas investment is to earn a satisfactory rate of return as translated into and measured in the home currency.* Many intermediate objectives like expanding market share, increasing profit margins, and minimizing political and economic risk will feature in management's decisions. But the translated rate of return is the "bottom line." Thus, earning a satisfactory rate of return in the overseas currency is neither necessary nor sufficient in itself. A return of 5 percent per year in a currency that is appreciating by 20 percent against the home currency will produce an effective return of over 25 percent per year, which may well be satisfactory. A return of 40 percent in a currency depreciating by 50 percent is not satisfactory.

The best way to assess whether an overseas investment has been satisfactory is to measure the net *cash flows* generated by the investment, translate them into terms of the home currency, and discount them at the appropriate cost of capital to obtain a net present value. This computation, however, can only be performed at the *end* of an investment's life. The challenge for accounting, of course, is to give good indications of the progress of the investment at *interim* stages—annually, or perhaps more frequently. In this routine accounting, future benefits have to be represented by asset measurements rather than estimates of cash flows. Because asset measurements often serve only as a rough indicator of future cash flows, accounting reports must inevitably remain an imperfect guide to the success of an investment. Nevertheless, as we shall see, some accounting methods are better than others.

Let us now consider a simple example which serves to illustrate the issues involved in choosing between the two main alternative methods of foreign currency translation. We shall consider again a company owned in Britain and operating in the United States, and we shall further assume that the exchange rate moved from exactly £1 = $2.50 at the start of the year to £1 = $2.00 at the end of the year. This means that the dollar effectively gained 25 percent against the pound: $100 increased in value from £40 to £50. The income statement and balance sheet (in dollars) of this hypothetical American subsidiary are shown in Table 1 and the income computation is shown in Table 2.

Our company has earned $700 during the year, a return of 10 percent on the $7,000 of equity capital employed. When results are translated into pounds, and if the accounting measure is to be consistent with economic reality, the outcome should be a rate of return of about 35 percent—the dollar return of 10 percent combined with the effect of the

TABLE 1

Illustrative Statement of Net Assets

	At Start	At End
Fixed Assets		
Cost	$20,000	$20,000
Depreciation	8,000	9,000
	$12,000	$11,000
Cash	—	1,700
	$12,000	$12,700
Less Debt	5,000	5,000
Equity	$ 7,000	$ 7,700

TABLE 2

Income Statement

Sales		$29,000
Depreciation Expense	$1,000	
Interest Expense	400	
Other Expenses	26,900	28,300
Income		$ 700

appreciation of the dollar at 25 percent. (Strictly, the return should be 37.5 percent, the product of 1.10 times 1.25 less 1.00.)

THE TEMPORAL METHOD

The two most frequently advocated methods of foreign currency translation are known as the "temporal" method and the "current" method. The temporal method was the basis for FAS 8, the U.S. standard on foreign currency translation issued by the Financial Accounting Standards Board in 1975. The temporal method takes the view that each component of the financial statements should be translated at the exchange rate that matches the timing of the accounting measurement of that component. For example, fixed assets and the related depreciation are measured at historical cost in conventional accounting. Under the temporal method, accordingly, they are translated at an historical exchange rate (the rate at the date of acquisition). Debt, however, is normally carried in the balance sheet at an amount that represents the current extent of the obligation. Consequently, under the temporal method, debt is translated at the current exchange rate.

To obtain the results of applying the temporal method to our numerical example, we need to know the exchange rate at the date of acquisition of the fixed assets. Let us truncate history and assume a historical rate of $4 to £1. The computations are set out in Tables 3 and 4.

TABLE 3

Net Worth Converted into £—Temporal Method

	At Start			At End		
	$	$/£	£	$	$/£	£
Fixed Assets						
Cost	$20,000	4.00	£ 5,000	$20,000	4.00	£ 5,000
Depreciation	8,000	4.00	2,000	9,000	4.00	2,250
	$12,000		£ 3,000	$11,000		£ 2,750
Cash	—		—	1,700	2.00	850
	$12,000		£ 3,000	$12,700		£ 3,600
Debt	5,000	2.50	2,000	5,000	2.00	2,500
Equity	$ 7,000		£ 1,000	$ 7,700		£ 1,100

TABLE 4

Income Measured in £—Temporal Method

	$	$	$/£	£	£
Sales		$29,000	2.00		£14,500
Depreciation Expense	1,000		4.00	250	
Interest Expense	400		2.00	200	
Other Expenses	26,900	28,300	2.00	13,450	13,900
Operating Income		$ 700			£ 600
Translation Adjustment (Loss)		—			(500)
Total Income		$ 700			£ 100

The first step is to convert net assets at the start of the year into pounds. Fixed assets in dollars are divided by four to obtain the number in pounds; debt is divided by 2.5. Next, net assets at the end of the year are converted into pounds. We then can see that net assets (equity) increased from £1,000 to £1,100. Since no dividends were paid and no new equity capital was raised, income is equal to the increase in net assets, i.e., £100.

Direct translation of sales and expenses gives income of £600; this is reduced to £100 by the loss of £500 on translation. The loss arises because the translation rate for the loan is changed from 2.5 to 2, causing the amount of the loan in pounds to increase from £2,000 to £2,500. The computations are recognizing, in effect, that repayment of the loan will be more expensive if it is made in pounds.

The main shortcomings of the temporal method are apparent from our example. First, the method seems to produce a significant distortion in the ratio of debt to total capital employed. The ratio is 41.6 percent in the dollar report at the start of the year. In the corresponding statements in pounds, the ratio is 66.6 percent. This distortion results from the use of different rates for the translation of fixed assets and debt. A similar problem afflicts the computation of income. A loss is recognized on the debt but no offsetting gain is claimed on the fixed assets as a result of the appreciation of the dollar. The rate of return on equity, far from being the 37.5 percent we expected, is shown as 10 percent (£100/£1,000).

TABLE 5

Net Worth Converted into £—Current Method

	At Start			At End		
	$	$/£	£	$	$/£	£
Fixed Assets						
Cost	$20,000	2.50	£8,000	$20,000	2.00	£10,000
Depreciation	8,000	2.50	3,200	9,000	2.00	4,500
	$12,000		£4,800	$11,000		£ 5,500
Cash	—		—	1,700	2.00	850
	$12,000		£4,800	$12,700		£ 6,350
Less Debt	5,000	2.50	2,000	5,000	2.00	2,500
Equity	$ 7,000		£2,800	$ 7,700		£ 3,850

TABLE 6

Income Measured in £—Current Method

	$	$	$/£	£	£
Sales		$29,000	2.00		£14,500
Depreciation Expense	1,000		2.00	500	
Interest Expense	400		2.00	200	
Other Expenses	26,900	28,300	2.00	13,450	14,150
Operating Income		$ 700			£ 350
Translation Adjustment (Gain)		—			700
Total Income		$ 700			£ 1,050

The disparate treatment of fixed assets and debt has been the main reason for criticism of the temporal method. As businessmen have been quick to point out, loans are usually raised to finance purchase of the fixed assets, and such loans are likely to be repaid in the foreign currency rather than in home currency. Assets and loans effectively hedge each other, at least to some extent, and any translation method that treats the two items differently fails to reflect economic reality.[1]

The difficulties described are bad enough when currency exchange rates move steadily in the anticipated direction. When the rates fluctuate sharply around a trend, however, the effects on income can be dramatic. Indeed, the measurement of income can come to seem like the result of a lottery. Criticism directed at these arbitrary effects, and at the resulting distortions of real overseas operating performance, caused the Financial Accounting Standards Board to reconsider FAS 8 and the problem of foreign currency translation.

THE CURRENT METHOD

The idea that assets and loans should be translated at the same rate led naturally to the consideration of the current method. This method calls for translation of *all assets and liabilities at the exchange rate prevailing at the balance sheet date.* The results of applying this method to our example are shown in Tables 5 and 6. The computations follow the same process as before with one exception: net assets are translated at $2.50 at the start of the period, but at $2.00 at the end.

A comparison of net asset numbers shows that net income for the period is £1,050. The income statement shows this to be made up of operating income of £350 plus a translation *gain* of £700. In effect, the current rate method recognizes a gain on translation of the fixed assets. At the start of the year, the fixed assets are measured at £4,800, and £500 is deducted for depreciation during the year to leave £4,300; however, with the fall in the exchange rate, end-of-year assets are measured at £5,500 and a gain of £1,200 results. The gain of £1,200 less the loss (which still arises) of £500 on the loan gives net translation gain of £700.

The current rate method thus gives us a rate of return measured at 37.5 percent (£1,050/£2,800), which accords with the economic reality as identified above.

To the extent that we can generalize from this example, the current method is a major

TABLE 7

Net Worth Converted into £; Revised Case—Current Method

	At Start			At End		
	$	$/£	£	$	$/£	£
Fixed Assets						
Cost	$20,000	2.50	£8,000	$20,000	2.00	£10,000
Depreciation	8,000	2.50	3,200	9,000	2.00	4,500
	$12,000		£4,800	$11,000		£ 5,500
Cash	—		—	1,000	2.00	500
	$12,000		£4,800	$12,000		£ 6,000
Less Debt	5,000	2.50	2,000	5,000	2.00	2,500
Equity	$ 7,000		£2,800	$ 7,000		£ 3,500

improvement over the temporal method. However, the users of accounts need to keep in mind that the usefulness of both methods is limited by the accounting convention of valuing assets at historical cost. Furthermore, if assets are measured at historical acquisition costs, translation of fixed assets at the current exchange rate will produce a number that is hard to interpret. Historical cost multiplied by the historical exchange rate produces a number that at least can be recognized as the sacrifice of funds of the "home currency" required to pay for the asset at the date of acquisition. Historical cost multiplied by the current exchange rate, however, produces a number that lacks any economic significance.

The implications of this situation can be illustrated by modifying slightly our above example. The result is a case that is less favourable to the current rate method. Suppose that the effective return in dollars remains at 10 percent but that, during the year under review, the return is earned partly in an increase in fixed asset values, reflecting an expected increase in future cash flows: the current cost of fixed assets (net of depreciation) is $11,700 compared to the historical cost of $11,000 in our previous illustration, but sales are only $28,300 and cash at the end of the year only $1,000 (a decrease of $700). The accounts based on historical cost measurements (see Tables 7 and 8) show income of zero in dollars, and £700 in sterling.

TABLE 8

Income Measured in £; Revised Case—Current Method

	$	$	$/£	£	£
Sales		$28,300	2.00		£14,150
Depreciation Expense	1,000		2.00	500	
Interest Expense	400		2.00	200	
Other Expenses	26,900	28,300	2.00	13,450	14,150
Operating Income		$ 0			£ 0
Translation Adjustment (Gain)		—			700
Total Income		$ 0			£ 700

TABLE 9

Net Worth Converted into £; Revised Case—Temporal Method

	At Start			At End		
	$	$/£	£	$	$/£	£
Fixed Assets						
Cost	$20,000	4.00	£5,000	$20,000	4.00	£5,000
Depreciation	8,000	4.00	2,000	9,000	4.00	2,250
	$12,000		£3,000	$11,000		£2,750
Cash	—		—	1,000	2.00	500
	$12,000		£3,000	$12,000		£3,250
Less Debt	5,000	2.50	2,000	5,000	2.00	2,500
Equity	$ 7,000		£1,000	$ 7,000		£ 750

The return of 25 percent (£700/£2,800) now shown by the current method fails to match the "real" return of 37.5 percent; and the fixed asset measurement, still £5,500, now is simply historical cost times the current exchange rate and fails to represent any real economic magnitude.

In this same case, however, use of the temporal method of translation would actually show a loss (see Tables 9 and 10). Thus, even though the current method is inadequate here, it still represents an improvement over the temporal alternative.

To strengthen further the correspondence between accounting and economic "reality," it would be necessary to use current cost measurements of all assets and liabilities. In that event, both the current and the temporal method would call for translation at the current exchange rate.

In practice, when accounting measurements reflect historic costs, we cannot generalise about the relationship between the choice of translation method and the usefulness of the accounting rate of return as an indicator of economic performance. In some cases, the temporal method may produce a better approximation of the actual return than the current rate method. For example, an unrecorded increase in the current cost of fixed

TABLE 10

Income Measured in £; Revised Case—Temporal Method

	$	$	$/£	£	£
Sales		$28,300	2.00		£14,150
Depreciation Expense	1,000		4.00	250	
Interest Expense	400		2.00	200	
Other Expenses	26,900	28,300	2.00	13,450	13,900
Operating Income		$ 0			£ 250
Translation Adjustment (Gain)		—			(500).
Total Income		$ 0			£ (250)

assets may be offset by the failure, under the temporal method, to recognise the effect on the value of the assets of a fall in the value of the foreign currency. We do not know the average effect, based on empirical data. A preference for the current rate method rests on a belief in the desirability of eliminating one cause of the divergence of accounting reports from economic reality. Further improvement requires the adoption of current measurements for assets and liabilities.

It is difficult to say what effect the distortions caused by accounting currency translations have on the stock prices of multinationals. The stock market, under the guidance of sophisticated investment analysts, may see through most of these distortions. Investors, after all, use information about the company's past mainly as a basis for predictions of future performance. They may use a variety of disclosures to draw inferences about the real value of a multinational's foreign assets. If such is the case, the choice of method of currency translation would have little importance for investors—though use of a poor method may increase their costs of analysis. In a reasonably sophisticated market, however, management's main responsibility should be to provide investors with the fullest possible disclosure (of accounting methods as well as results) of their international operations, and leave interpretation to the markets.

Failure to use the best accounting methods may be more important for other uses, such as government economic policy decisions. For corporate purposes, however, greatest importance attaches to the application of these accounting methods to internal evaluation of overseas performance, which may in turn affect management compensation and capital investment decisions. Part of the problem of evaluating overseas managers can be dealt with by using local rates of interest and inflation as standards for assessing the adequacy of rates of return measured in the *local currency*. For the purpose of capital allocation, however, the home country financial management must attempt to estimate the effects of currency changes on the long-run profitability of proposed international investments; and control procedures will need to focus on a comparison of actual and estimated returns in the home currency. Management thus would benefit from knowing the current value of net assets employed, translated at the current exchange rate. This measures the amount in a way that gives a useful basis for assessing home currency rates of return.

Consequently, we find that the foreign currency translation problem cannot be resolved in a satisfactory manner until we have dealt with the logically prior deficiency of historical cost measurements. To the extent that fixed assets are valued at or near their current values on the balance sheet, translation at the current exchange rate will provide a useful picture of profitability. The fact that large multinationals like Phillips N.V., TRW, and GE have chosen to make current measurements, at least for internal purposes, suggests that recognition of their usefulness may be spreading. If such adjustments are not practicable, or cost too much to produce, then historical cost measurements may offer the most reliable, cost-effective estimate of the current worth of resources within the conventions of accounting (which place heavy store on the use of reliable measurements). Under these conditions, the translation of our best measurement of current worth in dollars at our best estimate of the value of the dollar—i.e., the current exchange rate—then seems quite reasonable.

Such, at any rate, was the thinking of the Financial Accounting Standards Board when they chose to adopt the current rate method in Statement No. 52, *Foreign Currency Translation*, issued in December 1981 as a revision to Statement No. 8. The U.K. Accounting Standards Committee has issued a statement in the last few months. It is the first U.K. standard on foreign currency translation and it also adopts the current rate method.

THE MEASUREMENT OF INCOME

Apart from the limitations of historical cost conventions, can we conclude that the difficult problem of foreign currency translation has now been solved in a satisfactory manner and that the issue can be allowed to rest? The answer, unfortunately, is "No." One small provision, included in both the US and the UK standard, means that the translated income statements still fail to capture the essence of overseas operations: "Translation adjustments shall not be included in determining net income but shall be reported separately and accumulated in a separate component of equity" (FASB Statement No. 52, paragraph 13). As a result of this provision, reported income in our basic numberical example would be determined under the current rate method to be only £350, a rate of return of 12.5 percent (See Tables 5 and 6).

The standard setters were probably led to exclude the translation adjustment from the income statement because of a wish to preserve, as far as possible in the translation process, all financial ratios at their levels in foreign currency statements. The observed distortion in the debt-to-equity ratio had helped to discredit the temporal method, and it was no doubt felt that distortion should be similarly avoided in the income statement. Also, the recognition of the gain on translating fixed assets may have been seen as akin to the recognition of an unrealized profit.

Both of these concerns, however, seem unrelated to the main purpose of financial reporting. Gains and losses on foreign currency are intrinsic parts of the reality of overseas investment, and that reality should be reflected in financial reports. This point may be illuminated by considering the likely cause of changes in exchange rates. A depreciation of the £ against the dollar is likely, over long periods of time, to reflect the existence of a higher rate of inflation in the U.K. than in the U.S. For example, a depreciation of 25 percent would be expected if the rate of inflation were zero in the U.S., but 25 percent in the U.K. This change in the exchange rate would keep the relative prices of goods in the two countries constant.

Suppose those circumstances actually held, and the rate of return net of inflation was 10 percent (as in our illustration) according to the dollar measurements. If the translation gain were excluded from income, the rate of return would be represented as 12.5 percent in sterling (as computed above), and the return net of inflation would appear to be regstive. Inclusion of the translation adjustment in income would give a return of 37.5 percent in sterling, high enough to show that the investment overseas is worthwhile inspite of the high rate of inflation in the U.K.

From this perspective, the translation process can be seen in part as an adjustment of income numbers to reflect operating rates of return in the home country currency *gross of any adjustment for inflation*. Such a process effectively takes account of differences between the inflation rates of the countries ccrcerned. Or so it would, if changes in exchange rates always perfectly reflected changes in relative rates of inflation.

Foreign currency exchange rates, however, do not perfectly reflect differences in rates of inflation, particularly over short periods of time. Short-term capital flows associated with differences in interest rates and other factors can cause significant changes in exchange rates independently of prices. Only over the long run can it be said that exchange rate changes are determined largely by differences in inflation rates.

Most importantly for our purposes, however, changes in exchange rates do make businesses better or worse off. They are prices that determine the ultimate worth, in the home country, of cash flows generated by the overseas business. An income computation should reflect, as far as possible, all factors that make a business more or less profitable.

The performance of an overseas manager may best be judged in terms of the results measured in overseas currency, and set against standards of performance in the country concerned. The performance of the whole business—that is, its contribution to the value of the parent company and stockholders' investment—must be measured in the home currency. For that purpose exchange gains and losses are a part of the performance. It may be reasonable to recognize the volatility of exchange rates by showing gains and losses on translation in a special section of the income statement, perhaps grouped with extraordinary items. If the intent is to measure real economic performance, however, it is not fitting to exclude them from income altogether.

24

Currency Changes and Management Control: Resolving the Centralization/Decentralization Dilemma*

Donald R. Lessard and Peter Lorange

Effective control systems for decentralized operations require that operating management has a significant degree of control over the variables affecting the performance on which they are evaluated. Changes in exchange rates are one set of variables which affect the performance of foreign divisions. Many multinationals' policies to cope with changes in exchange rates are set at the corporate level and, thus, are not under control of the foreign divisional manager.

This situation reflects a complex organizational dilemma. On the one hand, pressures of time, distance, market and product differentials, as well as complex business-government relations, point toward the advantages of a decentralized organizational structure.[1] On the other hand, many normative models suggest that an appropriate response to fluctuating exchange rates, taxation differentials, controls on currency flows and variations in financial markets require highly centralized financial decision making[2] (for example, Horst [1971]: Lietaer [1970]: Robbins and Stobaugh, [1973]: Rutenberg [1970]: and Shapiro [1973]). If centralized financial decisions are imposed on operating managers and if the effects of such decisions are not somehow eliminated from the reported operating results, accounting profits will not provide accurate guides for control, and the motivational consequences may be undesirable. On the other hand, if operating managers are given the responsibility for financial decisions, it is unlikely that they will follow policies which are optimal from a corporate viewpoint,[3] even though the policies may

*This article is reprinted, with permission, from *Accounting Review,* July 1977, pp. 628–637.

[1]A marked evolution of corporate structure towards decentralized operations has taken place over the last four decades. For the classical discussion of this development, see Chandler [1962]; for the case of multinational corporations, see Stopford and Wells [1972] and Channon [1973]; for a summary of planning and control tools in decentralized corporations, see Lorange and Vancil [1977].

[2]Although Robbins and Stobaugh [1973] provide extensive examples and analyses supporting the benefits of centralized financial decision making, they find that the largest corporations have backed off from complete centralization of this function. This may be due to the difficulties of coordinating it with the management control process.

[3]The idea of holding operating managers responsible only for anticipated exchange rate fluctuations and assigning responsibility for unanticipated fluctuation to the financial function is valid whether operating decisions are centralized or decentralized. However, centralized operations will not encounter the same difficulties as decentralized operations where the operating divisions are evaluated on a performance measure that may be influenced not only by currency changes but also by corporate financial decisions which are outside the control of these operating managers.

decrease their own profits. In addition, they may overreact to risks of potential exchange rate fluctuations which appear large from their limited perspective.

In this article, first we introduce the question of an appropriate exchange rate for use in the budgeting process and through a simple example illustrate the effects of alternative approaches on management decisions. Then we discuss the benefits of using the same set of exchange rates in both setting the budget and tracking performance relative to the budget. We conclude with a discussion of how such rates should be set and whether and how often they should be updated to reflect new information. Throughout the discussion we focus on the control process over the operating cycle, with a time horizon of one year or less.

EXCHANGE RATES AND THE CONTROL PROCESS

Implicit in the control process of firms with foreign operations are assumptions about the future course of exchange rates and their impact on the firm. Operating decisions in any particular time period reflect a manager's anticipations regarding future exchange rates and their impact on performance. Exchange rates are incorporated in the control process at two points: (1) in setting the operating budget for a particular time period and (2) in tracking realized performance relative to the budget. When setting the operating budget, two sets of exchange rates can be used: the actual (spot) rates at that time or rates projected at that time for the end of the period. Further, if the budget is updated when exchange rates change, the actual rate at the end of the period can be used for the budget. In tracking performance relative to the budget, three sets of rates can be used: the actual rate when the budget was set, the rate projected at that time for the end of the period and the actual rate at the end of the period. The range of logical combinations of these rates is outlined in Table 1. Four cells are shaded out since they appear to be undesirable combinations.

In combination A-1, the exchange rate existing at the time the budget is developed is used in the budget as well as in tracking results relative to the budget. The implicit assumption is that the exchange rate will not change, but if it does, it will have no effect on the evaluation of the manager's performance. Combination A-3, where the exchange rate used to develop the budget is the actual rate at that time, while the actual rate at the end of the period is used to track results, excludes exchange rate forecasts from budgeting but places the full effect of any changes that take place on the operating manager. Combination P-2 involves a projected exchange rate both for budget preparation and for subsequent tracking of performance. Thus, P-2 introduces exchange rate forecasts into budgeting and holds the manager responsible for performance defined at that rate regardless of the actual outcome. We refer to the projected rates used in this fashion as internal forward rates (IFRs) since their use is analogous to the treasurer acting as a banker and "buying forward" receipts in foreign currencies at guaranteed rate.

Combination P-3 makes use of projected exchange rate when determining the budget and the actual rate at the end of the period rate for tracking performance. This again incorporates a projection but holds the manager responsible for the impact on performance of deviations from the projected rate. Thus, in this case the treasurer does not "guarantee" the forward rate. Combination E-3 employs the actual exchange rate at the end of the period, both for determining the budget as well as for tracking actual performance relative to the budget. Consequently, E-3 does not incorporate a projection of

TABLE 1

Possible Combinations of Exchange Rates in the Control Process

Rate Used for Determining Budget \ Rate Used to Track Performance Relative to Budget	*Actual at Time of Budget*	*Projected at Time of Budget*	*Actual at End of Period*
Actual at time of budget	A-1	A-2	A-3
Projected at time of budget	P-1	P-2	P-3
Actual at end of period (through updating)	E-1	E-2	E-3

exchange rate in the budget, but neither does it hold the manager responsible for any exchange rate fluctuation since the budget is always updated as the exchange rate changes.

The three shaded cells in the lower left of Table 1 (P-1—projected rate for setting the budget, actual rate at the time of the budget for tracking subsequent performance; E-1—actual end-of-period rate for setting the budget and actual rate at the time of budget preparation for tracking performance; E-2—actual rate at the end of the period for budget determination and projected rate at budget determination time for performance tracking) require exchange rate forecasts or updates for determining the budget but ignore these when tracking performance relative to the budget. The other shaded cell, A-2, requires the use of a projected rate (set at the time of the budget preparation) in measuring actual performance but does not use this rate for the preparation of the budget. Instead, the actual rate at that time is used. Hence, these four combinations are ruled out as inefficient.

A recent study of ten multinational corporations [Traver, 1975] showed that five used variants of P-3 (budgeting with a projected rate but tracking performance with the actual rate at end of period), three used variants of P-2 (projected rate at time of budget preparation both for preparing the budget and for performance tracking), and two had systems resembling A-3 (actual rate at beginning of period for budgeting and actual rate at end of period for tracking).

An Illustration

The likely effect of each of these different approaches on the decisions of managers of foreign responsibility centers can be illustrated with a simple example. Assume that the current dollar price of the foreign local currency (LC) is $0.10 and that there are two equally likely possibilities for the dollar value of the local currency in the next period—a 50 percent chance that it will move to $0.0833 and a 50 percent chance that it will remain the same, $0.10. Thus the expected dollar value of the local currency is $0.09165.[+] Assuming for the moment that the firm requires no risk-premium for bearing the risk of foreign exchange fluctuations, we can use the expected rate of $0.09165 as an appropriate

[+]Throughout the paper we use the dollar as the parent company's home currency. All other currencies are lumped under the heading local currency (LC).

TABLE 2

Budgeted Performance at Different Exchange Rates

	Option A	*Option B*	*Option C*
Local Currency Budget (stated in LC terms)			
Sales	80,000	100,000	150,000
Cost of goods sold	60,000	80,000	125,000
Operating expenses	4,000	5,000	7,500
Profit	16,000	15,000	17,500
[Exposed assets]	[75,000]	[100,000]	[200,000]
Dollar Budget I (LC 1 = $0.10)			
Sales	8,000	10,000	15,000
Cost of goods sold	6,000	8,000	12,500
Operating expenses	400	500	750
Profit	1,600	1,500	1,750
Dollar Budget II (LC 1 = $0.0833)			
Sales	6,664	8,333	12,495
Cost of goods sold	4,998	6,664	10,413
Operating expenses	333	417	625
Loss on exposed assets*	1,252	1,670	3,340
Profit	81	−418	−1,883
Dollar Budget III (LC 1 = $0.09165)			
Sales	7,332	9,165	13,748
Cost of goods sold	5,499	7,332	11,456
Operating expenses	367	458	687
Loss on exposed assets**	625	835	1,670
Profit	841	540	−65

*Loss on exposed assets for budget II are calculated as follows:

Option A: (75,000 × 0.10) − (75,000 × 0.0833) = 7.500 − 6.248 = 1.252

Option B: (100,000 × 0.10) − (100,000 × 0.0833) = 10.000 − 8.330 = 1.670

Option C: (200,000 × 0.10) − (200,000 × 0.0833) = 20.000 − 16.660 = 3.340

**Losses on exposed assets for budget III are calculated as follows:

Option A: (75,000 × 0.10) − (75,000 × 0.09165) = 7.500 − 6.874 = 625

Option B: (100,000 × 0.10) − (100,000 × 0.09165) = 10.000 − 9.165 = 835

Option C: (200,000 × 0.10) − (200,000 × 0.09165) = 20.000 − 18.330 = 1.670

IFR. Further assume that the manager is faced with an operating decision regarding three options which are not mutually exclusive. As is typically the case, the computations of adjustments to dollar profit due to currency fluctuations will involve adjustments of the foreign asset values as well as adjustment of foreign operating profits. Finally, we assume that the accounting results of the foreign responsibility center are translated from local currency into the parent company's currency according to the monetary/nonmonetary method.[5]

In Table 2, option "A" involves sales of LC 80,000 and requires LC 75,000 of "exposed" assets.[6] Option "B" gives sales of LC 100,000 and requires LC 100,000 of exposed assets. Option "C" eives sales of LC 150,000 but requires LC 200,000 of exposed assets. The remaining details of each option as well as the budgeted performance at each of the possible exchange rates are shown in Table 2. For simplicity, we assume that changes in the exchange rate will have no impact on LC operating results. Therefore, the actual performance at each rate will equal the budgeted performance for that rate. Also for simplicity we ignore the effect of taxes. It is easy to see how the treatment of foreign exchange fluctuations will affect a manager's budgeted and reported profits and, therefore, his or her incentives. If, at the one extreme, the budget implicitly assumes that there will be no exchange rate change, and if foreign exchange fluctuations are considered to be outside of the realm of the operating manager (as is the case with combination A-1 in Table 1), the results will be recorded as if the beginning and ending exchange rate is LC1=$0.10 (Budget 1 of Table 2), regardless of the actual outcome. All three options will appear profitable, including C which involves an expected loss. At the other extreme, if possible exchange rates are ignored in the budget but actual exchange fluctuations are imposed on the manager (case A-3 in Table 1), he or she probably will avoid option B as well as option C because of the high probability of a very poor performance relative to the budget (Budget II, Table 2). However, B has an expected profit and therefore is a sound option for all but the most risk-averse firms.

If the budget and reported profit are based on the internal forward exchange rate, LCI=$0.09165 (Case P-2, Table 1), the division manager clearly will accept Plans A and B and avoid Plan C (Budget III, Table 2). If the budget is based on the internal forward exchange rate but if performance is measured at the actual rate at the end of the period, the manager will clearly accept Plan A and reject Plan C, but the decision regarding Plan B will depend upon the extent to which the manager is averse to taking risks. The differences between actual and budgeted profits for the various budget-rate/tracking-rate combinations are illustrated in Table 3. Note that in all combinations along the diagonal, that is, those in which the same type of rates are used in both budget preparation and performance tracking, there will be no deviations due to exchange rate variations. However, the various combinations along the diagonal do have quite different implications for operating decisions. The combinations involving actual rates at the time of the budget or the actual rates at the end of the period for both budgeting and tracking (A-1 and E-3)

[5]In this paper we are not concerned with the definition of expousre, although the adjustments in our example are consistent with the latest FASB statement [1975]. Our proposal can be used in conjunction with a wide variety of exposure definitions, many of which would reflect economic reality more closely than current accounting conventions. See, for example, Dufey [1972] and First National City Bank [1975].

[6]"Exposed assets" under the monetary/nonmonetary translation method are defined as the *excess* of cash plus LC receivables plus other LC financial assets over all forms of LC obligations.

TABLE 3

Effects on Performance in Our Example from Possible Combinations of Exchange Rates in Budgeting Process

Rate Used for Determining Budget \ *Rate Used to Track Performance Relative to Budget*	*Actual at Time of Budget*		*Projected at Time of Budget*		*Actual at End of Period*	
	Actual Outcome LC1 = \$.10	*Actual Outcome* LC1 = \$.0833	*Actual Outcome* LC1 = \$.10	*Actual Outcome* LC1 = \$.0833	*Actual Outcome* LC1 = \$.10	*Actual Outcome* LC1 = \$.0833
Actual at time of Budget (LC1: \$.10)	*A-1*				*A-3*	
Option A Profit	1600	1600			1600	81
Budget	1600	1600			1600	1600
Deviation	0	0			0	−1519
Option B Profit	1500	1500			1500	−418
Budget	1500	1500			1500	1500
Deviation	0	0			0	−1918
Option C Profit	1750	1750			1750	−1883
Budget	1750	1750			1750	1750
Deviation	0	0			0	−3633
Projected at time of Budget (LC1: \$.09165)			*P-2*		*P-3*	
Option A Profit			841	841	1600	81
Budget			841	841	841	841
Deviation			0	0	+759	−760
Option B Profit			540	540	1500	−418
Budget			540	540	540	540
Deviation			0	0	+960	−958
Option C Profit			−65	−65	1750	−1883
Budget			−65	−65	−65	−65
Deviation			0	0	+1815	−1818
Actual rate at end of Period (LC1: \$.10 or LC1: \$.0833)					*E-3*	
Option A Profit					1600	81
Budget					1600	81
Deviation					0	0
Option B Profit					1500	418
Budget					1500	418
Deviation					0	0
Option C Profit					1750	−1883
Budget					1750	−1883
Deviation					0	0

allow the manager to ignore the effect of both anticipated and unanticipated fluctuations in exchange rates.

The combination of actual beginning of period rates for budgeting and actual end of period rates for tracking, A-3, although used in practice, appears to represent the worst of all possible worlds [Traver, 1975]. In the budgeting stage, no account will be taken of possible exchange fluctuations, yet their full impact will be attributed to the manager at the tracking stage. The harmful effects of such a system can be expected to include "padding" of budgets or decentralized hedging actions by managers to reduce exchange risks which are likely to loom very large from their narrower local perspective.

Combination P-2, involving IFRs at the budgeting and tracking stages, excludes unplanned exchange fluctuations but acknowledges expected fluctuations at the budgeting stage. Thus, it will dominate the other alternatives which expose managers to unforeseen exchange fluctuations but fail to force managers to consider them at the budgeting stage. These dominated combinations are A-1 and E-3. Based on these observations, we believe that combination P-2 generally will be superior to all others. Combination P-3 may appear equally attractive in situations where operating plans should and can be changed in response to exchange rate shifts. However, in a later section we argue that even under these circumstances P-2 is superior.

The suggested procedure of using internal forward exchange rates as the basis for decision making and performance evaluation goes a long way towards satisfying two major criteria for good management control systems, goal-congruence and fairness. Goal-congruence is restored because a corporate-wide point of view has been brought to bear on the currency exchange rate, eliminating decisions taken on the basis of the expectations and risk-preferences of local managers who necessarily will have a narrower horizon on the currency risk problem than the corporate headquarters. Fairness is restored, at least in regard to the exchange rate fluctuations, by the establishment of a standard under which the local decision maker gets no blame or credit for currency fluctuations outside of the division manager's control.

An examination of the foreign operations of the ten corporations referred to above confirms our approach. For those firms where both operating and financial decisions were decentralized, imposing exchange risk fluctuations on operating managers by tracking performance at actual end of period rates seemed to cause little concern since local management had authority to control the risk. However, of those firms with decentralized operations which attempted to centralize financial management, the ones which were most successful in eliciting local management behavior consistent with corporate goals combined consistent budgeting and tracking rates in their control systems.

SETTING INTERNAL FORWARD EXCHANGE RATES

One possible objection to the use of IFRs is the need for exchange rate forecasts. This requirement may appear to be particularly onerous in view of evidence that current exchange rate fluctuations are large relative to fundamental factors such as inflation differentials and interest rate differentials. Also, exchange markets appear to be efficient; therefore the fluctuations can be characterized as a random process [Giddy and Dufey, 1975; Kohlhagen, 1976]. However, forcasts of some type, whether implicit or explicit, are required for proper planning regardless of the particular control system. Further, in precisely this type of environment, in which there are large random exchange rate fluctuations, it is important to shield operating managers from these unforeseeable exchange rate variations.

Even in this environment some forecasting of exchange rates, at least in terms of long-term trends, is possible, and forecasts are available from major banks and econometric firms. Rather than dwell on the issue of forecasting exchange rates, we focus here on how IFRs should relate to the firms' forecasts. The value to a firm of flows in a particular currency in the future will not necessarily be equal to the expected value of the currency. Many firms seek to limit exchange rate risk by hedging their exposure through actions such as restructuring their financial assets and liabilities, changing the timing of international cash flows or entering into forward exchange contracts. Further, the value of currency flows to or from particular units of the firm depends upon their tax treatment. This will be a function of the firm's overall tax position as well as the range of mechanisms it has at its disposal for shifting profits and/or funds among subsidiary firms.[7]

A further question regarding IFRs is to what extent operating managers should have a role in setting them.

The most important reason for involving operating managers in setting IFRs is that these rates not only will reflect the corporation's best estimates of future exchange rate movements, but also they will reflect the extent to which the corporation can alter its business or financial decisions in anticipation of or in response to exchange rate changes. Decisions open to the firm might include changing prices or currencies in which sales are invoiced, sources of inputs, production schedules, markets for outputs and borrowing sources, in addition to hedging as a means of shifting some funds from one currency to another or leading and lagging certain receipts and or disbursements. That is, IFRs cannot be determined properly without a schedule of receipts and disbursements because of the simultaneous nature of the problem. This problem can be modelled formally as a decomposed mathematical programming problem which allows a centralized finance function and decentralized control over operations. However, we consider the most realistic method to be the use of one or more iterations between the two related problems. Beginning with a set of provisional IFRs, operating managers could prepare rough, highly aggregated sets of operating plans for their divisions. In turn, these would serve as input for a first solution of the centralized funds management problem. Then the resulting IFRs could be used to produce a final set of operating plans and budgeting rates to guide subsequent decisions. This iterative process points out the need for close coordination between the two activities.

Of course, another important consideration is to incorporate all relevant information

[7]It might be useful to think of the IFRs as shadow prices from a model for centralized international funds management. Scott [1973] provides a concise description of the key elements in this type of model. Robbins and Stobaugh [1973] formulate it as a linear programming problem. Lietaer [1970] describes it as a quadratic programming problem, and Rutenberg [1970] depicts it as a network problem. The inputs into such a model include the schedules of current and anticipated exposure as well as cash budgets which reflect variables such as planned activity, tax rates, interest rates, current and forecasted exchange rates and internal and external constraints on financial alternatives. Such a model should reflect the firm's willingness to bear exchange rate risks either through constraints limiting total risk exposure or through more explicit risk-reward tradeoffs. Since the objective of the model is to maximize the value of future flows or minimize the cost of funding future requirements, taking risk preferences into account, the shadow prices associated with future flows in various currencies may be interpreted as IFRs, representing the best estimate of their value to the firm.

available on a timely basis. To the extent that operating managers in particular countries have access to information not available to central financial personnel, they must be drawn into the process. This is unlikely for most major currencies, but it may be significant for smaller or less-developed countries about which information is not readily available. A final consideration is that managers should be incorporated in the process to assure understanding and acceptance of the IFRs, which are important inputs into business plans as well as reported performance. An honored convention for minimizing dysfunctionalities in control systems is that managers should have a role in the negotiation of any performance budget relevant to their own units. Confidence in the system undoubtedly would be strengthened if there were a procedure for appealing unacceptable IFRs to a higher level of management and a procedure for revising the IFRs when unforeseen events dramatically change the exchange rate.

ADJUSTING TO EXCHANGE RATE CHANGES WITHIN THE OPERATING CYCLE

To this point we have avoided the question of whether IFRs should be adjusted within the operating cycle if exchange rates change dramatically. The need for adjustment will depend on several factors, including the volatility of exchange rates and the relative sizes of exposed assets and LC earnings streams within the corporate total. Most critically, it will depend on the extent to which operating decisions can be changed in response to the new exchange rates. Clearly, if the operating cycle corresponds to a period over which decisions are not reversible, IFRs should not be changed under even the most extreme circumstances. Such a change would violate the basic concept of insulating operating managers from random exchange rate shifts. In other cases, decisions may be reversible at some cost. These cases call for new operating plans with some adjustment in the manager's reported profits to offset the costs involved. If the operating cycle is sufficiently long relative to the duration of particular operating decisions, IFRs can and should be updated. However, even here the change should apply only to the remainder of the period—the period for which new operating decisions can be made. In all cases, it would appear that updating the IFRs when appropriate would be preferable to making the operating subsidiaries responsible for actual exchange rate outcomes, whether reflected in the IFRs or not. Further, the coordination required for adjusting IFRs would create an environment of "sharing" the results of unforeseen developments instead of capriciously imposing them on operating units.

SUMMARY

We have outlined an approach for handling the treatment of currency changes within the multinational corporation's planning and control systems. This approach incorporates decentralized operating control of individual foreign subsidiaries and centralized control of the firm's finances. A set of currency rates which reflect the best judgment of not only currency developments but also the corporation's position vis-a-vis these changes, called IFRs, were suggested to be an appropriate basis for the development of budgets, as well as for tracking the operating performance of the foreign subsidiaries relative to the budget. Local management will be expected to take actions congruent with corporate objectives on the basis of these rates and will be held responsible for their performances relative to these rates. At the same time, financial decisions can be handled centrally, allowing a more effective and coordinated set of policies without impinging on the decentralized operating decisions.

The logic of using IFRs to deal with foreign exchange risks can be extended readily to other risks including price and interest rate fluctuations. As some form of inflation accounting is adopted, for example, a similar treatment of domestic price level risks will be called for. We have singled out exchange risks because we believe that their current treatment is a major source of conflict and distortion in decentralized multinational organizations.

REFERENCES

Chandler, A. D., *Strategy and Structure* (M.I.T. Press, 1972).

Channon, D. F., *The Strategy and Structure of British Enterprise* (Division of Research, Harvard Business School, 1973).

Dufey, G., "Corporate Finance and Exchange Variations," *Financial Management* (Summer 1972), pp. 51–57.

Financial Accounting Standards Board, Statement No. 8: *Accounting for the Translation of Foreign Currency Transactions and Foreign Currency Financial Statements* (1975).

First National City Bank. *Corporate Foreign Exposure Management* (1975).

Giddy, I. and G. Dufey, "The Random Behavior of Flexible Exchange Rates: Implications for Forecasting," *Journal of International Business Studies* (Spring 1975), pp. 1–32.

Horst, T., "The Theory of Multinational Firm: Optimal Behavior Under Different Tariffs and Tax Rates," *Journal of Political Economy* (September-October 1971), pp. 1059–1072.

Kohlhagen. S. W., "The Foreign Exchange Markets—Models, Tests, and Empirical Evidence" working paper (U. C. Berkeley, 1976).

Lietaer, B. A., *Financial Management of Foreign Exchange: An Operational Technique to Reduce Risk* (M.I.T. Press, 1970).

Lorange, P. and R. F. Vancil, *Strategic Planning Systems* (Prentice-Hall, 1977).

Robbins, S. M. and R. B. Stobaugh, *Money in the Multinational Enterprise* (Basic Books, 1973).

Rutenberg, D. P., "Maneuvering Liquid Assets in a Multinational Company: Formulation and Deterministic Solution Procedures," *Management Science* (June 1970), pp. 671–684.

Scott, G. M., *An Introduction to Financial Control and Reporting in Multinational Enterprises* (University of Texas at Austin, 1973).

Shapiro, A. C., "Exchange Risk Management for the Multinational Corporation," paper presented at Financial Management Association (1973).

Stopford, J. and L. T. Wells, *Managing the Multinational Enterprise: Organization of the Firm and Ownership of the Subsidiaries* (Basic Books, 1972).

Traver, S., "Setting 'Smart' Budgeting Rates in the Control Process" (Masters' Thesis, M.I.T., Sloan School of Management, 1975).

25

A Proposal for Measuring International Performance*

G. Bennett Stewart

INTRODUCTION

In principle, there should be no difference between the evaluation of foreign and domestic operations. The central issues are the same: Has the operation added to the value of our shareholders investment? To what extent is local operating management responsible for the unit's success or lack of it? Can additional capital be invested profitably?

Resolving these issues for foreign operations is more difficult, however, for several reasons. First, inflation rates overseas often are orders of magnitude higher than those in the United States. This renders conventional, historical-cost accounting statements nearly meaningless. When inflation is high, profits are overstated due to illusory holding gains, while assets, and thus the capital base, are carried at values well below current replacement cost.

Of course, this problem is not unique to foreign operations, just more pronounced. While the tendency has been for management to ignore the effects of inflation when evaluating performance in dollar terms (witness the general lack of interest in FAS #33 inflation-adjusted figures), this oversight becomes critical when evaluating foreign performance. For, differences in rates of inflation between countries are the primary reason—at least over the long run—why currencies change in value relative to each other. Currency translation and inflation accounting are thus inextricably linked. To measure performance properly, the effect of inflation must be built into local financial statements *before* it can be offset by currency translation.

The second problem is caused by exchange rate fluctuations that distort the income from, and thus the value of, foreign investments when translated into dollar terms. While local management may believe it is performing quite well, a sudden realignment of currency values can produce an entirely different impression for home country management. At other times, local performance may be exaggerated by translation gains that are unlikely to recur.

Corporate managers are understandably concerned that investors will penalize their company with a lower stock price because of the earnings volatility caused by currency fluctuations. The natural reaction is thus to hedge accounting exposure, and to shy away from foreign investments where there is a great likelihood of currency instability. Such a reaction, however, is clearly not always in the best economic interest of the firm, or its stockholders. In order to explain why this concern with accounting exposure is misplaced—whether under FAS #8 or the newly adopted FAS #52—we need to begin with an understanding of (1) what causes exchange rates to fluctuate and (2) how influential investors really appraise the performance and value of foreign operations.

Exchange rates tend to fluctuate around an "intrinsic" value. They may be overvalued

---

*This article is reprinted, with permission, from *Midland Corporate Finance Journal,* vol. 1, no. 2, 1983, pp. 56–71, published by Stern, Stewart, Putnam and Macklis, Ltd., Corporate Financial Consultants.

for a period of time, and then experience a dramatic devaluation that merely offsets the accumulation of past inflation. At other times exchange rates can move in *anticipation* of coming changes in economic conditions that will not affect the foreign unit's performance until some time in the future. Only some fluctuations in any given year will reflect changes in the intrinsic value of the currency. The majority of currency movements are temporary and likely to reverse themselves with the passage of time.

Investors consequently try not to place too much emphasis on any given year's exchange rate movements. Consider, for example, the following exchange between The Dexter Corporation's chairman, David Coffin, and the president of a leading investment advisory house:

David L. Coffin: [Foreign investment is] complex and frustrating. We have a number of successful foreign businesses that do well in local currencies but have suffered on a yearly comparison basis because of the stronger dollar of the past two years.

Edward M. Giles: It's frustrating for investors, too. It is difficult to make appropriate adjustments for currency-related change, whether positive or negative, and to determine whether the effects are transitory *or* fundamental.[1]

Sophisticated investors attempt to separate the fundamental from the transitory in order to pay for enduring value. This means, for one thing, that currently employed accounting methods of currency translation do not capture or simulate the process of valuation. If certain, but not all, exchange rate changes matter to price-setting investors, then accountants must inevitably fail to provide a measure of performance that reflects economic reality. They must choose between a technique like FAS #8, that places currency translation gains and losses on the income statement as if all exchange rate movements matter to investors; and one like FAS #52, that buries all adjustments in an equity reserve as if no currency fluctuations matter. Since the truth lies in between, reported results must be adjusted before meaningful measures of performance are possible.

The situation in Mexico over the past decade or so illustrates many of the problems encountered in measuring performance for international operations (and it will serve as the basis for the case study presented later in this article). Mexico experienced a much higher rate of inflation than the United States in the early 1970's, and yet the peso's value held steady at 12.5 to the dollar. This meant that, at some point, those economic forces that maintain purchasing power parity throughout the world would inevitably bring about a correction in the value of the peso. In 1976, the peso suffered a devaluation (of over 60 percent) to 20 pesos to the dollar. Thus, instead of gradual adjustment, most of the accumulated inflation differential between the U.S. and Mexico was reflected in a single day's change in the rate of exchange. This drastic translation loss was not a real economic loss; it simply compensated for the overvaluation of the Mexican currency—and thus the overstatement of returns from Mexican operations—in prior years.

Much the same pattern was repeated over the period 1976–1982. The Mexican authorities pursued economic policies designed to keep the peso fundamentally overvalued in order to achieve the dual objectives of a favorable balance of trade and rapid expansion in economic growth. For some time they were able to sustain this policy by borrowing against future oil revenues. The day of reckoning came when the market lost confidence

[1]The Dexter Corporation Annual Report, 1982.

in Mexico's ability to further mortgage its oil wealth. While the precise date of the devaluation was not foreseeable, it was widely anticipated by investors and considered necessary to offset past inflation.

Those companies that made long-term investment decisions predicated on the continuation of the unrealistically high peso of recent years now find themselves in a difficult position. This problem might have been avoided by translating results from Mexico into dollars using a more realistic exchange rate, one that reflects the fundamental economic forces that eventually determine a currency's value. In this way home country management would have been made aware that the performance in Mexico was overstated, and that a large translation loss was inevitable.

In this article, I will propose an alternative accounting framework that combines adjustments for local inflation with a method of currency translation using "normalized" exchange rates. Such a framework should provide a much more realistic picture of the economic realities of international operations than either unadjusted FAS #8 or FAS #52 results. Although not likely to be adopted soon by the Accounting Standards Board, this framework has a number of important internal uses, serving potentially as the basis for corporate decisions affecting capital allocation, the hedging of currency risk, and management compensation.

THE DETERMINANTS OF EXCHANGE RATES

Before approaching these questions, it is important to begin with at least a crude theory of exchange rates on which performance measures can be based.

Broadly speaking, exchange rate fluctuations can be attributed to one of three causes: (1) differences in rates of inflation, expected as well as actual; (2) relative economic competitiveness; and (3) government policy. Over any short interval of time, say, one-to-three years, changes in economic competitiveness and government policy may be the dominant factors affecting exchange rates. Hence, anticipating business cycles, fluctuations in interest rates, and election winners may be very useful in predicting short-term exchange rate movements. Over the longer term, however, these factors tend to cancel out, leaving inflation differentials the dominant force.

The impact of inflation on exchange rates is seen most clearly in those countries with consistently high or low rates of inflation. In Brazil and Argentina, for example, where inflation regularly runs in excess of 100 percent a year, their currencies suffer regular, indeed often programmed, devaluations. By contrast, the Swiss franc typically appreciates against other currencies due to the perennially low inflation enforced by conservative Swiss bankers. The same is generally true in Germany, where memory of the hyperinflation of the 1920s is the dominant psychological force leading the country to low inflation and a strong currency.

In countries like the U.S., which have had inflation rates between these two extremes, or where the level of inflation is not as readily predictable, exchange rate movements are not as visibly linked to differences in inflation rates. From year to year, the influence of business cycles and changes in government policies will be a major determinant of currency appreciation or depreciation. Nevertheless, for almost all countries, the cumulative exchange rate movements over a, say, five-year time horizon can be explained largely by inflation differentials.

Purchasing Power Parity

The tendency of exchange rate changes to offset inflation differentials between any two currencies is known as Purchasing Power Parity (PPP). The theory of PPP relies on the simple notion that similar products will sell at roughly the same price at any given point in time throughout the world. This happens because astute international traders buy where goods are cheap and sell where expensive, thus ensuring that similar goods in geographically isolated markets do not differ in price when translated at current exchange rates. If prices of the same goods are identical at current exchange rates, and if they are to remain so in the future (when converted at future exchange rates), then the *change* in price levels over time must be offset by a corresponding equal and opposite *change* in exchange rates.

The theory of PPP maintains, for example, that if the rate of inflation is 20 percent in one country while only 10 percent in another, the country with the 20 percent inflation will see its currency depreciate by 10 percent against the other currency. Otherwise, the price of identical products would not be the same, and profit opportunities would abound. PPP, then, far from being an arcane, unrealistic economic supposition, is simply the predictable outcome of more or less inevitable actions by businessmen to exploit profit opportunities.

How, then, can exchange rates ever deviate from PPP? Why is it not possible for international traders to maintain the same price for the same product at all times, thus ensuring that exchange rates continuously conform to PPP? Deviations from PPP occur, for one thing, because certain "frictions" reduce the profitability and increase the risk of international trade. These frictions include the costs of transportation, taxes, and financing, restrictions such as import quotas, exchange and capital controls, and lack of good information about prices and profit opportunities.

The presence of these frictions means that exchange rates can fluctuate in a "band" around the level dictated by PPP without creating opportunities to profit through trade. If, for example, the cost of financing, taxes, and transportation came to 20 percent of the value of the trade, exchange rates could deviate as much as 20 percent from their intrinsic value without setting in motion corrective market forces.

International Competitiveness

Another cause of temporary deviations from PPP are changes in the underlying competitiveness of an economy in international markets. If the world operated strictly on a barter basis for trade, then the exchange rate would be the ratio at which exported goods were traded for imported goods. Any change in this ratio would lead to a revaluation in the fundamental value of the currency.

In the real world, changes in the supply and demand, and thus in the "relative prices," of certain goods can dominate exchange rate movements over considerable periods of time. One of the best examples of this in recent years was the British pound. For several years after 1976, the pound appreciated against the dollar even while Britain was experiencing a higher rate of inflation than the United States. This was partly attributable to the increasing value of North Sea oil as petroleum prices continued to rise. The pound, acting much like a share of stock in the British economy, rose in line with the general increase in British wealth. So closely did the pound's value seem to be tied to oil that the *Economist* of London dubbed the currency, "The Petro-Pound." Now that oil prices have weakened, the pound, along with other oil-driven currencies, has lost its premium value in exchange markets.

An increase in the pound's value due to oil, however, should not affect the value of other British investments. To remain competitive in international markets, businessmen in Britain would have to hold down their prices in pounds to maintain the same cost to foreigners. But by so doing, the price charged to pound consumers will be reduced, thus lowering reported profits in pounds. In this case the translation gain arising from the initial appreciation in the pound offsets a subsequent return shortfall, leaving foreign investors equally well off on net. Thus, the change in the value of the pound did not, in fact, represent an exchange risk.

It could be argued, then, that the ideal framework for evaluating foreign performance should include exchange gains or losses arising from changes in relative prices as part of the return earned from a foreign operation. My proposal for evaluating foreign operations does not, however, explicitly account for the effects of deviations from PPP caused by such changes in relative prices for several reasons. First, the initial gain recorded in the example above is potentially misleading to management. It does not reflect the difficulty local management subsequently will have to remain competitive in pound terms, and so could communicate a confusing signal to corporate management about the desirability of investing additional capital. Second, there is no practicable way to ascertain whether deviations from PPP are caused by changes in relative prices, or by those changes in government policy which, as I shall argue, should be excluded from the evaluation of performance. Finally, and most important, evidence indicates that such changes in relative prices tend to average out over a period of 5 years or longer, leaving PPP as a valid long term predictor of exchange rate movements. Even a unified and dominant cartel like OPEC could not indefinitely maintain an artificially high price for oil against the economic forces of conservation, the development of substitutes, and the entry of new competitors. It is precisely these competitive forces that will drive exchange rates towards PPP over time.

Government Policy Affects Exchange Rates

Probably the most important reason why exchange rates fluctuate around their fundamental PPP value is government policy. Governments manipulate exchange rates to spur economic growth and employment, to cushion economic shocks, and, occasionally, to lead the country to painful, but necessary adjustments. Not surprisingly, the policies are frequently designed to help win elections. And while such policies can be successful for a short period of time (the benefits need last only through the next election), economic forces ultimately move the exchange rate back towards PPP.

By not allowing their currencies to depreciate to offset inflation differentials, governments preserve the prestige associated with stable currencies. More important, an overvalued exchange rate allows businessmen to import raw materials and consumers to import products at a lower cost than otherwise. But, while this may spur economic growth for a time, the free lunch cannot last forever.

The consequence of maintaining a currency artificially high is that payments due to foreigners for imports exceed payments received from foreigners for exports, and the government is thus forced to make up a balance of payments deficit. It will do so by using its own limited foreign exchange reserves to buy its currency in the forward exchange market. This provides its countrymen with the foreign currencies they collectively require to pay for the excess of imports over exports. At some point, however, the government will run out of money to subsidize the import spree, and the exchange rate will decline to the point where a balance will be achieved between desired imports and exports.

The day of reckoning can be further deferred by international borrowing, but only as long as the country has good credit in the capital markets. From 1976 to 1982, Mexico was able to maintain an overvalued peso by borrowing against its future oil revenues. In this way the country obtained the foreign reserves needed to subsidize its overvalued exchange rate. When the price of oil fell, the market's assessment of Mexico's creditworthiness was drastically reduced, the borrowing window closed, and the exchange rate plummeted.

Precisely the opposite economic policy is now being followed in Mexico. Mexico's recently elected government is forcing austerity by maintaining an exchange rate that is undervalued relative to its PPP value. In effect, the country is now being taxed through an undervalued exchange rate in order to pay for past excesses. The Mexican authorities used the exchange rate at first to subsidize and now to tax in a way that is not apparent to the ordinary citizen.

Management should not let itself be fooled by such manipulation of exchange rates. When the local currency is purposely overvalued, the results of local performance when translated into dollar terms will be *exaggerated* by the exchange rate subsidy. When the currency is undervalued, the results of foreign operations will be artificially *depressed* by the exchange rate tax. The result of government changes in policy transmitted through exchange rates is a potentially large and troublesome disparity in perception between corporate and local management.

INTEREST RATES AFFECT EXCHANGE RATES

Through monetary policies implemented by their central banks, governments can affect interest rates and, thus indirectly, exchange rates. Exchange rates are tied even more directly to interest rates than to the prices of goods and services, so that when interest rates change, exchange rates follow—even though this may temporarily require a deviation from PPP.

Exchange rates are related to interest rates in an economic relationship known as Interest Rate Parity (IRP). IRP is based on the simple principle that identically risky investments must offer investors everywhere the same underlying real rate of return, or else financial traders will find a way to make a sure profit. For this reason, exchange rate movements over time will be expected to offset differences between interest rates on similarly risky bonds denominated in different currencies. The principle of IRP holds that, for example, a country with a 15 percent interest rate should expect a 5 percent annual devaluation in its exchange rate relative to another currency where the interest rate on similarly risky bonds is only 10 percent.

Like PPP, the condition of Interest Rate Parity is the inevitable result of the profit motive. But also like PPP, IRP is subject to frictions that limit its efficacy as a predictor of exchange rates. These frictions, however, are much smaller. Information about interest rates is much more readily available than information about goods and services. The transportation of funds to arbitrage interest rates requires just the cost of a telex. The existence of offshore markets circumvents regulations and taxes. For all these reasons financial market arbitrage (IRP) is more effective than goods market arbitrage (PPP) in determining exchange rate movements. Even casual observation confirms that interest rates respond immediately to the announcement of a change in the money supply, whereas businessmen adjust prices of goods and services only after the effect of money growth on demand is clear. This means deviations from PPP will arise when there are sudden changes in interest rates. These deviations will reverse themselves, however, as businessmen eventually adjust prices and exchange rates to PPP.

Governments, then, can dramatically change interest rates, thereby manipulating exchange rates, by unexpectedly easing or tightening monetary policy. When the money supply expands, for example, interest rates initially will fall due to the greater availability of credit. But because IRP must hold, capital will flow to seek higher returns available overseas, causing the local currency to depreciate in value.

But these are only the immediate consequences of a more rapid growth in the money supply. What happens next is even more important. Since yields on similarly risky bonds must be equilibrated by arbitrage in the financial markets, the currency will be expected to *appreciate* somewhat over time so that the total return from holding local debt is equivalent to that available overseas.

This is not to imply that the currency will appreciate to a higher value *on net* as a result of a shift to a more expansionary monetary policy. The appreciation I refer to merely corrects for the initial devaluation that itself is a reaction to the temporary lowering of interest rates. The final result of an expansive monetary policy is higher inflation, higher interest rates, and a lower currency value, all in conformity with PPP and IRP. But where the expected higher inflation and interest rates may take as long as 18 months to materialize, the exchange rate response is likely to be swift. Therefore, today's exchange rate depreciation often presages tomorrow's higher inflation. A devaluation now for inflation later means a temporary, but eventually self-correcting, deviation from PPP.

This poses a major problem for international performance measurement. The immediate devaluation of the currency will produce a translation loss in dollar-reported performance. But it is a loss that may have little economic significance. In following periods the foreign unit's return will be boosted by the additional inflation expected to follow. The higher (nominal) return in local currency combined with the subsequent currency appreciation will offset the already recorded translation loss so that, provided the company is able to raise prices sufficiently to match local inflation, there is no net economic loss. Such temporary deviations from PPP thus cause accounting statements to misrepresent true corporate performance.

This example illustrates another important aspect of exchange rates: namely, they are forward looking in much the same way that common stock prices are. As a dramatic example, the expectation alone of the socialist victory in France began driving down the exchange rate before the new (ultimately inflationary) policies had even been announced, much less put into effect. It would have been inappropriate for American or British multinationals to penalize their managers in France for the effect of an anticipated inflation that had not yet affected their reported results. But this, of course, is what the accounting system does.

To continue with our discussion of interest rates, let's consider what will happen when monetary policy is unexpectedly tightened. The effect of reduced credit availability is higher interest rates now, but lower interest rates later when inflation eventually subsides. As the real interest rate climbs, foreign capital is attracted, thus boosting the exchange value of the currency. Currency appreciation now presages lower inflation tommorrow.

This is precisely what has taken place in the U.S. as a result of "Reaganomics." With the tightening of Fed policy came the predictable increase in interest rates. Foreign investors, attracted by higher yields in the U.S., shifted their portfolios into dollars and away from other currencies; and the value of the dollar appreciated in anticipation of the actual decline in U.S. inflation. In fact, the dollar appreciated so much that a partial depreciation of the dollar can now be expected to restore parity between yields on German mark and U.S. dollar investments.

Accounting, as a result, is now distorting performance measures for American operations abroad. The tightening of U.S. credit has temporarily raised the dollar above PPP, thus producing artificial exchange losses. As the dollar subsides in exchange markets the value of foreign investments will be restored through exchange gains. The results of foreign operations also will compare favorably with the lower interest rates that will ensue in the U.S.

The message for management should be clear: exchange rates are more closely tied to interest rates *in the short run* than to the prices of goods and services that determine corporate profits. This means that any accounting technique that uses current exchange rates to measure translation gains or losses will either reward or penalize local managers for the effect of economic forces that have not yet affected reported profits. Translating past performance using current exchange rates thus has the effect of mixing expectations for the future with the reality of the past.

A more accurate measure of performance is obtained when results are translated using a "normalized" exchange rate that filters out the impact of temporary deviations from PPP—whether due to changes in monetary policy or to a shift to a more lenient or restrictive exchange rate policy. The "normalized" rate follows the path dictated by the fundamental economic forces experienced to date. The use of such a rate has the virtue of neither penalizing nor rewarding local management for exchange rate fluctuations beyond their control. It may also provide a more reliable basis for judging whether additional capital can be profitably invested.

THE ENCHILADA FOOD COMPANY: A CASE STUDY

I will illustrate my proposal for evaluating international operations by considering the performance of a hypothetical Mexican subsidiary of an American multinational, The Enchilida Food Company.

Let us assume that the company was formed in Mexico at the beginning of 1977, and that we want to evaluate its operating performance through 1982. The major task facing home country management is to resolve the seeming paradox that the performance of Enchilada appeared to be quite attractive up until 1982, at which time a large peso devaluation appeared, virtually overnight, to substantially reduce the dollar value of the investment. The Enchilada case, an experience common to a number of American and European multinationals, raises issues like the following: Do such large devaluations, which are largely predictable, really represent a risk to U.S. corporations and their investors? Do translated results have any connection with economic reality when exchange rates fail to reflect past relative rates of inflation? If not, how can conventional accounting statements be made to reflect economic reality?

Before addressing these questions, let's go back a little farther into Mexico's economic history. (Information concerning the actual and intrinsic value of the peso is presented in the table below.)

TABLE 1

	71-75	1976	1977	1978	1979	1980	1981	1982
Exchange Rates (peso/dollar)								
Actual Yr. End	12.5	20.0	22.7	22.7	22.8	23.3	26.2	100.5
"Normalized"	17.7	19.5	23.9	26.2	28.0	31.6	37.2	56.1
Peso Value								
Mexican Inflation	96.1%	15.8%	29.1%	17.3%	18.2%	26.4%	27.9%	57.0%
U.S. Inflation	38.7	5.8	6.5	7.5	11.3	13.5	10.4	6.0
Normlzd. Ex. Rte. Chng.	44.1%	10.0%	22.6%	9.8%	6.9%	12.9%	17.5%	51.0%
Actual Ex. Rte. Chng.	0.0	(60.0)	(13.5)	(0.0)	(0.4)	(2.2)	(12.4)	(283.6)
Deviations From PPP	44.1%	(50.0%)	9.1%	9.8%	6.5%	10.7%	5.1%	(232.6%)
Cumulative Deviations	44.1%	(5.9%)	3.2%	13.0%	19.5%	30.2%	35.3%	(197.3%)

Over the period 1971–75, cumulative peso inflation exceeded dollar inflation by 44 percent, yet the peso's value was maintained, largely through Mexican central bank intervention, at 12.5 to the dollar. In 1976, the peso devalued from 12.5 pesos to 20 pesos to restore Purchasing Power Parity. The exchange rate adjusted in a single stroke to the cumulative excess of Mexican inflation over U.S. inflation.

This pattern repeated itself in the following period, 1976–1982. Over this period, cumulative Mexican inflation was some 285 percent higher than U.S. inflation, but the Mexican government insulated the currency through capital controls and borrowings, and only small devaluations in the peso occurred. Then, in 1982, a dramatic peso devaluation caught up with and even overcompensated for the cumulative difference in inflation rates. (This pattern is portrayed in Exhibit 1.)

EXHIBIT 1

Normalized and Actual Exchange Rate (Pesos per U.S. Dollar)

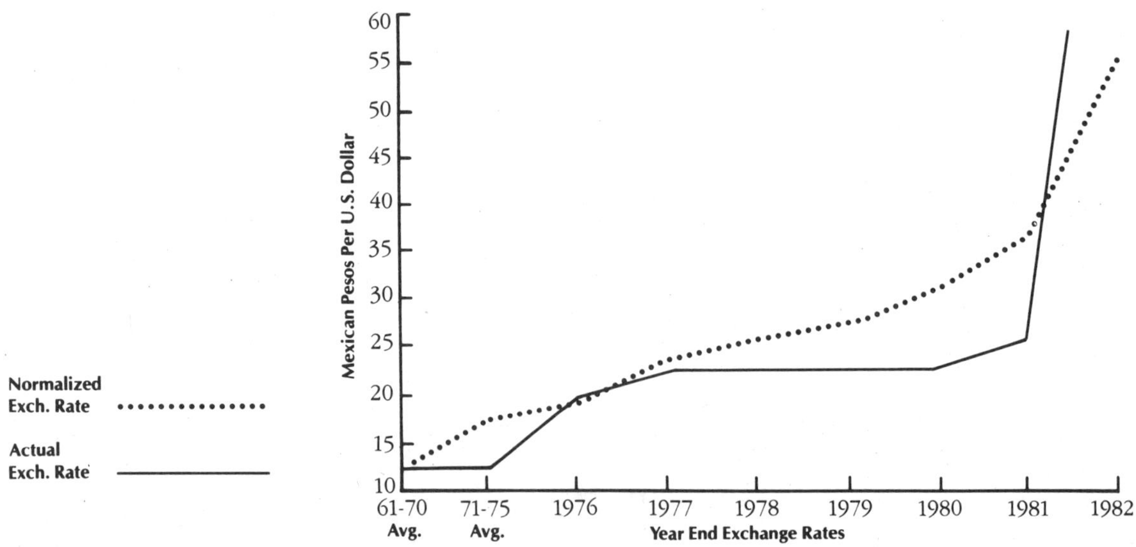

The characteristic, step-like movement of the peso is apparent as it suffers large devaluations after periods of relative stability. The "normalized" peso (plotted in the broken line) shows the exchange rate that would have resulted had devaluations been permitted to offset exactly the excess of Mexican inflation over U.S. inflation. By contrast, the "normalized" exchange rate depreciates each year in line with the excess of Mexican over American inflation. The actual peso value "plays leap-frog" with the normalized rate, falling behind when the government erects barriers to defend the peso, and then jumping ahead, even overshooting its mark, when the government surrenders to market forces.

The Standard Accounting Method

With this as a background, let's begin by showing how the current accounting technique, as prescribed in FAS #52, would translate the results of Enchilada into dollars.[2]

Before doing so, however, we should agree upon a basis for measuring and evaluating corporate performance. If performance is to be appraised in terms of contribution to share value, the procedure adopted should closely parallel the approach sophisticated investors employ to evaluate the quality of foreign investments. They take returns earned from both dividends and capital appreciation in local currency and translate them into dollars for comparison with the performance of similarly risky investments. In similar fashion, management should evaluate international investments by measuring rates of return on invested capital in terms of local currency, and then translate those returns into dollar terms. The final stage of the evaluation process should then review the adequacy of the rate of return earned in dollars against the opportunity cost of that capital, also expressed in dollars. Those investments that earn more than their cost of capital, in relevant cash flow terms, will increase stock price; those that do not will detract from shareholders' wealth.

I also recommend that the rate of return be calculated on the *total* amount of debt and equity capital rather than on equity alone. The rate of return so calculated will be unaffected by fluctuations in interest rates and differences in capital structure between subsidiaries (which are generally determined by centralized financial management).

I calculated three different accounting Rates of Return (RORs) for the Enchilada Food Company over the years 1977–1982, in each case dividing Net Operating Profit before taxes (NOP) by Total Capital employed at the beginning of the year. The first is the rate of return *in pesos* using conventionally reported income statements and balance sheets. The second is the rate of return as reported in dollars using FAS #52, but excluding any translation gain or loss.[3] The third rate of return is calculated in dollars including any translation gain or loss.[4] These all are plotted in Exhibit 2, along with the corresponding

[2]The company's results over this entire period are translated into dollars using FAS #52, even though FAS #52 was adopted only last year and Mexico, because of its hyper-inflation, would be required to use FAS #8 conventions for translation into dollars. To further simplify our analysis, I assume that the company pays no taxes and that the company is financed using only equity capital.

[3]Briefly, FAS #52 requires that the balance sheet, with the exception of the net worth account, be translated using year end exchange rates, and the income statement be translated using average exchange rates. See Bryan Carberg's article preceding.

[4]Under FAS #52, a translation gain or loss is credited directly to net worth without passing through the income statement. A translation gain or loss is calculated in order to balance net worth with the difference between the translated value for assets and liabilities. Part of the justification offered for this is that currency gains and losses will tend to balance out over time, so there is no need to include on the income statement something that is expected to contribute nothing over time. In fact, this rationale is erroneous. Currencies that consistently

actual devaluation in the peso from year-end-to-year-end. The following observations are noteworthy:

- After a temporary decline in 1978, the peso rate of return steadily improved, even through 1982.
- Up to 1982, the dollar returns closely tracked the peso return. This occurred because the peso was relatively stable against the dollar over this period. In 1982, the dollar return *before* translation loss, although lower than prior years, was still in excess of 10 percent, in spite of the dramatic peso devaluation.
- In 1982, Enchilada's translation loss was equal to approximately 74 *percent* of capital employed! The return in dollars *including* this loss was approximately −63 percent in 1982.
- The difference between peso returns and U.S. dollar returns each year roughly equals the actual percentage devaluation in the peso.

These results reveal several shortcomings of current accounting procedures. First, the reported peso results bear no relation to the real economic conditions in Mexico. Second, in those years in which the peso devalued only modestly, the returns reported in dollars are *overstated* because they reflect the higher rate of inflation experienced in Mexico without showing the offsetting effect of the inevitable, although deferred, devaluation. Finally, the return in dollars *including* translation loss is misleading because it concentrates the effect of the extreme devaluation in the peso into a single year. In reality, the devaluation is compensating for a cumulative overstatement of returns over the past five years.

Peso Performance Adjusted for Inflation

As stated earlier, the problems of currency translation and inflation accounting are inseparable. Consequently, before demonstrating how the use of "normalized" exchange rates would remedy this problem of currency translation, we must first deal with the prior problem of adjusting local currency numbers for inflation.

The results reported in pesos are severely distorted by inflation. Over the period 1976 to 1982, cumulative inflation in Mexico was more than 350 percent. This meant that a peso spent in 1982 had *less than one-fourth* the purchasing power of a peso in 1976. Yet the accounting statements mixed the two pesos as if they had equal value. When there is a large difference between the historic and current cost of foreign assets, then translated

---

appreciate over time due to conservative monetary policies will have a net translation gain even after the passage of many years. Ignoring the gains passed to the translation reserve when evaluating performance means that an important and consistent part of the return available to U.S. investors is overlooked. Managers in these countries may be unfairly penalized, and potentially attractive investments may be rejected if management worries about potential future accounting returns.

In contrast, countries such as Mexico that are inclined towards inflationary policies will experience a consistent devaluation over time and a net translation loss. Without considering the effect of such losses, the return available to U.S. shareholders may be overstated. Managers may be given bonuses where none is deserved, and investments may be accepted that are not attractive to investors. For this reason a rate of return was calculated using dollar reported results according to FAS #52, but including the translation gain or loss as part of the return.

EXHIBIT 2

The Enchilada Food Company—Mexico (Reported Peso and FASB 52 Returns)
Actual Peso Devaluation (In U.S. Dollars per Peso)

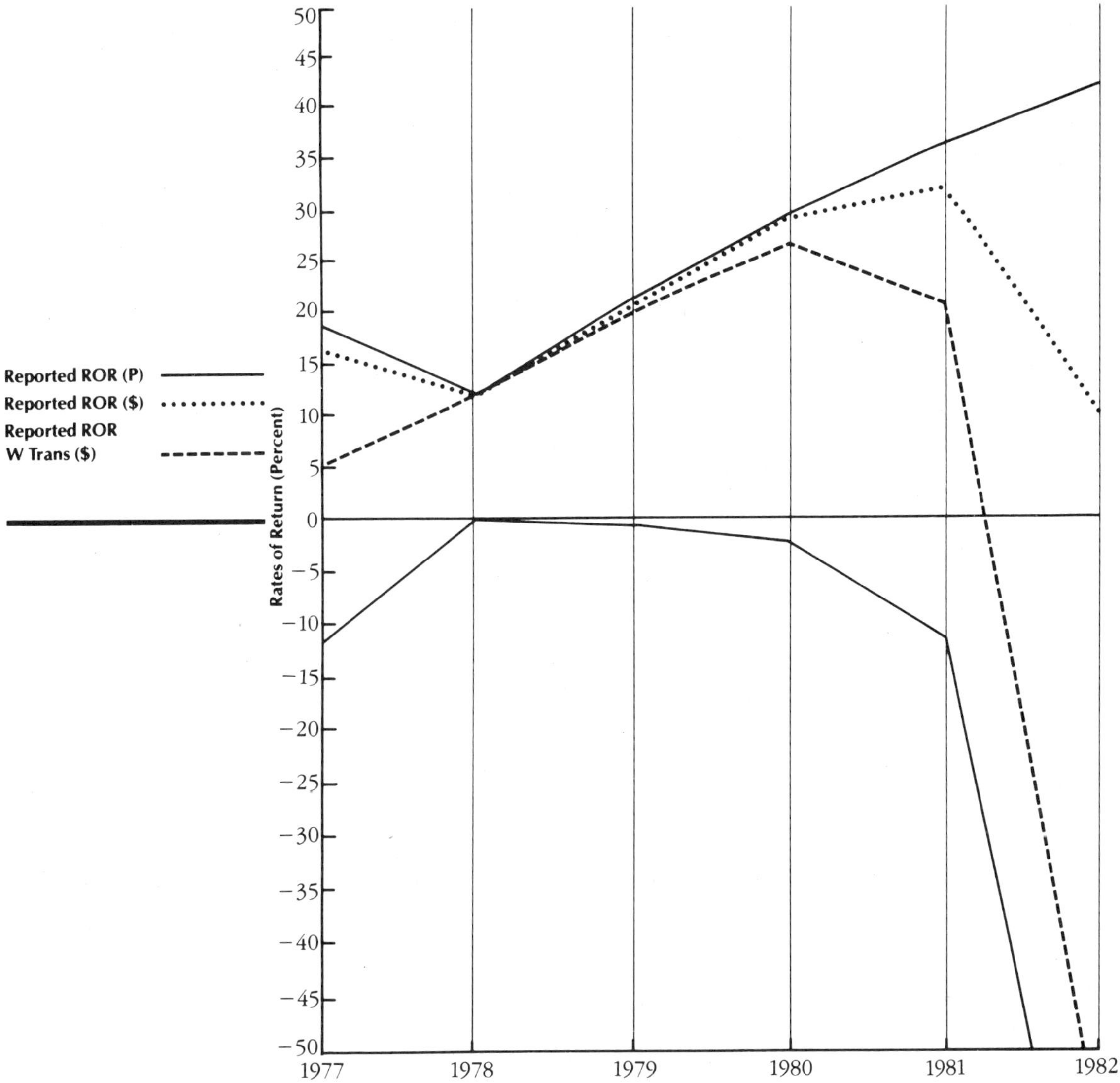

accounting rates of return, whether using FAS #8 or FAS # 52, will be all but meaningless.

In order to eliminate the distortions of inflation on reported earnings, standard financial statements can be adjusted as follows:

- No change is necessary for monetary assets (cash and receivables) because their face value represents their realizable value in current pesos.

EXHIBIT 3

The Enchilada Food Company—Mexico (Beginning Capital Employed)

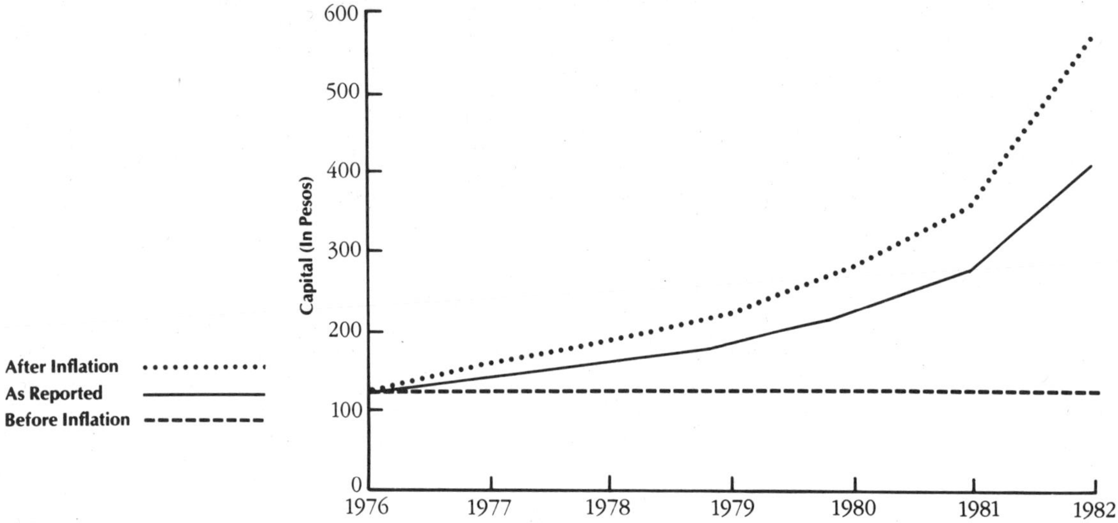

- The FIFO value of inventory, provided it turns quickly, can be employed as a close approximation of their value in current pesos.
- The current value of plant can be estimated by writing up the accounting value at the rate of peso inflation each year.

The resulting estimate of capital employed at current peso prices (which I will call *Capital with Inflation*) and capital as reported are plotted in Exhibit 3.

By 1982, reported capital understates current value by about 30 percent. The dashed line portrays current value capital deflated by the Mexican price index to constant 1976 pesos. It reveals that the "real" amount of capital employed by Enchilada did not change over this period. Capital investment served only to replace depreciation and to meet working capital requirements at higher peso prices. The difference between capital deflated to constant 1976 pesos and current peso value capital represents the cumulative amount of inflation gains.

The next step involves adjusting reported income for the effect of inflation. To do so, I computed Net Operating Profit (NOP) both before and after holding gains due to inflation. NOP *before Inflation* is calculated by subtracting operating costs at current peso prices from sales. Specifically, Cost of Goods Sold is computed on a LIFO basis and Depreciation Expense is based on the estimated current peso value of PPP. To calculate NOP *after Inflation, all* holding gains arising from inflation are added to NOP *before Inflation*. The inflation gain on inventories is estimated by the difference between LIFO and FIFO Cost of Goods Sold. The inflation gain on plant is estimated by multiplying the beginning of year value for net plant (at current prices) by the inflation rate over the year. There is no inflation gain on monetary assets. The NOPs so calculated are shown in Table 2 below along with reported NOP (in millions of pesos):

TABLE 2

	1977	1978	1979	1980	1981	1982
NOP Before Inf	10.9	5.8	19.3	28.0	43.3	25.0
NOP As Reported	23.6	15.5	35.0	55.0	82.2	118.6
NOP After Inf	40.0	28.2	47.0	75.2	106.5	190.0

The accounting profits consistently fall between profits *before* and *after Inflation* because *some, but not all,* of the holding gains arising from inflation are recorded. Inflation gains are realized on inventory sold and accounted for under FIFO accounting, but are expensed for LIFO inventories. Gains also are realized on plant insofar as depreciation charges based on historical acquisition costs understate true depreciation at current prices. The majority of holding gains on plant, however, are not recorded as long as plant is carried at a value well below its current peso cost.

Rates of Return can now be calculated by dividing NOP Before and After Inflation by the current value of capital employed at the beginning of the year. The Rate of Return *Before* Inflation is a "real" return. Subtracting costs at current prices means that enough funds have been set aside on the income statement to replace assets expended on the balance sheet at higher prices. Thus, the Real Return can be distributed to investors without impairing the company's ability to remain in business.

The Rate of Return *After* Inflation represents the "total" return available to investors in pesos from a combination of "real" operating profits *and* appreciation in the value of assets over the course of the year. The Total Return cannot be distributed to investors because that portion of the return due to inflation gains must be reinvested to replace assets at higher prices. Thus, the Total Return is available to investors only through a liquidation of the business.

What, then, is the justification for including asset appreciation as a component of return? Is it that every asset appreciates with inflation? Obviously not. The important point is that all assets will be worth more with inflation than they would be worth in the absence of that inflation. Stated differently, holding gains arise not because assets appreciate in value, but because money depreciates in value, so that even assets of unchanged value are worth more in money terms after inflation. But even this is not wholly correct. All that is necessary is that the level of profits the assets generate is increased by inflation, so that if price-to-earnings ratios are constant, the capitalized value of profits, and hence the value of assets, will appreciate with inflation. Since investors realize inflation gains through higher stock prices, the corresponding holding gain on assets should be included in measures of corporate performance.

The Real and Total Rates of Return (ROR), along with the conventional accounting ROR, are reproduced in the table following (All RORs in pesos).

As would be expected, Enchilada's Real RORs parallel economic growth rates in Mexico, while Total RORs mirror peso inflation. Reported accounting RORs fall between Total and Real RORs in each year. All three RORs followed the same pattern except in 1982, when both accounting and Total RORs increased while the Real ROR declined.

TABLE 3

	1977	1978	1979	1980	1981	1982
Real ROR	8.7%	3.6%	10.2%	12.5%	15.3%	6.9%
Acctg. ROR	18.9%	12.1%	21.6%	29.8%	36.7%	42.6%
Total ROR	32.0%	17.4%	24.8%	33.6%	37.6%	52.5%
Mex. Grwth.	4.2%	3.4%	8.3%	9.2%	8.3%	2.0%
Inflation	29.1%	17.3%	18.2%	26.4%	27.9%	57.0%

These results have several implications for performance measurement. It should again be apparent that the accounting ROR is meaningless as a performance measure. It will generally fall between the Real and the Total Return, but there is no guarantee even of this. Of the three RORs, the Real Return is the best reflection of the true performance of the operation. It tracks most closely with those general economic conditions in Mexico that directly affect profitability.

The Real Return, however, does suffer from one important shortcoming. It fails to reflect the effect of "real" holding gains and losses that are important to investors. A real holding gain or loss arises when an asset appreciates by more or less than the general rate of inflation experienced across the entire economy. Normally it makes sense to exclude real holding gains or losses from performance measures because they arise from unpredictable changes in the value of assets that cannot be expected to continue. For example, a company that buys and sells gold jewelry will realize holding gains or losses on its inventory as the price of gold fluctuates. These price fluctuations cannot be expected to contribute consistently to profits. As a rule, holding gains and losses represent one-time adjustments to value rather than a continuing source of income that investors will capitalize at a multiple into the company's stock price. And, therefore, to the extent that stock prices reflect the capitalized value of an expected, normalized cash flow; real holding gains and losses should be excluded from internal performance measures.

One important exception to this rule are monetary assets like cash and receivables. The value of monetary assets is fixed in terms of the currency of their denomination. Inflation in the currency diminishes the real value of net monetary assets and creates a holding loss for investors in direct proportion to the rate of inflation.

In 1982, for example, Enchilada's *Total Return* of 52.5 percent was less than the 57 percent rate of inflation in Mexico, indicating that the actual real return to investors was negative, even though the computed Real Return was *positive*. Investors suffered a real loss despite the fact that the business produced a real profit. This apparent contradiction is explained by recognizing that the company sustained a real holding loss on its net monetary assets—cash and receivables—that offsets the Real Return earned in the business. Therefore, *the best overall measure of performance in local currency is the Total Return deflated for local inflation*. This measure will incorporate both the real business performance and the real holding losses on monetary assets.

The same evaluation of performance and value also can be reached by comparing the Total Return with the cost of capital. Since both lenders and shareholders expect to be compensated in real purchasing power terms, the cost of obtaining debt and equity capital implicitly incorporates inflation. Consequently, a comparison of the Total Return with the "nominal" cost of capital will produce the same result as a comparison of the deflated return with the "real" cost of capital. In either case, when managers are evaluated according to these benchmarks, they will have an incentive to increase prices sufficiently to cover the loss incurred by holding monetary assets that lose value due to inflation.

Perhaps the most important advantage to using the Total Return, however, is that it produces the most meaningful result when translated into dollars. The holding gains included in the Total Return offset translation losses, leaving a net gain in dollars commensurate with the level of U.S. inflation.

Conversion to Dollars Using "Normalized" Exchange Rate

The next and final stage of the analysis, then, is to calculate Enchilada's rate of return translated into dollars. While it would be possible to appraise the performance of foreign operations in terms of the deflated Total Return measured in local currency, it is important that multinationals be able to review the results of all foreign operations expressed in the home currency.

In the case of Enchilada, the peso inflation-adjusted income statement (i.e., including holding gains) and balance sheet (at current peso prices) would be translated into dollar terms using FAS #52 conventions, *but substituting a "normalized" exchange rate for the actual rate.* As stated, the normalized exchange rate is that which would prevail if the peso conformed precisely to Purchasing Power Parity. Year-to-year changes in the normalized exchange rate would thus reflect only the differences in inflation between Mexico and the U.S.[5]

The translated statements can then be used to determine the Total ROR in dollars after Translation, which is calculated by dividing the dollar amount of total income, *including both peso holding gains and the translation loss*, by the translated value of Capital with Inflation. This return is shown in Exhibit 5, together with the Total ROR in pesos shown earlier in Exhibit 4.

As a graph makes clear, Enchilada's Total ROR in dollars including Translation Loss is *consistently* less than the Total ROR in pesos. Recall, by contrast, that in every year except 1982, the reported accounting RORs in dollars tracked the peso ROR because the peso did not depreciate against the dollar in accordance with inflation differentials.

By using the normalized exchange rate the company implicitly charges the operation each year for the translation loss that will eventually take place. It is like establishing a reserve against future translation losses that can be expected with a high degree of confidence. Then when the actual loss itself takes place, no great surprise is in store for management. Moreover, this encourages investment decisions to be made on the basis of the expected, rather than actual, currency values.

Another major advantage of this method is its consistent treatment of the dual consequences of Mexican inflation. The holding gains that arise from Mexican inflation are included in the peso Total Return, thus offsetting the translation loss that is also due to local inflation. The net effect is to record an inflation gain in dollars commensurate with the level of inflation experienced in the U.S.

One way to see this is to note (in Table 4 below) that the Total Return in pesos, after

[5]In the process, an exchange loss would be recognized to balance equity translated at the historical normalized rate with assets translated at the current normalized rate.

EXHIBIT 4

The Enchilada Food Company—Mexico (Rates of Return in Mexican Pesos)

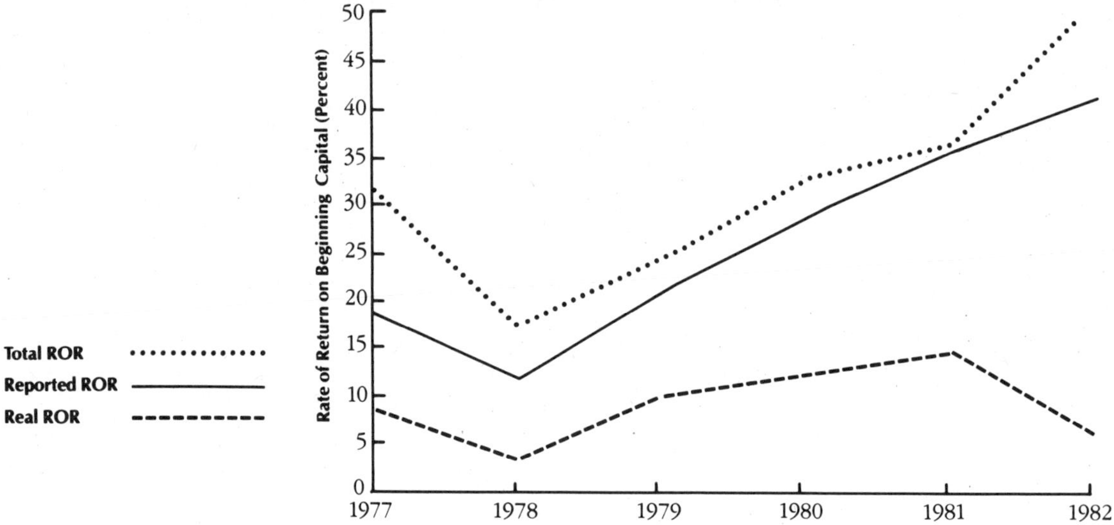

subtracting the percentage devaluation in the "normalized" exchange rate, is approximately equal to the Total Return in dollars after Translation Loss. This same relationship can be seen by noting that the percentage devaluation in the normalized exchange rate, plotted in Exhibit 6, explains the difference between the peso and dollar returns. Currency translation thus takes out of the Mexican return the difference between Mexican and U.S. inflation, leaving behind gains to compensate dollar investors for dollar inflation.

TABLE 4

	1977	1978	1979	1980	1981	1982
Total ROR (p)	32.0%	17.4%	24.8%	33.6%	37.6%	52.5%
Normalized Ex. Rte. Chng.	22.6%	9.8%	6.9%	12.9%	17.5%	51.0%
Difference	9.4%	7.6%	17.9%	20.7%	20.1%	1.5%
Total ROR Aft Trans ($)	7.6%	7.1%	16.8%	18.4%	16.7%	1.0%

An important implication is that historical cost accounting systems that do not recognize holding gains, but do record translation losses based on current exchange rates, will invariably report net losses where none in fact may exist. A more precise understanding of this can be gained by inspecting the table shown below.

TABLE 5

	1977	1978	1979	1980	1981	1982
Infl Gain (p)	29.1	22.4	27.7	47.2	63.2	164.9
Infl Gain ($)	1.22	0.85	0.99	1.49	1.70	3.02
Tran Loss($)	−1.18	−0.59	−0.46	−0.91	−1.36	−3.29
Net Gain ($)	0.04	0.26	0.52	0.58	0.34	−0.27

The first line is the inflation gain in pesos arising from the appreciation in value of both inventories and net plant. In the second line, the peso inflation gain has been translated to dollars. In the third line, the foreign exchange loss arising from a change in the "normalized" exchange rate is subtracted to arrive at the Net Gain (Loss) appearing in the dollar statements. *In every year except 1982 the translation loss has been more than offset by inflation gains,* leaving investors unaffected by the devaluation. Without recording the holding gain, however, a potentially misleading loss would be recorded in each year.

In 1982, the inflation gain on assets was insufficient to cover the exchange loss. It would be a mistake, however, to interpret this as exchange risk. The net loss is attributable instead to the purchasing power loss sustained on monetary assets denominated in pesos in Mexico. The failure of these assets to appreciate along with inflation in Mexico means that their value translated to dollars has fallen. But this simply is saying that monetary assets have sustained a real holding loss due to Mexican inflation. What appears as an

EXHIBIT 5

The Enchilada Food Company—Mexico (Inflation-Adjusted Returns—Pesos and Current Dollars)

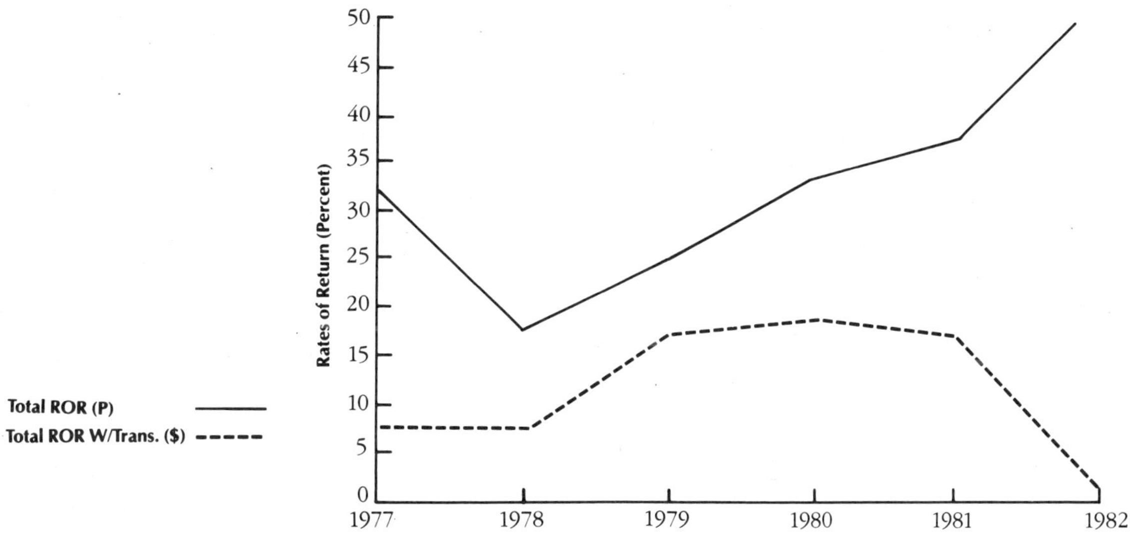

EXHIBIT 6

The Enchilada Food Company—Mexico ("Normalized" Peso Devaluation—In U.S. Dollars per Peso)

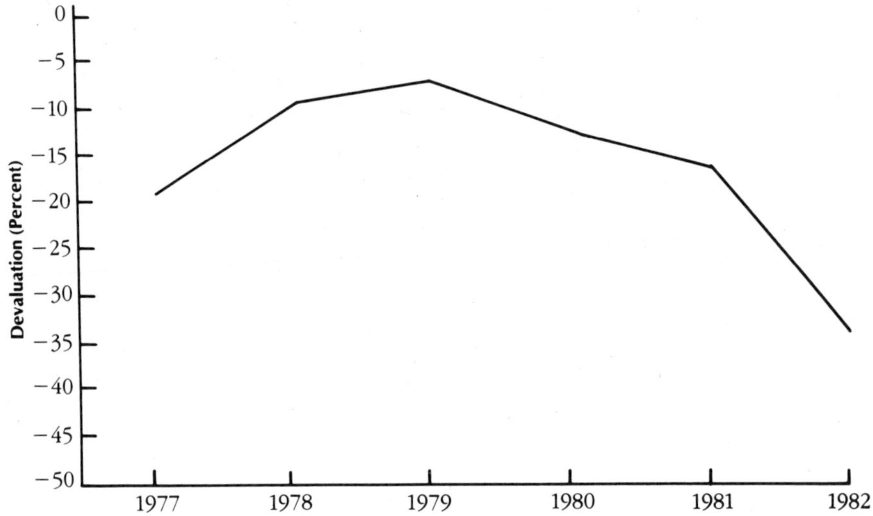

EXHIBIT 7

The Enchilada Food Company—Mexico (FASB 52 Return and Inflation Adjusted Return in U.S. Dollars)

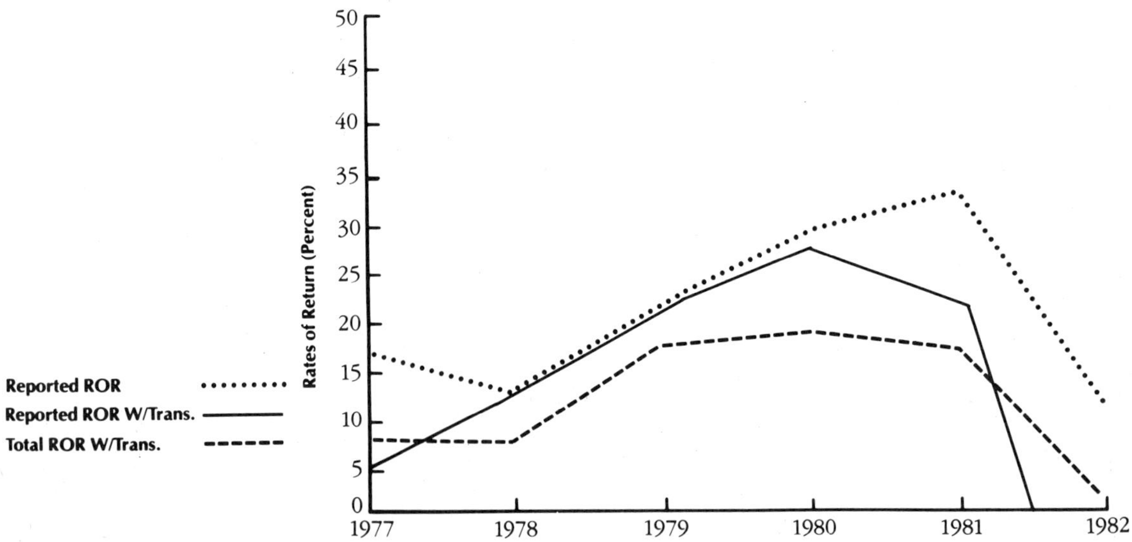

exchange loss, then, is no more than an inflation-induced holding loss. *The exchange loss has merely transmitted the inflation loss into its dollar equivalent.* The most effective way to hedge this loss is to pass on the costs of Mexican inflation to consumers through higher prices.

The contrast between the results reported under FAS #52 procedures and my inflation-adjusted, exchange-rate normalized method is illustrated by the plots appearing in Exhibit 7.

The translated ROR reported according to FAS #52 is represented by the dotted line. In each year it overstates the true economic performance of Enchilada because no adjustment is ever made for the higher rate of inflation in Mexico. (Of course the opposite would happen in a country that consistently had low inflation. Rates of return reported in dollars would miss the appreciation in translated value of capital invested overseas that is an important component of the return to investors in these countries.)

By including the FAS #52 translation loss in the calculation of ROR, one problem is solved, but two are created. The problem solved is that eventually, as PPP reasserts itself, the overstatement of returns is adjusted for by the translation loss. FAS #52 would thus accurately measure the return earned from a foreign investment, *but only on average and over time.* As a period-by-period measure of performance, it can be extremely misleading—especially, as in the Enchilada case, when a currency depreciates in one year to compensate for the excessive inflation of several prior years. The other problem introduced is that the translation loss is assessed without recognizing the offsetting holding gains. This means that losses will be recorded and accumulated on accounting statements where none may exist for investors.

The Total Return that includes both peso holding gains and currency translation losses (or gains), calculated using normalized exchange rates, avoids these shortcomings and thus provides the most meaningful measure of performance in dollar terms. *The use of the normalized exchange rate shifts the burden of adjustment from the year in which the currency revaluation actually takes place to those years in which the economic forces first arise that cause a change in the fundamental value of the currency.* Management therefore is charged or credited for exchange rate movements that correspond to the actual conditions of the local operating environment. Furthermore, by including the holding gains due to local inflation as part of the return to be converted to dollars, the loss incurred through translation is properly accounted for as just another consequence of the inflation itself. The graphs in Exhibit 7 together show that this is the return in dollars that corresponds most closely to the real return experienced by the local operating manager. The internal adoption of this measure by multinationals will accordingly bring about greater agreement between local management and corporate headquarters about the performance and fundamental value of a foreign operation.

SUMMARY

FAS #52 will provide a realistic measure of foreign operating performance only under the following conditions:

- Assets are carried on accounting balance sheets at values close to their current value.
- Exchange rates move in accordance with purchasing power parity.
- Translation gains and losses are included in the measure of profits.

In inflationary economies, of course, there will be a significant divergence between accounting values and current values. Furthermore, exchange rates deviate regularly, and often dramatically, from the course dictated by inflation differentials. This can be due to government intervention or changes in a country's competitiveness in international markets. Experience suggests that such deviations generally even out over time, leaving inflation differentials as the predominant force determining exchange rates over the long haul.

The real, economic performance of a foreign operating unit may be overstated or understated when the returns earned are translated at unrealistically high or low exchange rates. A more accurate appraisal of results is possible by using exchange rates that chart the fundamental course of currency values over time.

Specifically, the procedure I recommend involves first building inflation and inflation gains into the foreign unit's income statement and balance sheet. Without this, any currency translation procedure is likely to fail. Second, the results of the foreign operation can be translated to dollars using FAS #52 conventions, provided the translation gain or loss is included as part of the return. The exchange rate used for translation, however, should not be the actual exchange rate, which can be unduly influenced by government policy or temporary shifts in interest rates. Instead, a normalized rate—one that reflects inflation differentials and conforms to Purchasing Power Parity—should be substituted. The rate of return so calculated can then be compared with the cost of capital expressed in terms of dollar financing costs. In this way management has a common basis for comparing the performance of all foreign and domestic operations.

I contend that the Total Return in Dollars (adjusted for local inflation and including Translation Loss) using "normalized" exchange rates is the most appropriate measure of foreign operating performance for the following reasons: (1) it reflects the underlying real performance of the local economy and of local operating managers; (2) it reflects the cost of sustaining real holding losses on monetary assets that must be compensated for by a higher return in the business; (3) it includes holding gains which, after translation, would be commensurate with U.S. inflation, making it directly comparable to costs of capital expressed in dollars (which, of course, implicitly incorporate U.S. inflation); (4) it is equally applicable for countries that experience appreciating exchange values over time because the translation gain will be included as a systematic component of the return realized by investors; and, finally, (5) the use of normalized exchange rates forces management, both local and corporate, to see through distortions caused by the temporary suspension of fundamental economic forces and to incorporate anticipated currency changes into forward planning.

Taxation and Financial Logistics

26

Transfer Prices, Taxes, and Financial Markets: Implications of International Financial Transfers Within the Multinational Corporation*

Donald R. Lessard†

INTRODUCTION

The ability of multinational corporations (MNCs) to shift funds and accounting profits among their component units through internal channels raises interesting questions regarding the reasons for and welfare impacts of these firms' operations and, as a result, about appropriate public policies toward them. Popular critiques characterize the MNC as an "octopus," which, through its internal transfers disrupts exchange and credit markets, avoids both home-and host-country taxes, increases its monopoly power, gains an "unfair" competitive advantage relative to local firms, and hides its "excessive"profits to avoid public scrutiny and regulation.[1] While many such charges undoubtedly are overstated and often contradictory, there remain the questions of whether the MNC's ability to internalize financial transactions favors the MNC relative to national firms, whether it has an impact on the location of production, and whether it changes the distribution of income among consumers, suppliers of factors, and governments, both within and among countries. More specifically, each of the following might be asked:

- Do governments intentionally or unintentionally encourage the growth of multinationals relative to national firms by adopting tax policies or financial market regulations that favor MNCs by raising the cost of market transfers of goods, real factors, and especially capital between independent firms and investors?
- Do MNCs shift profits internally and as a result reduce total taxes and/or alter the distribution of tax revenues for a given distribution of real activities? Further, does this profit shifting alter the distribution of real investment, production, and trade itself?
- Do MNCs disguise their true profitability in various countries and as a result distort public policy toward them?

This paper reviews and synthesizes available research regarding the relevance of MNC internal financial mechanisms and the actual use of these mechanisms. Its primary purpose is to determine what, if any, guidance this research provides for policymakers. Since the relevant literature is fragmented, a major part of the paper is devoted to presenting a framework within which the impact of internal financial transfer may be analyzed. Three broad groups of purposes for which the internal financial mechanism

*This article is reprinted, with permission, from *International Business and Finance,* vol. 1, JAI Press, 1979, pp. 101–135.

†The author is grateful for the comments of Gene Carter, Ian Giddy, Thomas Horst, and Jim Paddock.

may be relevant are identified. These are minimizing taxes, circumventing barriers within and between financial markets, and disguising true profitability as a means to influence public policy.

The internal financial system is deemed relevant if its use increases the value to the firm and its shareholders of a particular operation relative to what it would be if all its financial transactions were at arms-length through external financial channels. By implication, internalizing any financial transfer than can be replicated at no greater cost by an independent single-country firm or individual investor through financial markets will provide no advantage, and hence be irrelevant. Relevant financial transfers may provide MNCs with absolute advantages over national competitors, or in cases where there are unique costs to international financial transfers on an arms-length basis, they may simply offset these costs and put the MNC on equal footing with a local competitor in a particular market.

This review is organized into four parts. The first two sections outline the characteristics of the MNC's financial system and describe the circumstances under which such a system provides significant advantages to the MNC. The third section provides a more in-depth review of theoretical arguments and empirical evidence regarding the role of internal financial systems in minimizing taxes. arbitraging financial markets, and influencing public policy, respectively. The fourth section relates the MNC financial advantages to the "generally accepted" theory of direct foreign investment. And the final section draws conclusions regarding the desirability and feasibility of controlling the MNC's financial system as well as the implications of taking into account its existence in formulating financial, tax, and industrial policies.

THE MULTINATIONAL FINANCIAL SYSTEM

Rutenberg (1970) and Robbins and Stobaugh (1973) aptly characterize the MNC as a financial system with myriad linkages for transferring funds and/or profits among its various units. Figure 1 illustrates the nature of these potential links. All of these links can and do exist among separate, independent firms, but their potential use is very different within a fully *controlled* corporate system. The differences result from two factors; greater discretion in the *choice of channels* through which financial transfers are made and in the *timing of transactions* within a controlled system.

In considering the financial transfers within an MNC, it is useful to also keep track of the internal real transactions that give rise to many of these financial claims. Any transfer of real goods or factors, ranging from finished product to vaguely defined intangible factors such as management skills, if not paid for immediately at an arms-length (market value) price, is accompanied by a financial transfer giving rise to some type of financial claim. Financial transfers within an MNC also may support real transfers to a component of the MNC from outside the corporate system. In this case, the MNC is acting as a financial intermediary.

Discretionary Choice of Channels

The MNC has considerable latitude in selecting the choice of financial channels, especially for transactions that arise from internal transfers of real goods or factors of production. For example, intangible factors of production are transferred to the subsidiary by the parent and can give rise to a wide range of different implicit and explicit financial

FIGURE 1

The Multinational Corporate Financial System

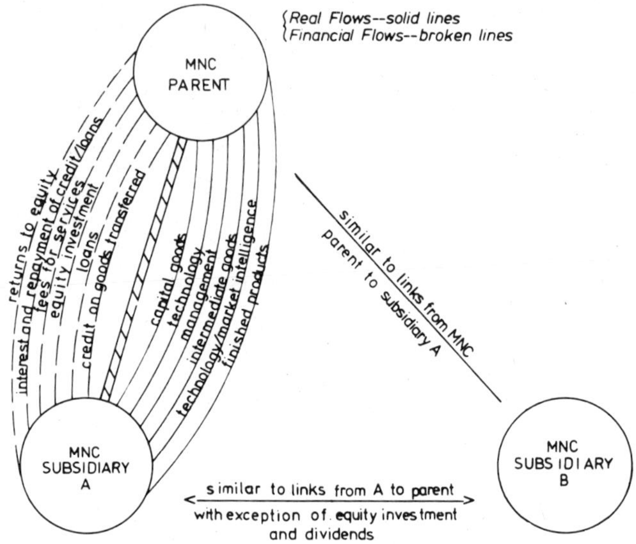

claims. If sold outright at an arms-length price, no claim is generated. If transferred in return for arms-length royalty fees, then they give rise to an explicit long-term financial contract similar to that which would be entered into by unrelated firms. However, if the cash price or market value of the royalty claims are below an arms-length price, then part of the financial claim will be an implicit (and unregistered) equity claim. If the transferred factors are underpriced relative to the market standards, subsidiary profits (other things equal) will be higher than those of an independent firm, and the parent's equity claim will be more valuable. If overpriced, the parent will be reducing equity by disguising the transfer as a payment on current account for factor transfers.

For financial transfers not arising from internal real transfers, the MNC still has many options. Intracompany financial transfers may be denominated as loans with considerable latitude regarding interest rate, currency, and repayment schedule. They also may be denominated as equity transfers. If the interest rate on a loan differs from market rates for loans with similar risk or if the amount loaned exceeds the subsidiary's contribution to the corporation's total debt capacity, there is an implicit equity transfer. This is also true of parent guarantees of subsidiary borrowing. Implicit or explicit equity claims may be recovered directly through dividend remittances or indirectly through the other types of transfers discussed above.

All of these mechanisms often are lumped together under the term "transfer pricing." Clearly, however, this includes much more than fiddling prices on intracompany transfers of goods.

Discretionary Timing

Although certain types of financial claims incorporate a specific schedule of payments, many mechanisms used by the MNC allow for leading or lagging of intracompany transfers. Trade credit, an open account, can be used quite flexibly. The flexibility of fees or royalties resulting from previous or concurrent transfers of factors of production may be limited by the contractual terms, but since both parties are related, the terms often can be altered. The most flexible of all, of course, are the equity claims. The MNC parent has considerable discretion regarding remittance of its equity claim or "rolling it over" into a new larger claim by reinvesting profits.

Even when timing is limited by contractual terms or government regulations, there is almost always a degree of latitude over the exact nature and timing of the flows. This flexibility is enhanced by the discretion the MNC has regarding the timing of internal transfers of goods and real factors of production.

The Relevance of Internal Financial Systems

While much has been made of the MNC's ability to select channels for and change the timing of internal financial transfers, little has been done to identify expressly those conditions under which these degrees of freedom represent an advantage for the MNC relative to single-country firms operating on an arms-length basis. After all, a purely domestic firm with several operating units has a similar system; yet such systems generally are not the object of the same type of criticism leveled at the MNC. For a domestic firm it does not appear that such a system provides an advantage relative to a set of smaller firms relying on arms-length external financial transactions. For example, for a multi-unit firm operating within a single country to engage in leading and lagging of intracompany payables would provide no special advantage, since the same results could readily be obtained by short-term external borrowing or lending transactions by the various units. Similarly, for one unit to borrow funds and relend them to another would have little economic impact. The ability to internalize financial transactions is relevant only to the extent to which there are barriers or costs to transfers of funds through external channels or differences in taxes depending on how revenues and costs are allocated among the various subunits of the firm.

The internal financial system of a multidivision firm within a single country such as the U.S. is largely irrelevant for two reasons. First, financial markets are quite efficient. Thus the cost of funds (equity and debt) for any particular investment can be expected to reflect the risk of the investment rather than whether it is being undertaken by a large diversified corporation or a smaller firm operating in a single industry. Further, transactions costs for transfers via financial markets will not exceed the costs of comparable internal transfers. Under such circumstances, mechanisms that allow for internal transfers of funds between operating units of a firm provide little or no advantage, since similar transfers could be replicated by independent firms or investors at little or no additional cost. In fact, most corporate financial transactions, including decisions regarding the structure of claims issued by the firm and whether earnings are retained or paid out as dividends, are shown by Modigliani and Miller (1958, 1961, 1963) to be irrelevant in efficient markets. Specific features of the tax system provide the strongest exceptions to the irrelevance arguments in the domestic case,[2] and even some of them are eliminated if *both* corporate and individual taxation are considered (Miller, 1976).

Second, the taxes associated with a particular operating unit are, under most circumstances, independent of whether it is part of a large conglomerate firm or separately incorporated. A single tax rate applies to the profits of all major corporations. Although the system is asymmetrical with respect to tax losses, these can be carried backward or forward, and besides, there exists an external "market" for tax losses through leases and other tax shelters. In extreme cases, unusable losses can be "sold" by merging the losing firm with a profitable one. As a result, there is little to be gained from spreading losses throughout a series of related firms.

There are several reasons for believing that the internal financial system is more likely to be relevant to a firm operating internationally. Often there are tax costs and other restrictions to financial transfers across national boundaries and many governments impose restrictions on domestic financial transactions. Both provide advantages to firms that can circumvent them through internal financial transfers. Tax rates differ across countries. Conflicting claims by various governments sometimes give rise to double taxation and there are limits to which losses or taxes paid in one country can be applied against profits or tax liabilities in another. As a result of these factors, the ability to allocate revenues and costs internally will affect global tax payments, as well as the distribution of these payments. Thus the value of a venture may depend on the nature of the firm that owns it.

Financial Tariffs and Quotas

One way to view the conditions under which having an internal financial mechanism will make a difference is to think of the multinational financial system as a network of linkages (as depicted in Figure 4-1) where transfers along some or all of the channels face tariffs or quotas. For example, within the accepted rules of the game for the international payments system, capital account transfers may be restricted (they may face quotas) while current transactions such as payments for goods or intangible factors of production are unrestricted. In such a case, there is a clear advantage to a firm having discretion over the type of channel through which it operates. In other cases, financial transfers classified as capital account transactions will face tariffs (transfer taxes or dual exchange rate systems) while current transactions will not.

Access to particular domestic financial markets also may be restricted to local firms. The MNC, through its local subsidiaries, can gain access to these markets and shift the funds elsewhere within its global systems through one of the many available mechanisms. In this way, it circumvents a barrier that would prevent international financial transfers by national firms or individual investors based in other countries.

Most importantly, by appropriate internal transfers the MNC can reduce overall taxes and can avoid taxes on specific financial transfers. This may bring them below the level that would have to be paid by national firms or individuals operating at arms-length, or it may simply offset double taxation, putting it on par with local competitors. In the case of the U.S. deferral provisions, for example, to the extent that the parent can shift funds from one subsidiary to another without passing them through the U.S. as remitted profits, taxes are postponed and hence their economic impact is reduced.

The major types of costs or restrictions that make internal financial transactions attractive are summarized in the box below.

Gains to MNCs from being able to circumvent these barriers can be grouped under two headings: *financial market arbitrage* and *tax system arbitrage*, although there clearly is an overlap between the two. Further, the ability to shift profits internally and thus disguise true profitability may be advantageous to the MNC in cases where profits are a function of bargaining or regulation, rather than competitive forces. Such potential gains do not appear to fit readily into the framework outlined above, but as we shall show, they

Formal Barriers to International Transactions

- Quantitative restrictions (exchange controls) and direct taxes on international movements of funds.
- Differential taxation of income streams according to nationality and global tax situation of the owners.
- Restrictions by nationality of investor and/or investment on access to domestic capital markets.

Informal Barriers to International Transactions

- Costs of obtaining information.
- Difficulty of enforcing contracts across national boundaries.
- Transaction costs.
- Traditional investment patterns.

Imperfections in Domestic Capital Markets

- Ceilings on interest rates.
- Mandatory credit allocations.
- Limited legal and institutional protection for minority shareholders.
- Limited liquidity because of thinness of markets.
- High transaction costs attributable to small market size and/or monopolistic practices of key financial institutions.
- Difficulty of obtaining information needed to evaluate securities.

are similar in nature to those resulting from tax system arbitrage. We shall refer to this class of gains as *regulatory system arbitrage*.

STUDIES OF MNC FINANCIAL BEHAVIOR

The questions of ultimate interest in this review are to what extent real investment, production, and trade decisions and the distribution of benefits resulting from these decisions are changed because of the MNC's ability to shift funds and profits internally. There are few studies that provide any direct evidence on these questions. As a result, we are forced to rely on less direct evidence, either in the form of models that show what behavior we should expect from MNCs under certain conditions or on general observations of the financial behavior of MNCs and its apparent impact on their real decisions.

In the following three sections, we review models and empirical observations of MNC financial behavior in terms of minimizing taxes, circumventing financial barriers, and disguising true profitability. A few of these models have been developed in order to draw positive inferences about MNC financial behavior and its impact on real variables, but the majority are normative models focusing either on the optimal exploitation of a firm's financial system, generally taking real variables as givens, or on the evaluation of individual investments, taking into account the impact of the financial variables. Although the former are of more direct interest, the latter also are of interest, since they typically involve more detailed and complex treatments of corporate financial behavior.

Both types of models serve two basic purposes in the study of the relevance of MNC financial systems. First, they provide concrete specifications of the nature of advantages provided by such systems and of the conditions under which they are relevant. Second, they provide some idea of the importance of these effects relative to other factors that influence real decisions. Given the difficulty of empirically verifying the role of various factors in the expansion of multinational enterprise, this is very important.

Empirical studies of MNC financial behavior face many problems. In particular, most are plagued with measurement difficulties. This is to be expected, since the essence of exploiting an internal financial system involves using internal channels for transferring funds and profits, many of which are unregistered either in the firm's reported results or in country data.

The MNC Financial System and Tax System Arbitrage

Clearly, differences in tax systems among countries have an impact on decisions regarding the location of production. Interactions exist between host-country income and withholding taxes, home-country corporate taxes on foreign source income including the effects of credits and deferrals, and home-country taxes at the investor level on either distributed or undistributed corporate profits. Thus total taxes paid on the profits of a particular venture will depend, to some extend, on the nationality of the investing firm. To that extent, taxes become relevant to the ownership decision. These effects have been reviewed by Horst (1975, 1977b), Hufbauer and Foster (1976), Kopits (1976a), and Musgrave (1975), among others. The scope of this review is more limited, concentrating on changes in the effect of taxes on location and production decisions that result from the MNC's ability to engage in internal transfers. We begin with the positive models that incorporate real decisions.

Positive Models of MNC Tax Arbitrage

Horst (1971) provides one of the first concrete models of direct foreign investment that takes into account the impact of the MNC's ability to manipulate transfer prices. He focuses on the production (and hence trade) decision of a monopolistic firm selling the same good to two different countries, allowing for various combinations of scale economies and ability to price independently in the two markets. Since the only financial transfer he allows is manipulation of transfer prices on intracompany trade, such transfers will have an effect on tariffs as well as the tax bill. As a result, he concludes that the firm will always be choosing between the largest and smallest possible transfer price for its exports, pricing goods as low as possible when

$$\pi_2 > \frac{t_2 - t_1}{1 - t_2} \tag{1}$$

where π_2 is the tariff rate charged by the improting country and t_1 and t_2 are the total tax rates (including home-country taxation of foreign source income, etc.) imposed by the exporting and importing countries, respectively. He further argues that since tariff rates generally will exceed tax differentials, both because tax systems appear to converge around a common rate and because U.S. firms can consolidate income from high-tax and low-tax countries and thus diminish any remaining differentials in effective tax rates, minimum transfer prices for exports to affiliates will be the rule. As a result, he concludes that tax increases by high-tariff countries will have little or no impact on the real decisions of firms, but will change the distribution of tax revenues in favor of these countries. If he had allowed for internal profit transfers that have no effect on tariffs, such as royalties on intangible factors of production or internal financing, this latter question would have been much more complicated. One would expect even less impact of taxes on real decisions, but conclusions regarding the impact of tax changes on the distribution of tax revenues would be much harder to draw.

In his most recent research on this subject, Horst (1975, 1977b) concentrates on the potential impact of changes in U.S. tax laws, such as the elimination of deferral, requiring country-by-country computation of the credit, and replacing the credit with a deduction, on the real investment and production decisions of U.S.-based MNCs and on the distribution of income between firms and the tax authorities of home and host countries. His model incorporates several financial variables that have an impact on taxes: headquarters charges (royalties and fees), the proportion of earnings remitted as dividends, and the debt/equity mix in intrafirm financing. For purposes of exposition, he concentrates on the effect of changes in the intrafirm debt/equity mix, taking dividend remittance and headquarters charges as fixed. However, since their profit-shifting effects are for the most part similar to those of royalties and fees, his results can be interpreted as if they apply to the full range of profit-shifting techniques. He concludes that certain changes in tax policy such as eliminating deferral or grossing-up LDC-source income would have little impact on real MNC activities, although they would shift revenues to the U.S. because they would remove old and create new incentives for profit shifting. If this profit shifting is unconstrained, he finds that even such drastic change in U.S. tax policy as replacing the credit with a deduction would have little impact on the real decisions of multinationals, but would have drastic effects on the distribution of tax revenues. His analyses and conclusions are much too complex to discuss in detail here, but they provide a strong case that the MNC's ability to make internal financial transfers must be taken into account in any analysis of the effects of current or proposed taxation of MNCs or their activities on various countries' tax revenues. Hufbauer and Foster (1976), and Sato and Bird (1975), in exploring similar issues, also conclude that internal financial transfers must be considered in examining tax effects.

Vaitsos (1974a,b) provides an extensive and provocative discussion of the welfare impact of MNC's ability to set nonmarket transfer prices for internal transfers of goods and services. He focuses on a seeming anomaly—the overpricing of goods and services to LDC manufacturing subsidiaries by their developed country parents in spite of the fact that most of these subsidiaries face relatively low local tax rates, liberal deferral provisions *vis-à-vis* home-country taxes, and, in many cases, relatively high tariffs. These factors, as shown by Horst and others, would be expected to result in a shift in reported taxable profits from parents to subsidiaries and not the other way around! He identifies a set of possible explanations, including transfer pricing as a means for: disguising local profitability to decrease political exposure and improving the firm's position in bargaining for tariff, subsidy, and other benefits; minimizing global taxes *even if* local tax rates are lower than parent rates; bypassing restrictions on remittances; and taking advantage of local joint-venture partners.

Vaitsos' tax argument is that a firm whose revenues from home and unaffiliated export sales are smaller than its costs in the home country, including those of supporting the global operation, will shift profits "upstream" to the parent in order to avoid tax losses. This undoubtedly is true. However, Kopits (1976a, p. 27) points out that there are few firms in this situation. A more likely scenario is that U.S.-based firms would shift profits "downstream" to use up excess foreign tax credits generated from operations in relatively high-tax countries. Clearly, generalizations are dangerous, but it appears unlikely that the phenomenon observed by Vaitsos can be explained in terms of tax minimization.

Normative Models of MNC Tax Arbitrage

Rutenberg (1970) provides a general model for optimizing MNC financial transactions, but he excludes from his model most real investment and production decisions, assuming that these have already been made. His aim is to show how the general tax minimization (and financial arbitrage) problem can be formulated as a linear program incorporating a host of constraints on the extent to which transfer prices, fees, royalties, and financial charges can be manipulated. As such his model sheds little light on the impact of these transfers on real decisions, but it does serve to make explicit many of the different channels available. He does discuss one real decision, the location of production for "high-margin" products, focusing on products with low transportation costs where current production costs are low relative to selling price, as a result of rents from previous R & D, advertising, or a monopoly position. Implicitly, what this involves is an unregistered transfer of the "patent" or "market franchise" at a zero price.

Robbins and Stobaugh (1973) employ a linear programming model developed by Daniel Schydlowsky to trace the potential benefits to a hypothetical firm of exploiting different aspects of the internal financial system. In their example, they vary constraints to allow for: alterations in transfer prices on intrafirm product flows by plus or minus 20 percent; shifting internal credit terms from 0 to 180 days with interest rates varying from 0 to 8 percent; varying maturities and rates on intracompany loans; and varying both the timing and amount of royalty and fee flows. They conclude that by optimizing, their hypothetical firm could increase the parent firm's profits by 16 percent from the base level where each unit is financially autonomous. While most of this gain is attributed to financial market arbitrage, a point we discuss below, tax minimization also plays an important role. The critical determinants of the extent of gains are the volume of intrafirm transactions of all types and the leeway the firm has in altering the terms on each transaction.

In addition to external constraints on "transfer pricing," firms may place internal constraints on such manipulations either because of considerations of social responsibility or because of distortions that such practices introduce into internal control systems. Shulman (1967), for example, stresses the costs in terms of internal distortions of altering transfer prices for tax purposes. However, Arpan (1971), Salmi (1975), Nieckels (1976) and others show that firms can and many do have separate transfer-pricing systems for internal and external purposes. Of course, this increases the complexity of international management and, presumably, gives an advantage to those firms with scale and experience sufficient to cope with it. Both Salmi (1975) and Nieckels (1976) develop optimizing models for tax-oriented transfer pricing that are quite rich in operational detail. There appears to be little question that under realistic assumptions tax arbitrage should provide advantages to the MNC.

Other normative models that one would expect to incorporate tax considerations are those focusing on MNC investment decisions. In reviewing the capital budgeting literature, however, we found that while tax factors were included, differences in taxes for MNCs and national firms were not treated explicitly. Exceptions are Adler (1974) and Adler and Dumas (1976), who focus on differences between required returns for MNCs and national firms. They show that taxes are relevant, but they emphasize distortions in financial markets as the basis for most of these differences.

Empirical Studies of MNC Tax-Related Behavior

Kopits (1972, 1976b) concentrates on a limited but complex set of internal financial decisions—the choice of royalties or dividends for remittances to the parent firm. In the 1972 paper, he estimates the reaction of dividends to differentials between home- and host-country tax rates and to split-rate tax systems in host countries that discriminate between retained and remitted earnings. He finds that taxes did have a significant effect on dividend remittances from developed countries and from this concludes that taxes may have a substantial influence on real investment flows. However, these results cannot be interpreted as showing whether the tax effects differ for MNCs, nor that they change real decisions. At best they show that taxes affect the percentage of profits remitted as dividends, and, without including other transfer channels as well as explicit estimates of the firms' investment opportunities, provide only limited evidence in this regard. In the later paper, Kopits (1976b) focuses on royalty remittances. He shows that the choice cannot be based simply on the relative tax rates in the home and host country, but also on the firms' ability to offset excess tax credits in high-tax countries against income generated from low-tax countries, a point also made by Ness (1972). Kopits again obtains significant results for developed countries, lending support to the notion that taxes do matter. To the extent that royalty arrangements are more flexible among related firms than unrelated firms, these results have a more direct bearing on the issue of whether taxes have a differential impact on MNCs. The results are again limited by the fact that the set of financial variables considered is small, a point that Kopits recognizes. Kopits (1976a) reviews a variety of similar efforts by other authors and concludes that there is some support for the notion that MNC financial decisions reflect tax factors. In general, however, he concludes that most tests are of limited value given the complexity of the underlying behavior and the extreme difficulty of capturing the effects empirically.

Descriptive Studies of MNC Tax Arbitrage

Robbins and Stobaugh (1973) provide an extensive description of MNC practices based on interviews with thirty-nine U.S.-based MNCs. In describing corporate transfer-pricing behavior, they conclude that tax minimization is an important consideration, but that exchange-rate restrictions provide even stronger motivation. Citing published figures on intracompany trade, they argue that by varying transfer prices by only 10 percent, U.S. MNCs would generate financial transfers larger than total actual royalty payments and approximately equal to actual dividend remittances. They believe that financial transfers are smaller than this figure, but nevertheless of considerable importance. One of the major points addressed by Robbins and Stobaugh is whether the extent to which a firm exploits its internal financial system is a function of firm size. Using a logistic regression model, they conclude that it is, with small firms making relatively little use of the system, medium firms substantial use of the system, and large firms moderate use of the system. They conclude that the reduced integrative focus of the large firms reflects external and internal constraints resulting from firm size.

Arpan (1971, 1972) reports on transfer-pricing practices of U.S. and non-U.S. MNCs. For most firms, he finds that managements viewed transfer prices as mechanisms for minimizing taxes and/or circumventing remittance restrictions. Effects on the degree of management control also were considered to be important, but many firms avoided conflict between the two objectives by using different transfer-pricing practices, apparently as the result of incentives provided by home-country tax systems.

The MNC Financial System and Financial Market Arbitrage

In this section, we focus on the circumstances in financial markets that would present MNCs, with their internal financial systems, with advantages relative to national firms or individual investors. In order to do so, it is necessary to identify in each case the nature of the advantage to be gained, the mechanism through which the MNC gains it, and the reason the same advantage is not generally available to non-MNC investors. The latter consideration is particularly important, since, as noted above, any access to financial markets that can be replicated readily by firms not possessing extensive internal mechanisms for transferring funds and/or profits or to individuals operating through financial markets is irrelevant to the differential valuation of the firm and its activities. For purposes of discussion, we divide MNC behavior aimed at profiting from financial market distortions into *exchange control arbitrage*, *credit market arbitrage*, and *equity market arbitrage*.

Exchange Control Arbitrage

If a country imposes exchange controls in order to maintain its exchange rate at a particular level, firms or investors able to circumvent these controls can engage in profitable arbitrage. One would expect MNCs, with their multiple channels for funds transfers to be favored in such cases. In a project valuation model, such gains would appear as a higher cash flow for the MNC than for an alternative investor firm lacking the mechanisms to circumvent the barriers. This source of gains appears to be a major element of MNC transfer pricing behavior *vis-à-vis* LDC subsidiaries as observed by Vaitsos (1974a,b) and Lall (1973). Both Arpan (1971, 1972) and Robbins and Stobaugh (1973) confirm this with their surveys of MNC behavior.

Leading and lagging is a major factor in exchange control arbitrage in those cases where governments intervene in exchange markets or impose restrictions temporarily to stave off a devaluation or revaluation. Firms that can accelerate or delay financial transfers clearly can gain. MNCs often will have a unique advantage, since they can alter current account transfers so as to avoid capital account restrictions. This type of exchange arbitrage is most likely under an exchange rate system with occasional large changes in currency parities. In fact, this ability of MNCs to beat the system may be a strong argument in favor of flexible exchange rates.

While exchange controls are generally thought of as binding on profit remittances, they also may interfere with the ability to invest in a particular project, as was the case with the U.S. OFDI controls. The MNC's ability to underprice real transfers and to guarantee external borrowing by foreign subsidiaries, both of which amount to unregistered outflows of equity, undoubtedly were a major factor in reducing or eliminating any impact of the controls on their real investment patterns.

Credit Market Arbitrage

A closely related potential source of gains is the ability of MNCs, through internal financial transfers, to take advantage of distortions in interest rates or escape the effects of restrictions on the availability of credit. Distortions in interest rates may result from a failure of market rates to adjust to an international equilibrium level due to (1) restrictions on the rates themselves—presumably resulting in credit rationing and allocation through nonmarket channels; (2) restrictions on access to domestic markets that shift the domestic equilibrium; and (3) restrictions on international financial transactions, including but not limited to exchange controls, that prevent international forces from acting on the domestic equilbrium.

The MNC, possessing at once the nationality of its home country and of the country in which the investment is located, will at worst have no disadvantage with domestic firms in obtaining subisidiary financing and gaining access to local financial markets. It should have a clear advantage in circumventing restrictions in international financial transactions, enabling it to borrow funds where available and shift them to countries where national investors face credit rationing.

Robbins and Stobaugh (1973) describe various mechanisms available to MNCs to circumvent restrictions separating capital markets. However in demonstrating these mechanisms, they employ the optimizing model discussed above in an unrealistic fashion. They assume that the firm knows future exchange rates with certainty, but that interest rates in various currencies do not reflect this knowledge. Thus their model generates large, sure gains from shifting currencies, gains that are limited only by restrictions placed on external corporate borrowing in various countries. Such a situation could only persist because of effective barriers to capital transfers, in which case the MNC would have to possess mechanisms for circumventing the barriers not available to others.

Macaluso and Hawkins (1977) provide some evidence that MNCs are able to avoid domestic credit restrictions to a greater extent than domestic firms. In four out of the six countries they examine, the MNC share of total investment rises when credit is tight. They also show that in tight credit periods, the share of MNC investment financed from internal sources increases, adding further credence to the view that MNCs actively circumvent domestic financial policies.

Equity Market Arbitrage

An argument similar to that applied to credit markets can be made for equity markets. Again, the MNC can engage in arbitrage if it has an advantage relative to domestic firms or investors in overcoming explicit or implicit barriers or minimizing taxes on international transfers of capital. The source of gains to equity market arbitrage is the reduction of risk through diversification. In the presence of barriers that inhibit international portfolio diversification by individual investors, the required rate of return for a given project may be lower for the MNC than for the national firm.

The logic of diversification is well known. Since the outcomes of different projects are not subject to exactly the same risks—i.e., the returns generated by several projects are not perfectly correlated—the risk of a portfolio of projects or securities will be less than the average risk of the individual projects. Lessard (1976) and Solnik (1974) show that the benefits of international diversification of equity securities investments are particularly strong. Equity returns within individual countries exhibit substantial covariation, placing a lower limit on the risk of a diversified portfolio of equity holdings. For large developed countries, this lower bound is around 50 percent of the risk (measured in terms of standard deviation) of the average individual security. However, since variations in returns on equity in various countries are substantially less than perfectly correlated, this lower bound falls to roughly 30 percent for an internationally diversified portfolio.

In an integrated international capital market without barriers or costs to capital transfers, individual investors can diversify their holdings of securities broadly, thereby averaging out much of the risk of individual projects themselves. As a result, the rate of return required on a particular venture will reflect only its contribution to the risk of a fully diversified portfolio, which is substantially smaller than its total risk. Since investors can diversify their own portfolios readily, firms need not concern themselves with their degree of diversification and can judge a venture's expected rate of return in relation to its systematic risk. As Adler and Dumas (1976) show, diversification at the corporate level will be relevant only when there are costs or barriers to such diversification at the investor level.

Many discussions of the diversification motive for DFI, including Prachowny (1972) and Stevens (1973), overlook this point, concentrating instead on the risk-reducing benefits of diversification without specifying why these are uniquely realized through the MNC. Ragazzi (1973), in contrast, stresses imperfections in non-U.S. equity markets, arguing that these may make the MNC the preferred channel for international diversification by U.S. investors. These considerations suggest that MNCs should not be concerned with forming corporate portfolios of activities with efficient mixes of total risk and return. Rather, they should seek to extend the frontier available to individual investors by investing more heavily, relative to the level justified by real and tax advantages, in those countries where investors cannot readily diversify for themselves. There are no direct tests of the relevance of the diversification motive for MNC expansion. Agmon and Lessard (1976b) suggest this is because of the difficulty of separating its effects from those of real market imperfections. Partial support, however, is provided by Hughes, Logue, and Sweeney (1976) and Agmon and Lessard (1977), who show that MNC security price behavior does reflect corporate international diversification. In order to confirm or reject the equity arbitrage hypothesis, empirical tests are required that relate direct foreign investment flows as a proportion of total investment flows between paris of countries to differences in barriers to portfolio capital flows.

Internal Financial Transfers as Means to Disguise Profits and Influence Public Policy Several authors, including Robbins and Stobaugh (1973), Lall (1973), and most notably Vaitsos (1974a,b), argue that MNCs often use internal transfers to disguise the profitability of local operations for political or social reasons. If a country pursues an industrial policy that explictly or implicitly focuses on profit rates, there clearly is a motivation to do so. This is likely to be particularly important for LDCs that seek to develop local industry by granting monopolies protected by high tariffs and often supported by direct or indirect subsidies. Profit-maximizing MNC behavior in such a case calls for shifting profits out of the local subsidiary, similar to that motivated by limitations on profit remittances. Further, although it might appear that such a strategy would increase an MNC's global taxes, since the LDCs in question often have relatively low tax rates, the tax effects can be offset if the profits are shifted to another low-tax jurisdiction. Therefore, determining which factors dominate is as yet an unanswered empirical question. Vaitsos' results for Colombia, for example, which showed a pattern of overpricing by MNCs in the pharmaceutical industry, could have reflected the considerations of either circumventing exchange controls or influencing industrial policy. A similar analysis for another country with a similar industrial policy but no exchange controls, such as Venezuela, could be extremely instructive.

A related argument is that MNCs use discretionary transfer prices as a means to increase monopoly gains by allowing them to either undercut competition or gouge consumers. There appears to be little direct basis for this argument, since the MNC's ability to discriminate between countries in its pricing depends upon tariff barriers and other forms of market barriers. Weston (1973) discusses this point at some length and dismisses it as having little merit. On an indirect level, however, if reported profitability is a factor in the determination of tariff protection, internal profit shifting will affect consumer prices as well as government revenues.

FINANCIAL MARKET IMPERFECTIONS AND THE THEORY OF DIRECT FOREIGN INVESTMENT

It is generally acknowledged that in order to justify foreign investments, the multinational corporation must have some advantage relative to local firms in the countries in which it invests that allowed it to overcome the costs imposed by cultural and geographical distance not borne by them. Most economists have argued that the primary sources of advantages by MNCs relative to local firms are imperfections in markets for products and factors of production.[3] Financial factors generally are excluded, presumably because financial markets are deemed to be more efficient than markets for real goods and services and hence less likely to give rise to advantages from internal transfer mechanisms. However, the above discussion suggests that imperfections in financial markets, including the ability to arbitrage tax systems, do exist and hence may give rise to an advantage for MNCs relative to local firms. In order to illustrate the potential relationship of these gains to the more traditional advantages of multinationalism, we outline the key factors affecting the value of investment projects facing the MNC in a partial equilibrium setting.

Project Valuation in a Multinational Context

The pattern of international investment, both in terms of the location of production and the ownership of firms, can be viewed as resulting from the interaction of a supply of investment opportunities occurring through time in different countries and the demand of potential bidders for these opportunities. The successful bidder can be either a domestic firm, defined as a firm located in the country where the investment takes place, or a foreign firm. Assuming complete information about the prospective return on investment opportunities, the successful bidder will be the one to whom the project is worth most. Successful bidders will be those who can generate larger or less risky cash flows over time from a given investment opportunity. This superiority may arise primarily as the result of imperfections in goods or factor markets. But it also may reflect some financial market imperfections. Alternatively, the successful bidders may have been able to capitalize the uncertain future cash flows at relatively lower required rates of return, again the result of imperfections in financial markets.

One firm may have higher cash flows than another because it has lower current costs because of control over intangible factors of production such as special knowledge not available in the market, a preferred market position, or other mechanisms that generate rents.[4] It may have lower total risks because of its control of the market, its special knowledge, and many other in the factors that also produce higher returns. Direct investment, foreign or local, can be viewed as a way to capitalize on these potential advantages either in the absence of markets in which the source of the advantage can be sold and the capitalized value of rents obtained directly or in the case where the "sale" of the advantage would destroy its rent-producing character.

Financial factors that could increase real project cash flows for the MNC relative to the level obtainable by a domestic firm include the ability to circumvent exchange rate barriers that maintain the exchange rate at a disequilibrium level and the ablility to reduce total taxes by appropriate choice of the channels through which the flows are transferred to the parent.

These same financial market imperfections may result in lower required rates of return for a given level of total project risk. Risky projects are most attractive to those investors able to diversify the largest proportion of the project's total risk. When there are costs or barriers to portfolio capital flows, MNCs are able to accept lower rates of return on projects than single-country firms because of their ability to diversify investment risks internationally.[5] A closely related potential financial advantage of the MNC is its ability to engage in arbitrage between financial markets where restrictions on capital flows or direct government intervention distort the cost of debt capital.

The value of a project from the perspective of a particular firm is the present value of estimated future cash flows discounted at the required rate of return which reflects the project's risk:

$$V = \sum_{t=0}^{\infty} \frac{CF_t}{(1 + \rho_*)^t} \tag{2}$$

where

V = total project value

CF_t = annual after-tax project cash flow to parent firm (prior to financing charges and related tax adjustments)

ρ_* = the overall cost of capital reflecting the required rate of return on equity, an opportunity cost, as well as the explicit costs of other sources of funds.

If the cash flows are perpetual and equal in all years, this reduces to:

$$V = \frac{\overline{CF}}{\rho_*} \tag{3}$$

In general, real imperfections will be reflected in the cash flows, while financial market imperfections will be reflected in the discount rate.

The various financial effects can be made more explicit by using a more generalized present-value formula where the tax impacts of the discretionary use of alternative financial channels, the financial structure, and other financial effects are treated individually.[6] The value of the project can be viewed as the sum of the present values of the project cash flows to a single-country firm located in the same country as the project after taxes but prior to financing costs, discounted at a rate reflecting the business risk of the project; the present value of tax savings relative to the taxes paid by the domestic firm as the result of internal financial transfers within the MNC; and savings resulting from being able to exploit specific distortions in credit markets:

$$V = \sum_{t=0}^{\infty} \frac{CF_t}{(1 + \rho)^t} + \sum_{t=0}^{\infty} \frac{\Delta T_t}{(1 + r)^t} + \sum_{t=0}^{\infty} \frac{\Delta I_t}{(1 + r)^t} \tag{4}$$

where

V = total project value

CF_t = annual after-tax flows of the project if all-equity financed by a domestic firm (*i.e.*, prior to any financing effects).

ρ = discount rate appropriate from parent perspective to the entire after-tax-cash flow stream prior to any financing effects.

ΔT_t = tax savings (penalties) relative to the level which would be paid by a domestic firm if the project were financed entirely by equity.

ΔI_t = annual savings (penalties) on interest costs of debt financing due to direct subsidies, differential access to repressed markets, or international arbitrage relative to what the firm would have to pay for unsubsidized borrowing obtained on an arms-length basis.

r = interest rate on debt as approximation to relevant discount rate for relatively certain streams of tax shields and interest savings.

Thus, differences in project value as a result of financial factors will be captured by differences in CF, the after-tax project flows; in ρ, the discount rate appropriate to the all-equity stream; by differences in ΔT, reflecting tax effects of the MNC's integrated financial system; and by differences in ΔI, reflecting differential abilities of firms to take advantage of financial market distortions. Of course, MNCs commonly possess other advantages *vis-à-vis* local firms resulting from imperfections in the markets for technology and managerial skills, but they also face the disadvantage of operating at a distance without an intimate knowledge of the domestic, political, social, and economic setting. Thus at times the financial advantages of MNCs may be the decisive factors.

IMPLICATIONS FOR PUBLIC POLICY

The studies reviewed in the third section, although not conclusive about the magnitude of internal financial transfers within MNCs or their impact on real decisions, leave little doubt that there are incentives for such transfers and that they do take place. Few aspects of MNC behavior evoke as much outrage as transfer pricing, broadly defined, and there are numerous proposals for cracking down on these practices and enforcing arms-length transfers. However, many profit-shifting practices are not heinous deeds, but are legal and would be considered by many as ethical. Further, even when this is not the case, the difficulty of controlling profit-shifting behavior would appear to argue in favor of reducing incentives for internal transfers rather than trying to control them directly.

should respond accordingly, within ethical and legal bounds. If they fail to do so, they are not behaving economically, at which point their very existence should be called into question. Of course, some profit-shifting practices involve misrepresentations of fact and violate the letter as well as the spirit of the law and should not be condoned. Many, however, are legal in a literal sense and many fall within the range in which reasonable observers would disagree as to whether they were ethical or unethical. Almost by definition, the activities of an MNC involve transfers of intangibles or even goods that have no objective arms-length price. Many of these are joint products and often their costs cannot be defined with certainty even within the firm. Further, in many cases the intangible factors, in particular technology and managerial knowhow, are goods that can be applied in one unit of the firm without detracting from their value elsewhere. Thus, in many cases, there is no objective economic solution and the allocation of profits within the MNC is totally arbitrary.

Financial transactions within the firm can be denominated in a variety of currencies and, given the illusion implicit within most tax systems that the national currency has constant purchasing power, a firm can reduce taxes by careful use of this mechanism. Is this illegal? Clearly not. Immoral or unethical? I do not know. And the list of such possibilities goes on.

Another argument in favor of concentrating on reducing incentives for internal profit transfers as opposed to controlling transfers themselves is that anything less than perfect control will favor MNCs relative to national firms. In fact, the recognition that differences in tax systems, barriers to capital flows, and regulated economies often provide advantages to MNCs able to take advantage of or circumvent these factors gives rise to a number of public policy considerations.

Implications for the "Efficiency" of MNCs

The central issue in the broad debate surrounding MNCs is whether they are vehicles of international economic efficiency, facilitating transfers of goods and factors of production that otherwise would not take place, or whether as suggested by Hymer (1970) they are vehicles for extending monopoly power, by removing from market channels transfers in certain critical goods or factors. Stated another way, the issue is whether the imperfections in goods and factor markets that are the sources of MNCs's advantages are "natural" barriers (largely due to the difficulty of transferring certain specialized intangibles) or are barriers created by the MNCs themselves to gain and hold monopolistic advantages. In the former case, the argument is that MNCs are "good," since they enable exchange, and hence welfare gains, that otherwise would have been impossible. In the second case, they are "bad," since they simply represent an extension of monopoly power. Since the two are difficult to distinguish in practice, the conclusions of most students of MNCs follow from their prior beliefs regarding the importance of "natural" and "created" barriers.

The recognition that the internal financial system of an MNC also may provide it with advantages further complicates the debate. To the extent that multinationalism is encouraged by tax systems that impose higher taxes on independent ventures than on the same ventures when part of an MNC, it does not represent an increase in efficiency, but neither can it be considered a monopolistic act. Rather, the MNC is largely a passive beneficiary of government policies and, to the extent that there are economic or political costs to corporate bigness, the costs are borne by society at large. Of course, it is possible that one country gains politically while others lose. This will be the case if economic control is shifted to MNCs based predominantly in one country. U.S. tax policy, in fact, appears to encourage such concentration.

If MNCs gain from their ability to circumvent barriers in financial markets, it might be argued that they contribute to a more efficient allocation of capital and risk. However, the barriers they overcome are in large part created by national governments to serve some social objective. The end result of the barriers and of MNC efforts to circumvent them is unlikely to be efficient from a domestic or international perspective. Nor is it likely to be politically desirable, since it implies greater concentration of economic activity (Agmon and Lessard, 1976a).

It is ironic that many barriers erected by countries to increase their economic independence may encourage the growth of MNCs which can bypass the affected markets. Similar arguments apply to incentives to multinationalism created by regulatory or bargaining situations which favor firms able to disguise profits through internal transactions.

The literature reviewed in this paper provides little hard empirical evidence regarding the importance of financial factors as incentives for multinationalism. However, the arguments presented suggest that these factors must be given greater weight in future studies, both because they provide a potentially important motivation for multinationalism and because they distort reported flows of investments and profits that form the basis for many conclusions regarding the desirability of MNCs.

Implications for Tax Policy

The discussion of tax policy toward MNCs by either home or host countries typically is couched in terms of economic efficiency, although it sometimes boils down to a "neo-mercantilist" approach of maximizing revenues for the country in question with little regard for international efficiency or equity. The typical efficiency criteria, capital import neutrality and capital export neutrality, seek to avoid tax-induced distortions in the international allocation of investment, production, and trade. A type of tax-induced distortion missed by both criteria is the favoring of MNCs relative to national firms or individual investors in those cases where internal profit transfers or global consolidation will reduce total taxes. This suggests a third efficiency criterion, which might be termed "octopus neutrality" or, more seriously but somewhat less accurately, "transfer price neutrality." Basically, it would call for the same tax treatment for a particular investment regardless of whether it was part of a multinational conglomerate or a stand-alone venture owned directly by individual investors. Examples of departures from this criterion from a U.S. perspective include the current system of limiting foreign tax credits to the U.S. tax that would be due on the foreign-source income, but allowing firms to use an overall limitation. This clearly favors those U.S. firms with low-tax foreign operations to offset against operations generating excess credits. It would appear that this advantage could be eliminated by requiring a country-by-country computation of tax credits. However, this would increase the incentives for profit shifting among high- and low-tax countries and would continue to favor the MNC—Catch-22. Only in the case where tax authorities are able to enforce arms-length prices for all transactions would this not be the case. Further, although the U.S. Firm with an extensive system of high- and low-tax operations has an advantage over the U.S. firm with few overseas operations, both will be at a disadvantage relative to domestic firms in the low-tax country and, at best, will be only on par with domestic firms in the high-tax country. Thus, transfer-price neutrality will conflict with the other efficiency criteria.[7]

The one case in which transfer-price neutrality will always coincide with both capital import and capital export neutrality, of course, is when all countries employ the same tax system, including a common unit of account. Several studies reviewed in this paper provide support for moving in this direction. They suggest that the effect of internal financial transfers, if unconstrained, is to neutralize the influence of tax factors on real decisions, but to magnify the effects of differences in tax systems on the distribution of tax revenues. It is precisely in such a world where countries would retaliate quickly against any competitive tax change, and the only stable solution would be a common system. Such a step would also eliminate all tax-related incentives for profit shifting, thus reducing the need for controls over intracompany transactions.

Implications for Financial Policies

A similar set of conclusions can be drawn regarding the implications of the MNC's internal financial system for a particular nation's financial policies. We assume that a country does not wish to restrict MNC operations if these are viewed as contributing to efficiency, but that it does not want to encourage growth of the MNC where this is not justified by natural conditions in goods and factor markets. In this case, the country will attempt to insure that national firms can bid successfully against MNCs for projects where they expect at least the same operating cash flows. Thus, the government will wish to insure equal access to credit resources and to world equity markets where the project's risks will be evaluated in the context of well-diversified portfolios. Elimination of financial restrictions of all sorts would appear to lead to this ideal, although for a variety of institutional reasons which are beyond the scope of this review, additional intervention on behalf of national firms in LDCs might be required.

Implications for Regulation and Bargaining

This is the area in which conclusions appear to follow most clearly. As stated by Streeten:

The allocation of large overhead and joint costs . . . is bound to be arbitrary within wide limits and a policy of maximizing global post-tax profits from the world-wide system of operations of the firm will greatly reduce the significance of declared prices, capital values and rates of return for purposes of national policy (Streeten, 1974, *p.* 264).

Little more need be said, except that the comment is applicable to developed countries as well as to LDCs. Vernon (1971a) makes this point, and it has been reiterated by many others, yet researchers continue to draw conclusions based on reported financial flows which tell only part of the story. One presumes that policymakers are not significantly different in this regard.

In all three areas—tax policy, financial policy, and regulatory policy—the ability of MNCs to shift funds and profits internally represents a constraint on national policies, a constraint that must be observed if governments do not wish to encourage the growth of MNCs beyond levels justified by natural conditions in goods and factor markets. In this regard, at least, MNCs do challenge national sovereignty.

NOTES

1. Barnet and Muller (1974) provide a provocative but often contradictory recital of the key charges leveled at MNCs for their financial behavior.

2. The major exception within the U.S. is the differential tax treatment at the investor level of dividends and retained earnings, which favors internal transfers from "cash rich" to "cash poor" operations as opposed to transfers through financial markets that would entail payment of dividends by one firm and the issue of new securities by another.

3. Reviews of the theory of direct investment are provided by Dunning (1973), Kindleberger (1969), Ragazzi (1973), Stevens (1974). The "generally accepted theory" appears to be that direct foreign investment can be explained in terms of wealth-maximizing behavior by firms that derive advantages from imperfections in markets for intangible factors of production. These imperfections may be "natural," reflecting special charac-

teristics of the factors being transferred (Magee, 1976) or may be created by the firms themselves through monopoly power (Hymer, 1960; Vaitsos, 1974a).

4. These rents, of course, may represent returns on previous R & D investment as suggested by Magee (1977a).

5. The benefits of international diversification to lower risk were extended to direct foreign investment by Ragazzi (1973), Rugman (1975), and Stevens (1974). Aliber (1970) also presents a financial rationale for direct investment, but bases it on a preference for the currency of the base country firm.

6. This approach is similar to that of Myers (1974), who shows that the additive relationship will hold within an integrated, efficient capital market. It will not hold strictly in the more general case where markets in different countries are to some extent segmented by barriers and where there are distortions within particular markets. Nevertheless, it is a useful way to identify the various elements in the process.

7. I am indebted to Thomas Horst for bringing this point to my attention.

REFERENCES

Adler, M. [1974], "The Cost of Capital and Valuation of a Two Country Firm," *Journal of Finance*, March 1974.

——— and B. J. Dumas, [1975], "The Long-term Financial Decisions of the Multinational Corporation," in Elton and Gruber, Eds., *International Capital Markets*, Amsterdam: North-Holland.

Aliber, R. Z., [1970] "A Theory of Direct Foreign Investment," in Kindleberger, Ed., *The International Corporation*, Cambridge, Mass.: The MIT Press, 1970.

Agmon, T. and D. R. Lessard, [1976a], "Investor Recognition of Corporate International Diversification," forthcoming, *Journal of Finance*.

———, [1976b], "The Multinational Firm as Vehicle for International Diversification: Implications for Capital Importing Countries," *Revista Brasileira de Mercados de Capitais*, Dec. 1976.

———, [1977], "Financial Factors and the International Expansion of Small Country Firms," M.I.T. volume edited by C. P. Kindleberger and T. A. Agmon, forthcoming, 1977.

Arpan, J. S., [1971], *International Intracorporate Pricing: Non-American Systems and Views*, New York: Praeger, 1971.

———, [1972], "Transfer Pricing in Multinational Financial Management, *EFA Financial Review*, Vol. 2, No. 2, 1972.

Barnet, R. J. and R. E. Muller, [1974], *Global Reach: The Power of the Multinational Corporations*, New York: Simon and Schuster, 1974.

Copithorne, L. W. [1971], "International Corporate Transfer Prices and Government Policy," *Canadian Journal of Economics*, Vol. 4, 1971.

Dunning, J. H., [1973], "The Determinants of International Production," *Oxford Economic Papers*, January 1973.

Grubel, H. G. [1968], "Internationally Diversified Portfolios," *The American Economic Review*, December 1968.

Hawkins, R. G., and D. Macaluso, [1976], "The Avoidance of Restrictive Monetary Policies in Host Countries by Multinational Firms," unpublished working paper, 1976.

Horst, T. O. [1971], "The Theory of the Multinational Firm: Optimal Behavior Under

Different Tariff and Tax Rates," *Journal of Political Economy*, Vol. 79, September 1971.

_____ [1975], "Tax Issues," Chapter 6 in Bergsten, C. F., T. O. Horst, and T. H. Moran, *American Multinationals and American Interests*, forthcoming, Brookings Institution.

_____ [1977a], "The Overall Versus Per-Country Limitation in the U.S. Foreign Tax Credit," unpublished working paper, Jan. 1977.

_____ [1977b], "American Taxation of Multinational Corporations," *American Economic Review*, June 1977.

Hufbauer, G., and D. Foster, [1976], "U.S. Taxation of the Undistributed Income of Controlled Foreign Corporations," mimeo, prepared by the Office of International Tax Affairs, U.S. Treasury for consideration by the House Ways and Means Committee Task Force on the Taxation of Foreign Income, April 1976.

Hymer, S. [1960], "The International Operations of National Firms: A Study of Direct Foreign Investment," MIT Press, 1976.

Kindleberger, C. P. [1969], *American Business Abroad: Six Lectures on Direct Investment*, New Haven: Yale University Press, 1969.

Kopits, G. F. [1972], "Dividend Remittance Behavior Within the International Firm: A Cross-Country Analysis," *Review of Economics and Statistics*, Vol. 54, August 1972.

_____ [1976a], "Taxation and Multinational Firm Behavior: A Critical Survey," unpublished, I.M.F., March 1976.

_____ [1976b], "Intrafirm Royalties Crossing Frontiers and Transfer-Pricing Behavior," *The Economic Journal*, December 1976.

Lall, S. [1973], "Transfer Pricing by Multinational Manufacturing Firms," *Oxford Bulletin of Economics and Statistics*, Vol. 35, August 1973.

Lessard, D. [1976], "World, Country and Industry Relationships in Equity Returns: Implications for Risk Reduction Through International Diversification," *Financial Analysts Journal*, Jan./Feb. 1976.

Magee, S. P. [1976], "Jobs and the Multinational," in this volume.

Miller, M. H. [1976], "Debt and Taxes," forthcoming, *Journal of Finance*.

Modigliani, F. and M. H. Miller, [1958], "The Cost of Capital, Corporation Finance, and the Theory of Investment," *American Economic Review*. Vol. 48, June 1958.

_____ [1961], "Dividend Policy, Growth and the Valuation of Shares," *Journal of Business*, Volume XXXIV, No. 4, Oct. 1961.

_____ [1963], "Corporate Income Taxes and the Cost of Capital—A Correction," *American Economic Review*, Vol. 53, No. 3, June 1963.

Musgrave, P. B. [1975], *Direct Investment Abroad and the Multinationals: Effects on the U.S. Economy*, prepared for the Subcommittee on Multinational Corporations of the Committee on Foreign Relations, U.S. Senate, Washington, D.C.: U.S. Government Printing Office, 1975.

Myers, S. C. [1974], "Interactions of Corporate Financing and Investment Decisions—Implications for Capital Budgeting," *Journal of Finance*, March 1974.

Ness, W. L. [1972], "A Linear Programming Approach to Financing the Multinational Corporation," *Financial Management*, Winter 1972.

_____ [1975], "U.S. Corporate Income Taxation and the Dividend Remittance Policy of Multinational Corporations," *Journal of International Business Studies*, Spring 1975.

Nieckels, L. [1976], *Transfer Pricing in Multinational Firms*, New York: Halstead Press, 1976.

Prachowny, M. F. J. [1972], "Direct Investment and the Balance of Payments of the United States: A Portfolio Approach," in F. Machlup *et al.*, ed., *International Mobility and Movement of Capital*, New York: Columbia University Press, 1972.

Ragazzi, G. [1973], "Theories of the Determinants of Direct Foreign Investment," *IMF Staff Papers*, Vol. 20, July 1973.

Robbins, S. M. and R. B. Stobaugh, [1973], *Money in the Multinational Enterprise: A Study in Financial Policy*, New York: Basic Books, 1973.

Rugman, A. R. [1975], "Motives for Foreign Investment: The Market Imperfections and Risk Diversification Hypothesis," *Journal of World Trade Law*, Sept./Oct. 1975.

Rutenberg, D. P. [1970], "Maneuvering Liquid Assets in Multinational Companies: Formulation and Deterministic Solution Procedures," *Management Science*, June 1970.

Salmi, T. [1975], *Joint Determination of Trade, Production, and Financial Flows in the Multinational Firm Assuming Risky Currency Exchange Rates*, Doctoral Thesis, Helsinki School of Economics, 1975.

Sato, M. and R. M. Bird, [1975], "International Aspects of the Taxation of Corporations and Shareholders," *IMF Staff Papers*, Vol. 22, July 1975.

Shulman, J. [1967], "When the Price is Wrong—By Design," *Columbia Journal of World Business*, May/June 1967.

Solnik, B. H. [1974], "Why Not Diversify Internationally?" *Financial Analysts Journal*, July 1974.

Stevens, G. V. G. [1972], "Capital Mobility and the International Firm," in F. Machlup et al., eds., *International Mobility and Movement of Capital*, New York: Columbia University Press, 1972.

_____ [1974], "The Determinants of Investment," in J. H. Dunning, ed., *Economic Analysis and the Multinational Enterprise*, London: Allen and Unwin, 1974.

Streeten, P. [1974], "Theory of Development Policy," in J. H. Dunning, ed., *Economic Analysis and the Multinational Enterprise*, London: Allen and Unwin, 1974.

Vaitsos, C. V. [1974a], *Intercountry Income Distribution and Transnational Enterprises*, Oxford: Clarendon Press, 1974.

_____ [1947b], "Welfare Considerations and the Multinational Firm, in J. H. Dunning, Ed., *Economic Analysis and the Multinational Enterprise*, London: Allen and Unwin, 1974.

Vernon, R. [1971], *Sovereignty at Bay: The Multinational Spread of U.S. Enterprise*, New York: Basic Books, 1971.

Weston, J. F. [1973], "Are MNC's Using Market Power to Overprice?" prepared for National Conference on Multinational Corporations, Washington, D.C., 1973.

27

Case of the Tangled Transfer Price*

M. Edgar Barrett

The scene is a conference room in the head office in Geneva of Universal Data Corporation's European operations. The time is shortly after lunch on a winter day in 1977. Three men are finishing cups of coffee which have been served by a secretary.

Seated at the head of the table is Clive Price, age 45, British by nationality and president of UDC-Europe. The other two are David Simmons, 39, Swiss and vice president—finance, and Clinton Salter, 48, American and vice president in charge of sales. [Two other officers of UDC-Europe mentioned in the conversation that follows are William O'Shaughnessy, general manager of the British Isles subsidiary, and Christian van Rhijn, general manager of the Belgian subsidiary.] UDC—its operations and its management control system—is briefly described in the ruled insert that appears on page 451.

Price: You chaps know why we're here. We've got problems related to pricing at our British and Belgian subsidiaries, and both of them require our immediate attention.

Simmons: I'm familiar with the Belgian matter, but not with the British one. What's wrong in England?

Salter: It's that recent shipment of U-645 to Amalgamated Metals, the one we invoiced directly from our Spanish plant as a means of getting around the British Price Commission.

Simmons: And a fine idea at that! Any time we can pick up an extra $200,000 by using Continental European prices, I shall support it. I wish we had thought of it earlier. What is the problem? Are the machines printing in Spanish?

Price: No. But apparently they're having service problems with them. Carlos Navarro, at our Spanish subsidiary, rang up yesterday. He says that the people at Amalgamated telephoned him to say it's been almost impossible to get anyone in England to service the machines.

Salter: The same old story.

Price: I rang up O'Shaughnessy right away. He admits that there's been a delay. However, he claims that his systems engineers have been tied up at ICI on a new project. Besides, he said, if Carlos was so concerned, he could have sent one of his own men down. After all, the Spanish subsidiary got credit for the sale.

Simmons: I beg to differ, Clive. We charged a commission against Spain's recorded profit, and we showed the same amount of commission as an additional revenue item on Britain's monthly operations report.

---

*This article is reprinted, with permission, from *Harvard Business Review,* May–June 1977, pp. 30–36, 176–178.

Salter: Maybe O'Shaughnessy missed that line on the report. What's the story in Belgium?

Simmons: We received a telex from the controller of the Belgian subsidiary this morning. Here, I made a copy for each of you.

(He gives Price and Salter each a sheet of paper, which they read. The text of the telex follows.)

ATTN: D P SIMMONS

PAPERWORK ON FIRST SHIPMENT U82/15 ENROUTE FROM IRELAND RECEIVED TODAY, FIVE MACHINES ENROUTE TO BRUSSELS AT FOB $41,000 EACH

WE DO NOT WANT TO CLEAR THESE MACHINES THROUGH CUSTOMS AS SHIPMENTS FROM FRANCE HAVE BEEN ARRIVING AT FOB $32,000 AND FROM USA AT FOB $35,200. PLEASE INSTRUCT IRELAND TO ISSUE REVISED INVOICES AT FOB $32,000 EACH SO WE CAN CLEAR THIS SHIPMENT WITHOUT CREATING VERY DANGEROUS SITUATION WITH LOCAL CUSTOMS.

WE AWAIT URGENT REPY TO REQUEST.

DAG ERICSSON
UDC-BRUSSELS

Simmons: You see, our Belgian controller is worried about the reaction of the customs authorities. He thinks they won't understand why the same model is arriving from three different sources at three different prices.

Price: Pardon me, David, but doesn't the real risk involve dumping? After all, seeing the same model come in at three prices may lead customs to conclude that some of the machines were dumped—particularly the American ones. If that happens, wouldn't we be slapped with higher duty charges on the American machines?

Simmons: I fear you're right, Clive. They might decide to put higher duty charges on all our American-made imports. With a duty on them of 8.4%, it would take little change in the assessed value of the goods to rack up a substantial tax bill. And it could get worse. We think that the Belgian officials trade data with their counterparts in other countries. Imagine the mess if all the Common Market countries began to investigate our transfer pricing.

Salter: Well, the answer to this one seems simple enough. Let's lower the incoming price to the French level. It's only a bookkeeping entry anyway.

Price: It's not that simple. The machines were diverted to Brussels at the request of the Belgian subsidiary. Christian van Rhijn agreed to take the machines, at $41,000 each, from the Irish plant.

Salter: I'm confused. Why would he do that?

Simmons: The story goes back several months now. During the spring, Clive received a telephone call from Christian demanding to know whether we actually planned to allow Galway to bill Belgium at an above-budget price for these extra machines. In addition, he complained about the 10% premium he had had to pay in order to get several extra machines from the United States.

Price: David and I explained to him that the high price resulted from three things—the increased demand for this model, higher than usual start-up costs in Galway, and the favorable tax deal we obtained from the Irish government. As you remember, we have a 16-year exemption from income tax on all export sales.

Simmons: Christian wasn't exactly enthralled with our explanation. He thought the Irish were taking advantage of the tight supply situation. He saw no reason why Belgium should absorb Galway's production inefficiencies. Moreover, he insisted that his reported results and his own annual bonus should not be affected by some quirk in the tax laws.

Price: So I rang up O'Shaughnessy and asked whether he could bring the price down. He mentioned the tax arrangement, saying it would be sheer folly to transfer any more profit to a high-tax area like Belgium. Then he reminded me that Belgium had no alternative source and Ireland could place the machines elsewhere. Besides, he said, the Brussels operation would still show a small profit on the transactions.

Simmons: I finally telexed Brussels that the final decision on price was up to them and O'Shaughnessy's group. I did note, however, that the Irish tax savings were substantial. They settled on the price of $41,000 each, FOB Brussels.

Salter: You know, I'm not wild about your explanation either. It seems to me that this creative transfer pricing is bound to blow up in our faces. In fact, my eyebrows feel a little warm right now.

Price: Now now, Clint, tax minimization is part of the game. You know very well that the decision to locate in Galway was heavily influenced by its cash flow advantages.

Simmons: Clive's right, Clint. We all agreed to the Galway plant decision. Besides, we're in business to earn a profit for our shareholders. Contributing corporate cash to the British or Belgian government is not high on UDC's list of priorities.

Salter: Well, I'm still not convinced. Don't you think we ought to forget the fancy footwork and stick to what we know best—building and selling computers?[1]

It is a reflection of the complexities of operating in a multinational environment that our four commentators agree fully on only one point. They all believe that a primary issue for UDC-Europe is determining its business objectives. Each makes a statement on what those objectives should be.

"Let's start by stating the responsibilities of the executives in this case," writes Earl F. Brown, managing partner, Arthur Young & Company (Continental Europe). "Nothing they do should violate either U.S. or local country laws, but they still must take whatever action they can, within the law, to maximize the return on shareholders' investment. This

[1]This case is derived from the author's knowledge of actual situations faced by U.S. corporations operating in Europe. Before reading the commentaries that follow, you may wish to jot down what you believe to be the major issues involved and the steps that UDC-Europe should take next. Exhibit I and Exhibit II summarize the financial effects of the transfer price actions.

Facts About UDC-Europe

The company, founded in 1967, is a U.S.-based manufacturer of minicomputers and peripheral hardware. It sells, leases, and services its equipment worldwide. Of its $800 million in revenues, the European operations contribute $185 million.

UDC-Europe, a wholly owned subsidiary, was founded in 1971. It is very profitable and enjoys a great deal of autonomy from the parent company. General managers of its ten geographically organized subsidiaries are administrative umbrellas for two or more legal entities created to meet national legal and tax requirements. Four subsidiaries (the Spanish, the French, the British, and the Irish) have manufacturing as well as marketing operations.

UDC-Europe treats each subsidiary as a profit center for purposes of managerial control and evaluation. It sets annual budgets in terms of pretax profit and judges local managers largely on their ability to meet or beat the targeted figures. UDC-Europe prices intracompany transfers at levels determined at the annual budget meeting except under special circumstances, such as unexpectedly higher volume or a complex tax situation. In the former case, the subsidiary manager is expected to negotiate a price. In the latter case, management at Geneva may set the price.

means that, when given a legally viable option, they should aim to maximize the profit of the parent company."

Alfred W. Cook, group controller and director of administration in the International Craft, Game & Toy Group of General Mills, Inc., takes the same position on compliance with local laws and notes: "Either each of the units in question should operate independently and realize the best possible performance in each country, or the company enters the gray area between the obligation to optimize profits for shareholders and behavior that borders on the unethical."

William W. Teeple, controller of the Container Division of International Paper Company, characterizes UDC's apparent business policy in Europe in three facets:

- *UDC is in business to serve customer needs; profitably, to its best ability, and certainly better than competition.*
- *Through a profit-center orientation, UDC wants to optimize the returns on its individual businesses on a 'stand alone' basis.*
- *The company looks at capital investment on the basis of local government incentives, particularly in the area of taxes.*

Derek Seddon, distribution manager of the Agricultural Division of Imperial Chemical Industries, Ltd., doubts the wisdom of trying to optimize returns on a stand-alone basis. In his view, the transfer-pricing problem "is only a symptom of a more deep-seated problem related to the definition and operation of profit centers. Transfer pricing can be viewed as a mechanism for allocating profit between profit centers.

"Properly used, it should motivate autonomous units to take independent decisions that lead to an optimum result for the organization. With the present organization of

UDC, suboptimum results appear more likely. The 10 so-called profit centers appear to have very little control over their selling or transfer prices. I would therefore argue that they are not profit centers."

FOR CENTRALIZATION

To deal with what he believes to be the fundamental control problem, Seddon suggests a restructuring of the organization: "A central product marketing team located in Geneva would be responsible for trading profit, with the different national subsidiaries acting as sales and after-sales service agents. The manufacturing units would be cost centers reporting to a production manager located in Geneva; product sourcing would be a marketing responsibility.

"Management accounting (the information required for commercial operation) should be separated from financial accounting (taxation, foreign currency cover, overnight balances) so that production, sales, and marketing can, in Salter's words, 'stick to what we know best.'"

Brown concurs with this recommendation. The UDC managers are entangled, he insists, not by the transfer price, but by the "intertwining of two information systems—that required for tax minimization and that needed for management control." UDC management should be convinced, Brown adds, that the company has only one profit center here; the entire European division.

"The basic mistake," he writes, "is to judge managers simply on the measurement of before-tax income as recorded on the legal (tax) books of their companies. These results should be ignored when assessing management's performance and determining annual bonuses.

"Sales branches should be measured against sales performance only, including such measures as percentage of growth, share of market, and the ratio of selling expenses to sales. Manufacturing operations should be controlled against a standard cost of production and by comparison of one plant's performance against the others, allowing, of course, for differences in wage rates and plant technology."

Both Brown and Seddon favor removing from the subsidiaries all responsibility for setting intracompany transfer prices. Brown states his case this way: "Transfer prices within Europe should be legally acceptable but should maximize company profits. Each product should have only one transfer price, and local management should not be allowed to negotiate these prices unilaterally."

Transfer-pricing decisions, Seddon asserts, cannot be made by UDC's subsidiaries, "especially in the complex European market, where cross-border duties and different tax rates influence marketing decisions."

FOR DECENTRALIZATION

Neither Cook nor Teeple agrees with the idea of centralizing decision making in respect to UDC's European transfer-pricing policies.

"Mechanically speaking," Cook writes, "it would be conceivable to centralize the responsibility and authority for all European business at the Geneva office of UDC and have it rule on all intercompany prices—and, as a corollary, centralize all bonus calculations. This would almost inevitably violate the intent of the law in each country. Thus the very matter of UDC's integrated European operations can be questioned.

EXHIBIT I

Profitability of British Sales (Estimated per Unit of Model U-64*)

General Data		
Manufactured in	Spain	United Kingdom
Sold to customer in	United Kingdom	United Kingdom
Selling subsidiary	Spain	Britain
UDC-Europe		
Retail price	$62,000	$42,000
Cost of goods sold	23,000	24,500
Gross margin	$39,000	$17,500
All other expenses†	18,000	16,000
Profit before tax	$21,000	$ 1,500
Tax‡	1,520	780
Profit after tax	$19,480	$ 720
British Subsidiary Only		
Retail price or sales commission earned	$11,000	$42,000
Cost of goods sold	0	24,500
Gross margin	$11,000	$17,500
All other expenses	10,000	16,000
Profit before tax	$ 1,000	$ 1,500
Tax‡	520	780
Profit after tax	$ 480	$ 720
Spanish Subsidiary Only		
Retail price	$62,000	NA
Cost of goods sold	23,000	
Gross margin	$39,000	
Sales commission paid	11,000	
All other expenses	8,000	
Profit before tax	$20,000	
Tax‡	1,000	
Profit after tax	$19,000	

*Data are on a per-machine basis. Actual exchange rates and cost figures from most recent monthly operations reports are employed. The Amalgamated Metals order was for 10 machines.

†A combination of freight charges, duty charges, and differences in national cost structures accounts for the disparity between the two columns.

‡Based on local tax rates. Funds are not expected to be repatriated to parent for many years. Spanish figures reflect a tax rate of 35% and the benefits of a 15% export incentive computed on the Spanish added value of goods exported from Spain.

EXHIBIT II

Profitability of Belgian Sales (Estimated per Unit of Model U-82/15*)

General Data		
Manufactured in	Ireland	Ireland
Sold to customer in	Belgium	Belgium
Selling subsidiary	Belgium	Belgium
	High Transfer Price	Low Transfer Price
UDC-Europe		
Retail price	$60,000	$60,000
Cost of goods sold	27,000	27,000
Gross margin	$33,000	$33,000
All other expenses†	18,000	17,700
Profit before tax	$15,000	$15,300
Tax‡	2,400	6,900
Profit after tax	$12,600	$ 8,400
Belgian Subsidiary Only		
Retail price	$60,000	$60,000
Transfer price in	41,000	32,000
Gross margin	$19,000	$28,000
All other expenses†	14,000	13,700
Profit before taxes	$ 5,000	$14,300
Tax‡	2,400	6,900
Profit after tax	$ 2,600	$ 7,400
Irish Subsidiary Only		
Transfer price out	$41,000	$32,000
Cost of goods sold	27,000	27,000
Gross margin	$14,000	$ 5,000
All other expenses	4,000	4,000
Profit before tax	$10,000	$ 1,000
Tax‡	0	0
Profit after tax	$10,000	$ 1,000

*Data are on a per-machine basis. Actual exchange rates and cost figures from most recent monthly operations reports are employed. This shipment involved 5 machines. The agreement between the two subsidiaries covered a total of 40 machines.

†Differences in incoming duty payments account for the disparity between the two columns. The duty payments are based on the invoiced (transfer) price.

‡Based on local tax rates.

"The case in question and remarks by the three executives involved illustrate clearly the kind of thinking that is at the root of the public's negative attitude toward multinational corporations (MNCs). They imply that an MNC is justified in operating as if national boundaries and national sovereignties are nonexistent. The facts are obviously the reverse, and unless MNCs comply fully with the intent and spirit of the laws in each country, ethics violations occur.

"Ideally, the correct position would be one that complies with the national intent and law in each country. Geneva headquarters would be able to operate only with such flexibility as remains available after such compliance."

Teeple proposes a transfer-pricing system based on market prices. "UDC needs a transfer price policy rather than day-to-day decisions based on tax opportunities," he says. "The question is, what type of a system should be used? In general, a market transfer-pricing system for UDC would offer a number of advantages.

"First, the accounting practices of many multinational corporations today have come under increased scrutiny by host governments, which often view them as mechanisms for avoiding taxation, exchange fluctuations, and the like. Consequently, a sound, consistent, straightforward transfer-pricing policy would put UDC in a good light with the fiscal authorities of each country it does business in.

"Second, market transfer pricing supports the decentralized profit-center concept and allows bottom-line measurement on a stand-alone basis consistent with the competitive environment of that country.

"Moreover, it allows future incremental investment to be viewed on the basis of what the real cash flow would be to the subsidiary, as well as to the parent company. It also avoids cash flow problems in subsidiaries.

"Finally, market transfer pricing encourages local management to reprice products in the marketplace on a consistent and competitive basis, while aiming at making an acceptable return. From a moral or ethical point of view, UDC would come off with a much better image using a consistent policy such as this."

UNITED KINGDOM AND BELGIUM

Two commentators had recommendations in respect to the service problems experienced by Amalgamated Metals. "Service by engineers from Britain," Cook states, "should be provided against fair compensation from Spain. The imaginary commission charged against Spain and credited to Britain escapes legal administration in both countries. The bookkeeping entry should be avoided."

Brown would remind the manager in Britain of the importance of after sales service. "Amalgamated Metals could be beneficial to future U.K. business," he writes. "Furthermore, Amalgamated's unhappiness with after-sales service will spread and affect the profitability of the U.K. subsidiary."

In regard to the Irish sale to Belgium, Seddon calls for the issuance of a new invoice, using the French price of $32,000 per machine. "Otherwise," he notes, "the tax authorities can legitimately claim that transfer pricing is being used as a means of avoiding tax. While tax minimization is allowed, tax avoidance is illegal."

UDC's tax burden, Seddon adds, could be minimized by nontransfer price means as well. He suggests reorganizing UDC to permit invoicing of sales of Irish-manufactured machines by the manufacturing subsidiary, with payment of a sales commission to the selling subsidiary at commercial rates.

FOUR KEY ISSUES

This case and the commentators' responses to it provide a clear illustration of the complexity of the issues involved in setting a transfer price policy for a multinational enterprise. The major issues are:

1. Profit maximization vs. profit satisfaction.
2. Centralization vs. decentralization.
3. One set of books vs. multiple sets.
4. The letter of the law vs. its intent.

A decision to follow the profit maximization route would almost certainly lead to some central review of transfer prices within Europe. As suggested by Brown and Seddon, it could easily result in the reorganization of the European division as one profit center. Conversely, a decision to strive for a satisfactory level of profits allows for the possibility that each national unit will be allowed to stand alone, with transfer prices based on the market price that would prevail in an arm's-length transaction.

In regard to the centralization question, market-based or negotiated transfer prices are viewed by many as a prerequisite to meaningful application of the profit center concept. Profit centers, in turn, are a vehicle for encouraging decentralized decision making and decisions that are more in tune with local circumstances. The commentators, while divided in their opinion as to how and where transfer pricing decisions should be made, agree that centralized decisions on transfer pricing are inconsistent with the existence of multiple profit centers.

Two of the commentators, noting that UDC is trying to make one set of books serve multiple roles, recommend that the company set up separate sets of books for fiscal and management control purposes. As many readers of this journal are aware, this is common practice in large U.S. companies, domestic or multinational.

A more complex question has to do with the responsibility, if any, of a multinational corporation to obey the intent as well as the letter of the various national laws. Naturally, as all the commentators stressed, every action must comply with the law.

"Intent," however, is a very elusive concept. For example, the Irish government clearly intends to provide temporary export subsidies for companies locating in Ireland. Does the government also "intend" to attract companies because of the possibility that these exports will carry a price high enough to minimize taxes in, say, Belgium? Does the EEC "intend" to look the other way when corporations are attracted by tax incentives to its underdeveloped parts, such as Western Ireland? Obviously, intention is not easy to ascertain.

Finally, there is the question, what is a market-based transfer price? To many people, it is the price that would be arrived at in an arm's-length transaction. Yet this could be said to be what happened when the Irish and Belgian managers settled on the price of $41,000 for each machine. Perhaps multinational corporations, whether they wish to be or not, are in the "gray area" to which Alfred Cook refers.

28
Maneuvering Liquid Assets
D. Rutenberg

1. INTRODUCTION

This chapter is concerned with moving funds between subsidiaries. The purpose of such moves is to get liquidity to each subsidiary when it needs it, in a way that minimizes total taxes paid by the corporation.

Corporations differ in the guidelines they impose on subsidiaries for handling liquid assets, but three patterns predominate, each corresponding to one of the archetypes of headquarters-subsidiary relationships introduced by Perlmutter [12]: ethocentric, policentric, and geocentric. Some headquarters feel uneasy about subsidiary managers holding liquid assets from year to year and insist on their declaring dividends to headquarters. This assures control of the foreign managers by the ethnocentric headquarters, although at a high cost in taxes. Geographically organized corporations tend to view each subsidiary as totally independent (which it legally is) and have little involvement in the management of liquid assets; this policy has the fewest negative behavioral consequences, although it results in a high level of total short-term assets. Between these two extremes, the geocentric corporation moves liquidity to subsidiaries when needed by manipulating transfer prices, managerial fees and royalties, dividends, and intersubsidiary loans in order to maximize interest received on liquid assets minus total taxes paid on a worldwide basis. As Robbins and Stobaugh (1973) noted:

Make no mistake about it—even though these large enterprises seemingly are decentralized, their worldwide network of units and intercompany links are in fact controlled indirectly by their rule books, or "bibles" from headquarters. The "bibles" are in the form of standard procedures, sometimes consisting of several volumes, that specify such items as the limits of local borrowing, standard terms of payment of intercompany accounts, and standard rules for management fees.

Clearly, such headquarters intervention may weaken incentive systems built on the profit center concept. Whether manuevering is worth the effort can be determined best by building a model; the difference between current and model after-tax profit provides a benchmark against which to judge the behavioral costs of headquarters intervention.

If deemed prudent, maneuvering liquid assets can enable a multinational to react to anticipated changes in exchange rates, currency controls, and other such risks and opportunities. Forecast exchange rates are a necessary input to the model explained in this chapter. Where several possible scenarios of the future environment have been envisioned, maneuvers for each can be evaluated.

2. THE MODEL

The subject of this article is the optimal use of tax havens, bilateral tax treaties, nonuniform treatments of income received from abroad, and national differences in income tax rates, import duties, and border taxes. This is a partial analysis for tactical planning because it takes as given the planned operations of each national subsidiary, and hence whether the subsidiary is to be a net source or recipient of funds in each year.

Suppose there are N subsidiaries around the world, and the analysis will be carried out over T years. A real problem deals with all N subsidiaries; for simplicity we deal with only three subsidiaries: i, j, and k. The analysis begins by forecasting the net cash surplus/deficit for each subsidiary for each period b_i^t, and by setting the safe levels below which bank deposits $K_i^{t,t+1}$ and other liquid asset holdings $G_i^{t,t+1}$ must not fall. From there, a linear program is developed as a guide to the optimal maneuvering of liquid assets between the subsidiaries. The linear program can be solved on a computer.

For each major product line or industry in a nation, a planner can plot the desired growth rate against the cash generation capability of the product line subsidiary in question.

Even within the strategic deployment of each product line in each nation, hard work is required to forecast the cash inflow requirements or cash outflow. Inflation of input prices must be forecast. Revenue must be estimated from pricing plans and market expansion intentions. The most probable rates of taxation must be forecast to yield after-tax income plus depreciation.

It is far more revealing to forecast *pro forma* cash flows and interest income in nominal, rather than what economists call "real," terms. Deflating these values with anticipated inflation obscures the possible conduits that can channel required liquidity to where it is needed at the most advantageous exchange rates. Forecast exchange rates are used in each year of the program.

The transaction's demand for cash in each subsidiary should also be estimated, for changes in this inventory affect the net availability for funds. Also associated with each subsidiary in each year is its profit π_i, its subpart F income (as defined in the U.S. Internal Revenue Code), and the effective rate of foreign income tax. Liquid funds can be held by

FIGURE 1

A Network Representing Flows Between Subsidiaries *i*, *j*, and *k*

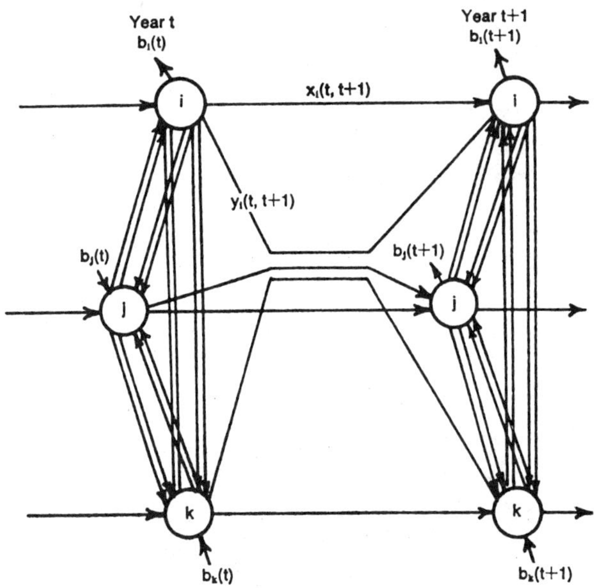

a subsidiary from one year to the next. This holding is represented as a flow through the arc connecting a subsidiary in one year to the same subsidiary in the succeeding year. If there is a significant term structure to the best interest rates obtainable by a subsidiary, then two year arcs can be added to take advantage of the higher interest rates obtainable on longer term loans. However, to simplify exposition we shall use only one year arcs. A peculiar feature of U.S. banks must also be depicted: If any part of the company has obtained a loan from a U.S. bank, then the company will be required to keep on deposit in branches of that bank no less than a specified "compensating balance." If each subsidiary maintains a dollar account in the U.S. bank, then the sum of these accounts can be used to satisfy the compensating balance requirement (even though the individual accounts are members of different OFDI class nations). Thus an aggregated compensating balance is an effective way to make intersubsidiary loans. The compensating balance requirement is depicted by the bunched parallel y arcs in Figure 1; the sum of flow through these arcs must be greater than or equal to the compensating balance requirement.

In Figure 1, operations in country i drain the system of $b_i(t)$ and $b_i(t + 1)$ in years t and $t + 1$ respectively, whereas in country j the local subsidiary is forecast to be a net generator of funds $b_j(t) < 0$ in year t, but a net user of funds $b_j(t + 1) > 0$ in year $t + 1$. A feasible solution is one which gets funds to the subsidiaries that need them. For a given pattern of intersubsidiary ownerships, there are at least four ways to transmit liquid assets from one national subsidiary to another. These control variables are:

$p_{ij}(t)$	Adjust the transfer prices on shipments between subsidiaries i and j.
$f_{ij}(t)$	Charge legal and managerial fees and royalties on technical knowledge supplied to subsidiary i by subsidiary j.
$l_{ij}(t)$, $l_{ji}(t + 1)$	Make new intersubsidiary loans, and repay old ones with interest. Delayed invoicing is a loan.
$d_{ij}(t)$	Remit dividends from subsidiary i to its legal stockholder subsidiary j.

There are N subsidiaries, and the analysis is done over time periods O, $\cdots$, T. The state of the system is specified by the amount of liquid assets held by each subsidiary:

$x_i(t, t + 1)$	Amount of liquid assets employed in their most profitable manner by subsidiary i in the one year period from t to $t + 1$.
$y_i(t, t + 1)$	Amount of cash held by subsidiary i (usually in a dollar account in a U.S. bank) that can satisfy compensating balance requirements.

In order to simplify modeling, it will be assumed that fund flow is averaged over the year, and only this average flow will be depicted. Of course, the time periods can be made as short as desired to more accurately depict reality. In each year N compensating balances must be specified, as must N − 1 dividend flows, N(N − 1) transfer price flows, and N(N − 1) loan flows. The number of managerial fee flows will be either N(N − 1) or N − 1, depending on whether or not fees and royalties have to follow the ownership pattern. Thus at most $T(3N^2 - N - 1)$ flows will have to be calculated.

3. COSTS AND BOUNDS ON FLOW THROUGH THE ARCS

There is a cost on flow through an arc, say the arc $p_{ij}(t)$ from i to j in year t depicting manipulated transfer prices. This cost depends on the pair of nations i and j, and can be expected to vary with time. Hence it would be formally correct to let the cost function be $P_{ij}(t)[p_{ij}(t)]$. This notation would be very cumbersome, however, so $P[p_{ij}(t)]$ will be used instead; it must be understood that P is a function of i, j, and t. The four methods of transferring funds between nations will be discussed first.

3.1 Adjusted Transfer Prices $P[p_{ij}(t)]$

Suppose subsidiary i manufactures subassemblies which are shipped to subsidiary j. If the transfer price is lower than "normal" then there occurs a net flow of funds from i to j. If the transfer price is set higher than "normal," then the flow of funds is from j to i.

There is a direct cost to flow through a p_{ij} arc. A lower transfer price reduces the revenue appearing in subsidiary i, and this usually reduces income tax and value added tax in country i. Any *ad valorum* export duty on subassemblies imposed by country i, or import duty imposed by country j will be reduced by the lower transfer price (so long as the invoices are believed). A lower transfer price will increase profits and value added appearing in country j. Hence the direct cost of sending funds through arc p_{ij} is:

Marginal rate of income and value added tax of subsidiary in country j, *minus marginal rate of income and value added tax of subsidiary in country* i *minus* ad valorum *tariff on exports by country* i *and on imports by country* j

There are two internal indirect costs to flow through a p_{ij} arc. If each subsidiary is a semi-autonomous profit center, then there will be a bilateral monopoly relationship between i and j. An imposed transfer price will work so long as producing to demand remains in the self interest of subsidiary i. One indirect cost lies in the required efforts to persuade i to produce. Another indirect cost lies in the profits foregone by subsidiary j as it tailors its promotional efforts to its cost of goods, partly the manipulated transfer price. Clearly these costs of acrimony over negotiated and imposed transfer prices are greatly reduced if unit sales and production quotas are set centrally. The external indirect costs arise from government inquiries. If the price is too low both governments will intervene. The tax authorities of country i will see tax revenues foregone (in USA, I.R.S., Section 482: see the recent case of Eli Lilly [5]). The import tariff commission of country j will see dumping. If the transfer price is too high, income tax will be foregone to country j. These external indirect costs have to be paid in bribes, time and effort at investigatory hearings, additional advertising to counter ill-will, and actual settlements. Section 482 of the U.S. Revenue Code confers great power to the Secretary of the Treasury. Its full text is:

In any case of two or more organizations, trades or, business (whether or not incorporated, whether or not organized in the United States, and whether or not affiliated) owned or controlled directly or indirectly by the same interests, the Secretary or his delegate may distribute, apportion, or allocate gross income, deductions, credits, or allowances between or among such organizations, trades, or businesses, if he determines that such distribution, apportionment, or allocation is necessary in order to prevent evasion of taxes or clearly to reflect the income of any of such organizations, trades, or businesses.

In light of such regulatory power by the U.S. government, and similar power by most other governments, it appears to be current industrial practice to abide by standard transfer prices on standard items. However, the continual introduction of new products requires that new transfer prices be established, and this is done with an eye to the considerations of this paper. Nonstandard items such as rejects, returned goods, and contaminated scrap can have any transfer price between zero and the standard price of a good item, and can easily be manipulated. One final technique used in practice is to invoice the goods through a chain of subsidiaries, each of which adds its commission.

3.2 Fees and Royalties $F[f_{ij}(t-1), f_{ij}(t)]$

Managerial advice, allocated headquarters overhead, and royalties on patents and trademarks are very elusive and difficult to price. Hence they appear to be very suitable conduits through which to move funds.

There is a direct cost. If these fees and royalties are a tax deductible business expense in country i, then a tax saving occurs. However, this need not be so, and there may be a withholding tax. If fees and royalties received from abroad are taxable as income in country j, then there is a tax cost.

There will likely be an indirect cost to any increase in fees and royalties. A treasury official in country i, struggling for foreign exchange, will be more likely to intervene the larger the increase. Hence the cost is a nonlinear (quadratic perhaps) function of $[(f_{ij}(t) - f_{ij}(t-1)]$. Many governments have become very strict about allocating foreign exchange for fees and royalties [18].

3.3 Intersubsidiary Loans $L_{ij}[l_{ij}(t)]$

The most prevalent form of intersubsidiary loan is a speed-up or delay in invoicing shipments between a pair of subsidiaries because normal terms of payment differ between regions of the world. In addition, actual shipping schedules can be accelerated in one direction and decelerated in the other so that one subsidiary carries inventory for both. Outright loans may also be possible. The danger in any intersubsidiary loan is that it will be deemed to constitute a dividend by the governments of the countries involved (especially the U.S. government). Hence, ritualistically, loans are made for 364-½ days and are then repaid with interest; a new loan is regranted immediately if desired.

There are direct costs. Let the interest rate on the loan be r (presumably reasonable to both governments). The loan $l_{ij}(t)$ departed from country i and arrived (presumably intact) at country j. At the end of the year $(1 + r)l_{ij}(t)$ must be repaid. If interest is a business expense in country j then the income tax payment will be reduced. Hence the net outflow from subsidiary j is $(1 + r - rT_j)l_{ij}(t)$, where T_j is the marginal rate of taxation in country j (including withholding). If there is no withholding tax on interest leaving country j, then $(1 + r)l_{ij}(t)$ will be repaid to subsidiary i. If interest received from abroad is taxable income in country i, then the inflow to subsidiary i (net of tax) will be $1 + r - rT_i)l_{ij}(t)$. A constraint that the loan must be repaid (with interest) must be added to the formulation.

3.4 Dividends $D[d_{ij}(t)]$

There are N wholly owned subsidiaries. The intersubsidiary ownership pattern is fixed, hence the $N - 1$ dividend arcs are known. The problem is to estimate the cost function $D[d_{ij}(t)]$ for each arc. The cost function (if nonlinear) and restrictions on dividend flow depend upon the tax base. It is presumed that aspects of the tax base internal to each country have been optimized, so that in this formulation we need consider only intersubsidiary allocations of the tax base, such as manipulations to transfer prices and fees, and the receipt of interest on intersubsidiary loans.

First we shall sketch a few foreign taxes on dividends, starting with the uncomplicated tax laws of Liechtenstein. Though they will not be examined here, local taxes imposed by states, counties and cantons are substantial enough that they should be included in the cost functions. Brief mention will be made of tax treaties between pairs of nations; their intimate details should be studied, especially when a company operates with a foreign corporate charter in a nation.

Secondly, we shall examine in detail the U.S. laws that pertain to dividends received from abroad. Due to the U.S. Revenue Act of 1962, all cost functions (even on dividends which do not flow to the U.S.A.) must be somewhat augmented. Due to the 1968 Office of Foreign Direct Investment, minimum bounds are imposed on certain groups of dividends.

3.4.1 $D[d_{ij}(t)]$ When j is not USA

Liechtenstein Corporations pay income tax (Ertragssteuer). Dividends paid by resident corporations pay a 3 percent coupon tax. This is never refunded, or permitted to be credited as a cost of doing business. There is no tax on dividends received. No tax treaties are currently in force which change these provisions.

Belgium Corporations pay income tax (impôt des sociétés) at the rate of 30 percent, but income going into retained earnings above 5,000,000 Belgian francs is taxed at the rate of 35 percent (model this as a 5 percent incentive for paying dividends until retained earnings drop to 5,000,000 Belgian francs). Dividends paid by a resident corporation are subject to a 18.2 percent withholding tax, which is never refunded nor permitted to be credited as a cost of doing business (deduct this from the incentive for paying dividends). Of dividends received into Belgium (after any withholding taxes by the government of the sending country) the tax imposed by the Belgian government is 18.7 percent (15 percent Belgian withholding tax plus 30 percent Belgian income tax on 15 percent of the 85 percent that survived Belgian withholding tax). By tax treaty, dividends received from an Italian corporation are exempt from Belgian withholding tax.

Germany Income tax (Körperschaftsteuer) and business tax (Gewerbesteuer) are imposed on corporations doing business in Germany. A 25 percent withholding tax is made on dividends paid. Profits not distributed to shareholders are taxed at 51 percent, but profits distributed to shareholders are taxes at only 15 percent. Dividends received by a German corporation are given a credit against company income tax, but not business tax. The effective tax rate depends, as before, on whether or not these profits from abroad will be distributed to shareholders.

3.4.2 U.S. Controls on $d_{i,USA}$

While planning a base company in the popular tax haven countries of Surinam, Panama, Liechtenstein, Switzerland, Bermuda and the Barbados, usually the most applicable laws are the U.S. Revenue Act of 1962, the U.S. Foreign Investors Tax Act of 1966, and the U.S. Foreign Direct Investment Program administered by the Office of Foreign Direct Investments (OFDI). The combination of these three laws is so complicated that it would not be trivial for a company to prepare a computer simulation for its tax position. Interestingly, however, (assuming all subsidiaries are 100% owned, and that subsidiaries in less developed countries are not legal parents to subsidiaries in advanced countries) U.S. law ignores patterns of legal intersubsidiary ownership so that subsidiaries can be regrouped annually at the discretion of the company. "Where there are many such foreign corporations and branches, this [regrouping] will provide ample opportunity for the exercise of ingenuity, alone or in connection with an electronic brain." [13, p. 15,203]

The OFDI regulations impose *lower* bounds on four sums of dividends. The four sums are defined by the geographical schedules:

U.S.A. and Canada

A. Underdeveloped, from Aden to Zambia

B. Developed, from Abu Dhabi to United Kingdom

C. Most of Europe plus South and South-West Africa, from Andorra to Switzerland

Let π_i be the annual profits (net transfer of capital plus reinvested earnings) in subsidiary i; this will be negative for subsidiaries which lost money. For a small company the applicable OFDI regulations (Section 503 allowables) impose four constraints on dividends, limiting the retained earnings to \$200,000.

$$\Sigma_{i,j}d_{ij} - \Sigma_{i,j}d_{ji} + \Sigma_{i,j}p_{ij} - \Sigma_{ij}p_{ji} + \Sigma_{i,j}f_{ij} - \Sigma_{i,j}f_{ji} + \Sigma_{i,j}l_{ij}r_{ij} - \Sigma_{i,j}l_{ij}r_{ji} \geqq \Sigma_i\pi_i - 2000{,}000.$$

For $i \in A$, $j \in A$

The other three constraints are for $i \in B$, $j \notin B$, for $i \in C$, $j \notin C$, and a worldwide formula $i \notin$ U.S. or Canada, $j \in$ U.S., Canada. These Section 503 allowables, if not used in any year, may not be carried forward for use in later years.

If the company so chooses, and it probably will unless it is a small company that is new abroad, it can replace the set of four equations (Section 503) with \$200,000 annual limits by three equations (Section 504). One cannot have the benefit of both Sections. In the Section 504 allowables there is no single worldwide constraint. In the three geographical schedule constraints:

In A, \$200,000 is replaced by 110% of average direct investment (net capital plus reinvested earnings) of company aggregated over all A countries during 1965 and 1966.

In B, \$200,000 is replaced by 65% of average 1965, 1966 direct investment in all B subsidiaries.

In C, \$200,000 is replaced by the smallest of (1) 35% of average 1965, 1966 direct investment in all C countries (2) average reinvested earnings in 1964, 1965, 1966 of all C subsidiaries. Use 0 if either (1) or (2) is negative.

3.4.3 U.S. Revenue Act of 1962

In attempting to calculate $D[d_{i,\mathrm{USA}}(t)]$ it is convenient to categorize three sources of dividends, (a) less developed countries, (b) foreign subsidiaries which have been organized into Western Hemisphere Trade Corporations, China Trade Act Corporations, and special corporations which can operate only in Puerto Rico or U.S. possessions, (c) all other countries.

Subsidiaries in less developed countries (the list is not quite identical with Schedule A countries of the OFDI regulations) are exempt from U.S. taxation on their retained earnings, and are subject to a low tax on dividends received into the U.S.A. The low tax results from the fact that U.S. tax *credit* is granted on the base of before-foreign-tax-income, whereas U.S. tax is calculated on the dividend received, which is net of foreign taxes. If the subsidiary pays its *entire* earnings as dividends $d_{i,\mathrm{USA}}$, then the total tax rate will be

$$D[d_{i,\mathrm{USA}}(1969)] = [T_{\mathrm{USA}} - T_i T_{USA} + T_i^2]d_{i,\mathrm{USA}}$$

If $T_{\mathrm{USA}} = 48$ percent, then a 5.76% saving is the most that can be achieved by paying dividends from a subsidiary in a less developed country that has a 24 percent tax rate.

The incentive to use Western Hemisphere Trade Corporations, China Trade Act Corporations, and Section 931 Corporations operating in Puerto Rico and other U.S. possessions was greatly increased by the Revenue Act of 1962. For a company which has already planned its physical operations, these special U.S. laws operate much as tax treaties: they reduce $D[d_{i,\mathrm{USA}}(1969)]$.

Most subsidiaries are not in less developed countries, nor are they qualified as Western Hemisphere Trade Corporations. Their U.S. parent is therefore liable to U.S. tax on the Subpart F income of such subsidiaries, even if it is retained abroad. Subpart F income consists of nonmanufacturing income (rents, royalties, licensing fees, dividends), income from services performed for related persons outside the nation, and income from the sale of property to related persons outside the nation.

Subpart F income is precisely defined in Internal Revenue Code Sections 951 (a) (1) (A) (i) and 952. Legal counsel competent in this portion of the code should be consulted, for carefully reading the definitions of these sections is like trying to debug someone else's computer program that was written compactly with layers of nested DO loops. Nevertheless, a Subpart F income figure is required. Manipulations to transfer prices and fees will be magnified by a factor of 2.5 in their influence on Subpart F income because of the "70–30" rule of Section 954 (b) (2) (B), but only within these 70–30 limits.

The 1962 Revenue Act offers significant tax relief under the "minimum distribution provisions" of Section 963. Section 963 (b) (3) provides a table, associating with each effective foreign tax rate a required percentage minimum distribution of earnings and profits.

To avoid misunderstanding Figure 2 it would be helpful to examine the total tax to be paid as a function of the subsidiary dividend payout rate. For example, consider a subsidiary with an effective foreign tax rate of 35 percent. From Figure 2 (or IRC 963 (b) (3)), this effective foreign tax rate calls for a minimum distribution of earnings and profits of 63 percent. The U.S. government grants a tax credit for taxes paid abroad, so that the total tax does not exceed the U.S. rate of income tax of 48 percent (ignoring the current surtax).

Unless a minimum distribution is made, the *entire* Subpart F income of the subsidiary

FIGURE 2

Graph of IRC Section 963(b) (3)

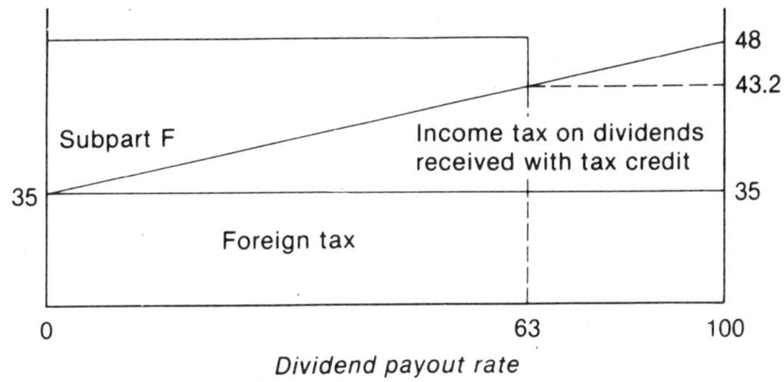

is taxed. Figure 3 implies that for dividends in excess of the minimum distribution the per unit cost is the slope of the total tax line. The figure applies to each year; if liquidity must be built up in a subsidiary, a sensible strategy would be to alternate minimum distribution years with zero dividend years. Unfortunately this may run afoul of the OFDI minimum repatriation regulations, referred to in the previous section. In fact, most U.S. corporations are finding that the OFDI regulations are so stringent that the dividends they must pay exceed the Subpart F minimum distributions. The network model of this paper can be applied ignoring Subpart F taxation, then re-run constraining insufficient flows to equal or exceed their minimum distribution. Alternatively, a minimum distribution can be applied to a chain of subsidiaries (a different consolidation to that required by OFDI A, B, and C country schedules) that the *sum* of dividend flows exceed a prescribed minimum. Such a consolidation is permitted by the U.S. Internal Revenue Code:

963 *(c) (2) AMOUNTS TO WHICH SECTION APPLIES—CHAIN OF CONTROLLED FOREIGN CORPORATIONS*

Subsection (a) (2) shall apply to amounts which (but for the provisions of this section) would be included in the gross income of the United States shareholder under section 951 (a) (1) (A) (i)—

FIGURE 3

Total Taxes as a Function of Dividend Payout Rate

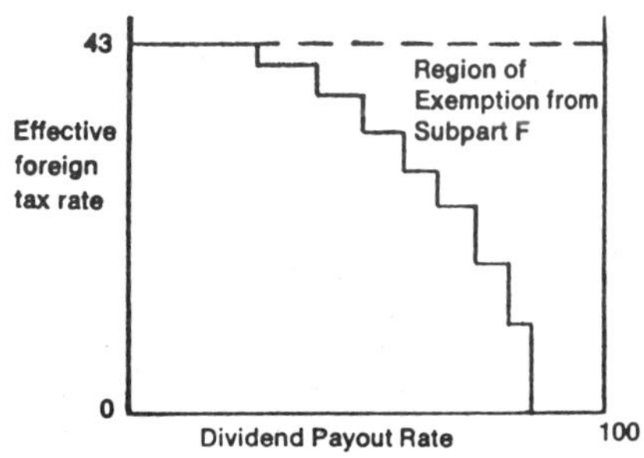

(A) *by reason of its ownership, within the meaning of section 958 (A) (1) (A) of stock of a controlled foreign corporation, and*

(B) *to the extent that the United States shareholder so elects, by reason of its ownership, within the meaning of section 958 (a) (2), of stock of any other controlled foreign corporation (an account of its ownership of the stock described in subparagraph (A) or of stock described in the subparagraph), but only if there is taken into account the earnings and profits of each foreign corporation, whether or not a controlled foreign corporation, by reason of which the United States shareholder owns, within the meaning of section 958 (a) (2), stock of such controlled foreign corporation.*

For a given pattern of intersubsidiary ownership there are numerous possible chains of subsidiaries. If a corporation has such generous OFDI constraints that it is liable for Subpart F taxation unless it increases dividends, it might consider searching for optimal chains of subsidiaries. Though this subject will not be explored in detail in this paper, the company could organize chains whose average effective foreign tax rate is *just* above each of the breaks in IRC 963 (b) (c), so that the tax saving is greatest. Unfortunately, for most companies the OFDI regulations preclude such considerations, and furthermore IRC 964 (a) (a safety net provision) deems that no chain or group may pay less than 90 percent of the U.S. tax rate.

3.5 $X[x_i(t, t+1)]$ Liquid Assets Held in Country i

Section 203 (c) of the OFDI regulations stipulates that a direct investor whose total liquid foreign balances exceeds $25,000 is required "to reduce the amount of liquid foreign balances (other than direct investment liquid foreign balnaces) held by such direct investor to an amount not in excess of the average end-of-month amounts of the same so held by such direct investor (whether or not a direct investor at that time) during 1965 and 1966". That is to say

$$\sum_{x=1}^{N} x_i \leqq a$$

where a is greater of $25,000 and average during 1965 and 1966.

If a company wants to hold liquid assets abroad totalling more than a, then it must confine them to less liquid or less desirable assets such as those specified in Section 203 (a) (2). Then $X[x_i(t, t-1)]$ is the effective interest rate earned by a less desirable asset such as OFDI Section 203 (c) (ii)

bank deposits, negotiable instruments, non-negotiable instruments, commercial paper and securities with a period of more than 1 year remaining to maturity when acquired by the direct investor and which are not redeemable in full at the option of the direct investor within a period of 1 year after such acquisition

If the multi-national company has raised money abroad then the "direct investment liquid foreign balances" are exempt. Then marginal changes to liquid balances in country i would presumably be held in the unrestricted foreign raised funds, for which $X[x_i(t, t-1)]$ is higher.

3.6 $Y[y_i(t, t + 1)]$ Cash Held in the U.S. Dollar Account of the Subsidiary

Foreign banks commonly grant loans on an overdraft basis, so that the borrowing company pays interest only on the amount of the granted loan which it has in use, much as a U.S. bank grants a line of credit. Nevertheless, when a U.S. bank actually grants a loan the borrowing company pays interest on the entire amount of the granted loan (whether or not withdrawn from the bank) and furthermore must keep specified compensating balances on deposit in the bank. As the company has to keep transaction and precautionary cash, the compensating balance requirement is not as onerous as it would be in a deterministic world, though it should be reflected in a slight upwards adjustment in U.S. interest rates to make them comparable with foreign "overdraft" interest rates.

U.S. dollar accounts held in the bank by the many corporate subsidiaries around the world are generally considered to count towards the compensating balance requirement:

$$\sum_{i=1}^{N} y_i(t, t + 1) \geq R_{t, t+1}$$

Loan officers generally refer only to the average balance through the preceding period, and would generally be unaware of the variance of the daily balance through the period. Furthermore, the fact that attention is focused on the sum of subsidiary balances permits the company to arrange a costless partial movement of funds between subsidiaries as the composition of the compensating balances is charged. Unless interest can be obtained for compensating balances $Y[y_i(t, t + 1)] = 0$.

Example

Most confusion appears to arise over dividend taxation, so this will be illustrated. Let the parent company in Liechtenstein own a subsidiary in Germany, which has a subsidiary of its own in Belgium.

Let us work up the ownership tree. The Belgian subsidiary declares a dividend of 100 to its German parent. The Belgian government withholds 18.20, so that 81.80 arrives in Germany. The German business tax (Gewerbesteuer), based on the *entire* dividend of 100, is 13.50 percent, so income net of business tax is 86.50. Company income tax (Körperschaftsteuer) is 51 percent of income net of business tax, so is $0.51 \times 86.50 = 44.11$ (this rate assumes income will be retained within the firm; income destined for dividends is taxed at only 15 percent). Only at this point is credit granted for the Belgian withholding tax, so that German company income tax due is $44.11 - 18.20 = 25.91$. The Belgian withholding tax was 18.20, the German business tax was 13.50, and the German company income tax is 25.91; their total is 57.61. That is to say, only 42.39 percent of the dividend gets through from the Belgian subsidiary to its German parent. That is to say $D[d_{BG}(1970)] = 0.5761$.

The German company now declares a dividend of 100 units to its parent in Liechtenstein. In Germany, the company income tax is 51 percent for retained earnings, but is only 15 percent for earnings paid out as dividends. The simplest way to model this is that the company income tax is 51 percent on all earnings, but that the German government gives the German company an income tax rebate of 36 percent on dividends paid out. Thus $100-36 = 64$ units leave the German company. However, the German Government imposes a 25 percent (of 100) withholding tax on dividends leaving Germany, so that 75 units arrive in the Liechtensteinian subsidiary. Thus 117.18 percent of the dividend gets through from the German subsidiary to its parent in Liechtenstein. That is to say $D[d\text{GL}(1970)] = -0.1718$. Naturally a constraint must be added that total dividends do not exceed earnings!

4. SOLUTION PROCEDURE AS A GENERALIZED NETWORK

Refer back to Figure 1 which presents the problem of manuevering liquid assets in a multi-national company as a network problem. The costs on each arc are actually reductions in liquidity (even government chafing has to be paid for with legal fees and "political contributions"). Consider flow through one of the ij arcs. If liquidity at source node i is reduced by p_{ij} units, liquidity at node j will be increased by less than p_{ij} units; only $p_{ij} - P[p_{ij}(t)]$ will get through to subsidiary y. The factor of attenuation on the arc $p_{ij}\,(t)$ is $.1 - P[p_{ij}(t)]/p_{ij}(t)$.

If deductions from liquidity are handled automatically by factors of attenuation, then the objective of the problem becomes to maximize the sum of liquid assets remaining after periot T (this could be a weighted sum if one can guess desirable countries in which to hold assets). Naturally, all requirements for funds must be satisfied. The problem is a generalized network (also called weighted distribution, or machine loading problem). Dantzig [2, Ch. 21] presents an excellent discussion of the generalized network problem, as does Eisemann [4]. The nonlinear aspects of the indirect costs can be charged as costs [11].

Computational procedures for the generalized network problem assume that all nodes could be connected, and that there are no constraints on arc flows other than node material balance equations. It appears sensible to decompose the problem. There are T subproblems, each an annual p, l, f, d maneuver around N nodes. The master problem consists of the material balance equations on the x and y arcs, the intertemporal constraints that loans must be repaid with interest, and that a cost of government chafing be imposed on any *change* in the f flow of fees.

5. SOLUTION AS AN ORDINARY NETWORK

There are the fewest conceptual problems if one solves the problem as a generalized network sketched in §4 above. However, another approach would be to solve the problem as an ordinary network in which the costs are costs on flow through arcs. After all, the problem has $T(3N^2 - N - 1)$ arcs, and an ordinary network is quicker to solve than a generalized network.

Two conceptual problems arise if an ordinary network is used. Firstly, at what interest rate should future costs be discounted to get their present value? The interest rates in each country are different. Secondly, costs on all arcs flowing into a node must be deducted from the availability of funds of the subsidiary in that year. To do so is to presuppose the optimal flows. Both of these problems *might* be surmounted by an iterative procedure. Run the problem and study the flows that occur. Represent taxes by deducting liquidity from nodes with inflows. Discount all the costs according to the route of flows. Then rerun the problem.

6. SYSTEMS WITHIN SYSTEMS

Maneuvering liquid assets reallocates revenue from high tax rate nations to the multi national company and low tax rate nations. If this were all this model did, it would represent a somewhat dubious contribution to mankind's knowledge. Fortunately the model can be run to evaluate effects of people's ideas by simulating parts of a larger reality. Four areas of current interest to international managers will be mentioned:

1. Short Term Loan Negotiations, Both Local and Multi National

The model presented in this paper is a linear program, and, therefore, has dual variables associated with each constraint. If the problem is formulated as a weighted distribution problem, the dual variable associated with the constraint that funds be available in a subsidiary in a certain year represent the value of taking a small loan and keeping it until the end of period T. All T of these dual variables for a given subsidiary can be translated into a term structure of interest rates from which the year to year value of additional money can be calculated. This data provides a very clear guideline for making short and medium term loans in that nation [1].

Some banks are themselves multi national. In one nation the bank may ration credit because of a high demand for loans within the permitted interest rate. In another part of the world the bank may be short of deposits as it strives to expand. In exchange for depositing money in one part of the bank, the multi-national company can achieve loan priority in another part of the bank. The rationale behind this is that most currencies are blocked and it may be easier for a company to move money than a foreign bank. The worthwhileness of such induced swap transactions can be evaluated with this model.

2. Raising Long Term Capital

Long term capital can be raised in most nations of the world, usually after negotiations with the host government and promises that local investments will result. To support such negotiations, worldwide manufacturing models must be supplemented by worldwide financial models such as this on which to simulate the consequences of different financing schemes. Similarly one can evaluate the benefits of mergers intended to qualify as a Western Hemisphere Trade Corporation, or to buy OFDI exemptions.

3. Restructuring the Pattern of Legal Ownership

If the company has N subsidiaries, there are $(N - 1)^2$ different patterns of intersubsidiary ownership possible even if each subsidiary is restrained to have just one legal parent. In theory one could use the theory of optimal spanning trees [3] to iterate to a worldwide tax minimizing legal structure a pattern of dividend conduits. If one removes the restriction that a subsidiary have one legal parent (but require that the percentage of ownership by each legal parent be constant once reorganization has occurred) then the problem is computationally much simpler and much more difficult for tax authorities to unsnarl. Unfortunately, the tax data required for cases of partial ownership is appreciably more complicated and vague than for cases of complete ownership. In practice the model presented in this paper, by taking some drudgery out of creativity, should stimulate new patterns of intersubsidiary ownership. A subcalculation, about which tax lawyers are well informed, is the benefit of operating in nation i with a corporate charter granted in nation j.

4. Inserting High Profit Products

The Swiss pharmaceutical companies prefer to produce their high profit products in the nations where they incur their largest cash drains to research and dividends. This practice, a vivid example of Vernon's product cycle theory [15], reduces the need to flow funds between nations, though at a high production and transportation cost. Ideally, one would like to simulate the effect of inserting a high profit product into any subsidiary technically sophisticated enough to manufacture it.

In a multi-national company there are many opportunities for maneuvers that take advantage of the fact of being multi national. Most of these do not appear to be used for fear of causing confusion and computational chaos. Hopefully, mathematical models provide a rational framework within which analysis can take place, and it is with this hope that the article was written.

REFERENCES

1. Calman, Robert F., *Linear Programming and Cash Management: CASH ALPHA*, Cambridge; The MIT Press, 1968.
2. Dantzig, George B., *Linear Programming and Extensions*, Princeton; Princeton University Press, 1963.
3. Edmonds, Jack, "Optimum Branching," *Journal of Research, National Bureau of Standards B*, Vol. 71B, No. 4 (October–December 1967), pp. 233–240.
4. Eisemann, Kurt, "The Generalized Stepping Stone Method for the Machine Loading Problem," *Management Science*, Vol. 11, No. 1. (September 1964), pp. 154–176.
5. *Eli Lilly & Company v. The United States*, 372 F. 2d 990, 178 Court of Claims, [No. 293–61, Decided February 17, 1967], pp. 666–733.
6. Hellawell, Robert, "United States Income Taxation and Less Developed Countries: A Critical Appraisal," *Columbia Law Review*, Vol. 66, No. 8. (December 1966), pp. 1393–1427.
7. *Information Guide for U.S. Corporations Doing Business Abroad*, New York; Price Waterhouse & Co., July, 1967.
8. *Information Guide for U. S. Direct Investors*, New York; Price Waterhouse & Co., November, 1968.
9. Kushner, Harold J. and F. C. Schweppe, "A Maximum Principle for Stochastic Control Systems," *Journal of Mathematical Analysis and Applications*, Vol. 8 (March 1964), pp. 287–302.
10. Lichtman, Paul B., "Taxation of Intercorporated Dividends Received in Europe," *European Taxation*, (August 1964), pp. 135–156.
11. Rutenberg, David, "Generalized Networks, Generalized Upper Bounding, and Decomposition of the Convex Simplex Method," *Management Science*, Vol. 16, No. 5 (January 1970).
12. ——, "Organizational Archetypes of a Multi-National Company," *Management Science*, Vol. 16, No. 6 (February 1970).
13. Seghers, Paul D., "How to do Business Abroad at Least Tax Cost," *Transaction Tax Guide*, Englewood Cliffs; Prentice-Hall, 1964.

14. Shulman, James, "When the Price is Wrong—By Design," *Columbia Journal of World Business*, (May–June 1967), pp. 69–76.

15. Vernon, Raymond, "International Investment and International Trade in the Product Cycle," *Quarterly Journal of Economics* (May 1966).

16. Walkup, D. W., and R. J. B. Wets," Stochastic Programs with Recourse," *SIAM Journal of Applied Mathematics*, Vol. 15, No. 5 (September 1967), pp. 1299–1314.

17. Wentz, Roy A., "Corporate Transfers of Intangibles Abroad," *The Tax Executive* (April 1967), pp. 142–159.

18. Zenoff, David B., "Remitting Funds from Foreign Affiliates," *Financial Executive* (March 1968).

19. _____ and J. Zwick, *International Financial Management*, New York, Prentice-Hall, 1969.

29

American Taxation of Multinational Firms*

Thomas Horst

Taxation of the multinational firm's foreign income has been debated continually over the last fifteen years. In the early 1950's the U.S. Treasury proposed to eliminate the deferral of U.S. taxes on foreign subsidiaries' retained earnings, in order to discourage the flow of direct investment capital abroad and to hasten the repatriation of direct investment income.[1] The Congress was unwilling to take so large a step, but in the Tax Reform Act of 1962 did require dividend income from developed countries to be "grossed up" and did limit the taxhaven abuse of deferral.[2] In the late 1960's the AFL-CIO grew increasingly concerned that U.S. multinationals were "exporting jobs" and called for the repeal of deferral and the foreign tax credit.[3] The New Economic Policy announced by President Nixon on August 15, 1971 sought to improve the balance of payments through a variety of measures including a tax preference for export income, the Domestic International Sales Corporation (*DISC*).[4] A primary argument in convincing Congress of the merits of *DISC* was that export income should enjoy a tax deferral comparable to foreign investment income. Although the union-backed Burke-Hartke Bill to repeal deferral and the foreign tax credit was voted down decisively in 1973, the Senate version of the Tax Reduction Act of 1975 would have eliminated deferal. Although this provision was dropped by the House-Senate conference committee, a special subcommittee chaired by Congressman Rostenkowski of the House Ways and Means Committee was established to study deferral and related issues more thoroughly. Finally, the Treasury implemented new guidelines for Sections 861 864 of the Internal Revenue Code which will create a strong tax incentive for U.S. investors to charge their foreign subsidiaries more for research and development undertaken by the parent. In opposing all these changes in U.S. policy, the multinationals have argued that higher taxes would undermine their competitiveness in world markets without helping U.S. exports, employment or the balance of payments.

This paper analyzes the profit-maximizing behavior of a multinational firm and explores the impact on that behavior of repealing deferral, compelling higher charges for *R & D* to foreign subsidiaries, and eliminating the foreign tax credit. My model is limited in

---

*This article is reprinted, with permission, from *American Economic Review,* June 1977, pp. 376–389.

[1]"Deferral" means taxing the dividends, but not the retained earnings, of a subsidiary. The evolution of U.S. taxation of foreign-source income is more fully described in the forthcoming study by C. Fred Bergster. Thomas Horst, and Theodore Moran, ch. 6. Gary Hufbauer and David Foster provide a thorough analysis of deferral and its relationship to other aspects of current U.S. tax policy.

[2]"Grossing up" means basing the tentative U.S. tax (i.e., before deducting the tax credit) on subsidiaries' dividends inclusive of the foreign income taxes allocable to those dividends.

[3]The foreign tax credit allows U.S. investors to reduce their U.S. income tax liability by the amount of foreign income and withholding taxes paid to foreign governments: see below.

[4]A *DISC* is essentially a dummy corporation established to receive tax-sheltered export income; half of that income must be paid out as a dividend and thereby subject to U.S. taxation, but half may be reinvested in export-related assets, such as export accounts receivable.

obvious respects: the analysis is static, not dynamic; the "multinational" invests at home and in one foreign country; and exports between parent and subsidiary are ignored. Higher U.S. taxes on foreign investment income may encourage the firm to invest more at home and less abroad, but that substitution is not necessarily matched by an increase in the parent's exports or a decrease in its imports. The model's primary virtue is incorporating several complex features of U.S. tax policy into a coherent analysis of multinational investment behavior. I explore not only the location of real investment, but also the options for financing that investment. As I shall show, U.S. tax policy affects firms' financial behavior, and that behavior in turn mitigates the impact of tax policy on the location of new investment. Finally, I have kept the analysis simple enough to be able to construct rough estimates of its parameters and simulate the possible impact of various tax changes. In the following sections I set forth the basic model, describe the impact of various tax changes, and summarize the more important conclusions. To aid the reader, the mathematical notation is summarized in Appendix Table A1.

1. THE BASIC MODEL

It is assumed that a multinational firm starts with an existing stock of foreign and domestic investment and seeks the optimal change in its position over the next year. Because the earnings generated by existing investments are an important source of capital for new investment, we cannot ignore the role of the past in shaping the present. To be specific, assume that current revenues (net of labor and material costs, but gross of interest expenses and income taxes) R and on the existing stock of investment I_o, plus new investment undertaken during the current period I.

$$R = R(I_0 + 1) \tag{1}$$

$$R^* = R^*(I_0^* + I^*) \tag{2}$$

An asterisk differentiates the parent's domestic investment from its foreign subsidiary's. Presumably, the marginal and average return on investment at home or abroad declines as the level of investment expands.

The analysis focuses not only on the levels of foreign and domestic investment, but also on the financing of that investment. For simplicity's sake we ignore the market for new equity and concentrate on that for debt. Rather than exploring directly the determinants of an optimal debt-equity ratio for the parent, subsidiary, and/or consolidated enterprise, it is merely assumed that new funds are available at home and overseas at increasing rates of interest. These increasing interest rates could reflect either the thinness of local capital markets or lenders' fears of the insolvency of the borrower. In either event, total borrowing costs B consist of those incurred by past borrowing L_o, plus those resulting from new borrowing, L:

$$B = B(L_0 + L) \tag{3}$$

$$B^* = B^*(L_0^* + L^*) \tag{4}$$

The levels of investment and borrowing are linked by balance sheet constraints. For the foreign subsidiary new investment I must equal new borrowing L, plus new funds obtained from the parent F, and the subsidiary's own retained earnings E_R:

$$I = L + F + E_R \tag{5}$$

The parent's new investment I^* must equal its own new borrowing L^*, less new funds advanced to the subsidiary F, plus its own retained earnings:

$$I^* = L^* - F + E_R^* \tag{6}$$

It is also assumed that the foreign subsidiary can deduct from its taxable income interest on *intra*firm debt as well as royalties, headoffice charges and other such payments for intrafirm services. Although I want to postpone for the moment the role of tax avoidance in determining such payments, let me note here that intrafirm interest expenses depend on the intrafirm interest rate i_p, and the ratio of debt to total intrafirm transfer of capital (debt plus equity) f. Total intrafirm interest payments equal those on past borrowing, $i_{P0}f_0F_0$, plus those on new borrowing, i_pfF. Likewise, it will be assumed that royalties, headoffice, and other intrafirm charges vary at least in the short run in proportion h to the foreign subsidiary's total investment, $I_0 + I$. Thus, the foreign subsidiary's taxable income E_B equals the revenues from investment R, minus the interest paid to outside lenders, B, the interest paid to the U.S. parent $i_{P0}f_0F_0 + i_pfF$, and payments for royalties, headoffice services, and the like, $h(I_0 + I)$:

$$E_B = R - B - (i_{P0}f_0F_0 + i_PfF) - h(I_0 + I) \tag{7}$$

Next it is assumed that the subsidiary pays income taxes at the rate t, and that the dividends paid to the parent D are some proportion p of income after taxes:

$$D = p(1 - t)E_B \tag{8}$$

Thus, the retained earnings available for reinvestment by the foreign subsidiary E_R, as shown in equation (5) above, are

$$E_R = (1 - p)(1 - t)E_B \tag{9}$$

Most foreign governments collect not just an income tax, but also withholding taxes (a typical rate would be 10 to 15 percent) on dividends, interest, royalties, and other payments to U.S. investors. Total withholding taxes paid W, equal:

$$W = w_DD + w_B(i_{P0}f_0F_0 + i_PfF) + w_Hh(I_0 + I) \tag{10}$$

where w_D, w_B, and w_H are the withholding tax rates for dividends, interest, and royalties, headoffice charges, etc., respectively.

We can now turn to U.S. tax policy. Rather than taxing foreign investment income net of foreign income and withholding taxes, the United States bases its tax on foreign-source income gross of foreign taxes and then grants a tax credit for foreign taxes paid. In my notation U.S. taxable income E_B^* equals domestic income net of interest costs $R^* - B^*$, plus interest, royalties, or other such receipts for intrafirm services and dividends:

$$E_B^* = R^* - B^* + (i_{P0}f_0F_0 + i_PfF) + h(I_0 + I) + D/(1 - t) \tag{11}$$

Note that intrafirm income receipts are *not* reduced by the withholding tax and that dividends have been grossed up to include the foreign income taxes "deemed paid" on those dividends.[5] Foreign-source income for the purposes of determining U.S. taxes exceeds the cash actually received by the parent. Note further that U.S. taxable income

[5]Legally speaking, the foreign subsidiary pays the income tax, and the U.S. parent is only deemed to have paid those taxes.

includes the dividends, but not the retained earnings of the foreign subsidiary. That is the essence of deferral.

The taxes paid to the U.S. Treasury T^*, equal the U.S. tax rate t^* times taxable income E_B^*, less the foreign tax credit T_C^*:

$$T^* = t^* E_B^* - T_C^* \tag{12}$$

The U.S. Investor can claim a foreign tax credit equal to the *lesser* of two amounts: 1) the withholding taxes on dividends, interest, royalties, etc. plus the income taxes deemed paid on the dividends: and 2) the U.S. tax rate[6] times total foreign-source income:

$$T_C^* = min\left\{W + \frac{tD}{1-t},\ t^* \cdot [i_{P0} f_0 F_0 + i_P f F + h(I_0 + I) + D/(1-t)]\right\} \tag{13}$$

If foreign taxes paid or deemed paid are less than the maximum creditable—the U.S. taxes which would have been due on the foreign-source income—the investor is said to have a deficit of tax credits. Using the withholding tax formula (10), we can prove that the investor will have a deficit of foreign tax credits if and only if the shareweighted average of foreign tax rates is less than the U.S. income tax rate:

$$s_B w_B + s_H w_H + s_D[w_D(1 - t) + t] < t^* \tag{14}$$

where s_B, s_H, and s_D sum to unity and are the shares of interest, royalties, and other such fees and dividends, respectively, in the U.S. investor's foreign-source income. Condition (14) indicates that even if the foreign tax burden on dividend income $w_D(1 - t) + t$ exceeds the U.S. tax rate t^*, the investor may yet avoid having surplus foreign tax credits by making sufficiently large interest and royalty payments. Let us rewrite the formula for the foreign tax credit as:

$$T_C^* = W + \frac{tD}{1-t} - x\{(w_B - t^*)(i_{P0} f_0 F_0 + i_P f F) + (w_H - t^*)h(I_0 + I)$$
$$+ [w_D(1 - t) + t - t^*]D/(1 - t)\} \tag{15}$$

where x is a binary variable equal to zero if and only if the investor has a deficit of foreign tax credits, i.e., condition (14) is satisfied. While equation (15) looks messier than (13), it is more tractable analytically.

The U.S. parent's after-tax income E_A^* equals its before-tax income E_B^*, less its U.S. taxes T^*, and the foreign taxes included in its taxable income:

$$E_A^* = E_B^* - T^* - [W + tD/(1 - t)] \tag{16}$$

The consolidated, after-tax income of the multinational enterprise equals the parent's after-tax income (which includes dividend income from its foreign subsidiary) plus the subsidiary's retained earnings:

$$E_C^* = E_A^* + E_R \tag{17}$$

To close out the model, we need to specify the parent's dividends and consequently its earnings available for reinvestment. It is assumed that the dividends paid to the ultimate shareholders D^* are some constant proportion p^* of *consolidated* after-tax earnings:

[6]Actually the foreign tax credit is limited not by the statutory tax rate but by the ratio of the firm's tentative U.S. taxes (i.e., before tax credits) to its total taxable income. If the firm has capital gains or certain other favorably taxed income, the statutory rate may exceed its average tax rate.

$$D^* = p^* E_C^* \tag{18}$$

The parent's retained earnings are the difference between its after-tax income and its dividends:

$$E_R^* - E_A^* - D^* = (E_C^* - E_R) - p^* E_C^* = (1 - p^*)E_C^* - E_R \tag{19}$$

From (19) it is apparent that consolidated after-tax earnings E_C^* are proportionate to consolidated retained earnings available for investment:

$$E_C^* = \frac{1}{1 - p^*}(E_R^* + E_R) \tag{20}$$

It is assumed that the multinational firm seeks to maximize either consolidated after-tax earnings or, equivalently, consolidated retained earnings available for investment. I have little direct evidence on what, if anything, a multinational strives to maximize and have chosen consolidated after-tax earnings E_C^* because it seems to be as reasonable and as convenient an objective as any. I should note, however, that this objective function does *not* discount the value of earnings retained abroad despite the probable tax cost of repatriating those funds as dividends. Thus the behavioral assumption would most aptly characterize a management-controlled firm whose primary objective was the growth of the firm and for whom dividends to shareholders are comparable to a tax on consolidated earnings.

What should the firm do to maximize its consolidated earnings? To begin to answer this question, let us substitute several of the earlier formulas into equations (17) and (20) and rewrite consolidated after-tax earnings as:

$$\begin{aligned} E_C^* = \frac{E_R^* + E_R}{1 - p^*} &= (1 - t^*)(R^* - B^*) + (1 - t)(R - B) \\ &- [t^* - t + x(w_B - t^*)](i_{P0} f_0 F_0 + i_P f F) \\ &- [t^* - t + x(w_H - t^*)]h(I_0 + I) \\ &- [t^* - t - x(w_D(1 - t) + t - t^*)]pE_R/(1 - t)(1 - p) \end{aligned} \tag{21}$$

The multinational firm has *seven* degrees of freedom in maximizing consolidated income. It can set four intrafirm financial parameters—i_p, f, h, and p—plus the rates of new domestic and foreign investment I^* and I, and the rate of transferring new capital to its subsidiary F. All other variables in equation (21) are either predetermined or will be determined by these seven values.

We distinguish the four intrafirm financial parameters, i_p, f, h, and p, from the three remaining controls, I^*, I, and F, because the former should be minimized or maximized according to straightforward, tax-avoidance criteria, while the latter must satisfy standard first-order conditions. Let us look first at the intrafirm financial parameters, for their optimal values can be determined by a close inspection of equation (21). We obviously need to differentiate between cases where an investor has a deficit, rather than a surplus, of foreign tax credits.

Deficit Case A deficit of tax credits obtains when foreign tax rates are comparatively low, condition (14) can be satisfied, and thus $x = 0$. In this case the firm should *minimize* royalties, interest, dividends, and all other forms of repatriating income. Foreign investment should be financed insofar as possible out of retained earnings rather than new funds obtained from the parent. If funds must be repatriated in one form or another, the investor will, so far as taxes are concerned, be indifferent among interest, royalties, headoffice charges, or dividends. Each generates the same increase in total tax payments.

Surplus Case A surplus of tax credits obtains when foreign tax rates are comparatively high, condition (14) is violated, and thus $x = 1$. In this case the firm should *maximize* royalties, headoffice charges, interest payments, and all other intrafirm charges deductible from the foreign subsidiary's income and *minimize* dividend payments. By substituting one form of income repatriation for another, the investor can reduce its foreign income taxes without a corresponding increase in its U.S. taxes. A multinational firm, in short, has a clear tax incentive to manipulate its intrafirm accounts to avoid generating excess tax credits.

Let me hasten to add that multinational firms have less than full flexibility in manipulating intrafirm accounts and that in actual practice tax avoidance is not the only criterion affecting the firm's behavior. National tax authorities strive to protect the local tax base: foreign governments may limit deductible payments to parent firms, and the United States applies its "arm's-length" standard to intrafirm interest rates, royalties, etc..[7] Likewise, foreign exchange authorities frequently limit intrafirm transactions to improve the balance of payments—witness the U.S. balance-of-payments guidelines affecting dividend repatriation in the late 1960's. Furthermore, the multinational may be willing to pay higher taxes in order to withdraw its income from weak-currency countries or to minimize its exposure to expropriation. But taxes do matter. Sidney Robbins and Robert Stobaugh (pp. 28–29 and 77) found that intrafirm debt-equity ratios and the methods of income repatriation reflected tax considerations. George Kopits (1972, 1974) found that subsidiaries' dividend payout rates were higher the lower the tax cost of paying dividends and that royalty rates were manipulated to offset excess tax credits generated by dividends.

Consolidated income depends also on the rates of new domestic and foreign investment I^* and I, and new funds advanced to the foreign subsidiary F. The first-order condition obtained by taking the partial derivative of E_C^* with respect to domestic investment I^* is:[8]

$$r^* = b^* \tag{22}$$

The marginal revenue from new domestic investment r^* should equal the marginal cost of newly borrowed funds in the United States, b^*. The analogous condition with respect to new foreign investment I is slightly more complicated:

$$r = b + \frac{(t^* - t_f)h}{(1 - t_f)} \tag{23}$$

where t_f is defined to be the effective rate of global (foreign plus U.S.) taxation of the foreign subsidiary's income. Assuming the investor succeeds in avoiding a surplus of

[7]The arm's length standard obligates an American investor to use transfer prices equal to those which would have prevailed between an independent buyer and seller.

[8]The derivations of the first-order conditions and the equations of change are straightforward, but exceedingly cumbersome. Because they will be published in the Mathematical Appendix to Bergsten, Horst, and Moran, ch. 6, and are available from the author on request, they are not reproduced here.

foreign tax credits, this effective rate of taxation is simply a weighted average of the foreign and U.S. income tax rates:

$$t_f = pt^* + (1 - p)t = t + p(t^* - t) \tag{24}$$

The portion of foreign subsidiary earnings paid out as dividends p, is taxed at the U.S. rate t^*, while that portion retained by the subsidiary $1 - p$, is taxed at the foreign rate t. The second term on the right-hand side of condition (23) recognizes that increased foreign investment generates higher headoffice and other such charges and that such income will be taxed at the U.S., rather than the foreign, rate. Practically speaking, this second term on the right-hand side of condition (23) is small, and the foreign subsidiary equates the marginal revenue from new investment to the marginal cost of locally borrowed funds.

The third and most interesting first-order condition is obtained from the derivative of consolidated income with respect to new funds advanced to the subsidiary F:

$$(1 - t^*)b^* = (1 - t_f)b - (t^* - t_f)i_p f \tag{25}$$

The significance of this condition is grasped more readily if we contrast two extreme cases, the equity-only and the debt-only investor. Suppose, first, that an American company invests overseas, borrows in local capital markets, but limits its own investment in its subsidiary to equity participation. That is to say, there is no intrafirm debt, only equity. This method of financing foreign investment is certainly encouraged by current U.S. tax policy, since debt gives rise to interest payments and thereby shifts income to the more highly taxed U.S. parent. In this equity-only case, $f = 0$, and condition (25) reduces to:

$$(1 - t^*)b^* = (1 - t_f)b \tag{26}$$

The optimal transfer of new funds to the subsidiary equates the after-tax return on equity in the two countries. If the U.S. income tax rate t^* exceeds the foreign income tax rate t, it will also exceed t_f, and the foreign investor will have an implicit tax incentive to invest abroad rather than in the United States.

Suppose for the sake of contrast that the American investor disregards the tax advantages of equity and relies exclusively on debt to finance new foreign investment. Suppose further that it was willing and able to charge interest equal to the subsidiary's marginal cost of newly borrowed funds b. In this case, $f = 1$, $i_p = b$, and condition (25) reduces to:

$$b^* = b \tag{27}$$

The multinational has no tax incentive to favor foreign investment over domestic, for *at the margin* they both generate equal tax payments. While deferral may reduce U.S. taxes and thus leave the multinational with additional funds for global investment, it would not bias the location of that investment. Although condition (27) represents a hypothetical extreme, it points up an important conclusion: deferral encourages an American investor to favor foreign over domestic investment 1) the lower the foreign income tax rate, 2) the lower the rate of dividend repatriation, 3) the lower the ratio of debt to new capital (debt plus equity) transferred to the subsidiary, and 4) the lower the interest charged on intrafirm debt. Deferral thus encourages the American investor to use equity rather than debt in financing foreign investment, and the more equity used, the greater is the implicit bias towards foreign and against domestic investment.

II. THE IMPACT OF CHANGING U.S. TAX POLICY

A. Repealing Deferral

In this section we will explore the impact of three proposed changes in current U.S. tax policy: repealing deferral: increasing *R & D* charges to foreign subsidiaries: and eliminating the foreign tax credit. If deferral were repealed, U.S. taxable income would include the grossed-up value of the foreign subsidiary's retained earnings $E_R/(1 - t)$ in addition to the income shown in equation (11) above. The U.S. taxable income and consolidated before-tax income now become one and the same:

$$E_B^* = (R^* - B^*) + (R - B) \tag{28}$$

Assuming the foreign tax credit would be extended to include all foreign income taxes paid, not just those associated with dividends, consolidated after-tax income would equal:

$$E_C^* = (1 - t^*)(R^* - B^* + R - B) - x\Big\{(w_B - t^*)(i_{P0}f_0F_0 + i_PfF) + (w_H - t^*)h(I_0 + I) + [w_Dp(1 - t) + t - t^*]\frac{E_R}{(1 - p)(1 - t)}\Big\} \tag{29}$$

As long as foreign income and withholding tax rates are low enough, or royalties, interest, and other such charges can be kept high enough to avoid a surplus of tax credits, $x = 0$, and the multinational firm has no further tax incentives to minimize or maximize the use of debt, intrafirm interest rates, royalties, dividends, or the like. The only tax consideration affecting the intrafirm accounts would be the desire to avoid excess tax credits.

Turning from the intrafirm financial parameters to the rates of new domestic and foreign investment and new capital transferred to the subsidiary, the first-order conditions for maximizing consolidated income are:

$$r^* = b^* \tag{30}$$

$$r = b \tag{31}$$

$$b^* = b \tag{32}$$

All the tax terms have cancelled each other out. Without deferral marginal revenue from new investment should equal the marginal cost of newly borrowed funds both within and between the two countries. Gone would be the implicit tax incentive to invest abroad rather than in the United States.[9]

To determine the amounts by which foreign and domestic investment might change, we must take the total derivatives of the original first-order conditions, (22), (23), and (25). Assuming for the moment that the intrafirm financial ratios i_p, f, h, and p remain fixed, we obtain three equations in three unknowns (dI^*, dI, and dF) and one known $dt_f = (1 - p)(t^* - t)$. Rather than presenting the messy formulas,[10] let me describe the nature of the

[9]In actual practice, various nonneutralities would remain. For example, the U.S. investment tax credit does not apply to foreign investment, and state and local income taxes are only deductible from U.S. federal income taxes, while analogous foreign taxes would be creditable. These remaining nonneutralities are carefully evaluated by Hufbauer and Foster.

[10]See fn. 8 above.

calculations and then proceed to some numerical examples. The impact of eliminating deferral can be decomposed into a *substitution* and *liquidity* effect. When U.S. taxes due on foreign investment income increase, the investor diverts fewer funds to foreign investment and more to domestic. This is the substitution effect. The liquidity effect derives from higher taxes: with fewer funds available for reinvestment and with outside funds becoming increasingly costly, the multinational cuts back on its global investment. The substitution and liquidity effects both reduce the rates of new foreign investment and new funds transferred to the foreign subsidiary. New domestic investment will increase if the positive substitution effect outweighs the negative liquidity effect.

My numerical examples are based upon the 1974 experience of American-owned manufacturing subsidiaries, see Appendix Table A2. Most of our model's parameters were roughly estimated from published statistical sources. For example, the average foreign income tax of 39 percent and average dividend payout rate of 42 percent implied an effective rate of global taxation of foreign subsidiary income of 42.8 percent. Thus, eliminating deferral would raise the effective rate of taxation from 42.8 percent to the U.S. rate of 48 percent, an increase of 5.2 percent. The parameters I could *not* estimate from any published sources were the elasticities of investment demand or borrowing costs implicit in equations (1) through (4) above. Accordingly, I arbitrarily assumed that the elasticities of the marginal revenue from new investment and marginal cost of new borrowing were equal to two and then compared those results with others based on higher or lower elasticities.

The numerical calculations of the impact of eliminating deferral are summarized in Table 1. Notice that I have scaled my example to make it appear that all new investment by foreign manufacturing affiliates of U.S. corporations in 1974 was undertaken by the sole subsidiary of a large U.S. manufacturer. In Case 1 (where all investment and borrowing elasticities are assumed to equal two) eliminating deferral would increase the

TABLE 1

Estimated Impact of Repealing Deferral: On New Domestic and Foreign Investment, New Funds Advanced to Subsidiaries, Consolidated After-Tax Income, and Domestic and Foreign Taxes Paid by U.S. Manufacturers, 1974

		Case 1		Case 2 (More Elastic Investment)		Case 3 (Less Elastic Borrowing)	
	Initial Value	Absolute Change	Percentage Change	Absolute Change	Percentage Change	Absolute Change	Percentage Change
Domestic Investment	36,400	1,429	3.9	3,613	9.9	1,360	3.7
Foreign Investment	18,300	−1,549	−8.5	−3,789	20.7	−1,579	−8.6
New Funds for Subsidiary	2,710	−2,466	−91.0	−4,642	−171	−2,028	−75
Consolidated After-Tax Income	15,194	−532	−3.5	−477	−3.1	−534	−3.5
U.S. Taxes Paid	6,005	545	9.1	501	8.3	532	8.9
Foreign Taxes Paid	5,001	−80	−1.6	−148	−3.0	−65	−1.3

Note Initial Values and Absolute Changes expressed in millions of dollars. Case 1 assumes the values for parameters shown in Appendix Table A2. Case 2 assumes the same values except the values of r^* and r' are two-fifths as large as those shown in Appendix Table A2. Case 3 assumes the same values as shown in Table A2 except the values of b^* and b' are twice as large as those shown.

parent's investment by 3.9 percent and reduced the subsidiary's by 8.5 percent in 1974. Because of lost liquidity the rate of global investment would have been slightly lower than it actually was. The substantial reduction in intrafirm funds transferred reflects our implicit assumption that eliminating deferral would encourage multinational firms to borrow more abroad and less at home than they now do. That is to say, taxes affect the location of borrowing as well as the location of investment. Consolidated after-tax income would have been \$532 million less than it was, which would represent a 3.5 percent decline for the large multinational manufacturer. These lowered earnings are the by-product, of course, of the higher taxes paid to the U.S. government. Foreign tax payments ease slightly because of the lower rate of new foreign investment and the higher rate of new borrowing by the foreign subsidiary.

In Case 2 all the parameters are identical to Case 1 except that we have assumed that new domestic and foreign *investment* are *more elastic* with respect to changes in the cost of capital than they were in Case 1 (the elasticities are equal to five rather than two). As can be seen, the more elastic domestic and foreign investment are, the greater is the substitution of domestic for foreign investment resulting from the loss of deferral. Case 3 differs from Case 1 only in assuming that new domestic and foreign *borrowing* are *less elastic* with respect to changes in the interest rate. As one can see, foreign investment falls by more and domestic rises by less than they did in Case 1. In short, the more elastic investment demand the greater the substitution effect is, and the more elastic the supply of external funds the smaller the liquidity effect is.

The estimates in Table 1 all assume that the intrafirm financial ratios i_p, f, h, and p remain fixed at their current values. As we noted above, however, eliminating deferral might also encourage investors to rely more on debt and less on equity in financing their foreign investment, to raise intrafirm interest and royalty rates, to expand charges for *R & D* and other headoffice expenses and to increase dividend payout rates. In the absence of deferral, all these changes except higher dividends would shift tax revenues from the foreign country to the United States. The statistics in Table 1 could thus understate the impact of eliminating deferral on both domestic and foreign tax revenues.[11]

Our findings are summarized in Table 2. Because there is no way of knowing how great the increase in intrafirm charges might be, we have arbitrarily assumed that all charges except for interest would be doubled. That is to say, headoffice, royalties, and all other intrafirm charges would increase from their current 1.1 percent to 2.2 percent of foreign subsidiaries' assets. Case 1 in Table 2 assumes that the foreign government would allow the multinational to deduct all such charges from the foreign subsidiaries' taxable income. As can be seen, the estimated impact on domestic and foreign investment would be minimal. The primary consequence would be a shift of taxable income from the foreign subsidiary to the U.S. parent. Foreign tax payments would fall by 12 percent while U.S. tax payments would increase by 11 percent. Because the U.S. income tax rate is higher than the foreign income tax rate, the global tax burden would rise and consolidated after-tax income would fall slightly.

This impact contrasts sharply with that in Case 2 where we have assumed that the foreign government would *not* allow increased deductions from the subsidiary's taxable

[11]Of course, factors which we have ignored could reverse this conclusion. For example, foreign governments might retaliate by raising their taxes on U.S.-owned subsidiaries' income, which would increase their parents' U.S. tax credit and decrease their tax payments.

TABLE 2

Estimated Impact of Doubling Headoffice, *R&D*, and Other Intrafirm Service Charges: On New Domestic and Foreign Investment, New Funds Advanced to Subsidiaries, Consolidated After-Tax Income, and Domestic and Foreign Taxes Paid by U.S. Manufacturers, 1974

		Case 1 (Deductions Allowed)		Case 2 (Deductions Disallowed)	
	Initial Value	Absolute Change	Percentage Change	Absolute Change	Percentage Change
Domestic Investment	36,400	149	0.4	1,393	3.8
Foreign Investment	18,300	−332	−1.8	−3,087	−16.9
New Funds for Subsidiary	2,710	444	16.4	−2,718	−100
Consolidated After-tax Income	15,194	−142	−0.9	−991	−6.5
U.S. Taxes Paid	6,005	688	11.5	981	16.3
Foreign Taxes Paid	5,001	−592	−11.8	−84	−1.7

Note Initial Values and Absolute Changes expressed in millions of dollars. Both cases assume that headoffice and other such charges are raised from 1.1 to 2.2 percent of the foreign subsidiaries' total assets. In Case 1 the foreign government allows higher deductions from the subsidiaries' taxable income; in Case 2 they do not.

income. The key to understanding this latter situation is recognizing that the new guidelines would subject foreign investment in

B. Increasing *R & D* Charges to Foreign Subsidiaries

As noted in the introduction, the Treasury has issued new guidelines for Sections 861–864 of the Internal Revenue Code. These new guidelines will require the multinationals to allocate a higher portion of their domestic *R & D* expenses to their foreign affiliates when determining their maximum allowable tax credit. Unless the investor has a deficit of tax credits, its U.S. tax payments will rise. The Treasury hopes that the multinationals would increase their *R & D* charges to avoid double taxation of this portion of their income. The multinationals claim that foreign tax authorities will not allow any additional deductions from the subsidiaries' income, so the disputed expenses would give rise to double taxation. We have used our microeconomic model to determine the impact of increasing *R & D* or other intrafirm charges, assuming first that the foreign government would, and second that it would not, permit come to a disguised form of double taxation. Foreign investment would be cut by 17 percent, or twice the reduction from eliminating deferral. Likewise, U.S. taxes would increase by 16 percent, a gain based on the direct impact of the new guidelines and the induced cutback in funds advanced to the subsidiary (if more investable funds are retained by the parent, U.S. borrowing and interest expenses can be cut proportionately). But in this second case U.S. tax revenues gain at the expense of the American investor and not the foreign treasury. In short, by disallowing higher deductions for *R & D* expenses, the foreign government can protect its tax base. But in doing so, it permits the double taxation which inhibits new investment by American-owned subsidiaries.

C. Repealing the Foreign Tax Credit

Several critics of U.S. tax policy have proposed the repeal of the foreign tax credit as well as deferral. Taxable income in the United States would include all foreign investment income net of foreign income and withholding taxes:

$$E_B^* = (R^* - B^*) + (R - B - T - W) \tag{33}$$

U.S. taxes would equal the U.S. tax rate times the taxable income with no foreign tax credit:

$$T^* = t^* E_B^* \tag{34}$$

Consolidated after-tax income would equal:

$$\begin{aligned} E_C^* = {} & (1 - t^*)(R^* - B^*) + (1 - t^*)(1 - w_D p)(1 - t)(R - B) \\ & + (1 - t^*)(t + w_D p(1 - t) - w_B) \quad (i_{P0} f_0 F_0 + i_P f F) \\ & + (1 - t^*)(t + w_D p(1 - t) - w_H) h(I_0 + I) \end{aligned} \tag{35}$$

Note the heavy taxation, $(1 - t^*)(1 - w_D p) \cdot (1 - t)$, of foreign investment income $R - B$. As is apparent from a close inspection of equation (35), the American investor can raise its consolidated after-tax earnings by increasing its use of intrafirm debt f, the rate of interest on that debt, i_p, or the rate of charging headoffice and other such expenses back to its subsidiary. Each of these measures shifts income from the subsidiary to the parent and relieves the double taxation of foreign investment income.

The new first-order conditions for maximizing after-tax income are:

$$r^* = b^* \tag{35}$$

$$r = b - \frac{t + w_D p(1 - t) - w_H}{(1 - t)(1 - w_D p)} h \tag{37}$$

$$b^* - (1 - t)(1 - w_D p) b + (t + w_D p(1 - t) - w_B) i_P f \tag{38}$$

Once again, the most interesting of these first-order conditions is the third, and its significance becomes more apparent by contrasting an equity-only with a debt-only investor. If an American investor ignored the obvious tax incentives to finance foreign investment with debt and advanced only equity funds to its subsidiary, $f = 0$ and equation (38) becomes:

$$b^* = (1 - t)(1 - w_D p) b \tag{39}$$

This is the mathematical formula for the AFL-CIO's dream and the multinationals' nightmare! Because of the double taxation of foreign equity income, the American manufacturer discriminates heavily against foreign investment and in favor of U.S. investment. By contrast, if an investor could rely wholly on debt in financing new investment and charge interest equal to its subsidiary's marginal cost of borrowing, $i_p f = b$ and equation (38) reduces to:

$$b^* = (1 - w_B) \text{b} \tag{40}$$

Although the American investor would still discriminate against foreign investment, that discrimination would be much less than above. The firm's ability to substitute debt for

TABLE 3

Estimated Impact of Repealing Deferral and the Foreign Tax Credit and Allowing Only a Deduction for Foreign Taxes Paid: On New Domestic and Foreign Investment, New Funds Advanced to Subsidiaries, Consolidated After-Tax Income, and Domestic and Foreign Taxes Paid by U.S. Manufacturers, 1974

		Case 1 (Initial Parameters)		Case 2 (Reliance on Debt)	
	Initial Value	Absolute Change	Percentage Change	Absolute Change	Percentage Change
Domestic Investment	36,400	9,291	25.5	3,970	10.9
Foreign Investment	18,300	−10,283	−56.2	−4,997	−27.3
New Funds for Subsidiary	2,710	−15,725	−580.3	−8,060	−297.4
Consolidated After-Tax Income	15,149	−2,974	−19.6	−3,107	−20.5
U.S. Taxes Paid	6,005	3,028	50.4	2,953	49.2
Foreign Taxes Paid	5,001	−504	−10.1	−144	−2.9

Note Initial Values and Absolute Changes expressed in millions of dollars. Estimates include the repeal of deferral—see first three columns of Table 1. Both cases assume that the foreign tax credit is replaced by a deduction from taxable income. In Case 1 all parameters are as shown in Appendix Table A2; in Case 2 the investor raises the ratio of new debt to new funds *f* to unity, and the interest on that debt to equal the subsidiary's marginal cost of borrowing.

equity in financing foreign investment will limit the substitution of domestic for foreign investment.

Our numerical examples bring out this point quite clearly. The estimates presented in Table 3 show the impact of repealing deferral and the foreign tax credit and allowing only a deduction for foreign taxes. In Case 1 the firm continues its traditional mix of debt and equity in financing foreign expansion; in Case 2 it uses only debt in financing new foreign investment and charges interest equal to the subsidiary's marginal cost of borrowing. The substitution of domestic for foreign investment is far greater in Case 1 (where the firm relies on its traditional debt-equity mix) than in Case 2 (where it shifts from equity to debt). Notice the substantial increase in U.S. taxes and the consequent decrease in consolidated corporate earnings and new investment. In fact, had the elasticities of investment demand and loanable funds been less than we supposed, the lost liquidity could more than offset the substitution effect, and domestic investment would *fall* with the repeal of the foreign tax credit. Finally, we note that the intrafirm flow of funds, already diminished by the repeal of deferral, would reverse its direction. The subsidiary either advances funds to the U.S. parent or repatriates previously received capital. In actual practice, this backflow of foreign direct investment might be blocked and the substitution of domestic for foreign investment diminished.[12]

III. CONCLUSION

We have explored the effects of U.S. taxation of foreign investment income on foreign and domestic investment, the financing of that investment, the mix of debt and equity in advancing funds to a foreign subsidiary, and dividends, royalties, and other such intrafirm

[12]The foreign tax authorities, for example, might treat the repatriation of capital as dividends paid out of past earnings and thus subject to a withholding tax. Likewise, foreign subsidiaries' access to local capital markets might be curtailed if local borrowing exceeded local investment.

payments. Under existing U.S. policy, corporate income taxes on foreign income are deferred until the subsidiary formally pays a dividend to its U.S. parent, and the parent can claim a tax credit for income and withholding taxes paid to the foreign government. This policy encourages the use of equity rather than debt in financing foreign expansion and discourages the repatriation of foreign investment income; if income is repatriated, investors may want to make minimal interest, royalty, and other such payments to offset the excess tax credits generated by dividends. Current policy also offers an implicit tax incentive to investing overseas, and the size of the incentive increases the lower the foreign income tax, the lower the subsidiary's dividend payout rate, the less debt and the more equity used in financing foreign investment, and the lower the interest on intrafirm debt.

If deferral were repealed, so too would most of the tax incentives to invest abroad or to manipulate intrafirm accounts to avoid taxes. The impact of this and other tax changes can be disaggregated into a substitution and a liquidity effect. If the elasticities of investment opportunities at home and abroad are low, so too will be the induced substitution of domestic for foreign investment. Likewise, if the elasticities of the supply of outside funds are small, any tax increase will exercise a larger drag on the firm's rate of global investment.

We also explored the effects of compelling U.S. investors to charge their foreign subsidiaries with a higher proportion of current *R & D* expenses and of repealing the foreign tax credit. If foreign governments will allow higher deductions from the subsidiaries' taxable income, the United States would gain tax revenues at the expense of the foreign government. If higher deductions are disallowed, foreign investment income is subject to a disguised form of double taxation, U.S. tax payments rise, corporate after-tax income falls, and the rate of foreign investment contracts. Repealing the foreign tax credit would have a profound impact on a multinational's profitability and, if its ability to compensate for the lost liquidity with increased borrowing is small, on its rate of global investment. The substitution of domestic for foreign investment depends not only on the elasticities of investment opportunities, but also the firm's ability to substitute debt for equity in its internal financing of foreign investment.

This analysis can be extended in several directions. Additional foreign countries could be included; intrafirm exports might be taken into explicit account; other aspects of U.S. and foreign tax policy (for example, depreciation allowances, investment tax credits) could be explored; and better numerical estimates of the model's parameters could be developed. The analysis should incorporate the dynamics of investment planning even though the mathematics could become formidable. Finally, our characterization of a multinational's financial behavior was rudimentary. But the analysis showed that tax policy affects financial behavior, and financial behavior in turn mitigates the impact of tax policy on investment spending. This interaction between tax policy and multinational finance surely deserves further attention.

APPENDIX

TABLE A1

Summary of Mathematical Notation

Symbol	Meaning
R	Total return on investment net of labor and material costs, but gross of interest expense and income taxes
I	Investment
B	Total interest paid on external debt
L	Borrowing in external capital market
F	Transfer of investable funds (debt plus equity) from parent to subsidiary
E_R	Retained earnings available for new investment
i_p	Interest rate applied to intrafirm debt
f	Proportion of F which is debt rather than equity
h	Ratio of $R\&D$ and other headoffice charges to total foreign investment $I_0 + I$
E_B	Taxable income
T	Income taxes paid
t	Income tax rate
D	Dividends paid
p	Ratio of dividends paid to earnings after income taxes
E_A	Earnings after income taxes
W	Withholding taxes paid
w_D, w_B, w_H	Withholding tax rates applied to intrafirm dividends, interest, and headoffice charges, respectively
T_C	Foreign tax credit allowed
s_D, s_B, s_H	Relative shares of dividends, interest and headoffice charges in total foreign-source income
x	Binary variable equal to unity if and only if the investor has paid more foreign income and withholding taxes than are creditable
E_C^*	Consolidated (i.e., parent plus subsidiary) after-tax income
t_f	Effective global (i.e., foreign plus *U.S.*) rate of taxation of foreign-subsidiary income
r	Marginal revenue from additional investment, i.e., dR/dI
b	Marginal cost of additional outside borrowing, i.e., dB/dL

Notes The * denotes the parent's *U.S.* operations, the lack of one the subsidiary's foreign operations. The 0 subscript indicates a predetermined stock, the lack of one the current flow.

TABLE A2

Values and Sources of Parameter Estimates Used in Simulations

Parameter	Value	Definition and Source
b, b^*	.09	Assumed marginal cost of externally borrowed funds for parent or affiliate.
p	.42	Subsidiary's dividend payout ratio. According to the U.S. Office of Business Economics (1975), Table 4, p. 51, manufacturing affiliates had a gross dividends-earnings ratio of .40 in 1974. I have raised this estimate marginally to approximate a four- or five-year moving average.
p^*	.33	Parent's dividend payout ratio. This is the ratio of all *U.S.* manufacturing firms' dividends to after-tax earnings. See U.S. Office of Business Economics (1975), p. S-20.
t	.391	Foreign income tax rate. This estimate is based on Kyrouz's realized tax rates; see Bergsten, Horst, and Moran, Table 6-2, col. 1.
t^*	.48	*U.S.* statutory income tax rate.
E_B	10.67	Affiliate's before-tax earnings. According to the U.S. Office of Business Economics (1975), Table 11, p. 51, the after-tax earnings of manufacturing affiliates in 1974 was $6.498 billion. Since this is net of income taxes, I have grossed this figure up by dividing it by 1 – .391.

TABLE A2 (*Continued*)

Parameter	Value	Definition and Source
h	.011	Ratio of fees and royalties to total affiliate investment. According to the U.S. Office of Business Economics (1975), Table 10, p. 49, manufacturing affiliates paid fees and royalties amounting to $1.855 billion in 1974. There is no reliable estimate of the total assets of *U.S.* manufacturing affiliates to use in deflating this figure. I consulted the U.S. Senate Committee on Finance, Table 12, p. 432 and obtained the estimate for $78 billion in total assets in 1970. I assumed that total assets grew at an annual growth rate of 16.7 percent per annum (the rate of growth of affiliate sales) between 1970 and 1974, which gives an estimated total assets for 1974 of $170 billion. Dividing the $1.85 billion in royalties and fees by the $170 billion total assets yields the value for h of .011.
w_D, w_H, w_B	.15	Withholding tax rates applied to dividends, fees, and interest payments, respectively. I have assumed that a 15 percent rate is applied to each type of payment.
F	2.71	Net capital outflow from parent to affiliate. See U.S. Office of Business Economics (1975), Table 3, p. 47.
$R^* - B^*$	12.73	Parent's domestic income before taxes. According to Bergsten, Horst, and Moran, Table 6-1, 24 multinational manufacturers reporting sufficient statistics earned 54.4 percent of their book income before taxes from domestic operations. The $12.73 billion equals 54.4 percent of $12.73 billion plus $10.67 billion (the latter being my estimate of the affiliate's pre-tax earnings above).
r'	−.0025	The slope of the marginal revenue from new investment by the foreign affiliate. This slope was chosen because it implied that an elasticity of 2 for the marginal-revenue-from-new-affiliate-investment schedule.
$r^{*\prime}$	−.0012	The slope of the marginal revenue from new investment by the *U.S.* parent. Lacking any more reliable estimate, I assumed that the elasticity of investment demand at home, 2, was the same as that abroad.
b'	.0049	The slope of the marginal cost of outside capital schedule for the foreign affiliate. Once again, lacking any better estimate I assumed a slope which would make the elasticity of the schedule equal to 2.
$b^{*\prime}$	.0024	Slope of the marginal cost of outside capital schedule for the *U.S.* parent. I chose a slope such that the elasticity would once again equal 2.
I_0	170.	Foreign affiliate's total assets. See note for h above.
F_0	34.	Total capital transferred from parent to affiliate. Robbins and Stobaugh, Table 4-1, Table 2, indicate that 20 percent of manufacturing affiliates' sources of funds between 1966 and 1969 came from their parents. My $34 billion estimate for F_0 is 20 percent of the $170 billion estimate for I_0.
f, f_0	.64	Ratio of intrafirm debt to total capital transfer for new and existing investment, respectively. Estimate obtained directly from U.S. Office of Business Economics (1975), Table 3, p. 47 for incorporated manufacturing affiliates.
i_p, i_{p_0}	.031	Intrafirm interest rate. James Nunns and Gary Hufbauer, Table 2, and U.S. Office of Foreign Direct Investment allows us to calculate the ratio of intrafirm interest payments to intrafirm debt. This low average interest rate reflects the use of interest-free trade credits.
I	18.3	Subsidiary's new investment in 1974. The U.S. Office of Business Economics (1976) Table 1, p. 21 indicates that manufacturing affiliates capital expenditures were $11.7 billion in 1974. This figure includes only property, plant, and equipment expenditures, so I have increased this figure by 56 percent to include short-term capital formation. This 56 percent increase is based on the ratio of the estimated increase in total assets between 1970 and 1974 (see note for h above) and the total value of property, plant, and equipment expenditures over that same interval.
I^*	36.4	According to the U.S. Senate Committee on Finance, Table 12, p. 432, the increase in the total assets of the *U.S.* parents between 1966 and 1970 was 1.99 times as large as that of their foreign affiliates. My value of I^* is 1.99 times 18.3, my estimate of the value of I.

REFERENCES

C. Fred Bergsten, Thomas Horst, and Theodore Moran, *American Multinationals and American Interests*, Washington, forthcoming.

G. C. Hafbauer and D. Foster, "U.S. Taxation of the Undistributed Income of Controlled Foreign Corporations," Office of International Tax Affairs, Dept. of Treasury, Apr. 1976.

G. F. Kopits, "Dividend Remittance Behavior Within the International Firm: A Cross Country Analysis," *Rev. Econ. Statist.*, Aug. 1972, 54, 339–42.

______, "Intrafirm Royalties Crossing Frontiers and Transfer Pricing Behavior," unpub. manuscript, Nov. 1974.

M. E. Kyrouz, "Foreign Tax Rates and Tax Bases," *Nat. Tax. J.*, Mar. 1975, 28, 61–80.

J. R. Nunns and G. C. Hufbauer, "The United States Balance of Tax Payments on Foreign Investment and Employment," *Colum. J. World Bus.*, Summer 1975, *10*, 12–20.

Sidney M. Robbins and Robert V. Stobaugh, *Money in the Multinational Enterprise*, New York 1973.

U.S. Congress, Senate, Committee on Finance, *Implications of Multinational Firms for World Trade and Investment and for United States Trade and Labor*, Washington 1973.

U.S. Office of Business Economics, "U.S. Direct Investment Abroad in 1974," *Surv. Curr. Bus.*, Oct. 1974, 55, 43–63.

______, "Capital Expenditures by Majority-Owned Foreign Affiliates of U.S. Companies: 1975 and 1976 and 1966–76 Trends," *Surv. Curr. Bus.*, Mar. 1976, 56, 20–29.

U.S. Office of Foreign Direct Investment, *Foreign Affiliate Financial Survey*, Washington 1971.

30
Imputation Systems of Corporation Tax Within the EEC*

C. W. Nobes

The design of the present UK system of corporation tax is sometimes misunderstood. It becomes clearer when it is compared to the systems operated in other countries. This article contrasts the workings of imputation in our own and other systems. Also, one of the Meade Committee's proposals for reform is examined. Then, the behaviour of our system during an inflationary period is briefly discussed. Finally, the purposes and current progress of the harmonisation of corporate taxation in the EEC are looked at.

SYSTEMS OF CORPORATION TAX

Systems of corporation tax are often divided[1] into three types: imputation, classical and split-rate. The UK system in 1965–73 was a classical system. Under such systems, company profits are taxed without a deduction for dividends paid; then the dividends are fully taxed as investment income in the hands of the shareholders. The United States and the Netherlands are examples of countries which still have classical systems. These are described by other writers.[2]

The other two types of system (imputation and split-rate) are designed to mitigate the above 'economic double taxation' of dividends for the reasons mentioned below. Imputation systems approach this mitigation by imputing to the shareholders some or all of the tax paid by companies. For example, taxpayers in the UK are deemed to have paid tax at the basic rate on their dividends grossed up at the basic rate. Split-rate systems tax distributed profits at a lower rate than retained profits. Such systems have a similar effect to imputation systems. Indeed, the present UK imputation system can be redesigned to look like a split rate system with exactly the same corporation tax and income tax burdens (see the appendix).

There are other adjustments that can be made to mitigate double taxation. For example, in the USA the classical system is modified in that the first $100 of dividends received by an individual each year are exempted from personal income tax. Alternatively, the 'primary dividend' system allows companies to deduct some proportion of dividends in the calculation of their taxable incomes. Such a system has operated in Sweden and Iceland. We will return to different systems in the section on harmonisation. Meanwhile, attention will be directed to imputation systems.

The introduction of an imputation system in the UK in 1973 seems to have been the

---

*This article is reprinted, with permission, from *Accounting and Business Research*, Spring 1980, pp. 221–231.

[1] A. J. van den Tempel, *Corporation Tax and Individual Income Tax in the EEC*, Brussels, 1970; International Bureau of Fiscal Documentation, *European Taxation*, vol 12, nos 5 and 6, 1972; OECD, *Theoretical and Empirical Aspects of Corporate Taxation*, Paris, 1974.

[2] C. F. McCarthy, W. M. Mann and W. A. Gregory, *The Federal Income Tax*, Prentice-Hall, Englewood Cliffs, NJ, latest edition; J. F. Chown, *Taxation and Multinational Enterprise*, Longman, London, 1974, ch. 4; M. R. Saunders, *Tax Planning for Businesses in Europe*, Butterworth, London, 1977, ch. 8.

result of three main factors. First, there was the need to harmonise practice within the EEC. This will be discussed later. Second, there was an equity argument against the economic double taxation of dividends. This argument, also considered later, involves a comparison of incorporated and unincorporated businesses. The nature of the inequity depends on whether one is considering retained or distributed profit. This second argument was closely linked with a third: that an imputation system would encourage effective investment by reducing the classical system's bias against distribution of profits.

The purpose behind this third argument was a desire to improve the *quality* of investment. The theory is that there should be larger payments of dividends once economic double taxation is eased. This should lead to the movement of resources away from the many averagely profitable companies towards profit-maximising investors. These should direct the funds on to those companies which, because of their profit records, are most attractive and can use resources most effectively. Even if these larger dividend payments lead to smaller total investment, due to leakage into taxation and consumption, it can be argued that this should be more than compensated for by better quality investment.[3]

Unfortunately, it has not been possible to establish whether the imputation system in the UK would lead to greater dividends, because of such complicating factors since 1973 as high inflation and dividend restrictions. Also, it is not at all clear that it is possible for investors to tell which companies will make the best use of investment funds. A company's past record of profit does not reliably show that it will continue to be a more efficient user of investment resources.[4]

Having briefly introduced the imputation system, we should now look at how it works in the UK, France and West Germany.

THE WORKINGS OF THE UK IMPUTATION SYSTEM

One way of illustrating the workings of imputation is to make a comparison with the classical system. Suppose that a company earns net profits before tax of 10,000 every year. Suppose also that the rate of corporation tax under the UK classical system was 40% and under the imputation system is 52%. In each case, the basic rate of income tax is 33%. The tax credit *imputed* to unincorporated shareholders is linked to the basic rate of income tax for administrative simplicity. For this example, it is 33/67 of the cash dividend, as in 1978/79. Income tax is not deducted at source from dividends in the imputation system. (See box on next page).

This shows that, for the basic rate taxpayer, the payment of dividends causes no extra tax to be paid by either the company or the shareholder. (Advance Corporation Tax, ACT, is discussed below.) Consequently, when the tax on both company and shareholders is considered, companies with large payout ratios suffer less tax than they would under a classical system. This is despite the higher rate of corporation tax under the imputation system. The precise proportion of dividend payout above which this is true depends on the levels of corporation tax and income tax.

So far, shareholders have been assumed to be unincorporated. For corporate shareholders, there is a *full* imputation of the corporation tax borne by the paying company on

[3]OECD, *Theoretical and Empirical Aspects of Corporate Taxation*, Paris, 1974.

[4]G. Whittington, *The Prediction of Profitability*, Cambridge University Press, 1971, chs 4 and 5.

		Classical System		Imputation System	
Company:	Net profit before tax	10,000		10,000	
	less Corporation tax (40%)	4,000	(52%)	5,200	
	Profit available for distribution	6,000		4,800	
	Dividends (say)	2,000		1,340	
	Undistributed profit	4,000		3,460	
The 2,000 gross dividend under the classical system is equivalent to the 1,340 cash dividend under the imputation system:					
Shareholder:	Dividend	2,000		1,340	
	less Basic rate income tax deducted at source (33%)		660		0
	Cash received		1,340		1,340
	Tax credit imputed (33/67 × 1340)	—		660	
	Income to be taxed	2,000		2,000	
	Tax at basic rate (33%)	660		660	
	less Tax already paid	660		—	
	less Tax credit imputed	—		660	
	Tax due		0		0
	Net dividend after tax		1,340		1,340

the profits out of which the dividends are paid. That is, the receiving company pays no tax on its dividend income.

Returning to unincorporated shareholders, those who pay no income tax because of low taxable incomes can claim 'repayment' of the tax credit. Those whose marginal rates are above the basic rate pay income tax on the 2,000 of the above example and can claim the tax credit. The effect on higher rate taxpayers is interesting. Let us use the above example but take 98% marginal income tax rate (i.e. 83% income tax and 15% investment income surcharge; the highest rates in 1978/79).

Shareholder:		
Cash dividend		1,340
Imputed credit (33/67)	660	
	2,000	
Income tax (98%)	1,960	
Tax credit	660	
Tax to pay		1,300
Post-tax receipt		40

The tax rate here on the cash dividend is 97% (i.e. 1,300/1,340). This means that the so called 'tax credit' has merely reduced the individual's tax rate by 1%. Note that for basic rate taxpayers, the effective rate of income tax on *cash* dividends is 0%; but for 98% taxpayers it is 97% (rather than 98% less 33% as might appear at first sight). For these latter taxpayers, there is little useful imputation of the 5,200 corporation tax borne by the paying company. There is full corporate taxation of the company's taxable profit, followed by 97% taxation on the cash dividend paid out of that taxed profit.

Under the 'classical' system of 1965–73, the 98% taxpayer would have been treated as follows, using the same basic rate of income tax:

Gross dividend		2,000
Tax deducted at source (33%)		660
Net dividend received		1,340
Tax on 2,000 at 98%	1,960	
Tax already deducted	660	
Tax to pay		1,300
Post-tax receipt		40

This shows that, despite the remarks in the preceding paragraphs, the present partial imputation system is better for dividend recipients than the classical system, even for high rate taxpayers. To achieve a post-tax receipt of .40 under a classical system, the company has to pay out 2,000 rather than 1,340. Therefore, the bias against distribution has been lessened by the change to the imputation system. However, it has certainly not been removed, unless none of the shareholders pays tax at above the basic rate. As will be shown later, the bias *can* be removed by such an imputation system as that of West Germany.

If similar calculations to those above are performed for other rates of income tax, the table below can be constructed. It shows how the imputation system becomes steadily less useful as higher rates of personal taxation are reached. The general relationship is that the 'effective rate' is given by (m–b)/(l–b), where m is the marginal rate and b is the basic rate.[5]

Individual Marginal Tax Rate (m) %	Effective Rate on Cash Dividend %
33	0
50	25
70	55
98	97

This 'effective rate' is *negative* for those paying 0% or 25% marginal tax rates. This rate is relevant for dividend policy. Assuming that the company can reclaim ACT (see below), the 'effective rate' is the one that determines the extra tax which will be borne by the company-plus-shareholders as a result of the payment of dividend. In the case of non-taxpayers, the total tax borne by company-plus-shareholders will actually *fall* as a result of a payment of dividends.

It should be noted in summary that a partial imputation system *can* totally remove double taxation and the bias against distribution when the tax credit cancels the personal liability. Alternatively, the double taxation can be removed by imputing all the corporation tax to shareholders; but even if there is no double taxation because there is no effective liability to corporation tax, there could still be some bias against distribution if personal income tax is larger than the underlying corporation tax and only operates when dividends are paid.

[5] i.e. $\left(\frac{Dm}{1-b} - \frac{Db}{1-b}\right) + D$, where D is the cash dividend.

ADVANCE CORPORATION TAX

A source of some confusion is the Advance Corporation Tax (ACT). This is an advance on the later payment of corporation tax (9–21 months after a company's year-end). It is not an essential part of an imputation system, as will be shown. It was designed mainly to improve the government's cash flow by speeding up tax payments. A second reason for it relates to those cases where there is no corporation tax liability (CTL) for there to be an advance of. This reason is discussed later.

ACT is related in size to the level of dividend payments: in 1978/79 it amounted to 33/67 of the dividend, when the basic rate of income tax was 33%. Any ACT paid[6] causes a set-off against the eventual CTL leaving only the difference (mainstream corporation tax) to be paid. ACT is *not*, therefore, an extra tax on dividends, assuming that there is an adequate CTL.

One supposes that, when the imputation system was planned, it was not clear that there would often be inadequate corporation tax liabilities to allow a full ACT set-off. This problem of 'unrelieved' ACT occurs because of low profits and high tax allowances. Particularly in inflationary periods, capital allowances and stock reliefs may greatly reduce taxable profits. In addition, despite low taxable profits, dividends have been rising in money terms. As far as has been possible within a period of dividend restraint, dividend policy seems to have been based on a desire to compensate shareholders for a fall in the real value of dividends rather than on estimates of changes in 'real' profit.[7] Therefore, there have been many examples of unrelieved ACT.[8]

This illustrates the second reason for ACT. That is, it ensures that imputation credits are not granted to recipients of dividends when there has been no underlying payment of corporation tax to impute. ACT is paid on dividends irrespective of a company's taxable profits and can normally only be relieved against CTL. Consequently, the shareholders' tax credits will always have been paid for.[9] In order to make this operate more exactly, the ACT set-off in any year is limited to the amount of ACT that would relate to a dividend that, when 'grossed up' for the ACT, would absorb all the taxable income. To reduce the harshness of this, unrelieved ACT can be carried back for 2 years or forward indefinitely against other years' CTL.

A prevalent misconception is that the reason there are tax credits in the UK imputation system is because there is an ACT. We have seen that, for the above two good reasons, the tax credits amount to the same size as the ACT. However, in theory, the tax credits are not due to ACT but are a partial imputation of the CTL in order that double taxation of dividends is mitigated. This general point about imputation systems is made clear by two aspects of the French and German systems. These are that, in each case, the imputation tax credits are based on the rates of *corporation* tax and that there are no general equivalents of ACT. Perhaps even more revealing is the fact that the Irish imputation system, although it has a tax credit based on the basic rate of income tax and operates in other ways similarly to the UK system, also has no ACT.[10]

[6]ACT is paid using a quarterly accounting system. The need to pay ACT is cancelled out to the extent that the company has received franked investment income which has caused ACT to be paid by the paying company.

[7]P. R. A. Kirkman and C. W. Nobles, 'Dividend policy and inflation', *Accountancy*, October, 1976.

[8]e.g. 'Now institutional shareholders hit back', *Accountancy*, August, 1975.

[9]Either by the paying company or another company; see note 6.

[10]*Corporation Tax Act 1976 (Ireland)*; SSAP, CCAB Accountancy Bodies, 1977, Appendix 3.

Having outlined the UK system, it is now time to draw contrasts with the French and German systems. In each case, the rules relating to the determination of taxable income, capital gains, tax collection, etc. are interestingly different from UK practice.[11] However, our present purpose requires that attention be directed to the methods of imputation.

THE FRENCH IMPUTATION SYSTEM

Corporation tax in France is levied at a rate of 50% on taxable profit. Dividends are not deductible in the calculation of taxable profit; they are paid out of taxed profit. Also, these dividends are subject to personal income tax in the hands of the recipients. However, there is a tax credit (*avoir fiscal*) which imputes to the shareholders some of the tax paid by the company. So far, the system is similar to the Uk partial imputation system. An important difference is that the size of the tax credit is not linked to the basic rate of income tax, but is one half of the underlying corporation tax on the dividends. An example follows.

Company:	Taxable profits	10,000
	Corporation tax	5,000
	Distributable profit	5,000
	Dividend	4,000
	Undistributed profit	1,000
Shareholder:	Dividend	4,000
	Avoir fiscal	2,000
	Taxable income	6,000
	Tax credit available	2,000

This 50% imputation is of a similar size to the UK imputation (see section on harmonisation). However, because the top rates of French income tax are low compared to those in the UK, the imputation remains very useful for all unincorporated shareholders.

The French treatment of *corporate* shareholders is very different from UK practice. Instead of full imputation of corporation tax, the treatment depends on whether or not the recipient is a 'holding' company (one that owns at least 10% or FF 10m in the paying company). Holding companies pay tax on 5% of (grossed up) dividend income and take the tax credit appropriate to that proportion. Other companies pay corporation tax on all dividends. These dividends are grossed up by the tax credit which is then available to the company. In the above example, if the shareholder were a non-holding company, the corporation tax due on the 'net' dividend income of 4,000 would be 1,000 (i.e. 6,000 × 50% less 2,000 tax credit).

As can be seen from the definition of a holding company, this disadvantageous tax treatment, under which dividends may partially bear corporation tax several times, only applies to small holdings, not to subsidiaries or important trade investments. These latter holdings receive approximately full imputation, as mentioned above.

It should be noted that there is no general equivalent of ACT in the French imputation system. However, in cases where no French corporation tax has been borne on income out of which dividends are paid, a *précompte* of 33⅓ is deducted at source from the

[11] J. F. Chown, *op. cit*, ch. 4; M. R. Saunders, *op. cit.*, chs 2 and 3.

dividend. This is charged in order to cover the net cost to the Revenue of the *avoir fiscal* available to the recipients. An example of this occurs where a French company receives dividend or branch income from abroad and has chosen to pay corporation tax on income from French sources only.[12] (An analogous option is not available to UK companies; and a *précompte* would not be necessary anyway because of ACT.)

THE WEST GERMAN IMPUTATION SYSTEM

By the corporation tax reform law of 1976, the split-rate system of corporation tax was replaced by an imputation system from 1st January 1977. However, the German imputation system continues to include different rates for distributed and undistributed profits: 36% for the former and 56% for the latter. Credit for the *full* amount of the underlying corporation tax is given to the recipients of dividends. There is also a withholding tax of 25% on dividends, which is a deduction of tax at source by the paying company on behalf of the Revenue authorities. It is designed to make evasion more difficult. Resident shareholders can claim credit for the withholding tax. These various points can be illustrated:

Company:	1.	Taxable income		10,000	
	2.	Normal rate corporation tax (56%)		5,600	
	3.	Balance before relief		4,400	
	4.	Retained profit (e.g. ¼)		1,100	
	5.	Distribution (¾)		3,300	
	6.	Reduction of corporation tax		1,500	i.e. (56% less 36%) of ¾ of 10,000
	7.	Total distribution		4,800	
	8.	Withholding tax (25%)		1,200	
	9.	Net distribution		3,600	
Shareholder:	10.	Net distribution		3,600	
	11.	Tax credits: withholding	1,200		
	12.	imputed	2,700		i.e. 36% of ¾ of 10,000
				3,900	
	13.	Taxable income		7,500	
	14.	Income tax (e.g. 40%)		3,000	
	15.	Tax credits		3,900	
	16.	Refund		900	

Note that the reduction in corporation tax in line 6 means that distributed income bears only 36% tax. The shareholders receive the net distribution after a withholding tax (line 8), which can be treated as a tax credit (line 11). The imputed tax credit in line 12 is the full amount of corporation tax borne on the distributed income. The result of all this is that the company has paid 4,100 (i.e. 5,600 less 1,500) in corporation tax and has also deducted and paid 1,200 in withholding tax on the distribution. The shareholders pay no

[12] M. R. Saunders, *op. cit.*, ch 2.

further tax and, moreover, they receive a refund of 900. The total received by the shareholders is, therefore, 4,500 (i.e. 3,600 + 900). This is 60% (because 40% has gone in income tax) of 7,500 (i.e. the distribution of $\frac{3}{4}$ of the income of 10,000).

This demonstrates that, as a result of full imputation, dividends bear no corporation tax but only income tax. The double taxation of dividend income has been completely removed for all unincorporated shareholders. This is very different in its effects from the UK system. Indeed, unlike a split-rate system, this German dual-rate imputation system cannot be re-expressed in order to behave identically to the British or French imputation systems. It is essentially a different kind of system. Ironically, although a move to an 'imputation' system appears to be a harmonising action, the previous German split-rate system was closer in effect to the British or French systems.

Turning to corporate shareholders, they also receive full imputation because dividend income is exempt from corporation tax when received by holding companies (those with at least a 25% holding). Alternatively, when the recipient is not a holding company, the treatment is similar to that for unincorporated shareholders. This includes the charging of a withholding tax and the process of imputation. The net result is that the dividend income only bears corporation tax once.

Again there is no ACT. However, there is a similar German provision to the French *précompte* in those cases where income paid out as dividends has not borne German corporation tax due to double taxation treaties or other reasons.

THE MEADE COMMITTEE

The Meade Committee[13] devoted some attention to the major problem in corporate taxation which imputation is designed to solve, that is the different taxation of retained and distributed profits. On the one hand, it might be argued that any double taxation of income (on the company and on the shareholder) is inequitable when comparisons are made with unincorporated businesses. This argument is used to justify imputation of corporation tax to the shareholders. On the other hand, it is argued that it is inequitable, again compared to unincorporated businesses, to allow companies to accumulate retained profits which have not borne tax at the shareholders' marginal rates. This argument may justify a separate corporation tax at a higher rate than basic rate income tax, if shareholders are assumed to pay higher rates of tax.

One approach to solving these problems is that of the split-rate systems, which have a lower rate of corporation tax for distributed income than for retained income. Other approaches seen above are to tax corporate profits at fairly high rates and then to impute all or part of this tax to shareholders with their distributions.

The Meade Committee reasonably proposed that the theoretically correct solution is for retained profit to be apportioned to shareholders just as if they were partners ploughing profit back. This apportionment would be taxed with the dividends at the shareholders' marginal tax rates. There would be a full imputation of corporation tax via a tax credit on both distributed and apportioned profit. In this way, the company would effectively bear no tax, and corporation tax would be a sort of withholding tax. This would solve the problems of double taxation and retained profits. Incidentally, it would be necessary to

[13]Meade Committee. *The Structure and Reform of Direct Taxation*, IFS/Allen and Unwin, London, 1978, chs 7 and 12.

adjust capital gains tax in order to avoid a double taxation of the gains arising from retained profits.

Clearly, there would be some administrative problems with this system and some unfortunate implications for the cash flow of shareholders of companies which retain a high proportion of profits. However, the idea is very attractive theoretically. The present German system's treatment of *distributed* income is close to the Meade suggestions; and it taxes retained profits at a rate (56%) which is also the top marginal rate of income tax. The UK provisions that require close companies to apportion about half of their profits to shareholders so that they may bear income tax are also concerned with this problem.

INFLATION

There are numerous detailed differences between the operations of the different corporation taxes discussed in this article. These are not so much differences of broad *system* but alternative ways of measuring taxable income, treating income from abroad, and so on. These matters are vital for many companies but must be left for tax books[14] and tax professionals. However, there are two particular differences between UK and Franco-German practice which might be said to amount to a difference of system with respect to inflation adjustments.

The first difference is that there has been a system of stock relief[15] in the UK since 1973, which approximately subjects taxable profit to a 'cost-of-sales adjustment'[16] by removing part of the holding gain on stocks. This is a very important adjustment (see Table A). In a similar way, US companies are allowed to use a last-in first-out (LIFO) system of inventory valuation as a partial correction. However, in France and Germany (and other continental European countries) there is no adjustment for stock holding gains.

The second difference is that in France and Germany (and indeed in most of the rest of the EEC and in the USA) depreciation is an allowable expense for tax purposes. Depreciation rates are generally prescribed and based on estimated useful lives of the appropriate assets. In contrast to this, the UK system of capital allowances means that the whole cost of plant and machinery and 54% of industrial buildings can be charged against profit in the year of purchase. In the year of purchase, the historic cost *is* the current cost. In this sense, there is also a 'depreciation adjustment'[16] to taxable profit (see Table A).

As a result of these two factors, the UK corporation tax system adjusts taxable income in a very approximate way towards a current cost operating profit figure. This reduces (or possibly even eliminates) the extent to which taxation is based on unrealistically high profit figures during inflationary periods. This is not the case with the French and German corporation taxes.

HARMONISATION

The Treaty of Rome calls for the elimination of customs duties between member states, the introduction of common tariffs with third countries, and the removal of barriers to the free movement of persons, capital, goods and services. The interest in taxation shown by the EEC Commission, which is the guardian of the Treaty of Rome, stems from this

[14]J. F. Chown, *op. cit.*: M. R. Saunders, *op. cit.*

[15]S. R. James and C. W. Nobes, *The Economics of Taxation*, Philip Allan, Oxford, 1978, ch. 12.

[16]Accounting Standards Committee. *Current Cost Accounting, ED18*, London, 1976.

TABLE A

The Value of Tax Allowances to UK Companies £m

	1974	1975	1976
Capital allowances	2,981	3,589	4,149
Stock relief	720	1,490	940
Taxes on company income	1,957	1,955	2,316

Sources *National Income and Expenditure 1966–1976*. Central Statistical Office HMSO, 1978, pp 39 and 132; *Times Business News*, 30 March 1977, page 21; *Accountancy Age*, 3 March 1978, page 3.

Notes The 'value' of the capital allowances is taken to be 52% of their size. The figures for stock relief relate to fiscal years rather than calendar years. The table is drawn from several sources and, therefore, should be taken to give only a broad indication of magnitudes.

desire to promote the free movement of persons, capital, goods and services. The free movement of goods and services implies particularly the harmonisation of indirect taxes. Similarly the free movement of people and capital implies the harmonisation of direct taxes. If there were no harmonisation of taxes and if barriers to movement were eliminated, there might then be encouragement or obstruction of flows of people, capital and so on to particular countries within the EEC for purely fiscal reasons.

It is the aim of harmonisation[17] that the conditions of competition and the returns to capital and effort should not be significantly affected by differences in effective tax burdens. Just by having looked at the corporate taxation systems in three EEC countries, it should be clear that the scope for harmonisation is considerable. However, there are much larger differences—for example, the Netherlands and Luxembourg have classical systems of corporation tax. The EEC Commission's activity in this area of tax harmonisation will now be charted.

In 1962, the Neumark Committee[18] recommended to the Commission that a split-rate system should be adopted. As has been said, this is similar to the pre-1977 German system and is designed to mitigate the effects of 'economic double taxation' of dividends by including a lower rate of corporation tax on distributed profits. In 1970, the van den Tempel Report[19] described the three types of corporation tax systems, and recommended the classical system.

However, the Commission's draft Directive[20] of 1975 on the harmonisation of corporate taxation proposes the imputation system. This must be due partly to the fact that a majority of EEC countries were already using such a system or had plans to introduce one. In 1975, Belgium, France and the UK were using an imputation system. Since then,

[17]D. Dosser, *British Taxation and the Common Market*, Charles Knight, London, 1973, ch. 1, 4 and 6; and R. Burke, 'Harmonisation of Corporation Tax' *Intertax*, June–July, 1979.

[18]Neumark Committee, *EEC Reports on Tax Harmonisation*, International Bureau of Fiscal Documentation, Amsterdam, 1963.

[19]A. J. van den Tempel, *Corporation Tax and Individual Income Tax in the EEC*, Brussels, 1970.

[20]EEC Commission, *Proposal for a Directive concerning the Harmonization of Systems of Company Taxation and of Withholding Taxes on Dividends*, COM(75) 392 final, Brussels, 1975.

TABLE B

EEC Imputation Systems in 1979

Country	Imputation Introduced	National Corporation Tax Rate %	Tax Credit as Proportion of Dividend	Tax Credit as % of Underlying CT
Belgium	1963	48	57·5	62·29
France	1965	50	50	50
UK	1973	52	42.9 (i.e. 30/70)	39·56
Ireland	1976	45	42.9 (i.e. 30/70)	52·38
W. Germany	1977	56 & 36	56.25	100
Denmark	1977	37	15	25·54
Italy	1977	25[1]	33.33	100

Source for columns 3 and 4: Sections E of *The Taxation of Private Investment Income*. International Bureau of Fiscal Documentation.

Note Withholding taxes have been ignored throughout.

[1]There is also a deductible local income tax of 15°, making a total of 36.25%.

Germany, Denmark, Ireland and Italy have introduced one. For rates of tax and tax credit see Table B.

Some of the reasons[21] for choosing an imputation system have been mentioned. They include the fact that the tax credit reduces the bias against distribution and favours small investors (lower rate taxpayers). Also, the system should reduce the incentive for evasion by lowering the effective marginal rate of tax on dividends. In addition, since the corporation tax rate tends to be higher under an imputation system, there is a fairer comparison between the rates of tax borne on company retained profits and partnership profits.

The draft Directive proposes that there shall be imputation systems in operation with a single rate of tax between 45% and 55% (Article 3).[22] Also, Article 8 proposes that imputation credits shall be between 45% and 55% of the corporation tax that would have to be paid on a sum equal to the taxable income out of which the dividend could be paid (i.e. on the dividend increased by the corporation tax). For example, looking at the UK system in 1978/9:

Taxable income	1,000
Corporation tax	520
	480
Dividends	480
Undistributed profit	0
Recipients' income	480.00
Tax credit (33/67)	236.42
'Grossed up' dividend	716.42

[21]International Bureau of Fiscal Documentation, *European Taxation*, Vol. 16, Nos. 2,3,4, 1976, pp. 41–51.

[22]C. W. Nobes, 'EEC imputation systems of corporation tax', *Journal of Business Law*, July 1979.

$$\frac{\text{Tax credit}}{\text{Corporation tax}} = \frac{236.42}{520.00} = \qquad 45.47\%$$

Full distribution has been chosen so that it is easy to see that '520' is the corporation tax that would be paid on the dividends 'grossed up' at the corporation tax rate. The level of distribution will not affect this percentage.

It can be seen that, with the credit at 33/67, the UK system satisfies the above requirements. However, as was mentioned earlier, there are strong administrative reasons for linking the imputation credit directly with the basic rate of income tax. The lowering of the rate of 30% for 1979/80 reduces the credit percentage to 39·56% which falls below the Directive's guidelines.

Another requirement of the draft Directive is that the corporation tax and imputation credits should not be discriminatory between companies or shareholders in different member states (Article 4). For example, the tax credit should be available to all. Further, the costs of the tax credit should be borne eventually by the state of the distributing corporation, even though another state may lose income tax revenue initially. There is to be a clearing house arrangement for settling such claims.

There was a discussion above on the usefulness of ACT as a means of ensuring that imputation credits cannot be granted without the payment of underlying corporation tax by the distributing company. The draft Directive is concerned with this area, and Article 9 proposes a *précompte* (or compensatory tax) for distributions where there is insufficient taxed profit in the present or preceding *five* years.

Also, Articles 14 to 17 propose a withholding tax of 25% on dividends. This is designed to discourage tax evasion by arranging for deduction of tax at source. The tax can be treated as a credit by EEC shareholders. This presents a significant disadvantage to investors in third countries. It is hoped that this problem will be alleviated before the Directive is passed.

The draft Directive has been criticised on many grounds. The omission of a proposed treatment for capital gains is important. Unless their taxation is also harmonised, there will be much wasteful manoeuvring in order to create capital gains in favourable member States rather than *income* in any State or capital gains in unfavourable States. Another criticism is that other corporate taxes, like net worth, turnover and local taxes, must be included in the harmonisation. More generally, the different rules relating to the calculation of taxable income need attention if total effective tax burdens are to be harmonised. A further criticism is that some countries in the EEC are intrinsically less attractive to companies for economic, geographical and political reasons; and that these countries need advantageous corporate tax regimes if they are to encourage investment and employment. Therefore, to harmonise taxation without altering these other factors might give rise to unpleasant regional side-effects.

The 'opinion' of the European Parliament[23] on the draft Directive has stressed the need to include the problem of different tax bases as well as tax systems. Partly as a result of this and partly because member states are not enthusiastic about changing their tax systems or losing flexibility, the 1975 draft Directive (and that of 1978 concerning the

[23] *Official Journal*, 1979, C 140.

taxation of financial institutions)[24] have been delayed and may need considerable amendment.

Meanwhile, little notice seems to have been taken of the draft Directive. For example, the new German system goes outside the proposals in a number of ways.[25] It has two rates rather than a single rate, both of which are outside the proposed range. Also, the tax credit is outside the range. Indeed, as far as rates are concerned, Table B shows that three out of the seven EEC countries with imputation systems had corporation tax rates outside the proposed range in 1979, and five out of the seven had tax credits outside the proposed range. These five include three of the systems introduced after the draft was issued.

So, harmonisation will probably be a slow process, and it needs to advance on a wider front than at present proposed. However, the proposals should give an indication of the direction of future changes in corporate taxation in the EEC.

SUMMARY

Corporation tax systems may be divided into three types with respect to their approaches to the taxation of distributed income. Imputation and split-rate systems are both designed to mitigate the economic double taxation of dividends which is inherent in classical systems. The former two systems can be viewed as different expressions of the same system. This article is mainly concerned with imputation systems, particularly those of the UK, France, West Germany and Ireland. Of these, only the German involves the full imputation to the shareholders of the corporation tax paid by the company. The others, therefore, still entail some double taxation of distributed income for higher rate taxpayers. In the UK for the highest rate taxpayers, there is almost complete double taxation.

The UK system is the only one in the EEC to include a general ACT. It is also unusual in that the tax credit attached to dividends is linked to the basic rate of income tax and has been contrived to be the same size as the ACT.

The French have one of the oldest imputation systems. It involves a tax credit of half the underlying rate of corporation tax. Unlike the UK system, the French system entails less than full imputation for incorporated shareholders. There is a *précompte* to pay for the tax credit where no French corporation tax has been paid.

The recent West German imputation system has two rates of tax, and full imputation to shareholders. This completely removes the economic double taxation of dividends. There is a similar provision to the *précompte*.

The Meade Committee recommended a system that would tax both distributed and retained profits at the shareholders' marginal rates of income tax. There would be full imputation of corporation tax. In this way, retained profits would not be allowed to accumulate without bearing income tax, but no profits would suffer economic double taxation.

An important difference between the UK and continental imputation systems is that the former is approximately adjusted for the effects of inflation.

Proposals for harmonisation of corporate taxation within the EEC date back almost as

[24]EEC Commission, *Proposal for a Directive on the Application to Collective Investment Institutions* [of the 1975 draft Directive]. COM(78) 340 final. Brussels.

[25]R. T. Bartlett, 'The harmonization of company taxation within the EEC'. *Journal of Business Law*, July 1977.

far as its foundation. The most recent proposals are contained in a draft Directive of 1975, which has yet to be approved by the Council of Ministers. It proposes an imputation system with rates and tax credits within certain bands. However, there seems little prospect of immediate progress in this area. The four EEC imputation systems introduced since the draft have all gone against it in some way. Also, the major differences in the determination of taxable income mean that the draft Directive would not harmonise tax burdens even if it harmonised some aspects of tax systems.

APPENDIX

THE RESTATING OF THE UK IMPUTATION SYSTEM TO RESEMBLE A SPLIT-RATE SYSTEM

Taking the same corporation tax rate as that used to illustrate the imputation system in the second section of the paper, let us redesign the system to make it look like a split-rate system without ACT.

	Imputation System	
Net price before tax	10,000	
less Corporation tax (52%)	5,200	(ACT = 660, MCT = 4540)
Distributable profits	4,800	
Dividends (say)	1,340	
Undistributed profits	3,460	
Cash dividends received by shareholder	1,340	
Tax credit imputed (33/67)	660	
Income to be taxed	2,000	
Tax at basic rate (33%)	660	
Tax credit	660	
Tax due	0	
or		
Tax at higher rate (e.g. 50%)	1,000	
Tax credit	660	
Tax due	340	

	Split-Rate System		
Net profit before tax	10,000		
For distribution	2,000		2,000
	8,000	tax deducted at source (33%)	
Tax at 52% on 8,000 = 4,160			660
		net cash dividend	1,340
Tax at 19% on 2,000 = 380			
	4,540		
Undistributed profit	3,460		
Gross taxable dividend	2,000		
Tax at basic rate (33%)	660		
Tax deducted at source	660		
Tax due	0		
Tax at higher rate (e.g. 50%)	1,000		
Tax deducted at source	660		
Tax due	340		

Let us now postulate a split-rate system with a corporation tax rate of 52% on undistributed profit, and 19% on distributed profit. Basic rate income tax is deducted at source under this system. Note that real split-rate systems usually work in the way illustrated, that is with the tax on the distributed income being paid out of the more highly taxed income (see above).

Notice that, in each case, the total tax paid by the company to the Revenue is 5,200. Also, the timing of the payments will be the same. The 660 paid in the split-rate system will be equivalent to ACT. The 4,540 will be equivalent to Mainstream Corporation Tax. Also, the net income tax due is the same for both 'systems'.

More generally, let

C_r = nominal rate applicable to retained profit
C_d = nominal rate applicable to distributed profit
t = rate of tax credit as proportion of dividend
m = marginal rate of income tax paid by shareholders
b = basic rate of income tax
Y = taxable income
D = cash dividend

Imputation System: $(C_r = C_d)$. Corporation tax liability (CTL) $= C_r \cdot Y$

(i) $\text{ACT} = D \cdot \dfrac{b}{1 - b}$

Tax credit $= Dt$

(ii) Total income tax paid later $= m \cdot D \cdot (1 + t) - Dt$

(iii) $MCT = CTL - ACT = C_r \cdot Y - D \cdot \frac{b}{1 - b}$

Split-Rate System: Gross dividend $= D \cdot \frac{1}{1 - b}$

(iii) Total corporation tax $= C_r \cdot \left(Y - D \cdot \frac{1}{1 - b}\right) + C_d \cdot D \cdot \frac{1}{1 - b}$

(i) Total income tax deducted at source $= D \cdot \left(\frac{1}{1 - b}\right) \cdot b = D \cdot \frac{b}{1 - b}$

(ii) Total income tax paid later $= mD \frac{1}{1 - b} - D \cdot \frac{b}{1 - b}$

Now, let particular rates be chosen so that $C_r = C_d + b$. Also, let us set $t = \frac{b}{1 - b}$ as in the UK. A little algebraical manipulation will prove that the payments made at the same time are the same under both systems, that is (i) is the same under both systems, (ii) is the same, etc.

Part IV
Investment and Long-Term Financing

INTRODUCTION

The primary determinants of long-term strategic decisions are conditions in product and factor markets that a firm can profitably exploit given its experience and organizational skills. Financial considerations are of critical importance in the evaluation of alternative product/market/technology opportunities but seldom are major sources of value in their own right. This is due to the fact that financial markets, by and large, are relatively efficient. As a result, various types of financial contracts are likely to be fairly priced, and many financial choices are of limited relevance.

There are exceptions, of course. In the domestic U.S. setting, appropriate financing choices can add value by reducing taxes or by exploiting implicit or explicit financial grants provided by governmental agencies. Internationally, opportunities for adding value through financing choices are more widespread, reflecting complex interactions of various national tax systems, barriers or controls on financial transfers, gaps in financial markets, and much greater government involvement in the financing of industry in certain countries.

The evaluation of projects is also substantially more complex in an international context because of these currency, tax, and financing considerations. Thus, in making investment and financing decisions internationally, the manager must contend with a larger number of considerations that are relevant and must be able to cut through the confusion and complexity resulting from many of these same factors.

Part IV is organized in two sections. The first group of articles focuses on the financing of the firm doing business internationally, the second on the evaluation of foreign projects.

Financing Decisions and Techniques

Lessard and Shapiro (Article 31) discuss the various factors that distinguish financing choices in a multinational context from those in the single-country case and argue that most issues are related to one of three objectives: minimizing taxes, exploiting financial market distortions, and managing risks. Their discussion abstracts from the problem of selecting the overall debt-equity mix since there is little theory to suggest that this problem is drastically different in the multinational as compared to single-country case. Not surprisingly, they suggest that tax minimization is the major source of value added from appropriate financing decisions, but also suggest that given the types of credit and foreign exchange controls often in place, firms are likely to encounter distortions in financial markets that they can exploit profitably given sufficient internal financing latitude. Finally, they argue that arranging a firm's financing to lay off key exogenous risks such as foreign exchange risks is likely to add value because of various organizational complications arising from undue volatility of cash flows and profits.

Dufey and Giddy (Article 32) describe a variety of recent innovations in international financial markets including new trade financing techniques such as forfeiting, credit transactions denominated in currencies other than that of jurisdiction in which the transactions take place, options and a series of swaps and parallel loans, and foreign exchange options. They explain these innovations in terms of changing conditions that allow institutions or markets to supply them and, most importantly, explain demands for these innovations in terms of the types of benefits that individuals or corporations can gain from them. The authors present a picture of considerable financing flexibility with innovations that allow the separation of many different attributes previously bundled together on a standardized basis.

Capital Budgeting

The scope of the section dealing with project evaluation is limited to the financial evaluation of the project cash flows and does not include the rich and complex economic and strategic factors that give rise to these cash flows. (Articles 4 and 5 provide an overview of the relevant economic theory.) In the first article, Shapiro (Article 33) identifies the key considerations that distinguish project evaluation in the international setting from its domestic counterpart and suggests how these factors can be incorporated in a standard capital budgeting framework. Lessard (Article 34) outlines an approach for treating each of these differentiating factors separately and explicitly. He also provides suggestions for simplified treatments of currency adjustments based on the equilibrium tendencies outlined in Part II and links the discount rates used in evaluating foreign projects to the concepts of international asset valuation introduced in Part I.

Financing Decisions and Techniques

31

Guidelines for Global Financing Choices*

Donald R. Lessard and Alan C. Shapiro

INTRODUCTION

The financing choices of a firm operating within a single country are typically limited to the type of instruments it issues and the timing of those issues. Multinational corporations (MNCs) are faced with other financing choices as well. They must decide on the currency of issue, the jurisdiction of issue, and the corporate legal vehicle through which the issue is made. Also, if funds are raised by a legal unit other than the one where they are needed, the MNC must select the form of inter-affiliate transfer of the funds. In making these choices, management must consider the availability of funds, their relative costs, and the extent to which such financing either increases or offsets the firm's operating risks.

Besides choosing the best financing vehicles, financial executives of multinationals must address a number of other important financing issues. One concerns the firm's global financial structure. Should each affiliate have a capital structure based on local norms, or instead attempt to mirror the firm's worldwide debt-equity target? And to what extent should this decision be influenced by the tax deductibility of interest payments and also by considerations of "agency costs"—those potential problems associated with the incentives and the accountability of local subsidiary management that can be affected by 'the firm's' method of financing its subsidiaries?

Another issue concerns the cost and risk associated with debt denominated in different currencies. For example, should Volkswagen finance its U.S. operations with deutschemark debt at 8 percent or dollar debt at 12 percent? This choice will be influenced by expectations about future movements in the deutschemark/dollar exchange rate relative to the 4 percent interest differential, and also by the nature and degree of exchange risk facing Volkswagen.

The possibility of credit and exchange controls and other forms of political risk will also influence the firm's choice of how to finance its overseas operations. For example, political risk considerations will determine, in part, whether firms investing in Mexico will do so with parent equity or debt, or by borrowing from Mexican banks. Such considerations will also affect the extent to which the parent's investment will be guaranteed by an agency of the MNC's home government.

As a general rule, the corporate financing decision reduces to a trade-off between two objectives: minimizing the expected after-tax cost of financing and keeping risks within acceptable levels. Evaluating this trade-off may be a much more complicated exercise for multinationals than for purely domestic companies. For not only do tax laws vary from country to country, but the risks can also be of a kind and magnitude not encountered at home. Finance theory, to be sure, has contended that stockholders can benefit only from

***This article reprinted, with permission, from *Midland Corporate Finance Journal,* Spring 1984, published by Stern, Stewart, Putnam and Macklis, Ltd., Corporate Financial Consultants.**

the firm's reduction of so-called "systematic" or market risk (the risk of the firm as part of the market portfolio of stocks). In the case of multinationals especially, however, we argue that financial executives must take account of the potential effects of idiosyncratic or "unsystematic" risks—those associated specifically with the industry, the country of operations, and with the firm itself—in determining how to fund its activities.

Establishing a worldwide financial policy is thus an extraordinarily complex undertaking. It is made more so by the lack of an explicit analytical framework for quantifying these trade-offs. International finance scholars have proposed partial solutions to the problem,[1] but few comprehensive solutions have even been attempted. Further, those "total system" mathematical programming approaches that have been proposed are far too complex for practical application. They also typically omit important aspects of the problem.[2]

Unfortunately, it is not currently within our power (if indeed it will ever be) to quantify the impact on shareholder wealth of the various factors involved in designing such a plan. And how these factors interact with each other seems even less amenable to measurement. Thus, our objective in this article is necessarily modest. We seek to develop a set of reasonable guidelines for multinationals in evaluating their financing options. Such guidelines are "reasonable" in the sense that they are based on our understanding of how financial markets function.

Our proposed approach for evaluating global financing choices breaks down the overall problem into three largely separable objectives:

1. minimizing taxes;
2. managing currency and political risks; and
3. exploiting financial market distortions.[3]

These three objectives can be pursued through financing strategies that can be classified either as "passive" or "active." Passive financing strategies are those based on the assumption that management has no special information or forecasting skills; active strategies are based on an assumed ability to systematically "beat the market" in forecasting prices or exchange rate movements. In this sense, both arbitrage and hedging are passive strategies, while speculation is active.

The remainder of this article is organized in six parts. We begin by discussing the basic considerations inherent in all financing choices. In the next three sections, we explore the three major considerations of multinational financing: minimizing taxes, managing risks, and exploiting market distortions. In the fifth section we discuss how these three objectives relate to the firm's overall capital structure. Finally, we identify the conditions under which each of these three financing considerations are truly separable.

BASIC CONSIDERATIONS IN INTERNATIONAL FINANCING CHOICES

In line with mainstream financial theory, we assume that the goal of the firm is to maximize the market value of its shares. The market value of the shares, in turn, is said to reflect the present value of the firm's expected future after-tax cash flows, discounted at a rate which reflects the market's assessment of the firm's systematic or non-diversifiable risk—that is, the risk of the firm from the perspective of a well-diversified stockholder.[4]

What evidence do we have that the market "prices" risk in this way? Research on capital markets demonstrates that, on average and over time, stockholders expect and receive returns on their investment commensurate with the risks they bear. The higher the risks the higher the average returns. And as the bulk of the evidence also suggests, average returns on investment correlate most strongly (as predicted by the Capital Asset Pricing Model (CAPM)) with measures of systematic or non-diversifiable risk. This systematic or "market" risk, generally measured by "beta," is the sensitivity of a firm's stock price to market wide and general economic developments. The CAPM thus implies that stock market investors are concerned, for the most part, *not* with the total variability (i.e., "total risk") of the firm's cash flows, but only with the "co-variability" of those flows with the performance of the economy as a whole.

Finance theory thus maintains that, in general, reducing corporate risks which are diversifiable at the portfolio level does not benefit stockholders. Most company specific risks, provided they do not significantly raise the possibility of bankruptcy, can be managed more efficiently by stockholders.

In this article, however, we are going to depart somewhat from the implications of the CAPM for risk management to argue that the total risk of the firm's equity (that is, diversifiable as well as nondiversifiable risks) must be taken into account in multinational financial decision-making. We are not arguing that the presence of firm- and country-specific risks raises the market's discount rate, but rather that such diversifiable risks, if unmanaged, may have significant effects on the expected *level* of the firm's cash flow. Excessive earnings variability, for example, may affect a firm's access to credit and, hence, its ability to benefit from interest tax shields. It may also restrict its ability to raise money for attractive projects (especially if the alternative of an equity issue requires the firm to disseminate information of value to its competitors). Also, it may influence the willingness of suppliers, customers, and employees to commit themselves to relationships with the firm. Finally, and perhaps most important, the uncertainty created by volatile earnings and cash flows may hinder management's ability to take a long view of the firm's prospects and make the most of opportunities.

With these considerations in mind, we have "rewritten" the objective function of the firm as follows:

$$\text{Maximize } V_F = \Sigma V_i - P(\sigma) \tag{1}$$

where V_i is the present value of each of the firm's activities (divisions, business units, or projects) and $P(\sigma)$ is a penalty factor that reflects the impact on expected after-tax cash flows of the total risk of the firm's equity. According to this formulation, the value of the firm *is reduced* by an increase in the expected variability of cash flow.

The crucial implication of this inclusion of a penalty factor for total risk is that the multinational might want to "lay off" those "unsystematic" risks which, by contributing substantially to the expected variability of its cash flow, may endanger the financing and operating flexibility of the company. For example, it may want to purchase insurance against major casualties, provided the insurance is fairly priced to reflect the expected probability and size of the loss. It also may want to hedge major risks associated with changes in commodity prices and foreign exchange—again, provided the relevant contracts are fairly priced according to the CAPM. Although such hedging transactions will have a zero present value in their own right, they will reduce this penalty factor associated with total risk at the level of the corporation.

A further rationale for hedging at the level of the corporation is that limited information and incomplete markets can prevent investors from replicating the firm's hedging activities at an equivalent cost. This is especially likely in the case of political risks, which the firm can sometimes reduce or shift through appropriate financing decisions.

In the case of very large, well-capitalized multinationals like IBM, with operations spread throughout the world, the probability of such idiosyncratic risks causing financial distress is small. Under these conditions, this penalty factor should probably be valued at zero. For, at any given time, such multinationals are taking many small, partly offsetting bets on exchange rates, inflation rates, political stability, etc. And when viewed relative to the capitalization of the company, such risks may add up to a very low risk profile.

In such cases, the multinational's financing choices would depend only on the additive present values of each transaction. The only choices which would matter under such circumstances are those that reduce taxes or those that are "bargains"—that is, financing options priced at below market rates. Bargains can be the result of concessional financing policies, distortions due to restrictions imposed on transactions, or information not yet reflected in market prices.

Passive Versus Active Policies

Financing choices often involve taking advantage of perceived bargains as well as reducing taxes or risks. Using an analogy from investment management, we can draw a distinction between "passive" and "active" financing decisions. Passive financing decisions or strategies are those that don't involve any special information; they are based on the assumption that all financing options are fairly priced—that is, there are no bargains because markets work well. Active financing strategies depend on the ability to spot bargains and to exploit them by taking positions.

Passive strategies include tax arbitrage, riskless financial market arbitrage, and hedging. In contrast, active considerations assume market inefficiency or distortion, and they lead to speculation.[6] This category includes those risky financing opportunities that depend on government-induced market distortions. But, as we shall argue later, exploiting such opportunities may not necessarily depend on special information or forecasting skill possessed by the firm.

Passive choices logically precede active choices. Thus, in any situation a firm should first determine what choices it would make if it had no special information. Only then should it consider altering its financing choices to exploit a perceived bargain. This would mean weighing the present value of the bargain, taking into account its systematic risk, against its impact on the total risk of the firm. For example, a firm may decide that, all other things equal, it should finance its affiliate with yen debt in order to reduce its yen exposure. Suppose, however, that the firm has access to French francs at a below market rate. Its choice, then, would depend on the trade-off between lower expected financing costs and the higher penalty associated with increased exchange risk. Arbitrage opportunities are the exception to the rule here, since they have positive net present values without having any impact on corporate risk.

MINIMIZING TAXES

The asymmetrical tax treatment of various components of financial cost, such as the treatment of dividend payments versus interest expense and of exchange losses versus exchange gains, often means that equality of before-tax costs will lead to inequality of after-tax costs. Moreover, the U.S. and many European countries impose withholding taxes on dividends and interest paid to foreign investors by domestic corporations. And this has led inevitably to a proliferation of foreign finance subsidiaries designed to avoid this additional tax burden.

Financing choices aimed at reducing taxes typically have two components: 1) selecting the tax-minimizing investment, currency, jurisidiction, and favored vehicle and currency for *internal* (inter-affiliate) financial transfers that minimize and position profits or losses in the jurisdiction which minimizes overall income taxes.

Structure of External Claims

Choice of Investment

Because interest payments on debt are tax-deductible and dividends are not, there is an incentive to increase the firm's financial leverage. In addition, because interaffiliate dividend payments may lead to different tax consequences than interest and principal payments, parent company financing of its affiliates in the form of debt rather than equity has tax advantages under certain circumstances. (These and other factors are discussed later.)

Choice of Currency

International covered interest arbitrage normally ensures that the annualized forward exchange premium or discount equals the nominal yield differential between debt denominated in different currencies. For example, if the one-year U.S. dollar interest rate is 12 percent while the equivalent pound sterling interest rate is 17 percent, the pound should be selling at a one-year forward discount relative to the dollar equal to 5 percent. Otherwise, an arbitrage opportunity would present itself. Moreover, a rational expectations approach to exchange rates implies that the forward premium or discount equals the expected rate of change in the exchange rate adjusted by an appropriate risk premium.[7] This means that, holding risk constant, the difference in interest rates should equal the expected change in the exchange rate during the term of the loan. Thus, in the example cited above, the pound is predicted to devalue by about 5 (17–12) percent during the coming year. To the extent that these theories hold, as a good deal of empirical evidence suggests, a firm unconcerned with the total risk of its cash flows would be indifferent between issuing debt in one currency or another.

The presence of taxes, however, may distort the interest arbitrage relationship from the perspective of the firm because its tax situation may differ from that of the marginal transactors in the market. For example, Shapiro [1982a] has shown that if arbitrage and speculation equilibrate real yields before tax, then the classic corporate prescription to issue weak-currency debt will minimize expected after-tax financing costs. There are exceptions, of course. For example, a firm operating under the laws of a country like Sweden is permitted to recognize unrealized exchange losses on foreign currency immediately for tax purposes, while taxes on exchange gains are deferred until realized.[8] Although this doesn't mean that it is always cheaper for firms based in Sweden to issue hard-currency debt, the fact that Swedish tax law accelerates tax credits for foreign exchange losses shifts the balance towards borrowing in currencies likely to appreciate relative to the krona. By contrast, England is a special case where government regulations reinforce the rule to borrow in the local currency when it is weak. This is because England's Inland Revenue will not permit the deduction for tax purposes of exchange losses on the principal amount of foreign currency loans—while the higher interest rate on pound debt, which reflects the expected pound devaluation, is fully tax deductible.

In general, where there is asymmetrical tax treatment of foreign exchange gains and losses or where interest expenses are subject to one tax rate and exchange gains and losses are subject to a different rate, the expected after-tax cost of borrowing will differ across currencies even if their expected before-tax costs are the same.

Choice of Jurisdiction

To the extent that the choice of currency to be borrowed can be separated from the choice of the country in which the borrowing takes place or in which the borrowing firm is domiciled, the firm will want to borrow so as to maximize its tax deductions. So long as national tax systems are not indexed for inflation, a firm typically will benefit most by borrowing in the country with the highest inflation and nominal interest rates. In so doing, the firm maximizes its interest deductions, provided interest charges and gains or losses on currency movements are treated equivalently.[9] To take full advantage of these tax deductions, the firm should use internal financial transfer mechanisms to shift funds throughout the system.

Choice of Vehicle

In the U.S. the withholding tax rate on dividend and interest payments to foreign investors varies between zero and 30 percent, depending on the bilateral tax treaty with the foreign country to which these payments are made. Even though this tax is nominally paid by the foreign recipient, foreign investors demand a higher before-tax rate of return as compensation, thus shifting the incidence of the tax to the security issuer.[10]

The approach taken by many American multinationals to avoid these taxes is to establish offshore finance subsidiaries. An offshore finance subsidiary is a wholly-owned affiliate incorporated overseas, usually in a tax haven country, whose function is to issue securities abroad for use in either the parent's domestic or foreign business.[11]

Structure of Internal Transfers

To the extent that tax minimization requires the firm to issue claims in countries other than where the funds are required, it must transfer the funds internally. The way this is done has important tax implications. If internal financial transfers are at "arm's length," reflecting external financing costs, then the potential advantages outlined in the previous section are largely negated. However, by choosing the appropriate instrument—and in the case of debt claims, the appropriate currency and interest rate—withholding taxes on transfers within the firm can be reduced or avoided, and revenues or costs can be shifted to jurisdictions where they have the most favorable tax consequence.[12]

MANAGING RISKS

In principle, firms should not try to minimize risks. Rather, they should take risks whenever they expect to be rewarded for doing so. This risk-return trade-off is captured in the investment rule derived from the capital asset pricing model: namely, invest in all projects where the expected returns exceed the required return (which is a function of interest rates and the projects' *systematic* risks only). Recall, however, that earlier we added to the firm's objective function a penalty factor associated with *total* risk or variability. And, as suggested, this has very different implications for corporate risk management. To the extent that a particular element of risk contributes materially to the firm's total risk, management will want to lay off that risk as long as the expected excess return associated with bearing that risk is not large. Or, putting it the other way around, it will want to lay off such risks unless the cost of doing so is too great.

This implies that the firm will want to lay off those risks that contribute materially to its total risk but are priced fairly in relation to the CAPM. Those risks which are most likely to be fairly priced are those for which substantial, specialized markets have developed. Such markets exist for risks that are faced by large numbers of firms, especially when many of them hold offsetting positions. Examples of such risks include interest rate risks, currency risks, commodity price risks, certain political risks and funding risks.

Foreign Exchange Risks

If financing opportunities in various currencies are fairly priced, firms can structure their liabilities so as to reduce their exposure to foreign exchange risk at no cost to the value of the firm. In the case of contractual items, i.e., those fixed in nominal terms, this simply involves matching net positive positions in each currency with borrowings of similar maturity. The goal is to offset unanticipated changes in the home currency value of operating cash flows with identical changes in the home currency cost of servicing its liabilities. With non-contractual operating cash flows the same principle applies. But perfect hedging is more difficult due to the great uncertainty in estimating the expected effects of currency changes on operating flows. Further, special contracts are required exactly to offset currency risk because changes in relative prices across countries measured by the real exchange rate are associated, but not perfectly correlated, with variations in the nominal exchange rate.[13]

Quite often, however, simple rules of thumb will suffice. For example, a firm that has developed a sizable export market should hold a portion of its liabilities in the currency of determination of its export revenues—often but not always the currency of that country. This would allow any reduction in operating cash inflows due to an exchange rate change to be offset by a reduction in the debt service cash outflows. To illustrate this principle, a company such as Volkswagen, which exported almost half its output to the U.S. prior to 1971, should have financed about half its assets with dollar debt. Failure to do so almost bankrupted Volkswagen following the sharp appreciation of the deutschemark beginning in August of 1981. In 1974 alone, Volkswagen lost over $310 million by lowering its deutschemark price in an attempt to maintain its market share.

Political Risk

In the hedging of exchange risks, the firm should seek financing that will offset risks inherent in the business. The use of financing to reduce political risks typically involves mechanisms to avoid or at least reduce the impact of certain risks, such as those of exchange convertibility. It may also involve financing mechanisms that actually change the risk itself, as in the case of expropriation or other direct political acts.

Firms can sometimes reduce the risk of currency inconvertibility by appropriate inter-affiliate financing. Methods for dealing with such risks include investing parent funds as debt rather than equity, arranging back-to-back and parallel loans which interpose a bank between the parent and the subsidiary, and using local financing to the extent possible. Of course, such arrangements will be most valuable when the banks or local investors face significantly fewer restrictions or smaller risks—especially if the risk in question involves possible discrimination against direct foreign investors. While local investors may often have an advantage in this regard, it cannot be taken as a general rule. Even if a particular political risk cannot be modified by shifting it from one firm or investor to another, a firm with substantial exposure will benefit by laying off such risks to firms or investors with less exposure. This is the economic basis for commercial political risk insurance. Another approach used by MNCs to reduce their political risk exposures is as follows: instead of supplying subsidiaries with direct or guaranteed capital, the parent company may want to raise capital for a foreign investment from the host and other governments, international development agencies, overseas banks, or even from customers. Because repayment is tied to the project's success, the firm(s) sponsoring the project can create an international network of banks, government agencies, and customers with a vested interest in the fulfilment of the host government's contract with the sponsoring firm(s). In such a case, any expropriation threat is likely to upset relations with customers, banks and governments worldwide.[14]

Again, this type of financing arrangement is beneficial to the extent that the expected gain from shifting these political risks exceeds the risk premium charged by lenders. This will be the case if the political risks facing external lenders are lower than those facing the firm. International banks, for example, to the extent that they maintain close relationships with the countries in which they do business, are likely to possess substantially more leverage with local governments than MNCs.[15]

Product Market Risk

In a well-functioning market a firm can lay off currency risks at no cost and thus reduce the penalty term in the objective function (Eq. 1). It also can arrange its financing so as to shift certain key business risks to well-diversified investors concerned only with the systematic component of these risks. A firm engaged in the extraction and processing of minerals, for example, is overwhelmingly exposed to product price fluctuations. And though these risks may be largely diversifiable for investors, the company will clearly want to protect against such risks. Examples of instruments used to shift product market risks, besides the relatively short-term commodity futures contracts, are the silver-linked bonds issued by the Sunshine Mining Corporation and the oil-linked bonds issued by Mexico. Financing linked to advance sales contracts (known as "take-or-pay" contracts) or to production shares (common in the oil industry) also plays a similar role. In all these instances, payments to investors rise and fall with the fortunes of the company, thus stabilizing the company's earnings and cash flow.

Securing Access to Funds

A continuing concern of firms, both domestic and multinational, is to secure a stable source of funds. Two elements of this strategy include diversification of fund sources and buying insurance through excess borrowing.

Diversification of Fund Sources

A key element of any MNC's global financial strategy should be to gain access to a broad range of fund sources to lessen its dependence on any one financial market. A further benefit is that the firm broadens its sources of economic and financial information, providing a useful supplement to its domestic information sources and aiding in its financial decision-making process.

An interesting example of this strategy is provided by Natomas, the San Francisco-based oil producer. In 1977, Natomas sold a $30 million, seven-year Eurobond issue even though it could have obtained funds at a lower cost by drawing on its existing revolving credit lines or by selling commercial paper. According to Natomas, the key purpose of this Euroissue was to introduce the company's name to international investors as part of its global financial strategy.[16] By floating a Eurobond, the firm was able to make the acquaintance of some of the largest non-U.S. financial institutions in the world, including Swiss Bank Corporation, the issue's lead manager. Each lead underwriter was handpicked by the company, with an eye to its overall financing needs. For example, a Swiss bank was selected as manager because Natomas felt that European banks, and Swiss banks in particular, have greater placing power with long-term investors than do U.S. underwriters operating in Europe. In addition, these European institutions were expected to serve Natomas as a source of market and economic information to counterbalance the input it already was receiving from U.S. banks.

For similar reasons, a number of Japanese firms have recently begun to sell equity shares in the United States. In 1976, for example, Pioneer raised over $27 million in the United States through the sale of 4 million shares of Pioneer common stock. This was in keeping with its multilateral financing strategy, designed to familiarize U.S. investors with its name.[17] In conjunction with this sale, Pioneer had previously applied for listing of its stock on the New York Stock Exchange.

Excess Borrowing

Most firms have lines of credit with a number of banks which give them the right to borrow up to an agreed upon credit limit. Unused balances carry a commitment fee, normally on the order of .5 percent per annum. In order not to tie up funds unnecessarily, most banks periodically review each credit limit to see whether the customer's account activity level justifies that credit line. Some firms are willing to borrow funds that they do not require (and then place them on deposit) in order to maintain their credit limit in the event of a tight money situation. In effect, they are buying insurance against the possibility of being squeezed out of the money market. One measure of the cost of this policy is the difference between the borrowing rate and the deposit rate, multiplied by the average amount of borrowed funds placed on deposit. Another cost may be considerable banker ill will if a corporation borrows when money is tight (i.e., when the firm is worried about financial sources) and does not use the money productively.

EXPLOITING CAPITAL MARKET DISTORTIONS

Government credit and capital controls can lead to deviations from the equilibrium tendencies of interest rate parity, forward parity, and international Fisher parity. As a result, the firm may encounter financing choices that are not fairly priced. Some of these can be exploited through riskless arbitrage, which requires no special forecasting skills. Others may require speculation on uncertain future outcomes. Further, even in the absence of government intervention, firms may be able to identify instances where there are opportunities for arbitrage or speculation. In fact, opportunistic financing by firms is a key factor in assuring that the various equilibrium conditions hold. The most consistent opportunities, though, will result either from credit and exchange controls or explicit financial subsidies.

The condition for covered interest arbitrage is

$$\frac{F}{S} = \frac{1 + R}{1 + R^*} \tag{2}$$

where R and R^* are the nominal interest rates in the home and foreign currencies respectively, and F and S are the forward and spot rates in terms of direct quotes (home currency price of foreign currency).[18] Arbitrage opportunities are most likely to be available between controlled or subsidized domestic rates and freely determined offshore rates, in which case a comparison of the two rates in a single currency is all that is necessary.

The condition for speculation is

$$1 + R = (1 + R^*) \times E(S)/S \tag{3}$$

where E(S) is the expected value of the future spot rate.[19] In 1981, for example, Pacific Southwest Airlines borrowed yen rather than dollars on the speculation that the dollar would not fall enough relative to the yen to offset the percent interest differential between borrowing rates in the two currencies.[20] As of the end of 1983, they had gained substantially from this position. However, because PSA's revenues had little to do with movements in the yen/dollar rate, this choice did increase the firm's overall risk and undoubtedly weakened the position of its creditors. Had the dollar dropped sharply relative to the yen, as it did for example in 1978–79, the firm would have faced a large loss due to its financing choice with no corresponding business gain.

Government Credit and Capital Controls

Governments often intervene in domestic financial markets to achieve goals other than economic efficiency. For example, a government might limit corporate borrowing to hold down interest rates, thereby providing its finance ministry with a lower-cost source of funds to meet a budget deficit. Or overseas investment flows may be restricted, as they were in the United States from 1968 to 1974 under the Overseas Foreign Direct Investment (OFDI) regulations.

Where governments restrict access to local credit markets, local interest rates are usually at a lower-than-equilibrium level on a risk-adjusted basis. If there is an effective offshore market for the currency, the controls will result in a difference between domestic and offshore rates and thus give rise to an arbitrage opportunity. The firm can borrow in the domestic market and, to the extent that the short position exceeds its desired passive position in that currency, the firm can lend the same currency in offshore markets. Or equivalently, it can transform the short position to a position in another currency through forward or swap transactions linked to the offshore rate. As a result, the firm should borrow as much as possible in the credit-rationed market. In many instances, the MNC with its multiple citizenship has greater access to these lower-cost funds. Moreover, it has a greater ability to shift these funds through its internal financial transfer system.

If there is no offshore market, the mispriced credit can be exploited only by taking a risk. As a result, the firm will have to trade off the positive net present value against the effect on its total risk. As a result, the firm will not necessarily borrow as much as possible.

Government Subsidies

Many governments offer incentives to MNCs to influence their production and export sourcing decisions. Direct investment incentives include interest rate subsidies, very long loan maturities, loan guarantees, official repatriation guarantees, direct grants related to project size, favorable prices for land and favorable terms for the building of plants. The Canadian government, for example, provides firms with grants of up to $30,000 for each job created in areas characterized by high unemployment and slow economic growth—

and also with direct loans and loan guarantees. Similarly, new investments located in the Mezzogiorno region of Italy can qualify for cash grants which cover up to 40 percent of the cost of plant and equipment, as well as low interest rate loans, cheaper electricity, and reduced rail charges. Governments will also often agree to build transportation, communications and other links to those factories. Some indirect incentives include corporate income tax holidays, accelerated depreciation, and a reduction or elimination of the payment of other business taxes and import duties on capital equipment and raw materials.[21] Perhaps the best-known example of such tax relief is the case of the Republic of Ireland, which does not tax profits on exports of locally-manufactured goods during the first fifteen years of operation. In addition, Ireland permits firms to write off 100 percent of the cost of new plant and equipment in the first year, without deducting state grants toward the cost of the equipment.

Strictly speaking, most of the above are examples of subsidies which affect *investment* rather than *financing* decisions. But, in many cases, the value of the subsidy will depend on how the investment is financed. For example, in the case of investment in countries granting tax holidays, a multinational might wish to shift the financing of that investment to a different jurisdiction in order to benefit from the tax shield provided by interest payments.

In addition, governments of developed nations have export financing agencies whose purpose is to boost local exports by providing long repayment periods, low interest rates, and low-cost political and economic risk insurance. These export credit programs can often be used to advantage by multinationals. The form of use will depend on whether the firm is looking to export or import goods or services. But the basic strategy remains the same: shop around among the various export credit agencies for the best possible financing arrangement.

Firms engaged in projects that have sizable import requirements may be able to finance these purchases on attractive terms from various export financing agencies. To do this, the firm must compile a list of goods and services required for the project and relate them to potential sources by country. Where there is overlap among the potential suppliers, the purchasing firm (or country) may be able to extract more favorable financing terms from the export credit agencies involved. Perhaps the clearest application of this strategy in recent years was the financing of the Soviet gas pipeline to Western Europe. The Soviet Union played off various European and Japanese suppliers and their export financing agencies against each other and managed to get extraordinarily favorable credit and pricing terms.

INTERACTIONS WITH THE FIRM'S OVERALL FINANCIAL STRUCTURE

In our discussion of specific financing choices, we have implicitly assumed that the firm has somehow determined its overall mix of debt and equity and is merely deciding where, in which currencies, and through which legal vehicle it should borrow or lay off specific risks. These individual financing choices can be treated as independent of the firm's overall debt-equity determination as long as two conditions hold: 1) financial distress and agency factors which enter into this determination depend only on the firm's consolidated debt-equity structure, and 2) the firm can, at zero cost, offset over- or underborrowing in one jurisdiction elsewhere in the system. Clearly, these conditions do not hold exactly but it appears that, in many cases, they hold closely enough to allow separation of the issues of the overall debt-equity mix and the selection of specific financing sources. In this section, we explore some of the constraints on subsidiary financial structure. We do not deal with the determination of the overall mix because it is discussed amply, though inconclusively, in the literature.[22]

A problem that has long perplexed financial executives of multinational corporations is how to arrange the capital structures of their foreign affiliates and what factors are relevant in making this decision. Specifically, the problem is whether subsidiary financial structures should a) conform to parent company norms; b) conform to the capitalization norms established in each country; or c) vary so as to take advantage of opportunities to minimize taxes, offset risks, or exploit distortions in financial markets.

What is often overlooked, however, when deciding on a wholly-owned subsidiary's funding is that any accounting rendition of a separate capital structure for the subsidiary is illusory *unless* the parent is willing to allow its affiliate to default on its debt or unless external factors such as credit controls limit the enforceability of cross-border controls. As long as the rest of the MNC group has a legal or moral obligation to prevent the affiliate from defaulting, the individual unit has no independent capital structure.[23] In such a case, its true debt/equity ratio is equal to that of the consolidated group.

Some evidence on parent willingness to guarantee (implicitly if not explicitly) their affiliates' debts is provided by two surveys, one by Stobaugh (1970) and the other by Business International (1979). In the survey by Stobaugh, not one of a sample of twenty medium and large multinationals (average annual foreign sales of \$200 million and \$1 billion, respectively) said it would allow its subsidiaries to default on debt which did not have a parent company guarantee. Of the small multinationals interviewed (average annual sales of \$450 million), only one out of seventeen indicated it would allow a subsidiary to default on its obligations under some circumstances. The 1979 survey by Business International of eight U.S.-based MNCs had similar findings.[24] The majority of firms interviewed said they would make good the non-guaranteed debt of a subsidiary that defaulted on its borrowings.

It is likely that the market has already incorporated this practical commitment in its estimate of the parent's worldwide debt capacity. An overseas creditor, on the other hand, may not be as certain regarding the firm's intentions. The fact that the parent doesn't guarantee its subsidiaries' debt may convey the information that under certain circumstances the parent will choose to walk away from its subsidiary.

Many multinationals view subsidiary financial structures as having little relevance. In the 1979 survey by Business International, for example, most of the firms expressed little concern with the debt-equity mixes of their foreign affiliates. One possible reason for this lack of concern is the fact that, for most of the firms interviewed, their affiliate debt ratios had not significantly raised their consolidated debt ratios. Again, however, they focused on their worldwide rather than individual subsidiary's capital structures.

The third option, therefore, to vary affiliate financial structures so as to take advantage of local financing opportunities, appears to be the best choice. There are, however, several constraints to such an approach. These constraints arise from the fact that a firm's operations in different jurisdictions have different groups of noncorporate stakeholders—governments, managements, workers, lenders, joint venture partners, suppliers, customers—whose interests are affected by subsidiary capital structures.

Capital Structure Requirements

Many jurisdictions require that locally incorporated firms maintain particular levels of equity capitalization or equity ratios. In some cases, these are simply holdovers of national incorporation laws which apply imperfectly to multinationals. In others, they are express attempts to require potentially footloose multinationals in effect to "post bond" against future actions considered undesirable by local authorities. However, as long as a nation does not simultaneously apply capital controls, the firm still has substantial freedom of choice regarding the currency and tax consequences of its financing, given the array of potential offshore and interaffiliate financing options.

Management Control

Despite the logic of the argument that a subsidiary's capital structure is relevant only insofar as it affects the parent's consolidated worldwide debt ratio, some companies still follow a policy of not providing parent financing beyond the initial investment. Their rationale for this policy, which is to avoid "giving local management a crutch," can best be understood in the context of agency theory. By forcing foreign affiliates to stand on their own feet, the parent firm is tacitly admitting that its powers of surveillance over foreign affiliates are limited, due to physical and/or cultural distance. In effect, the parent is turning over some of its monitoring responsibilities to local financial institutions. At the same time, affiliate managers will presumably be working harder to improve local operations, thereby generating the internal cash flow that will help replace parent financing.

The existence of agency costs can also affect corporate policy regarding parent guarantees. As Robbins and Stobaugh have commented, when a firm provides an affiliate with a loan guarantee, it "lose[s] the bank as your [its] partner in controls."[25] Because the bank will be repaid regardless of the affiliate's profitability, it will have less incentive to monitor the affiliate's activities.

While financial autonomy may be a useful control device, its costs in the form of constraints on global financing and operation should be carefully monitored. For example, in the absence of a guarantee, the local bank will probably insist on inserting various complicating covenants in its loan agreement with the subsidiary. These restrictive covenants could result in a significant loss in operational and financial flexibility. If the costs imposed by these constraints are high, alternatives should be sought—for example, a more effective system for controlling local operating management.

One possibility is to allocate only certain financing decisions and responsibilities to local management, and retain the rest under central corporate control. For example, local management might be held responsible for financing its local currency working capital requirements, while home country management would make all other financing decisions. Such differentiation, of course, requires a considerable degree of sophistication in performance measurement and control. The costs of such a control system must be traded off against the gains in financial flexibility.

Jurisdictional Matching

Even if legal requirements and control considerations do not cause the financial structures of an MNC's subsidiaries to differ significantly from one another, a firm may wish to limit cross-border commitments, including direct parent financing or parent guarantees, because of the difficulty of enforcing its cross-border claims. The threat of currency controls or outright expropriation in one jurisdiction, for example, may expose the parent to financial distress if it borrows against these anticipated revenues in another jurisdiction.

Even if local lenders face the same political risks and incorporate them in their lending rates, local borrowing without a parent guarantee may reduce the "financial distress penalty." To protect lenders from the risk of subsidiary bankruptcy, however, the parent usually will provide a conditional guarantee in the form of a comfort letter obligating the parent to make good on its subsidiary's debts except in the event of expropriation.[26]

These considerations do not apply equally to all countries. In the case of relatively stable jurisdictions with open capital and currency markets, firms are likely to be willing to issue guarantees and engage in other necessay cross-border transactions to minimize taxes or risks or exploit distortions. In countries more apt to impose limits on cross-border transactions, though, firms will have to weigh carefully the benefits of financial flexibility against the costs of cross-border exposure.

Joint Ventures

Because many MNCs participate in joint ventures, either by choice or necessity, establishing an appropriate financing mix for this form of investment is an important consideration. Our previous assumption that affiliate debt is equivalent to parent debt in terms of its effect on perceived default risk may no longer be valid. This assumption was based on the increased risk of financial distress associated with more highly leveraged firms. In countries such as Japan and Germany, however, increased leverage does not necessarily lead to increased financial risks because of the close relationship between the local banks and local corporations. Thus, debt raised by a joint venture in Japan, for example, may not be equivalent to parent-raised debt with respect to its impact on default risk. The assessment of the effects of leverage in a joint venture is a judgmental factor which requires an analysis of the partner's ties with the local financial community, particularly with the local banks.

Unless the joint venture can be isolated from its partners' operations, however, there are likely to be some significant agency problems associated with this form of ownership. Transfer pricing, establishment of royalty and licensing fees, and allocation of production and markets among plants are just some of the areas where each owner has an incentive to engage in activities that will harm its partners. This probably explains why bringing in outside equity participants is generally such an unstable form of external financing. In recognition of their lack of complete control over a joint venture's decisions and its profits, most MNCs will, at most, guarantee joint venture loans in proportion to their share of ownership.

SUMMARY AND CONCLUSIONS

In this article, we have attempted to provide a framework for multinational firms to use in arranging their global financing. We have broken down the international aspects of the problem into three largely separable objectives: minimizing taxes, managing risks, and exploiting market distortions. The first two of these rely on passive considerations in that they do not rely on any superior forecasting skills, whereas the third may or may not have an active component. In either case, these functions are largely separate. Tax minimization typically can be pursued without altering the currency risk position of the firm. Overall risk management can be carried out without any special information about capital market opportunities. Once the firm has established its desired passive position, it then can decide by how much it is willing to alter its risk exposures to exploit perceived bargains. Arbitrage opportunities, of course, are simple to deal with because they have no overall risk implications.

Following this discussion, we described how each of these three financing considerations influences the firm's choice of overall financial structure. Clearly, parent and affiliate structures must be allowed to differ if the firm is to exploit the special opportunities of being multinational. However, it may wish to constrain the extent to which it distorts the financing of a particular subsidiary because of undesired behavioral effects on local managers, or in the case of joint ventures, conflicts with local shareholders.

Although there are many areas in which our recommendations are qualitative rather than quantitative, our approach to developing a financing strategy should be useful in a domestic as well as international context. The remaining limitations of our approach are common to both domestic and international financial management because they reflect the limitations of financial theory in general.

NOTES

1. For a review of early studies in this area see Naumann-Etienne [1974]. More recently, Shapiro [1975] has examined the impact of taxes on financial choices, Remmers [1980] has extended Shapiro's work to include uncertainty, Dufey and Giddy [1978] have emphasized the implications of efficient international financial markets for financing choices.

2. These include Ness [1972] who incorporates various financial constraints in a cost-minimizing linear program, Schydlowsky (in Robbins and Stobaugh [1973]) who develops a similar model, Lietaer [1971] who incorporates uncertainty in a quadratic programming model but does not address taxes, and most recently Kornbluth and Vinso [1981] who stress system versus local country capital structures but whose treatment of currency expectations is highly simplified. Several commercial models have been developed, but most have fallen into disuse.

3. This breakdown of the problem follows Lessard [1979b], pp. 349–351.

4. In this paper we ignore the more complex issues of valuation in a multicurrency, multicountry environment where different investors may display different currency preferences. We believe that this is not a serious problem since investors can readily offset the currency component of a firm's equity returns in their own portfolios as long as they know what that component is. This view outlined in Lessard and Stulz [1984] contradicts the position taken by Wihlborg [1980].

5. Adler and Dumas [1977] employ a similar objective function.

6. Although it is impossible to differentiate between the hedging and speculative motives either in theory or practice, we assume for purposes of this paper that hedging involves the desire for pure risk reduction whereas speculation involves the willingness to trade off risk and return.

7. Major contributions to the evolving discussion of currency risk premiums include Solnik [1978], Frankel [1979], and Stulz [1982].

8. See Levi [1977] for a discussion of the simultaneous arbitrage opportunities for investors of two countries that arise when interest and currency movements receive differential tax treatment in each country.

9. This prescription assumes that international Fisher parity holds before tax.

10. This assumes that the supply of funds facing a firm is much more elastic than its demand for those funds.

11. The Netherlands Antilles (N.A.) is a particularly attractive location for such a venture since the bilateral tax treaty between the U.S. and N.A. specifically exempts interest payments by the finance subsidiary to foreign bondholders from U.S. withholding tax, even where 100 percent of the finance subsidiary's gross income is derived from U.S. sources (because proceeds were lent to the parent).

12. See Lessard [1979a] and Shapiro [1982b] for overviews of the role of internal financial transactions. Horst [1977] and Adler [1979] provide more in-depth analyses on the impact of inter-affiliate financial structures on taxes.

13. See Lessard and Lightstone [1983] for further discussion of this point.

14. Moran [1973] shows how this strategy was used successfully by Kennecott to finance a major copper mine expansion in Chile. Despite the subsequent rise to power of Salvador Allende, who promised to expropriate all foreign holdings in Chile with "ni un centavo" in compensation, Allende was forced to honor prior government commitments to Kennecott.

15. See, for example, Lax and Sebenius [1981].

16. "Diversifying Sources of Financing," *Business International Money Report*, September 23, 1977, pp. 297–298.

17. Why Japanese Firms Float Equity Abroad, *Business International Money Report*, February 11, 1977, pp. 44–45.

18. Forward parity need not hold in the presence of political risk (see Aliber [1973]) or forward contract default risk (see Adler and Dumas [1977]) so that deviations thereof need not indicate bargains.

19. Strictly speaking, E(S) should be replaced with CE(S), the certainty equivalent of the future spot rate. The certainty equivalent will differ from the expected spot rate if S has non-zero systematic risk (beta) or if the currency in question is that of a country which is a significant net borrower. See references in note 7 above.

20. "Turning to Japan for Cut-rate Loans," *Business Week*, November 23, 1981.

21. For a discussion of how these financial incentives should be incorporated in project analyses see Lessard [1981].

22. See, for example, Stewart C. Myers, "The Search for Optimal Capital Structure," *Midland Corporate Finance Journal*, Vol. 1 No. 1.

23. This point is made by Adler [1974] and Shapiro [1978].

24. "Policies of MNCs on Debt/Equity Mix," *Business International Money Report*, September 21, 1979, pp. 319–320.

25. Robbins and Stobaugh [1973], p. 67.

26. Hodder (1982) discusses the relationship between political risk and financing choices at greater length.

REFERENCES

Adler, M., (1974), "The Cost of Capital and Valuation of a Two-Country Firm," *Journal of Finance* (March).

_____ (1979), "U.S. Taxation of U.S. Multinational Corporations," in M. Sarnat and G. Szego (eds.), *International Trade and Finance* Vol. IV. Ballinger.

_____ and B. Dumas (1977), "The Microeconomics of the Firm in an Open Economy," *American Economic Review* (February).

_____ and _____ (1977), "Default Risk and the Demand for Forward Exchange," in H. Levy and M. Sarnat, (eds.), *Financial Decision Making Under Uncertainty*. Academic Press.

Aliber, R. Z. (1973), "The Interest Rate Parity Theorem: A Reinterpretation," *Journal of Political Economy* (November/December).

Barnea, A., R. Haugen, and L. Senbet (1981), "Market Imperfections, Agency Problems, and Capital Structure: A Review," *Financial Management* (Summer).

Cohen, B. (1972), "Foreign Investment by U.S. Corporations as a Way of Reducing Risk," Yale University Economic Growth Center Discussion Paper No. 151, September.

Dufey, G. and I. Giddy (1878), "International Financial Planning," *California Management Review* (Fall).

Fama, E. (1980), "Agency Problems and the Theory of the Firm," *Journal of Political Economy* (April).

Frankel, J. (1979), "The Diversifiability of Exchange Risk," *Journal of International Economics* (August).

Hodder, J. (1982), "Hedging International Exposure Capital Structure Under Flexible Exchange Rates and Expropriation Risk," Stanford University Working Paper.

Horst, T. (1977), "American Taxation of Multinational Firms," *American Economic Review* (June).

Jensen, M. and W. Meckling (1976), "Theory of the Firm: Managerial Behavior, Agency Cost, and Ownership Structure," *Journal of Financial Economics* 3.

Kornbluth, J. and J. Vinso (1981), "Financial Planning for the Multinational Corporations: A Fractional, Multiobjective Approach," *Journal of Financial and Quantitative Analysis* (December).

Lax, D. and J. Sebenius (1981), "Insecure Contracts and Resource Development," *Public Policy*, (Fall).

Lessard, D. (1979a), "Transfer Prices, Taxes and Financial Markets: Implications of Internal Financial Transfers within the Multinational Firms," in R. B. Hawkins (ed.), *Economic Issues of Multinational Firms*. JAI Press.

_____ (1979b), "Financial Management of International Operations," in D. Lessard (ed.), *International Financial Management*. Boston Warren, Gorham, and Lamont.

_____ (1981), "Evaluating International Projects: An Adjusted Present Value Approach," in R. Krum and F. Derkinderen (eds.), *Capital Budgeting under Conditions of Uncertainty*, Hingham, MA Martinus Nijhoff.

_____ and R. Stulz (1984), "Currency Considerations in International Equity Investment," unpublished manuscript, M.I.T. May.

_____ and J. Lightstone (1983), "The Impact of Exchange Rates on Operating Profits New Business and Financial Responses," unpublished MS.

Levi, M. (1977), "Taxation and 'Abnormal' International Cash Flows," *Journal of Political Economy* (June).

Lietaer, B. (1971), *Financial Management of Foreign Exchange*, Cambridge, MA: M.I.T. Press.

Modigliani, F. and M. Miller (1958), "The Cost of Capital, Corporation Finance, and the Theory of Investment," *American Economic Review* (June).

Moran, T. (1974), *The Politics of Dependence: Copper in Chile*, Princeton, N.J. Princeton University Press.

Nauman-Etienne, R. (1974), "A Framework for Financial Decisions in Multinational Corporations—A Summary of Recent Research," *Journal of Financial and Quantitative Analysis* (November).

Ness, W. (1972), "A Linear Programming Approach to Financing the Multinational Corporations," *Financial Management* (Winter).

Remmers, L. (1980), "A Note on Foreign Borrowing Costs," *Journal of International Business Studies* (Fall).

Robbins, S. and R. Stobaugh (1972), *Money in the Multinational Corporation*. New York Basic Books.

Rugman, A. (1979), *International Diversification and the Multinational Enterprise.* Health Lexington.

Shapiro, A. (1975), "Evaluating Financing Costs for Multinational Subsidiaries," *Journal of International Business Studies* (Fall).

_____ (1978), "Financial Structure and Cost of Capital in the Multinational Corporation," *Journal of Financial and Quantitative Analysis* (June).

_____ (1982a), "The Impact of Taxation on the Currency-of-Denomination Decision for Long-Term Foreign Borrowing and Lending," *Journal of International Business Studies,* forthcoming.

_____ (1982b) *Multinational Financial Management.* Boston Allyn & Bacon.

Solnik, B. (1978), "International Parity Conditions and Exchange Risk," *Journal of Banking and Finance* 2.

Stobaugh, R. (1970), "Financing Foreign Subsidiaries," *Journal of International Business Studies* (Summer).

Stonehill, A. and T. Stitzel (1969), "The Financial Structure of Multinational Corporations," *California Management Review* (Fall).

Stulz, R. (1982), "The Forward Exchange Rate and Macroeconomics," *Journal of International Economics,* 12.

Wihlborg, C. (1980), "Exposure Management of Foreign Subsidiaries," *Journal of International Business Studies* (Winter).

32

Innovation in the International Financial Markets*

Gunter Dufey and Ian H. Giddy

New financial techniques and instruments are created when both the demand for and the supply of those instruments become sufficiently large. New financial instruments appear almost always to represent new combinations or packages of a relatively small number of financial services. In the international context these packages are designed to cope with controls on international financial transactions and with the peculiar interest and exchange risks faced by international firms and banks. This approach, when applied to a wide range of new international instruments, seems to explain why some have failed and others have succeeded.

INTRODUCTION: A THEORY OF INTERNATIONAL FINANCIAL INNOVATION

Innovations in international financial markets arise when firms, usually financial institutions, find it profitable to offer or employ a technique or instrument which better fulfills one of the four functions provided by the international financial sector: 1) liquid and standardized instruments for effecting payments in individual currencies; 2) mechanisms for conducting monetary exchange between different currencies; 3) institutions and markets for channeling savings into investments across national boundaries; and 4) mechanisms for allocating, diversifying, and compensating for risk. The objective of this paper is to develop a theory of innovation in financial markets and to focus on factors which determine the creation and likelihood of success of such innovative instruments.

Generation of New Information

Innovation of any kind involves, among other things, the production of new information. The conditions for the socially optimal level of information generation and the optimal subsequent pricing of that information have been considered by Arrow [1], Demsetz [19], and Johnson [32], as well as others. While often costly to produce, new information can be used by any number of people without additional cost: it is a public good. The socially optimal price of a public good is zero. Indeed, the more easily new information is disseminated, the more likely its price will quickly fall to zero, thus reducing or eliminating private incentive to produce easily duplicated innovations. This is Arrow's "appropriability problem." [1] Three ways to reconcile this dilemma have been proposed: the government can create the information itself; the government can award prizes[1] to innovating firms in exchange for the right to disseminate the information freely; or private firms may be able to appropriate the returns through the creation of patent-protected

---

*This article reprinted with permission, from *Journal of International Business Studies,* Fall, 1981, pp. 33–51.

temporary monopolies. Where government intervention is absent or patent laws provide poor protection (as is often the case in international business), there is either little incentive for innovation or the market for innovation is internalized and the value of innovations exploited within the firm[2] (hence the existence of large, multinational firms in information-generating industries). In either case there will be welfare losses: in the former case, from inadequate innovation, and in the latter, from the reluctance of monopolistic firms to share the new information they have generated.

Innovative Financial Instruments and Techniques

Two strands of thought can be discerned in the meager literature on innovation of financial instruments and techniques.[3] One view holds that the spur to innovation comes mainly from an increased demand; the other view emphasizes changes in supply. To our knowledge, the first consistent framework was supplied by Greenbaum and Haywood [27] who stress rises in nonhuman wealth per capita as the primary, "demand" stimulus to innovation. Extending the Gurley-Shaw [28] hypothesis, Greenbaum and Haywood argue that because of fixed costs involved in portfolio management, increases in individuals' and firms' nonhuman wealth will result in a greater demand for a wider diversification of financial claims. Supply, in the Greenbaum-Haywood model, is largely a function of improvement in information over time.

In contrast, Ben-Horim and Silber [6] stress supply factors, particularly those associated with external constraints (regulatory or otherwise) imposed on financial intermediaries, and the availability of institutional support. They find some evidence that major U.S. financial innovations (such as negotiable Certificates of Deposit) occur in response to significant increases in the costs of financial constraints on banks. These increases alter the relative costs of various factors in financial service production and so lead to a search for new financial techniques or instruments with a less costly factor mix.

Both studies, then, hold the view that innovations result from changes in the financial environment and from responses aimed at maintaining or increasing profit or income. Although innovations can be "defensive" as well as "aggressive," environmental changes seem to provide the necessary incentive for innovation. (Whether the level and price of financial innovations are socially optimal remains unresolved.) On the other hand, the environment may also act as a disincentive to innovate. In any industry, the incentive for innovation will decline when patent protection is less effective, when the industry is potentially more competitive, and when product imitation is easier. Financial innovations are extremely easy to imitate because the instruments possess a limited number of attributes,[4] each of which is characterized by degree of risk and expected return. These in turn are functions of maturity, liquidity, the guarantor, and so forth.[5] Thus, we view most financial innovations, except those designed to circumvent regulations, as no more than a change in the combination of features of existing instruments. If this is correct, all an imitating firm need do is observe the particular arrangement of attributes in a competitor's contract and replicate them. Because of the technical ease of imitation and the difficulty of proving any financial contract to be unique rather than a variant of some existing combination, there can be no patent system for financial instruments or techniques.

In light of these environmental disincentives, one might suppose that the innovation rate in financial markets would be relatively low. Yet observations of the U.S. and international markets indicate that new instruments and techniques—successful and unsuccessful—have appeared frequently over the past two decades. To understand why this is the case, and which firms find it possible to retain profits from their financial innovations, a brief excursion into the literature from the advertising field is necessary.

A distinction has been drawn by Nelson [42] between "search" goods and "experience" goods. The qualities of the former are evident on inspection; advertising need only be factual. The qualities of experience goods, on the other hand, can be determined only by consuming them. Physical product innovations are search goods; any firm that can produce them can also sell them. This ease of entry is what makes patent protection necessary in such industries.

Services, however, including complex financial services, are experience goods, at least when first introduced. Because the risks and returns are hard to ascertain, customers will tend to purchase new financial instruments and services only from firms that have a sound reputation. Hence, there is an economic rationale for certain highly reputable financial institutions to specialize in the repeated development, marketing, and support of new financial contracts. These institutions will enjoy a temporary monopoly advantage that enables them to appropriate returns from investment in financial innovation. Even where the imitation lag is zero, innovation will continue, because new entrants with less prestigious names will normally be unable to appropriate the returns from innovation directly. The market for their talents will be internalized; inventive individuals or firms will tend to be absorbed by those who command the most confidence.

The higher the costs of introducing financial techniques or instruments, the more strongly this conclusion holds. Silber [52] has observed that, because financial instruments are held for their returns rather than for their direct utility, the ease with which a secondary market can be established strongly affects the likelihood of early success for new financial instruments. In some cases, the innovating firm may have to create the secondary market. The development and maintenance of such support constitutes a fixed cost, creating economies of scale and an obvious "free rider" problem.[6] Only a large firm with an efficient distribution network will be able to reduce such fixed costs, and only one with a reputation-induced temporary monopoly will be able to recover such costs as remain.

Inducements to Financial Innovation

Given an institutional mechanism for the continual generation of financial innovations, the theoretical problem remaining is to be able to predict what kind of innovations will appear, under what circumstances. As was observed in the previous section, innovations can be of two kinds: "aggressive" innovations, which are developed by firms specializing in new financial product introduction; and "defensive" innovations, which arise in response to changes in customer needs or in relative costs.[7] The former are presumably random and, in the financial industry, relatively infrequent. The latter, however, should be predictable. The hypothesis of this paper is that all defensive innovations are of two types: (a) changes aimed at circumventing government regulations of the price or quantitiy of financial services (either the regulations themselves change, or their effective costs change); or (b) adaptive changes resulting from changes in relative prices or relative risks that give rise to a "gap" in the range of available financial instruments.

The first type has been discussed frequently in the past. (See for example [27].) Silber [52] generalizes the notion to other constraints, including self- and market-imposed constraints. Many such innovations involve altering the jurisdiction or legal form of contracts without changing their riskiness or return.

The second type of defensive innovations, those that arise from newly emerged gaps in the range of financial services offered,[8] usually involves either unbundling or combining existing financial services. Unbundling of various services allows each to be priced and sold on its own merits, whereas combining services often reduces total transactions costs. Thus one might expect "combining" instruments to emerge in retail markets, and "isolating" instruments to appear in wholesale financial markets. Instruments that serve purely to transfer risk will likely emerge when risk in the financial environment increases.

Financial Innovation in an International Context

Some special conditions in the international financial environment have a bearing on financial innovation: (a) the regulatory environment is multinational, (b) the competitive conditions differ, and (c) exchange rate changes constitute an additional risk. Each feature will be considered in turn.

Institutions that have the flexibility to conduct business outside particular national jurisdictions can also design financial contracts that place the legal location of the contracts in favorable jurisdictions. Many international financial innovations, such as, Eurobonds, are structured to minimize government interference and to reduce taxes or other regulatory costs. In general, however, it is an oversimplification to claim that international financial transactions are exempt from government regulation and control.

Indeed, the general rule is that controls on transborder transactions—such as, transfer of financial instruments from one jurisdiction to another—are more severe than those on internal transfers. Whether the regulatory environment is more or less restrictive cannot be determined a priori. In some instances, the greater relative freedom has permitted the creation of new instruments, not available domestically; in other cases, greater restriction on international transfers of funds has produced innovations designed solely to circumvent the controls. In the absence of patent protection, some degree of monopolistic control is necessary for a firm to capture the returns from financial innovation. Because a greater number of large, experienced financial institutions participate aggressively in the international markets than in domestic markets, the degree of competition and the probability of rapid imitiation is heightened. The incentive for innovation should accordingly be reduced. Yet, the opposite extreme—the protected, domestic, cartel-like banking system—is not conducive to innovation, either. Arrow [1] has shown that the gains from cost-reducing innovations are smaller to a monopolist than to the competitive firms which can appropriate those gains. This confirms what intuition would suggest: monopolists or oligopolists face less pressure to innovate than do competitive firms. It is not clear, however, whether an innovation is likely to spread faster in a competitive market than in an oligopoly. Whereas competitive firms facing a high elasticity of demand will be forced to copy a cost-reducing innovation quickly, it is also true that oligopolists and cartel members tend to undertake major changes in concert. These considerations aside, it seems clear that, on balance, the rate of production and spread of financial innovations is greater in international than in domestic markets. One reason is simply the wider range of needs for specialized financial techniques. Another is that the greater variety of institutions and ideas in the international market leads to cross-fertilization of concepts and techniques which can be incorporated in new instruments. More participants also ensure better secondary markets. Most important, however, is the fact that the potential market for cost- or risk-saving techniques is much larger, even if the imitation lag is shorter.

Finally, the international environment involves fluctuating exchange rates, which not only create new risks and new types of transactions, but also require that financial institutions intermediate between entities which have different base currencies and different degrees of access to foreign exchange markets. As exchange rates and other financial variables have become less stable, the risks of international business have increased and the scope for financial innovation has expanded.

INTERNATIONAL FINANCIAL INNOVATION: A RESPONSE TO A RISKIER ENVIRONMENT

Changes in regulation and changes in the economic environment that produce a different set of risks and returns have been the inducements to defensive innovation in the international context. During the 1960s, rapid economic growth and increasing capital mobility in the industrial countries led governments to establish capital controls to defend their monetary policies and the fixed exchange rate system. The banks quickly responded by implementing techniques designed to circumvent these and other regulatory constraints. This was the decade in which Eurobonds, Eurodollars, and parallel loans were introduced.

By the mid-1970s, in contrast, the regulatory incentives for financial innovation were overshadowed by new economic incentives and changes in the competitive structure of financial markets. Floating exchange rates freed governments from the need to defend misvalued currencies. The financial systems of many major countries became more flexible: interest rate and credit controls had begun to lose their effectiveness. Governments themselves took advantage of the innovations of the previous decade by placing, borrowing, and recycling funds through the Euromarkets.

With greater mobility and flexibility, however, came greater financial interdependence and a period of adjustment to a changed system. Governments, attempting to compensate for the dissipated effects of traditional stabilization policies, increased their intervention in the money and foreign exchange markets; yet all that resulted was a less stable system, evidenced by the increased instability and volatility of exchange rates, interest rates, and inflation rates during the early seventies. The decade of the 1970s produced innovations to cope with exchange and interest rate risks and led to a boom in trading Eurodollars, Eurobonds, and floating rate notes. The remainder of this paper examines these and other innovations, and the reason for their success or failure.

INTERNATIONAL FINANCIAL INSTRUMENTS: SUCCESSES AND FAILURES

The Success Stories

This section describes the international financial innovations that must be considered successful, if only by virtue of the magnitude they have attained. The sequence moves from variations of traditional trade financing techniques to more exotic combinations. Then some examples of techniques and instruments that were not successful will be discussed, and an attempt will be made to draw some conclusions as to the distinguishing factors.

(a) Trade Financing Techniques Recycled

The first example illustrates how an age-old technique—export financing through bankers' acceptances—can be successfully adapted to take advantage of new opportunities provided by changes in the external environment. The factors that gave rise to *Forfaiting*[9] are closely linked to the activist role played by many governments in the economic development of their countries—particularly, but by no means exclusively, by the socialist countries. There, government-owned enterprises frequently import capital goods, often in the form of turn-key plants, from suppliers in industrialized countries on extended payment terms related to the life of the project. Such maturities, which may range anywhere from 3 to 12 years, cannot be handled through the institutions that traditionally undertake export financing. From the point of view of the exporters who may finance such transactions by borrowing in the markets, this would be costly. More important, technologically oriented capital goods manufacturers feel very uncomfortable with the economic and political risks associated with loans to foreign political entities. Forfaiting solves the exporter's problems, and it is also advantageous to the borrower—that is, the importer.

A typical transaction involves four parties: the exporter and the importer, the importer's bank (which also tends to be a government entity) and the forfaiter, usually a special purpose subsidiary of one of the large Swiss, West German, or Austrian banks which have pioneered this technique.

When the exporter's negotiations with the importing organization are nearly complete, the exporter obtains a commitment for the forfaiter to finance the transaction at a firm interest cost. This cost is the discount at which the forfaiter will purchase at the time the deal is completed. The forfaiter also charges a fee as compensation for the cost of assuming availability of funds, which may require him to borrow funds on a long-term basis and reinvest them on a short-term basis during the commitment period. [43] When the transaction is completed, the importer's organization gives the exporter a series of promissory notes with maturities staggered according to the repayment terms, usually in 6-month intervals reflecting the installments. Most important, these promissory notes are endorsed by the importer's bank which becomes the primary obligor in the transactions, just as in the case of a banker's acceptance.

The forfaiter will purchase the total bundle from the exporter without recourse, thus assuming the risk of the state-owned bank and, ultimately, of the government of the importer's country. The essence of forfaiting involves shifting the country's risk to an institution that specializes in assessing such risks. But the forfaiter is also an international market specialist. Usually the package of notes is broken up and sold to various investors who prefer different maturities. The forfaiter endorses the notes, thus collecting the risk premium in addition to the difference in yield between the value of the individual note and the discount which he obtained when he bought the package. Thus, the forfaiter exploits both differences in perceived political risk and also, possibly, imperfections in international money markets arising from transactions costs.

While it is fairly obvious why government banks will endorse the notes[10]—they obtain funds which contribute to the economic development of their country—it is not so obvious why they do not borrow directly in international credit markets. Here we encounter another market imperfection: the government banks believe—rightly or wrongly—that the obligations stemming from their endorsements, which are contingent liabilities, will count very little (if at all) against their credit limits in international markets. Because it is next to impossible to set objective credit limits for government borrowers, international lending institutions and their supervisory authorities frequently use arbitrary ratios in lieu of judgment. As the great majority of forfaiting transactions involve East European countries and some Middle Eastern and Latin American governments, forfaiting may represent a device for evading credit rationing in the western banking system.

A different twist on an old trade financing technique is the "domestication" of securities issued by foreign borrowers in national markets. For example, several Brazilian borrowers have gained access to the U.S. commercial paper market by having a domestic bank open a letter of credit on their behalf. [2] From a legal perspective this makes the bank the primary obligor and the paper becomes an acceptable investment for institutional investors which normally face externally or self-imposed restrictions on holdings of foreign securities.

(b) Eurobonds

The market for these instruments represents an example of the phenomenon of external markets that coexist and compete with their domestic counterparts. The concept is by now well accepted: an international instrument, identical to the domestic instrument in all respects except location of issue, will be free from certain costs or constraints. In practice, not all such instruments succeed, because not all serve a genuinely unsatisfied need in the most efficient fashion. Indeed, the supply of Eurobonds was for a long time inhibited by the high cost of issue and of organizing a secondary market. The basis of the Eurobond's success is an inconsistency in regulation: governments tend to limit the access of foreign issuers of bonds to their national markets, but have less stringent or noneffective controls on domestic investors who purchase foreign bonds. Internationally active investment banking firms can therefore issue bonds and similar debt instruments in such a way that national markets are bypassed. The issues are given the legal form of private placement and/or placement in nonresident investment accounts.[11]

The history of the Eurobond sheds an interesting light on the process of financial innovation. Although the pattern of regulation has been in existence for a long time, the market for Eurobonds did not develop until 1964 when the U.S. balance of payments program, particularly the Interest Equalization TAX (IET), closed the U.S. market to foreign borrowers. Until that time, this market had been reasonably open to all borrowers who were able to comply with SEC accounting and disclosure requirements—largely public entities from developed countries. No doubt a major factor preventing the earlier emergence of the market and contributing to its subsequent erratic growth was the difficulty of developing an organized secondary market for bonds sold in a variety of countries and lacking an integrated mechanism for trading. Substantial sales bagan only in the mid 1970s, 10 to 15 years after the first Eurobonds were issued. By that time, the volume of bonds outstanding had reached a critical point at which economies of scale in the secondary market came into play. Also, the gradual entry of institutional investors who trade in response to relatively small incentives contributed to the development of an active secondary market.[12] Indeed, when the IET was reduced to zero in January 1974, the Eurobond market continued to flourish, side by side with the revival of the market for foreign bonds in the United States.[13] By this time the instruments developed in the Eurobond market had spawned features distinct from those of the foreign bonds issued in the U.S. market. They are now quite different from bonds issued in any of the national markets.[14]

(c) Eurocurrencies

This paper would be incomplete without a brief consideration of the most eminently successful of postwar international financial innovations: the Eurocurrency, or external money market, competes directly with the domestic wholesale money markets of many countries.[15] The necessary condition for the existence of an external money market is that certain regulatory costs affecting both deposits and loans can be avoided by placing time deposits and loans on the books of financial institutions operating in jurisdictions that do not impose costly regulations, such as, reserve requirements, portfolio restrictions. The relaxation of comprehensive exchange controls on both residents and nonresidents has facilitated the international transfer of funds that arises in the course of transactions related to external intermediation.

This innovation has contributed significantly to the ease with which savers' and borrowers' needs can be reconciled, regardless of geographical location. Funds of great magnitude can be intermediated in a context of unrestricted competition, virtually free of administrative credit controls affecting either price or quantity. In essence, the Eurocurrency market has performed an important "unbundling" service by permitting the separation of country of jurisdiction from the currency of denomination of financial instruments.

(d) Eurodollar Certificates of Deposit

The Eurocurrency market has itself stimulated the development of several new instruments. As occurred in the U.S. money market, a successful market for negotiable certificates of deposit (CDs) has been created in London. These instruments, known as London Dollar CDs or Euro CDs, have been called "the first new negotiable instrument created under English Law since 1896." [58, p. 608] Their function is obvious: they represent Eurodollar deposits with negotiability and potential liquidity. Unlike Eurodollars per se, Euro CDs were created not by regulation, but by the desire of the issuing banks to have assured availability of funds while providing the depositor with the liquidity of an actively traded negotiable instrument. The key to the success of the Euro CD was therefore the development of a viable secondary market in London.

Two financial institutions undertook the initial investment in hopes of gaining a sufficiently high return before competition began to deprive them of the rewards for innovating. With hindsight it can be said that they were disapppointed.[16] Other banks quickly began writing similar paper in order to obtain funds at lower rates than were available through deposit taking. Many lenders prefer CDs which provide them with liquidity[17] and are therefore satisfied with a lower yield.

The innovators in the secondary market did not fare much better. Apart from White, Weld, & Co. (whose strength was in the underwriting), the secondary market in Euro CDs was dominated by the British discount houses that began dealing in these instruments as a sideline to their main business in short-dated governments, acceptances, local authority bonds, and so on.

When the volume of CDs outstanding had reached approximately $5 billion, the large U.S.-based money market dealers, using their extensive information and retail networks to good advantage, began outcompeting the London discount houses and—to a lesser extent—the brokers, in both the new issue business and much of the secondary market.

[53, p. 422] Today, the U.S. dealers play an important role in the Euro CD market, just as they do in the domestic CD market. At present the liquidity of the Euro CD secondary market is less than that of the U.S. market, largely because of the difference in volume. At the end of 1980 the value of Euro CDs outstanding was approximately one fourth of the volume of the domestic CDs.

(e) Roll-over Credits

Domestic banks, as a rule, have a wider range of stable sources of funds, ranging from demand deposits to equity capital. To the extent that these funds are insensitive to interest rate changes, domestic banks can afford to make loans at fixed rates. Eurobanks, in contrast, are specialized wholesale banks that rely on a sole funding source—large external time deposits, mostly from highly interest-sensitive depositors. The Eurobanks' cost of funds therefore varies directly with the level of short-term interest rates. How could they make term loans without facing considerable interest rate risk?

The answer was the roll-over credit, or revolver. Under this arrangement, funds are committed to the borrower for medium-term periods, such as 3 years; but the interest rate changes every 3 or 6 months in direct relation to prevailing short-term rates in the Eurodollar interbank market. Thus the availability of funds could now be assured for longer periods than the interest-commitment period, and medium-term loans could be safely funded by obtaining three- or six-month time deposits.

As interest rates began to fluctuate more widely, the advantage of distinguishing the loan agreement period from the interest rate period became increasingly important to the banks. Customers found these arrangements acceptable, because they were able to avoid the risk of loan nonrenewal. Nonfinancial enterprises are, as a rule, more willing than banks to bear an interest rate risk, especially if their net operating cash flow exhibits some positive correlation with interest rates. Today, the overwhelming majority of Euro-lending is done on a floating-rate basis, as is appropriate for periods in which inflation and interest rates fluctuate widely.

(f) Floating Rate Notes

From the revolving loan it was only a small step to the floating rate note (FRN), introduced in 1969. The FRN allowed some corporate borrowers to obtain funds directly from nonbank sources at interest rates that varied with short-term bank rates. These instruments allowed investors greater flexibility to focus on real interest rates in an environment characterized by unprecedented uncertainty about future movements of rates. The growth of FRNs has been impressive. In the first year of issue, the volume was approximately U.S. $15 million; in 1976, the volume was well over $1 billion.[18]

During the "Herstati Crisis" of 1974, banks learned to appreciate the fact that whereas the overall volume of funds available for deposits may be quite stable, or even expanding, individual institutions are not immune to a funding risk. Hence, the introduction of the bank FRN and the floating rate CD (which differ only in terms of subordination) provided the banks with the same "unbundling" of risks that the "revolver" had provided to their customers.[19] Floating rate CDs enable banks to be assured of the longer-term availability of funds, while allowing the interest rates on their liabilities to vary periodically with market rates. In addition, appropriate placement policies allow the issuing bank to broaden and diversify its sources of funds. As compared with banks, relatively few corporate borrowers use this vehicle, preferring instead revolving loans from banks and the commercial paper market. [49] Interestingly, occasional experiments with more complex clauses—such as, provisions for early redemption at the holder's option at declining discounts from par, or issues with declining spreads over the interbank deposit rate—have not been successful. Investors seem to have a strong preference for instruments which are conceptually simple.[20]

(g) Multicurrency Option Facilities

As corporations became aware of the different forms of loans and currencies available in the Eurocurrency market, a logical step was to structure loan agreements that would allow them to "draw down" funds on their borrowings in one or more stipulated currencies. The choice tends to be limited to those currencies which are "convertible" and for which external deposit markets[21]—or active forward markets—exist. The pricing is based on the London interbank rate, plus or minus a currency adjustment factor equal to the forward premium or discount prevailing in the foreign exchange market.

Multicurrency option facilities represent just one example of a whole class of instruments that reflect the intimate linkage between interest rates and exchange rates in a multinational market. The instruments differ in how they bundle and unbundle credit and currency transactions, the precise configuration being determined by transactions costs, regulation, and other market imperfections.

(h) Forward and Futures Contracts in Foreign Exchange

The basic instrument in foreign exchange is the forward exchange contract, where two parties agree to exchange currencies at a predetermined rate at a specific time in the future.[22] While the forward foreign exchange contract is, of course, not new, there are two variants that warrant notice. The first is the well-publicized futures contract, in effect a standardized forward foreign exchange contract that is negotiable, salable prior to maturity, and guaranteed to be relatively free of default risk. These features, together with the small denominations in which they are available, make the risks and returns of exchange rate changes accessible to the small investor. Such investors have therefore been willing to pay the higher transactions cost of the organized futures market. Despite such differences, empirical evidence reveals no statistically significant differences between forward and futures prices. [12]

(i) Swaps and Parallel Loans

The second variant of interest is the use of a forward exchange contract in conjunction with a credit arrangement which effectively changes the currency of denomination of that deposit or loan. A number of these combinations will be reviewed below; however, the general principle is that the currency of denomination of an asset can be "converted" by contractually selling the future cashflows from that asset for another currency. Similarly, the currency denomination of a liability may be altered by contractually purchasing the foreign currency necessary to liquidate that obligation. The remarkable feature of this use of forward contracts in the Eurocurrency market, for example, is that it enables banks to offer deposits or loans in any currency for which there is a forward exchange market, even if no external money market exists in that currency. The result is that the Eurodollar is the only full-fledged external money in existence; other Eurocurrencies are often simply Eurodollars linked to forward exchange contracts.

Currency Swaps

While the term swap has come to refer to almost any arrangement that incorporates a forward foreign exchange contract, currency swaps simply denote an agreement to exchange certain amounts of currencies on a spot basis and to reverse the transaction later at a specified time and rate. Currency swaps are used widely by foreign exchange traders who wish to limit their risk over time. When the regulatory environment compels it, corporations sometimes find (long-term) currency swaps useful.

The simultaneous spot purchase and forward sale of a foreign currency serves to lock in any difference between the spot and forward exchange rates. The difference, often referred to as the "swap rate," represents the change in value of funds at two separate points in time, and is therefore the equivalent of an interest rate. Because a currency swap locks in the nominal cost or return of a temporary conversion of funds into a second currency, it can be used to compare the rates of return in two currencies.

Credit Swaps

This instrument explicitly ties together a credit transaction and a forward contract, or their equivalents. A typical transaction would involve a firm in country A providing (hard) currency funds for its affilitate in a weak-currency country. The parent company, for example, would lend dollar funds to an intermediary—a commercial bank, or even the central bank of the weak currency country—which, in turn, lends local currency funds to the foreign affiliate. At a predetermined date in the future, the transaction will be reversed. The cost of the transaction is the interest rate on the dollar funds less the interest rate on the local currency funds, adjusted for the swap rate: the difference between the exchange rates used to convert the parent's funds into, and later out of, the affiliate's currency. Because of these contractural relationships, the intermediary (local or foreign central bank) bears the burden of the exchange risk on the (dollar) principal. The interest on the local currency loan, however, is subject to exchange risk in dollar terms.

Market imperfections provide the rationale for firms and intermediaries undertaking such complex deals instead of simpler alternatives, such as borrowing in the local money market, or lending dollar funds covered with a forward contract. Neither forward cover nor access to local credit markets may be available at reasonable rates. For the intermediaries, such credit swaps are a means of bolstering their foreign exchange reserves, using the financial needs of captive foreign affiliates to obtain these reserves at a lower cost than might be available through outright borrowing. Moreover, because they are close to the political powers that determine extent and timing of devaluations, they may be able to assess the foreign exchange risk better than private companies. Indeed, the intermediary bank is frequently the central bank itself.

A special form of credit swap is an arrangement whereby a claim is denominated in one currency (say, dollars) but the amount of principal and interest to be paid each period is determined by variations in the dollar exchange rate of another currency (such as yen). Thus if, one year after the issue of such a bond, the yen has risen by 5 percent, the dollar amount of principal and interest to be paid also rises by 5 percent. The purpose of this instrument, which is effectively a yen-denominated claim, is merely to avoid taxes and restrictions on securities denominated in particular currencies, such as yen. [60].

Arbi-Loans

This variation of the credit swap occurs when one unit of an integrated firm transfers funds to another unit to take advantage of capital market imperfections. The first affiliate borrows locally, at an advantageous interest rate and passes the funds to the second affiliate for use in the latter's currency. The loan is covered with a forward contract. In effect, the first unit acts as an intermediary, undertaking arbitrage between two financial markets. It is able to do so only if it has both access to cheap local funds and a means to move them out—say, via dividends or other intracompany payments. The funds are cheap in the sense that the difference between the local interest rate and the interest rate in the foreign currency exceeds the swap rate.

Parallel Loans

This is an arrangement under which two corporations (or other institutions) in different countries make loans to each other in their own countries and currencies. The classic example is that of an American firm making a dollar loan to the U.S. subsidiary of a British company, while the British firm simultaneously makes a sterling loan to the British subsidiary of the American firm. Such dollar/sterling parallel loans are concluded at an interest rate differential reflecting the difference between long-term interbank rates.

Each loan serves as collateral for the other and bears an interest rate related to local credit conditions plus the putative cost of a long-term forward exchange contract. Unlike some of the earlier examples, this technique is purely a by-product of regulation; it enables firms to avoid capital (and perhaps also credit) controls.[23] In concept, it is a costly and clumsy arrangement: two parties with matching needs have to be brought together, and the agreement is a combination of three financial contracts (two loans and one implicit forward transaction). Only regulations which constrain credit allocation or prevent free capital flows justify its existence.[24]

Apparent Failures

Our contention is that international financial innovations are likely to succeed only if they offer (1) a means of circumventing regulation, (2) an "unbundling" of previously linked financial services, or (3) a combination of services with relatively low transactions costs. Moreover, even if they fulfull one or more of these conditions, their success is likely to be hindered unless a secondary market or the institutional framework for such a market is already in place.

(a) Currency-Combination Instruments

A prime example of this concept is the "currency-basket Eurobond," much touted by international bankers and officials in past years. The intention was sensible: by offering a bond whose value was linked to a weighted average of several currencies, issuers provided investors with ready-made-currency diversification.[25] Some have even been denominated in Special Drawing Rights (SDRs)—a basket of currencies "backed by the IMF." Yet compared with total Eurobond issues, currency-combination bonds have failed dismally.[26] Why?

Banking practitioners claim that some of these currency baskets have been expensive to administer, and that they included minor currencies in which the investor had no interest; it has also been said that investors simply did not understand them. Although there may be some truth to this, the true reason is probably much simpler: the portfolio of the typical international investor is sufficiently large to allow him to obtain currency diversification tailored to his specific needs at little extra cost—for example, through the purchase of different bonds denominated in single currencies. This contention is supported by the fact that not only did complex, multicurrency formulae fail, but simpler units, based on only a few major currencies, also fared poorly. [11].

(b) Eurocommercial Paper and Euroequities

In the early 1970s, about a dozen U.S. multinational companies were persuaded to issue dollar-denominated commercial paper in London as an alternative to borrowing Eurodollars, largely to comply with U.S. foreign investment restrictions. What the promoters of the "innovation" overlooked was that the spread between deposit rates and borrowing rates is necessarily narrower in the Euromarket than in the domestic banking markets, and therefore the cost of intermediation was very low. Borrowers could save very little by going directly to investors for funds. This fact, together with the cost of issue and distribution, made the advantages of the instrument minimal, and the volume of Eurocommercial paper issued was very small.

Euroequities were an innovation that existed only in the minds of fast-working financial writers, who saw in the success of the Eurobond market the possibility of a similar opportunity for equities. As quickly became apparent, however, only fixed-interest Eurosecurities (for example, Eurobonds) can be sufficiently differentiated from their domestic counterparts to make possible issuing techniques that circumvent those restrictions and tax effects common to issues in national markets. Euroequities, wherever issued, would give a claim on the residual income of a subsidiary in an integrated corporation and so would not differ from parent-firm equities. Thus, one of the major preconditions for Euroequities—their regulatory advantage over and distinction from national equities—never existed. The few issues were actually either fixed-interest securities with an equity feature, similar to convertible bonds, or internationally distributed shares that were in no way different from those issued in a national market, and the end result was that many drifted back through arbitrage as soon as prices showed the slightest difference.

(c) Index-Linked Financial Instruments

During periods of monetary and economic instability, there is an obvious need for financial contracts that allocate equitably among borrowers and lenders windfall gains and losses arising from sizable, unexpected interest rate movements. Because nominal interest rates are determined largely by expected rates of inflation over the term of the contract, it is tempting to try to insulate financial contracts from unexpected changes in the price level by tying the yield to some index that represents this inflation factor. Yet a survey of the world's financial markets shows that index-linked financial assets are few and far between; even where they have been tried, they were often no more than relatively short-lived experiments. [45] Why have they consistently failed, given that the basic concept appears to be sound?[27]

The fact that we do not find indexation in the unregulated international markets suggests that there must be problems other than governmental opposition. One possible obstacle is that of finding an acceptable index. The usual price indices (consumer-, wholesale-, and GNP deflator) are not universally acceptable; the various goods that make up an index (or the weights assigned to them) may or may not be relevant for particular borrowers, or lenders, or both. Another problem is that the index must be objective and verifiable. Price indices in many countries are often not credible, because they are believed to consist of political numbers manipulated by the government.

Whereas it may be possible to overcome these technical difficulties (though at some cost), there is a more cogent reason why index-linked financial contracts are very rare: there exists a ready alternative, which is to shorten the maturity of the pricing contract.

Floating rates capture most of the variation in inflation, and they may have succeeded where index bonds have failed because market interest rates are objective and verifiable.

(d) Commodity-Linked Bonds

Even more rare than index-linked bonds are those where the principal (and possibly the interest rate) is tied to the price of a commodity. These instruments, more properly termed commodity equities because they are bonds only in the sense of seniority of claims, might provide an issuer with the assurance that his liability would rise or fall in line with his revenues. Thus, this instrument has been suggested as a solution to the debt problems of developing countries that rely for export receipts on one or two commodities.[28]

From the international investor's perspective, commodity equities (if objectively indexed) provide a means of participating in the risks and returns of primary producers.[29] Yet the fact that very few of these instruments have been floated suggests there may be problems on the supply side. First, the issuer is protected only on the revenue side. Should his costs increase by a similar amount, the burden of servicing the increased liability will be considerable. Second, rising prices for the commodity may coincide with a decrease in volume, further affecting net revenues from which the liability must be repaid. From the investor's perspective, changes in the value of his asset (the particular commodity) may not be linked to the cost of his consumption basket. It is not surprising that few of these instruments have actually been issued.

(e) Forward Forwards

During the late 1960s a market appeared in London that anticipated the now-thriving interest rate futures market, but itself never took off. A forward forward, or more correctly, a forward Eurodollar CD, is a contract to issue a Eurodollar CD at a fixed interest rate at a given date in the future. Such contracts, in conjunction with the issue of ordinary (spot) CDs, effectively constituted CDs of longer term than were at that time legally permitted in the UK. However, since the same effect can now be achieved as easily by simultaneously buying and selling CDs of different maturities, participants in the Eurodollar market have not employed this technique to any great extent. Whether the introduction of standardized Eurodollar futures contracts traded in organized markets will be able to capture the advantage of unbundling of two financial services (a pure interest rate plus a forward contract) remains to be seen.

(f) Foreign Exchange Options

Finally, several authors have pointed out the apparent need for puts and calls in spot foreign exchange. Shapiro and Rutenberg predicted in 1976 that "they will be available soon." [51, p. 53] These contracts involve two parties (a firm and a bank, for example), one of which has the right to purchase a currency at an agreed-upon exchange rate any time between two given dates. It has been shown that call option prices are tied to interest rates on single-currency and currency-option bonds. [24]

Conceivably, a firm could employ foreign currency options whenever it faces future cash flows that are fixed in amount but of uncertain timing or execution. Standardized contracts could make them accessible even to small investors on the organized futures markets; indeed, commodity options have attracted some investor interest. Such contracts do exist [30, p. 57; 3] but have never attained the status of an established market with publicly known prices. The reason may lie in part in the specialized nature of such instruments and the consequent difficulty of establishing a secondary market. A more persuasive reason, however, is that a bank offering an open options contract exposes itself

TABLE 1

International Financial Innovations in the Postwar Era

Instrument or Technique and Date of Introduction	Environmental Factor or Need To Be Filled	Supply Factor	Degree of Success
Swaps (late 1950s)	Currency flexibility in loans, deposits in a single money market	Potentially higher cost than alternative	High
Eurobonds (1958)	Domestic taxes and issue regulations	Severe secondary market difficulties at first	High
Eurodollars (1959)	Domestic bank regulation	Easy to issue	High
Currency basket bond (1961)	Ready-made diversification	Minimal secondary market	Minor
Roll-over credits (early 1960s)	Lenders match assets to liabilities	Transfer of interest rate risk	High
Parallel loans (early 1960s)	Credit and exchange controls	High cost of matching participants' needs	Modest
Currency option bond (1965)	Investor desire for probable gains but not losses from exchange rate changes	Highly risky for borrower	Minor
Dual-currency convertible bonds (mid-1960s)	Issue controls and exchange controls	Thin secondary market	Minor
London dollar CDs (1967)	Liquidity	Secondary market slow to grow at first	Modest
Forward forward CDs (late 1960s)	Transfer of interest rate risk	No secondary market; available in different form	Minor
Forfaiting (late 1960s)	Transfer of country risk to specialist institution	Adaptation of traditional technique	Modest

to considerable risk. Such risks are difficult to offset,[30] and a bank entering into a large number of option contracts would likely face regulatory constraints. In the absence of evidence to the contrary, therefore, we attribute the slow growth of foreign exchange options to government intervention in bank portfolio decisions.

CONCLUSION: A ROUGH TAXONOMY

Despite the fact that the decade of the 1970s appears to have been demonstrably more conducive than previous decades to the generation and support of international financial innovations, a number of well-publicized innovations have not met their proponents' expectations. The cost and success rates of past innovations are important determinants of the future fate of innovation. In the authors' view, the probability of success can be enhanced by drawing on the lesson of past failures—which is, that in order to succeed the innovation must involve a genuinely new combination of standard financial elements and

TABLE 1 *Continued*

International Financial Innovations in the Postwar Era

Instrument or Technique and Date of Introduction	Environmental Factor or Need To Be Filled	Supply Factor	Degree of Success
Floating rate notes (1970)	Transfer of interest rate risk	Small secondary market	Modest
Eurocommercial paper (1971)	None under existing regulatory system	Secondary market difficulties	Minor
Multicurrency option loan	Provides borrower flexibility	Increases risk for banks	Modest
Negotiable Eurocurrency loan participation notes (early 1970s)	Standardization potential liquidity	No assured secondary market	Minor at present
Currency futures (1973)	Standardization, negotiability; transfer of default risk	Institutional framework in place	High
Floating rate CDs (1977)	Transfer of commitment period risk	Small secondary market	Minor so far
Foreign exchange options (1970s)	Hedge currency risk of uncertain cash flows	Regulatory obstacles	Minor
Eurodollar interest futures (introduction under discussion)	Standardization, negotiability; transfer of default risk	Institutional framework exists	NA
Euroequity (never)	None at present	Secondary market assured	None
Index-linked bonds (rare)	Avoiding risk from unexpected inflation	No objective index available/secondary market difficulties	Minor
Commodity-linked bonds (rare)	Price fluctuation of reference commodity	Unrelated to cash flow of issuer	Minor

must bridge a gap arising from some change in the regulatory or economic environment. Judging the degree of success of a new technique is tricky: demand for some instruments is low merely because they successfully fill a narrow market need; and most innovations with an identifiable likelihood of failure never see the light of day. These reservations notwithstanding, Table 1 summarizes the major innovations and their characteristics. Next to each technique have been identified the major facilitating factors, such as regulatory circumvention, and the primary supply constraints or influences.

Several public policy implications emerge from the theory and this survey of financial techniques. Innovation is a public good, and as a rule there is a presumed rationale for the public production of public goods; where, as in the case of financial innovation, it appears that government agencies would be inadequate, there exists a case for patent protection or subsidy of innovators. Patents, however, are impractical for financial contracts, and the government cannot easily determine the appropriate subsidy for a financial contract. One form of subsidy might be in the support of secondary markets; government might commit itself to absorbing part of the losses of market-makers. Whereas this is done to some extent (through the tax system) by governments seeking to develop domestic capital markets, it is difficult to conceive of a mechanism for secondary market support on an international scale.

This leaves the risks and rewards of financial innovation largely in private hands, and especially in the hands of those financial institutions whose reputation allows them to appropriate the returns from financial produce development. Whether the rate of innovation that occurs in this fashion is socially optimal or not is impossible to say, although it seems probable that society as a whole would have gained from the earlier development of secondary markets for some instruments such as Eurobonds.

In conclusion, therefore, the public policy implications are primarily negative ones. First, it is contrary to the public interest, at least in this context, to seek to inhibit the risk-taking behavior of resourceful, reputable financial institutions: it is precisely they that have a comparative advantage in gaining a return from investments in new financial ventures. Second, the fewer the regulations that are placed on individuals' or firms' access to the full range of financial contracts, the greater the gain from, and reward to, innovation; the fewer the resources devoted to circumventing regulation; and the more resources alloted to the task of devising contracts that fully match investors' and borrowers' needs.

NOTES

1. See [33], pp. 341–343. The value of the prizes would be related to the net present value of the monopoly profits accruing to a patent-protected private innovator, if this value could be reasonably estimated.

2. For a detailed discussion of internalized versus patent-protected innovation, see [9], esp. Ch. 2.

3. In addition to the studies that follow, see [18] and [56].

4. The attributes, the last two of which are unique to international instruments, include: promised yield, expected rate of return, rate of return risk, liquidity or marketability, maturity or duration, assurance of availability of funds or claims, divisibility, currency of denomination, and country of jurisdiction.

5. Tobin has suggested that most of the relevant properties of assets can be classified under the headings of "liquidity," "reversibility," "divisibility," "predictability of value," "yield," "return," and "acceptability in exchange." See [27], p. 572.

6. The thinness of the secondary markets, for example, created a serious barrier to the acceptance of Eurobonds and Eurodollar certificates for deposit.

7. As with many such distinctions, this one is somewhat arbitrary; but it highlights some contrasts between innovations in stable and in unstable financial environments.

8. Holland [29] called this category "transcendental innovation" and cites fee-based services and negotiable certificates of deposit as examples. However, he argues that "transcendental innovation has slowed both absolutely and relative to circumventive innovation during the current period of economic difficulty." (p. 163).

9. The term comes from the French word "a forfait," meaning "without recourse."

10. Endorsement of the notes by a government-owned financial institution is very important. First, history has shown that, for a given government, the obligations of its financial institutions tend to have a higher priority than those of its commercial enterprises. Second, and more important, the endorsement (or "aval") makes each note a pure financial instrument, separated from the underlying economic transaction and free from any counterclaims of the importer against the exporter.

11. A typical example is a bond issue of a Norwegian municipality, that is managed by an underwriting group based in London, who places a portion of dollar-denominated instruments in the investment accounts that

French (or Italian, or Belgian, etc.) investors maintain in Switzerland (or Holland, or the United Kingdom, or Luxembourg).

12. Eurobond turnover cleared through the two dominant clearing systems, Cedel and Euro-clear, increased more than tenfold during the 1970s: see [7], p. 319.

13. For data, see OECD, *Capital Market Study—Statistical Annex* (OECD: Paris, periodic); Morgan Guaranty Trust Company, *World Financial Markets*, various issues; and U.S. Federal Reserve Board, *Federal Reserve Bulletin*, various issues.

14. For a detailed discussion of Eurobond issuing and underwriting techniques, see [23].

15. For recent surveys see [39] and [20].

16. Citicorp and White, Weld, & Co. were the institutions that introduced the instrument. They spent 15 months in tortuous discussions and legal inquiries; yet the first buyer of a $25,000 London CD was Chemical Bank in London, which promptly began printing its own in blatant imitation! On the other hand, several of the most prominent U.S. banks allowed 7 or 8 years to pass before entering the market. See [59], p. 608.

17. Sometimes this liquidity is illusory, as the issuance of a CD is accompanied by an informal agreement that the CD will not be traded; indeed, the paper is typically held in safekeeping by the issuing bank who will pay a higher rate. The buyer, in turn, can show on his balance sheet dollar assets that are not only safe, but appear to be liquid. Fifty percent of the total volume of Euro-CDs is believed by market observers to consist of "lock-up CDs" see [53], p. 420.

18. For year-by-year data, see *Kredietbank Weekly Bulletin*, 17 June 1977, pp. 6–7.

19. A further unbundling has been achieved by some syndication managers, who have divided syndicated Eurocredits into negotiable short-term instruments, sometimes called loan participation certificates. They are regarded as a hybrid of Eurocredits and floating rate notes, and are unique to the external markets because issuing them in the United States would subject them to S.E.C. requirements. For an example see [47].

20. This also holds to a recent "innovation" the drop-lock bond, which starts its life as an FRN. If the LIBOR Rate falls below a trigger rate, the FRN is automatically and permanently converted into a fixed-rate bond. [35] A similar fate befell a FRN that incorporated a deferred put option which allowed note holders to redeem the note at face value after 3 years. [48]

21. As bankers have learned to understand the interaction between external and national financial markets, some agreements have given the borrower an additional choice of drawing funds in a chosen currency in either the external or the internal market. Of course, the pricing differs and the agreements become rather complex. See, for example, [8].

22. If that date is 2 business days or less, the exchange is considered a spot transaction.

23. Another possible market imperfection is the banks' failure to offer long-term forward contracts at reasonable spreads, perhaps because the market is too "thin." In that case the corporation might as well undertake to find one of the contracting parties directly.

24. A variant of the parallel loan across currencies involves 2 offsetting transactions in the domestic and the external (Euro-) sector of the credit market in a single currency.

25. For an analysis of currency basket formulas, see [50].

26. For data, see *Kredietbank Weekly Bulletin*, 29 June 1979, p. 5.

27. Stanley Fischer has presented models of the demand for index bonds under several sets of conditions and concludes that "reasons for the nonexistence of indexed bonds in the U.S. economy do not emerge clearly from the analysis." [25], p. 527.

28. The most recent discussion of this proposal is in [36]. Mexico has issued five "Petrobonds" between April 1977 and April 1980, and a few (domestic), French issues have been linked to gold. In 1980 a silver mining company issued notes the value of which was linked to the price of silver [54].

29. An added advantage is the avoidance of the moral hazard problems associated with portfolio investment in markets lacking appropriate disclosure rules and other investor protection laws, which is typical for many LDCs.

30. Feiger and Jacquillat [24] have argued that foreign exchange puts and calls are redundant, in that by using a portfolio of currency option and conventional bonds one can "create" currency puts or calls. This implies that banks could create an offset, given that a sufficiently broad and deep currency option bond market existed.

REFERENCES

1. Arrow, Kenneth J. "Economic Welfare and the Allocation of Resources for Investment." In *The Rate and Direction of Inventive Activity: Economic and Social Factors*, Princeton: Princeton University Press, 1962. (A Report of the National Bureau of Economic Research.)
2. "A Way Out for Brazil." *Institutional Investor, International Edition*, December 1980, pp. 96, 97.
3. Babble, David F. "The Rise and Decline of Currency Options." *Euromoney*, September 1980, pp. 141–149.
4. "The Back-to-Back Loan: Intercompany Financing Via a Bank Intermediary." *Business International Money Report*, 3 June 1977, pp. 169–170.
5. "Banks as Borrowers." *The Banker*, January 1977, pp. 61–65.
6. Ben-Horim, Moshe, and Silber, William L. "Financial Innovation: A Linear Programming Approach." *Journal of Banking and Finance* 1 (1977), pp. 277–296.
7. Bolusset, Ivan. "Euro-clear et Cedel." *Banque*, March 1981, pp. 313–319.
8. *Business International Money Report*, 14 February 1975, p. 3; and 7 March 1975, p. 11.
9. Casson, Mark. *Alternatives to the Multinational Enterprise*. London: Holmes and Meier, 1979.
10. "Chicago BofT Developing Futures Pack for 90-Day Eurodollar CDs." *American Banker*, 3 July 1978, p. 1.
11. "Cocktail Hour in the Euromarkets." *Institutional Investor, International Edition*, December 1980, p. 122.
12. Cornell, Bradford, and Reinganum, Marc. "Forward and Futures Prices: Evidence from the Foreign Exchange Markets." Graduate School of Management, UCLA, Working Paper 7–80.
13. Craven, John A. "The Supersonic Rise of the Floating Rate Note." *Euromoney*, October 1976, pp. 80–91.
14. "The Currency Deals behind the Market's Spree." *Business Week*, 22 May 1978, p. 152.
15. "Currency Swap Outstrips Parallel Loan as Hedging, Financing Device." *Business International Money Report*, 30 September 1977, pp. 305–306.
16. "Currency Swapping: Attractive Financing Option for Consenting Firms." *Business International Money Report*, 24 June 1977, pp. 193–194.
17. Dempsey, James P. "The Mexican Back-to-Back Loan." *Euromoney*, May 1978, pp. 69–75.
18. Demsetz, Harold. "The Cost of Transacting." *Quarterly Journal of Economics*, February 1968, pp. 33–53.
19. ______. "Information and Efficiency: Another viewpoint." *Journal of Law and Economics*, 1969, pp. 1–22.
20. Dufey, Gunter, and Giddy, Ian H. *The International Money Market*. Englewood Cliffs: Prentice-Hall, 1978.

21. "Eurodollar Contract Puts BOT in World Futures." *Chicago Sun Times*, 21 June 1978.

22. "Euromarkets: At Last—the Floating Rate CD." *The Banker*, June 1977, pp. 35–37.

23. *Euromoney*, various articles, April 1978, pp. 21–121.

24. Feiger, George, and Jacquillat, Bertrand. "Currency Option bonds, Puts and Calls on Spot Exchange and the Hedging of Contingent Foreign Earnings." *Journal of Finance*. December 1979, pp. 1129–1139.

25. Fischer, Stanley. "The Demand for Index bonds." *Journal of Political Economy*, June 1975, pp. 509–534.

26. "Floating Rate Notes, A Novel Investment Formula." *Kredietbank Weekly Bulletin*, 17 June 1977, pp. 1–6.

27. Greenbaum, Stuart I., and Haywood, Charles F. "Secular Change in the Financial Services Industry," *Journal of Money, Credit and Banking*, May 1971, pp. 571–589.

28. Gurley, John G., and Shaw, Edward S. "Financial Aspects of Economic Development." *American Economic Review*, September 1955, pp. 515–538.

29. Holland, Robert C. "Speculation on Future Innovation." In *Financial Innovation*, edited by William L. Silber. Lexington: D. C. Heath, 1976, p. 163.

30. Hudson, Nigel R. L. *Money and Exchange Dealings in International Banking*. London: Macmillan, 1979.

31. Hutchins, Warren C. "Problems in Eurocurrency Credits." In *Financial Crisis: Institutions and Markets in a Fragile Environment*, edited by Edward I. Altman. New York: Wiley, 1977, pp. 226–229.

32. Johnson, Harry G. "The Efficiency and Welfare Implications of the International Corporation." In *The International Corporation*, edited by Charles P. Kindleberger. Cambridge, MA: MIT Press, 1978, pp. 35–56.

33. Kindleberger, Charles P. "Comment." In *The New International Economic Order*, edited by Jagdish N. Ghagwati. Cambridge, MA: MIT Press, 1977, pp. 341–343.

34. Lehman Brothers. "Currency Swaps." *Euromoney*, August 1976, pp. 109–111.

35. ______. "Multicurrency Convertibles." *Euromoney*, February 1976, p. 107.

36. Lessard, Donald R., and Wellons, Philip A. "Financing Development: Innovation in Private Capital Markets." Joint Study on International Industrial Cooperation prepared for United Nations Industrial Development Organization, April 1979.

37. "London Chooses the Wrong Option." *The Economist*, 25 March 1978, pp. 101–106.

38. "Market Innovation." *The Banker*, July 1979, p. 121.

39. McKinnon, Ronald I. "The Eurocurrency Market." *Essays in International Finance*, no. 125, Princeton University.

40. Mitchell, Richard, "How the Drop-Lock Bond Fits into Place." *Euromoney*, June 1979, pp. 149–151.

41. "Multinationals Seek Revolving Credits, Combining for Currency, Dollar Lines." *American Banker*, 18 July 1978, p. 1.

42. Nelson, P. "Information and Consumer Behavior." *Journal of Political Economy* 78, 1970, pp. 311–329.

43. Neuhaus, Walther. "Quoting for Long Commitment Periods." *Euromoney*, May 1978, pp. 77–84.

44. "No more." *The Economist*, 25 March 1978, pp. 39–40.

45. Organization for Economic Cooperation & Development. *Indexation of Financial Assets: Further Material on Problems and Experiences*. Paris: OECD, 1975.

46. "Parallel Loans and Long Term Currency Swaps." *Multinational Business*, no. 3 (1977), pp. 29–30.

47. Pearlman, Ellen. "Euronotes Hit The Big Time." *Institutional Investor, International Edition*, February 1981, pp. 29–30.

48. ______. "The Premiere of the Perpetual Put." *Institutional Investor, International Edition*, June 1980, p. 15.

49. Potter, David R. W. "New Cards and New Players." *The Banker*, January 1978, pp. 61–69.

50. Robichek, Alexander A., and Eaker, Mark R. "Debt Denomination and Exchange Risk in International Capital Markets." *Financial Management*, Autumn 1976, pp. 11–18.

51. Shapiro, Alan C., and Rutenberg, David P. "Managing Exchange Risks in a Floating World." *Financial Management*, Summer 1976, p. 53.

52. Silber, William L. "Towards a Theory of Financial Innovation." In *Financial Innovation*, edited by William L. Silber. Lexington: D. C. Heath, 1976, pp. 53–85.

53. Stigum, Marcia. *The Money Market: Myth, Reality and Practice*. Homestead, IL: Dow Jones-Irwin, 1978.

54. "Sunshine Mining Fashions Silver-Backed Certificates to Garner Big Savings." *Business International Money Report*, 21 March 1980, pp. 93, 94.

55. Teichman, Thomas. "Forfaiting." *The Banker*, March 1977, p. 41–44.

56. Tinic, Seha M. "The Economics of Liquidity Services." *Quarterly Journal of Economics*, February 1972, pp. 79–93.

57. "U.K. Banks Have Free Hand to Develop Imaginative Parallel Loan Deals." *Business International Money Report*, 5 May 1978, pp. 137–138.

58. "U.K. Portfolio Managers Trigger Second-Generation Currency Swap Deals." *Business International Money Report*, 9 June 1978, pp. 178–179.

59. von Clemm, Michael. "London Dollar CD: 10th Anniversary." *The Banker*, May 1976, pp. 607–609.

60. "Yen Issue Comes in Disguise." *Euromoney*, January 1981, pp. 150–151.

Capital Budgeting

33

International Capital Budgeting*

Alan C. Shapiro

INTRODUCTION

Multinational corporations evaluating foreign investments are forced to confront several capital budgeting issues that are rarely, if ever, encountered by wholly domestic firms. Here are just a few: How do foreign tax regulations affect the expected profitability of international investments? Should management evaluate projected cash flows from the standpoint of a foreign subsidiary, and in terms of local currencies, or from the home currency perspective? How can the use of foreign sources of financing be reflected in investment analysis? Should the required rate of return on international investments be raised to reflect risks like expropriation, currency controls, and exchange rate fluctuations? Are there significant benefits to investors from international portfolio diversification? and if so, how does this affect the value of foreign investment by multinationals?

My purpose in this article is to address these issues in the context of modern finance theory, and to present a practical framework that incorporates the special complications of international investment into the standard discounted cash flow (DCF) capital budgeting method. By reducing to a common denominator the effects of these complex factors on the expected profitability of contemplated foreign investments, the framework enables management to evaluate international projects on a uniform basis and, thus, to compare them directly with all other investment opportunities. The principle aim of the framework is to make the greatest possible use of available information about the expected risks and returns of foreign investment. At the same time, it eliminates some of the arbitrary adjustments of cost of capital and cash flow that are now common practice in multinational capital budgeting.

Before turning to the subject of international investment, I want to review the standard DCF method that most companies use to evaluate their capital investment alternatives. Then I will discuss the modifications of the standard DCF framework necessary to accommodate the special features of foreign project appraisal. This is followed by a discussion of the required rate of return, or cost of capital, for foreign investments. Finally, having proposed a financial framework for quantifying the value of investments, I offer a theoretical rationale for direct foreign investment that attempts to identify the characteristics most likely to distinguish—*prior* to any detailed, systematic financial analysis—profitable from unprofitable foreign projects. Such a rationale should serve as a basic guide for multinational strategic thinking; it can also be used to furnish the criteria for the first screening of foreign investment opportunities.

THE DISCOUNTED CASH FLOW FRAMEWORK

The standard capital budgeting analysis has two steps. The first, and ordinarily the most time-consuming, is the estimation of expected after-tax cash flows associated with a

---

*This article reprinted, with permissiom, from *Midland Corporate Finance Journal,* Vol. 1, no. 1, Spring 1983, pp. 26–45, published by Stern, Stewart, Putnam and Macklis, Ltd., Corporate Financial Consultants.

prospective investment. The second is the discounting of those cash flows back to the present using the company's weighted average cost of capital. If the resulting number, known as the net present value (NPV) of those cash flows, is positive, the investment should be undertaken; if negative, it should be rejected.

The weighted average cost of capital (WACC) is conceptually simple and easy to apply. Recall that the calculation of WACC involves weighting the after-tax cost of each component of capital by its proportional representation in the company's (target) capital structure. For a company with only debt and equity in its capital base, its overall cost of capital and, hence, its required rate of return on normal investments, would be expressed as follows:

$$\text{WACC} = (\text{Cost of Debt} \times \text{Debt/Total Capital}) + (\text{Cost of Equity} \times \text{Equity/Total Capital})$$

The use of the weighted cost of capital is thus predicated on the assumption of a specific financing structure, or debt-equity ratio, *for each individual project*. Consequently, the indiscriminate, corporate-wide use of a single rate is appropriate only when the financial structures and commercial risks are similar for all investments considered. The costs of debt and equity will vary with different project risks. Furthermore, because projects with different risks are likely to have different debt capacities, their required rates of returns should be calculated using not the company's capital structure, but rather the financial structure supported by the project standing apart from the company.

Another objection to the use of a single corporate-wide discount rate—one especially pertinent to foreign investments—is its failure to reflect the availability of project-specific loans at concessionary rates. There also may be cases where the multinational (MNC) may choose to use foreign source funds having a higher cost due to home country exchange controls. The benefits or costs of these unusual sources of financing should be reflected in the analysis.

An Adjusted Present Value Approach

One way to reflect these deviations from the company's typical investment and financing policy is to adjust the company's weighted average cost of capital. But, for some companies, such as those in extractive industries, there is no norm. Project risks and financial structure vary by country, raw material, production stage, and position in the life cycle of the project. Such problems can be dealt with by using an alternative procedure, known as the "adjusted present value" (APV) approach. Developed by Stewart Myers[1] in the early 1970s, the APV approach involves discounting cash flows at a rate that by removing the effects of financing, reflects only the business risks of the project. This rate, called the *all-equity* rate (also known as the "cost of capital for business risk"), represents the required rate of return on a project financed entirely with equity.

The all-equity rate, c, can be used in capital budgeting by viewing the value of a project as the sum of the following components: (1) the present value of project cash flows after taxes but before financing costs, discounted at c; (2) the present value of the tax savings on debt financing, discounted at the company's normal domestic borrowing rate, b; and (3) the present value of any savings on (or penalties from) interest costs associated

[1]Myers, Stewart C. (1974), "Interactions of Corporate Financing and Investment Decisions," *Journal of Finance*, March, pp. 1–26.

with project-specific financing, discounted also at b.[2] This latter differential would generally be due to government regulations and/or subsidies that caused interest rates on restricted funds to diverge from domestic interest payable on unsubsidized, arm's-length borrowings.

In equation form, the APV of a project can be expressed as follows:

$$APV = -I + \underset{(1)}{\frac{X}{c}} + \underset{(2)}{\frac{(b \times D) \times t}{b}} + \underset{(3)}{\frac{(b - b') \times D'}{b}}$$

where:

- I is the initial investment, assuming a one-time initial outlay
- X is the expected annual operating after-tax cash flow, assuming the project is financed with all equity (and has an infinite life)
- c is the risk-adjusted required rate of return on the specific project, assuming the project is financed solely with equity
- b is the company's normal domestic borrowing rate
- D is the amount of debt financing supported by the project (assumed to be constant throughout the project's life)
- t is the company's marginal tax rate
- b' is the rate of interest (translated into its domestic equivalent) on special foreign source financing
- D' is the amount of special foreign source debt financing used (also assumed to be constant throughout)

It should be emphasized that the all-equity cost of capital equals the required rate of return on a *specific* project; this in turn can be broken down into the riskless rate of interest plus an appropriate risk premium based on the project's particular risk. Thus c varies according to the risk of the specific project.

Recall also that, in accordance with the capital asset pricing model (CAPM), the risk reflected in c is only "systematic risk." As measured by "beta," systematic risk reflects not the total variability of a company or project's expected returns, but rather its co-variability with market-wide (e.g., S&P 500) average returns. It is a measure of investors' exposure to "non-diversifiable" or market risk and, as such, reflects the sensitivity of an investment's return to general economic conditions which affect all stock prices.

For project analysis, this means that a project's risk and, thus, its minimum required

[2]In a paper published in 1979, Donald Lessard discusses these issues in his extention of the APV approach to foreign project appraisals. See Donald R. Lessard, "Evaluating Foreign Projects: An Adjusted Present Value Approach," in Donald R. Lessard, ed. *International Financial Management*, Boston: Warren, Gorham & Lamont.

rate of return should reflect its correlation only with overall market returns. The interaction of the project's returns with the returns of the company's other investments is largely irrelevant, and thus should be ignored, in the valuation and capital budgeting process. The message of modern finance is that, in well-functioning capital markets, *corporate* diversification does not add value. Why, after all, should investors pay premiums for diversified companies when they can privately and cheaply accomplish the same end by buying a mutual fund? Casual observation, combined with what evidence we have on this question, says that the market doesn't reward companies for diversification it can easily duplicate at the same or lower cost.

In short, each individual project should be viewed as having its own required return; and this risk-adjusted minimum return, or "cost of capital," is completely unaffected by the composition of the company's portfolio of present and prospective investments.

ISSUES IN FOREIGN INVESTMENT ANALYSIS

With this review of the principles of valuation as background, let's turn to two troublesome issues confronting foreign project analysts:

1. Should expected cash flows be measured from the standpoint of the project (or the foreign subsidiary's managers) or from that of the parent company?
2. Should the uniquely foreign economic and political risks be reflected by raising the required rate of return (or the discount rate) or by adjusting expected cash flows?

Parent Versus Project Cash Flows

Because of tax regulations and exchange controls, a substantial difference can exist between the cash flow of a project and the amount that can be remitted to the parent multinational corporation. Also, many project expenses, such as management fees and royalties, are actually returns to the parent company. And, yet another source of this discrepancy, the *incremental* revenue contributed to the parent MNC by a project can differ from total project revenues if, for example, the project involves substituting local production for parent company exports, or if transfer price adjustments shift profits elsewhere in the system. (It is only incremental revenues, of course, that should be credited to the project.)

Given the appreciable differences between parent and project cash flows likely to exist, what, then, are the relevant cash flows to use in evaluating a foreign project? The managers of a foreign subsidiary can be expected to focus only, of course, on those project cash flows accruing locally. Unless compensated for doing otherwise, they will tend to ignore the consequences of their investment policies on the economic situation of the rest of the MNC.

Partly because of the impracticability of expecting local management to take a global view, and partly out of a desire to decentralize decision-making and offer foreign managers greater autonomy, some have suggested that the effect of restrictions on repatriation be ignored. According to economic theory, however, the value of a project is determined by the net present value of future cash flows *back to the investor*. Thus, the parent MNC should value only those cash flows (net of any transfer costs such as taxes) that are—or, more precisely, *can be*—repatriated. Only remittable funds can be used to pay dividends and interest, to amortize the firm's debt, and to reinvest.[3]

To overcome the problem caused by the difference between project and parent cash flows, I recommend that the financial analysis of foreign investments proceed in three stages. In the first stage, project cash flows are computed solely from the subsidiary's standpoint, as if it were a separate national corporation. In the second stage, the perspective shifts to that of the parent company. This step requires specific forecasts of the amounts, forms, and timing of transfers (assuming all repatriable cash is actually remitted) to headquarters. It also involves gathering information about taxes and other expenses incurred in the transfer process. Third and last, the parent company should take into account the indirect benefits and costs this investment confers or imposes on the rest of the system, such as an increase or decrease in export sales by another affiliate. This, of course, may not be easy to do. In some cases, management may be able to estimate incremental cash flows to the parent only by subtracting worldwide parent company cash flows (without the investment) from post-investment parent company cash flows.

While the principle of adjusting and valuing incremental cash flows is conceptually simple, it can become quite complicated in its actual application. Let's look at how this recommended procedure might be applied, with special attention to the tax question.

Incorporating Tax Factors

Because only after-tax cash flows are relevant, it is necessary to determine when and what taxes must be paid on foreign-source profits. On the basis of existing tax laws, taxes paid are a function of the time of remittance (are profits remitted immediately or are they reinvested?), the form of remittance (whether as dividends, loan repayments, or transfer price adjustments), the foreign income tax rate, the existence of withholding taxes, the treaties between home and host countries, and the existence and usability of foreign tax credits.

Because of these complexities in estimating actual after-tax cash flows back to the parent, I propose a simpler approach for calculating the tax liabilities on the foreign investment. This approach makes two conservative assumptions: first, the maximum amount of funds available for remittance in each year is actually remitted; second, the tax rate applied to these cash flows is the higher of the home or host country rate. This means that a project is evaluated as if the maximum allowable amount of dividends were repatriated each year. (See box on following page).

The fact that there are substantial tax savings from reinvesting locally instead of repatriating can be ignored at this initial stage of the investment analysis. The recognition of excess foreign tax credits and alternative, lower-cost remittance channels should also be deferred. Finally, in order to avoid understating the parent's tax liability (by understating remitted cash flow), all funds expected to be transferred back to the parent in the form of management fees, royalties, and licensing fees are included in this initial stage of the analysis.

The reasoning behind this division of the investment analysis procedure into these stages is straightforward: if the investment is acceptable under conservative assumptions, then it will be acceptable under a more liberal set of circumstances, and it will not be

[3]This principle also holds, of course, for a domestic firm. For example, dividends received by a parent firm from an unconsolidated domestic subsidiary (less than 80% ownership) are taxed at a 15% rate and, hence, should be valued at only 0.85 of the original dividend paid.

A simple calculation of an MNC's marginal tax rate on remitted foreign-source earnings illustrates the procedure. Suppose after-tax earnings of \$120,000 will be remitted by an affiliate to its U.S. parent in the form of a dividend. Assume the foreign tax rate is 40%, the withholding tax on dividends is 4%, and excess foreign tax credits are unavailable. The marginal rate of additional taxation is found by adding the local withholding tax to the U.S. tax owed on the dividend. Withholding tax in this case would equal \$4,800 (\$120,000 × .04), while U.S. tax owed would be \$7,200. (The U.S. tax is calculated as follows. With a before-tax local income of \$200,000 (\$200,000 × (1 − .4) = \$120,000), the U.S. tax owed before foreign tax credits would equal \$200,000 × .46, or \$92,000. The firm would receive foreign tax credits equal to \$84,800, for the \$80,000 in the local tax paid and the \$4,800 dividend withholding tax. This leaves a net of \$7,200 owed the IRS.) The incremental taxes on the MNC's remitted foreign-source earnings would thus equal \$12,000 (\$4,800 + \$7,200) and the marginal tax rate would be 10% (\$12,000/\$120,000).

necessary to calculate all the additional tax savings possible. If the initial net present value is negative under these conservative assumptions, then the additional tax savings can be estimated and added back.

Political and Economic Risk Analysis

All else being equal, multinational companies prefer to invest in countries with stable currencies, healthy economies, and minimal political risks. But because all else is usually not equal, management must carefully evaluate the consequences of various political and economic risks for the viability of potential investments.

There are presently, to my knowledge, four practical (though not necessarily correct) methods of incorporating international political and economic risks, such as the risks of currency fluctuations and expropriation, into foreign investment analysis. They are:

1. Shortening the minimum payback period.
2. Raising the required rate of return of the investment.
3. Adjusting cash flows for the costs of risk reduction; e.g., charging a premium for overseas political risk insurance.
4. Adjusting cash flows to reflect the specific impact of a given risk.

Adjusting the Discount Rate or Payback Period

The additional risks confronted abroad are usually discussed in general terms rather than in direct relation to specific investments. This rather vague view of risk probably explains the popularity of two questionable approaches to account for the added political and economic risks of overseas operations. One is to use a higher discount rate for foreign operations, the other to require a shorter payback period. For example, if exchange restrictions are anticipated, a normal required return of 15% might be raised to 20%, or, alternatively, a five-year payback standard may be shortened to three years.

Neither of these approaches lends itself to careful evaluation of the actual impact of a particular risk on expected investment returns. Thorough risk analysis requires an assessment of the magnitude and timing of such risks, and their implications for the projection of cash flows. For example, an expropriation expected five years hence is likely to be much less threatening than one anticipated next year, even though there is a higher probability associated with the former. Using a uniformly higher discount rate to reflect these quite different expropriation risks only serves to distort the meaning of the *present value* of a project by penalizing future cash flows relatively more heavily than current ones. It is not a good substitute for careful risk evaluation.

Furthermore, the choice of a risk premium (or risk premiums, if the discount rate is allowed to vary over time), whether 2% or 10%, is an arbitrary one. Adjusting cash flows instead of assigning some more or less arbitrary risk premium makes it possible to make fuller, more specific use of the information available about the effects of a specific risk on the future returns from an investment.

The two principal methods for adjusting cash flow estimates to reflect international risks are: (1) uncertainty absorption and (2) adjustment of expected values of future cash flows.

Uncertainty Absorption

Uncertainty absorption is used to quantify the effect of international risk by charging against each year's flows a premium for political and economic risk insurance, whether or not such insurance is actually purchased.[4] Political risks like currency inconvertibility or expropriation can be covered by insurance bought through the Overseas Private Investment Corporation, a U.S. government agency. Economic risks like currency fluctuations can be hedged in the forward exchange market. In the latter case, the uncertainty absorption approach involves adjusting each period's dollar cash flow by the cost of a hedging program (again, regardless of whether the program is put in place).

There is, however, a problem with the uncertainty absorption method: it does not accurately measure the effect of a given political or economic risk on the present value of a project. In the case of expropriation, political risk insurance normally covers only the book value, not the economic value, of expropriated assets. The relationship between the book value of a project's assets and the economic value of a project, as measured by its future cash flows, is at best tenuous. It is worthwhile, of course, to compare the cost of political risk insurance with its expected benefits. But insurance is no substitute for a careful evaluation of the impact of political risk on the expected profitability of a specific project.

As a method for dealing with exchange risk, the uncertainty absorption technique is fine if local currency cash flows are fixed, as in the case of interest on a foreign currency-denominated bond. But, where income is generated by an ongoing business operation, the operating cash flow in local currency will itself be affected by changes in the exchange rate.[5] This effect is entirely ignored by the uncertainty absorption technique.

Adjusting Expected Values

In 1978, I published a paper recommending that the expected cash flows, not the discount rate, of a project be adjusted to reflect the *specific* impact of each perceived risk. The argument was based largely on my firsthand observation that management typically has more and better information about the effect of a given risk on a project's cash flows than

[4]This is the approach recommended by Arthur Stonehill and Leonard Nathanson in "Capital Budgeting and the Multinational Corporation," *California Management Review*, Summer 1968, pp. 39–54.

[5]As pointed out by Ian Giddy (1976) and a number of others, there is a set of equilibrium conditions in an efficient foreign exchange market that generally cause exchange rate changes and inflation to have only a minimal impact—at least over the long run—on real cash flows. To be more specific, the relative version of purchasing power parity states that changes in the ratio of domestic and foreign prices will equal changes in the equilibrium exchange rate. This means, for example, that the effect on cash flows of a foreign currency depreciation should be largely offset by a higher rate of foreign inflation.

about its effect on shareholders' required return. Such cash flow adjustments, by assigning probabilities to various economic and political events, will generate an *expected* value for the project; that is, the value resulting from this adjustment will reflect the expected "mean" or average outcome of a number of possible effects on cash flow caused by specific international risks.

In adjusting expected cash flow downward and allowing the discount rate to remain unchanged, this procedure does not assume that shareholders have a neutral attitude toward risk. What it does assume, however, is that either (1) risks such as expropriation, currency controls, inflation, and exchange rate changes are unsystematic or (2) the diversification provided by foreign investment may actually *lower* a firm's systematic risk. If the latter is true (and, as I will argue later, there is some persuasive evidence to support this belief), adjusting only the expected values of future cash flows will yield a *lower bound* on the value of the investment to the firm.

According to modern capital asset pricing theory, adjusting expected cash flows, instead of the discount rate, to reflect incremental risks is justified so long as the systematic risk of a proposed investment remains unchanged. To the extent that these international political and economic risks are unsystematic, there is no theoretical reason to adjust the cost of capital of a project to reflect those risks. The possibility that foreign investments may actually reduce a firm's systematic risk by providing international diversification means that this approach, if anything, underestimates the present value of a project to the parent corporation.[6]

The Impact of Political Risk

In recent years, there has been a significant increase, in developing and developed countries alike, in the kinds and magnitude of political risks that multinational companies have historically faced. Currency controls, expropriation, changes in tax laws, requirements for additional local production or expensive pollution control equipment—these are just some of the more visible forms political risk can take. The common denominator of such risks, however, is not hard to identify; government intervention into the workings of the economy that affects, for good or ill, the value of the firm. While the consequences are usually adverse, changes in the political environment can provide opportunities. The imposition of quotas on autos from Japan, for example, was undoubtedly beneficial to U.S. auto manufacturers.

Measuring Political Risks

A number of commercial and academic political risk forecasting models are available today. These models typically supply country indices that attempt to quantify the level of political risk in each nation. Most of these indices rely on some measure(s) of the stability

[6]Although the suggestion that cash flows from politically risky areas be discounted at a rate that ignores those risks is contrary to current corporate practice, the difference may be more apparent than real. In 1979, Donald Lessard observed that most firms evaluating foreign investments discount most likely ("modal") rather than expected ("mean") cash flows at a risk-adjusted rate. If an expropriation or currency blockage is anticipated (though with a probability well under .50), then the mean value of the probability distribution of future cash flows will be significantly below its mode. Thus, the negative effect of the widespread practice of raising the discount rate may, in the typical case, be offset by the perhaps equally popular practice of using most likely rather than average cash flows. From a theoretical standpoint, of course, cash flows should always be adjusted to reflect the change in the mean or expected values caused by a particular risk. But such flows, to repeat, should be further discounted only in cases where the attending international risks can be shown to be systematic.

of the local political regime. Such measures may include the frequency of changes of government, the level of violence in a country (for example, violent deaths per 100,000 population), number of armed insurrections, conflicts with other states, and so on. The basic function of these stability indicators is to determine how long the current regime will be in power and, equally important, whether that regime will also be willing and able to enforce its foreign investment guarantees.

Other popular indicators of political risk include various economic factors such as inflation, balance of payments deficits or surpluses, and the level and growth rate of per capita GNP. The intention behind these measures is to determine whether the economy is in good shape or requires a "quick fix." Foreign governments with sagging economies often resort to expropriations to increase government revenues, or to measures blocking currency conversions to improve their balance of payments.

Despite the increased sophistication of these models, there is little evidence of their success in forecasting political risk. For one thing, political instability by itself does not necessarily contribute to political risk. Changes of government in Latin America, for example, are quite frequent; yet, most multinationals continue to go about their business undisturbed.

The most important weakness of these indices, however, is their implicit assumption that each firm in a country faces the same degree of political risk. As indicated by the empirical evidence on the post-World War II experiences of U.S. and British MNCs, this assumption is manifestly untrue. The data clearly show that, except in those countries that went Communist, companies differ in their susceptibilities to political risk according to their industry, size, composition of ownership, level of technology, and degree of vertical integration with other affiliates.[7] For example, expropriation—or, its more prevalent form, creeping expropriation—is more likely to occur in the extractive, utility, and financial service sectors of an economy than in the manufacturing sector.[8] Also, the expected effect of currency controls will probably not be the same over the life of an investment. It is only when a project is throwing off excess cash that restrictions on profit repatriation generally become a problem.

Because political risk has a different meaning for, and effect on, each firm, it is doubtful that any index of generalized political risk will be of much value to a company selected at random. The specific operating and financial characteristics of a company will largely determine its susceptibility to political risk and, hence, the effects of that risk on the present value of its foreign investment.

Managing Political Risk

Once a firm has assessed the political environment of a country, it must then decide whether to invest and, if so, how to structure its investment to minimize political risk. The important point to keep in mind, once again, is that political risk is not independent

[7]See, for example, Truitt, J. Frederick (1970), "Expropriation of Private Foreign Investment: Summary of the Post-World II Experience of American and British Investors in the Less Developed Countries," *Journal of International Business Studies*, Fall, pp. 21–34. Also Hawkins, Robert G.; Mintz, Norman; and Provissiero, Michael (1976), "Government Takeovers of U.S. Foreign Affiliates," *Journal of International Business Studies*, Spring, pp. 3–15.

[8]See David Bradley (1977), "Managing Against Expropriation," *Harvard Business Review*, July–August, pp. 75–83. Bradley argues that companies whose inputs and services are more easily replaced are more likely to be subject to expropriation.

of the firm's activities. The substance and form of the firm's investments will, in large measure, determine their susceptibility to changing government policies. For example, a multinational can reduce the risk of expropriation by keeping the project dependent on affiliated companies for markets, supplies, transportation, and technology. Another defensive ploy is to offer local foreign investors or government agencies a stake in the venture's success.[9] Similarly, a firm can reduce the impact of currency controls by investing in the form of debt rather than equity (because governments are more hesitant to restrict loan repayments than dividends), borrowing locally, and setting high transfer prices on goods sold to the subsidiary while buying goods produced by the subsidiary at lower prices where legally possible.[10] Obviously, it is important to incorporate these methods into a capital budgeting and planning procedure that is completed *before* the initial commitment of funds.

One other point: the automatic inclusion of depreciation in computing cash flows from domestic operations is questionable when evaluating a foreign project. Dividend payments in excess of reported profits will decapitalize the enterprise, thereby inviting closer host government scrutiny. Using depreciation cash flows to service parent company debt, however, is generally more acceptable. Thus, while parent company funds—whether called debt or equity—require the same return, the cash flow from foreign projects could very well be affected by the form of the investment.

Cash Flow Adjustments for Political Risks

To make the greatest possible use of available information, political risks should be incorporated into foreign investment analysis by adjusting the expected cash flows of a project, not its required rate of return. In this section, I want to demonstrate the application of my proposed cash-flow adjustment method using the extreme case of political risk: an expropriation. The aim of this exercise is to illustrate how a multinational investment analyst could quantify the effect of an expropriation (or any other form of political risk) on the present value of a contemplated foreign investment.

Let's assume that, in the absence of expropriation, the expected cash flow of a given project over a specified period is $1 million. Assume also that if expropriation occurs prior to that time, the expected cash flow is zero. If we can assign a probability of expropriation of .25, the expected cash flow during that period would be $750,000 ((.76 × $1,000,000) + (.25 × 0)).[11]

[9]In a paper published in 1981, I provided a framework for the assessment and management of political risk, concentrating on the methods available to reduce the risk of expropriation. See Alan C. Shapiro (1981), "Managing Political Risk: A Policy Approach," *Columbia Journal of World Business*, Fall, pp. 63–70.

[10]Numerous other mechanisms available for accessing or otherwise using blocked funds are described in my own paper, "Managing Blocked Currency Funds," University of Southern California Working Paper (1980). They include swap, parallel, and back-to-back loans, leading and lagging, purchase of commodities and local services for use abroad, conducting research and development locally, and hosting corporate conventions and business meetings locally.

[11]In the event of an expropriation, the expected return is not likely to be zero. Thus, it is also necessary to estimate the expected value of the net compensation provided in such a case. While difficult to foresee with any precision, such post-expropriation compensation can be expected to come from several sources:

- Direct Compensation paid to the firm by the local government. (This compensation can be delayed, as in Chile, for example, where many MNCs were expropriated by the Allende government with little or no

Calculating the probability of expropriation with any level of confidence is, of course, difficult, if not impossible. In cases of extreme uncertainty about the timing of a possible expropriation, an alternative to assigning probabilities is to use a form of break-even analysis. Suppose, for instance, that management is reasonably certain that expropriation will occur either in the third year of the project or not at all. If no expropriation occurs, the project's net present value (NPV) is estimated to be \$3 million. If an expropriation does occur, however, the expected NPV is −\$2 million. In this case, the expected NPV (in millions) equals $-2p + 3(1-p)$, where p is the unknown probability of expropriation. The value of p at which the project breaks even can be found by solving for p^* where $-2p^* + 3(1-p) = 0$, or $p^* = .6$. Thus, if the probability of expropriation is less than .6, the project will have a positive expected net present value. This probability break-even analysis is often more easily applied because it is normally easier, and certainly requires less information, to ascertain whether p is less or greater than .6, than to decide on the absolute level of p.[12]

Cash Flow Adjustments for Exchange Rate Changes and Inflation

Projected cash flows can be stated in any combination of nominal (current) or real (constant) domestic or foreign currency terms. To ensure comparability among the various cash flows and with today's home currency outlays, however, all cash flows must finally be expressed in real terms; i.e., in units of constant purchasing power. Nominal cash flows can be converted to real cash flows by adjusting either the cash flows or the discount rate. That is, nominal cash flows can be discounted at the nominal discount rate or real cash flows can be discounted at the real discount rate. Both methods yield the same results.[13]

In order to assess the effect of exchange rate changes on expected cash flows, it is first necessary to remove the effect of offsetting changes in inflation and exchange rates. Over the long run, purchasing power parity (or the "law of one price") is a reasonably good

---

compensation. When Allende was overthrown, however, his successors began returning property and otherwise compensating these MNCs.)

- Indirect compensation, such as the management contracts received by oil companies whose properties were nationalized by the Venezuelan government.
- Payment received from political risk insurance. (Insurance payments may lag expropriation by several years as well.)
- Tax deductions in the home country associated with such an extraordinary loss.
- A reduction in the amount of capital that must be repaid by the project equal to the unamortized portion of any local borrowing. It is inconceivable that a firm which has had a foreign operation expropriated would pay back any local borrowing except as part of a total compensation package worked out with the government. Suppliers of capital from outside the host country would normally be repaid by the parent company (whether or not loans were guaranteed) in order to preserve the parent's credit reputation.

[12]In 1978, I published a paper developing a variety of analytical formulas to deal with the impact of expropriation and currency controls on a project's expected NPV. See Alan C. Shapiro (1978), "Capital Budgeting for the Multinational Corporation," *Financial Management*, Spring, pp. 7–16. In this article, I provide a more complex and less artificial illustration of how such cash flow adjustments for expropriation could be made.

[13]See Lessard, Donald R. (1979). "Evaluating Foreign Projects: An Adjusted Present Value Approach." In Donald R. Lessard, ed. *International Financial Management*, Boston: Warren, Gorham & Lamont: or Shapiro, Alan C. (1982). *Multinational Financial Management*, Boston: Allyn and Bacon.

approximation of economic reality; and thus, these changes tend to be almost completely offsetting.

But because there is often a lag between a given change in relative rates of inflation and the exchange rate change necessary to maintain international equilibrium, it is worthwhile to analyze each effect separately. This is particularly true when government intervention occurs, such as in a fixed-rate system or a managed float. Furthermore, local price controls may not allow the normal adjustment of internal prices to take place. This will result in relative price changes, leading to deviations from purchasing power parity.

The possibility of relative price changes within a foreign economy can be incorporated easily by altering projected nominal local currency project cash flows. To capture the effect of exchange rate fluctuations, the MNC should list for each period the various possible exchange rates along with the anticipated local currency (LC) cash flow associated with each particular currency scenario. By assigning probabilities to these different exchange rates, management can then calculate for each period an expected home currency cash flow. This can be done by first converting each LC cash flow into its home currency equivalent, and then multiplying by the probability assigned to that scenario.[14]

Thus, the present value of future cash flows from a foreign project can be calculated in a two-stage procedure: (1) convert nominal foreign currency cash flows into nominal home currency terms; and (2) discount those nominal flows at the nominal expected domestic required rate of return. This procedure, to reiterate, will yield the same results as first converting nominal foreign currency cash flows into *real* home currency terms, and then discounting them at the *real* domestic required rate of return.

THE COST OF CAPITAL FOR FOREIGN INVESTMENTS

A central question that must be addressed by the multinational corporation is whether the required rate of return or foreign projects should be higher, lower, or the same as that for comparable domestic projects. To answer this question, it is necessary to examine one of the most complex issues in international financial management: the cost of capital for multinational firms.

Recall that the opportunity cost of capital for a given investment is the minimum risk-adjusted return required by shareholders of the firm for undertaking that investment. As such, it is the basic standard of corporate performance. Unless the investment generates sufficient funds to provide suppliers of capital with their expected returns, the firm's value will suffer. This return requirement is met only if the net present value of future project cash flows, using the project's cost of capital as the discount rate, is positive. An alternative, and generally equivalent, investment criterion is to use the cost of capital as a cut-off rate for the internal rates of return on proposed investments.

The development of appropriate cost-of-capital measures for multinational firms is tied to how those measures will be used. When used as discount rates to aid in the global resource allocation process, they should reflect the value to firms of engaging in specific activities. Thus, the emphasis here is on the cost of capital for specific foreign projects rather than for the firm as a whole. As pointed out earlier, unless the financial structures and commercial risks are similar for all projects considered, the indiscriminate use of an

[14]It is impossible to do justice to the complex question of exchange risk management in the allotted space. In the third issue of this journal, Brad Cornell and I will present an extended treatment of this issue alone.

overall cost of capital for project evaluation is inappropriate. Different discount rates should be used to value prospective investments that are expected to change the risk complexion of the firm.

My approach to determining the project-specific required return on equity is based on modern capital market theory.[15] According to this theory, an equilibrium relationship exists between an asset's required return and its associated risk. This relationship is formulated by the Capital Asset Pricing Model (CAPM). As mentioned earlier, the CAPM is based on the notion that intelligent risk-averse shareholders will seek to diversify their risks and, as a consequence, the only risk that will be rewarded with a risk premium is systematic or "non-diversifiable" risk. Systematic risk, as measured by beta, is the sensitivity of an investment's value to changes in general economic conditions. Statistically, it is the covariance of a security's (or any investment's) returns with broad, market-wide average returns.

Discount Rates for Foreign Investments

The importance of the CAPM for the international company is that the relevant component of risk in pricing a firm's stock is its systematic risk; in other words, that portion of return variability that cannot be eliminated through diversification, whether by investors or corporations. Much of the systematic or general market risk affecting a company, at least as measured using a domestic stock index such as the S&P 500 or the NYSE index, is caused by the cyclical nature of the national economy in which the company is operating. For this reason, it is highly possible that multinationals, by having operations in a number of countries whose economic cycles are not perfectly in phase, may be reducing the variability of their earnings through international diversification.

A number of studies suggest this is, in fact, the case.[16] Such studies suggest that there is little correlation among the earnings of the various national components of MNCs. Thus, to the extent that foreign cash flows are not perfectly correlated with those of domestic investments, the total risk (systematic and unsystematic) associated with variations in cash flows appears to be *reduced*, not increased, by international investment. Furthermore, most of the economic and political risks faced by the multinational corporation appear to be unsystematic and can, therefore, be eliminated through stockholders' diversification.

Rather surprisingly, it is the less-developed countries (LDCs), where political risks are greatest, which are likely to provide the greatest diversification benefits. This is because the economies of LDCs are less closely tied to the U.S., or to any other Western, industrialized, economy. By contrast, the correlation among the economic cycles of developed countries is considerably stronger; and the diversification benefits from investing in industrialized countries, from the standpoint of an American or Western European MNC, are proportionately less.

It should be noted, however, that the systematic risk of projects, even in relatively isolated LDCs, is unlikely to be far below the average for all projects, because these

[15]For a good review of this theory, see William F. Sharpe (1978), *Investments*, Englewood Cliffs, NJ: Prentice-Hall.

[16]See, for example, Benjamin I. Cohen, *Multinational Firms and Asian Exports*, New Haven, Conn.: Yale University Press, 1975; and Alan Rugman, "Risk Reduction by International Diversification," *Journal of International Business Studies*, Fall 1976, pp. 75–80.

countries are still tied into the world economy. The important point about LDCs, then, is that their ratio of systematic to total risk is generally quite low; their systematic risk, while perhaps slightly lower, is probably not significantly less than that of industrialized countries.[17]

Even if a nation's economy is not closely linked to the world economy, the systematic risk of a project located in that country might still be rather large. For example, a foreign copper mining venture will probably face systematic risk very similar to that faced by an identical extractive project in the United States, regardless of whether the foreign project is located in Canada, Chile, or Zaire. The reason is that the major element of systematic risk in any extractive project is related to variations in the price of the mineral being extracted, which is set in a world market. The world market price is in turn a function of world-wide demand, which itself is systematically related to the state of the world economy. By contrast, a market-oriented project in an LDC, whose risk depends largely on the evolution of the domestic market in that country, is likely to have a systematic risk that is small, both in relative and absolute terms.

One of the major issues in selecting a discount rate for foreign investments is choosing the relevant market portfolio for evaluating a project's systematic risk, or its beta coefficient. Is the relevant base portfolio against which covariances are measured the domestic portfolio of the investor or the world market portfolio? Selecting the appropriate portfolio is important because a risk that is systematic in the context of the home country market portfolio may well be diversifiable in the context of the world portfolio. If this is the case, then using the domestic market portfolio to calculate beta will result in a higher required return than if risk were measured using the world market portfolio. On the other hand, a risk that is unsystematic in a domestic context may be systematic in a global context, with corresponding implications for the measurement of beta. Thus, the choice of a base portfolio could well affect the present value of a project and, hence, its acceptability.

Which market, then, domestic or global, is the relevant context for measuring the risks of international investment? The appropriate market portfolio to use in measuring beta depends largely on one's view of world capital markets. More precisely, it depends on whether world markets are integrated or not. If they are, then the world portfolio is the correct choice. If they are not, the correct choice is the domestic portfolio. The test of capital markets' integration is whether international assets are priced in a common context; that is, world capital markets are integrated to the extent that security prices offer all investors worldwide the same trade-off between systematic risk and real expected return. In a perfectly integrated market, the risk premium expected by investors for holding a foreign stock would reflect that stock's risk relative only to a globally-diversified portfolio.

The truth probably lies somewhere in between.[18] Capital markets are now integrated to a great extent, and can be expected to become ever more so with time. But, due to various government regulations and other market imperfections, that integration is not complete.

Accordingly, my present recommendation to American managers is to measure the betas of international projects against the U.S. market portfolio. My reasons for this are three:

[17]This point was made by Fischer Black.

[18]Michael Adler and Bernard Dumas discussed this and related issues at great length in "International Portfolio Choice and Corporation Finance: A Survey," a CESA working paper soon to be published in *The Journal of Finance*.

1. It ensures comparability of foreign with domestic projects which are evaluated using beta calculated relative to a U.S. market index.
2. There is as yet no readily accessible global market index.
3. The relatively minor amount of international diversification attempted (as yet) by U.S. investors suggests that the relevant portfolio from their standpoints is the U.S. market portfolio.

International Capital Market Integration and Corporate International Diversification

To the extent that international investments actually reduce the systematic risk of the firm, management is justified in using proportionately lower hurdle rates in evaluating such investments. If, in addition to this condition, capital markets are not fully integrated internationally (so that, say, an American investor seeking to invest in the Brazilian economy could do so only by buying the shares of an American multinational with Brazilian operations), then international diversification by multinationals could be providing investors with benefits they cannot achieve simply by buying foreign securities. This means that where there are barriers to international portfolio investments, MNCs could accept lower rates of return than firms operating only locally because of their ability to diversify investment risks internationally.

The net effect of such financial market imperfections, then, may be to enable MNCs to undertake overseas projects that would otherwise be unattractive. But if international portfolio diversification can be accomplished as easily and as cheaply by individual investors, then although the required rates of return on MNC securities would be lower to reflect the reduced co-variability of MNC earnings caused by international diversification, there would no further reduction of the discount rate to reflect investors' willingness to pay a premium for the indirect diversification provided by the shares of MNCs.

The fact is, though, very little foreign portfolio investment is actually undertaken by U.S. investors. This lack of investment in foreign securities is normally explained by various legal, informational, and economic barriers that serve to segment national capital markets, deterring investors seeking to invest abroad.[19] These barriers include currency controls, specific tax regulations, relatively less efficient and less developed capital markets abroad, exchange risk, and the lack of readily accessible and comparable information on foreign securities. The lack of adequate information can significantly increase the perceived riskiness of foreign securities, giving investors an added incentive to keep their money at home.

Furthermore, no other country in the world has the breadth or depth of industry that the United States has. Hence, to diversify adequately within foreign economies, it will usually be necessary to acquire shares of multinational firms in industries where indigenous firms do not exist. Diversifying into the computer industry in Venezuela, for example, means buying the shares of IBM or some other multinational computer manu-

[19]For a good description of the various barriers to international portfolio diversification, see Gunter Dufey's "Institutional Constraints and Incentives on International Portfolio Investment," *International Portfolio Investment*, U.S. Department of the Treasury OASIA, 1976.

EXHIBIT 1
Risk Measures for Foreign Market Portfolios[a]

Country	Annualized Standard Deviation of Returns (%)[b]	Correlation with U.S. Market[c]	Market Risk (beta) from U.S. Perspective
France	26.4	.50	.71
West Germany	20.4	.43	.47
Japan	20.1	.40	.43
The Netherlands	21.9	.61	.72
Switzerland	22.7	.63	.77
Great Britain	41.0	.51	1.13
United States	18.5	1.00	1.00

Source Donald R. Lessard, "An Update on Gains from International Diversification," 1977. This table appeared in Donald R. Lessard, "Evaluating Foreign Projects: An Adjusted Present Value Approach," in Donald R. Lessard, ed., *Interntional Financial Management* (Boston: Warren, Gorham & Lamont, 1979), p. 590. Reprinted by permission of the author.

aAll figures estimated form data for 1973–1977 period

bMeasured in U.S. dollars

cThe S&P 500 Stock Index is used to represent the U.S. market

facturer with Venezuelan operations. To the extent that their international investment opportunities are so restricted, U.S. investors may be able to achieve low-cost international diversification only by purchasing the shares of U.S.-based MNCs. Moreover, investors in countries like France and Sweden that restrict overseas portfolio investment would appear to benefit even more by being able to purchase shares in domestically-based multinationals. All these conditions would lead investors to pay a premium for the international diversification provided by the shares of multinational corporations.

Because the world's economies are not perfectly synchronized, and also because of these imperfections in world capital markets, the value of international diversification to investors appears to be significant. Donald Lessard[20] and Bruno Solnik,[21] among others, have presented evidence that national factors have a stronger impact on security returns than any common world factor, In addition, they find that returns from the different national equity markets have relatively low correlations with each other. (See Exhibit 1.)

In short, Lessard and Solnik's results suggest that international diversification signifi-

[20]Lessard, Donald R. (1974). "World, National, and Industry Factors in Equity Returns," *Journal of Finance*, May, pp. 379–391.

[21]Solnik, Bruno H. (1974). "Why Not Diversify Internationally?" *Financial Analysts Journal*, July–August, pp. 48–54.

EXHIBIT 2
The Potential Gains from International Diversification

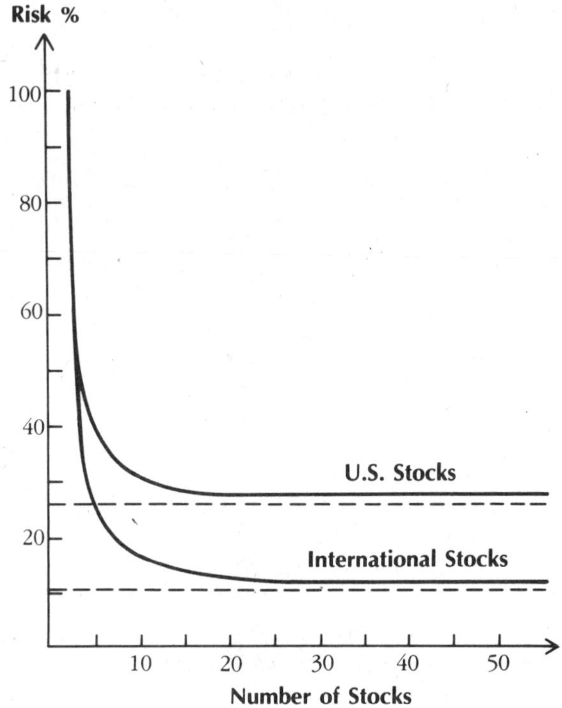

Source Bruno Solnik, "Why Not Diversify Internationally Rather Than Domestically?," *Financial Analysts' Journal*, July–August 1974, p. 51. Reprinted by permission of publisher.

cantly reduces the risk of portfolio returns. In fact, the variance of an internationally diversified portfolio appears to be as little as 33 percent of the variance of individual securities (as compared to 50 percent for a diversified portfolio of U.S. securities alone). In other words, the risk of an internationally-diversified portfolio is about one third less than the risk of a domestically-diversified portfolio. (See Exhibit 2.)

Thus, the ability of multinationals to provide an indirect means of international diversification should be an important advantage to international investors. As noted earlier, however, such corporate diversification will prove beneficial to MNC shareholders only if there are barriers to direct international portfolio diversification by individual investors.

Nevertheless, regardless of whether investors are internationally diversified or not, the apparently lower degree of systematic risk of foreign investments means that the required returns on such projects will still probably be lower, not higher, than required returns on comparable domestic projects. At the very least, therefore, when evaluating prospective foreign investments, executives of multinational firms should seriously question the use of a risk *premium* to account for the added political and economic risks of overseas operations.

INTERNATIONAL CAPITAL BUDGETING AND CORPORATE STRATEGY

The capital budgeting process typically involves calculation of the net present values of the various investment opportunities, domestic and foreign, facing the firm. Those projects with positive net present values (excess returns) are accepted; those that fail this test are rejected. The emphasis is on estimating future cash flows and required rates of return.

Only rarely, however, is the issue raised as to the origin of investments yielding excess returns. It is taken for granted that they do exist and can be found using fairly straightforward capital budgeting techniques. Yet, it should be recognized that identifying positive net present value projects in this way is very similar to (and as unreliable as) selecting under-valued securities on the basis of fundamental analysis. The latter can only be done with confidence if financial market imperfections exist which prevent asset prices from reflecting their equilibrium values. Similarly, the existence of economic rents—excess returns that lead to positive net present values—results largely from imperfections in real markets. Such imperfections take the form of monopolistic control over product or factor supplies. In less technical terms, companies can have a distinctive superiority in knowledge of specific markets, technological expertise, trademarks, patents—all of which exist in the real as distinguished from the financial sector of the business.

The imperfections that presently characterize world capital markets are not likely to be around for long. But, unlike the financial sector where prices are continuously and rapidly adjusting to reflect new information, and where all companies can expect to get a fair deal based on their expected risks and returns, imperfections in the real markets may last for some time. Technological edges, production cost efficiencies, superior management capability, vertical integration—all these factors can enable companies to earn consistently abnormal returns. In the long run, though, even such differences can be expected to be neutralized by the inevitable forces of competition.

But, over the short- to intermediate-term, the availability of positive NPV projects depends largely on a company's ability to exploit imperfections in real markets. The essential focus of the corporate planner should thus be on identifying, strengthening, and then capitalizing on those comparative advantages which distinguish it from its competitors, both actual and potential. A thorough understanding of such imperfections, and the company's ability to exploit them, should provide the qualitative basis for determining—prior to any systematic financial analysis—which foreign investments are likely to have positive net present values.

Various studies of the phenomenon of direct foreign investment[22] have helped to identify those market imperfections that have allowed, or encouraged, firms to become multinational. Among those market imperfections contributing to the rise of the multinational are government regulations and controls, such as tariffs and capital controls, that impose barriers to free trade and private portfolio investment.

Real market imperfections, however, in the areas of firm-specific skills and information are probably the most important single reason for the rise of multinationals. This is

[22]Direct foreign investment, or DFI, is defined as the acquisition abroad of physical assets such as plant and equipment.

the explanation provided by Richard Caves (1971),[23] who sought to understand not only why firms engage in direct foreign investment, but also why they choose that option over licensing or exporting. Caves's work on multinationals, which relies on the theory of industrial organization, points to certain general circumstances under which each approach—exporting, licensing, or local production—will be the preferred alternative for exploiting foreign markets.

According to Caves, multinationals have intangible capital in the form of trademarks, patents, general marketing skills, and other organizational abilities. If this intangible capital can be embodied in the form of products without much adaptation, then exporting will generally be the preferred method of market penetration. Where the firm's knowledge takes the form of specific product or process technologies that can be written down and transmitted objectively, then foreign expansion will usually take the licensing route.

Often, however, this intangible capital takes the form of organizational skills. Among these specialized skills are knowledge about how best to service a market (including new product development and adaptation), quality control, advertising, distribution, after-sales service, and the general ability to read changing market desires and translate them into salable products. Because it is difficult, if not impossible, to separate these services and sell them apart from the firm, we expect this form of market imperfection to lead to corporate attempts to exert control directly through the establishment of foreign affiliates. There will also, of course, be added costs in establishing and administering an operation overseas. Consequently, as Ian Giddy has pointed out, "The market in an intermediate good (product, factor, service or knowledge) will be internalized if and only if the benefits from circumventing imperfections outweigh the administrative and other costs of central control."[24]

Because local firms have an inherent cost advantage over foreign investors (who must bear the costs of operating in an unfamiliar environment together with the stigma of being foreign), multinationals can succeed abroad only if their monopolistic advantages cannot be purchased or duplicated by local competitors. Eventually, however, all barriers to entry erode, and the multinational firm must find new sources of competitive advantage to defend itself against the inevitable increase in competition both at home and abroad.

My approach to international strategic planning can be reduced to the following four interrelated propositions:

1. Effective corporate planning should be directed toward identifying those investments likely to provide the most profitable returns. (Without suggesting that the firm adopt a myopically short-run view, profitability should be regarded as the prerequisite, not merely a by-product, of multinational survival and expansion.) The strategic response of a firm to a competitive threat, which includes the decision to invest in operations overseas, should be designed to exploit its distinctive advantages. Such advantages will stem, in large part, from imperfections in international product or factor markets. Effective corporate planning, accordingly, should be grounded in a thorough understanding of the company's competitive advantages, and on the associated barriers to entry that would prevent competitors from eroding those advantages.

[23]Caves, Richard E. (1971), "International Corporations: The Industrial Economics of Foreign Investment," *Economica*, February, pp. 1–27.

[24]Giddy, Ian H. (1978), "The Demise of the Product Cycle Model in International Business Theory," *Columbia Journal of World Business*, Sp., p. 93.

2. The global approach to investment planning requires a systematic evaluation of individual entry strategies in foreign markets, a comparison of the options, and selection of the best method of entry. Many multinationals seem to disregard the fact that a market's sales potential, and thus its profitability, is at least partly a function of the entry strategy.[25]
3. Investment planning requires a continuous audit of the effectiveness of current entry methods. As knowledge about a foreign market increases, or sales potential grows, the optimal market penetration strategy will likely change.
4. A systematic investment analysis requires the use of appropriate evaluation criteria. Despite the added complexities of overseas investment evaluation (and perhaps *because* of the difficulties they present), most multinationals continue to use simple rules of thumb in making international investment decisions. Analytical techniques are used only as a rough screening device or as a final checkoff before project approval. While simple rules of thumb are obviously easier and cheaper to use, there is a danger of obsolescence and misuse as the fundamental assumptions underlying their applicability change.

The use of the theoretically sound and recommended present value analysis is anything but straightforward. The strategic rationale underlying many investment proposals can be translated into traditional capital budgeting criteria, but it is often necessary to look beyond the returns associated with the project itself to determine its true impact on the overall, worldwide risk and return of the multinational. For example, an investment made to save a market threatened by competition or trade barriers must be judged on the basis of the sales that would otherwise have been lost. As another example, export creation and direct investment often go hand in hand, ICI, the British chemical company, found that its exports to Europe were enhanced by its strong market position there in other product lines—a position due mainly to ICI's local manufacturing facilities. Such cash flow synergies should be reflected in the capital budgeting analysis.

SUMMARY AND CONCLUSIONS

Because of the length of this article, I want to review a few of the major issues in multinational capital budgeting it examines, and to offer an outline of the solutions it proposes.

The first major complication of international investment addressed is accounting for the significant differences that can arise between project (or foreign subsidiary) and parent cash flows. To deal with this problem, I offered a three-stage procedure for incorporating such differences into the traditional discounted cash flow framework. The first involves the projection of expected after-tax cash flows, strictly from the perspective of the local project or subsidiary managers. The second step was to estimate the timing and magnitude

[25]For example, a study by the Conference Board in 1966 (*U.S. Production Abroad and the Balance of Payments*, New York: The Conference Board) showed that 62 percent of firms surveyed made no attempt to determine the net profits from their existing foreign licensing agreements. Instead, they simply treated these agreements as a free good, ignoring the opportunity costs that would have been revealed by a comparison of alternatives. Similarly, a survey by David Rutenberg ("Shunning the Risks of Eastern Europe," Queens University Paper (1978)) of 120 companies disclosed that, on average, these companies accepted only about 11% of the joint venture proposals they received, rejecting 83% out of hand without evaluating them. Also, only one-third had a policy of actively searching for joint venture opportunities.

of both actual and allowable repatriations (which also gives the multinational's management a means of estimating their marginal tax rate on foreign-source earnings). The final phase attempts to project any effect that the given investment would have on worldwide corporate cash flows.

Next, I offered a rationale for adjusting project cash flows instead of the discount rate to reflect the key political and economic risks that MNCs face abroad. Cash flow adjustments are preferred on theoretical grounds: most distinctively foreign risks are unsystematic or diversifiable, and thus do not raise investors' required rates of return. Adjustments of cash flows are also preferred because management generally has access to more and better information about the specific effect of such risks on cash flow projections. The popular practice of adjusting a foreign project's required rate of return to reflect incremental risk does not usually allow for adequate consideration of the time pattern and magnitude of the risk being evaluated. Using a uniformly higher discount rate to reflect additional risk indiscriminately penalizes future cash flows relative to less distant ones.

Some investments, however, do entail more systematic risk than others, and such risks should be reflected in project discount rates. The key question, therefore, in setting discount rates for foreign projects is whether the incremental risks are systematic. The use of an international risk premium ignores the fact that the risk of an overseas investment (which should be viewed in the context of all other investments of the firm's shareholders, domestic as well as foreign) may be considerably lower than the total risk of the project. For this reason, the automatic inclusion of a premium for risk when evaluating foreign projects is not a necessary element of conservatism. It is instead a management shortcut that may penalize the firm's shareholders by causing management to reject positive net present value foreign investments.

Unlike the diversification sought by wholly domestic conglomerates (especially in the 60s), there may be significant benefits to multinationals from international diversification. The theoretical justification for such benefits depends on the extent to which international capital markets are imperfectly integrated, thus preventing investors from achieving such diversification on their own. On the assumption that world capital markets are not fully integrated, multinational managers may be justified in actually *lowering* the required rates of return on foreign projects that offer significant additional diversification.

Finally, the article offers a theoretical rationale for the multinational firm, one which should serve as the basis for international strategic planning. Such a rationale should provide the qualitative criteria for the initial screening of foreign investment opportunities. The existence and success of multinationals is attributed largely to their success in defending and exploiting barriers to entry created by product and factor market imperfections. Multinational corporate planning, accordingly, should be based on identifying and preserving those competitive advantages that distinguish it from its competitors. Given the inevitability of competition, and of the eventual lowering of barriers of entry, corporate planners must continually reassess both their competitive vulnerabilities and strengths.

REFERENCES

Adler, Michael and Bernard Dumas, "International Portfolio Choice and Corporation Finance: A Survey," CESA Working Paper (1981), forthcoming *Journal of Finance*.

Caves, Richard E., "International Corporations: The Industrial Economics of Foreign Investments," *Economica*, (February 1971), 1–27.

Cohen, Benjamin I., *Multinational Firms and Asian Exports*, New Haven, Conn.: Yale University Press (1975).

Dufey, Gunter, "Institutional Constraints and Incentives on International Portfolio Investment," *International Portfolio Investment*, U.S. Department of the Treasury OASIA (1975).

Giddy, Ian H., "An Integrated Theory of Exchange Rate Equilibrium," *Journal of Financial and Quantitative Analysis* (December 1976), 883–892.

Giddy, Ian H., "The Demise of the Product Cycle Model in International Business Theory," *Columbia Journal of World Business*. (Spring 1978), 90–97.

Hawkins, Robert G., Norman Mintz, and Michael Provissiero, "Government Takeovers of U.S. Foreign Affiliates," *Journal of International Business Studies*, (Spring 1976), 3–15.

Lessard, Donald R., "World, National, and Industry Factors in Equity Returns," *Journal of Finance*, (May 1974), 379–391.

Lessard, Donald R., "Evaluating Foreign Projects: An Adjusted Present Value Approach," in Donald R. Lessard (ed.), *International Financial Management*, Boston: Warren, Gorham & Lamont (1979).

Rugman, Alan, "Risk Reduction by International Diversification," *Journal of International Business Studies*, (Fall 1976), 75–80.

Rutenberg, David P., "Shunning the Risks of Eastern Europe," Queens University Working Paper (1978).

Shapiro, Alan C., "Capital Budgeting for the Multinational Corporation," *Financial Management*, (Spring 1978), 7–16.

Shapiro, Alan C., "Managing Blocked Currency Funds," University of Southern California Working Paper (1980).

Shapiro, Alan C., "Managing Political Risk: A Policy Approach," *Columbia Journal of World Business*, (Fall 1981), 63–70.

Shapiro, Alan C., *Multinational Financial Management*, Boston: Allyn and Bacon (1982).

Solnik, Bruno H. "Why Not Diversify Internationally?" *Financial Analysts Journal*, (July–August 1974), 48–54.

Truitt, J. Frederick, "Expropriation of Private Foreign Investment: Summary of the Post-World War II Experience of American and British Investors in the Less Developed Countries," *Journal of International Business Studies*, (Fall 1970), 21–34.

34

Evaluating International Projects: An Adjusted Present Value Approach*

Donald R. Lessard

In evaluating projects that cut across national boundaries, firms must deal with a variety of issues seldom encountered within a single country that affect the distribution of net operating cash flows available to the parent, as well as the valuation of these cash flows.[1] Factors influencing the statistical distribution of net operating cash flows, in addition to differences in fundamental economic and political conditions in various countries, include differing rates of inflation and volatile exchange rates that may or may not cancel each other, differences in tax rules and tax rates, and restrictions or taxes on cross-border financial transactions. Factors that may influence the valuation of operating cash flows with a given statistical distribution include incomplete and often segmented capital markets that result from controls on financial transactions both within and among countries; the dependence of net of tax cash flows available to the parent on the firm's overall tax and cash-flow position in various countries; the availability of project-specific concessional finance—loans, guarantees, or insurance against commercial or political risks; and, on occasion, requirements to issue securities—especially equity—within markets partially or totally isolated by barriers to internal or cross-border financial transactions. Further, the available cash flows and their value to the firm often depend on the specific financing of the project, not only because of concessional financing opportunities, but also because the costs or limits on cross-border transfers often depend on the nature of the financial transaction involved, e.g., interest or principal, fees, dividends, or payment for goods.

As a result of these various factors, it is often necessary to distinguish project and parent cash flows, to recognize interactions between the financing and valuation of a project, to take into account dependencies between project valuation and the corporation's overall tax and cash-flow situation, and to incorporate in the valuation criterion the perspectives of multiple investors not sharing a common capital market. Thus traditional weighted-average cost of capital rules that implicitly separate investment and financing decisions often are inapplicable or misleading,[2] as well as exceedingly complex.[3] A variety of alternative approaches have been put forward,[4] some involving multiple investment criteria,[5] others requiring the consideration of the "full-system" effects of the project in question,[6] and others providing relatively complex criteria reflecting the existence of multiple investors based in less than fully integrated capital markets.[7]

This paper seeks to show that an adjusted present value approach (APV), based on the

---

*This article is reprinted, with permission, from Crum and Derkinderen (eds.), *Capital Budgeting under Conditions of Uncertainty,* Martinus Nijhoff Publishing, 1981, pp. 118–137.

An earlier version of this paper was published in D. R. Lessard, ed., *International Financial Management* (New York: Warren, Gorham & Lamont, 1979). I am grateful to a large number of persons who have commented on the earlier versions of this paper, including Fischer Black, Gene Carter, Rich Cohn, Gunter Franke, Christine Hekman, Stewart Myers, Joel Ornstein, Jim Paddock, Alan Shapiro, and Kirit Vora. All remaining errors and arbitrary choices are, of course, my responsibility.

value additivity principle (VAP) that holds for independent projects in complete capital markets, provides a relatively simple framework for evaluating most international projects consistent with state-of-the-art financial practice. It is restricted to projects wholly owned by the parent or whose equity is shared by investors having access to the same relatively complete capital markets. It does not address the valuation of projects by joint ventures in which equity is shared by investors based in markets segmented by barriers[8] or the relative valuation of particular projects by firms based in countries with relatively complete markets and by local firms operating in a more restricted capital market—a potential motivation for direct foreign investment.[9]

Special attention is given to the valuation of operating cash flows that are not denominated in any specific currency but that reflect the interaction of inflation rates and exchange rates and of nominal cash flows, such as depreciation tax shields and debt service that are contractually denominated in a specified currency.

The paper is organized in six sections. The second section describes the APV approach and discusses the circumstances under which it is applicable. The third section discusses the valuation of operating and contractual cash flows. The fourth section presents a general APV formula for foreign projects that distinguishes between operating and contractual cash flows and takes into account the effects of differing tax systems, exchange and credit restrictions, and concessional financing opportunities, together with their interactions with the structure of the project's cross-border interaffiliate financing, as well as with the local subsidiary and parent firm's external financing. The fifth section discusses briefly the risk premiums applicable to the various cash flows, and the last section discusses the implementation of the APV approach, especially with regard to approaches involving multiple cash-flow estimates and simulation.

THE ADJUSTED PRESENT VALUE APPROACH

As a result of the "cost of capital revolution" of the 1960s, the dominant approach to project evaluation is to discount expected after-tax project cash flows by a weighted-average cost of capital,

$$\text{NPV} = \sum_{t=0}^{T} \frac{\overline{\text{CF}}_t}{(1 + \rho^*)^t}, \tag{1}$$

where NPV is net present value, $\overline{\text{CF}}_t$ is the expected total after-tax project cash flow in period t, and ρ^* is the weighted-average cost of capital. ρ^* in turn is usually defined as

$$\rho^* = (1 - \lambda\ \rho^{\text{E}} + \lambda r(1 - \tau), \tag{2}$$

where λ is the weight of debt in the total capital structure, r is the pretax interest rate on debt, τ is the corporate tax rate, and ρ^{E} is the required rate of return on equity.

The advantage of the traditional approach is its simplicity. It imbeds in a single discount rate all financing considerations, thus enabling planners to focus on the project's investment characteristics. However, different discount rates are required for projects that differ from a firm's typical project in terms of either business risk or contribution to debt capacity, and equation (2) provides little guidance since ρ^{E} will be changed by an unspecified amount. Both conditions are the rule rather than the exception for foreign projects. Further, when the financing complications of foreign projects are introduced, the weighted-average approach becomes complex and cumbersome, removing its major advantage. In fact, when financing sources for foreign projects include limited amounts of restricted funds or project-specific concessionary credit, there will be different weighted-average costs for projects that differ only in scale. With capital structures that vary over time—which is typical of projects financed independently of the parent to minimize taxes, to take advantage of project-specific financing subsidies, or to minimize political risks—a different weighted average will be required in different years of the project's life.

Differences in project debt capacity can be incorporated via the alternative weighted-average formula developed by Modigliani and Miller:

$$\rho^* = \rho[1 - \tau\lambda], \tag{3}$$

where ρ is the "all-equity" required rate of return reflecting the project's business risk. Further, it can be generalized to situations where business risk differs as well. The *project* required rate of return, ρ_j^*, is given by

$$\rho_j^* = [r + \beta_j(\rho_m - r)]\,[1 - \tau\lambda], \tag{4}$$

where β_j is the project's beta coefficient (adjusted to remove the effect of leverage) and $(\rho_m - r)$ is the risk premium on the market portfolio.

As noted by Myers [16], however, formulas (2) and (4) are exactly correct only if the cash flows are perpetual and λ is constant over time. In many cases where projects are financed from a common corporate pool, the errors are not serious. However, if the financial structures of specific foreign projects differ from those of the parent firm or vary over the project lives because of the availability of concessional finance, tax considerations, or efforts to reduce political or currency risks, even the generalized formula (4) is likely to be misleading.

To deal with the problem, Myers [16] suggests a return to the basic Modigliani-Miller equation underlying (3). Rather than implicitly incorporating financial factors in ρ^*, the approach values them explicitly in an adjusted present value equation:

$$\text{APV} = \sum_{t=0}^{T} \frac{\overline{\text{CF}}_t}{(1 + \rho_j)^t} + \sum_{t=0}^{T} \frac{TS_t}{(1 + r)^t}, \tag{5}$$

where the first term is the present value of the total expected operating cash flows discounted by ρ_j, the "all-equity" discount rate reflecting the project's business risk, and the second term is the present value of the tax shields arising from debt, discounted at the before-tax cost of debt, r. This is a direct application of the value additivity principle (VAP)—that in equilibrium the market value of any set of "risk-independent" cash flows available for distribution to security holders (after corporate taxes) is equal to the sum of the values of the individual components.[10]

Applicability of VAP to International Projects

Value additivity is a robust concept. Haley and Schall [11, pp. 230–237] show that it applies without exception for securities (claims to income streams) issued in complete, competitive capital markets with neutral personal taxes. Further, they argue that because of clientele effects, VAP will hold in general for individual firms even if personal taxes are not neutral in their treatment of interest, dividend, and capital gain income. Most importantly, they point out that even if markets are not complete (i.e., that there is no perfect substitute for one or more of the income streams provided by the firm or project), the potential for investor arbitrage will generally maintain value additivity. It breaks down when certain transactions are restricted or costly, and as a result the potential for investor arbitrage is impaired.

At first glance, this latter condition appears to rule out VAP for projects with income streams subject to cross-border costs or restrictions or to projects in countries with capital markets isolated by such barriers. However, VAP requires only that investors can engage in arbitrage among the various income streams available for distribution by the parent firm after corporate taxes. Thus any restrictions or taxes on cross-border transfers to the parent must be reflected in the income stream components, but will not affect the ability to combine or divide these remittable, net of corporate tax streams for valuation.

The fact that local capital markets are not competitive because of internal controls or lack of the necessary institutional infrastructure or are isolated from other markets by barriers to cross-border transactions is irrelevant in the valuation of projects by wholly owned ventures in such countries by firms based in countries with relatively open, competitive capital markets. These conditions may change the investment opportunity set facing the firm through their impact on the competition for projects resulting from differences in project valuation by local and international firms, but the appropriate context for the valuation of these flows is the base country capital market. Even in the case of joint ventures, these conditions will have no effect on the valuation of a given set of income streams by the international firm, although they may lead to different valuation criteria for the local firm and hence to lack of agreement between the participants regarding investment and financing decisions.[11]

RECOGNITION OF INFLATION AND EXCHANGE RATE CHANGES

An individual international project may involve cash flows in several different currencies, some proportion of which will be contractually denominated in those currencies and the remainder of which will be determined by the interactions of future business conditions and changes in relative prices, price levels, and exchange rates. These flows can be viewed from four different perspectives as illustrated in Table 1: either in the base currency or the local currency valuation is that the discount rates used are consistent with the way the cash flows are stated—i.e., if current values are used, the discount rates must incorporate the relevant inflation premiums; if constant, the discount rates should not include inflation premiums.

Common practice in estimating and evaluating cash flows can be characterized as follows: Firms first project expected revenues and expenses in constant terms, linking present unit costs and revenues with future unit sales projections. These flows are trans-

TABLE 1
Alternative Cash-Flow Perspectives

	Treatment of Inflation	
Currency	Constant	Current
Local	I	II
Base	III	IV

formed into current terms by inflating them at the anticipated general rate of inflation. If the flows are not already stated in the base currency, they then are translated into current base currency units using projected exchange rates. This process involves moving from quandrant I in Table 1 to quadrant II and then to quadrant IV. Although there is nothing necessarily incorrect with this approach, it often is applied inconsistently, and important interdependencies between inflation and exchange rates and their impacts on operating and contractual cash flows are often overlooked. Further, it is difficult to extend this approach to accommodate a range of operating cash-flow estimates generated by simulation. Each scenario must incorporate explicit assumptions regarding inflation rates, exchange rates, and cash flows, while a simulation requires the joint distribution of the three sets of variables.

The basis for a simpler, yet more transparent approach is provided by the set of equilibrium relationships between interest rates, rates of inflation, and changes in exchange rates that (tend to) hold in efficient markets—purchasing power parity and the (domestic and international) Fischer effect.[12] Even when these relationships do not hold precisely, they serve to highlight the impact on cash flows of the interactions between inflation and exchange rates and to provide insights regarding the valuation of these flows.

It is useful to separate cash flows into two groups: (1) operating cash flows that are not contractually denominated in nominal terms and whose value in constant terms is relatively independent of inflation, and (2) contractual flows denominated in a particular currency whose value in current terms is relatively independent of inflation. A different treatment is appropriate for each of the two classes of flows.

Operating Cash Flows

The home currency value of operating cash flows in another currency is given by

$$V = \sum_{t=1}^{T} \frac{\overline{CF}\ (\text{current})_t * \bar{S}_t}{(1+\rho)^t} = \sum_{t=1}^{T} \frac{\overline{CF}\ (\text{constant})_t (1+\bar{I})^t * \bar{S}_t}{(1+\rho)^t}, \tag{6}$$

where $\overline{CF}$ (current) are expected cash flows in current local terms and $\overline{CF}$ (constant) are the expected flows in constant terms, and ρ is the all-equity rate appropriate for flows in the home currency with the project's risk.

This formula can be simplified substantially if the two key equilibrium relationships—purchasing power parity (PPP) and the Fisher effect (IFE)—are assumed to hold.[13] PPP implies that exchange rate changes and relative rates of inflation offset each other. As a result, the expected spot exchange rate for foreign currency (stated in terms of units of the base currency per unit of foreign currency) at time t is

$$\overline{S_t} = S_0\,(1 + I)^t/(\bar{I} + \bar{I}^*)^t, \tag{7}$$

where S_0 is the current spot rate, I the expected base currency inflation rate, and I^* the expected foreign currency inflation rate.[14,15] IFE implies that the nominal riskless interest rate, r, for a given currency, incorporates a premium for anticipated inflation. Thus $(1 + \rho)$ can be restated as

$$(1 + r_{real})\,(1 + I)\,(1 + RP) \tag{8}$$

when r_{real} is the real interest rate and RP is the risk premium.

Substituting into (6)[16]

$$V = \sum_{t=1}^{T} \frac{\overline{CF}\ (\text{constant})_t (1+\bar{I}^*)^t S_0 (1+\bar{I})^t/(1+\bar{I}^*)^t}{[(1+\rho_{real})(1+\bar{I})]^t} \tag{9a}$$

$$= S_0 \sum_{t=1}^{T} \frac{\overline{\text{CF}} \text{ (constant)}^t}{(1 + \rho_{\text{real}})} \tag{9b}$$

The problem of cash flows in different currencies and discount rates appropriate for each one collapses into a single currency calculation where the current exchange rate simply scales the flows to a common base.

Departures from PPP and IFE

Of course, PPP does not hold exactly, and interest rates do not provide exact guides to future exchange rate changes. However, there is little evidence for major currencies subject to market forces that deviations from these key relationships are persistent or that they can be forecast.[17] As a result, the simplified approach to cash-flow estimation and valuation based on these equilibrium tendencies is quite robust for single-point expected cash-flow estimates. If various distributions of cash flows are considered, the problem becomes more complex. *Ex post* deviations from IFE will have no effect on valuation if PPP continues to hold. However, departures from PPP are likely to alter cash flows stated in constant local terms, as well as the real exchange rate at which they can be converted into the base currency. This is because they result in changes in the relative prices of inputs or outputs sold or sourced in different countries. Further, the deviations themselves are likely to reflect changes in relative prices within countries, with important implications for cash flows.

It is much more likely that firms can forecast trends in relative prices of certain inputs and outputs as opposed to overall deviations from PPP, since relative price changes hinge on microlevel changes in productivity, scarcity, or substitutability of the good or factor in question. Furthermore, given the evidence that PPP holds quite well over the long run, these relative price shifts are likely to result in larger impacts on project values than divergences from PPP. These relative price shifts can be incorporated readily by changing project cash flows in either (9a) or (9b), but (9b) is more transparent since it abstracts from offsetting inflation and exchange rate changes.

Where exchange rates are forecast to diverge from PPP because of exchange controls or trade barriers, explicit joint estimates of the local currency cash flows and exchange rates are required. These can be stated in either real or nominal terms since the key element is the change in the real exchange rate (deviation from PPP) and not the absolute exchange rate and level of inflation. Typically, the impact of PPP deviations in such cases will not be symmetric, since price controls or other market interventions are likely to be systematically related to the PPP departures.

Contractual Cash Flows

Contractual nominal cash flows including interest on debt and tax rebates based on historical cost depreciation can be discounted at a nominal rate appropriate to the currency in question and converted to the base currency by multiplying the resulting present value by the current spot rate,

$$V = S_0 \sum_{t=1}^{T} \frac{\overline{\text{CF}} \text{ (current)}_t}{[(1 + r)(1 + \text{RP})]^t}, \tag{10}$$

where $(1 + r) = (1 + r_{\text{real}})(1 + I)$ and I is the rate of inflation for the currency in which the flows are denominated.

For major currencies, where interest rate parity and the Fisher effect tend to hold, market interest rates are appropriate. Where market interest rates do not reflect generally held inflation and exchange rate expectations as a result of credit controls or exchange restrictions, an offshore rate (if available) or an estimated rate must be used.

Deviations from IFE

Any unanticipated change in exchange rates, whether it represents a departure from PPP or not, changes the present value of contractual flows. Anticipated changes reflected in the interest rate will have no effect on the value of interest-bearing contractual claims, but will change the value of non-interest-bearing claims, such as depreciation and other tax shields based on historical cost allocations.

APPLYING APV TO FOREIGN PROJECTS

The APV approach, outlined earlier, provides a "divide and conquer" approach to capital budgeting. Financial contributions to a project's value are recognized separately and explicitly, the total present value is the sum of the present values of the basic project cash flows, and the treatment of the various financial effects can be generalized to incorporate the special situations encountered in evaluating foreign projects. In particular, the cash flows can be separated into operating and contractual components, as well as into those components that can be estimated independently for the project and those that depend on systemwide cash-flow and tax interactions. This breakdown is illustrated in the following general equation:

Adjusted present value APV (11)

=

Noncontractual operating flows:

Capital outlay

$$\sum_{i=1}^{N} S_0^i \sum_{t=0}^{T} \frac{I_t^i}{(1+\rho_1)^t} \tag{11a}$$

+

Remittable after-tax operating cash flows

$$\sum_{i=1}^{N} S_0^i \sum_{t=1}^{T} \frac{\overline{CF}_t^i(1-\tau)}{(1+\rho_2)^t} \tag{11b}$$

+

Contractual flows:

Contractual operating flows

$$\sum_{i=1}^{N} S_0^i \sum_{t=1}^{T} \frac{CONT_t^i(1-\tau)}{(1+\rho_3)^t} \tag{11c}$$

Depreciation tax shields

$$\sum_{i=1}^{N} S_0^i \sum_{t=1}^{T} \frac{DEP_t^i(\tau)}{(1+\rho_4)^t} \tag{11d}$$

+

Tax shields due to normal borrowing

$$\sum_{i=1}^{N} S_0^i \sum_{t=1}^{T} \frac{INT_t^i(\tau)}{(1+\rho_5)^t} \tag{11e}$$

+

Financial subsidies or penalties

$$\sum_{i=1}^{N} S_0^i \sum_{t=1}^{T} \frac{\Delta INT_t^i}{(1+\rho_6)^t} \tag{11f}$$

$$+$$

Operating flows dependent on firm's overall tax and cash-flow position

Tax reduction or deferral via interaffiliate transfers $$\sum_{i=1}^{N} S_0^i \sum_{t=1}^{T} \frac{TR_t^i}{(1+\rho_7)^t} \tag{11g}$$

$$+$$

Additional remittances via interaffiliate transfers $$\sum_{i=1}^{N} S_0^i \sum_{t=1}^{T} \frac{REM_t^i}{(1+\rho_8)^t} \tag{11h}$$

where superscript i denotes currency i and S_0^i is the current spot rate for currency i.

Each of the terms is discussed in greater detail below. We assume that operating flows are stated in constant terms and hence discounted at a real rate, while the contractual flows are stated in current terms and hence are discounted at the relevant nominal rate. Appropriate risk premiums for the various components are discussed later.

Capital Outlay (11a)

The elements of this term are unambiguous for items purchased by the firm, but are more complex for capital items sourced internally. The major obstacle in the latter case is calculating the true incremental cost to the system, which may differ substantially from the registered book value of the item in question. Contractual capital costs should be distinguished from noncontractual costs and discounted at nominal rates.

Capital expenditures often are paid out of accumulated funds from existing operations whose use is restricted by exchange controls or because special tax advantages will be forfeited or additional U.S. taxes imposed if the funds are remitted rather than reinvested. The APV framework lends itself readily to incorporating the incremental value of a project resulting from its ability to employ such funds. Since the operating cash-flow term already captures project cash flows that will be available for remittance, taxed as if they are remitted, the use of restricted funds simply reduces the investment outlays (11a) by the difference between their face value and the present value of these funds if remitted via the best alternative mechanism.

Operating Cash Flow (11b).

In the domestic case, there is little difficulty in defining after-tax operating cash flows. They are the total project cash flows less U.S. taxes. Whether they are reinvested in the project or not makes no difference, since all flows are deemed available to the corporate cash pool. With foreign projects, there are two major issues in defining operating cash flows: (1) whether to use project cash flows or only those flows remitted to the parent, and (2) what taxes to assume, since these will be a function of financing and remittance decisions. The first distinction arises because of foreign exchange restrictions and ceilings on profit remittances; the second because of the interactions of various national tax systems.

Clearly, the only cash flows of value to the parent are those available for remittance in one form or another, not necessarily those actually remitted. Furthermore, after-tax flows must take into account the incremental taxes to the entire corporation. However, the specific choice of ways to deal with the two issues is a question of managerial art—the solution should be straightforward, easy to apply, and likely to bring to management's attention the most critical issues.

There are two basic approaches. One is to begin with the most favorable set of assumptions regarding taxation and remittability and, in later terms of the APV equation, to subtract the present values of reductions due to specific restrictions or international tax interactions. The other is to start with conservative assumptions regarding remittability and taxation, later adding the present value of gains resulting from various mechanisms for circumventing restrictions or deferring taxes. I prefer the second alternative for the pragmatic reason that if a project is attractive under conservative assumptions, there is no need to proceed with the far more complex set of calculations regarding tax and remittance adjustments that require consideration of the total corporate cash flow and tax situation.[19]

The conservative approach includes in the first term only those cash flows available for remittance through normal channels—for example, amortization of investment and repatriation of earnings—but not those that can be obtained only through transfer pricing or other mechanisms for circumventing restrictions. The tax rate applied to these flows is either the parent rate or the foreign rate, whichever tax system imposes the largest tax liability. This implicitly assumes that all operating cash flows are remitted immediately to the United States and that the parent has no excess foreign tax credits. Any additional value derived by circumventing restrictions on cash remittances, deferring U.S. taxes, or offsetting excess foreign tax credits can be incorporated in additional terms. Since depreciation tax shields are captured in a separate term, after-tax cash flows are simply pretax flows multiplied by one minus the relevant tax rate.

A further and perhaps more serious issue in the computation of operating cash flows is the difficulty of measuring the true incremental cash flows of a project in an interdependent multinational system. For example, the establishment of a manufacturing plant in a country previously served by exports will result in an erosion of profits elsewhere in the system, but it may also create new profit opportunities for other parts of the system that provide intermediate or complementary products. This difficulty is exacerbated by departures from arm's length transfer pricing among units, some of which may result from conscious manipulation of tax and exchange control systems, but most of which result from the near impossibility of allocating the joint costs and benefits associated with "soft" factors of production, such as technology and managerial expertise used by more than one unit of the corporation. Clearly, an attempt should be made to measure incremental cash flows to the total system. Further, in keeping with conservative tax and remittance assumptions, interaffiliate flows should be valued as closely to an arm's length value as possible.[20]

Contractual Operating Flows (11c)

Some elements of operating costs or revenues, as well as capital costs, may be set contractually. Typically, this will be true only for a relatively short period, and the distinction is thus immaterial for capital budgeting. However, where long-term sourcing or sales contracts are involved, explicit recognition of the contractual cash flows is called for.[21]

Depreciation Tax Shields (11d)

This contractual cash flow is deterministic, subject to the corporation's ability to use or to sell the tax shield, given investment outlays. The relevant tax rate and set of tax rules that should be used are those binding at the margin, as noted above.

Interest Tax Shields (11e).

For a variety of reasons, including the availability of concessionary credit, the existence of tax or exchange considerations that favor remittances in the form of interest payments, and the desire to hedge currency or political risks, foreign projects are often financed with a different and typically higher proportion of debt than the corporation as a whole.

Further, the debt issued to finance the project often exceeds the increment to overall debt capacity provided by the project. Thus approaches that directly utilize the project capital structure in computing a weighted-average cost of capital are likely to overstate the worth of the project, but a weighted average based on the total firm's capitalization also is likely to be misleading. In the APV equation, in contrast, the second term captures the tax shields associated with a project's incremental contribution to corporate debt capacity. The costs or benefits of "overborrowing" at the project level for reasons of currency risk, concessionary credit, or remittance restrictions are treated explicitly in later terms.

Financial Subsidies or Penalties (11f)

The value of subsidies in the form of concessionary credit or penalties resulting from local financing requirements can be computed by comparing the present value of the total pretax payments on the debt, including interest and principal, discounted at the rate that would apply if the same debt were issued to competitive capital markets with the face value of the debt. For example, if a project is eligible for a concessionary loan at 6 percent instead of a market rate of, say, 9 percent, (11f) would be the difference between the present value of the total pretax payments on the 6 percent debt discounted at 9 percent, and the face value of the debt.[22]

Ability to Reduce or to Defer Taxes (11g)

The base case operating cash flows, term (11b), incorporate conservative assumptions regarding the taxation of project cash flows—that they will be taxed at the U.S. rate or the local rate in the foreign country, whichever results in the greater tax liability. In many cases, an MNC can reduce taxes from this level by combining profits from countries with relatively low and high taxes, by shifting expenses and revenues among its affiliates, or simply by reinvesting profits in low-tax countries and deferring the additional U.S. taxes. In principle, the present value of these tax changes can be readily incorporated in an APV term, although computing them may require a complex corporate tax model. However, reversing the analysis to calculate a "break-even" value for term (11g) may show that a readily attainable degree of tax reduction is all that is required. Thus the full analysis can be avoided.

Ability to Circumvent Restrictions on Remittances (11h)

The base case operating flows, term (11b), include only those operating flows available for remittance. Thus they will be less than project flows whenever there are binding remittance restrictions. In many cases, however, the restricted flows can be transferred out through interaffiliate pricing, management fees, special export programs, or other mechanisms. The value of these remittances, typically less than the face value of the funds in question, can be incorporated in another APV term. Again, a major advantage of the "divide and conquer" approach is that it makes explicit the impact on project value of remittance restrictions and alternative ways around them. Even where the exact possibilities for transferring restricted funds are not known, a "break-even" value for term (11h) can be computed, thus showing what proportion, in present value terms, of the restricted profits would have to be transferred to make the project marginally attractive.

RISK PREMIUMS FOR FOREIGN PROJECTS

Although the APV approach does not require that the effects of financial structure be reflected in the discount rate, the discount rate for each term must reflect both the rate of interest (real in the case of operating flows, nominal in the case of nominal flows) and a risk premium. According to current capital market theory, this risk premium should reflect only the systematic risk of the project. Depending on the openness of the base country capital market, this systematic risk should be measured relative to the firm's home country market portfolio or relative to the world market portfolio. As shown by Lessard [13], the systematic risk of projects in various countries differs substantially from U.S. and world perspectives, but much more so for other single-country versus world perspectives. From a single-country perspective, foreign projects will tend to have less systematic risk than domestic projects, although this may not be true if the more appropriate world base is used. In countries where local conditions are extremely uncertain, but not highly dependent on the world economy, the total risk of the project will be substantially greater than its systematic risk from any perspective other than the local one. Thus even apparently risky projects may not require greater than normal risk premiums.

The suggestion that cash flows from projects in politically unstable countries should not require large risk premiums is at odds with general practice. Many firms attach large risk premiums to such projects. However, the difference is often more semantic than real. A common approach to evaluating foreign projects is to discount most likely (modal) rather than expected (mean) cash flows at a risk-adjusted rate. For projects with a significant risk of expropriation or large losses due to changes in the economic structure of a country, the mean will be substantially lower than the mode. Thus the discount rate is being used to shift cash flows toward their expected values to discount them by a risk premium. Such "risk adjustments," however, introduce biases, and the more explicit approach that captures the effect of risks on expected cash flows, as well as on their valuation, is preferable.[23]

Appropriate discount rates for each major category of the APV terms are discussed below.

Noncontractual Flows (ρ_1 and ρ_2): Capital Outlays

Since these flows are not contractually fixed in any currency, but vary depending on the interactions of inflation and exchange rates, as well as on a host of other factors, I have argued that they should be stated in terms of units of constant purchasing power and discounted at the real rate of interest plus a risk premium reflecting their systematic risk. However, determining this systematic risk represents a major challenge. In many cases, there are no host country firms in the same industry with shares traded in an active market to provide beta estimates. Furthermore, formal or informal approaches for estimating fundamental betas are likely to be hampered by a lack of experience with similar projects. In addition, beta estimates estimated empirically will relate the volatility of equity values, reflecting both operating and contractual cash flows. Hence it is necessary to "back out" the relevant betas for the various components. This is not an insurmountable task, though, since the contractual flows are relatively safe and can be assumed to be discounted at a rate close to the riskless rate. Thus the adjustment involves "unlevering" beta, not only for financial leverage, but also for depreciation tax shields.

Contractual Flows (ρ_3–ρ_6)

The critical element in discounting these flows is determining the appropriate nominal interest rate for (near) riskless debt. Undoubtedly there is some risk of default associated with the various contractual flows, and hence a risk premium may be required. Nevertheless, as a first approximation, the corporation's borrowing rates in unregulated markets can be used. Technically, the depreciation tax shields are subject only to the risk that the firm cannot make use of them. This may be serious in certain cases, but in general if the firm cannot take the deductions directly, it can carry them forward or backward in time or, in the ultimate case, transfer them to another firm through mergers. Roughly speaking, then, ρ_4 will involve only a small risk premium and can be approximated by the interest rate on the firm's debt in the currency in question. Similar arguments apply to interest tax shields and financial subsidies.

System-Dependent Operating Flows (ρ_7 and ρ_8)

Although part of these flows are tax savings due to transfer pricing or earnings retention decisions, they are not contractually denominated except to the extent that the profit shifting also changes depreciation tax shields. Thus in practice it might be necessary to separate the term into an operating and contractual component, with the appropriate inflation and risk adjustments for each element. The amount available for remittance through these channels will depend directly on project operating cash flows and thus, although the risks of being able to remit these additional funds are unlikely to be highly systematic, the discount rate applicable to operating flows, ρ_2, appears to be a reasonable choice.

CONCLUSIONS

The APV approach provides a generalized framework capable of incorporating most of the special financial considerations that arise in evaluating foreign projects. Its attractiveness vis-à-vis traditional approaches, which attempt to force all these factors into a single term, rests only in part on its conceptual superiority. Much of its attraction lies in its transparency and simplicity of use in certain situations.

In practice, capital budgeting involves a great deal of trial and error with various "what if" questions. Furthermore, many uncertain outcomes are never reduced to specific cash flows, but instead are dealt with by testing the sensitivity of cash flows to changes in a particular assumption and by judging whether a particular variable is likely to exceed a "break-even" value. The ability to separate the various terms greatly facilitates such analyses. In most cases, only the operating cash-flow streams will need to be run under a variety of scenarios. Similarly, if there is uncertainty with respect to the appropriate discount rates, most of it will center on the risk premium for the operating cash flows, and thus sensitivity analysis can concentrate on these flows. The distinction between real and nominal flows allows a substantially simplified treatment of inflation and exchange rates, but it also serves to highlight the differential impact of these factors on the two types of flows.

While the assumptions of purchasing power parity and interest rate parity undoubtedly break down for certain countries or currencies, they provide the best set of base case single-point estimates. If deviations from these relationships are explicitly considered, a careful attempt to model the effect of these deviations on the cash flows themselves is called for. Treating them as independent in either a scenario or simulation approach is fallacious and is likely to result in more serious errors than assuming that the naive parity conditions hold. The explicit separation of contractual and noncontractual cash flows in various currencies lends itself to sensitivity or simulation approaches for determining the impact of exchange rate changes or a project's present value, valuable both for capital budgeting and foreign exchange exposure analysis.

While these considerations clearly favor the APV approach, they do not call for its use in all situations. Little will be lost in using a single discount rate that is roughly consistent with APV solutions for small, recurring projects with few or no financing interactions. However, even in this case, the APV framework provides the ideal basis for computing these hurdle rates for decentralized use. Any strategic decision that involves financial complexities, though, should be evaluated in the more complete fashion outlined.

NOTES

1. See Eiteman and Stonehill [6], Rodriguez and Carter [22], Shapiro [25], and Folks [7] for summaries of the factors distinguishing domestic and foreign projects. An early paper that raised most of these questions was Stonehill and Nathanson's [29].

2. Rodriguez and Carter [22] demonstrate how weighted-average measures using project or subsidiary capital structures are misleading when there is financial "layering" within the corporation.

3. Shapiro [26] provides a detailed derivation of a weighted-average rule for international projects that takes many of these factors into account. However, it is exceedingly complex, and the resulting hurdle rate is likely to differ across projects and over time.

4. Naumann-Etiene [17] provides a good review of the early literature on this topic.

5. Eiteman and Stonehill [6] suggested a dual hurdle rate approach. Although they have dropped it in their subsequent edition, it continues to be advocated by others.

6. See, for example, Pomper [20].

7. Alder [1] provides the most complete treatment of this issue.

8. See Adler [1] and Adler and Dumas [2] for a discussion of valuation in such cases. Although the APV from the viewpoint of a single investor will not in general be the appropriate investment criterion for the joint venture, it will be appropriate for valuing that project from the single investor's viewpoint. In practice, there may be no rule that satisfies both participants in the joint venture. In such cases, project acceptance depends on bargaining among the participants, where each may use an APV measure to evaluate their share.

9. See, for example, Adler and Dumas [2, 3], Agmon and Lessard [4], and Stapleton and Subrahmanyan [28].

10. The VAP, an extension of the first Miller-Modigliani proposition, was introduced by Schall [24] and, although not given the same name, by Myers [16]. For an excellent statement, see Haley and Schall [11, pp. 202–208].

11. In practice, virtually all international ventures can be considered joint ventures in the sense that the local government's income taxes are risky equity claims and locally issued debt typically carries some project-related risks. In these cases, the local government's valuation of a venture may differ from that of the international firm, but these effects will usually be swamped by other adjustments, such as shadow prices for foreign exchange and labor and the recognition of positive and negative externalities.

12. For a succinct definition of these relationships, see Giddy [9], Frenkel [8], and Solnik [27]. See Dornbusch [5] for a more complete discussion of the underlying economic theory.

13. For an excellent review of the theory and evidence regarding purchasing power parity, see Officer [18]. Levich [15] reviews the evidence regarding the degree to which the forward rate is an unbiased predictor of future spot exchange rates and of interest rate parity, conditions that jointly imply IFE.

14. The classical PPP relationship is defined in terms of certain, contemporaneous variables. Giddy [10] and Solnik [27] discuss the expectational form.

15. This formula can be altered readily to accommodate varying rates of inflation over time.

16. If PPP does not hold exactly, equation (9a) includes the covariances among cash flows, inflation, and exchange rates and does not reduce to (9b). However, if the cash flows in constant terms are (relatively) independent of inflation and the exchange rate, the approximation is satisfactory.

17. Roll [23], for example, finds no evidence that deviations from PPP persist or can be forecast.

18. The value of riskless contractual flows is unaffected by uncertainty regarding the exchange rate since it can be locked in by borrowing or lending an equivalent flow at the nominal market interest rate.

19. This assumption is analogous to the "default value" approach suggested by Folks [7].

20. Vernon and Wells [3] and Robbins and Stobaugh [21] provide further illustration of the difficulty of measuring incremental cash flows at a system level.

21. See Lessard [12, pp. 354–356] for a discussion of contractual and noncontractual cash flows and their implications for corporate exposure to exchange rate changes.

22. Pretax cash flows are used since it is assumed that the use of concessionary debt will require a matching reduction in other corporate borrowings. Thus the additional interest tax shields of the concessionary debt will be offset by reduced interest tax shields on corporate borrowing at market rates. The tax shields gained and lost will not match exactly if debt capacity is defined in terms of book values. Even if defined in terms of (net present value of) cash flows, the offset will be inexact since the proportion of the debt service flows that is interest will differ for the concessionary debt and borrowings at the market rate with the same present value. In most cases, however, the error is small.

23. Eiteman and Stonehill [6] follow a third approach, "adjusting" cash flows until they are of equivalent risk to those of domestic projects and then discounting them by the domestic "cost of capital." This is similar to taking certainty equivalents of cash flows and discounting them by the riskless rate. While in many ways it is theoretically more appealing than to discount expected cash flows by a risk-adjusted rate, there are no operational, yet reasonably precise ways to do this.

REFERENCES

1. Adler, M. "The Cost of Capital and Valuation of Two-Country Firm," *Journal of Finance* (March 1974).
2. Adler, M., and Dumas, B. "Optimal International Acquisitions," *Journal of Finance* (March 1975).
3. Adler, M., and Dumas, B. "The Microeconomics of the Firm in an Open Economy," *American Economic Review* (February 1977).
4. Agmon, T., and Lessard, D. R. "Financial Factors and the International Expansion of Small-Country Firms," in Agmon and Kindleberger, eds., *Multinationals from Small Countries*. Cambridge, Mass.: M.I.T. Press, 1977.
5. Dornbusch, R. "Monetary Policy under Exchange Rate Flexibility," in *Managed Exchange Rate Flexibility*. Boston: Federal Reserve Bank of Boston, Conference Vol., No. 20, 1979.
6. Eiteman, D. K., and Stonehill, A. I. *Multinational Business Finance*, 2nd ed. Reading, Mass.: Addison-Wesley Publishing Company, 1979.
7. Folks, W. R., Jr. "Critical Assumptions in Evaluating Foreign Investment Projects," paper submitted at Nijenrode conference, August 1979.
8. Frenkel, J. A. "A Monetary Approach to the Exchange Rate: Doctrinal Aspects and Empirical Evidence," *Scandinavian Journal of Economics* (May 1976).
9. Giddy, I. "The Cost of Capital in the International Firm," unpublished working paper, Columbia University, 1976.
10. Giddy, I. "An Integrated Theory of Exchange Rate Equilibrium," *Journal of Financial and Quantitative Analysis* (December 1976).
11. Haley, C. W., and Schall, L. D. *The Theory of Financial Decisions*. New York: McGraw-Hill Book Company, 1979.
12. Lessard, D. R., ed. *International Financial Management*. New York: Warren, Gorham, & Lamont, 1979.
13. Lessard, D. R., "World, Country and Industry Relationships in Equity Returns:

Implications for Risk Reduction through International Diversification," *Financial Analysts Journal* (January/February 1976).

14. Lessard, D. R., "Transfer Prices, Taxes, and Financial Markets: Implications of Internal Financial Transfers within the Multinational Firm," in R. B. Hawkins, ed., *Economic Issues of Multinational Firms*, JAI Press, 1979.
15. Levich, R. M. "The Efficiency of Markets for Foreign Exchange," in Lessard, ed., *International Financial Management*.
16. Myers, S. C. "Procedures for Capital Budgeting under Uncertainty," *Industrial Management Review* (Spring 1968).
17. Naumann-Etiene, R. "A Framework for Financial Decisions in Multinational Corporations—A Summary of Recent Research," *Journal of Financial and Quantitative Analysis* (November 1974).
18. Officer, L. H. "The Purchasing Power Theory of Exchange Rates: A Review Article," *IMF Staff Papers* (March 1976).
19. Ornstein, J., and Vora, K. T. "Foreign Investment Projects in Multinational Firms," Master's thesis, Sloan School of Management, M.I.T., December 1978.
20. Pomper, C. B. *International Investment Planning: An Integrated Approach*. Amsterdam: North-Holland Publishing Company, 1976.
21. Robbins, S. M., and Stobaugh, R. B. *Money in the Multinational Corporation*. New York: Basic Books, 1973.
22. Rodriguez, R. M., and Carter, E. E. *International Financial Management*. Englewood Cliffs, N.J.: Prentice-Hall, 1979.
23. Roll, R. "Violations of Purchasing Power Parity and Their Implications for Efficient International Commodity Markets," in M. Sarnat and G. P. Szego, eds., *International Finance and Trade*, Vol. 1. Cambridge, Mass.: Ballinger Publishing Company, 1979.
24. Schall, L. D. "Asset Valuation, Firm Investment, and Firm Diversification," *Journal of Business* (January 1972).
25. Shapiro, A. C. "Capital Budgeting for the Multinational Corporation," *Financial Management* (May 1978).
26. Shapiro, A. C. "Financial Structure and the Cost of Capital in the Multinational Corporation," *Journal of Financial and Quantitative Analysis* (November 1978).
27. Solnik, B. "International Parity Conditions and Exchange Risk," *Journal of Banking and Finance* (August 1978).
28. Stapleton, R. C., and Subrahmanyan, M. G. "Market Imperfections, Capital Market Equilibrium, and Corporation Finance," *Journal of Finance* (May 1977).
29. Stonehill, A. I., and Nathanson, L. "Capital Budgeting and the Multinational Corporation," *California Management Review* (Summer 1968).
30. Taggart, R. A., Jr. "Capital Budgeting and the Financing Decision: An Exposition," *Financial Management* (Summer 1977).
31. Vernon, R. A., and Wells, L. T. *Manager in the International Economy* 3rd ed. Englewood Cliffs, N.J.: Prentice-Hall, 1976.

Author Index

Boldface entries indicate where an article by an author in this book is found

Subject Index